INEQUALITY

IN THE

21ST CENTURY

A READER

EDITED BY

David B. Grusky

AND

Jasmine Hill

WESTVIEW
PRESS

Westview Press was founded in 1975 in Boulder, Colorado, by notable publisher and intellectual Fred Praeger. Westview Press continues to publish scholarly titles and high-quality undergraduate- and graduate-level textbooks in core social science disciplines. With books developed, written, and edited with the needs of serious nonfiction readers, professors, and students in mind, Westview Press honors its long history of publishing books that matter.

Copyright © 2018 by Westview Press
Published by Westview Press,
An imprint of Perseus Books, LLC,
A subsidiary of Hachette Book Group, Inc.
2465 Central Avenue
Boulder, CO 80301
www.westviewpress.com

Every effort has been made to secure required permissions for all text, images, maps, and other art reprinted in this volume.

Westview Press books are available at special discounts for bulk purchases in the United States by corporations, institutions, and other organizations. For more information, please contact the Special Markets Department at 2300 Chestnut Street, Suite 200, Philadelphia, PA 19103, or call (800) 810-4145, ext. 5000, or e-mail special. markets@perseusbooks.com.

A CIP catalog record for the print version of this book is available from the Library of Congress
PB ISBN: 978-0-8133-5064-6
EBOOK ISBN: 978-0-8133-5065-3

10 9 8 7 6 5 4 3 2 1

*To a more perfect union, justice, domestic tranquility,
and the general welfare*

CONTENTS

PART III: THE ONE PERCENT

PART IV: POVERTY AND THE UNDERCLASS

PART V: MOBILITY AND THE AMERICAN DREAM

The Division of Labor

How Much Discrimination Is There?

How Gender Intersects

A Stalling Out?

PART VIII: HOW INEQUALITY SPILLS OVER

PART IX: MOVING TOWARD EQUALITY?

PREFACE AND ACKNOWLEDGMENTS

For the first time in many decades, there is ongoing public discussion of income inequality and the legitimacy of taxing the rich; indeed the 2016 presidential election was partly a mandate on just such issues. The Occupy Wall Street movement, which was the first explicitly anti-inequality movement in recent US history, initially receded in the aftermath of the Great Recession but was then very explicitly invoked and reinvigorated by Bernie Sanders during his campaign. We also have a new term, the "one percent," to denote the elite within the United States, a term with a valence that is not as straightforwardly worshipful as the elite have perhaps come to expect. The study of poverty and inequality is no longer a sleepy little enterprise confined to the halls of academia.

This growing public interest in matters of poverty and inequality make it especially important to bring to the public the best available scholarly research in a readable and distilled form. The simple purpose of this book is to do just that.

This is of course no small order. For all its virtues, academic writing is not known for its brevity and succinctness, and our task was thus to excerpt in ways that eliminated all inessential material while still preserving the integrity of the contributions. We have excised many clarifying and qualifying footnotes, almost all decorative theorizing and literature reviews, and much analysis that was not crucial in advancing the argument. Understandably, some of our readers and contributors would no doubt oppose all excerpting, yet the high cost of implementing such a radical stance would be a substantial reduction in the number of readings that could be reproduced. We apologize to our authors for being unable to present the selections in their entirety and encourage our readers to consult the original and full versions of our excerpted pieces. In some cases, we have alternatively asked the authors themselves to provide trimmed versions of articles that were originally published elsewhere, an approach that can yield more cohesive pieces when the excerpting would otherwise have to be very heavy.

The editing rules adopted here were in most cases conventional. For example, ellipses were used to indicate when content from the original was excised, and brackets were used to mark off a passage that was inserted for the purpose of clarifying meaning. It should be noted that in some cases ellipses were not used when the excised text was a footnote or when relatively minor phrases were omitted and ellipses proved too distracting. When necessary, tables and footnotes were renumbered, and all articles that were cited in excised passages were likewise omitted from the list of references at the end of each chapter. The spelling, grammar, and stylistic conventions of the original contributions were otherwise preserved.

This book is, as is typically the case for anthologies, the output of a complicated division of labor with many contributors. In selecting the new contributions, we relied on our own trusted advisors, especially Michelle Jackson. Over the course of a long production process, we also drew extensively on the excellent Westview staff, including Marco Pavia and Krista Anderson. Most importantly, we thank our Westview Press senior editor, James Sherman, for his spot-on advice at every stage of the process.

David B. Grusky and Jasmine Hill
Stanford, California 2017

INEQUALITY
IN THE
21ST CENTURY

1. Poverty and Inequality in the 21st Century

DAVID B. GRUSKY AND JASMINE HILL

It was not so long ago that many social scientists subscribed to a version of "modernization theory" in which racial inequalities, gender inequalities, and class-based discrimination were seen as premodern residues that were destined to wither away. Although there were always prominent dissenters, this benign understanding of history was the driving force behind much of the research on inequality until the late 1970s.

But that was then. Over the last twenty years, this benign understanding has been largely discredited, and a wide variety of alternative accounts are now contending to become the new lens through which we understand the forces making for change in inequality.

How did such a dramatic reversal in our understanding of the logic of history come about? It will be useful to organize our introduction to current research on inequality around a description of these forces that led to an unravelling of modernization theory and the rise of new worries about extreme income inequality, growing joblessness, persistent racism, and the stalling-out of historic declines in gender inequality.

The Modernization Narrative

It should not be too surprising that the modernization narrative of the 1950s, 1960s, and 1970s was a largely optimistic narrative about the inevitability of progress. The narrative of the day was likely to be benign, after all, because many of the key trends in inequality were in fact quite reassuring. This is especially so for trends in income inequality up to the mid-1970s. As is well known, there was a precipitous decline in income inequality in the 1930s, and thereafter the United States experienced approximately thirty years of stability in income inequality (Saez, Ch. 6; Piketty, Ch. 7).

As important as this decline in income inequality was, the modernization narrative was more concerned with trends in inequalities of *opportunity*. In the United States and other liberal welfare regimes, even extreme inequalities in income were seen as quite palatable insofar as the opportunities for getting ahead were widely available to children from all families, even relatively poor ones. The "race to get ahead" was the commonly used metaphor of this time: If that race was fairly run, then the resulting inequalities in outcomes were viewed as altogether legitimate.

The featured claim of the modernization narrative was precisely that this race was becoming ever fairer. This decline in "inequalities of opportunity" was partly attributed to the expansion of secondary and post-secondary schooling and the associated diffusion of loan and aid programs, such as the G.I. Bill, that reduced financial constraints on access to schooling. Although some scholars indeed emphasized this pathway, others showed that college was a "great equalizer" in the sense that *all* college graduates, those from rich and poor families alike, did equally well in the labor market (see Torche, Ch. 34). When a child from a poor family goes to college, the resulting degree becomes a "shield" of sorts, in effect protecting that child from class-based discrimination.

The more general point is that competitive market economies should work to reduce all forms of discrimination based on gender, race, or social class. In his "taste for discrimination" model, Gary Becker (1957) argued that such discrimination will gradually disappear because it entails paying a premium to the preferred class of labor, a premium that non-discriminating employers do not have to bear (thus giving them a competitive advantage). The latter economic account works in tandem with a sociological one that emphasizes the diffusion of modern personnel practices in the form of universalistic hiring practices (e.g., open hiring, credentialism) and bureaucratized pay scales and promotion procedures. The essence of such bureaucratic personnel practices is a formal commitment to universalism (i.e., treating all workers equally) and to meritocratic hiring and promotion (i.e., hiring and promoting on the basis of credentials).

The final component of the modernization narrative has one's social class becoming a less important and encompassing identity. The "working class" within the early-industrial economy was an especially prominent identity because political parties and unions carried out the ideological work needed to convert the working class into a culturally coherent community. The key claim, however, is that this identity became less central as (a) political parties abandoned class-specific platforms in favor of "issue politics," and (b) unions became narrowly instrumental by focusing on tangible benefits rather than some transformative and politicized class narrative. In the absence of organizations that explicitly trained members into a class-based worldview, social classes increasingly become purely statistical categories deployed by social scientists, not the deeply institutionalized communities of the past (see Weeden and Grusky 2005).

New Narratives

We have laid out the modernization narrative in some detail because it still plays the important role of a discredited approach lurking in the background. It also remains prominent partly because an alternative with all the reach of the old narrative has not yet emerged. In this sense, the contemporary literature remains unsettled and inchoate, with many accounts vying for the role of successor to modernization theory. We review some of these competing accounts below.

Rent and Income Inequality

The most prominent alternative to modernization theory, an account featuring "rent" and other forms of competition-restricting regulation, has as its backdrop the spectacular takeoff in income inequality in the United States. As Saez (Ch. 6) discusses, income inequality increased dramatically in the US in the late 1970s, with it now reaching levels as high as those prevailing in the 1920s.

There are, of course, many prominent accounts that understand this development as simply the expected playing-out of competitive market forces when confronted with the "exogenous shock" of computers and other technological innovations that raised the demand for skilled labor (see Goldin and Katz, Ch. 8). The theory of skill-biased technical change, for example, implies that the demand for skilled workers is rapidly increasing because of these innovations, that the existing supply of skilled workers cannot meet this rising demand, and that the resulting disequilibrium bids up the price for skilled labor and leads to an increase in inequality. Although the higher productivity of skilled workers will lock in some of this inequality, we should eventually see a reversal or slowdown in the trend because the high wages going to skilled workers should induce more workers to invest in skill (by going to college), which in turn increases the competition for skilled jobs and ultimately drives down the pay going to those jobs. The competitive market should, by this logic, correct some of the problem.

The "rent narrative" instead rests on the view that extreme inequality should be partly attributed to the many opportunities to collect rent. We adopt here the usual definition of rent as returns on an asset (e.g., labor) in excess of what is necessary to keep that asset in production in a fully competitive market. By this definition, rents exist (a) when demand for an asset exceeds supply, *and* (b) when the supply of that asset is fixed through "natural" means (e.g., a shortage of talent) or through social or political barriers that artificially restrict supply. The first condition implies that those holding some "asset," like being tall and agile enough to be a center for a professional basketball team, are in short supply and that employers are therefore in pitched competition to secure that asset. The second condition, the "fixed supply" stricture, implies that labor cannot readily respond to the price increases that arise when demand exceeds supply. It is difficult, for example, for workers to respond to the high salaries paid to professional basketball centers by willing themselves to grow seven feet tall (and to become extraordinarily agile). We, of course, care more about rent that is generated by changing social institutional constraints than rent that is generated by largely constant and enduring genetic constraints. In contemporary labor markets, the former type of rent takes on many forms, including the wage premiums associated with the minimum wage, the wage premiums associated with the union wage, and the capacity of chief executive officers (CEOs) to extract better remuneration packages (see Red Bird and Grusky 2015; Piketty, Ch. 7; Hacker and Pierson, Ch. 10).

How does a rent-based account explain the takeoff? The story is a twofold one focusing on (a) a declining capacity to extract rent at the bottom of the income distribution, and (b) a growing capacity to extract rent at the top of the income distribution. At the bottom of the distribution, the weakening of labor unions and the decline in the real value of the minimum wage means that workers are less likely to benefit from rent, thus lowering their wages and increasing inequality (see Western and Rosenfeld, Ch. 11). The growing capacity to extract rent at the top arises because of the spread of competition-restricting norms and regulations. The returns to education are increasing, for example, because those with college degrees are increasingly protected from the competition that would occur under a system in which everyone, no matter how poor they were, had full and complete access to higher education. The highly educated are further advantaged insofar as they are in occupations that have increasingly erected barriers to entry (e.g., licensure, certification) that then protect them from competition. Finally, CEO pay takes off because board members are sitting on the board at the behest of the CEO, a setup that lends itself to board members favoring ample compensation packages (see Bebchuk and Fried, Ch. 73).

It follows that rent-destruction and rent-creation are asymmetric forces. That is, just as rent is gradually being destroyed for workers at the bottom of the income distribution, it is also gradually being created at the top of the distribution. By this logic, rent is a driving force behind the rise of inequality and an intrinsic part of modern economies, certainly not the simple vestige that modernization theorists typically assume.

The Perverse Effects of Slow Growth

The rent account thus locates the contemporary dilemma as proceeding from our relentless commitment to destroying rent at the bottom of the income distribution while at the same time supporting, at least implicitly, its equally relentless expansion at the top. The second main narrative on offer, one that instead focuses on the dynamics of wealth, plays out without making any assumptions about possible changes in market competitiveness. The dynamic on which it rests could in fact unfold in the context of perfectly competitive markets.

The starting point for this account (see Piketty, Ch. 7) is the recent increase in the amount of private wealth relative to total national income. In the middle of the 20th century, private wealth in Britain and France equaled about two or three years of national income, a relatively low share. This share then rose sharply to about five or six years of national income by 2010. The main reason for this change is declining growth rates: In slowly growing economies, past wealth becomes ever more important, as even a small flow of new savings among the already-wealthy will increase their wealth substantially. This means that inherited wealth will come to dominate the wealth that workers can amass from a lifetime of labor. It is here, then, that we see a very explicit return to Marx's (Ch. 2) very famous worries about the growing concentration of wealth.

Why is this result so troubling? It is not that Piketty, like Marx, is pushing some iron law of accumulation that then culminates in an apocalyptic vision. Instead, Piketty is worried about the implications of this development for the legitimacy of capitalism, a legitimacy that rests in part on the premise that the race to get ahead should be a fair and open one. What Piketty (Ch. 7) shows is that this commitment can be undermined by relatively slow rates of economic growth. This is not, then, some conventional indictment of the unfair and "rigged" institutions (e.g., CEO pay institutions) by which labor is compensated. Although Piketty is also very troubled by such practices, his is instead an expose of the unanticipated consequences of slow economic growth.

It might be imagined that Piketty would therefore push for a pro-growth solution. The main problem with this solution, as Piketty stresses, is that there are real limits on the capacity of advanced economies to restore the high growth rates of the past. As a result, Piketty's fallback solution is a progressive annual tax on capital, a tax that will then allow for new instances of "primitive accumulation" among those who are not born into wealth.

The Perverse Effects of Rising Income Inequality

The foregoing narrative thus lays out the perverse and underappreciated effects of slow economic growth. As a natural complement, we might next consider a narrative that again calls into question the capacity of contemporary economies to deliver on their commitment to openness and equal opportunity, although in this case it is rising inequality rather than slowing growth that is potentially undermining that commitment.

The main worry here is that, by virtue of the rise in income inequality, there is an unprecedented infusion of additional resources among the higher reaches of the class structure, an infusion that will work to increase the amount of reproduction. By this logic, inequality of condition and of opportunity are now understood as varying together, even though scholars have typically been at pains to stress that they are analytically distinct.

How might parents in privileged classes use their newfound income? The available evidence (e.g., Putnam 2015) suggests that they will increase the human, cultural, and social capital of their children via high-quality childcare and preschool, educational toys and books, after-school training and test preparation, science-related summer camps, elite preparatory schools, prestigious college degrees, a "finishing-school" vacation in Europe, and stipends or allowances that free them from the need to work during high school and college. As the takeoff plays out, privileged parents can also more readily afford privileged residential neighborhoods, with accordingly improved access to high-quality public schools, neighborhood amenities that assist in human-capital formation (e.g., libraries), and peers that can provide all manner of career advantages (see Mitnik, Cumberworth, and Grusky 2015).

The implication of this "infusion at the top" is that it undermines the capacity of liberal welfare regimes to deliver on their commitment to equal opportunity. The standard liberal mantra, as has been so frequently rehearsed, is that extreme inequality is quite unproblematic as long as it is the result of a fair and open race. The central dilemma of our time: How can a fair and open race be delivered when high

incomes afford parents so many opportunities to assist their children? The readings in this book provide a range of approaches to resolving this defining conundrum of the 21st century.

Commodification

The "commodification narrative," to which we next turn, again takes rising income inequality as its starting point (see Grusky and MacLean 2015). It emphasizes that extreme inequality not only makes it difficult for the poor to buy opportunity but also disadvantages them in a growing range of markets for goods and services. The key problem here is that access to all manner of goods and services increasingly depends on the simple capacity to pay for them. It follows that those at the bottom of the income distribution are now doubly disadvantaged: It is not just that they have less money (relative to others), but it is also that access to goods, services, and opportunities increasingly requires precisely the money that they do not have. It may be said, then, that relentless commodification is what gives rising inequality its teeth.

This process is playing out very broadly. The market is gradually replacing the nuclear family, extended family, and neighborhood as the go-to source for delivering childcare, domestic services, after-school education, financial services, old-age care, health care, and much more. The resulting commodification is closely related to the relentless differentiation and specialization of the sort that modernization theorists, such as Talcott Parsons (1994), so frequently stressed. The marketization narrative emphasizes, however, the very special *way* in which such functions are differentiating: Namely, they are differentiating out of the family and into the *market*, thus making the capacity to pay for these functions all important.

It follows that rising inequality is especially consequential because those at the bottom of the distribution are disadvantaged in the competition for ever more services. If early childhood education has differentiated out of the family and is now mainly delivered on the market, how will poor families be able to pay for it? If access to high-quality primary and secondary schooling, although nominally "free," is in principle only available within rich neighborhoods with a high entry price, how will poor families be able to access them? If access to marriage (and the supplementary economic resources it provides) is increasingly a "luxury good" only available to the well-off, how will poor men and women gain access to those supplementary resources and the economies of scale that marriage affords? These are all simple – but consequential – examples of the growing neoliberal commitment to price goods and services at their market value rather than "give them away."

There are two solutions to this fundamental dilemma. The first entails capitulation to commodification: We can acquiesce to the process but insist that, insofar as the poor increasingly need money to buy goods and services, we must then commit to an aggressively redistributive tax system. We can make commodification work, in other words, only if there is enough money at the bottom of the distribution to enable the poor to purchase the goods and services that are increasingly only available on the market. The second solution entails reversing commodification rather than acquiescing to it. This approach proceeds by reinstalling various types of public goods, including free college education, free high-quality childcare, and integrated neighborhoods (which amounts to "giving away" neighborhood amenities rather than selling them). If this approach were taken, a relatively high level of income inequality becomes more palatable, as so-called "basic needs" are now met through direct delivery rather than market mechanisms.

Automation

The next narrative that we review, again one that is increasingly popular, starts with the very troubling decline in prime-age employment. Because many people who would like to work will stop looking for work during economic downturns (and thus no longer register as unemployed), the economy's capacity to provide jobs is best measured with the prime-age employment ratio, defined as the ratio of employed 25–54 year-olds to the population of that same age. For more than sixty years, the share of 25–54 year-old men in the labor force has been declining, with the current level (as of May 2016) down a full 10 percentage points from the peak of 98 percent in 1954 (see Council of Economic Advisors 2016). This "jobs problem," which is especially prominent among low-skilled men, has led to a sharp rise in the number of poor households without any working adults, a trend that reverses the earlier declines in nonworking poverty under welfare reform.

The looming question of our time is whether technology and automation may push this rate yet lower. The pessimists understand the technologies of the future as mainly job-destroying with "robots in the operating room, self-driving cars snaking through the streets, and Amazon drones dotting the sky" (Thompson 2015, p. 3; Karabarbounis & Neiman 2014). These new technologies, so it is argued, will replace drivers, clerks, and untold other occupations and accordingly drive down prime-age employment far lower than it is today. Even now, the leading firms (e.g., Apple) are formed around the control of intellectual property rights, such as patents, copyrights, and trademarks, and any tasks unrelated to the production of such rights are subcontracted and performed overseas. We can continue to have record-high profits and declining employment insofar as (a) the main comparative advantage of the US is ferreting out and exploiting these rent-generating opportunities, and (b) the resulting employment effects are mainly felt overseas.

What can be done? The rise of nonworking poverty and the decline in the prime-age employment ratio have led to (a) renewed calls to provide public-sector jobs of last resort, (b) new efforts to ensure that anti-poverty programs successfully promote labor force attachment, and (c) new experiments with unconditional cash transfers to those in poverty. These and other potential reforms will be discussed in several of the readings that follow.

Camouflaging Ideologies

We have focused to this point on narratives pertaining to inequalities in economic outcomes and opportunities. It is useful to conclude our review with a discussion of narratives that are instead focused on understanding the contemporary dynamics of racial, ethnic, and gender inequalities. These new narratives may be understood as efforts to come to terms with (a) the extreme forms of inequality that continue to flourish under late industrialism (e.g., extreme racial disparities in criminal justice), and (b) recent slowdowns in the pace of change in many key forms of gender and racial inequality (e.g., slowing declines in the gender pay gap). The latter developments are difficult to reconcile with the long-standing view that competitive market economies and bureaucratic forms of organization should work to reduce inequalities based on gender, race, or ethnicity. The simple question here: If bureaucracy and competition indeed have such equalizing effects, why is it taking so long for those effects to be fully expressed?

We cannot possibly review within this short essay the wide range of contemporary answers to that question. Although there are a host of relevant economic and institutional narratives that have recently emerged (and that will be discussed throughout this book), we focus here on some of the key cultural forces in play, if only because we have not made much of them to this point. We are referring in particular to the important role of "camouflaging ideologies" in legitimating inequality as a just and fair outcome. In the US, the main camouflaging ideology is the widespread view that we remain a land of opportunity in which talent, merit, and effort are decisive in determining who wins the competition to get ahead. Because the labor market is viewed by much of the public as winnowing out talent in this fair and impersonal way, those who tend to do relatively well in this competition, such as white males, are then seen as competent, meritorious, and hence deserving of their fate. This process leads us to have certain expectations or "priors" about the relative competence of different groups (see Ridgeway, Ch. 64). Put differently, we tend not only to treat the individual winners of the race as especially competent, but we also go on to assume that the groups of which they are members are intrinsically more competent and meritorious.

This dynamic, which has the effect of slowing the rate of equalizing change, plays out across various types of racial, gender, and ethnic inequalities. How, for example, does this camouflaging ideology make sense of the disproportionate number of male CEOs? It implies that men are simply more likely to be "CEO material" and that the labor market is fairly recognizing this gender difference in intrinsic capacities to make good decisions, exert authority, or otherwise be a successful CEO. It is in this sense that equal-opportunity ideologies not only legitimate individual inequality but also propagate beliefs about intrinsic *group differences* in competence. These beliefs in turn lend legitimacy to existing inequalities and make them less vulnerable to critique.

It is useful in this context to distinguish between (a) the modernization narrative as a story about how inequality is generated, and (b) the modernization narrative as an adequate characterization of the way in which inequality is truly generated. This narrative has arguably proven to be a better story than factual account: That is, its great success is its widespread diffusion as a popular *story* about inequality, while its great failure is that the story is very incomplete and does not provide an adequate characterization of the

actual processes in play. It is especially pernicious when a meritocratic story about the genesis of inequality is adopted without that story having adequate foundation in fact. This combination is pernicious because that story then serves to "lock in" illicit inequalities as if they were licit.

Conclusions

The foregoing narratives thus constitute a sea change relative to the sensibilities that prevailed after World War II and even into the 1960s and 1970s. To be sure, the standard-issue sociologist of the past also embraced the view that poverty and inequality were important social problems, but overlaid on that sensibility was an appreciation of various "logics of history" that operated in the main to reduce them, if only gradually and fitfully. The problem of inequality was understood, then, as a tractable moral problem, an unfortunate side effect of capitalism that would become yet more manageable with the transition into the increasingly affluent forms of advanced industrialism.

We have sought to show that the benign narrative of the past, which now mainly seems naive and quaint, has been supplanted by a host of new narratives that give far greater weight to the forces making for inequality of outcome and opportunity. As the above review reveals, there are a host of overlapping narratives in play, and it is unclear which of these, if any, will become an overarching narrative with all the force and sway of the earlier modernization narrative.

We cannot pretend to have exhausted all the pessimistic narratives under discussion (see Red Bird and Grusky 2016 for a wider discussion). We have focused on those pertaining to income, wealth, and opportunity only because they have proven to be especially prominent. The same pessimistic sensibility is, however, quite widely in play: We are referring, for example, to (a) narratives of "globalization" that describe how the liberalization of financial and capital markets has harmed poor countries (Cohen and Sabel, Ch. 71); (b) narratives of "deindustrialization" that describe the loss of inner-city jobs and the associated rise of an urban underclass (Wilson, Ch. 50); (c) narratives of "segmented assimilation" that describe the relatively bleak prospects for at least some new immigrant groups (Portes and Zhou, Ch. 45); (d) narratives of "opting out" that have highly trained women eschewing stressful careers in favor of recommitting to their children, spouses, and domestic responsibilities (see Percheski, Ch. 57); and (e) narratives of "essentialist segregation" that describe how sex-typed occupational ghettos continue to be built around presumed differences in male and female aptitudes (Levanon and Grusky, Ch. 58).

Although counternarratives of the more optimistic sort are also being developed, these seem not to be as frequently generated or as readily embraced; and the proponents of such narratives find themselves beleaguered, outnumbered, and on the defensive. Has the pendulum swung too far? It is child's play to posit any number of nonempirical sources of our fascination, some might say obsession, with the pessimistic narrative. It is surely plausible, for example, that our exaggerated taste for pessimism might lead us to downplay the good news, ferret out the bad, and only rarely consider the silver lining. As important as these biases may be, it is undeniable that there are many big inequality transformations underway, at least some of which are troubling regardless of one's normative priors.

REFERENCES

Becker, Gary S. 1957. *The Economics of Discrimination*. Chicago: University of Chicago Press.

Council of Economic Advisors. 2016. "The Long-Term Decline in Prime-Age Male Labor Force Participation." https://www.whitehouse.gov/sites/default/files/page/files/20160620_cea_primeage_male_lfp.pdf

Grusky, David B., and Alair McLean. 2016. "The Social Fallout of a High-Inequality Regime." *The Annals of the American Academy of Political and Social Science* 663, pp. 33–52.

Karabarbounis, L., and B. Neiman. "The Global Decline of the Labor Share." *Quarterly Journal of Economic* 129(1), pp. 61–103

Mitnik, Pablo A., Erin Cumberworth, and David B. Grusky. 2016. "Social Mobility in a High-Inequality Regime." *Annals of the American Academy* 663 (January), pp. 140-84.

Parsons, Talcott. 1994. "Equality or Inequality in Modern Society, or Social Stratification Revisited." Pp. 670–85 in *Social Stratification, Class, Race, and Gender in Socio-logical Perspective*, 1st edition, edited by David B. Grusky. Boulder, CO: Westview Press.

Putnam, Robert D. 2015. *Our Kids: The American Dream in Crisis*. New York: Simon & Schuster.

Red Bird, Beth, and David B. Grusky. 2015. "Rent, Rent-Seeking, and Social Inequality." In *Emerging Trends in the Social and Behavioral Sciences*, eds., Stephen Kosslyn and Robert Scott. Wiley. Available from http://onlinelibrary.wiley.com/book/10.1002/9781118900772.

Red Bird, Beth, and David B. Grusky. 2016. "Distributional Effects of the Great Recession: Where Has All the Sociology Gone?" *Annual Review of Sociology* 42, pp. 185–215.

Thompson, Derek. 2015. "A World Without Work." *The Atlantic* (July/August).

Weeden, Kim A., and David B. Grusky. 2005. "The Case for a New Class Map." *American Journal of Sociology* 111, pp. 141–212.

PART I

THE CLASSIC THEORY

The readings in this section make the case that class, race, and gender are the great fracturing forces of our time. Although we now often take it for granted that these are especially fundamental forms of inequality, it is revealing to return to the classic texts that were so instrumental in building that understanding.

Why, it might be asked, are class, race, and gender such prominent divides in industrial and late-industrial societies? The authors in this section—Karl Marx, Max Weber, W.E.B. Du Bois, and Charlotte Perkins Gilman—suggest that well-defined social groups based on class, race, or gender will emerge (a) when the groups play fundamentally different roles in the economy (the "division of labor"), (b) when these different roles allow one group to extract resources from another ("exploitation"); (c) when the groups enjoy different lifestyles, consumption practices, and patterns of association ("social inequality"), and (d) when the groups have different histories and worldviews ("cultural inequality").

These four "structuring forces" are not of course equally drawn on by the four contributors to this section. If Gilman's essay on gender focuses less, for example, on lifestyles as a differentiating force, it is no doubt because men and women often live together (and thus to some extent share a "lifestyle"), whereas blacks and whites or capitalists and workers are less likely to live in the same home or even neighborhood. At the same time, Gilman shows that other powerful forces work to produce well-defined "gender groups," most notably a strictly enforced occupational division of labor in which men work in the formal economy while women work at home.

If the authors draw on these four forces in different ways, they nonetheless share the view that class, race, and gender are social constructions that are neither natural or inevitable and that—as a result—could conceivably become less prominent in the future. The key sociological question, indeed one that has animated the field over the 100–150 years since these classic texts were published, is whether the forces of class, race, and gender contain the seeds of their own demise. Although the key tenet of modernization theory, as reviewed in our introductory essay, is that "ascription" based on class, race, and gender will gradually wither away, recent developments have called that assumption into question and suggested that these forms of inequality may be more resistant to change than had before been imagined.

The rise of such "pessimistic" accounts, which will be in evidence throughout this book, often entails returning to and building on the seminal works of Marx, Weber, Du Bois, and Gilman. We have thus provided selections from these works that anticipate some of these recent worries and that reveal some of the reasons why class, race, and gender inequalities have proven very adaptive and can flourish even today.

2. Karl Marx[*]

Classes in Capitalism and Pre-Capitalism

The history of all hitherto existing society[1] is the history of class struggles.

Freeman and slave, patrician and plebeian, lord and serf, guild-master[2] and journeyman, in a word, oppressor and oppressed, all stood in constant opposition to one another, carried on an uninterrupted, now hidden, now open fight, a fight that each time ended, either in a revolutionary re-constitution of society at large, or in the common ruin of the contending classes.

In the earlier epochs of history, we find almost everywhere a complicated arrangement of society into various orders, a manifold gradation of social rank. In ancient Rome, we have patricians, knights, plebeians, slaves; in the Middle Ages, feudal lords, vassals, guild-masters, journeymen, apprentices, serfs; in almost all of these classes, again, subordinate gradations.

The modern bourgeois society that has sprouted from the ruins of feudal society has not done away with class antagonisms. It has but established new classes, new conditions of oppression, and new forms of struggle in place of the old ones.

Our epoch, the epoch of the bourgeoisie, possesses, however, this distinctive feature: it has simplified the class antagonisms. Society as a whole is more and more splitting up into two great hostile camps, two great classes directly facing each other: Bourgeoisie and Proletariat.

From the serfs of the Middle Ages sprang the chartered burghers of the earliest towns. From these burgesses the first elements of the bourgeoisie were developed.

The discovery of America, the rounding of the Cape, opened up fresh ground for the rising bourgeoisie. The East-Indian and Chinese markets, the colonisation of America, trade with the colonies, the increase in the means of exchange and in commodities generally, gave to commerce, to navigation, to industry, an impulse never before known, and thereby, to the revolutionary element in the tottering feudal society, a rapid development.

The feudal system of industry, under which industrial production was monopolised by closed guilds, now no longer sufficed for the growing wants of the new markets. The manufacturing system took its place. The guild-masters were pushed on one side by the manufacturing middle class; division of labour between the different corporate guilds vanished in the face of division of labour in each single workshop.

Meanwhile the markets kept ever growing, the demand ever rising. Even manufacture no longer sufficed. Thereupon, steam and machinery revolutionised industrial production. The place of manufacture was taken by the giant, Modern Industry, the place of the industrial middle class, by industrial millionaires, the leaders of whole industrial armies, the modern bourgeois.

Modern industry has established the world-market, for which the discovery of America paved the way. This market has given an immense development to commerce, to navigation, to communication by land. This development has, in its turn, reacted on the extension of industry; and in proportion as industry, commerce, navigation, railways extended, in the same proportion the bourgeoisie developed, increased its capital, and pushed into the background every class handed down from the Middle Ages.

We see, therefore, how the modern bourgeoisie is itself the product of a long course of development, of a series of revolutions in the modes of production and of exchange.

Each step in the development of the bourgeoisie was accompanied by a corresponding political advance of that class. An oppressed class under the sway of the feudal nobility, an armed and self-governing association in the mediaeval commune[3]; here, independent urban republic (as in Italy and Germany), there taxable "third estate" of the monarchy (as in France), afterwards, in the period of manufacture proper, serving either the semi-feudal or the absolute monarchy as a counterpoise against the nobility, and, in fact, cornerstone of the great monarchies in general, the bourgeoisie has at last, since the establishment of Modern Industry and of the world-market, conquered for itself, in the modern representative State, exclusive political sway. The executive of the modern State is but a committee for managing the common affairs of the whole bourgeoisie.

[*]Karl Marx. "The Communist Manifesto," in *Selected Works, Vol. I* (Moscow: Progress Publishers, 1964), pp. 108–119. Reprinted by permission of International Publishers. *The Poverty of Philosophy* (New York: International Publishers, 1963), pp. 172–175. Reprinted by permission of International Publishers. "The Eighteenth Brumaire of Louis Bonaparte," in *Selected Works, Vol. I* (Moscow: Progress Publishers, 1963), pp. 478–479. Reprinted by permission of International Publishers. *Capital, Vol. III* (Moscow: Progress Publishers, 1967), pp. 885–886. Reprinted by permission of International Publishers. From THE MARX-ENGELS READER, SECOND EDITION by Karl Marx and Friedrich Engels, edited by Robert C. Tucker. Copyright© 1978, 1972 by W.W. Norton & Company, Inc. Used by permission of W. W. Norton & Company, Inc.

The bourgeoisie, historically, has played a most revolutionary part. The bourgeoisie, wherever it has the upper hand, has put an end to all feudal, patriarchal, and idyllic relations. It has pitilessly torn asunder the motley feudal ties that bound man to his "natural superiors," and has left remaining no other nexus between man and man than naked self-interest, callous "cash payment." It has drowned the most heavenly ecstasies of religious fervour, chivalrous enthusiasm, philistine sentimentalism, in the icy water of egotistical calculation. It has resolved personal worth into exchange value, and in place of the numberless indefeasible chartered freedoms, has set up that single, unconscionable freedom—Free Trade. For exploitation, veiled by religious and political illusions, it has substituted naked, shameless, direct, and brutal exploitation.

The bourgeoisie has stripped of its halo every occupation hitherto honoured and looked up to with reverent awe. It has converted the physician, the lawyer, the priest, the poet, the man of science, into its paid wage-labourers.

The bourgeoisie has torn away from the family its sentimental veil and has reduced the family relation to a mere money relation.

The bourgeoisie has disclosed how it came to pass that the brutal display of vigour in the Middle Ages, which Reactionists so much admire, found its fitting complement in the most slothful indolence. It has been the first to show what man's activity can bring about. It has accomplished wonders far surpassing Egyptian pyramids, Roman aqueducts, and Gothic cathedrals; it has conducted expeditions that put in the shade all former Exoduses of nations and crusades.

The bourgeoisie cannot exist without constantly revolutionising the instruments of production, and thereby the relations of production, and with them the whole relations of society. Conservation of the old modes of production in unaltered form, was, on the contrary, the first condition of existence for all earlier industrial classes. Constant revolutionising of production, uninterrupted disturbance of all social conditions, and everlasting uncertainty and agitation distinguish the bourgeois epoch from all earlier ones. All fixed, fast-frozen relations, with their train of ancient and venerable prejudices and opinions, are swept away, and all new-formed ones become antiquated before they can ossify. All that is solid melts into air, all that is holy is profaned, and man is at last compelled to face with sober senses, his real conditions of life and his relations with his kind.

The need of a constantly expanding market for its products chases the bourgeoisie over the whole surface of the globe. It must nestle everywhere, settle everywhere, and establish connexions everywhere.

The bourgeoisie has, through its exploitation of the world-market, given a cosmopolitan character to production and consumption in every country. To the great chagrin of Reactionists, it has drawn from under the feet of industry the national ground on which it stood. All old-established national industries have been destroyed or are daily being destroyed. They are dislodged by new industries, whose introduction becomes a life-and-death question for all civilised nations, by industries that no longer work up indigenous raw material, but raw material drawn from the remotest zones; industries whose products are consumed, not only at home, but in every quarter of the globe. In place of the old wants, satisfied by the productions of the country, we find new wants, requiring for their satisfaction the products of distant lands and climes. In place of the old local and national seclusion and self-sufficiency, we have intercourse in every direction and universal inter-dependence of nations. And as in material, so also in intellectual production. The intellectual creations of individual nations become common property. National one-sidedness and narrow-mindedness become more and more impossible, and from the numerous national and local literatures, there arises a world literature.

The bourgeoisie, by the rapid improvement of all instruments of production, by the immensely facilitated means of communication, draws all, even the most barbarian, nations into civilisation. The cheap prices of its commodities are the heavy artillery with which it batters down all Chinese walls and forces the barbarians' intensely obstinate hatred of foreigners to capitulate. It compels all nations, on pain of extinction, to adopt the bourgeois mode of production; it compels them to introduce what it calls civilisation into their midst, *i.e.*, to become bourgeois themselves. In one word, it creates a world after its own image.

The bourgeoisie has subjected the country to the rule of the towns. It has created enormous cities, has greatly increased the urban population as compared with the rural and has thus rescued a considerable part of the population from the idiocy of rural life. Just as it has made the country dependent on the towns, so it has made barbarian and semibarbarian countries dependent on the civilised ones, nations of peasants on nations of bourgeois, the East on the West.

The bourgeoisie keeps more and more doing away with the scattered state of the population of the means of production and of property. It has agglomerated population, centralised means of production, and has concentrated property in few hands. The necessary consequence of this was political centralisation. Independent, or loosely connected provinces, with separate interests, laws, governments, and systems of taxation, became lumped together into one nation, with one government, one code of laws, one national class-interest, one frontier, and one customs-tariff.

The bourgeoisie, during its rule of scarce one hundred years, has created more massive and more colossal productive forces than all preceding generations together. Subjection of Nature's forces to man, machinery, application of chemistry to industry and agriculture, steam-navigation, railways, electric telegraphs, clearing of whole continents for cultivation, canalisation of rivers, whole populations conjured out of the ground—what earlier century had even a presentiment that such productive forces slumbered in the lap of social labour?

We see then: the means of production and of exchange, on whose foundation the bourgeoisie built itself up, were generated in feudal society. At a certain stage in the development of these means of production and of exchange, the conditions under which feudal society produced and exchanged, the feudal organisation of agriculture and manufacturing industry, the feudal relations of property became no longer compatible with the already developed productive forces; they became so many fetters. They had to be burst asunder; and so they were burst asunder.

Into their place stepped free competition, accompanied by a social and political constitution adapted to it and by the economical and political sway of the bourgeois class.

A similar movement is going on before our own eyes. Modern bourgeois society with its relations of production, of exchange and of property, a society that has conjured up such gigantic means of production and of exchange, is like the sorcerer, who is no longer able to control the powers of the nether world whom he has called up by his spells. For many a decade past the history of industry and commerce is but the history of the revolt of modern productive forces against modern conditions of production, against the property relations that are the conditions for the existence of the bourgeoisie and of its rule. It is enough to mention the commercial crises that by their periodical return put on its trial, each time

more threateningly, the existence of the entire bourgeois society. In these crises a great part not only of the existing products, but also of the previously created productive forces, are periodically destroyed. In these crises, an epidemic emerges that, in all earlier epochs, would have seemed an absurdity—the epidemic of over-production. Society suddenly finds itself put back into a state of momentary barbarism; it appears as if a famine, a universal war of devastation had cut off the supply of every means of subsistence; industry and commerce seem to be destroyed; and why? Because there is too much civilisation, too much means of subsistence, too much industry, too much commerce. The productive forces at the disposal of society no longer tend to further the development of the conditions of bourgeois property; on the contrary, they have become too powerful for these conditions, by which they are fettered, and so soon as they overcome these fetters, they bring disorder into the whole of bourgeois society, endanger the existence of bourgeois property. The conditions of bourgeois society are too narrow to comprise the wealth created by them. And how does the bourgeoisie get over these crises? On the one hand by enforced destruction of a mass of productive forces; on the other, by the conquest of new markets, and by the more thorough exploitation of the old ones. That is to say, by paving the way for more extensive and more destructive crises, and by diminishing the means whereby crises are prevented.

The weapons with which the bourgeoisie felled feudalism to the ground are now turned against the bourgeoisie itself.

But not only has the bourgeoisie forged the weapons that bring death to itself; it has also called into existence the men who are to wield those weapons—the modern working class—the proletarians.

In proportion as the bourgeoisie, *i.e.*, capital, is developed, in the same proportion is the proletariat, the modern working class, developed—a class of labourers, who live only so long as they find work, and who find work only so long as their labour increases capital. These labourers, who must sell themselves piecemeal, are a commodity, like every other article of commerce, and are consequently exposed to all the vicissitudes of competition, to all the fluctuations of the market.

Owing to the extensive use of machinery and to division of labour, the work of the proletarians has lost all individual character, and, consequently, all charm for the workman. He becomes an appendage of the machine, and it is only the most simple, most monotonous, and most easily acquired knack that is required of him. Hence, the cost of production of a workman is restricted, almost entirely, to the means of subsistence that he requires for his maintenance and for the propagation of his race. But the price of a commodity, and therefore also of labour, is equal to its cost of production. In proportion, therefore, as the repulsiveness of the work increases, the wage decreases. Nay more, in proportion as the use of machinery and division of labour increases, in the same proportion the burden of toil also increases, whether by prolongation of the working hours, by increase of the work exacted in a given time or by increased speed of the machinery, etc.

Modern industry has converted the little workshop of the patriarchal master into the great factory of the industrial capitalist. Masses of labourers, crowded into the factory, are organised like soldiers. As privates of the industrial army, they are placed under the command of a perfect hierarchy of officers and sergeants. Not only are they slaves of the bourgeois class and of the bourgeois State; they are daily and hourly enslaved by the machine, by the overlooker, and above all, by the individual bourgeois manufacturer himself. The more openly this despotism proclaims gain to be its end and aim, the more petty, the more hateful and the more embittering it is.

The less the skill and exertion of strength implied in manual labour, the more modern industry becomes developed, the more is the labour of men superseded by that of women. Differences of age and sex have no longer any distinctive social validity for the working class. All are instruments of labour, more or less expensive to use, according to their age and sex.

No sooner is the exploitation of the labourer by the manufacturer, so far, at an end, and he receives his wages in cash, than he is set upon by the other portions of the bourgeoisie, the landlord, the shopkeeper, the pawnbroker, etc.

The lower strata of the middle class—the small tradespeople, shopkeepers, and retired tradesmen generally, the handicraftsmen and peasants—all these sink gradually into the proletariat, partly because their diminutive capital does not suffice for the scale on which Modern Industry is carried on, and is swamped in the competition with the large capitalists, partly because their specialised skill is rendered worthless by new methods of production. Thus the proletariat is recruited from all classes of the population.

The proletariat goes through various stages of development. With its birth begins its struggle with the bourgeoisie. At first the contest is carried on by individual labourers, then by the workpeople of a factory, then by the operatives of one trade, in one locality, against the individual bourgeois who directly exploits them. They direct their attacks, not against the bourgeois conditions of production, but against the instruments of production themselves: they destroy imported wares that compete with their labour, they smash machinery to pieces, they set factories ablaze, they seek to restore by force the vanished status of the workman of the Middle Ages.

At this stage the labourers still form an incoherent mass scattered over the whole country, and broken up by their mutual competition. If anywhere they unite to form more compact bodies, this is not yet the consequence of their own active union but of the union of the bourgeoisie, the class, in order to attain its own political ends, that is compelled to set the whole proletariat in motion, and is moreover yet, for a time, able to do so. At this stage, therefore, the proletarians do not fight their enemies, but the enemies of their enemies, the remnants of absolute monarchy, the landowners, the non-industrial bourgeois, and the petty bourgeoisie. Thus the whole historical movement is concentrated in the hands of the bourgeoisie; every victory so obtained is a victory for the bourgeoisie.

But with the development of industry, the proletariat not only increases in number; it becomes concentrated in greater masses, its strength grows, and it feels that strength more. The various interests and conditions of life within the ranks of the proletariat are more and more equalised, in proportion as machinery obliterates all distinctions of labour, and nearly everywhere reduces wages to the same low level. The growing competition among the bourgeois, and the resulting commercial crises, make the wages of the workers ever more fluctuating. The unceasing improvement of machinery, ever more rapidly developing, makes their livelihood more and more precarious; the collisions between individual workmen and individual bourgeois take more and more the character of collisions between two classes. Thereupon the workers begin to form combinations (Trades' Unions) against the bourgeois; they club together in order to keep up the rate of wages; they found permanent associations in order to make provision beforehand for these occasional revolts. Here and there the contest breaks out into riots.

Now and then the workers are victorious, but only for a time. The real fruit of their battles lies, not in the immediate result, but in the ever-expanding union of the workers. This union is helped by the improved means of communication that are created by modern industry and that places the workers of different localities in contact with one another. This contact was needed to centralise the numerous local struggles, all of the same character, into one national struggle between classes. But every class struggle is a political struggle. And that union, to attain the burghers of the Middle Ages, with their miserable highways, required centuries, the modern proletarians, thanks to railways, achieve in a few years.

This organisation of the proletarians into a class, and consequently into a political party, is continually being upset again by the competition between the workers themselves. But it rises up again, stronger, firmer, mightier. It compels legislative recognition of particular interests of the workers by taking advantage of the divisions among the bourgeoisie itself. Thus the ten-hours' bill in England was carried.

Altogether collisions between the classes of the old society in many ways further the course of development of the proletariat. The bourgeoisie finds itself involved in a constant battle. At first with the aristocracy and, later on, with those portions of the bourgeoisie itself, whose interests have become antagonistic to the progress of industry; at all times with the bourgeoisie of foreign countries. In all these battles, it sees itself compelled to appeal to the proletariat, to ask for its help, and thus, to drag it into the political arena. The bourgeoisie itself, therefore, supplies the proletariat with its own elements of political and general education, and it furnishes the proletariat with weapons for fighting the bourgeoisie.

Further, as we have already seen, entire sections of the ruling classes are, by the advance of industry, precipitated into the proletariat, or are at least threatened in their conditions of existence. These also supply the proletariat with fresh elements of enlightenment and progress.

Finally, in times when the class struggle nears the decisive hour, the process of dissolution going on within the ruling class, and within the whole range of old society, assumes such a violent, glaring character, that a small section of the ruling class cuts itself adrift and joins the revolutionary class, the class that holds the future in its hands. Just as in an earlier period, a section of the nobility went over to the bourgeoisie; so now a portion of the bourgeoisie goes over to the proletariat, and in particular, a portion of the bourgeois ideologists, who have raised themselves to the level of comprehending theoretically the historical movement as a whole.

Of all the classes that stand face to face with the bourgeoisie today, the proletariat alone is a really revolutionary class. The other classes decay and finally disappear in the face of Modern Industry; the proletariat is its special and essential product.

The lower middle class, the small manufacturer, the shopkeeper, the artisan, the peasant: all these fight against the bourgeoisie, to save from extinction their existence as fractions of the middle class. They are therefore not revolutionary, but conservative. Nay more, they are reactionary, for they try to roll back the wheel of history. If by chance they are revolutionary, they are only so in view of their impending transfer into the proletariat; they defend not their present, but their future interests, and they desert their own standpoint to place themselves at that of the proletariat.

The "dangerous class," the social scum, that passively rotting mass thrown off by the lowest layers of old society, may, here and there, be swept into the movement by a proletarian revolution; its conditions of life, however, prepare it far more for the part of a bribed tool of reactionary intrigue.

In the conditions of the proletariat, those of old society at large are already virtually swamped. The proletarian is without property; his relation to his wife and children has no longer anything in common with the bourgeois family-relations; modern, industrial labour, modern subjection to capital, the same in England as in France, in America as in Germany, has stripped him of every trace of national character. Law, morality, and religion, are to him so many bourgeois prejudices, behind which lurk in ambush just as many bourgeois interests.

All the preceding classes that got the upper hand sought to fortify their already acquired status by subjecting society at large to their conditions of appropriation. The proletarians cannot become masters of the productive forces of society, except by abolishing their own previous mode of appropriation, and thereby also every other previous mode of appropriation. They have nothing of their own to secure and to fortify; their mission is to destroy all previous securities for, and insurances of, individual property.

All previous historical movements were movements of minorities, or in the interests of minorities. The proletarian movement is the self-conscious, independent movement of the immense majority, in the interests of the immense majority. The proletariat, the lowest stratum of our present society, cannot stir and cannot raise itself up without the whole superincumbent strata of official society being sprung into the air.

Though not in substance, yet in form, the struggle of the proletariat with the bourgeoisie is at first a national struggle. The proletariat of each country must, of course, first settle matters with its own bourgeoisie.

In depicting the most general phases of the development of the proletariat, we traced the more or less veiled civil war, raging within existing society, up to the point where that war breaks out into open revolution, and where the violent overthrow of the bourgeoisie lays the foundation for the sway of the proletariat.

Hitherto, every form of society has been based, as we have already seen, on the antagonism of oppressing and oppressed classes. But in order to oppress a class, certain conditions must be assured to it under which it can, at least, continue its slavish existence. The serf, in the period of serfdom, raised himself to membership in the commune, just as the petty bourgeois, under the yoke of feudal absolutism, managed to develop into a bourgeois. The modern labourer, on the contrary, instead of rising with the progress of industry, sinks deeper and deeper below the conditions of existence of his own class. He becomes a pauper, and pauperism develops more rapidly than population and wealth. And here it becomes evident, that the bourgeoisie is unfit any longer to be the ruling class in society and to impose its conditions of existence upon society as an overriding law. It is unfit to rule because it is incompetent to assure an existence to its slave within his slavery, because it cannot help letting him sink into such a state, that it has to feed him, instead of being fed by him. Society can no longer live under this bourgeoisie, in other words, its existence is no longer compatible with society.

The essential condition for the existence, and for the sway of the bourgeois class, is the formation and augmentation of capital; the condition for capital is wage-labour. Wage-labour rests exclusively on competition between the labourers. The advance of industry, whose involuntary promoter is the bourgeoisie, replaces the isolation of the labourers, due to competition, by their revolutionary combination, due to association. The development of Modern Industry, therefore, cuts from under its feet the very foundation on which the bourgeoisie produces and appropriates products. What the bourgeoisie, therefore, produces, above all, is its own grave-diggers. Its fall and the victory of the proletariat are equally inevitable.

NOTES

1. That is, all written history. In 1847, the prehistory of society, the social organisation existing previous to recorded history, was all but unknown. [Note by Engels to the English edition of 1888.]

2. Guild-master, that is, a full member of a guild, a master within, not a head of a guild. [Note by Engels to the English edition of 1888.]

3. "Commune" was the name taken, in France, by the nascent towns even before they had conquered from their feudal lords' and masters' local self-government and political rights as the "Third Estate." Generally speaking, for the economical development of the bourgeoisie, England is here taken as the typical country; for its political development, France. [Note by Engels to the English edition of 1888.]

This was the name given their urban communities by the townsmen of Italy and France after they had purchased or wrested their initial rights of self-government from their feudal lords. [Note by Engels to the German edition of 1890.]

The Communist Manifesto, pp. 108–119

The first attempts of workers to associate among themselves always take place in the form of combinations.

Large-scale industry concentrates in one place as a crowd of people unknown to one another. Competition divides their interests. But the maintenance of wages, this common interest with which they have against their boss, unites them in a common thought of resistance—combination. Thus combination always has a double aim; stopping competition among the workers so that they can carry on general competition with the capitalist. If the first aim of resistance was merely the maintenance of wages, combinations, at first isolated, constitute themselves into groups as the capitalists in their turn unite for the purpose of repression, and in face of always united capital, the maintenance of the association becomes more necessary to them than that of wages. This is so true that English economists are amazed to see the workers sacrifice a good part of their wages in favour of associations, which, in the eyes of these economists, are established solely in favour of wages. In this struggle—a veritable civil war—all the elements necessary for a coming battle unite and develop. Once it has reached this point, association takes on a political character.

Economic conditions had first transformed the mass of the people of the country into workers. The combination of capital has created a common situation for this mass: common interests. This mass is thus already a class as against capital, but not yet for itself. In the struggle, of which we have noted only a few phases, this mass becomes united, and constitutes itself as a class for itself. The interests it defends become class interests. But the struggle of class against class is a political struggle.

In the bourgeoisie we have two phases to distinguish: that in which it constituted itself as a class under the regime of feudalism and absolute monarchy, and that in which, already constituted as a class, it overthrew feudalism and monarchy to make society into a bourgeois society. The first of these phases was longer and necessitated the greater efforts. This, too, began by partial combinations against the feudal lords.

Much research has been carried out to trace the different historical phases that the bourgeoisie has passed through from the commune up to its constitution as a class.

But when it is a question of making a precise study of strikes, combinations and other forms in which the proletarians carry out their organization as a class, some are seized with real fear and others display a transcendental disdain.

An oppressed class is the vital condition for every society founded on the antagonism of classes. The emancipation of the oppressed class thus implies necessarily the creation of a new society. For the oppressed class to be able to emancipate itself, it is necessary that the productive powers already acquired and the existing social relations should no longer be capable of existing side by side. Of all the instruments of production, the greatest productive power is the revolutionary class itself. The organization of revolutionary elements as a class supposes the existence of all the productive forces which could be engendered in the bosom of the old society.

Does this mean that after the fall of the old society there will be a new class domination culminating in a new political power? No.

The condition for the emancipation of the working class is the abolition of every class, just as the condition for the liberation of the third estate, of the bourgeois order, was the abolition of all estates[1] and all orders.

The working class, in the course of its development, will substitute for the old civil society an association which will exclude classes and their antagonism, and there will be no more political power properly so-called, since political power is precisely the official expression of antagonism in civil society.

Meanwhile, the antagonism between the proletariat and the bourgeoisie is a struggle of class against class, a struggle which carried to its highest expression is a total revolution. Indeed, is it at all surprising that a society founded on the opposition of classes should culminate in brutal contradiction, the shock of body against body, as its final dénouement?

Do not say that social movement excludes political movement. There is never a political movement which is not at the same time social.

It is only in an order of things in which there are no more classes and class antagonisms that social evolutions will cease to be political revolutions. Till then, on the eve of every general reshuffling of society, the last word of social science will always be:

"Le combat ou la mort; la lutte sanguinaire ou le néant. C'est ainsi que la question est invinciblement posée."[2]

NOTES

1. Estates here in the historical sense of the estates of feudalism, estates with definite and limited privileges. The revolution of the bourgeoisie abolished the estates and their privileges. Bourgeois society knows only classes. It was, therefore, absolutely in contradiction with history to describe the proletariat as the "fourth estate." [Note by F. Engels to the German edition, 1885.]

2. "Combat or death; bloody struggle or extinction. It is thus that the question is inexorably put." George Sand, Jean Ziska.

The Poverty of Philosophy, pp. 172–175

The small-holding peasants form a vast mass, the members of which live in similar conditions but without entering into manifold relations with one another. Their mode of production isolates them from one another instead of bringing them into mutual intercourse. The isolation is increased by France's bad means of communication and by the poverty of the peasants. Their field of production, the small holding, admits of no division of labour in its cultivation, no application of science, and therefore, no diversity of development, no variety of talent, and no wealth of social relationships. Each individual peasant family is almost self-sufficient; it itself directly produces the major part of its consumption and thus acquires its means of life more through exchange with nature than in intercourse with society. A small holding, a peasant and his family; alongside them another small holding, another peasant and another family. A few score of these make up a village, and a few score of villages make up a Department. In this way, the great mass of the French nation is formed by simple addition of homologous magnitudes, much as potatoes in a sack form a sack of potatoes. In so far as millions of families live under economic conditions of existence that separate their mode of life, their interests and their culture from those of the other classes, and put them in hostile opposition to the latter, they form a class. In so far as there is merely a local interconnection among these small-holding peasants, and the identity of their interests begets no community, no national bond, and no political organisation among them, they do not form a class. They are consequently incapable of enforcing their class interests in their own name, whether through a parliament or through a convention. They cannot represent themselves; they must be represented. Their representative must at the same time appear as their master, as an authority over them, as an unlimited governmental power that protects them against the other classes and sends them rain and sunshine from above. The political influence of the small-holding peasants, therefore, finds its final expression in the executive power subordinating society to itself.

The Eighteenth Brumaire of
Louis Bonaparte, pp. 478–479

The owners merely of labour-power, owners of capital, and landowners, whose respective sources of income are wages, profit and ground-rent, in other words, wage-labourers, capitalists and landowners, constitute then three big classes of modern society based upon the capitalist mode of production.

In England, modern society is indisputably most highly and classically developed in economic structure. Nevertheless, even here the stratification of classes does not appear in its pure form. Middle and intermediate strata obliterate lines of demarcation everywhere (although incomparably less in rural districts than in the cities). However, this is immaterial for our analysis. We have seen that the continual tendency and law of development of the capitalist mode of production is more to divorce the means of production from labour, and more to concentrate the scattered means of production into large groups, thereby transforming labour into wage-labour and the means of production into capital. And to this tendency, on the other hand, corresponds the independent separation of landed property from capital and labour, or the transformation of all landed property into the form of landed property corresponding to the capitalist mode of production.

The first question to be answered is this: What constitutes a class?—and the reply to this follows naturally from the reply to another question, namely: What makes wage-labourers, capitalists and landlords constitute the three great social classes?

At first glance—the identity of revenues and sources of revenue. There are three great social groups whose members, the individuals forming them, live on wages, profit and ground-rent respectively, on the realisation of their labour-power, their capital, and their landed property.

However, from this standpoint, physicians and officials, e.g., would also constitute two classes, for they belong to two distinct social groups, the members of each of these groups receiving their revenue from one and the same source. The same would also be true of the infinite fragmentation of interest and rank into which the division of social labour splits labourers as well as capitalists and landlords—the latter, e.g., into owners of vineyards, farm owners, owners of forests, mine owners and owners of fisheries.

Capital, Vol. III, pp. 885–886

---

3. Max Weber*
Class, Status, Party

Economically Determined Power and the Social Order

Law exists when there is a probability that an order will be upheld by a specific staff of men who will use physical or psychical compulsion with the intention of obtaining conformity with the order, or of inflicting sanctions for infringement of it.[1] The structure of every legal order directly influences the distribution of power, economic or otherwise, within its respective community. This is true of all legal orders and not only that of the state. In general, we understand by 'power' the chance of a man or of a number of men to realize their own will in a communal action even against the resistance of others who are participating in the action.

'Economically conditioned' power is not, of course, identical with 'power' as such. On the contrary, the emergence of economic power may be the consequence of power existing on other grounds. Man does not strive for power only in order to

*FROM MAX WEBER: ESSAYS IN SOCIOLOGY translated by Gerth & Wright Mills (1946): 6,664 words from pp. 180-195. © 1946, 1958, 1973 by H. H. Gerth and C. Wright Mills. By permission of Oxford University Press USA.

enrich himself economically. Power, including economic power, may be valued 'for its own sake.' Very frequently, the striving for power is also conditioned by the social 'honor' it entails. Not all power, however, entails social honor: The typical American Boss, as well as the typical big speculator, deliberately relinquishes social honor. Quite generally, 'mere economic' power, and especially 'naked' money power, is by no means a recognized basis of social honor, nor is power the only basis of social honor. Indeed, social honor, or prestige, may even be the basis of political or economic power, and very frequently has been. Power, as well as honor, may be guaranteed by the legal order, but, at least normally, it is not their primary source. The legal order is rather an additional factor that enhances the chance to hold power or honor; but it cannot always secure them.

The way in which social honor is distributed in a community between typical groups participating in this distribution we may call the 'social order.' The social order and the economic order are, of course, similarly related to the 'legal order.' However, the social and the economic order are not identical. The economic order is for us merely the way in which economic goods and services are distributed and used. The social order is, of course, conditioned by the economic order to a high degree, and in its turn reacts upon it.

Now: 'classes,' 'status groups,' and 'parties' are phenomena of the distribution of power within a community.

Determination of Class-Situation by Market-Situation

In our terminology, 'classes' are not communities; they merely represent possible, and frequent, bases for communal action. We may speak of a 'class' when (1) a number of people have in common a specific causal component of their life chances, in so far as (2) this component is represented exclusively by economic interests in the possession of goods and opportunities for income, and (3) is represented under the conditions of the commodity or labor markets. [These points refer to 'class situation,' which we may express more briefly as the typical chance for a supply of goods, external living conditions, and personal life experiences, in so far as this chance is determined by the amount and kind of power, or lack of such, to dispose of goods or skills for the sake of income in a given economic order. The term 'class' refers to any group of people that is found in the same class situation.]

It is the most elemental economic fact that the way in which the disposition over material property is distributed among a plurality of people, meeting competitively in the market for the purpose of exchange, in itself creates specific life chances. According to the law of marginal utility, this mode of distribution excludes the non-owners from competing for highly valued goods; it favors the owners, and in fact, gives to them a monopoly to acquire such goods. Other things being equal, this mode of distribution monopolizes the opportunities for profitable deals for all those who, provided with goods, do not necessarily have to exchange them. It increases, at least generally, their power in price wars with those who, being propertyless, have nothing to offer but their services in native form or goods in a form constituted through their own labor, and who above all are compelled to get rid of these products in order barely to subsist. This mode of distribution gives to the propertied a monopoly on the possibility of transferring property from the sphere of use as a 'fortune,' to the sphere of 'capital goods'; that is, it gives them the entrepreneurial function and all chances to share directly or indirectly in returns on capital. All this holds true within the area in which pure market conditions prevail. 'Property' and 'lack of property' are, therefore, the basic categories of all class situations. It does not matter whether these two categories become effective in price wars or in competitive struggles.

Within these categories, however, class situations are further differentiated: on the one hand, according to the kind of property that is usable for returns; and, on the other hand, according to the kind of services that can be offered in the market. Ownership of domestic buildings; productive establishments; warehouses; stores; agriculturally usable land, large and small holdings—quantitative differences with possibly qualitative consequences; ownership of mines; cattle; men (slaves); disposition over mobile instruments of production, or capital goods of all sorts, especially money or objects that can be exchanged for money easily and at any time; disposition over products of one's own labor or of others' labor differing according to their various distances from consumability; disposition over transferable monopolies of any kind—all these distinctions differentiate the class situations of the propertied just as does the 'meaning' which they can and do give to the utilization of property, especially to property which has money equivalence. Accordingly, the propertied, for instance, may belong to the class of rentiers or to the class of entrepreneurs.

Those who have no property but who offer services are differentiated just as much according to their kinds of services as according to the way in which they make use of these services, in a continuous or discontinuous relation to a recipient. But always this is the generic connotation of the concept of class: that the kind of chance in the *market* is the decisive moment which presents a common condition for the individual's fate. 'Class situation' is, in this sense, ultimately 'market situation.' The effect of naked possession *per se*, which among cattle breeders gives the non-owning slave or serf into the power of the cattle owner, is only a forerunner of real 'class' formation. However, in the cattle loan and in the naked severity of the law of debts in such communities, for the first time mere 'possession' as such emerges as decisive for the fate of the individual. This is very much in contrast to the agricultural communities based on labor. The creditor-debtor relation becomes the basis of 'class situations' only in those cities where a 'credit market,' however primitive, with rates of interest increasing according to the extent of dearth and a factual monopolization of credits, is developed by a plutocracy. Therewith 'class struggles' begin.

Those men whose fate is not determined by the chance of using goods or services for themselves on the market, e.g. slaves, are not, however, a 'class' in the technical sense of the term. They are, rather, a 'status group.'

Communal Action Flowing from Class Interest

According to our terminology, the factor that creates 'class' is unambiguously economic interest, and indeed, only those interests involved in the existence of the 'market.' Nevertheless, the concept of 'class-interest' is an ambiguous one: even as an empirical concept, it is ambiguous as soon as one understands it as something other than the factual direction of interests following with a certain probability from the class situation for a certain 'average' of those people subjected to the class situation. The class situation and other circumstances remaining the same, the direction in which the individual worker, for instance, is likely to pursue his interests may vary widely, according to whether he is constitutionally qualified for the task at hand to a high, to an average, or to a low degree. In the same way, the direction of interests may vary according to whether or not a *communal* action of a larger or smaller portion of those commonly affected by the 'class situation,' or even an association among them, e.g. a 'trade union,' has grown out of the class situation from which the individual may or may not expect promising results. [Communal action refers to that action which is oriented to the feeling of the actors that they belong together. Societal action, on the other hand, is oriented to a rationally motivated adjustment of interests.] The rise of societal or even of communal action from a common class situation is by no means a universal phenomenon.

The class situation may be restricted in its effects to the generation of essentially *similar* reactions, that is to say, within our terminology, of 'mass actions.' However, it may not have even this result. Furthermore, often merely an amorphous communal action emerges. For example, consider the 'murmuring' of the workers known in ancient oriental ethics: the moral disapproval of the work-master's conduct, which in its practical significance was probably equivalent to an increasingly typical phenomenon of precisely the latest industrial development, namely, the 'slow down' (the deliberate limiting of work effort) of laborers by virtue of tacit agreement. The degree in which 'communal action' and possibly 'societal action,' emerges from the 'mass actions' of the members of a class is linked to general cultural conditions, especially to those of an intellectual sort. It is also linked to the extent of the contrasts that have already evolved, and is especially linked to the *transparency* of the connections between the causes and the consequences of the 'class situation.' For however different life chances may be, this fact in itself, according to all experience, by no means gives birth to 'class action' (communal action by the members of a class). The fact of being conditioned and the results of the class situation must be distinctly recognizable. For only then the contrast of life chances can be felt not as an absolutely given fact to be accepted, but as a resultant from either (1) the given distribution of property, or (2) the structure of the concrete economic order. It is only then that people may react against the class structure not only through acts of an intermittent and irrational protest, but in the form of rational association. There have been 'class situations' of the first category (1), of a specifically naked and transparent sort, in the urban centers of Antiquity and during the Middle Ages; especially then, when great fortunes were accumulated by factually monopolized trading in industrial products of these localities or in foodstuffs, and furthermore, under certain circumstances, in the rural economy of the most diverse periods, when agriculture was increasingly exploited in a profit-making manner. The most important historical example of the second category (2) is the class situation of the modern 'proletariat.'

Types of 'Class Struggle'

Thus every class may be the carrier of any one of the possibly innumerable forms of 'class action,' but this is not necessarily so: In any case, a class does not in itself constitute a community. To treat 'class' conceptually as having the same value as 'community' leads to distortion. That men in the same class situation regularly react in mass actions to such tangible situations as economic ones in the direction of those interests that are most adequate to their average number is an important and after all simple fact for the understanding of historical events. Above all, this fact must not lead to that kind of pseudo-scientific operation with the concepts of 'class' and 'class interests' so frequently found these days, and which has found its most classic expression in the statement of a talented author, that the individual may be in error concerning his interests, but that the 'class' is 'infallible' about its interests. Yet, if classes as such are not communities, nevertheless class situations emerge only on the basis of communalization. The communal action that brings forth class situations, however, is not basically action between members of the identical class; it is an action between members of different classes. Communal actions that directly determine the class situation of the worker and the entrepreneur are: the labor market, the commodities market, and the capitalistic enterprise. But, in its turn, the existence of a capitalistic enterprise presupposes that a very specific communal action exists and that it is specifically structured to protect the possession of goods *per se*, and especially the power of individuals to dispose, in principle freely, over the means of production. The existence of a capitalistic enterprise is preconditioned by a specific kind of 'legal order.' Each kind of class situation, and above all when it rests upon the power of property *per se*, will become most clearly efficacious when all other determinants of reciprocal relations are, as far as possible, eliminated in their significance. It is in this way that the utilization of the power of property in the market obtains its most sovereign importance.

Now 'status groups' hinder the strict carrying through of the sheer market principle. In the present context they are of interest to us only from this one

point of view. Before we briefly consider them, note that not much of a general nature can be said about the more specific kinds of antagonism between 'classes' (in our meaning of the term). The great shift, which has been going on continuously in the past, and up to our times, may be summarized, although at the cost of some precision: the struggle in which class situations are effective has progressively shifted from consumption credit toward, first, competitive struggles in the commodity market, and then, toward price wars on the labor market. The 'class struggles' of antiquity—to the extent that they were genuine class struggles and not struggles between status groups—were initially carried on by indebted peasants, and perhaps also by artisans threatened by debt bondage and struggling against urban creditors. For debt bondage is the normal result of the differentiation of wealth in commercial cities, especially in seaport cities. A similar situation has existed among cattle breeders. Debt relationships as such produced class action up to the time of Cataline. Along with this, and with an increase in provision of grain for the city by transporting it from the outside, the struggle over the means of sustenance emerged. It centered in the first place around the provision of bread and the determination of the price of bread. It lasted throughout antiquity and the entire Middle Ages. The propertyless as such flocked together against those who actually and supposedly were interested in the dearth of bread. This fight spread until it involved all those commodities essential to the way of life and to handicraft production. There were only incipient discussions of wage disputes in antiquity and in the Middle Ages. But they have been slowly increasing up into modern times. In the earlier periods they were completely secondary to slave rebellions as well as to fights in the commodity market.

The propertyless of antiquity and of the Middle Ages protested against monopolies, pre-emption, forestalling, and the withholding of goods from the market in order to raise prices. Today the central issue is the determination of the price of labor.

This transition is represented by the fight for access to the market and for the determination of the price of products. Such fights went on between merchants and workers in the putting-out system of domestic handicraft during the transition to modern times. Since it is quite a general phenomenon, we must mention here that the class antagonisms that are conditioned through the market situation are usually most bitter between those who actually and directly participate as opponents in price wars. It is not the rentier, the share-holder, and the banker who suffer the ill will of the worker, but almost exclusively the manufacturer and the business executives who are the direct opponents of workers in price wars. This is so in spite of the fact that it is precisely the cash boxes of the rentier, the share-holder, and the banker into which the more or less 'unearned' gains flow, rather than into the pockets of the manufacturers or of the business executives. This simple state of affairs has very frequently been decisive for the role the class situation has played in the formation of political parties. For example, it has made possible the varieties of patriarchal socialism and the frequent attempts—formerly, at least—of threatened status groups to form alliances with the proletariat against the 'bourgeoisie.'

Status Honor

In contrast to classes, *status groups* are normally communities. They are, however, often of an amorphous kind. In contrast to the purely economically determined 'class situation' we wish to designate as 'status situation' every typical component of the life fate of men that is determined by a specific, positive or negative, social estimation of *honor*. This honor may be connected with any quality shared by a plurality, and, of course, it can be knit to a class situation: class distinctions are linked in the most varied ways with status distinctions. Property as such is not always recognized as a status qualification, but in the long run it is, and with extraordinary regularity. In the subsistence economy of the organized neighborhood, very often the richest man is simply the chieftain. However, this often means only an honorific preference. For example, in the so-called pure modern 'democracy,' that is, one devoid of any expressly ordered status privileges for individuals, it may be that only the families coming under approximately the same tax class dance with one another. This example is reported of certain smaller Swiss cities. But status honor need not necessarily be linked with a 'class situation.' On the contrary, it normally stands in sharp opposition to the pretensions of sheer property.

Both propertied and propertyless people can belong to the same status group, and frequently they do with very tangible consequences. This 'equality' of social esteem may, however, in the long run become quite precarious. The 'equality' of status among the American 'gentlemen,' for instance, is expressed by the fact that outside the subordination determined by the different functions of 'business,' it would be considered strictly repugnant—wherever the old tradition still prevails—if even the richest 'chief,' while playing billiards or cards in his club in the evening, would not treat his 'clerk' as in every sense fully his equal in birthright. It would be repugnant if the American 'chief' would bestow upon his 'clerk' the condescending 'benevolence' marking a distinction of 'position,' which the German chief can never dissever from his attitude. This is one of the most important reasons why in America the German 'clubby-ness' has never been able to attain the attraction that the American clubs have.

Guarantees of Status Stratification

In content, status honor is normally expressed by the fact that above all else a specific *style of life* can be expected from all those who wish to belong to the circle. Linked with this expectation are restrictions on 'social' intercourse (that is, intercourse which is not subservient to economic or any other of business's 'functional' purposes). These restrictions may confine normal marriages to within the status circle and may lead to complete endogamous closure. As soon as there is not a mere individual and socially irrelevant imitation of another style of life, but an agreed-upon communal action of this closing character, the 'status' development is under way.

In its characteristic form, stratification by 'status groups' on the basis of conventional styles of life evolves at the present time in the United States out of the traditional democracy. For example, only the resident of a certain street ('the street') is considered as belonging to 'society,' is qualified for social intercourse, and is visited and invited. Above all, this differentiation evolves in such a way as to make for strict submission to the fashion that is dominant at a given time in society. This submission to fashion also exists among men in America to a degree unknown in Germany. Such submission is considered to be an indication of the fact that a given man *pretends* to qualify as a gentleman. This submission decides, at least *prima facie,* that he will be treated as such. And this recognition becomes just as important for his employment chances in 'swank' establishments, and above all, for social intercourse and marriage with 'esteemed' families, as the qualification for dueling among Germans in the Kaiser's day. As for the rest: certain families resident for a long time, and of course, correspondingly wealthy, e.g. 'F. F. V., i.e.

First Families of Virginia,' or the actual or alleged descendants of the 'Indian Princess' Pocahontas, of the Pilgrim fathers, or of the Knickerbockers, the members of almost inaccessible sects and all sorts of circles setting themselves apart by means of any other characteristics and badges . . . all these elements usurp 'status' honor. The development of status is essentially a question of stratification resting upon usurpation. Such usurpation is the normal origin of almost all status honor. But the road from this purely conventional situation to legal privilege, positive or negative, is easily traveled as soon as a certain stratification of the social order has in fact been 'lived in' and has achieved stability by virtue of a stable distribution of economic power.

'Ethnic' Segregation and 'Caste'

Where the consequences have been realized to their full extent, the status group evolves into a closed 'caste.' Status distinctions are then guaranteed not merely by conventions and laws, but also by *rituals.* This occurs in such a way that every physical contact with a member of any caste that is considered to be 'lower' by the members of a 'higher' caste is considered as making for a ritualistic impurity and to be a stigma which must be expiated by a religious act. Individual castes develop quite distinct cults and gods.

In general, however, the status structure reaches such extreme consequences only where there are underlying differences which are held to be 'ethnic.' The 'caste' is, indeed, the normal form in which ethnic communities usually live side-by-side in a 'societalized' manner. These ethnic communities believe in blood relationship and exclude exogamous marriage and social intercourse. Such a caste situation is part of the phenomenon of 'pariah' peoples and is found all over the world. These people form communities, acquire specific occupational traditions of handicrafts or of other arts, and cultivate a belief in their ethnic community. They live in a 'diaspora,' strictly segregated from all personal intercourse, except that of an unavoidable sort, and their situation is legally precarious. Yet, by virtue of their economic indispensability, they are tolerated, indeed, frequently privileged, and they live in interspersed political communities. The Jews are the most impressive historical example.

A 'status' segregation grown into a 'caste' differs in its structure from a mere 'ethnic' segregation: the caste structure transforms the horizontal and unconnected coexistences of ethnically segregated groups into a vertical social system of super- and subordination. Correctly formulated: a comprehensive societalization integrates the ethnically divided communities into specific political and communal action. In their consequences they differ precisely in this way: ethnic coexistences condition a mutual repulsion and disdain but allow each ethnic community to consider its own honor as the highest one; the caste structure brings about a social subordination and an acknowledgment of 'more honor' in favor of the privileged caste and status groups. This is due to the fact that in the caste structure ethnic distinctions as such have become 'functional' distinctions within the political societalization (warriors, priests, artisans that are politically important for war and for building, and so on). But even pariah people who are most despised are usually apt to continue cultivating in some manner that which is equally peculiar to ethnic and to status communities: the belief in their own specific 'honor.' This is the case with the Jews.

Only with the negatively privileged status groups does the 'sense of dignity' take a specific deviation. A sense of dignity is the precipitation in individuals of social honor and of conventional demands which a positively privileged status group raises for the deportment of its members. The sense of dignity that characterizes positively privileged status groups is naturally related to their 'being' which does not transcend itself, that is, it is to their 'beauty and excellence.' Their kingdom is 'of this world.' They live for the present and by exploiting their great past. The sense of dignity of the negatively privileged strata naturally refers to a future lying beyond the present, whether it is of this life or of another. In other words, it must be nurtured by the belief in a providential 'mission' and by a belief in a specific honor before God. The 'chosen people's' dignity is nurtured by a belief either that in the beyond 'the last will be the first,' or that in this life a Messiah will appear to bring forth into the light of the world which has cast them out the hidden honor of the pariah people. This simple state of affairs, and not the 'resentment' which is so strongly emphasized in Nietzsche's much-admired construction in the *Genealogy of Morals,* is the source of the religiosity cultivated by pariah status groups. In passing, we may note that resentment may be accurately applied only to a limited extent; for one of Nietzsche's main examples, Buddhism, it is not at all applicable.

Incidentally, the development of status groups from ethnic segregations is by no means the normal phenomenon. On the contrary, since objective 'racial differences' are by no means basic to every subjective sentiment of an ethnic community, the ultimately racial foundation of status structure is rightly and absolutely a question of the concrete individual case. Very frequently a status group is instrumental in the production of a thoroughbred anthropological type. Certainly a status group is to a high degree effective in producing extreme types, for they select personally qualified individuals (e.g. the Knighthood selects those who are fit for warfare, physically and psychically). But selection is far from being the only, or the predominant, way in which status groups are formed: Political membership or class situation has at all times been at least as frequently decisive. And today the class situation is by far the predominant factor, for of course the possibility of a style of life expected for members of a status group is usually conditioned economically.

Status Privileges

For all practical purposes, stratification by status goes hand-in-hand with a monopolization of ideal and material goods or opportunities, in a manner we have come to know as typical. Besides the specific status honor, which always rests upon distance and exclusiveness, we find all sorts of material monopolies. Such honorific preferences may consist of the privilege of wearing special costumes, of eating special dishes taboo to others, of carrying arms—which is most obvious in its consequences—the right to pursue certain non-professional dilettante artistic practices, e.g. to play certain musical instruments. Of course, material monopolies provide the most effective motives for the exclusiveness of a status group; although, in themselves, they are rarely sufficient, and almost always they come into play to some extent. Within a status circle there is the question of intermarriage: the interest of the families in the monopolization of potential bridegrooms is at least of equal importance and is parallel to the interest in the monopolization of daughters. The daughters of the circle must be provided for. With an increased inclosure of the status group, the conventional preferential opportunities for special employment grow into a legal monopoly of special offices for the members. Certain goods become objects for monopolization by status groups. In the typical fashion these include 'entailed estates' and frequently also the possessions of serfs or bondsmen, and finally, special trades. This monopolization occurs positively when the status group is exclusively

entitled to own and to manage them; and negatively when, in order to maintain its specific way of life, the status group must *not* own and manage them.

The decisive role of a 'style of life' in status 'honor' means that status groups are the specific bearers of all 'conventions.' In whatever way it may be manifest, all 'stylization' of life either originates in status groups or is at least conserved by them. Even if the principles of status conventions differ greatly, they reveal certain typical traits, especially among those strata which are most privileged. Quite generally, among privileged status groups there is a status disqualification that operates against the performance of common physical labor. This disqualification is now 'setting in' in America against the old tradition of esteem for labor. Very frequently every rational economic pursuit, and especially 'entrepreneurial activity,' is looked upon as a disqualification of status. Artistic and literary activity is also considered as degrading work as soon as it is exploited for income, or at least when it is connected with hard physical exertion. An example is the sculptor working like a mason in his dusty smock as over against the painter in his salon-like 'studio' and those forms of musical practice that are acceptable to the status group.

Economic Conditions and Effects of Status Stratification

The frequent disqualification of the gainfully employed as such is a direct result of the principle of status stratification peculiar to the social order, and of course, of this principle's opposition to a distribution of power which is regulated exclusively through the market. These two factors operate along with various individual ones, which will be touched upon below.

We have seen above that the market and its processes 'knows no personal distinctions': 'functional' interests dominate it. It knows nothing of 'honor.' The status order means precisely the reverse, viz.: stratification in terms of 'honor' and of styles of life peculiar to status groups as such. If mere economic acquisition and naked economic power still bearing the stigma of its extra-status origin could bestow upon anyone who has won it the same honor as those who are interested in status by virtue of style of life claim for themselves, the status order would be threatened at its very root. This is the more so as, given equality of status honor, property *per se* represents an addition even if it is not overtly acknowledged to be such. Yet if such economic acquisition and power gave the agent any honor at all, his wealth would result in his attaining more honor than those who successfully claim honor by virtue of style of life. Therefore all groups having interests in the status order react with special sharpness precisely against the pretensions of purely economic acquisition. In most cases they react the more vigorously the more they feel themselves threatened. Calderon's respectful treatment of the peasant, for instance, as opposed to Shakespeare's simultaneous and ostensible disdain of the *canaille* illustrates the different way in which a firmly structured status order reacts as compared with a status order that has become economically precarious. This is an example of a state of affairs that recurs everywhere. Precisely because of the rigorous reactions against the claims of property *per se,* the 'parvenu' is never accepted, personally and without reservation, by the privileged status groups, no matter how completely his style of life has been adjusted to theirs. They will only accept his descendants who have been educated in the conventions of their status group and who have never besmirched its honor by their own economic labor.

As to the general *effect* of the status order, only one consequence can be stated, but it is a very important one: the hindrance of the free development of the market occurs first for those goods which status groups directly withheld from free exchange by monopolization, which may be effected either legally or conventionally. For example, in many Hellenic cities during the epoch of status groups, and also originally in Rome, the inherited estate (as is shown by the old formula for indication against spendthrifts) was monopolized just as were the estates of knights, peasants, priests, and especially the clientele of the craft and merchant guilds. The market is restricted, and the power of naked property *per se,* which gives its stamp to 'class formation,' is pushed into the background. The results of this process can be most varied. Of course, they do not necessarily weaken the contrasts in the economic situation. Frequently they strengthen these contrasts, and in any case, where stratification by status permeates a community as strongly as was the case in all political communities of antiquity and of the Middle Ages, one can never speak of a genuinely free market competition as we understand it today. There are wider effects than this direct exclusion of special goods from the market. From the contrariety between the status order and the purely economic order mentioned above, it

follows that in most instances the notion of honor peculiar to status absolutely abhors that which is essential to the market: higgling. Honor abhors higgling among peers and occasionally it taboos higgling for the members of a status group in general. Therefore, everywhere some status groups, and usually the most influential, consider almost any kind of overt participation in economic acquisition as absolutely stigmatizing.

With some over-simplification, one might thus say that 'classes' are stratified according to their relations to the production and acquisition of goods, whereas 'status groups' are stratified according to the principles of their *consumption* of goods as represented by special 'styles of life.'

An 'occupational group' is also a status group. For normally, it successfully claims social honor only by virtue of the special style of life which may be determined by it. The differences between classes and status groups frequently overlap. It is precisely those status communities most strictly segregated in terms of honor (viz. the Indian castes) who today show, though within very rigid limits, a relatively high degree of indifference to pecuniary income. However, the Brahmins seek such income in many different ways.

As to the general economic conditions making for the predominance of stratification by 'status,' only very little can be said. When the bases of the acquisition and distribution of goods are relatively stable, stratification by status is favored. Every technological repercussion and economic transformation threatens stratification by status and pushes the class situation into the foreground. Epochs and countries in which the naked class situation is of predominant significance are regularly the periods of technical and economic transformations. And every slowing down of the shifting of economic stratifications leads, in due course, to the growth of status structures and makes for a resuscitation of the important role of social honor.

Parties

Whereas the genuine place of 'classes' is within the economic order, the place of 'status groups' is within the social order, that is, within the sphere of the distribution of 'honor.' From within these spheres, classes and status groups influence one another and they influence the legal order and are in turn influenced by it. But 'parties' live in a house of 'power.'

Their action is oriented toward the acquisition of social 'power,' that is to say, toward influencing a communal action no matter what its content may be. In principle, parties may exist in a social 'club' as well as in a 'state.' As over against the actions of classes and status groups, for which this is not necessarily the case, the communal actions of 'parties' always mean a societalization, for party actions are always directed toward a goal which is striven for in planned manner. This goal may be a 'cause' (the party may aim at realizing a program for ideal or material purposes), or the goal may be 'personal' (sinecures, power, and from these, honor for the leader and the followers of the party). Usually the party action aims at all these simultaneously. Parties are, therefore, only possible within communities that are societalized, that is, which have some rational order and a staff of persons available who are ready to enforce it, for parties aim precisely at influencing this staff, and if possible, to recruit it from party followers.

In any individual case, parties may represent interests determined through 'class situation' or 'status situation,' and they may recruit their following respectively from one or the other. But they need be neither purely 'class' nor purely 'status' parties. In most cases they are partly class parties and partly status parties, but sometimes they are neither. They may represent ephemeral or enduring structures. Their means of attaining power may be quite varied, ranging from naked violence of any sort to canvassing for votes with coarse or subtle means: money, social influence, the force of speech, suggestion, clumsy hoax, and so on to the rougher or more artful tactics of obstruction in parliamentary bodies.

The sociological structure of parties differs in a basic way according to the kind of communal action which they struggle to influence. Parties also differ according to whether or not the community is stratified by status or by classes. Above all else, they vary according to the structure of domination within the community. For their leaders normally deal with the conquest of a community. They are, in the general concept which is maintained here, not only products of specially modern forms of domination. We shall also designate as parties the ancient and medieval 'parties,' despite the fact that their structure differs basically from the structure of modern parties. By virtue of these structural differences of domination it is impossible to say anything about the structure of parties without discussing the structural forms of social domination *per se*. Parties, which are

always structures struggling for domination, are very frequently organized in a very strict 'authoritarian' fashion. ...

Concerning 'classes,' 'status groups,' and 'parties,' it must be said in general that they necessarily presuppose a comprehensive societalization, and especially a political framework of communal action, within which they operate. This does not mean that parties would be confined by the frontiers of any individual political community. On the contrary, at all times it has been the order of the day that the societalization (even when it aims at the use of military force in common) reaches beyond the frontiers of politics. This has been the case in the solidarity of interests among the Oligarchs and among the democrats in Hellas, among the Guelfs and among the Ghibellines in the Middle Ages, and within the Calvinist party during the period of religious struggles. It has been the case up to the solidarity of the landlords (international congress of agrarian landlords), and has continued among princes (holy alliance, Karlsbad decrees), socialist workers, conservatives (the longing of Prussian conservatives for Russian intervention in 1850). But their aim is not necessarily the establishment of new international political, i.e. *territorial*, dominion. In the main they aim to influence the existing dominion.[2]

NOTES

1. *Wirtschaft und Gesellschaft*, part III, chap. 4, pp. 631–40. The first sentence in paragraph one and the several definitions in this chapter which are in brackets do not appear in the original text. They have been taken from other contexts of *Wirtschaft und Gesellschaft*.

2. The posthumously published text breaks off here. We omit an incomplete sketch of types of 'warrior estates.'

4. W.E.B Du Bois*
The Conservation of Races

The American Negro has always felt an intense personal interest in discussions as to the origins and

*W. E. Burghardt Du Bois. 1897. *The Conservation of Races*. *The American Negro Academy Occasional Papers*, No.2. Washington, D.C.: Published by the Academy. Accessed online at: http://www.gutenberg.org/files/31254/31254-h/31254-h.htm; W. E. Burghardt Du Bois. 1903. *The Souls of Black Folk*. Published by Tribeca Books.

destinies of races: primarily because back of most discussions of race with which he is familiar, have lurked certain assumptions as to his natural abilities, as to his political, intellectual and moral status, which he felt were wrong. He has, consequently, been led to deprecate and minimize race distinctions, to believe intensely that out of one blood God created all nations, and to speak of human brotherhood as though it were the possibility of an already dawning tomorrow.

Nevertheless, in our calmer moments we must acknowledge that human beings are divided into races; that in this country the two most extreme types of the world's races have met, and the resulting problem as to the future relations of these types is not only of intense and living interest to us, but forms an epoch in the history of mankind.

It is necessary, therefore, in planning our movements, in guiding our future development, that at times we rise above the pressing, but smaller questions of separate schools and cars, wage-discrimination and lynch law, to survey the whole questions of race in human philosophy and to lay, on a basis of broad knowledge and careful insight, those large lines of policy and higher ideals which may form our guiding lines and boundaries in the practical difficulties of every day. . . . The question, then, which we must seriously consider is this: What is the real meaning of Race; what has, in the past, been the law of race development, and what lessons has the past history of race development to teach the rising Negro people?

When we thus come to inquire into the essential difference of races, we find it hard to come at once to any definite conclusion. Many criteria of race differences have in the past been proposed, such as color, hair, cranial measurements, and language. And manifestly, in each of these respects, human beings differ widely. . . . Unfortunately for scientists, however, these criteria of race are most exasperatingly intermingled. Color does not agree with texture of hair, for many of the dark races have straight hair; nor does color agree with the breadth of the head, for the yellow Tartar has a broader head than the German; nor, again, has the science of language as yet succeeded in clearing up the relative authority of these various and contradictory criteria. . . .

Although the wonderful developments of human history teach that the grosser physical differences of color, hair, and bone go but a short way toward explaining the different roles which groups of men have played in Human Progress, yet there are differ-ences—subtle, delicate, and elusive though they may be—which have silently but definitely separated men into groups. . . . What, then, is a race? It is a vast family of human beings, generally of common blood and language, always of common history, traditions, and impulses, who are both voluntarily and involuntarily striving together for the accomplishment of certain more or less vividly conceived ideals of life.

Turning to real history, there can be no doubt, first, as to the widespread, nay, universal, prevalence of the race idea, the race spirit, the race ideal, and as to its efficiency as the vastest and most ingenious invention of human progress. We, who have been reared and trained under the individualistic philosophy of the Declaration of Independence and the laissez-faire philosophy of Adam Smith, are loath to see and loath to acknowledge this patent fact of human history. We see the Pharaohs, Caesars, Toussaints, and Napoleons of history and forget the vast races of which they were but epitomized expressions. We are apt to think in our American impatience, that while it may have been true in the past that closed race groups made history, that here in conglomerate America, *nous avons changer tout cela*—we have changed all that and have no need of this ancient instrument of progress. . . .

The question now is: What is the real distinction between these nations? Is it the physical differences of blood, color, and cranial measurements? Certainly we must all acknowledge that physical differences play a great part. . . . But while race differences have followed mainly physical race lines, yet no mere physical distinctions would really define or explain the deeper differences—the cohesiveness and continuity of these groups. The deeper differences are spiritual and psychical differences—undoubtedly based on the physical, but infinitely transcending them. The forces that bind together the Teuton nations are, then, first, their race identity and common blood, and secondly, and more important, a common history, common laws and religion, similar habits of thought, and a conscious striving together for certain ideals of life. . . .

The English nation stood for constitutional liberty and commercial freedom; the German nation for science and philosophy; the Romance nations stood for literature and art; and the other race groups are striving, each in its own way, to develop for civilization its particular message, its particular ideal, which shall help to guide the world nearer to that perfection of human life for which we all long, that "one far off Divine event.". . .

Manifestly some of the great races of today—particularly the Negro race—have not as yet given to civilization the full spiritual message which they are capable of giving. I will not say that the Negro-race has yet given no message to the world, for it is still a mooted question among scientists as to just how far Egyptian civilization was Negro in its origin; if it was not wholly Negro, it was certainly very closely allied. Be that as it may, however, the fact still remains that the full, complete Negro message of the whole Negro race has not as yet been given to the world: that the messages and ideal of the yellow race have not been completed, and that the striving of the mighty Slavs has but begun. The question is, then: How shall this message be delivered?; how shall these various ideals be realized? The answer is plain: by the development of these race groups, not as individuals, but as races. For the development of Japanese genius, Japanese literature and art, and Japanese spirit, only Japanese, bound and welded together, Japanese inspired by one vast ideal, can work out in its fullness the wonderful message which Japan has for the nations of the earth. For the development of Negro genius, of Negro literature and art, of Negro spirit, only Negroes bound and welded together, Negroes inspired by one vast ideal, can work out in its fullness that great message we have for humanity. We cannot reverse history; we are subject to the same natural laws as other races, and if the Negro is ever to be a factor in the world's history—if among the gaily-colored banners that deck the broad ramparts of civilizations is to hang one uncompromising black, then it must be placed there by black hands, fashioned by black heads, and hallowed by the travail of 200,000,000 black hearts beating in one glad song of jubilee.

For this reason, the advance guard of the Negro people—the 8,000,000 people of Negro blood in the United States of America—must soon come to realize that if they are to take their just place in the van of Pan-Negroism, then their destiny is not absorption by the white Americans. That if in America it is to be proven for the first time in the modern world that not only Negroes are capable of evolving individual men like Toussaint, the Saviour, but are a nation stored with wonderful possibilities of culture, then their destiny is not a servile imitation of Anglo-Saxon culture, but a stalwart originality which shall unswervingly follow Negro ideals.

It may, however, be objected here that the situation of our race in America renders this attitude impossible; that our sole hope of salvation lies in our being able to lose our race identity in the commingled blood of the nation; and that any other course would merely increase the friction of races which we call race prejudice, and against which we have so long and so earnestly fought.

Here, then, is the dilemma, and it is a puzzling one, I admit. No Negro who has given earnest thought to the situation of his people in America has failed, at some time in life, to find himself at these cross-roads; has failed to ask himself at some time: What, after all, am I? Am I an American, or am I a Negro? Can I be both? Or is it my duty to cease to be a Negro as soon as possible and be an American? If I strive as a Negro, am I not perpetuating the very cleft that threatens and separates Black and White America? Is not my only possible practical aim the subduction of all that is Negro in me to the American? Does my black blood place upon me any more obligation to assert my nationality than German, or Irish, or Italian blood would?

It is such incessant self-questioning and the hesitation that arises from it that is making the present period a time of vacillation and contradiction for the American Negro; combined race action is stifled, race responsibility is shirked, race enterprises languish, and the best blood, the best talent, the best energy of the Negro people cannot be marshalled to do the bidding of the race. They stand back to make room for every rascal and demagogue who chooses to cloak his selfish deviltry under the veil of race pride.

Is this right? Is it rational? Is it good policy? Have we in America a distinct mission as a race—a distinct sphere of action and an opportunity for race development, or is self-obliteration the highest end to which Negro blood dare aspire?

If we carefully consider what race prejudice really is, we find it, historically, to be nothing but the friction between different groups of people; it is the difference in aim, in feeling, in ideals of two different races; if, now, this difference exists touching territory, laws, language, or even religion, it is manifest that these people cannot live in the same territory without fatal collision; but if, on the other hand, there is substantial agreement in laws, language, and religion; if there is a satisfactory adjustment of economic life, then there is no reason why, in the same country and on the same street, two or three great national ideals might not thrive and develop, that men of different races might not strive together for their race ideals as well, perhaps even better, than in isolation. Here, it seems to me, is the reading of the riddle that puzzles so many of us. We are Americans, not only by birth and by citizenship, but by our political ideals, our language, our religion. Farther than that, our Americanism does not go. At that point, we are Negroes, members of a vast historic race that from the very dawn of creation has slept, but half awakening in the dark forests of its African fatherland. We are the first fruits of this new nation, the harbinger of that black tomorrow which is yet destined to soften the whiteness of the Teutonic today. We are that people whose subtle sense of song has given America its only American music, its only American fairy tales, its only touch of pathos and humor amid its mad money-getting plutocracy. As such, it is our duty to conserve our physical powers, our intellectual endowments, our spiritual ideals; as a race, we must strive by race organization, by race solidarity, by race unity to the realization of that broader humanity that freely recognizes differences in men, but sternly deprecates inequality in their opportunities of development.

...

After the Egyptian and Indian, the Greek and Roman, the Teuton and Mongolian, the Negro is a sort of seventh son, born with a veil, and gifted with second-sight in this American world, a world which yields him no true self-consciousness, but only lets him see himself through the revelation of the other world. It is a peculiar sensation, this double-consciousness, this sense of always looking at one's self through the eyes of others, of measuring one's soul by the tape of a world that looks on in amused contempt and pity. One ever feels his twoness, an American, a Negro; two souls, two thoughts, two unreconciled strivings; two warring ideals in one dark body, whose dogged strength alone keeps it from being torn asunder.

The history of the American Negro is the history of this strife, this longing to attain self-conscious manhood, to merge his double self into a better and truer self. In this merging he wishes neither of the older selves to be lost. He would not Africanize America, for America has too much to teach the world and Africa. He would not bleach his Negro soul in a flood of white Americanism, for he knows that Negro blood has a message for the world. He simply wishes to make it possible for a man to be both a Negro and an American, without being cursed and spit upon by his fellows, without having the doors of Opportunity closed roughly in his face.

This, then, is the end of his striving: to be a co-worker in the kingdom of culture, to escape both death and isolation, to husband and use his best powers and his latent genius. These powers of body

and mind have in the past been strangely wasted, dispersed, or forgotten.

5. Charlotte Perkins Gilman*
Women and Economics

We are the only animal species in which the female depends on the male for food, the only animal species in which the sex-relation is also an economic relation. With us an entire sex lives in a relation of economic dependence upon the other sex, and the economic relation is combined with the sex-relation. The economic status of the human female is relative to the sex-relation.

It is commonly assumed that this condition also obtains among other animals, but such is not the case. . . . The female bee and ant are economically dependent, but not on the male. The workers are females, too, specialized to economic functions solely. And with the carnivora, if the young are to lose one parent, it might far better be the father: the mother is quite competent to take care of them herself. With many species, as in the case of the common cat, she not only feeds herself and her young, but has to defend the young against the male as well. In no case is the female throughout her life supported by the male.

In the human species the condition is permanent and general, though there are exceptions, and though the present century is witnessing the beginnings of a great change in this respect. We have not been accustomed to face this fact beyond our loose generalization that it was "natural," and that other animals did so, too. . . .

In studying the economic position of the sexes collectively, the difference is most marked. As a social animal, the economic status of man rests on the combined and exchanged services of vast numbers of progressively specialized individuals. The economic progress of the race, its maintenance at any period, its continued advance, involve the collective activities of all the trades, crafts, arts, manufactures, inventions, discoveries, and all the civil and military institutions that go to maintain them. The economic status of any race at any time, with its involved effect on all the constituent individuals, depends on their

*Gilman, Charlotte Perkins. *Women and Economics*. Boston, MA: Small, Maynard & Company, 1898. Print.

world-wide labors and their free exchange. Economic progress, however, is almost exclusively masculine. Such economic processes as women have been allowed to exercise are of the earliest and most primitive kind. Were men to perform no economic services save such as are still performed by women, our racial status in economics would be reduced to most painful limitations. . . .

This is not owing . . . to any inherent disability of sex, but to the present condition of woman, forbidding the development of this degree of economic ability. The male human being is thousands of years in advance of the female in economic status. Speaking collectively, men produce and distribute wealth; and women receive it at their hands. . . .

Studied individually, the facts are even more plainly visible, more open and familiar. . . . The comfort, the luxury, the necessities of life itself, which the woman receives, are obtained by the husband, and given to her by him. And, when the woman, left alone with no man to "support" her, tries to meet her own economic necessities, the difficulties which confront her prove conclusively what the general economic status of the woman is. . . . But we are instantly confronted by the commonly received opinion that, although it must be admitted that men make and distribute the wealth of the world, women earn their share of it as wives. This assumes either that the husband is in the position of employer and the wife as employee, or that marriage is a "partnership," and the wife an equal factor with the husband in producing wealth.

Economic independence is a relative condition at best. In the broadest sense, all living things are economically dependent upon others. . . . But in the closest interpretation, individual economic independence among human beings means that the individual pays for what he gets, works for what he gets, gives to the other an equivalent for what the other gives him. I depend on the shoemaker for shoes and the tailor for coats, but, if I give the shoemaker and the tailor enough of my own labor as a house-builder to pay for the shoes and coats they give me, I retain my personal independence. I have not taken of their product, and given nothing of mine. As long as what I get is obtained by what I give, I am economically independent.

Women consume economic goods. What economic product do they give in exchange for what they consume? The claim that marriage is a partnership, in which the two persons married produce wealth which neither of them, separately, could produce, will not bear examination. A man happy and comfortable can produce more than one unhappy and uncomfortable, but this is as true of a father or son as of a husband. To take from a man any of the conditions which make him happy and strong is to cripple his industry, generally speaking. But those relatives who make him happy are not therefore his business partners and entitled to share his income.

Grateful return for happiness conferred is not the method of exchange in a partnership. The comfort a man takes with his wife is not in the nature of a business partnership, nor are her frugality and industry. A housekeeper, in her place, might be as frugal, as industrious, but would not therefore be a partner. Man and wife are partners truly in their mutual obligation to their children—their common love, duty, and service. But a manufacturer who marries, or a doctor, or a lawyer, does not take a partner in his business, when he takes a partner in parenthood, unless his wife is also a manufacturer, a doctor, or a lawyer. In his business, she cannot even advise wisely without training and experience. To love her husband, the composer, does not enable her to compose; and the loss of a man's wife, though it may break his heart, does not cripple his business, unless his mind is affected by grief. She is in no sense a business partner, unless she contributes capital or experience or labor, as a man would in like relation. Most men would hesitate very seriously before entering a business partnership with any woman, wife or not.

If the wife is not, then, truly a business partner, in what way does she earn from her husband the food, clothing, and shelter she receives at his hands? By house service, it will be instantly replied. This is the general misty idea upon the subject—that women earn all they get, and more, by house service. Here we come to a very practical and definite economic ground. Although not producers of wealth, women serve in the final processes of preparation and distribution. Their labor in the household has a genuine economic value.

For a certain percentage of persons to serve other persons, in order that the ones so served may produce more, is a contribution not to be overlooked. The labor of women in the house, certainly, enables men to produce more wealth than they otherwise could; and in this way women are economic factors in society. But so are horses. The labor of horses enables men to produce more wealth than they otherwise could. The horse is an economic factor in society. But the horse is not economically independent, nor is the woman. If a man plus a valet can perform more useful service than he could minus a valet, then the valet is performing useful service. But, if the valet is the property of the man, is obliged to perform this service, and is not paid for it, he is not economically independent.

The labor which the wife performs in the household is given as part of her functional duty, not as employment. The wife of the poor man, who works hard in a small house, doing all the work for the family, or the wife of the rich man, who wisely and gracefully manages a large house and administers its functions, each is entitled to fair pay for services rendered.

To take this ground and hold it honestly, wives, as earners through domestic service, are entitled to the wages of cooks, housemaids, nursemaids, seamstresses, or housekeepers, and to no more. This would of course reduce the spending money of the wives of the rich, and put it out of the power of the poor man to "support" a wife at all. . . . But nowhere on earth would there be "a rich woman" by these means. Even the highest class of private housekeeper, useful as her services are, does not accumulate a fortune. . . .

But the salient fact in this discussion is that, whatever the economic value of the domestic industry of women is, they do not get it. The women who do the most work get the least money, and the women who have the most money do the least work. Their labor is neither given nor taken as a factor in economic exchange. It is held to be their duty as women to do this work; and their economic status bears no relation to their domestic labors, unless an inverse one. . . .

Without going into either the ethics or the necessities of the case, we have reached so much common ground: the female of genus homo is supported by the male. Whereas, in other species of animals, male and female alike graze and browse, hunt and kill, climb, swim, dig, run, and fly for their livings; in our species the female does not seek her own living in the specific activities of our race, but is fed by the male. . . .

Knowing how important a factor in the evolution of species is the economic relation, and finding in the human species an economic relation so peculiar, we may naturally look to find effects peculiar to our race. We may expect to find phenomena in the sex-relation and in the economic relation of humanity of a unique character, phenomena not traceable to human superiority, but singularly derogatory to that superiority; phenomena so marked, so morbid, as to give rise to much speculation as to their cause. Are these natural inferences fulfilled? Are these peculiarities in the sex-relation and in the economic relation manifested in human life? Indisputably these are, so plain, so prominent, so imperiously demanding attention, that human thought has been occupied from its first consciousness in trying some way to account for them. To explain and relate these phenomena, separating what is due to normal race-development from what is due to this abnormal sexuo-economic relation, is the purpose of the line of study here suggested. . . .

We, as a race, manifest an excessive sex-attraction, followed by its excessive indulgence, and the inevitable evil consequence. It urges us to a degree of indulgence which bears no relation to the original needs of the organism, and which is even so absurdly exaggerated as to react unfavorably on the incidental gratification involved; an excess which tends to pervert and exhaust desire as well as to injure reproduction.

The human animal manifests an excess in sex-attraction which not only injures the race through its morbid action on the natural processes of reproduction, but which injures the happiness of the individual through its morbid reaction on his own desires.

What is the cause of this excessive sex-attraction in the human species? The immediately acting cause of sex-attraction is sex-distinction. The more widely the sexes are differentiated, the more forcibly they are attracted to each other. The more highly developed becomes the distinction of sex in either organism, the more intense is its attraction for the other. In the human species we find sex-distinction carried to an excessive degree. Sex-distinction in humanity is so marked as to retard and confuse race-distinction, to check individual distinction, seriously to injure the race. Accustomed as we are simply to accept the facts of life as we find them, to consider people as permanent types instead of seeing them and the whole race in continual change according to the action of many forces, it seems strange at first to differentiate between familiar manifestations of sex distinction, and to say, "This is normal and should not be disturbed. This is abnormal and should be removed." But that is precisely what must be done.

Normal sex-distinction manifests itself in all species in what are called primary and secondary sex-characteristics. The primary are those organs and functions essential to reproduction; the secondary, those modifications of structure and function which sub-serve the uses of reproduction ultimately, but are not directly essential, such as the horns of the stag, of use in sex-combat; the plumage of the peacock, of use in sex-competition. All the minor characteristics of beard or mane, comb, wattles, spurs, gorgeous color or superior size, which distinguish the male from the female, these are distinctions of sex. These distinctions are of use to the species through reproduction only, the processes of race-preservation. They are not of use in self-preservation. The creature is not profited personally by his mane or crest or tail-feathers: they do not help him get his dinner or kill his enemies.

On the contrary, they react unfavorably upon his personal gains, if, through too great development, they interfere with his activity or render him a conspicuous mark for enemies. Such development would constitute excessive sex-distinction, and this is precisely the condition of the human race. Our distinctions of sex are carried to such a degree as to be disadvantageous to our progress as individuals and as a race. The sexes in our species are differentiated not only enough to perform their primal functions; not only enough to manifest all sufficient secondary sexual characteristics and fulfil their use in giving rise to sufficient sex-attraction; but so much as seriously to interfere with the processes of self-preservation on the one hand; and, more conspicuous still, so much as to react unfavorably upon the very processes of race-preservation which they are meant to serve. Our excessive sex-distinction, manifesting the characteristics of sex to an abnormal degree, has given rise to a degree of attraction which demands a degree of indulgence that directly injures motherhood and fatherhood. We are not better as parents, nor better as people, for our existing degree of sex-distinction, but visibly worse. . . .

When, then, it can be shown that sex-distinction in the human race is so excessive as not only to affect injuriously its own purposes, but to check and per-vert the progress of the race, it becomes a matter for most serious consideration. Nothing could be more inevitable, however, under our sexuo-economic relation. By the economic dependence of the human female upon the male, the balance of forces is altered. Natural selection no longer checks the action of sexual selection, but co-operates with it. Where both sexes obtain their food through the same exertions, from the same sources, under the same conditions, both sexes are acted upon alike, and developed alike by their environment. Where the two sexes obtain their food under different conditions, and where that difference consists in one of them being fed by the other, then the feeding sex becomes the environment of the fed. Man, in supporting woman, has become her economic environment. Under natural selection, every creature is modified to its environment, developing perforce the qualities needed to obtain its livelihood under that environment. Man, as the feeder of woman, becomes the strongest modifying force in her economic condition. Under sexual selection the human creature is of course modified to its mate, as with all creatures. When the mate becomes also the master, when economic necessity is added to sex-attraction, we have the two great evolutionary forces acting together to the same end; namely, to develop sex-distinction in the human female. For, in her position of economic dependence in the sex-relation, sex-distinction is with her not only as means of attracting a mate, as with all creatures, but as means of getting her livelihood, as is the case with no other creature under heaven. Because of the economic dependence of the human female on her mate, she is modified to sex to an excessive degree. This excessive modification she transmits to her children; and so is steadily implanted in the human constitution the morbid tendency to excess in this relation, which has acted so universally upon us in all ages, in spite of our best efforts to restrain it. . . . This is the immediate effect upon individuals of the peculiar sexuo-economic relation which obtains among us.

PART II

THE GREAT TAKEOFF IN INCOME AND WEALTH INEQUALITY

This section addresses the rapid takeoff in economic inequalities in the US and many other countries. Although social scientists are often critiqued for failing to predict the recent market crash and the Great Recession that followed, in fact they also failed—just as spectacularly—to predict the takeoff in income inequality some four decades ago. The field has, however, been scrambling ever since, and we now have a good understanding of why the takeoff happened (see Saez, Ch. 6; Piketty, Ch. 7).

At the risk of some oversimplification, the main explanations on offer can be categorized into two key types: (a) those that understand rising inequality in terms of the operation of competitive market forces, and (b) those that instead understand it as the outcome of rent creation and destruction (see Hacker and Pierson, Ch. 10). Within the "competitive market" camp, the single most famous account starts with the claim that technological changes, like the computerization of the economy, were the key exogenous shock that started the takeoff. These technological changes were skill-biased in the sense that they increased the productivity of and demand for highly skilled workers. If the workplace is suddenly chock-full of computers, the employer now needs skilled workers to operate them, and those workers will of course be more productive than their pen-and-paper predecessors were.

How does this technological shock affect wages? The underlying mechanism is very simple: As the productivity of workers in the new computerized economy increases, and as the demand for these workers increases, their wages will increase as well. If this account is on the mark, we should expect further increases in inequality as long as educated workers continue to become more productive and the demand for them continues to outstrip the supply. The takeoff is in this sense expressing nothing more than the inexorable logic of a competitive market (see Goldin and Katz, Ch. 8, for details).

Although most scholars of the takeoff would agree that market forces are part of the story behind the takeoff, hardly anyone now regards this competitive-market account as full and complete. The key alternative accounts instead rely on the concept of rent. By "rent," we mean returns on an asset, like labor, that are in excess of what would be needed to keep that asset in production in a fully competitive market. If a chief executive officer (CEO), for example, is paid more than they would obtain in a truly competitive market, then that executive is securing rent.

Why might CEOs be overpaid? It is ultimately because those at the top have the power to extract more for themselves: The members of a CEO's pay-setting board might favor ample compensation packages for the CEO because their interests are served by pleasing someone who is so powerful (see Bebchuk and Fried, Ch. 73, for details). The CEO's capacity to extract rent is of course but one example of how contemporary economies, far from being highly competitive, are instead rife with opportunities for those at the top to secure ever more for themselves. If rent of this sort is indeed behind the takeoff, it means that extreme inequality is not simply the unfortunate price of running a competitive economy. It is instead an indirect signal of an uncompetitive economy.

These new opportunities for rent among managers, executives, and others at the top are, however, just one side of a rent-based account of the takeoff. It is also important to appreciate that many of the opportunities for less privileged workers to collect rent are withering away. When scholars refer, for example, to the "union wage," they are simply acknowledging the rent that is collected when those outside the union cannot compete for union jobs and thereby undercut that wage. Although the union wage is therefore a classic form of rent, it is also a declining form because the number of unionized workers is rapidly shrinking in the US (see Western and Rosenfeld, Ch. 11). The simple upshot: The takeoff in income inequality proceeds from the rise of rent at the top and the decline of rent at the bottom.

We do not mean to suggest that all accounts of the takeoff may be neatly characterized as either market-based or rent-based. Although some of the accounts presented in this section take a more hybrid form, this organizing frame is nonetheless useful in bringing some order to one of the richest and most complicated fields in social science.

6. Emmanuel Saez*

Striking It Richer: The Evolution of Top Incomes in the United States

The recent dramatic rise in income inequality in the United States is well documented. But we know less about which groups are winners and which are losers, or how this may have changed over time. Is most of the income growth being captured by an extremely small income elite? Or is a broader upper middle class profiting? . . .

I explore these questions with a uniquely long-term historical view that allows me to place current developments in deeper context than is typically the case.

Efforts at analyzing long-term trends are often hampered by a lack of good data. In the United States, and most other countries, household income surveys virtually did not exist prior to 1960. The only data source consistently available on a long-run basis is tax data. The U.S. government has published detailed statistics on income reported for tax purposes since 1913, when the modern federal income tax started. These statistics report the number of

* Saez, Emmanuel. 2016. *Striking It Richer: The Evolution of Top Incomes in the United States* (2015 Update). 3rd ed. Originally found in *Pathways Magazine: Fighting Poverty During Downturns*, Summer 2008.

taxpayers and their total income and tax liability for a large number of income brackets. Combining these data with population census data and aggregate income sources, one can estimate the share of total personal income accruing to various upper-income groups, such as the top 10 percent or top 1 percent.

We define income as the sum of all income components reported on tax returns (wages and salaries, pensions received, profits from businesses, capital income such as dividends, interest, or rents, and realized capital gains) before individual income taxes. We exclude government transfers such as Social Security retirement benefits or unemployment compensation benefits from our income definition. Therefore, our income measure is defined as cash market income before individual income taxes.

Figure 6.1 presents the pre-tax income share of the top decile since 1917 in the United States. In 2015, the top decile includes all families with market income above $124,800. The overall pattern of the top decile share over the century is U-shaped. The share of the top decile is around 45 percent from the mid-1920s to 1940. It declines substantially to just above 32.5 percent in four years during World War II and stays fairly stable around 33 percent until the 1970s. Such an abrupt decline, concentrated exactly during the war years, cannot easily be reconciled with slow technological changes and suggests instead that the shock of the war played a key and lasting role in shaping income concentration in the United States.

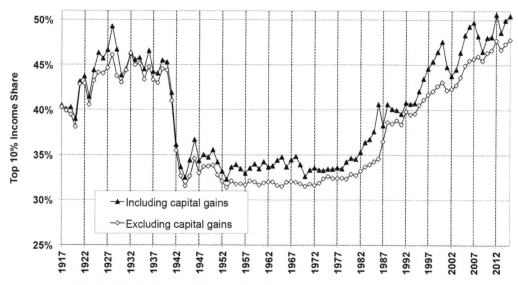

FIGURE 6.1   The Top Decile Income Share, 1917-2015

Note: [Much of the discussion in this note is based on previous work with Thomas Piketty. All the data described here are available in excel format at http://elsa.berkeley.edu/~saez/TabFig2014prel.xls.] Income is defined as market income (and excludes government transfers). In 2015, top decile includes all families with annual income above $124,800.

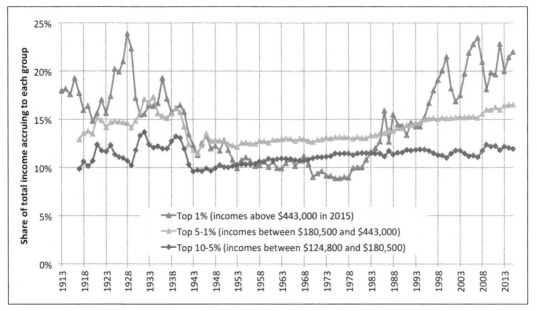

FIGURE 6.2   Decomposing the Top Decile US Income Share into 3 Groups, 1913-2015

Note: Income is defined as market income including capital gains.

After decades of stability in the post-war period, the top decile share has increased dramatically over the last twenty-five years and has now regained its pre-war level. Indeed, the top decile share in 2012 is equal to 50.6 percent, a level higher than any other year since 1917 and even surpasses 1928, the peak of stock market bubble in the "roaring" 1920s.

Figure 6.2 decomposes the top decile into the top percentile (families with income above $443,000 in 2015) and the next 4 percent (families with income between $180,500 and $443,000), and the bottom half of the top decile (families with income between $124,800 and $180,500). Interestingly, most of the fluctuations of the top decile are due to fluctuations within the top percentile. The drop in the next two groups during World War II is far less dramatic, and they recover from the WWII shock relatively quickly. Finally, their shares do not increase much during the recent decades. In contrast, the top percentile has gone through enormous fluctuations along the course of the twentieth century, from about 18 percent before WWI, to a peak to almost 24 percent in the late 1920s, to only about 9 percent during the 1960s–1970s, and back to almost 23.5 percent by 2007. Those at the very top of the income distribution therefore play a central role in the evolution of U.S. inequality over the course of the twentieth century.

The implications of these fluctuations at the very top can also be seen when we examine trends in *real*

income growth per family between the top 1 percent and the bottom 99 percent in recent years, as illustrated in Table 6.1. From 1993 to 2015, for example, average real incomes per family grew by only 25.7 percent over this 22-year period. However, if one excludes the top 1 percent, average real incomes of the bottom 99 percent grew only by 14.3 percent from 1993 to 2015. Top 1 percent incomes grew by 94.5 percent from 1993 to 2015. This implies that top 1 percent incomes captured 52 percent of the overall economic growth of real incomes per family over the period 1993–2015.

The 1993–2015 period encompasses, however, a dramatic shift in how the bottom 99 percent of the income distribution fared. Table 6.1 next distinguishes between five sub-periods: (1) the 1993–2000 expansion of the Clinton administrations, (2) the 2000-2002 recession, (3) the 2002-2007 expansion of the Bush administrations, (4) the 2007-2009 Great Recession, and (5) 2009-2015. During both expansions, the incomes of the top 1 percent grew extremely quickly by 98.7 percent and 61.8 percent respectively. However, while the bottom 99 percent of incomes grew at a solid pace of 20.3 percent from 1993 to 2000, these incomes grew only 6.8 percent percent from 2002 to 2007. As a result, in the economic expansion of 2002-2007, the top 1 percent captured two thirds of income growth. Those results may help explain the disconnect between the

TABLE 6.1 Real Income Growth by Groups

		Average Income Real Growth	Top 1% Incomes Real Growth	Bottom 99% Incomes Real Growth	Fraction of total growth (or loss) captured by top 1%
		(1)	(2)	(3)	(4)
Full period	1993-2015	25.7%	94.5%	14.3%	52%
Clinton Expansion	1993-2000	31.5%	98.7%	20.3%	45%
2001 Recession	2000-2002	-11.7%	-30.8%	-6.5%	57%
Bush Expansion	2002-2007	16.1%	61.8%	6.8%	65%
Great Recession	2007-2009	-17.4%	-36.3%	-11.6%	49%
Recovery	2009-2015	13.0%	37.4%	7.6%	52%

Computations based on family market income including realized capital gains (before individual taxes). Incomes exclude government transfers (such as unemployment insurance and social security) and non-taxable fringe benefits. Incomes are deflated using the Consumer Price Index. Column (4) reports the fraction of total real family income growth (or loss) captured by the top 1%. For example, from 2002 to 2007, average real family incomes grew by 16.1% but 65% of that growth accrued to the top 1% while only 35% of that growth accrued to the bottom 99% of US families.

Source: Piketty and Saez (2003), series updated to 2015.

economic experiences of the public and the solid macroeconomic growth posted by the U.S. economy from 2002 to 2007. Those results may also help explain why the dramatic growth in top incomes during the Clinton administration did not generate much public outcry while there has been a great level of attention to top incomes in the press and in the public debate since 2005.

During both recessions, the top 1 percent incomes fell sharply, by 30.8 percent from 2000 to 2002, and by 36.3 percent from 2007 to 2009. The primary driver of the fall in top incomes during those recessions was the stock market crash, which reduced realized capital gains, and, especially in the 2000–2002 period, the value of executive stock-options. However, bottom 99 percent incomes fell by 11.6 percent from 2007 to 2009 while they fell only by 6.5 percent from 2000 to 2002. Therefore, the top 1 percent absorbed a larger fraction of losses in the 2000-2002 recession (57 percent) than in the Great recession (49 percent). The 11.6 percent fall in bottom 99 percent incomes is the largest fall on record in any two-year period since the Great Depression of 1929–1933.

From 2009 to 2015, average real income per family grew by 13.0 percent (Table 6.1) but the gains were very uneven. Top 1 percent incomes grew by 37.4 percent while bottom 99 percent incomes grew only by 7.6 percent. Hence, the top 1 percent captured 52 percent of the income gains [over this period]. . . .

The top percentile share declined during WWI, recovered during the 1920s boom, and declined again during the Great Depression and WWII. This very specific timing, together with the fact that very high incomes account for a disproportionate share of the total decline in inequality, strongly suggests that the shocks incurred by capital owners during 1914 to 1945 (depression and wars) played a key role. Indeed, from 1913 and up to the 1970s, very top incomes were mostly composed of capital income (mostly dividend income) and to a smaller extent business income, the wage income share being very modest. Therefore, the large decline of top incomes observed during the 1914–1960 period is predominantly a capital income phenomenon.

Interestingly, the income composition pattern at the very top has changed considerably over the century. The share of wage and salary income has increased sharply from the 1920s to the present, and especially since the 1970s. Therefore, a significant fraction of the surge in top incomes since 1970 is due to an explosion of top wages and salaries. Indeed, estimates based purely on wages and salaries show that the share of total wages and salaries earned by the top 1 percent wage income earners has jumped from 5.1 percent in 1970 to 12.4 percent in 2007.

Evidence based on the wealth distribution is consistent with those facts. Estimates of wealth concentration, measured by the share of total wealth accruing to top 1 percent wealth holders, constructed by Wojciech Kopczuk and myself from estate tax returns for the 1916-2000 period in the United States, show a precipitous decline in the first part of the century with only fairly modest increases in recent decades. The evidence suggests that top incomes earners today are not "rentiers" deriving their incomes from past wealth but rather are "working rich," highly paid employees or new entrepreneurs who have not yet accumulated fortunes comparable to those accumulated during the Gilded Age. Such a pattern might not last for very long. The drastic cuts of the federal tax on large estates could certainly accelerate the path toward the reconstitution of the great wealth concentration that existed in the U.S. economy before the Great Depression.

The labor market has been creating much more inequality over the last thirty years, with the very top earners capturing a large fraction of macroeconomic productivity gains. A number of factors may help explain this increase in inequality, not only underlying technological changes but also the retreat of institutions developed during the New Deal and World War II—such as progressive tax policies, powerful unions, corporate provision of health and retirement benefits, and changing social norms regarding pay inequality. We need to decide as a society whether this increase in income inequality is efficient and acceptable and, if not, what mix of institutional and tax reforms should be developed to counter it.

---

7. Thomas Piketty*
Capital in the 21st Century

The distribution of wealth is one of today's most widely discussed and controversial issues. But what do we really know about its evolution over the long term? Do the dynamics of private capital accumulation inevitably lead to the concentration of wealth in ever fewer hands, as Karl Marx believed in the nineteenth century? Or do the balancing forces of growth, competition, and technological progress lead in later stages of development to reduced inequality and greater harmony among the classes, as Simon Kuznets thought in the twentieth century? What do we really know about how wealth and income have evolved since the eighteenth century, and what lessons can we derive from that knowledge for the century now under way?

These are the questions I attempt to answer. Let me say at once that the answers contained herein are imperfect and incomplete. But they are based on much more extensive historical and comparative data than were available to previous researchers, data covering three centuries and more than twenty

*CAPITAL IN THE TWENTY-FIRST CENTURY by Thomas Piketty, translated by Arthur Goldhammer, Cambridge, Mass.: The Belknap Press of Harvard University Press, Copyright © 2014 by the President and Fellows of Harvard College.

countries. . . . Before turning in greater detail to the sources I tried to assemble in preparation for this study, I want to give a quick historical overview of previous thinking about these issues. . . .

Marx: The Principle of Infinite Accumulation

The most striking fact of [Marx's] day was the misery of the industrial proletariat. Despite the growth of the economy, or perhaps in part because of it, and because, as well, of the vast rural exodus owing to both population growth and increasing agricultural productivity, workers crowded into urban slums. The working day was long, and wages were very low. A new urban misery emerged, more visible, more shocking, and in some respects, even more extreme than the rural misery of the Old Regime. . . .

In 1848, on the eve of the "spring of nations" (that is, the revolutions that broke out across Europe that spring), [Marx] published *The Communist Manifesto*, a short, hard-hitting text, whose first chapter began with the famous words, "A specter is haunting Europe—the specter of communism." The text ended with the equally famous prediction of revolution: "The development of Modern Industry, therefore, cuts from under its feet the very foundation on which the bourgeoisie produces and appropriates products. What the bourgeoisie therefore produces, above all, are its own gravediggers. Its fall and the victory of the proletariat are equally inevitable."

Over the next two decades, Marx labored over the voluminous treatise that would justify this conclusion and propose the first scientific analysis of capitalism and its collapse. . . . His principal conclusion was what one might call the "principle of infinite accumulation," that is, the inexorable tendency for capital to accumulate and become concentrated in ever fewer hands, with no natural limit to the process. This is the basis of Marx's prediction of an apocalyptic end to capitalism: either the rate of return on capital would steadily diminish (thereby killing the engine of accumulation and leading to violent conflict among capitalists), or capital's share of national income would increase indefinitely (which sooner or later would unite the workers in revolt). In either case, no stable socioeconomic or political equilibrium was possible. . . .

Like his predecessors, Marx totally neglected the possibility of durable technological progress and steadily increasing productivity, which is a force that can to some extent serve as a counterweight to the process of accumulation and concentration of private capital. He no doubt lacked the statistical data needed to refine his predictions. He probably suffered as well from having decided on his conclusions in 1848, before embarking on the research needed to justify them. Marx evidently wrote in great political fervor, which at times led him to issue hasty pronouncements from which it was difficult to escape. That is why economic theory needs to be rooted in historical sources that are as complete as possible, and in this respect Marx did not exploit all the possibilities available to him. What is more, he devoted little thought to the question of how a society in which private capital had been totally abolished would be organized politically and economically—a complex issue if ever there was one, as shown by the tragic totalitarian experiments undertaken in states where private capital was abolished.

Despite these limitations, Marx's analysis remains relevant in several respects. First, he began with an important question (concerning the unprecedented concentration of wealth during the Industrial Revolution) and tried to answer it with the means at his disposal: economists today would do well to take inspiration from his example. Even more important, the principle of infinite accumulation that Marx proposed contains a key insight, as valid for the study of the twenty-first century as it was for the nineteenth. . . . If the rates of population and productivity growth are relatively low, then accumulated wealth naturally takes on considerable importance, especially if it grows to extreme proportions and becomes socially destabilizing. In other words, low growth cannot adequately counterbalance the Marxist principle of infinite accumulation: the resulting equilibrium is not as apocalyptic as the one predicted by Marx but is nevertheless quite disturbing. Accumulation ends at a finite level, but that level may be high enough to be destabilizing. In particular, the very high level of private wealth that has been attained since the 1980s and 1990s in the wealthy countries of Europe and in Japan, measured in years of national income, directly reflects the Marxian logic.

From Marx to Kuznets, or Apocalypse to Fairy Tale

Turning from the nineteenth-century analyses of Marx to the twentieth-century analyses of Simon Kuznets, we might say that economists' no doubt overly developed taste for apocalyptic predictions gave way to a similarly excessive fondness for fairy tales, or at any rate happy endings. According to Kuznets's theory, income inequality would automatically decrease in advanced phases of capitalist development, regardless of economic policy choices or other differences between countries, until eventually it stabilized at an acceptable level. Proposed in 1955, this was really a theory of the magical postwar years referred to in France as the "Trente Glorieuses," the thirty glorious years from 1945 to 1975. For Kuznets, it was enough to be patient, and before long, growth would benefit everyone. The philosophy of the moment was summed up in a single sentence: "Growth is a rising tide that lifts all boats." A similar optimism can also be seen in Robert Solow's 1956 analysis of the conditions necessary for an economy to achieve a "balanced growth path," that is, a growth trajectory along which all variables—output, incomes, profits, wages, capital, asset prices, and so on—would progress at the same pace, so that every social group would benefit from growth to the same degree, with no major deviations from the norm. Kuznets's position was thus diametrically opposed to the Ricardian and Marxist idea of an inegalitarian spiral and antithetical to the apocalyptic predictions of the nineteenth century.

In order to properly convey the considerable influence that Kuznets's theory enjoyed in the 1980s and 1990s and to a certain extent still enjoys today, it is important to emphasize that it was the first theory of this sort to rely on a formidable statistical apparatus. It was not until the middle of the twentieth century, in fact, that the first historical series of income distribution statistics became available with the publication in 1953 of Kuznets's monumental Shares of Upper Income Groups in Income and Savings. Kuznets's series dealt with only one country (the United States) over a period of thirty-five years (1913–1948). . . .

What did he find? He noted a sharp reduction in income inequality in the United States between 1913 and 1948. More specifically, at the beginning of this period, the upper decile of the income distribution (that is, the top 10 percent of US earners) claimed 45–50 percent of annual national income. By the late 1940s, the share of the top decile had decreased to roughly 30–35 percent of national income. This decrease of nearly 10 percentage points was considerable: for example, it was equal to half the income of the poorest 50 percent of Americans. The reduction of inequality was clear and incontrovertible. This was news of considerable importance, and it had an enormous impact on economic debate in the postwar era in both universities and international organizations. . . .

In fact, Kuznets himself was well aware that the compression of high US incomes between 1913 and 1948 was largely accidental. It stemmed in large part from multiple shocks triggered by the Great Depression and World War II and had little to do with any natural or automatic process. In his 1953 work, he analyzed his series in detail and warned readers not to make hasty generalizations. But in December 1954, at the Detroit meeting of the American Economic Association, of which he was president, he offered a far more optimistic interpretation of his results than he had given in 1953. It was this lecture, published in 1955 under the title "Economic Growth and Income Inequality," that gave rise to the theory of the "Kuznets curve."

According to this theory, inequality everywhere can be expected to follow a "bell curve." In other words, it should first increase and then decrease over the course of industrialization and economic development. According to Kuznets, a first phase of naturally increasing inequality associated with the early stages of industrialization, which in the United States meant, broadly speaking, the nineteenth century, would be followed by a phase of sharply decreasing inequality, which in the United States allegedly began in the first half of the twentieth century.

Kuznets's 1955 paper is enlightening. After reminding readers of all the reasons for interpreting the data cautiously and noting the obvious importance of exogenous shocks in the recent reduction of inequality in the United States, Kuznets suggests, almost innocently in passing, that the internal logic of economic development might also yield the same result, quite apart from any policy intervention or external shock. The idea was that inequalities increase in the early phases of industrialization, because only a minority is prepared to benefit from the new wealth that industrialization brings. Later, in more advanced phases of development, inequality automatically decreases as a larger and larger fraction of the population partakes of the fruits of economic growth.

The "advanced phase" of industrial development is supposed to have begun toward the end of the nineteenth or the beginning of the twentieth century in the industrialized countries, and the reduction of inequality observed in the United States between 1913 and 1948 could therefore be portrayed as one instance of a more general phenomenon, which should theoretically reproduce itself everywhere, including underdeveloped countries then mired in postcolonial poverty. The data Kuznets had presented in his 1953 book suddenly became a powerful political weapon. . . .

The Sources Used in This Study

The World Top Incomes Database (WTID), which is based on the joint work of some thirty researchers around the world, is the largest historical database available concerning the evolution of income inequality; it is the primary source of data here.

The second most important source of data . . . concerns wealth, including both the distribution of wealth and its relation to income. Wealth also generates income and is therefore important on the income study side of things as well. Indeed, income consists of two components: income from labor (wages, salaries, bonuses, earnings from nonwage labor, and other remuneration statutorily classified as labor-related) and income from capital (rent, dividends, interest, profits, capital gains, royalties, and other income derived from the mere fact of owning capital in the form of land, real estate, financial instruments, industrial equipment, etc., again regardless of its precise legal classification). The WTID contains a great deal of information about the evolution of income from capital over the course of the twentieth century.

It is nevertheless essential to complete this information by looking at sources directly concerned with wealth. . . . In the first place, just as income tax returns allow us to study changes in income inequality, estate tax returns enable us to study changes in the inequality of wealth. . . . We can also use data that allow us to measure the total stock of national wealth (including land, other real estate, and industrial and financial capital) over a very long period of time. We can measure this wealth for each country in terms of the number of years of national income required to amass it. . . .

The Major Results of This Study

What are the major conclusions to which these novel historical sources have led me? The first is that one should be wary of any economic determinism in regard to inequalities of wealth and income. The history of the distribution of wealth has always been deeply political, and it cannot be reduced to purely economic mechanisms. In particular, the reduction of inequality that took place in most developed countries between 1910 and 1950 was above all a consequence of war and of policies adopted to cope with the shocks of war. Similarly, the resurgence of inequality after 1980 is due largely to the political shifts of the past several decades, especially in regard to taxation and finance. The history of inequality is shaped by the way economic, social, and political actors view what is just and what is not, as well as by the relative power of those actors and the collective choices that result. It is the joint product of all relevant actors combined.

The second conclusion . . . is that the dynamics of wealth distribution reveal powerful mechanisms pushing alternately toward convergence and divergence. Furthermore, there is no natural, spontaneous process to prevent destabilizing, inegalitarian forces from prevailing permanently.

Consider first the mechanisms pushing toward convergence, that is, toward reduction and compression of inequalities. The main forces for convergence are the diffusion of knowledge and investment in training and skills. The law of supply and demand, as well as the mobility of capital and labor, which is a variant of that law, may always tend toward convergence as well, but the influence of this economic law is less powerful than the diffusion of knowledge and skill and is frequently ambiguous or contradictory in its implications. Knowledge and skill diffusion is the key to overall productivity growth as well as the reduction of inequality both within and between countries. We see this at present in the advances made by a number of previously poor countries, led by China. These emergent economies are now in the process of catching up with the advanced ones. By adopting the modes of production of the rich countries and acquiring skills comparable to those found elsewhere, the less developed countries have leapt forward in productivity and increased their national incomes. The technological convergence process may be abetted by open borders for trade, but it is fundamentally a process of the diffusion and sharing of knowledge—the public good par excellence—rather than a market mechanism. . . .

Forces of Convergence, Forces of Divergence

I will pay particular attention in this study to certain worrisome forces of divergence—particularly worrisome in that they can exist even in a world where there is adequate investment in skills and where all the conditions of "market efficiency" (as economists understand that term) appear to be satisfied. What are these forces of divergence? First, top earners can quickly separate themselves from the rest by a wide margin (although the problem to date remains relatively localized). More importantly, there is a set of forces of divergence associated with the process of accumulation and concentration of wealth when growth is weak and the return on capital is high. This second process is potentially more destabilizing than the first, and it no doubt represents the principal threat to an equal distribution of wealth over the long run.

To cut straight to the heart of the matter: in Figures 7.1 and 7.2 I show two basic patterns that I will try to explain in what follows. Each graph represents the importance of one of these divergent processes. Both graphs depict "U-shaped curves," that is, a period of decreasing inequality followed by one of increasing inequality. One might assume that the realities the two graphs represent are similar. In fact, they are not. The phenomena underlying the various curves are quite different and involve distinct economic, social, and political processes. Furthermore, the curve in Figure 7.1 represents income inequality in the United States, while the curves in Figure 7.2 depict the capital/income ratio in several European countries (Japan, though not shown, is similar). It is not out of the question that the two forces of divergence will ultimately come together in the twenty-first century. This has already happened to some extent and may yet become a global phenomenon, which could lead to levels of inequality never before seen, as well as to a radically new structure of inequality. Thus far, however, these striking patterns reflect two distinct underlying phenomena.

The US curve, shown in Figure 7.1, indicates the share of the upper decile of the income hierarchy in US national income from 1910 to 2010. It is nothing more than an extension of the historical series Kuznets established for the period 1913–1948. The top decile claimed as much as 45–50 percent of national income in the 1910s–1920s before dropping to 30–35 percent by the end of the 1940s. Inequality then stabilized at that level from 1950 to 1970. We subsequently see a rapid rise in inequality in the 1980s, until by 2000 we have returned to a level on the order of 45–50 percent of national income. The magnitude of the change is impressive. It is natural to ask how far such a trend might continue.

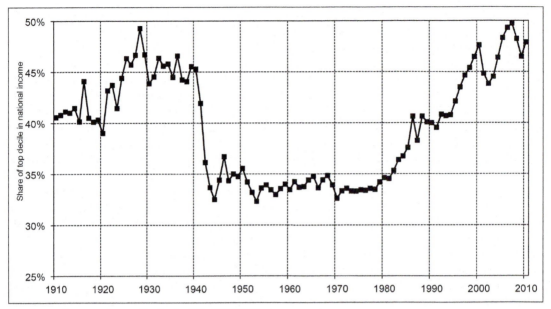

FIGURE 7.1 Income Inequality in the US, 1910-2010

The top decile share in U.S. national income dropped from 45-50% in the 1910s–1920s to less than 35% in the 1950s. (This is the fall documented by Kuznets); it then rose from less than 35% in the 1970s to 45-50% in the 2000s–2010s. *Sources and series*: see piketty.pse.ens.fr/capital21c.

This spectacular increase in inequality largely reflects an unprecedented explosion of very elevated incomes from labor, a veritable separation of the top managers of large firms from the rest of the population. One possible explanation of this is that the skills and productivity of these top managers rose suddenly in relation to those of other workers. Another explanation, which to me seems more plausible and turns out to be much more consistent with the evidence, is that these top managers by and large have the power to set their own remuneration, in some cases without limit, and in many cases without any clear relation to their individual productivity, which in any case is very difficult to estimate in a large organization. This phenomenon is seen mainly in the United States and to a lesser degree in Britain, and it may be possible to explain it in terms of the history of social and fiscal norms in those two countries over the past century. The tendency is less marked in other wealthy countries (such as Japan, Germany, France, and other continental European states), but the trend is in the same direction. . . .

The Fundamental Force for Divergence: *r > g*

The second pattern, represented in Figure 7.2, reflects a divergence mechanism that is in some ways simpler and more transparent and no doubt exerts greater influence on the long-run evolution of the wealth distribution. Figure 7.2 shows the total value of private wealth (in real estate, financial assets, and professional capital, net of debt) in Britain, France and Germany, expressed in years of national income, for the period 1870–2010. Note, first of all, the very high level of private wealth in Europe in the late nineteenth century: the total amount of private wealth hovered around six or seven years of national income, which is a lot. It then fell sharply in response to the shocks of the period 1914–1945: the capital/income ratio decreased to just 2 or 3. We then observe a steady rise from 1950 on, a rise so sharp that private fortunes in the early twenty-first century seem to be on the verge of returning to five or six years of national income in both Britain and France. (Private wealth in Germany, which started at a lower level, remains lower, but the upward trend is just as clear.)

This "U-shaped curve" reflects an absolutely crucial transformation. . . . In particular, the return of high capital/income ratios over the past few decades can be explained in large part by the return to a regime of relatively slow growth. In slowly growing economies, past wealth naturally takes on disproportionate importance because it takes only a small flow of new savings to increase the stock of wealth steadily and substantially.

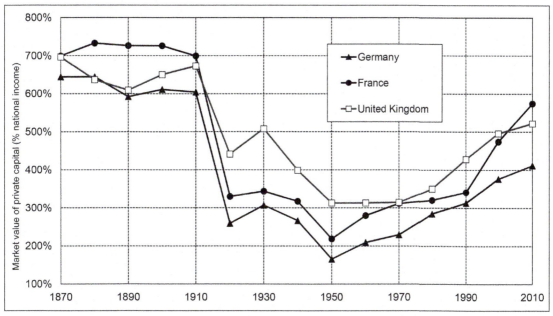

FIGURE 7.2 The capital/income ratio in Europe, 1870-2010

Aggregate private wealth was worth about 6–7 years of national income in Europe in 1910, between 2 and 3 years in 1950, and between 4 and 6 years in 2010. *Sources and series*: see piketty.pse.ens.fr/capital21c.

If, moreover, the rate of return on capital remains significantly above the growth rate for an extended period of time (which is more likely when the growth rate is low, though not automatic), then the risk of divergence in the distribution of wealth is very high.

This fundamental inequality, which I will write as $r > g$ (where r stands for the average annual rate of return on capital, including profits, dividends, interest, rents, and other income from capital, expressed as a percentage of its total value, and g stands for the rate of growth of the economy, that is, the annual increase in income or output), plays a crucial role. In a sense, it sums up the overall logic of my conclusions.

When the rate of return on capital . . . significantly exceeds the growth rate of the economy (as it did through much of history until the nineteenth century and as is likely to be the case again in the twenty-first century), then it logically follows that inherited wealth grows faster than output and income. People with inherited wealth need save only a portion of their income from capital to see that capital grow more quickly than the economy as a whole. Under such conditions, it is almost inevitable that inherited wealth will dominate wealth amassed from a lifetime's labor by a wide margin, and the concentration of capital will attain extremely high levels— levels potentially incompatible with the meritocratic values and principles of social justice fundamental to modern democratic societies. . . .

To sum up what has been said thus far: the process by which wealth is accumulated and distributed contains powerful forces pushing toward divergence, or at any rate toward an extremely high level of inequality. Forces of convergence also exist, and in certain countries at certain times, these may prevail, but the forces of divergence can at any point regain the upper hand, as seems to be happening now, at the beginning of the twenty-first century. The likely decrease in the rate of growth of both the population and the economy in coming decades makes this trend all the more worrisome.

My conclusions are less apocalyptic than those implied by Marx's principle of infinite accumulation and perpetual divergence (since Marx's theory implicitly relies on a strict assumption of zero productivity growth over the long run). In the model I propose, divergence is not perpetual and is only one of several possible future directions for the distribution of wealth. But the possibilities are not heartening. Specifically, it is important to note that the fundamental $r > g$ inequality, the main force of divergence in my theory, has nothing to do with any market imperfection. Quite the contrary: the more perfect the capital market (in the economist's sense), the more likely r is to be greater than g. . . .

Conclusion

The problem is enormous, and there is no simple solution. Growth can of course be encouraged by investing in education, knowledge, and nonpolluting technologies. But none of these will raise the growth rate to 4 or 5 percent a year. History shows that only countries that are catching up with more advanced economies—such as Europe during the three decades after World War II or China and other emerging economies today—can grow at such rates. For countries at the technological frontier—and thus ultimately for the planet as a whole—there is ample reason to believe that the growth rate will not exceed 1–1.5 percent in the long run, no matter what economic policies are adopted.

With an average return on capital of 4–5 percent, it is therefore likely that $r > g$ will again become the norm in the twenty-first century, as it had been throughout history until the eve of World War I. In the twentieth century, it took two world wars to wipe away the past and significantly reduce the return on capital, thereby creating the illusion that the fundamental structural contradiction of capitalism (r > g) had been overcome.

To be sure, one could tax capital income heavily enough to reduce the private return on capital to less than the growth rate. But if one did that indiscriminately and heavy-handedly, one would risk killing the motor of accumulation and thus further reducing the growth rate. Entrepreneurs would then no longer have the time to turn into rentiers, since there would be no more entrepreneurs.

The right solution is a progressive annual tax on capital. This will make it possible to avoid an endless inegalitarian spiral while preserving competition and incentives for new instances of primitive accumulation…. The difficulty is that this solution, the progressive tax on capital, requires a high level of international cooperation and regional political integration. It is not within the reach of the nation-states in which earlier social compromises were hammered out. Many people worry that moving toward greater cooperation and political integration within, say, the European Union only undermines existing achievements (starting with the social states that the various countries of Europe constructed in response to the shocks of the twentieth century) without constructing anything new other than a vast market predicated on ever purer and more perfect competition. Yet pure and perfect competition cannot alter the inequality $r > g$, which is not the consequence of any market "imperfection." On the contrary. Although the risk is real, I do not see any genuine alternative: if we are to regain control of capitalism, we must bet everything on democracy—and in Europe, democracy on a European scale. Larger political communities, such as in the United States and China, have a wider range of options, but for the small countries of Europe, which will soon look very small indeed in relation to the global economy, national withdrawal can only lead to even worse frustration and disappointment than currently exists with the European Union. The nation-state is still the right level at which to modernize any number of social and fiscal policies and to develop new forms of governance and shared ownership intermediate between public and private ownership, which is one of the major challenges for the century ahead. But only regional political integration can lead to effective regulation of the globalized patrimonial capitalism of the twenty-first century.

8. Claudia Goldin and Lawrence F. Katz*
The Race Between Education and Technology

Economic inequality since 1980 increased greatly. The earnings of college graduates rose at a far greater clip than did the earnings of those who stopped at high school graduation. The incomes of top managers and professionals increased at a much faster rate than did those of ordinary workers.

The increase in inequality was more all-encompassing than a widening *between* different education levels or occupational groups. The expanding gap also occurred *within* groups, even within educational levels. Among college graduates, for example, those with degrees from institutions with higher standards for admissions earned relatively more over time. Those who went to more prestigious law schools did better relative to other law school graduates. The widening occurred within virtually all groups in a manner that is not easily explained by the usual observable factors such as years of schooling. At

*THE RACE BETWEEN EDUCATION AND TECHNOLOGY, by Claudia Goldin and Lawrence Katz, Cambridge, Mass.: The Belknap Press of Harvard University Press, Copyright © 2008 by the President and Fellows of Harvard College.

almost all educational and experience levels, for example, the earnings for those near the top of the distribution increased considerably relative to those near the middle or close to the bottom.[1] The pervasive and rapid increase in economic inequality has led many to search for explanatory factors that are themselves pervasive and rapid. A key suspect is *skill-biased* technological change, particularly that involved in the use of computers.[2] Chief among other factors that have been mentioned are increased international trade and outsourcing, the greater immigration of low-wage workers, the decline in private-sector unionization, the erosion of the real value of the federal minimum wage, and changes in social norms concerning the pay of executives and other top-end earners. Here we mainly discuss the role of technological change.

The central idea concerning the role of technology in affecting inequality is that certain technologies are difficult for workers and consumers to master, at least initially. Individuals with more education and higher innate abilities will be more able to grasp new and complicated tools. Younger individuals are often better able to master new-fangled equipment than are older individuals. Employers, in turn, will be more willing to hire those with the education and other observable characteristics that endow them with the capacity to learn and use the new technologies. Existing employees who are slow to grasp new tools will not be promoted and might see their earnings reduced. Those who are quicker will be rewarded.

The type of technological change that is necessary to explain the pervasive and rapid increase in economic inequality in the latter part of the twentieth century and the early twenty-first century must meet various criteria. First, it must have affected a large segment of the workforce, both production line workers and those in the office, and both highly educated professionals and ordinary staff. As such, the innovation would probably have to be of the "general purpose technology" form.[3] A general purpose technology is one that is not specific to a particular firm, industry, product, or service. Instead, it is pervasive and omnipresent, cutting across various production methods and services. In addition, the technological innovation must have diffused during a fairly brief period. Finally, it must have required workers to think, adjust, and reconfigure the workplace. Computerization would seem to be the perfect culprit.

As we demonstrate in this chapter, it is clear that technological change—computerization in particular—is *part* of the explanation for rising inequality in the past twenty-five years. But, although computerization and other technological changes were culprits in fostering inequality, these "criminals" were not acting alone. The reasoning is simple.

New technologies alter the relative demand for different types of labor; however, the overall impact of a new technology on the wage structure reflects not only these demand shifts but also the supply responses by individuals attending various types of schools or obtaining skills on the job or in other ways. Just because a technology places increasing demands on the skill, education, and know-how of the workforce does not necessarily mean that economic inequality will rise and, if it does, that the increase will be sustained over a long period. If the supply of skills rises to accommodate the increase in demand for skill, then wage inequality need not change.

In other words, the evolution of the wage structure reflects, at least in part, a race between the growth in the demand for skills driven by technological advances and the growth in the supply of skills driven by demographic change, educational investment choices, and immigration.[4] This framework suggests that the rise in educational wage differentials and wage inequality since 1980 resulted from an acceleration in demand shifts from technological change, or a deceleration in the growth of the supply of skills, or some combination of the two.

The "computers did it" account also lacks historical perspective regarding technological change and inequality. Other critical moments existed in U.S. history when general purpose technologies swept the factory, office, and home. Consider, for example, the advent of motive power in the form of water wheels and later steam engines or, better yet, the electrification of the factory, home, and urban transportation. The notion that computerization provided the first or the most momentous instance in U.S. economic history of a complex technology that placed greater demands on the knowledge, ability, and flexibility of virtually all workers and consumers is gravely mistaken.

Lessons from History

In the early twentieth century, a wide range of industries, particularly the newer and more technologically dynamic ones, demanded more-educated workers. The workers to whom we refer, were not necessarily of the professional class and they were not all working in an office, a boardroom, or on the

TABLE 8.1 U.S. Educational Composition of Employment and the College/High School Wage Premium: 1950 to 2005

	Full-Time Equivalent Employment Shares (%) by Education				
	High School Dropouts	*High School Graduates*	*Some College*	*College Graduates*	*College/High School Wage Premium*
1950 Census	58.6	24.4	9.2	7.8	0.313
1960 Census	49.5	27.7	12.2	10.6	0.396
1970 Census	35.9	34.7	15.6	13.8	0.465
1980 Census	20.7	36.1	22.8	20.4	0.391
1980 CPS	19.1	38.0	22.0	20.9	0.356
1990 CPS	12.7	36.2	25.1	26.1	0.508
1990 Census	11.4	33.0	30.2	25.4	0.549
2000 CPS	9.2	32.4	28.7	29.7	0.579
2000 Census	8.7	20.6	32.0	29.7	0.607
2005 CPS	8.4	30.9	28.9	31.8	0.596

Sources: Data for 1950 to 1990 are from Autor, Katz, and Krueger (1998, table 1). Data for 2000 and 2005 are from the 2000 and 2005 Merged Outgoing Rotation Groups (MORG) of the CPS and 2000 Census IPUMS using the same approach as in Autor, Katz, and Krueger (1998).

Notes: The college/high school wage premium is expressed in logs. Full-time equivalent (FTE) employment shares are calculated for samples that include all individuals 18 to 65 years old in paid employment during the survey reference week for each census and CPS sample. FTE shares are defined as the share of total weekly hours supplied by each education group. The tabulations are based on the 1940 to 2000 Census IPUMS; the 1980, 1990, 2000, and 2005 CPS MORG samples. The log (college/high school) wage premium for each year is a weighted average of the estimated college (exactly 16 years of schooling or bachelor's degree) and post-college (17+ years of schooling or a post-baccalaureate degree) wage premium relative to high school workers (those with exactly 12 years of schooling or a high school diploma) for the year given. The weights are the employment shares of college and post-college workers in 1980. Educational wage differentials in each year are estimated using standard cross-section log hourly earnings regressions for wage and salary workers in each sample with dummies for single year of schooling (or degree attainment) categories, a quartic in experience, three region dummies, a part-time dummy, a female dummy, a nonwhite dummy, and interaction terms between the female dummy and quartic in experience and the nonwhite dummy. The levels of the log college wage premium can be compared across census samples and across CPS samples respectively. But the levels of the CPS and census wage differentials cannot be directly compared with each other due to differences in the construction of hourly wages in the two surveys. For further details see Autor, Katz, and Krueger (1998).

sales floor. That is, they were not always white-collar workers. Rather, they included ordinary production line workers who were using more complicated and valuable machinery. For these workers, having more education meant having some high school and possibly a high school diploma. For the professional positions, the more-educated individuals would have gone to college. Our point is that new and more complex technologies have had a long history of transforming the workplace, as well as everyday life, in ways that reward quick-thinking, flexible, often young, and educated individuals.

The most important historical point we want to make in this chapter concerns a unified explanation for long-term trends in inequality in America. The inequality story of the twentieth century contains two parts: an era of initially declining inequality, and a more recent one of rising inequality. But can the two parts of the inequality experience have a unified explanation in the context of a demand-side framework? If technological change was skill-biased in the latter part of the twentieth century so that the more skilled and educated did relatively better, was the opposite true of the earlier part of the century so that the less skilled and educated fared relatively better?

The answers lie in the fact that skill-biased technological change was far more rapid and continuous during most of the twentieth century than has been previously suspected. Similar amounts of "skill bias" can be measured during much of the twentieth century. Thus, the demand-side argument, *by itself,* cannot explain both parts of the twentieth century inequality experience. One cannot fully resolve the divergent inequality experiences of the two halves of the twentieth century by appealing to a recent acceleration in the degree of skill-biased technological change brought on by the computer revolution. Computers, to be sure, have given us much that is novel, time-saving, informative, entertaining, and convenient. Yet, in terms of the skill bias to technological change and the increase in the relative demand for skill, the era of computerization has brought little that is new. . . .

The evolution of the college wage premium and the educational composition of the US workforce from 1950 to 2005 are given in Table 8.1. The relative supply of college workers rose throughout the more than half-century era considered. The fraction of all full-time workers who were high school dropouts was almost 59 percent in 1950 and that for college graduates was barely 8 percent. In 2005, high school dropouts were 8 percent and college graduates were almost 32 percent. Those with some college rose from 9 percent to 29 percent. At the same time, however, the wage premium for college graduates relative to high school workers more than doubled, from 36.7 percent in 1950 to 86.6 percent in 2005. But most of the increase in the college premium occurred since 1980, with the decline in the college wage premium in the 1970s offsetting much of the earlier increases in the 1950s and 1960s.

The key implication of the two central facts of a rising college wage premium and rising relative supply of college workers since 1980 can be best understood with reference to Figure 8.1, which is a schematic representation of the market for skilled and unskilled labor.[5] In this simplified depiction, the workforce consists of two groups—the skilled or highly educated (Ls) and the unskilled or less educated (Lu). Relative wages for the two groups (w_s/w_u) are determined by the intersection of a downward-sloping relative demand curve and an upward-sloping relative supply curve. The short-run relative supply of more-skilled workers is assumed to be inelastic, since it is predetermined by factors such as past educational investments, immigration, and fertility.

Although one cannot directly observe the entire demand and supply functions, one can observe the equilibrium relative wages and relative skills employed, as given in Table 8.1. Figure 8.1 illustrates the recent changes using data from 1980 and 2000. The actual labor market outcomes from Table 8.1 shifted from point A (year 1980) to point B (year 2000). Thus, the relative supply function of more-skilled workers shifted outward from 1980 to 2000, from S_{1980} to S_{2000}. It is also the case—and this is a major point we would like to make—that the relative demand function must also have *shifted outward*. We have drawn such a shift in Figure 8.1 as from D_{1980} to D_{2000}.[6] But why did the relative demand curve shift outward?

Evidence on Skill-Biased Technological Change

Just because the relative demand for more highly skilled workers increased does not necessarily mean that there was skill-biased technological change. Another possibility, and one that has received considerable attention, is that the manufacturing jobs taken by the less well-educated in the United States have gone overseas. The relative demand for skill would then rise even if there had been no technological change. But there is very strong evidence for the technology explanation.

In the first place, relative employment of more-educated workers and of nonproduction workers increased rapidly *within* industries and *within* establishments during the 1980s and 1990s in the United States. The increased employment occurred despite the fact that the relative cost of hiring such workers greatly increased. Even though international outsourcing has been blamed for the decreased utilization of the less educated, the facts in this case argue against that explanation as being the primary factor. Large within-industry shifts toward more skilled workers occurred in sectors with little or no foreign outsourcing activity, at least in the 1980s and up to the late 1990s. Between-industry product demand shifts cannot be the main culprit. The magnitude of employment shifts to skill-intensive industries, as measured by between-industry demand shift indices, is simply too small.[7] New technologies and greater capital intensity, as shown in many studies, are strongly and positively associated with higher relative utilization of more-skilled workers in firms and industries.[8] A clear positive relationship has been found between the relative employment of more-skilled workers and measures of technology and capital, such as computer investments, the growth of employee computer use, R&D expenditures, the utilization of scientists and engineers, and increased capital intensity.[9] Case studies of the banking, auto repair, and valve industries show that the introduction of new computer-based technologies is strongly associated with shifts in demand toward more-educated workers.[10] Surveys of human resource managers reveal that large investments in information technology, particularly those that decentralize decision making and increase worker autonomy, increase the demand for more highly educated workers.[11] The evidence is consistent with the "computers did it" view of widening inequality. But we have more direct confirmation.

How have computers increased the relative demand for educated and skilled workers? A multitude of reasons exist and often differ by workplace. Computerized offices have routinized many white-collar tasks, and the simpler and more repetitive tasks are

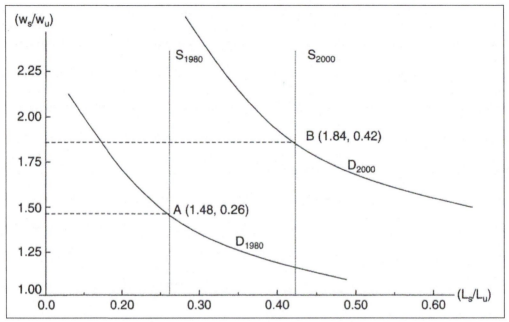

FIGURE 8.1 A Schematic Representation of the Relative Supply and Demand for Skill: 1980 and 2000

Point A is approximately the values for (w_s/w_u) and (L_s/L_u) from Table 8.1 (using the 1980 Census data and exponentiating the college/ high school wage premium) and point B is the same for 2000 (using the 2000 Census data), where L_s/L_u is the ratio of college graduates to those with less than a college degree as per the selection criteria given in Table 8.1. Thus, point A is $e^{0.391} = 1.48$ for (w_s/w_u) and 0.26 for (L_s/L_u).

more amenable to computerization than are the more complex and idiosyncratic. On the shop floor, microprocessor-based technologies have facilitated the automation of many production processes. Where hundreds of production workers once stood, often a handful remains together with a small team of workers operating the computer. Computers, the Internet, and electronic commerce have raised the returns to marketing and problem-solving skills.[12] The share of US workers directly using computers on the job increased from 25 percent in 1984 to 57 percent in 2003.[13] Even though computers have been easy for younger and highly educated workers to use, they have been daunting for many others, at least initially.

The empirical and logical case for skill-biased technological change, as a substantial source of demand shifts favoring more-educated workers since 1980, would appear very strong. But that does not necessarily mean that the driving force behind rising wage inequality since 1980 was an alteration in the type or a quickening in the rate of technological change. The reason is that capital-skill complementarity was present throughout the twentieth century as was rapid skill-biased technological change. These effects of technological change occurred even during periods of declining or stable educational wage differentials and narrowing economic inequality.

The evidence that skill-biased technological change has been ongoing for at least the last half century begins with a pioneering article by Zvi Griliches (1969), who found a substantial degree of capital-skill complementarity in US manufacturing during the 1950s. Other researchers following Griliches' path documented strong within-sector skill upgrading, even in the face of rising educational wage differentials during the 1950s and 1960s, and a strong positive correlation of industry skill demand with capital intensity and technology investments throughout the 1950s to the 1970s.[14] . . .

"It Isn't Just Technology—Stupid"

Great technological advances in recent decades have increased the relative demand for skill; but, surprising as it may seem, the early part of the twentieth century also experienced great advances that increased the relative demand for skill, possibly to an equal degree. Technological changes, however, were not always skill biased. We can locate a turning-point in the late nineteenth century when technological changes became, on net, skill biased.

Technological changes are not, in themselves, responsible for the increase in inequality in the recent period, just as they are not responsible for the decrease in inequality during the earlier part of the twentieth century. Thus the central point of this chapter, to paraphrase a mantra of the 1992 presidential campaign, is that "it isn't just technology—stupid." Since "it isn't just technology," the reason for rising inequality cannot be located solely on the demand side. The other important part of the answer can be found on the supply side.

REFERENCES

Autor, David H., Lawrence F. Katz, and Melissa S. Kearney. 2005. "Trends in U.S. Wage Inequality: Re-Assessing the Revisionists." NBER Working Paper no. 11627 (September).

Autor, David, Lawrence F. Katz, and Alan B. Krueger. 1998. "Computing Inequality: Have Computers Changed the Labor Market?," Quarterly Journal of Economics 113 (November), pp. 1169–213.

Autor, David H., Frank Levy, and Richard J. Murnane. 2003. "The Skill Content of Recent Technological Change: An Empirical Investigation," Quarterly Journal of Economics 118 (November), pp. 1279–333.

Bartel, A., Ichniowski, C., and K. Shaw. 2007. "How does Information Technology Really Affect Productivity? Plant-Level Comparisons of Product Innovation, Process Improvement, and Worker Skills." Quarterly Journal of Economics.

Borjas, George J., Richard B. Freeman, and Lawrence F. Katz. 1997. "How Much Do Immigration and Trade Affect Labor Market Outcomes?" Brookings Papers on Economic Activity, no. 1, pp. 1–90.

Bound, John, and George Johnson. 1995. "What Are the Causes of Rising Wage Inequality in the United States?" Economic Policy Review 1.1.

Bresnahan, Timothy F., Erik Brynjolfsson, and Lorin M. Hitt. February 2002. "Information Technology, Workplace Organization, and the Demand for Skilled Labor: Firm-Level Evidence," Quarterly Journal of Economics, Vol. 117, pp. 339–376.

Bresnahan, Timothy, and Manuel Trajtenberg. 1995. "General Purpose Technologies 'Engines of Growth?'" NBER Working Paper No. w4148.

Doms, Mark, Timothy Dunne, and Kenneth R. Troske. 1997. "Workers, Wages, and Technology," Quarterly Journal of Economics. 1997. CXII, 253–290.

Friedberg., L. 2003. The impact of technological change on older workers: evidence from data on computer use. Industrial and Labor Relations Review, 56(3), 511–529.

Griliches, Z. 1969. "Capital-skill Complementarity." The Review of Economics and Statistics, 51(4): 465–468.

Katz, Lawrence F., and David H. Autor. 1999. "Changes in the Wage Structure and Earnings Inequality," in Handbook of Labor Economics, Vol. 3, O. Ashenfelter and D. Card, eds. (Amsterdam: North-Holland).

Katz, Lawrence F., and Kevin M. Murphy. 1992. "Changes in Relative Wages, 1963–87: Supply and Demand Factors," Quarterly Journal of Economics 107 (February), pp. 35–78.

Lemieux, Thomas. 2006. "Postsecondary Education and Increased Wage Inequality," American Economic Review 96 (May), pp. 195–99.

Levy, Frank, and Richard J. Murnane. 2004. The New Division of Labor. New York: Russell Sage.

NOTES

1. See Autor, Katz, and Kearney (2005) and Lemieux (2006) on the recent patterns of the evolution of US residual (within-group) wage inequality.

2. Skill-biased technological change refers to any introduction of a new technology, change in production methods, or change in the organization of work that increases the demand for more-skilled labor (e.g., college graduates) relative to less-skilled labor (e.g., non-college workers) at fixed relative wages.

3. See Bresnahan and Trajtenberg (1995) on general purpose technologies and their contributions to economic growth.

4. The percentage college wage premium (adjusted for demographics) can be derived by exponentiating the log college/high school wage differential shown in the final column of Table 8.1, subtracting 1, and then multiplying by 100. The levels of the log college wage premium from the Census and CPS are not fully comparable due to differences in the construction of hourly wages in the two surveys. Thus, we add the 2000 to 2005 CPS change in the log college premium to the 2000 Census log college premium to get a 2005 log college premium that can be compared to the 1950 Census log college premium.

5. See Bound and Johnson (1995), Katz and Autor (1999), and Katz and Murphy (1992) for more detailed expositions of this framework.

6. Changes in institutional factors or norms of wage setting that lead to deviations from competitive labor market outcomes could have played a role, although the basic logic of the framework would still hold, as would the implication that the relative demand function shifted outward as long as firms remain on their labor demand curves. It is possible that institutional factors, such as unions, produced employment levels off the demand curve and that declines in union strength could have led to a reduction in the relative wage and employment of less highly educated workers even in the absence of demand shifts against them.

7. Autor, Katz, and Krueger (1998) find that growth in the employment and wage bill shares of more-educated workers from 1960 to 1996 is dominated by within in-

dustry changes using data on U.S. three-digit industries. Borjas, Freeman, and Katz (1997) illustrate that between industry labor demand shifts from international trade explain only a modest portion of the rise in the demand for more-skilled US workers from 1980 to 1995.

8. Doms, Dunne, and Troske (1997) provide a detailed plant-level analysis on the correlates of the adoption of new technologies in US manufacturing in the 1980s and 1990s.

9. Autor, Katz, and Krueger (1998) document strong positive correlations of skill upgrading with computer investments, increases in capital intensity, R&D investments, and increased employee computer usage for US industries.

10. On the banking sector, see Autor, Levy, and Murnane (2003) and Levy and Murnane (2004). Levy, Beamish, Murnane, and Autor (1999) examine auto repair and Bartel, Ichniowski, and Shaw (2007) study the valve industry.

11. Bresnahan, Brynjolfsson, and Hitt (2002) study these issues combining a detailed survey of senior human resource managers on organizational practices and labor force characteristics with detailed information on information technology investment for US companies in the mid-1990s.

12. Autor, Levy, and Murnane (2003) posit such an organizational complementarity between computers and workers who possess both greater cognitive skills and greater people skills.

13. Friedberg (2003) uses questions on computer use at work from a series of CPS Computer and Internet Use supplements to document the growth of US employee computer usage.

14. See, for example, Autor, Katz, and Krueger (1998).

---

9. Robert Frank*
Why Is Income Inequality Growing?

The bursting of the American housing bubble in 2008 sent the economy into free fall, with output and employment tumbling even more rapidly than during the early stages of the Great Depression in the 1930s. And as even free-market enthusiasts like former Federal Reserve chairman Alan Greenspan agreed, irresponsible lending practices by financial industry executives helped precipitate the crisis.

So it is little wonder that there was immediate and widespread public outrage over the billions of

*Original article prepared for the fourth edition of *Social Stratification: Class, Race, and Gender in Sociological Perspective*, edited by David B. Grusky. Copyright © 2014 Westview Press.

taxpayer dollars used to bail out large banks whose leaders had been receiving eight-figure annual bonuses. Nor should it be any surprise that with the economy still struggling and those bonuses again surging, populist anger continues.

By fall 2011 this anger had spawned the Occupy Wall Street movement. For the first time in more than eighty years, rising income inequality became a subject of widespread public discussion.

The specific public policy proposal offered most frequently in response to populist outrage has been a government-imposed cap on executive pay. In weighing this proposal, officials would do well to recall the words of Marcus Aurelius in *Meditations*: "How much more grievous are the consequences of anger than the causes of it."

Solving a problem requires an accurate diagnosis of its cause, and much of the received wisdom on the causes of rising inequality is spurious. Perhaps the most commonly held view is that inequality has grown because corporate miscreants have successfully suppressed competition. But although vivid examples of such abuses persist, most markets are in fact more competitive now than they have ever been.

In their influential book *Winner-Take-All Politics* (2010), the political scientists Jacob Hacker and Paul Pierson persuasively explain how a rising tide of campaign contributions has led Congress to enact lower tax rates for top earners and less stringent regulations for the corporations they own and manage.[1] It is a compelling story whose importance has been underscored by the US Supreme Court's decision in *Citizens United v. Federal Election Commission* in 2010. But although Hacker and Pierson are correct that the reductions in top tax rates won by campaign contributors have contributed to the growth of inequality, those reductions are of only secondary importance. Across a broad swath of markets, not just those in which regulation has been relaxed, the far more important dimension of the story has been the change in the distribution of pretax incomes.

For the first three decades after World War II, pretax incomes grew at roughly the same rate— slightly less than 3 percent a year—for households at all rungs of the income ladder. Since the mid-1970s, however, the pattern has been dramatically different. The inflation-adjusted median hourly wage for American men is actually lower now than it was in 1975. Real median household incomes have grown by roughly 15 percent since then, primarily because of large increases in female labor force participation. Only those in the top quintile, whose incomes have roughly doubled since the mid-1970s, have escaped the income slowdown.

That last statement is somewhat misleading, however, because the income growth picture is much the same within the top quintile as for the population as a whole. That is, those at the bottom of the top quintile have seen little real income growth, the lion's share of which has been concentrated among top earners in the group. Real incomes among the top 5 percent, for example, were more than two and a half times larger in 2007 than in 1979, whereas those among the top 1 percent were almost four times larger. In 1976 only 8.9 percent of the nation's total pretax incomes went to the top 1 percent of earners, but by 2007 that group was receiving 23.5 percent of the total.

The pattern is similar for virtually all groups. It is true for dentists, for example, and also for college graduates. In every group, pretax real incomes have been largely stagnant for all but the top earners.

Some of the most spectacular growth in top incomes has occurred in the financial services industry, where, as Hacker and Pierson explain, relaxed regulation has been an important reason. But deregulation and tax favors are not the central story for most of the economy.

Others argue that chief executive officer (CEO) pay has soared because executives pack their boards with cronies who gratefully grant them outsized salaries. That obviously has happened in specific cases. But because this is hardly a new phenomenon, it fails as an explanation of why CEO pay has risen so dramatically over time. Institutional investors and leveraged buyout specialists are now a much more powerful force in the market than they were three decades ago. Because these investors know that share prices fall when a CEO packs the board with cronies, they can profit by intervening when they see evidence of that happening.

In one celebrated instance, Kohlberg, Kravis, Roberts won the bidding for control of RJR-Nabisco at a time when the corporation was perceived to be severely underperforming under CEO Ross Johnson. KKR's first move was to fire Johnson. The buyout firm managed to break even on this transaction, even though it paid share prices twice as high as they had been under Johnson's leadership. In short, the growing influence of large outside investors has made executive misbehavior less widespread than it used to be.

Why, then, has CEO pay at the nation's largest companies risen more than tenfold during the past three decades? As Philip Cook and I argued in our 1995 book *The Winner-Take-All Society*, the simplest explanation rests on technological changes that not only have increased the value of the most talented business leaders, but also have resulted in more open competition for their services.[2] Falling shipping costs, advances in production technology, and the information revolution have combined to increase the scope of many markets in recent decades. Companies that were local became regional, then national, and now international. Scale matters. When a corporal errs, fewer soldiers suffer than when a general missteps. The same holds true in the corporate world. As enterprises have grown, the economic consequences of decisions made by top management have increased in tandem.

A simple numerical example illustrates the extent to which growing scale increases the leverage of executive talent. Measured by market capitalization, Apple is currently the world's largest company. Its future earnings growth depends heavily on its ability to ramp up production quickly enough to serve the rapidly growing demand for its smartphones and tablets. The company's current CEO, Tim Cook, is widely regarded as one of the world's most talented supply chain managers. Now suppose, conservatively, that Cook is just 3 percent better than the next best candidate Apple could have tapped for the same task. If Apple's fiscal 2012 earnings of approximately $40 billion were 3 percent higher because of Cook's performance, he was worth $1.2 billion more to the company's shareholders that year than the second-best CEO candidate would have been. Cook's 2012 pretax compensation package has been reported as $376 million—no small sum, to be sure, but only a fraction of even a conservative estimate of his value to the company.

But growth in executive leverage alone cannot explain the explosive increase in executive salaries. The decisions made by Charles Erwin Wilson, who headed General Motors from 1941 to 1953, had as great an impact on that company's annual bottom line as the corresponding decisions by today's average Fortune 500 CEO. Yet even after adjusting for inflation, Wilson's total career earnings at GM were just a fraction of what today's top CEOs earn every year.

This is so because a second factor necessary to explain explosive CEO pay growth—an open market for CEOs—did not exist in Wilson's day. Until recently, most corporate boards shared an implicit belief that the only viable candidates for top executive positions were those who had spent all or most of their careers with the company. There was usually a leading internal candidate to succeed a retiring CEO and seldom more than a few others who were even credible choices. Under the circumstances, CEO pay was a matter of negotiation between the board and the anointed successor.

That nearly exclusive focus on insiders has softened in recent decades, a change driven in no small part by one particularly visible outside hire. In 1993 IBM decided to hire Louis J. Gerstner away from RJR Nabisco. At the time outside observers were extremely skeptical that a former tobacco CEO would be able to turn the struggling computer giant around. But IBM's board thought that Gerstner's motivational and managerial talent were just what the company needed, and that subordinates could compensate for Gerstner's gaps in technical knowledge. The company's bet paid off spectacularly, of course, and in the years since then an existing trend toward hiring CEOs from outside has accelerated in most industries.

Most companies still promote CEOs from within, but even in those cases the spot market for talent has completely transformed the climate in which salary negotiations take place. Internal candidates can now credibly threaten to go elsewhere if they are not remunerated in accordance with the market's estimate of their value.

Critics point to examples of disastrously unsuccessful CEOs to support their claim that executive pay is completely divorced from performance. Certainly corporate boards never know for sure how much a given executive will add to or subtract from the company's bottom line. They are forced to rely on crude estimates, and hiring decisions based on them sometimes don't pan out. But even crude estimates are informative, and companies that did not gamble in accordance with them would eventually cede ground to rivals that did.

The simple fact is that in large organizations, even marginally better executive performance has an enormous impact on a company's bottom line. It is because executive labor markets are becoming more, rather than less, competitive that executive compensation in large American corporations has risen more than tenfold since 1980.

The winner-take-all perspective is by no means confined to the executive suite. The economist's traditional explanation of why some people earn more than others is that people are paid in rough proportion to their human capital: an amalgam of charac-teristics such as intelligence, training, experience, temperament, and the like. The human capital model directs our attention to the worker rather than the job. Yet a given level of human capital will realize its full value only if placed in a position with adequate scope and opportunity. For example, whereas having a slightly more talented salesperson may mean little if the task is to sell children's shoes, it will mean a great deal if the task is to sell securities to the world's largest pension funds.

An economist under the influence of the human capital metaphor might ask: Why not save money by hiring two mediocre people to fill an important position, instead of paying the exorbitant salary required to attract the best? Although that sort of substitution might succeed with physical capital, it does not necessarily work with human capital. Two average surgeons or CEOs or novelists or quarterbacks are often a poor substitute for a single gifted one.

Technology has greatly extended the power and reach of the planet's most gifted performers. The printing press let a relatively few gifted storytellers displace any number of minstrels and village raconteurs. Now that we listen mostly to recorded music, the world's best soprano can be everywhere at once. The electronic newswire allowed a small number of syndicated columnists to displace a host of local journalists. And the proliferation of personal computers has enabled a handful of software developers to replace thousands of tax accountants.

The result is that for positions in which additional talent has great value to the employer or the marketplace, there is no reason to expect that the market will compensate individuals in proportion to their human capital. For such positions—which confer the greatest leverage or "amplification" of human talent—small increments of talent may have enormous value and may be greatly rewarded as a result of the normal competitive market process. This simple insight lies at the core of the winner-take-all perspective on growing inequality.

Of course the mere fact that explosive pay growth at the top may have been largely a consequence of market forces does not make it an improper object of public policy concern. But neither does the mere fact that the highest salaries make some people feel angry and resentful mean that it would be a good idea for the government to cap executive pay. Any legislative action to abridge the freedom to negotiate mutually satisfactory contracts between executives and their employers must be predicated on a persuasive showing that existing freedoms impose undue costs on others.

As it turns out, that is relatively easy to demonstrate. As I have argued elsewhere, runaway income growth at the top has spawned changes in spending patterns that have made it more difficult for middle-income families to achieve basic life goals.[3] Consider, for example, the middle-income family whose goal is to send its children to a school of at least average quality. A good school is an inherently context-dependent concept. It compares favorably with other schools in the same area. In almost every jurisdiction, the better schools tend to serve children who live in more expensive neighborhoods. The upshot is that the median family must outbid 50 percent of other parents merely to send its children to a school of average quality.

Achieving that goal has become much more expensive in recent decades. Between 1970 and 2007, for example, the median size of a newly constructed single-family home in the United States increased by more than 50 percent. But if real median wages were essentially stagnant during that period, why did the median house grow so much bigger?

That question is difficult to answer without reference to an expenditure cascade launched by higher spending at the top. Top earners built bigger houses simply because they had so much more money. That changed the frame of reference that shapes demands among earners just below the top, who travel in similar social circles, so they, too, built bigger houses. And so on, all the way down the income ladder.

Similar cascades have influenced how much families must spend to celebrate special occasions. The average American wedding in 2009 cost $27,000, almost three times as much, in real terms, as its counterpart in 1980.

Capping executive pay would be an ill-considered response to the expenditure cascades that have made life more difficult for the middle class. It would undercut one of the most important functions of the labor market, which is to steer people to the jobs that will make the most productive use of their talents. Having a slightly more talented CEO improves corporate earnings by a larger amount in a big company than in a small one. So if each CEO candidate accepts the highest offer received, both total corporate earnings and total CEO earnings will be maximized. Executive pay caps would reduce those totals by eliminating the signals that steer people to the jobs that make best use of their talents. But why would anyone prefer a world with more,

say, personal injury lawyers and fewer corporate executives?

Fortunately, we can address the most important costs of runaway income inequality without compromising the labor market's ability to allocate talent efficiently. Beyond a certain point, what matters most in people's decisions to take particular jobs is relative pay, not absolute pay. If any one company were to reduce its CEO pay offer unilaterally, it would risk losing its best candidates to rival firms. But if all companies cut their salaries in half, most executives would end up in the same jobs as before. Companies cannot organize across-the-board pay cuts on their own, but the government can accomplish the same goal through the tax structure.

Higher tax rates on top earners would attenuate the expenditure cascades that have been making life so much more costly for middle-income families. With fewer after-tax dollars to spend, the additions to top earners' mansions and the expenses for their children's coming-of age parties would grow less rapidly. And because it is relative expenditure that beyond some point determines whether people achieve what they set out to do, top earners wouldn't sacrifice anything important by spending less.

Hacker and Pierson are right that the growing influence of money on politics has been pernicious. But although the campaign contributions of top earners have bought them lower tax rates and less stringent regulations on their companies, such political shenanigans have not been the most important cause of rising income inequality. The big story has been the explosive growth in pretax incomes of the top 1 percent, and in most sectors of the economy that growth has been largely a consequence of intensifying market forces.

Those forces have produced important social benefits, but have also generated enormous social costs. The good news is that simple changes in tax policy can curb those costs without sacrificing the most important benefits.

NOTES

1. Jacob Hacker and Paul Pierson, *Winner-Take-All Politics: How Washington Made the Rich Richer—and Turned Its Back on the Middle Class* (New York: Simon & Schuster, 2010).

2. Robert H. Frank and Philip J. Cook, *The Winner-Take-All Society* (New York: The Free Press, 1995).

3. Robert H. Frank, *The Darwin Economy* (Princeton, NJ: Princeton University Press, 2011).

10. Jacob S. Hacker and Paul Pierson*

Winner-Take-All Politics: Public Policy, Political Organization, and the Precipitous Rise of Top Incomes in the United States

The three salient trends [of our time]—that income has become hyper-concentrated at the top, that the increase in income hyperconcentration has been sustained, and that this hyperconcentration has produced few "trickle-down" benefits for the vast majority of American households—raise difficult problems for standard economic analyses of rising inequality that emphasize autonomous market changes that have widened the gap among broad skill and educational groups. They also call into question some central features of recent works that move beyond this economic emphasis to bring in politics.

By far the dominant economic explanation for rising inequality emphasizes "skill-biased technological change"—a shift toward greater emphasis on specialized skills, knowledge, and education—that has fueled a growing divide between the highly educated and the rest of American workers.[1] The evidence on the changing income distribution shows, however, that American inequality is not mainly about the gap between the well-educated and the rest, or indeed about educational gaps in general. It is about the extraordinarily rapid pulling away of the very top. Those at the top are often highly educated, but so too are those just below them who have been left behind. Put another way, the distribution of educational gains over the last twenty-five years—who finishes college or gains advanced degrees—has been much broader than the distribution of economic gains. Only a very small slice of the new educational elite has entered the new economic elite.

Another problem for the standard economic account is that the United States looks distinct from other nations, despite the fact that all these nations have presumably been buffeted by similar market and technological forces. American inequality is the highest in the advanced industrial world. Yet gaps in skills are not measurably larger in the United States than they are in other affluent nations. And while the return to schooling is higher in the United States, this explains only a trivial portion of American inequality relative to inequality in other nations.[2] American distinctiveness is particularly pronounced when it comes to the hyperconcentration of income at the top. Figure 10.1 shows the share of income, excluding capital gains, going to the top 1 percent in twelve rich nations. The first bar shows the share in the mid-1970s (1973–75); the second shows the share around the millennium (1998–2004). As the figure makes clear, the United States leads the pack with regard to both the level (16 percent) and increase (virtually a doubling) of the top 1 percent's share of income. Note that half of the nations in Figure 10.1—France, Germany, Japan, the Netherlands, Sweden, and Switzerland—experienced little or no increase. Note, too, that the United States was similar to many of these nations in terms of the share of income going to the top 1 percent in the 1970s—indeed, the shares in the United States and Sweden track very closely until around 1980.

It is true that the other English-speaking nations in this group—Australia, Canada, Ireland, New Zealand, and the United Kingdom—have followed a path more like the United States's, suggesting overlapping policy and political trends. Still, the United States stands out even among these nations, experiencing a doubling of the income share of the top 1 percent between the mid-1970s and 2000, compared with around half that in percentage terms in the other five nations. (The difference is smaller if 1980 is used as the base year, rather than the mid-1970s, but the United States still experienced a larger percentage increase—despite starting from a higher base.)

Moreover, the trajectory of the two countries that are most often compared to the United States's, the United Kingdom and Canada, cannot be viewed as wholly independent of the rise of America's winner-take-all economy. The rise in the compensation of the highest earners, especially corporate executives and financial managers, drives much of the outsized gains at the top in the United States. Companies in English-speaking Canada and the United Kingdom compete for these workers, and thus have faced the most pressure to match the massive salaries on offer in the United States. There is substantial evidence that much of the (considerably smaller) rise in executive compensation in Canada is driven by American developments, rather than reflecting an

*Republished with permission of Sage Publications, Inc. Journals, from "Winner-Take-All Politics: Public Policy, Political Organization, and the Precipitous Rise of Top Incomes in the United States," by Jacob S. Hacker and Paul Pierson, published in *Politics & Society* 38:2, Copyright © 2010; permission conveyed through Copyright Clearance Center, Inc.

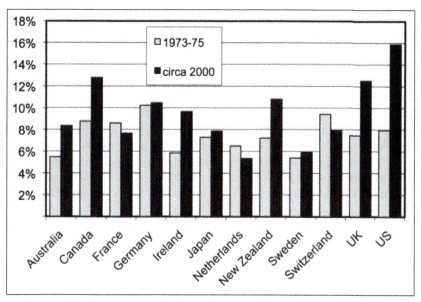

FIGURE 10.1 The Top 1 Percent's Share of National Income, Mid-1970s versus Circa 2000

Source: Andrew Leigh. "How Closely Do Top Incomes Track Other Measures of Inequality?" *Economic Journal* 117, no. 524 (2007): 619–33, http://econrsss.anu.edu.au/~aleigh/pdf/TopIncomesPanel.xls.

independent example of the same phenomenon.[3] While the contagion effect of the United States is difficult to quantify, some (and perhaps much) of the increase in top incomes in other English-speaking nations may reflect competitive pressure to match the more dramatic rise in the United States—a rise that we shall see has a great deal to do with US public policy.

Some economists have accepted that American inequality has been distinctly top-heavy but insist that the market still rules. The economist (and former Bush administration official) Gregory Mankiw has evocatively likened the American superrich to the winners of the golden ticket in *Charlie and the Chocolate Factory*.[4] Most of the educated receive only the chocolate bar; a lucky few find a ticket to vast riches within the bar's wrapper. But Mankiw's analogy is silent on the question *of how the tickets were placed in the chocolate bar and why some of the educated get the ticket and others do not.* It implies that both the presence of the tickets and the selection is market-driven, when in fact, as we shall see, Mankiw's "golden tickets" were in substantial part created by government, and their distribution has been deeply shaped by the political clout of their beneficiaries.

To be sure, market processes and technological changes have played a significant part in shaping the distribution of rewards at the top. Revolutionary changes in information technology have fostered more concentrated rewards in fields of endeavor—such as sports or entertainment—where the ability to reach large audiences is the principal determinant of economic return.[5] Computers, increased global capital flows, and the development of new financial instruments have made it possible for savvy investors to reap (or lose) huge fortunes almost instantaneously. Other examples of such technologically driven winner-take-all inequality can be found. But these accounts do not come close to explaining the concentrated gains at the very top of the American economic ladder, especially those driven by rising executive pay and financial market compensation. They do not explain why these trends have been much more pronounced in the United States than elsewhere. Nor do they explain why market structures conducive to such outcomes arose when they did, much less why, as we show, those structures were fostered by government.

An Organizational-Policy Perspective on Winner-Take-All Inequality

A convincing political account of American inequality must explain the defining feature of American inequality, namely, the stunning shift of income toward the very top. Equally important, it must explain how public policy has contributed to this trend. This means not only identifying public policies that can be linked to large increases in inequality; it also means providing an account of the political processes that have led to the generation of those policies.

These are not easy tasks. They require an understanding of the connections, often subtle, between policy structures and economic outcomes. Moreover, they require close examination of the political forces behind policy change. Depending on the policy involved, the relevant decision makers may be legislators, regulators, or presidents. New enactments may be required to shift policy. As we will see, however, policy change often occurs when groups with the ability to block change effectively resist the updating of policy over an extended period of time in the face of strong contrary pressure and strong evidence that policy is failing to achieve its initial goals—what we call policy "drift."[6] These complex connections between political action and social outcomes are not likely to be established without sustained attention to the evolving content of public policies.

Existing political accounts—while a vast improvement over the standard economic diagnosis—are not particularly successful in identifying plausible links among politics, policy, and rising inequality. McCarty, Poole, and Rosenthal focus on the way in which gridlock has prevented policy updating in a few areas (the minimum wage, public assistance policies, the estate tax), but for the most part say little about how public policy has influenced rising inequality—and virtually nothing about how it has fueled the meteoric rise of top incomes. Bartels, for his part, fails to show how partisan control of the executive by itself could plausibly be connected to the dramatic rise in winner-take-all outcomes that has occurred since the late 1970s.

At the root of these weaknesses, in our view, is a conception of politics that focuses overwhelmingly on the voter-politician relationship—a view we call "politics as electoral spectacle." By contrast, we believe the rise of winner-take-all inequality can only be convincingly explained with a very different perspective—which we call "politics as organized combat."

Government's Reshaping of the American Economy

If the politics of electoral spectacle is about winning elections, the politics of organized combat is about

transforming what government does. Did the shifting balance of organized interests lead to major changes in the governance of the American political economy? The answer is yes, and we document these changes in four crucial policy arenas: taxation, industrial relations, executive compensation, and financial markets.

We seek to make a plausible case for two claims. First, there is substantial evidence that policy developments of the past three decades—through both enactments and drift—have made a central contribution to the surge of winner-take-all economic outcomes in the United States. Second, there is also substantial evidence that organized interests were highly motivated, mobilized, and involved in many of these developments.

Taxes

Taxes represent perhaps the most visible way in which policy makers influence the distribution of income. Furthermore, even casual observers are aware that policy since the Reagan administration has often involved significant tax cuts for the well-to-do. Yet crucial questions remain unanswered—questions we will address with regard to all four of the policy areas we examine. How big has the policy shift been? Has it made a significant contribution to rising inequality? Who exactly has benefited? Moreover, what does the pattern of policy change suggest about political dynamics? When, and through what mechanisms, has policy changed?

Thanks to work by Thomas Piketty and Emmanuel Saez, we are now in a much better position to answer some of these questions.[7] Piketty and Saez have generated stunning data on the changing structure of federal taxation. The data allow Piketty and Saez to investigate tax *incidence*—not just changes in the marginal rates in the tax code but the actual tax levels that households pay once deductions and other maneuvers are taken into account.

Piketty and Saez's results, presented in Figure 10.2, are striking in several respects. First, they suggest that the role of taxes in rising inequality is much more pronounced if one concentrates on the very top income groups. The changes of the tax rate for those at the ninetieth percentile, and even the ninety-eighth percentile, have actually been quite modest over the past four decades. By contrast, there have been startlingly large changes for those in the top 1 percent. This is mostly because of the declining role of the corporate income tax and the estate tax. *Progressivity*

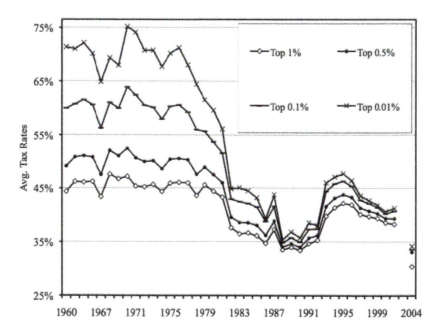

FIGURE 10.2 Average Tax Rates for Top Income Groups, 1960–2004

Source: Thomas Piketty and Emmanual Saez, "How Progressive Is the U.S. Federal Tax System? A Historical and International Perspective," *Journal of Economic Perspectives* 21, no. 1 (2007): 3–24.

used to be very pronounced at the very top of the tax code; now it is almost entirely absent. As Piketty and Saez summarize their findings, "The 1960 federal tax system was very progressive even within the top percentile, with an average tax rate of around 35 percent in the bottom half of the top percentile to over 70 percent in the top 0.01 percent."[8] Second, not only has the shift in policy been highly concentrated on the very affluent, the magnitude of the shift is quite large. Again, Piketty and Saez:

[T]he pre-tax share of income for the top 0.1 percent rose from 2.6 percent in 1970 to 9.3 percent in 2000. The rise in after-tax income shares was from 1.2 percent in 1970 to over 7.3 percent in 2000. In percentage point terms, the increase in pretax incomes is slightly greater than the increase in posttax incomes. But in terms of observing what those with very high incomes can afford to consume, the after-tax share of income for those in this income group multiplied by a factor of 6.1, while the pretax share of income multiplied by a factor of 3.5. The tax reductions enacted in 2001 and 2003 have further weakened the redistributive power of the federal income tax today.[9]

One can ask, counterfactually, what if the gap between pre- and post-tax income of the top 1 percent had not declined since 1970? According to Piketty

and Saez, the top 0.1 percent had about 7.3 percent of after-tax income in 2000. If the gap between their pre- and post-tax income had remained what it was in 1970, they would have had about 4.5 percent of after-tax income. In other words, *changes in tax incidence account for roughly one-third of the total gains in income share for the top 0.1 percent in the last four decades.* (Moreover, this is just the direct effect of the decline in effective taxation at the top. Many experts believe the rise in executive pay that we will discuss in a moment has been fostered indirectly by the decline, which has increased the confidence of compensation boards that executives will reap much of the astronomical salaries that boards grant.)

Equally striking is the enduring nature of the policy shift. Although the early years of the Reagan administration figure prominently, the change began in the 1970s. The initial drop came through large cuts in the capital gains tax and other taxes on the well-to-do passed, after very intense business lobbying, by a Congress composed of large Democratic majorities in both chambers and signed into law by a Democratic president.

Moreover, it is difficult to trace these developments to any straightforward shift in public opinion regarding taxation.[10] Research on both the tax cuts of the early 1980s and those of the past few years suggest that organized interests have played a prominent role, both in keeping tax cuts on the agenda and shaping policy to focus the gains of tax-policy changes on those at the very top of the income distribution.[11] The rise of supply-side economics, with its emphasis on the negative effects of high marginal tax rates on the well-off, surely helped the progress of tax cuts. Yet the supply-side rationale actually gained credence only *after* the initial flurry of tax cuts in the 1970s, and it was largely exhausted as a serious intellectual force by the time the Bush administration and congressional Republicans slashed upper-income taxes in the early 2000s.

A number of specific developments within the broad arc of tax policy making suggest an impressive focus on directing benefits not just to the very well-to-do (say, the bottom half of the top 1 percent), but to the superrich. David Cay Johnston provides copious evidence, for example, that there has been a steep decline, encouraged by Congress, in IRS oversight of high-income returns, combined with a politically induced shift of resources to oversight of Earned Income Tax Credit returns of the poor and lower middle class.[12] Studies of specific battles over the estate tax and the alternative minimum tax have suggested that policy makers repeatedly chose courses of action that strongly advantaged the very wealthy at the expense of the much larger group of the merely well-to-do.[13] In all these accounts, the influence of organized interests—particularly lobbyists representing business and the wealthy, conservative antitax groups such as Americans for Tax Reform, and free-market think tanks like the Cato Institute—loom much larger than the sway of voters or pull of general public sentiment.

Industrial Relations

The evolution of industrial relations in the United States provides the second crucial chapter in the tale of winner-take-all inequality's rise. Research in comparative political economy has long maintained that the organization of relationships between employers and workers is of fundamental significance for a wide range of economic interactions. For good reason: there are wide and highly consequential differences in these arrangements within the universe of affluent democracies that have been repeatedly linked to major distributional and market differences across nations.

The United States has always stood out on measures of union strength as a nation with a weak organized labor movement. Nonetheless, over the past three decades, the structure of American industrial relations has changed profoundly. Union density—the share of the workforce covered by collective bargaining—has fallen precipitously, especially in the private sector. From organizing roughly one-third of the workforce, union organization has fallen to under one-tenth of private sector employees. . . .

[There are] at least two important ramifications of union power. First, unions have the capacity to play an important role in corporate governance.[14] At least under certain institutional conditions, they have the resources and incentives necessary to provide a check on the scale of executive compensation, and to push for compensation designs that align executive incentives more closely with those of their firms. Indeed, even with their current weakness, American unions represent one of only two organized interests providing a potential check on managerial autonomy—the other being "investor collectives" like public employee pension systems and (more problematically) mutual funds.

Second, unions may play a significant role in political conflicts related to the distribution of income. On the one hand, they may push policy makers to address issues of mounting inequality. On the other, they may recognize, highlight, and effectively resist policy changes that further inequality. Consider just one example of how the contemporary weakness of organized labor shows up in recent policy developments. Well over a thousand registered lobbyists in Washington identify taxes as one of their areas of activity. Yet during recent fights over the estate tax—a policy issue with large and obvious distributional consequences—organized labor could supply only *one* union lobbyist to address the issue.[15] Amazingly, even this lobbyist was available only quarter-time to work on *all* tax issues. In fact, the biggest organized opposition to estate tax repeal came not from organized labor but from a group of billionaires led by William Gates Sr. (Bill Gates's father). It is hard to imagine a more telling illustration of the existing organizational inequalities in Washington on economic issues.

Even if one accepts labor's potential significance for politics and policy making, however, there is the issue of how to account for union decline. Many would maintain that the decline of unions in the United States is almost exclusively a market phenomenon. Unions are fading, it is often suggested, because of changes in the global economy that relentlessly send their jobs overseas. Yet as in so many

TABLE 10.1 Union Share of Wage and Salary Workers in the United States and Canada

	United States (%)	Canada (%)	Percentage point difference
1960	30.4	32.3	1.9
1970	26.4	33.6	7.2
1980	22.2	35.7	13.5
1990	15.3	34.5	19.2
2000	13.5	32.4	18.9
2005	12.5	32.0	19.5

Sources: David Card, Thomas Lemieux, and W. Craig Riddell, "Unionization and Wage Inequality: A Comparative Study of the U.S., the U.K. and Canada" (Working Paper 9473, National Bureau of Economic Research, Cambridge, MA, 2003); Sylvia Allegreto, Lawrence Mishel, and Jared Bernstein, *The State of Working America* (Ithaca, NY: Cornell University Press, 2008); and Statistics Canada, *Labour Force Historical Review* 2008 (Table Cd3T09an), Ottawa, Statistics Canada, 2009 (Cat. No. 71F0004XCB).

aspects of the subject of inequality, a comparative view casts doubt on the idea that market imperatives are the only story, and that extreme union decline in the private sector is inevitable. While unions have declined in significance in many Western nations, their presence has fallen little or none in others.[16] And one of those nations has the virtue for comparative analysis of being otherwise quite similar to the United States—namely, Canada. Once more limited in reach than their American counterparts, Canadian unions now enjoy much broader membership (about one-third of the nonagricultural workforce) and have seen little decline—despite similar worker attitudes toward unions in the two nations (Table 10.1).

The contrast with Canada suggests the possibility that fall in union density has been in significant part a political process. And indeed there is considerable evidence this is the case. Popular advocates of this view would stress events like Ronald Reagan's efforts to break the strike by air traffic controllers (PATCO), as well as changes in the composition of the National Labor Relations Board after his election. As Henry Farber and Bruce Western have cogently argued, however, a heavy emphasis on these overt initiatives is difficult to reconcile with a close examination of the timing and patterns of union decline.[17] Our own account would emphasize alternative policy mechanisms and focus on the consequences of government inaction rather than action. During the recent transformation of the American political economy, the evolution of industrial relations is perhaps the most consequential instance of policy drift. The absence of an updating of industrial relations policy has had brutal effects on the long-term prospects of organized labor. It is well understood that the American industrial relations system contained certain structural features that gravely threatened unions after the 1960s.[18] Well established in certain manufacturing industries in particular states, unions were acutely vulnerable to the movement of manufacturing jobs to states where labor rights were more limited, as well as shifts in employment to sectors that had not previously been organized.

An updating of industrial relations policy could have addressed some of these weaknesses. Careful

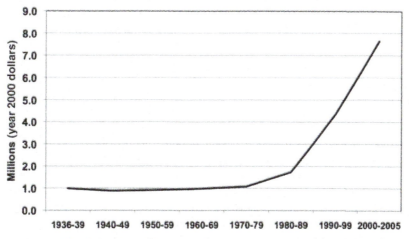

FIGURE 10.3 The Evolution of Executive Compensation (Mean Pay of Top Executives)

Source: Carols Frydman and Raven Saks, "Historical Trends in Executive Compensation, 1936–2003" (Working paper, Massachusetts Institute of Technology, Cambridge, MA, 2005).
Note: Sum of salaries, bonuses, long-term bonus payments, and the Black-Scholes value of stock option grants for the three highest-paid officers in the largest fifty firms in 1940, 1960, and 1990.

comparison with Canada is revealing. As Table 10.1 suggests, the two union movements diverged dramatically in their capacity to cope with a shifting economic environment. The Canadian economist W. Craig Riddell has found that little of the divergence can be explained by structural differences in the two nations' economies, or even by differing worker propensities to join a union.[19] Rather, the difference is due to the much lower (and declining) likelihood in the United States that workers who have an interest in joining a union will actually belong to one. There is considerable evidence that differences in labor law are a major part of the explanation. Prominent institutional differences include Canadian practices that allow for card certification and first-contract arbitration, ban permanent striker replacements, and impose strong limits on employer speech.[20] Meanwhile, aggressive antiunion activities by employers in the United States have met little resistance from public authorities.

In short, the severe decline of organized labor in the United States was in part a *political* outcome, driven by new antiunion enactments as well as the failure to update policy to reflect the increasing relative strength of employers in a more global, service-oriented economy. There were policy alternatives that would have reduced the decline, and that had advocates within the United States. The opponents of such reforms, possessing formidable and growing organizational resources, mobilized effectively to stop them. They then used their organizational resources to exploit the resulting drift and launch a vigorous assault on American labor, with effects felt not just in the economic sphere but also in American politics.

Corporate Governance and Executive Compensation

While changes in taxation and the reach of unions are obviously germane to inequality, the case for discussion of corporate governance requires some defense. No one disputes that rising executive pay has played a central role in mounting American inequality. Piketty and Saez suggest that perhaps half of the pretax gains of the top 1 percent reflect the explosion of executive compensation.[21] Figure 10.3 shows the development of total compensation for the top three executives at the nation's largest firms since the mid-1930s. As the figure shows, executive pay skyrockets after 1980, with the largest increases coming in the 1990s.

Here we enter a sphere that Americans have typically treated as outside of politics, but which comparative evidence suggest is strongly influenced by patterns of political contestation.[22] Cross-nationally there is tremendous variation in corporate governance practices and in economic outcomes. Rising executive compensation is much more evident in Anglo countries than in other rich democracies, and most evident of all in the United States. Compensation structures remain much different in most of the advanced industrial world than they are in the United States. For instance, where stock options are used, they are often linked to long-term rather than short-term performance, as well as to firm performance relative to industry norms. Thus, for example, when a rising price of oil drives up the share price of energy companies, CEOs would receive extra compensation only if their firm's performance exceeded industry averages.

The rise in executive pay seems related to a broader shift in structures of corporate governance, ostensibly toward maximization of "shareholder value" but arguably toward what Peter Gourevitch and James Shinn call "managerism," in which opportunities for well-positioned elites to extract resources increase. The hypothesis to consider is that the capacity of managers to engage in such extraction has increased.[23] The issue, as the financier John Bogle has recently put it, is whether the United States moved toward an "ownership society" in which managers serve owners or an "agency society" in which managers serve themselves.

A school of thought (prominent in the field of law and economics) sees the United States's and other systems of diffused ownership as representing the best protections for stockholders.[24] That view relies heavily on a principal-agent analysis that sees boards of directors as protecting shareholders through "arm's-length negotiations" with executives. Yet in many cases, boards are not playing the role outlined in this theory. Lucian Bebchuk and Jesse Fried provide many findings more consistent with a "board-capture" view, in which boards are so beholden to managers that they offer little countervailing authority.[25] Perhaps most telling, the design of CEO compensation often varies markedly from what one would expect if it were intended to encourage good performance. Indeed, in much the same way that our view of interest groups suggests opportunities to outflank disorganized "outsiders" (exploiting structural advantages under conditions of asymmetric information), Bebchuk and Fried demonstrate the prominence in corporate arrangements of what they call "camouflage." Patterns of executive compensation seem designed to mitigate public outrage rather than limit excessive pay or link it more closely to value.

Most accounts of American inequality, if they touch on these issues at all, regard them as matters of markets, not politics. At a minimum, however, policy makers (like police officers who studiously look the other way) have done little to constrain the dramatic shift that has taken place. This is in sharp contrast to the experience abroad, where—even though executive pay is much lower—there have been substantial efforts to monitor and impose limits on executive pay, and where sources of countervailing power appear to be much stronger. Again, the comparative evidence of American (or at least Anglo) exceptionalism with regard to executive pay suggests that there is nothing about the structure of modern capitalism that makes such extraordinary increases in executive salaries inevitable or even likely.

In fact, one can see strong links between American policy making and the explosion of executive compensation. The most direct, and consequential, concerns the development of stock options. This constitutes another highly significant example of policy drift. During the 1990s, stock options became the central vehicle for enhancing executive compensation—indeed, roughly 50 percent of executive compensation came through stock options by 2001. Although ostensibly a vehicle for linking pay to performance, these options were almost always structured in ways that lowered the visibility of high payouts (by removing them from financial accounts at the time they were granted). Moreover, options were granted without creating strong connections between payout and managerial effectiveness, even though instruments for establishing such links were well-known and widely used abroad.[26] The value of options simply rose along with stock prices, even if stock price gains were fleeting, or a firm's performance badly trailed that of other companies in the same sector. In the extreme but widespread practice of "backdating," option values were reset retroactively to provide big gains for executives—a practice akin to repositioning the target after the fact to make sure the archer's shot hits the bull's-eye.

The structure of American corporate governance—and its associated, distinctive patterns of executive compensation—is a prime contributor to American winner-take-all inequality. To a considerable if largely unrecognized extent, this is a *political* outcome. The policy alternative is not just hypothetical; other countries, including ones with market systems relatively similar to that of the United States', have moved to facilitate organized countervailing powers.[27] Yet in the United States, huge differences remain in the relative capacity for organized action of managers and shareholders. And there is substantial evidence that political authorities remain far more attentive to the interests of the former than the latter.

Financial Deregulation

With the pillars of high finance now battered, it is easy to forget how dramatic the rise of the American financial sector has been. Wages and salaries in US financial services roughly doubled their share in the economy over the past three decades, expanding from 5 percent to nearly 10 percent of all wages and salaries between 1975 and 2007. The percentage of the economy composed of financial industry activities exploded—from less than 2 percent just after World War II to more than 8 percent. Between 1980 and 2007, financial service companies expanded their proportion of company profits from around 13 percent to more than 27 percent. (In the early 2000s, the share nearly reached one-third of all corporate profits—despite the fact that employment in the sector was lower than it was thirty years ago.) Even staid corporate giants got into the act. In 1980, GE earned 92 percent of its profit from manufacturing. In 2007, more than half of GE's profits came from its financial businesses. The home address of the winner-take-all economy has been neither Hollywood nor Silicon Valley, but Wall Street.

The rise of finance is virtually synonymous with the rise of winner-take-all, since in no major sector of the economy are gains so highly (and increasingly) concentrated at the top. In part, this is just a chapter of the broader rise of executive pay. But the other part is the runaway rewards that have flowed into the pockets of the rich out of America's widening range of exotic new financial institutions—from boutique hedge funds to massive financial conglomerates crossing once-inviolable regulatory boundaries. These rewards have involved the development of complex new financial products that, for most Americans, offered limited benefits—and sometimes real economic risks—but which held out the prospect of big returns from every financial transaction and spectacular incomes for those within the industry.

At the very top, the gains were mind-boggling. In 2002 it took $30 million to make it to the top twenty-five hedge fund incomes; in 2004, $100 million; in 2005, $130 million. That year, five hedge fund managers made $500 million or more. These were just the biggest of the big winners, however: in the two years before they began reporting losses that dwarfed the profits of prior years and brought many of their stockholders to ruin, the venerable firms of Goldman Sachs, Merrill Lynch, Morgan Stanley, Lehman Brothers, and Bear Stearns paid their employees bonuses of $75 billion. Wages in the financial sector took off in the 1980s. But what were considered princely sums at that time simply set the floor for what was to follow. The pace of the rise actually accelerated in the 1990s, and again after the millennium. Current revelations about Wall Street excesses make abundantly clear that the central chapter in the chronicle of winner-take-all inequality is a tale of American finance.

As with executive compensation, attempts to discuss the political roots of this economic transformation were long dismissed out of hand. Until a few years ago, high finance was depicted as the purest of markets. When analysts referenced the preferences of "Wall Street," it was taken as almost a synonym for economic rationality itself, rather than as a set of specific economic interests. Yet financial markets, like others, are not pre-political. Our financial system has always rested on an extensive set of government interventions. Public policy establishes the legal environment for financial transactions, including such crucial issues as what constitutes insider dealing or an unacceptable conflict of interest, how much monitoring and transparency there will be in major financial transactions, and what levels of leverage and risk are acceptable given the potentially massive externalities associated with large-scale speculation. In response to market failures on all these dimensions in the run-up to the Great Depression, extensive new federal regulations were designed during the New Deal to ensure investor confidence and align private ambitions more closely with broad economic goals, such as financial stability. Regulations sought to limit conflicts of interest, encourage transparency, and discourage reckless risk-taking that placed the desire for private gain in conflict with the integrity and security of the financial system.

Over the last three decades, these relatively quiet and stable financial markets gave way to ones that were both far more dynamic and—for good or ill— had far more pervasive effects on the rest of the economy. Some of this dramatic shift was clearly driven by changes in the nature of economic activity and the possibilities for financial intermediation. Technological innovation made possible the development of new financial instruments and facilitated spectacular experiments with securitization. Moreover, as Robert Gordon and Ian Dew-Becker note, technology helped "shift Wall Street from million-share trading days in the 1980s to billion-share trading days since the late 1990s," which "must also have contributed to the multi-fold increase in real incomes of investment bankers and share traders."[28] Nonetheless, the gradual shredding of the post–New Deal rulebook for financial markets did not simply result from the impersonal forces of "financial innovation." Titans of finance are wont to airbrush the role of government out of their tales of individual economic success. Sanford Weill, the former chairman of Citigroup, put it this way: "People can look at the last 25 years and say this is an incredibly unique period of time. We didn't rely on somebody else to build what we built."[29] But Weill and the other financial chieftains who prospered so greatly during this "unique" period relied a great deal on supportive politicians in government. Weill, for example, helped lead the industry assault on the Glass-Steagall Act, stripping away key conflict-of-interest and transparency rules. These "reforms" legalized powerful financial conglomerates, such as the one produced by Weill's merger of Travelers Insurance and Citibank to form Citigroup (an entity that would become a ward of the American taxpayer only a decade later). . . .

Policy—both what government has done and what, as a result of drift, it has failed to do—has played an absolutely central role in the rise of winner-take-all economic outcomes. It is not the only thing that has mattered, but it has mattered a lot. Moreover, in the main areas where the role of government appears most significant, we see a consistent pattern: active, persistent, and consequential action on the part of organized interests that stood to gain from a transformation of government's role in the American economy. A winner-take-all politics accompanied and helped produce a winner-take-all economy.

Conclusion

Explaining the remarkable rise of a winner-take-all economy requires a true *political economy*—that is, a perspective that sees modern capitalism and modern electoral democracies as deeply interconnected. On the one side, government profoundly influences the economy through an extensive range of policies that shape and reshape markets. On the other side, economic actors—especially when capable of sustained collective action on behalf of shared material interests—have a massive and ongoing impact on how political authority is exercised.

Recent economic accounts have missed the first side of this relationship. Conceptualizing government's role in an excessively narrow way, they have attributed highly concentrated gains to impersonal technological forces. While this interpretation has some basis, neither the American experience nor comparative evidence suggests it can bear the weight that economists have placed on it.

Perhaps surprisingly, the limits of these accounts flow from a similar source. Too many [social scientists] have treated the American political economy as an atomized space, and focused their analysis on individual actors, from voters and politicians to workers and consumers. But the American political economy is an *organized* space, with extensive government policies shaping markets, and increasingly powerful groups who favor winner-take-all outcomes playing a critical role in politics. Finding allies in both political parties, organized groups with a long view have successfully pushed new initiatives onto the American political agenda and exploited the opportunities created by American political institutions to transform U.S. public policy—through new enactments and pervasive policy drift. In the process, they have fundamentally reshaped the relative economic standing and absolute well-being of millions of ordinary Americans. Politics and governance have been central to the rise of winner-take-all inequality.

NOTES

1. Eli Berman, John Bound, and Stephen Machin, "Implications of Skill-Biased Technological Change," *Quarterly Journal of Economics* 113, no. 4 (1998): 1245–79; and Claudia Goldin and Lawrence F. Katz, *The Race between Education and Technology* (Cambridge, MA: Harvard University Press, 2008).

2. Richard Freeman, *America Works: Critical Thoughts on the Exceptional U.S. Labor Market* (New York: Russell Sage, 2007).

3. Perhaps most telling, there is little sign of the same meteoric rise at the top among *French-speaking* portions of Canada, where executives do not appear to be competing in the same common labor market that has allowed American pay levels at the top to diffuse to the rest of Canada.

Emmanuel Saez and Michael R. Veall. "The Evolution of High Incomes in Northern America: Lessons from Canadian Evidence," *American Economic Review* 95, no. 3 (2005): 831–49.

4. Gregory N. Mankiw. "The Wealth Trajectory: Rewards for the Few," *New York Times,* April 20, 2008.

5. Phillip J. Cook and Robert H. Frank, *The Winner-Take-All Society* (New York: Free Press, 1995).

6. Jacob S. Hacker, "Privatizing Risk without Privatizing, the Welfare State: The Hidden Politics of U.S. Social Policy Retrenchment," *American Political Science Review* 98. no. 2 (2004): 243–60.

7. Thomas Piketty and Emmanual Saez, "How Progressive Is the U.S. Federal Tax System? A Historical and International Perspective." *Journal of Economic Perspectives* 21, no. 1 (2007): 3–24.

8. Ibid., 12.

9. Ibid., 15.

10. Hacker and Pierson, *Off Center,* chap. 3.

11. For tax cuts of the early 1980s, see Edsall, *New Politics of Inequality,* 226–33; Ferguson and Rogers, *Right Turn,* 119–24; and David Stockman, *The Triumph of Politics: Why the Reagan Revolution Failed* (New York: Harper & Row, 1987). For tax cuts in the past few years, see Hacker and Pierson, *Off Center,* chap. 3.

12 David Cay Johnston, *Perfectly Legal* (New York: Portfolio Books, 2003).

13. Michael J. Graetz and Ian Shapiro, *Death by a Thousand Cuts: The Fight over Taxing Inherited Wealth* (Princeton, NJ: Princeton University Press, 2005). Hacker and Pierson, *Off Center.*

14. Peter A. Gourevitch and James Shinn, *Political Power and Corporate Control: The New Global Politics of Corporate Governance* (Princeton, NJ: University of Princeton Press, 2005).

15. Graetz and Shapiro, *Death by a Thousand Cuts.*

16. According to the ICTWSS Database (Institutional Characteristics of Trade Unions, Wage Setting, State Intervention and Social Pacts), of the nineteen rich democracies for which data are available from the early 1970s through the mid-2000s, union density increased in four (Finland, Belgium, Denmark, and Sweden) and declined by less than 15 percent in four others (Norway, Canada, Italy, and Luxembourg). In seven nations (Switzerland, the United Kingdom, Denmark, Ireland, the Netherlands, Japan, and Austria), the decline was between one-third and one-half. In four more, it was greater than 50 percent: Australia (55 percent), New Zealand (59 percent), France (63 percent), and the United States (57 percent). Only France had lower union density at the end of the period, though in France, unlike in the United States, the effects of statutory bargaining extend to nearly the whole workforce. Jelle Visser, University of Amsterdam, http://www.uva-aias.net/208.

17. Henry Farber and Bruce Western, "Ronald Reagan and the Politics of Declining Union Organization," *British Journal of Industrial Relations* 40 (2002): 385–402.

18. Nelson Lichtenstein, *State of the Union* (Princeton, NJ: Princeton University Press, 2002); and Paul Osterman, *Securing Prosperity—The American Labor Market: How It Has Changed and What To Do about It* (Princeton, NJ: Princeton University Press, 1999).

19. W. Craig Riddell, "Unionization in Canada and the United States: A Tale of Two Countries," in *Small Differences that Matter: Labor Markets and Income Maintenance in Canada and the United States*, ed. David Card and Richard Freeman (Chicago: University of Chicago Press and National Bureau of Economic Research, 1993), 109–48.

20. John Goddard, "Do Labor Laws Matter? The Density Decline and Convergence Thesis Revisited," *Industrial Relations* 42. no. 3 (2003): 458–92.

21. Piketty and Saez, "How Progressive Is the U.S. Federal Tax System?" Also see Ian Dew-Becker and Robert J. Gordon, "Where Did the Productivity Growth Go? Inflation Dynamics and the Distribution of Income," *Brookings Papers in Economic Activity* 2 (2005): 67–150; and Robert J. Gordon and Ian Dew-Becker, "Controversies about the Rise of American Inequality: A Survey" (Working Paper 13982, National Bureau of Economic Research, Cambridge, MA, May 2008).

22. Mark Roe, *Political Determinants of Corporate Governance: Political Context, Corporate Impact* (Oxford, UK: Oxford University Press, 2003); and Gourevitch and Shinn, *Political Power and, Corporate Control.*

23. As noted earlier, there is a connection between the previous discussion of tax policy and the current discussion of executive compensation. The sharp fall in true tax rates on very high incomes may have stimulated the rise in executive pay since the recipients capture so much more of any rise in compensation. Carola Frydman and Raven Sax estimate that "had tax rates been at their year 2000 level for the entire sample period, the level of executive compensation would have been 35 percent higher in the 1950s and 1960s." "Executive Compensation: A New View from a Long-Term Perspective, 1936–2005" (Working Paper W14145, National Bureau of Economic Research, Cambridge, MA, June 2008). http://ssm. eom/abstract=1152686.

24. Kevin J. Murphy, "Politics, Economics, and Executive Compensation," *University of Cincinnati Law Review* 63 (1995): 714–46.

25. Lucian Bebchuk and Jesse Fried, *Pay without Performance: The Unfulfilled Promise of Executive-Compensation* (Cambridge, MA: Harvard University Press, 2004).

26. Arthur Levitt, *Take on the Street: How to Fight for Your Financial Future* (New York: Vintage, 2002).

27. Gourevitch and Shinn have an interesting argument about why the British system (similar in important respects to the American one) seems to be less vulnerable to regulatory capture by managers. They stress the majoritarian structure of political institutions, which puts greater checks on the political influence of highly concentrated interests.

28. Gordon and Dew-Becker, "Controversies about the Rise of American Inequalities," 25.

29. Louis Uchitelle and Amanda Cox, "The Richest of the Rich, Proud of a New Gilded Age," *New York Times,* July 15, 2007, A1.

11. Bruce Western and Jake Rosenfeld*
Unions, Norms, and the Rise in U.S. Wage Inequality

The decline of organized labor in the United States coincided with a large increase in wage inequality. From 1973 to 2007, union membership in the private sector declined from 34 to 8 percent for men and from 16 to 6 percent for women. During this time, wage inequality in the private sector increased by over 40 percent. Union decline forms part of an institutional account of rising inequality that is often contrasted with a market explanation. In the market explanation, technological change, immigration, and foreign trade increased demand for highly skilled workers, raising the premium paid to college graduates (for reviews, see Autor, Katz, and Kearney 2008; Gottschalk and Danziger 2005; Lemieux 2008).

Compared to market forces, union decline is often seen as a modest source of rising inequality (Autor et al. 2008). Scholars view unions' effects as indirect, mediating the influence of technological change (Acemoglu 2002); secondary to other institutions like the minimum wage (Card and DiNardo 2002; DiNardo, Fortin, and Lemieux 1996); and limited, accounting for only a small fraction of rising inequality and only among men (Card, Lemieux, and Riddell 2004).

We revisit the effects of union decline on inequality by examining union effects on nonunion wages, considering whether wage inequality is lower among nonunion workers in highly unionized regions and industries.

Union effects on nonunion workers can work in several ways. Nonunion employers may raise wages to avert the threat of union organization (Leicht 1989). We argue that unions also contribute to a moral economy that institutionalizes norms for fair pay, even for nonunion workers. In the early 1970s, when 1 in 3 male workers were organized, unions were often prominent voices for equity, not just for their members, but for all workers. Union decline marks an erosion of the moral economy and its underlying distributional norms. Wage inequality in the nonunion sector increased as a result.

Our analysis estimates union effects on wage inequality by decomposing the growth in hourly wage inequality for full-time workers in the private sector. Analyses of the Current Population Survey (CPS) show that union decline explains a fifth of the increase in inequality among men and none of the increase among women if only union wages are considered. The effect of union decline grows when we account for the link between unionization and nonunion wages. In this case, deunionization explains a fifth of the inequality increase for women and a third for men.

Unions and Nonunion Wages

Union wages have been a main focus of research on inequality, but organized labor also affects nonunion workers. Economists often contrast the effects of spillover and threat. When unions raise wages for their members, employers may cut union employment, forcing unemployed workers to find jobs in the nonunion sector. Spillover of workers into the nonunion labor market causes wages to fall. The threat effect results from nonunion employers raising wages to the union level to avert the threat of unionization. The two theories yield opposing predictions: unions reduce nonunion wages with spillover but increase nonunion wages with threat. Empirical studies tend to support the threat effect, showing that nonunion wages are higher in highly unionized industries, localities, and firms (Farber 2005; Leicht 1989; Neumark and Wachter 1995).

The theory of union threat has distributional implications. If unions threaten to organize low-wage workers, employers may raise wages, thereby equalizing the wage distribution. Testing this theory, Kahn and Curme (1987) estimated the effect of industry unionization on the variance of nonunion wages for detailed industries and occupations in the 1979 CPS. Consistent with the equalizing effect of union threat, they found less inequality among nonunion workers in highly unionized industries (cf. Belman and Heywood 1990).

Unions and the Moral Economy

The theory of union threat takes a rationalist view of employers and a minimalist view of labor market institutions. Employers minimize labor costs and only raise wages when threatened with even greater pay increases through unionization. Institutions are conceived minimally in the sense that unions are the key distortion in an otherwise competitive labor market.

We relax these assumptions, arguing that the labor market is embedded in a moral economy in which norms of equity reduce inequality in pay. The moral economy consists of norms prescribing fair distribution that are institutionalized in the market's formal rules and customs. In a robust moral economy, violation of distributional norms inspires condemnation and charges of injustice. We often think of the moral economy historically—determining, for example, fair prices for bread and flour under the British Corn Laws (Thompson 1971) or the relative rank and standing of English workers in the nineteenth century (Polanyi [1944] 1957).[1]

Unions are pillars of the moral economy in modern labor markets. Across countries and over time, unions widely promoted norms of equity that claimed the fairness of a standard rate for low-pay workers and the injustice of unchecked earnings for managers and owners (Hyman and Brough 1976; Webb and Webb 1911). Comparative researchers emphasize the role of distributional norms governing European industrial relations (Elster 1989b; Swenson 1989). The US labor movement never exerted the broad influence of the European unions, but US unions often supported norms of equity that extended beyond their own membership. In our theory of the moral economy, unions help materialize labor market norms of equity (1) culturally, through public speech about economic inequality, (2) politically, by influencing social policy, and (3) institutionally, through rules governing the labor market.

Culturally, industrial unions often use a language of social solidarity in public discourse and within firms. Politically, US unions have been frequent advocates for redistributive public policy. Institutionally, US industrial relations often extend union conditions to nonunion workers. Unions also helped establish pay norms in local labor markets. In some industries, union influence was amplified by law.

Data and Methods

We link union decline to rising inequality by decomposing the variance of log wages. The decomposition uses a variance function regression in which the mean and the variance of an outcome depend on independent variables, providing a model of between- and within-group inequality (Western and Bloome 2009).

The decomposition is based on a regression on the log hourly wage, y_i, for respondent i ($i=1, \ldots, N$) for a given year of the CPS. Our key predictors are an indicator for union membership, u_i, and a continuous variable, $\bar{u}_i$, that records for each respondent the unionization rate for the industry and region in which they work. Covariates, including schooling, age, race, ethnicity, and region, are collected in the vector, x_i. The model includes equations for the conditional mean of log wages,

$$\hat{y}_i = x_i \alpha_1 + u_i \alpha_2 + \bar{u}_i \alpha_3$$

and the conditional variance,

$$\log \sigma_i = x_i \beta_1 + u_i \beta_2 + \bar{u}_i \beta_3$$

We expect union membership and industry-region unionization to have positive effects on average wages, but negative effects on the variance of log wages. Economy-wide changes in average wages and within-group inequality, perhaps due to general shifts in norms or the macroeconomy, are captured through the regression intercepts.

We measure between-group wage inequality by the variance of the conditional means,

$$B = \sum_{i=1}^{n} w_i (\hat{y}_i - \bar{y})^2 \tag{1}$$

where w_i is the sample weight for respondent i, normed to sum to 1, and $\bar{y}$ is the grand mean of log wages. We measure within-group inequality by the residual variance,

$$W = \sum_{i=1}^{n} w_i \sigma_i^2 \tag{2}$$

That each respondent has a variance may be counterintuitive, but it is simply estimated by the squared residual from the regression on y_i. Because unions are mostly associated with within-group inequality, we expect deunionization to be closely associated with an increase in within-group variance, W. Summing within- and between-group components yields the total variance, a measure of overall inequality:

$$V = B + W.$$

We decompose the rise in inequality with two adjusted variances that fix in a baseline year either the coefficients or the distribution of some predictors. First, focusing on individual union membership, we calculate the level of inequality assuming unionization had remained at its 1973 level. We estimate this compositional effect by reweighting the data to preserve the 1973 unionization rate across all years, from 1973 to 2007. We then use the adjusted weights in Equations 1 and 2 to calculate adjusted variances for all years. Second, we add the effects of union threat and equitable wage norms on nonunion workers by calculating wage inequality assuming industry-region unionization and its coefficients remain constant at the 1973 level. Fixing industry-region unionization coefficients, and reweighting to hold union density constant, yields adjusted values of $\hat{y}_i$ and σ_i^2 that are plugged into Equations 1 and 2 to obtain adjusted measures of between- and within-group inequality.

We compiled data from the annual May files of the CPS from 1973 to 1981 and the annual Merged Outgoing Rotation Group files of the CPS from 1983 to 2007 (Unicon Research Corporation various years; U.S. Bureau of the Census various years). We exclude 1982, when union questions were omitted from the survey, and 1994 and three-quarters of 1995, when allocation flags for wages were missing. The analysis includes men and women working full-time (i.e., 30 hours a week or more) in the private sector.

The dependent variable is log hourly wages adjusted for inflation to 2001 dollars. Several adjustments improve the quality and continuity of the wage data. Nonresponse to wage and income questions increases over time, and by 2007, about a third of CPS workers did not report wages. The CPS imputes wages to nonrespondents, but regression coefficients for nonmatched criteria are attenuated and the residual variance for wages is sensitive to the imputed data (Hirsch 2004; Mouw and Kalleberg 2010). We thus omit imputed wages from the analysis.

Results

To study the effects of declining union membership on wage inequality, we fix the unionization rate at 1973 levels. Similar to earlier research, we find the

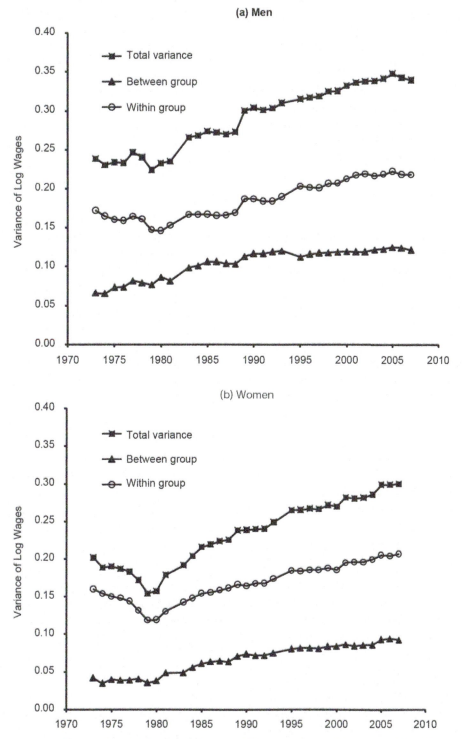

FIGURE 11.1 Observed and Adjusted Within- and Between-Group Variances of Log Hourly Wages, Full-Time, Private Sector Men and Women, 1973 to 2007; Adjusted Variances Fix Union Membership at the 1973 Level

largest effect of declining union membership on men's within-group inequality. The observed within-group variance increases by .046 points, but the adjusted variance (with the 1973 unionization rate) increases by only .028 points. Over a third of the increase in within-group inequality is associated with declining union membership ([.046–.028]/.046 = .40). Between-group inequality increases by .055 variance points and the adjusted series increases by almost as much, by .053, indicating that union decline explains little of the rise in men's between-group inequality. Summing the between- and within-group effects, the decline in unionization from 34 to 8 percent explains about a fifth of the rise in inequality in hourly wages among full-time, private sector men.

Among women, the effect of declining union membership on wage inequality is smaller. Inequality grew slightly more for women than for men, but increasing women's wage inequality is unrelated to union membership. Within-group inequality increased by about .047 points among women but the adjusted series, with 1973 unionization held constant, increases nearly as much, by .043 points. Similarly, between-group inequality increased by .051 points and the adjusted between-group variance, with union membership fixed, increased by .054 points. Consistent with other research, holding the unionization rate constant explains almost none of the rise in women's wage inequality.

Union decline explains more of the rise in wage inequality once we account for the link between unions and nonunion wages. The link between organized labor and nonunion workers is captured by the effects of industry-region unionization on the mean and variance of wages. The total effect of deunionization can be measured by fixing the 1973 unionization rate as before and also fixing industry-region unionization rates and their coefficients at 1973 values (see Figure 11.1). This adjustment indicates the strong relationship between union decline and rising within-group inequality. Among men, adjusted within-group inequality does not increase between 1973 and 2007, suggesting effects of union threat and eroding norms of equity on the wage distribution. Deunionization's effect on union and nonunion wages is associated with about a third of the rise in wage inequality. This accounting, which includes unions' effects on nonunion wages, is 50 to 100 percent larger than the union effects on inequality reported in other decompositions (cf. Card 2001; DiNardo et al. 1996).

Among women, the association between union decline and wage inequality is smaller, but greater than zero, once nonunion wages are taken into account (see Figure 11.1, panel b). Declining industry-region unionization accounts for over half of the increase in women's within-group inequality. Adding between and within-group effects together, union decline is associated with about a fifth of the rise in wage inequality among women.

Discussion

These results suggest unions are a normative presence that help sustain the labor market as a social institution, in which norms of equity shape the allocation of wages outside the union sector.

The key comparison implied by our analysis is fundamentally historical, from the early 1970s to the 2000s. In the earlier period, unions offered an alternative to an unbridled market logic, and this institutional alternative employed over a third of all male private sector workers. The social experience of organized labor bled into nonunion sectors, contributing to greater equality overall. As unions declined, not only did the logic of the market encroach on what had been the union sector, but the logic of the market deepened in the nonunion sector, too, contributing to the rise in wage inequality.

REFERENCES

Acemoglu, Daron. 2002. "Technical Change, Inequality, and the Labor Market." Journal of Economic Literature 40:7–72.

Autor, David H., Lawrence F. Katz, and Melissa S. Kearney. 2008. "Trends in U.S. Wage Inequality: Revising the Revisionists." Review of Economics and Statistics 90:300–323.

Belman, Dale and John S. Heywood. 1990. "Union Membership, Union Organization and the Dispersion of Wages." Review of Economics and Statistics 72:148–53.

Card, David. 2001. "The Effect of Unions on Wage Inequality in the U.S. Labor Market." Industrial and Labor Relations Review, 54: 296–315.

Card, David and John E. DiNardo. 2002. "Skill-Biased Technological Change and Rising Wage Inequality: Some Problems and Puzzles." Journal of Labor Economics 20:733–83.

Card, David, Thomas Lemieux, and W. Craig Riddell. 2004. "Unions and Wage Inequality." Journal of Labor Research 25:519–62.

DiNardo, James, Nicole M. Fortin, and Thomas Lemieux. 1996. "Labor Market Institutions and the Distribution of Wages, 1973–1992." Econometrica 64:1001–1044.

Elster, Jon. 1989a. "Social Norms and Economic Theory." The Journal of Economic Perspectives, 3(4): 99–117.

Elster, Jon. 1989b. "Wage Bargaining and Social Norms." Acta Sociologica 32:113–36.

Farber, Henry S. 2005. "Nonunion Wage Rates and the Threat of Unionization." Industrial and Labor Relations Review 58:335–52.

Gottschalk, Peter and Sheldon Danziger. 2005. "Inequality of Wage Rates, Earnings and Family Income in the United States, 1975–2002." Review of Income and Wealth 51:231–54.

Hirsch, Barry T. 2004. "Reconsidering Union Wage Effects: Surveying New Evidence on an Old Topic." Journal of Labor Research 25:233–66.

Hyman, Richard and Ian Brough. 1976. Social Values and Industrial Relations. Oxford, UK: Basic Blackwell.

Kahn, Lawrence M. and Michael Curme. 1987. "Unions and Nonunion Wage Dispersion." Review of Economics and Statistics 69:600–607.

Leicht, Kevin T. 1989. "On the Estimation of Union Threat Effects." American Sociological Review 54:1035–1057.

Lemieux, Thomas. 2008. "The Changing Nature of Wage Inequality." Journal of Population Economics 21:21–48.

Mouw, Ted and Arne Kalleberg. 2010. "Occupations and the Structure of Wage Inequality in the United States, 1980s to 2000s." American Sociological Review 75:402–431.

Neumark, David and Michael L. Wachter. 1995. "Union Effects on Nonunion Wages: Evidence from Panel Data on Industries and Cities." Industrial and Labor Relations Review 49:20–38.

Polanyi, Karl. [1944] 1957. The Great Transformation: The Political and Economic Origins of Our Time. Boston: Beacon Press.

Swenson, Peter. 1989. Fair Shares: Unions, Pay and Politics in Sweden and West Germany. Ithaca, NY: Cornell University Press.

Thompson, Edward Palmer. 1971. "The Moral Economy of the English Crowd in the 18th Century." Past and Present 50:76–136.

Unicon Research Corporation. Various years. CPS Utilities Merged Outgoing Rotation Group and May Files. Santa Monica, CA.

U.S. Bureau of the Census. Various years. Current Population Survey 1980 May File. ICPSR ed. Ann Arbor, MI: Inter-university Consortium for Political and Social Research [producer and distributor].

Webb, Sidney and Beatrice Webb. 1911. Industrial Democracy. London: Longmans, Green.

Western, Bruce and Deirdre Bloome. 2009. "Variance Function Regressions for Studying Inequality." Sociological Methodology 39:293–326.

NOTES

1. Thompson (1971) coined the term "moral economy." Elster (1989a) argued that distributional norms are departures from strict rationality, eliciting strong emotions in response to violation.

12. Richard B. Freeman*
(Some) Inequality Is Good for You

Imagine a world with no inequality of pay. Regardless of whether people work hard or take it easy, whether they work in sewers or palaces, do brain surgery or flip burgers, they are paid the same. Would many people work hard or choose the more onerous job and produce much in such a world? Economic analysis suggests that most people would not work hard. . . . Output would increase if the society paid more to those who would work harder or who would gain more skills or who would accept more onerous tasks—i.e., if the society accepted greater inequality. . . .

Generalizing from this, economists see efforts to reduce inequality below what the market produces as costing society in terms of output. The efficiency-equity trade-off creates a choice between (a) lower output and a more desirable distribution of income and (b) higher output and a less desirable distribution. If the gain in output from higher inequality is sizeable, the rate of poverty could be lower in a high-inequality society than in a low-inequality society. . . .

[Now] consider a world in which most inequality results from random chance. Society hands large sums of money to some people and little to others for no particular reason. You were born a Rockefeller or not, a superstar entertainer or not. You bought the winning lottery ticket or you got the ticket worth nada. To the extent that inequality is due to luck unrelated to incentives, it is hard to justify. . . . In sum, the critical issue in the debate over inequality is the extent to which it acts as an incentive and affects total production as opposed to the extent to which it reflects an uneven distribution of resources and consumption. . . .

The Relation Between Inequality and Output

Economic analysis suggests that the relation between output and inequality follows an inverse-U-shaped curve. At very low levels of inequality, increases in inequality generate greater social output. The equity-efficiency trade-off operates in that area: society gets

*Adapted from *The New Gilded Age: The Critical Inequality Debates of Our Time*. Edited by David B. Grusky and Tamar Kricheli-Katz. Copyright © 2012 by the Board of Trustees of the Leland Stanford Jr. University.

more output with more inequality. It chooses the most desirable point. But the gains in output from inequality decline and then drop. Beyond the level of inequality that maximizes output, increases in inequality reduce output.

Figure 12.1 illustrates this relation. The horizontal axis displays the level of inequality in an economy. The vertical axis shows output, defined as the sum of the production of each person in the economy based on the incentive determined by the level of inequality. When inequality is zero, output is zero: no incentive implies no production. At the maximal level of inequality, where all of the output goes to a single person, output is higher than zero but low. As inequality increases from zero incentives, output increases. People have an incentive to work harder or take on more onerous and productive tasks. As rewards go increasingly to the more productive, some less able workers might reduce their effort but total output would rise as those with greater chances of gaining the larger rewards produce more. Then the gains from inequality end and society reaches the output of I*, which is the output-maximizing level of inequality.

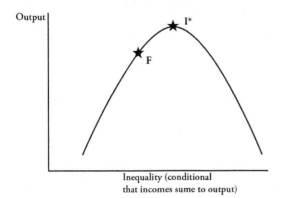

FIGURE 12.1 The inequality-output inverse-U curve

To the right of I*, output falls as inequality increases toward the maximum level. The higher inequality will induce a few "superstars" with a chance to reach the top of the income hierarchy to work harder and produce more, but it will demotivate everyone else. Since there are more normal workers than superstars, total output falls. At the extreme, where one person or entity earns nearly everything—the feudal lord, the slave owner, a small group of billionaires—and where most people earn subsistence wages, there is an incentive to become the dominant person or group but not to do much of anything. Run a golf tournament where there is a single prize, and Tiger Woods and a few other players will enter and try hard.

But most players, with little or no chance of gaining the prize, will drop out of the tour. In fact, of course, golf and other tournaments give prize moneys to people who rank tenth, twentieth, fiftieth, and so forth (in declining amounts) so that all players have an incentive to enter the tournament and do their best. . . .

To be sure, a numerical example can demonstrate only that something is possible. Assume more superstars capable of winning the tournament or a greater gap between the output of the more able and less able, and you can generate the result that, by rewarding those at the top of the distribution, all of the prizes produce greater output than giving incentives for persons throughout the distribution. Contrarily, assume more regular workers, and the less unequal reward system would have looked better than it did in my example. Both economic theory and evidence suggest that the inverse U-shaped inequality-output curve is a realistic representation of economic reality.

The relevant theory is the theory of prizes in tournaments when competitors vary in their abilities. Like much economic theory, the analysis is fairly mathematical but structured around a comprehensible idea that can be explained without any math. The analysis specifies the conditions under which it is better to give incentives to many people (multiple prizes in a tournament)—lower inequality—than to concentrate incentives for the top person in the income distribution (single prize in a tournament)—high inequality. The technical condition for multiple prizes to induce greater output than single prizes is that each worker's marginal productivity declines with effort or, equivalently, that their cost of effort rises with the level of effort so that the highly productive squeeze out less additional output when they are given increasingly large incentives compared to the more numerous less-productive workers.

The analysis depends greatly on the uncertainty of gaining greater rewards from increased effort. If there was no uncertainty, the top person would always win, and once everyone knew who the top person was, the other highly productive persons would give up; and similarly for persons lower in the distribution. That uncertainty or luck is a positive contributor to production in a tournament model shows that, contrary to the general view that luck is a nonproductive factor in the distribution of income, some uncertainty/luck is in fact productivity-motivating ex ante. . . .

The Maze Tournament

To illuminate the incentive-output relation, Alex Gelber and I undertook a set of maze experiments at the

Changes in numbers of mazes

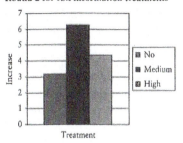

A: Mean score increase from Round 1 to
Round 2 for full information treatments

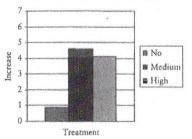

B: Mean score increase from Round 1 to
Round 2 for no information treatments

Changes in number of mazes, where person cheated

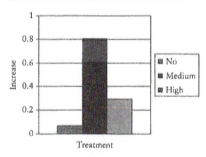

A: Increase in cheating per person from Round 1
to Round 2 for full information treatments

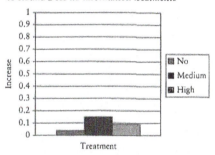

B: Increase in cheating per person from Round 1
to Round 2 for no information treatments

FIGURE 12.2 Changes in numbers of mazes solved and in numbers where people cheated, by incentive treatment and information (per person)

Harvard Business School Computer Lab for Experimental Research in 2004-2005. In each experiment, we gave six participants the task of solving packets of paper mazes in two rounds: a first round that would identify the participants' maze-solving ability and a second round in which we had subjects compete in a tournament with three incentive treatments, each of which distributed $30 in total prizes.

Our no-inequality treatment gave each participant $5 regardless of their performance. The only incentive was the intrinsic desire to do well, either absolutely or relative to others. Our high-inequality treatment gave $30 to the top scorer and nothing to anyone else. . . . In the medium-inequality condition, we gave out multiple prizes. There are many ways to do this. We chose a reward structure in which the winner received $15, the second-prize winner received $7, the third-prize winner received $5, the fourth-prize winner received $2, the fifth-prize winner received $1, and the sixth-prize winner received nothing. This gave incentives to persons in all parts of the distribution of first-round maze performances. . . .

We also varied the amount of information the subjects had about their relative standing in the distribution of maze-solving skills. At the end of Round 1, in half of the groups we informed subjects of the scores of all group members in the first round. Since individuals knew their own score, this enabled them to place themselves in the distribution and assess their chances of ranking high or low in the second round. We refer to this treatment as "full information." In the other half of the experiments, we said nothing about how others performed. . . .

The upper part of Figure 12.2 gives the main results from our experiment in terms of the change in the number of mazes solved per person from the first round to the second round in the three inequality incentives in the full information and no information conditions. . . . The results under full information show the inverted U-relation. There is a modest increase in the number of mazes solved for the no-inequality group (due presumably to learning); a large increase in the number of mazes solved for the middle-inequality group, and a moderate increase in the number of mazes solved for the high-inequality group. . . . When subjects have no information about their relative position in the distribution of maze-solving, they have no clear incentive to try harder under the different inequality treatments.

Because the experiment was conducted with paper and pencil mazes rather than with computer mazes, subjects had an opportunity to cheat or fudge on their answers. One way they could do so was to jump their pencil over a line and complete a maze incorrectly. Another way was to skip a maze and do additional mazes and count them in their total, even though the instructions said they could not count any mazes after an incomplete one. In the first round, twenty-six subjects fudged in maze-solving and counted forty-eight mazes as solved that they had not solved properly. . . . By contrast, in the second round, nearly three times as many people (76) fudged/cheated on 151 mazes, with a distinct pattern across the treatments. The bottom panel of Figure 12.2 shows that in the full-information case, the largest increase in fudging/cheating occurred for the middle-inequality incentive group, in which all subjects can gain by doing better. . . . In sum, in the maze tournament, when people know where they stand relative to others and can thus roughly estimate how much they might gain from doing better, inequality/incentives operate to produce the inverted-U pattern shown in Figure 12.1. . . .

Where Does the United States Stand?

The level of inequality is a social good about which individuals can have legitimate varying preferences. . . . Economists aside, the inequality in the income distributions suggests that the median voter is likely to prefer less inequality than the market generates and thus in a democracy the socially desired level of inequality will be less than the output-maximizing level. Figure 12.1 displays this relation by locating the desired (fair) level of inequality, F, to the left of I*. With this specification, society pays a price in efficiency for a "fairer" income distribution, giving the equity-efficiency trade-off. . . .

The natural question to ask next is how income inequality in the United States compares to the output-maximizing level and to the socially desirable level. This is difficult to answer. . . . What is clear is that the United States has the highest level of inequality among advanced countries. Indeed, the level of inequality in the United States exceeds that in many developing countries, [whereas] inequality tends to be higher than in advanced countries. My suspicion is that the level of inequality exceeds the [output-maximizing] level, and that many of the ways in which top earners make their money in response to incentives are counterproductive—giving them reasons to fudge financial reports, hide bad outcomes through financial chicanery, release good news when they can cash in their options, and otherwise exploit the incentive compensation system rather than to act productively. The recent financial crisis might be partly interpreted in just those terms.

One reason for my suspicion is that so much of recent inequality has taken the form of huge increases in earnings at the top of the income distribution, where incentives are already larger than for any other workers. It is hard to imagine that top CEOs need increasingly more pay to motivate them. Another reason is that some of the rise of inequality occurred through modes of payment that do not work as efficient incentives. Much of the high earnings of executives is in stock options that pay off if the firm share prices rises. They are designed to align the interests of executives with shareholders. But the options are written in ways that seem to raise executive pay regardless of their actual performance. . . .

I [thus] suspect but cannot prove that inequality has gone past the output-maximizing level. . . . If future US governments experiment with tax and fiscal policies favorable to the average citizen, shifting incentives down the income distribution as in the middle-inequality maze experiment, my guess is that the economy will grow as or more rapidly than it would with continued policies that privilege the wealthy few.

PART III

THE ONE PERCENT

The purpose of this section is to explore how power, privilege, and money may come together to form an elite at the top of the social hierarchy. In recent years, the "one percent" has become the preferred label for the elite, but few scholars would probably seriously believe that an arbitrary income threshold of that sort captures very well the structure of power and advantage at the top. The contributors to this section—C. Wright Mills, Alvin Gouldner, David Brooks, and Shamus Khan—develop a more rigorous vocabulary for understanding how power and advantage can be organized.

The simple question that cuts across these readings is whether late industrial societies tend to generate a powerful and solidary upper class. The "power elite" narrative (see Mills, Ch. 13) has it that economic, political, and military elites form a unitary class by virtue of co-residing in the same neighborhoods, attending the same schools, belonging to the same clubs, sharing a coherent political ideology, and interacting as approximate equals (see also Khan, Ch. 16). This small elite occupies positions of considerable power and can therefore "mightily affect the everyday worlds of ordinary men and women" (Mills, Ch. 13). As against this account, we might imagine that capitalists, by virtue of their economic power, have become the de facto "ruling force" (Marx, Ch. 2). Although some key leadership positions are of course formally filled by political or military elites, it is hardly radical anymore to suggest that they are acting largely at the behest of capitalists and corporations (who wield influence via lobbying, campaign funding, and the like). This Marxian account, unlike the contemporary "one percent" formulation, does not admit mere wage laborers into the elite (e.g., superstar athletes, top managers), no matter how high their incomes may be.

More recently, Gouldner (Ch. 14) has suggested that a third claimant to power, the "knowledge class," is in ascendancy as expert knowledge comes to be understood as a source of value and a prerequisite for responsible and successful leadership (also Brooks, Ch. 15). For Gouldner and other "new class" theorists, the main struggle of the contemporary period is not between capitalists and workers (as workers long ago lost out), rather it is found in the ongoing "civil war" (Gouldner, Ch. 14) between capitalists with the power to buy influence and intellectuals or technocrats who claim to have the knowledge to successfully wield it. The outcome of this civil war is far from obvious: While capitalists bring ever-growing economic power to the table, intellectuals and Silicon Valley technocrats rest their case on the efficiency of relying on results-driven scientific and expert knowledge.

The readings in this section, which draw mainly from long-standing classics in the field, nonetheless read as if they were quite fresh. Although there are inevitably rapid changes in the personnel filling elite positions, the underlying structure of the elite (as revealed in the relative power of economic, intellectual, or political leaders) would appear to change only in slow motion. This makes the classic analyses of the past still very relevant today.

13. C. Wright Mills*
The Power Elite

The powers of ordinary men are circumscribed by the everyday worlds in which they live, yet even in these rounds of job, family, and neighborhood, they often seem driven by forces they can neither understand nor govern. 'Great changes' are beyond their control but affect their conduct and outlook nonetheless. The very framework of modern society confines them to projects not their own, but from every side, such changes now press upon the men and women of the mass society, who accordingly feel that they are without purpose in an epoch in which they are without power.

But not all men are in this sense ordinary. As the means of information and power are centralized, some men come to occupy positions in American society from which they can look down upon, so to speak, and by their decisions mightily affect, the everyday worlds of ordinary men and women. They are not made by their jobs; they set up and break down jobs for thousands of others; they are not confined by simple family responsibilities; they can escape. They may live in many hotels and houses, but they are bound by no one community. They need not merely 'meet the demands of the day and hour'; in some part, they create these demands and cause others to meet them. Whether or not they profess their power, their technical and political experience of it far transcends that of the underlying population. What Jacob Burckhardt said of 'great men,' most Americans might well say of their elite: 'They are all that we are not.'[1] The power elite is composed of men whose positions enable them to transcend the ordinary environments of ordinary men and women; they are in positions to make decisions having major consequences. Whether they do or do not make such decisions is less important than the fact that they do occupy such pivotal positions: their failure to act, their failure to make decisions, is itself an act that is often of greater consequence than the decisions they

do make. For they are in command of the major hierarchies and organizations of modern society. They rule the big corporations. They run the machinery of the state and claim its prerogatives. They direct the military establishment. They occupy the strategic command posts of the social structure, in which are now centered the effective means of the power and the wealth and the celebrity which they enjoy.

The power elite are not solitary rulers. Advisers and consultants, spokesmen and opinion-makers are often the captains of their higher thought and decision. Immediately below the elite are the professional politicians of the middle levels of power, in the Congress and in the pressure groups, as well as among the new and old upper classes of town and city and region. Mingling with them in curious ways are those professional celebrities who live by being continually displayed but are never, so long as they remain celebrities, displayed enough. If such celebrities are not at the head of any dominating hierarchy, they do often have the power to distract the attention of the public or afford sensations to the masses, or, more directly, to gain the ear of those who do occupy positions of direct power. More or less unattached, as critics of morality and technicians of power, as spokesmen of God and creators of mass sensibility, such celebrities and consultants are part of the immediate scene in which the drama of the elite is enacted. But that drama itself is centered in the command posts of the major institutional hierarchies.

1

The truth about the nature and the power of the elite is not some secret which men of affairs know but will not tell. Such men hold quite various theories about their own roles in the sequence of event and decision. Often they are uncertain about their roles, and even more often they allow their fears and their hopes to affect their assessment of their own power. No matter how great their actual power, they tend to be less acutely aware of it than of the resistances of others to its use. Moreover, most American men of affairs have learned well the rhetoric of public relations, in some cases even to the point of using it when they are alone, and thus coming to believe it. The personal awareness of the actors is only one of the several sources one must examine in order to understand the higher circles. Yet many who believe that there is no elite, or at any rate none of any consequence, rest their argument upon what men of

*Adapted from THE POWER ELITE by Wright Mills (1956), pp.3-18, 20-23, 365-367. ©1956, 2000 by Oxford University Press, Inc. By permission of Oxford University Press, USA. As published in *Social Stratification: Class, Race, and Gender in Sociological Perspective,* 3rd edition, by David Grusky, copyright © 2009. Reprinted by permission of Westview Press, an imprint of Perseus Books, LLC, a subsidiary of Hachette Book Group, Inc.

affairs believe about themselves, or at least assert in public.

There is, however, another view: those who feel, even if vaguely, that a compact and powerful elite of great importance does now prevail in America often base that feeling upon the historical trend of our time. They have felt, for example, the domination of the military event, and from this they infer that generals and admirals, as well as other men of decision influenced by them, must be enormously powerful. They hear that the Congress has again abdicated to a handful of men decisions clearly related to the issue of war or peace. They know that the bomb was dropped over Japan in the name of the United States of America, although they were at no time consulted about the matter. They feel that they live in a time of big decisions; they know that they are not making any. Accordingly, as they consider the present as history, they infer that at its center, making decisions or failing to make them, there must be an elite of power.

On the one hand, those who share this feeling about big historical events assume that there is an elite and that its power is great. On the other hand, those who listen carefully to the reports of men apparently involved in the great decisions often do not believe that there is an elite whose powers are of decisive consequence.

Both views must be taken into account, but neither is adequate. The way to understand the power of the American elite lies neither solely in recognizing the historic scale of events nor in accepting the personal awareness reported by men of apparent decision. Behind such men and behind the events of history, linking the two, are the major institutions of modern society. These hierarchies of state, corporation, and army constitute the means of power; as such they are now of a consequence not before equaled in human history—and at their summits, there are now those command posts of modern society which offer us the sociological key to an understanding of the role of the higher circles in America.

Within American society, major national power now resides in the economic, the political, and the military domains. Other institutions seem off to the side of modern history, and, on occasion, duly subordinated to these. No family is as directly powerful in national affairs as any major corporation; no church is as directly powerful in the external biographies of young men in America today as the military establishment; no college is as powerful in the shaping of momentous events as the National Security Council. Religious, educational, and family institutions are not autonomous centers of national power; on the contrary, these decentralized areas are increasingly shaped by the big three, in which developments of decisive and immediate consequence now occur. . . .

Within each of the big three, the typical institutional unit has become enlarged, has become administrative, and, in the power of its decisions, has become centralized. Behind these developments there is a fabulous technology, for as institutions, they have incorporated this technology and guide it, even as it shapes and paces their developments.

The economy—once a great scatter of small productive units in autonomous balance—has become dominated by two or three hundred giant corporations, administratively and politically interrelated, which together hold the keys to economic decisions.

The political order, once a decentralized set of several dozen states with a weak spinal cord, has become a centralized, executive establishment which has taken up into itself many powers previously scattered, and now enters into each and every cranny of the social structure.

The military order, once a slim establishment in a context of distrust fed by state militia, has become the largest and most expensive feature of government, and, although well versed in smiling public relations, now has all the grim and clumsy efficiency of a sprawling bureaucratic domain.

In each of these institutional areas, the means of power at the disposal of decision-makers have increased enormously; their central executive powers have been enhanced; within each of them modern administrative routines have been elaborated and tightened up.

As each of these domains becomes enlarged and centralized, the consequences of its activities become greater, and its traffic with the others increases. The decisions of a handful of corporations bear upon military and political as well as upon economic developments around the world. The decisions of the military establishment rest upon and grievously affect political life as well as the very level of economic activity. The decisions made within the political domain determine economic activities and military programs. There is no longer, on the one hand, an economy, and, on the other hand, a political order containing a military establishment unimportant to politics and to money-making. There is a political economy linked, in a thousand ways, with military institutions and decisions. On each side of the world-split running through central Europe and around the Asiatic rimlands, there is an ever-increasing interlocking of economic, military, and political structures.[2] If there is government intervention in the corporate economy, so is there corporate intervention in the governmental process. In the structural sense, this triangle of power is the source of the interlocking directorate that is most important for the historical structure of the present.

The fact of the interlocking is clearly revealed at each of the points of crisis of modern capitalist society—slump, war, and boom. In each, men of decision are led to an awareness of the interdependence of the major institutional orders. In the nineteenth century, when the scale of all institutions was smaller, their liberal integration was achieved in the automatic economy, by an autonomous play of market forces, and in the automatic political domain, by the bargain and the vote. It was then assumed that out of the imbalance and friction that followed the limited decisions then possible a new equilibrium would in due course emerge. That can no longer be assumed, and it is not assumed by the men at the top of each of the three dominant hierarchies.

For given the scope of their consequences, decisions—and indecisions—in any one of these ramify into the others, and hence top decisions tend either to become coordinated or to lead to a commanding indecision. It has not always been like this. When numerous small entrepreneurs made up the economy, for example, many of them could fail and the consequences still remain local; political and military authorities did not intervene. But now, given political expectations and military commitments, can they afford to allow key units of the private corporate economy to break down in slump? Increasingly, they do intervene in economic affairs, and as they do so, the controlling decisions in each order are inspected by agents of the other two, and economic, military, and political structures are interlocked.

At the pinnacle of each of the three enlarged and centralized domains, there have arisen those higher circles which make up the economic, the political, and the military elites. At the top of the economy, among the corporate rich, there are the chief executives; at the top of the political order, the members of the political directorate; at the top of the military establishment, the elite of soldier-statesmen clustered in and around the Joint Chiefs of Staff and the upper echelon. As each of these domains has

coincided with the others, as decisions tend to become total in their consequence, the leading men in each of the three domains of power—the warlords, the corporation chieftains, the political directorate—tend to come together, to form the power elite of America.

2

The higher circles in and around these command posts are often thought of in terms of what their members possess: they have a greater share than other people of the things and experiences that are most highly valued. From this point of view, the elite are simply those who have the most of what there is to have, which is generally held to include money, power, and prestige—as well as all the ways of life to which these lead.[3] But the elite are not simply those who have the most, for they could not 'have the most' were it not for their positions in the great institutions. For such institutions are the necessary bases of power, of wealth, and of prestige, and at the same time, the chief means of exercising power, of acquiring and retaining wealth, and of cashing in the higher claims for prestige.

By the powerful we mean, of course, those who are able to realize their will, even if others resist it. No one, accordingly, can be truly powerful unless he has access to the command of major institutions, for it is over these institutional means of power that the truly powerful are, in the first instance, powerful. Higher politicians and key officials of government command such institutional power; so do admirals and generals, and so do the major owners and executives of the larger corporations. Not all power, it is true, is anchored in and exercised by means of such institutions, but only within and through them can power be more or less continuous and important. . . .

If we took the one hundred most powerful men in America, the one hundred wealthiest, and the one hundred most celebrated away from the institutional positions they now occupy, away from their resources of men and women and money, away from the media of mass communication that are now focused upon them—then they would be powerless and poor and uncelebrated. For power is not of a man. Wealth does not center in the person of the wealthy. Celebrity is not inherent in any personality. To be celebrated, to be wealthy, and to have power requires access to major institutions, for the institutional positions men occupy determine in large part their chances to have and to hold these valued experiences.

3

The people of the higher circles may also be conceived as members of a top social stratum, as a set of groups whose members know one another, see one another socially and at business, and so, in making decisions, take one another into account. The elite, according to this conception, feel themselves to be, and are felt by others to be, the inner circle of 'the upper social classes.'4 They form a more or less compact social and psychological entity; they have become self-conscious members of a social class. People are either accepted into this class or they are not, and there is a qualitative split, rather than merely a numerical scale, separating them from those who are not elite. They are more or less aware of themselves as a social class and they behave toward one another differently from the way they do toward members of other classes. They accept one another, understand one another, marry one another, tend to work and to think, if not together, at least alike.

Now, we do not want by our definition to prejudge whether the elite of the command posts are conscious members of such a socially recognized class, or whether considerable proportions of the elite derive from such a clear and distinct class. These are matters to be investigated. Yet in order to be able to recognize what we intend to investigate, we must note something that all biographies and memoirs of the wealthy and the powerful and the eminent make clear: no matter what else they may be, the people of these higher circles are involved in a set of overlapping 'crowds' and intricately connected 'cliques.' There is a kind of mutual attraction among those who 'sit on the same terrace'—although this often becomes clear to them, as well as to others, only at the point at which they feel the need to draw the line; only when, in their common defense, they come to understand what they have in common, and so close their ranks against outsiders.

The idea of such ruling stratum implies that most of its members have similar social origins, that throughout their lives they maintain a network of informal connections, and that to some degree there is an interchangeability of position between the various hierarchies of money and power and celebrity. We must, of course, note at once that if such an elite stratum does exist, its social visibility and its form, for very solid historical reasons, are quite different

from those of the noble cousinhoods that once ruled various European nations.

That American society has never passed through a feudal epoch is of decisive importance to the nature of the American elite, as well as to American society as a historic whole. For it means that no nobility or aristocracy, established before the capitalist era, has stood in tense opposition to the higher bourgeoisie. It means that this bourgeoisie has monopolized not only wealth, but prestige and power as well. It means that no set of noble families has commanded the top positions and monopolized the values that are generally held in high esteem; and certainly that no set has done so explicitly by inherited right. It means that no high church dignitaries or court nobilities, no entrenched landlords with honorific accouterments, no monopolists of high army posts have opposed the enriched bourgeoisie and in the name of birth and prerogative successfully resisted its self-making.

But this does *not* mean that there are no upper strata in the United States. That they emerged from a 'middle class' that had no recognized aristocratic superiors does not mean they remained middle class when enormous increases in wealth made their own superiority possible. Their origins and their newness may have made the upper strata less visible in America than elsewhere. But in America today there are in fact tiers and ranges of wealth and power of which people in the middle and lower ranks know very little and may not even dream. There are families who, in their well-being, are quite insulated from the economic jolts and lurches felt by the merely prosperous and those farther down the scale. There are also men of power who in quite small groups make decisions of enormous consequence for the underlying population.

The American elite entered modern history as a virtually unopposed bourgeoisie. No national bourgeoisie, before or since, has had such opportunities and advantages. Having no military neighbors, they easily occupied an isolated continent stocked with natural resources and immensely inviting to a willing labor force. A framework of power and an ideology for its justification were already at hand. Against mercantilist restriction, they inherited the principle of *laissez-faire;* against Southern planters, they imposed the principle of industrialism. The Revolutionary War put an end to colonial pretensions to nobility, as loyalists fled the country and many estates were broken up. The Jacksonian upheaval with its status revolution put an end to pretensions to monopoly of descent by the old New England families. The Civil War broke the power, and so in due course the prestige, of the antebellum South's claimants for the higher esteem. The tempo of the whole capitalist development made it impossible for an inherited nobility to develop and endure in America.

No fixed ruling class, anchored in agrarian life and coming to flower in military glory, could contain in America the historic thrust of commerce and industry, or subordinate to itself the capitalist elite—as capitalists were subordinated, for example, in Germany and Japan. Nor could such a ruling class anywhere in the world contain that of the United States when industrialized violence came to decide history. Witness the fate of Germany and Japan in the two world wars of the twentieth century; and indeed the fate of Britain herself and her model ruling class, as New York became the inevitable economic, and Washington the inevitable political capital of the western capitalist world.

4

The elite who occupy the command posts may be seen as the possessors of power and wealth and celebrity; they may be seen as members of the upper stratum of a capitalistic society. They may also be defined in terms of psychological and moral criteria, as certain kinds of selected individuals. So defined, the elite, quite simply, are people of superior character and energy.

The humanist, for example, may conceive of the 'elite' not as a social level or category, but as a scatter of those individuals who attempt to transcend themselves, and accordingly, are more noble, more efficient, made out of better stuff. It does not matter whether they are poor or rich, whether they hold high position or low, whether they are acclaimed or despised; they are elite because of the kind of individuals they are. The rest of the population is mass, which, according to this conception, sluggishly relaxes into uncomfortable mediocrity.[5] This is the sort of socially unlocated conception which some American writers with conservative yearnings have recently sought to develop. But most moral and psychological conceptions of the elite are much less sophisticated, concerning themselves not with individuals but with the stratum as a whole. Such ideas, in fact, always arise in a society in which some people possess more than do others of what there is to possess. People with advantages are loath to believe that they just happen to be people with advantages.

They come readily to define themselves as inherently worthy of what they possess; they come to believe themselves 'naturally' elite; and, in fact, to imagine their possessions and their privileges as natural extensions of their own elite selves. In this sense, the idea of the elite as composed of men and women having a finer moral character is an ideology of the elite as a privileged ruling stratum, and this is true whether the ideology is elite-made or made up for it by others.

In eras of equalitarian rhetoric, the more intelligent or the more articulate among the lower and middle classes, as well as guilty members of the upper, may come to entertain ideas of a counter-elite. In western society, as a matter of fact, there is a long tradition and varied images of the poor, the exploited, and the oppressed as the truly virtuous, the wise, and the blessed. Stemming from Christian tradition, this moral idea of a counter-elite composed of essentially higher types condemned to a lowly station, may be and has been used by the underlying population to justify harsh criticism of ruling elites and to celebrate utopian images of a new elite to come.

The moral conception of the elite, however, is not always merely an ideology of the overprivileged or a counter-ideology of the underprivileged. It is often a fact: having controlled experiences and select privileges, many individuals of the upper stratum do come in due course to approximate the types of character they claim to embody. Even when we give up—as we must—the idea that the elite man or woman is born with an elite character, we need not dismiss the idea that their experiences and trainings develop in them characters of a specific type. . . .

5

These several notions of the elite, when appropriately understood, are intricately bound up with one another, and we shall use them all in this examination of American success. We shall study each of several higher circles as offering candidates for the elite, and we shall do so in terms of the major institutions making up the total society of America; within and between each of these institutions, we shall trace the interrelations of wealth and power and prestige. But our main concern is with the power of those who now occupy the command posts, and with the role which they are enacting in the history of our epoch.

Such an elite may be conceived as omnipotent, and its powers thought of as a great hidden design.

Thus, in vulgar Marxism, events and trends are explained by reference to 'the will of the bourgeoisie'; in Nazism, by reference to 'the conspiracy of the Jews'; by the petty right in America today, by reference to 'the hidden force' of Communist spies. According to such notions of the omnipotent elite as historical cause, the elite is never an entirely visible agency. It is, in fact, a secular substitute for the will of God, being realized in a sort of providential design, except that usually non-elite men are thought capable of opposing it and eventually overcoming it.

The opposite view—of the elite as impotent—is now quite popular among liberal-minded observers. Far from being omnipotent, the elites are thought to be so scattered as to lack any coherence as a historical force. Their invisibility is not the invisibility of secrecy but the invisibility of the multitude. Those who occupy the formal places of authority are so check-mated—by other elites exerting pressure, or by the public as an electorate, or by constitutional codes—that, although there may be upper classes, there is no ruling class; although there may be men of power, there is no power elite; although there may be a system of stratification, it has no effective top. In the extreme, this view of the elite, as weakened by compromise and disunited to the point of nullity, is a substitute for impersonal collective fate; for, in this view, the decisions of the visible men of the higher circles do not count in history.

Internationally, the image of the omnipotent elite tends to prevail. All good events and pleasing happenings are quickly imputed by the opinion-makers to the leaders of their own nation; all bad events and unpleasant experiences are imputed to the enemy abroad. In both cases, the omnipotence of evil rulers or of virtuous leaders is assumed. Within the nation, the use of such rhetoric is rather more complicated: when men speak of the power of their own party or circle, they and their leaders are, of course, impotent; only 'the people' are omnipotent. But, when they speak of the power of their opponent's party or circle, they impute to them omnipotence; 'the people' are now powerlessly taken in.

More generally, American men of power tend, by convention, to deny that they are powerful. No American runs for office in order to rule or even govern, but only to serve; he does not become a bureaucrat or even an official, but a public servant. And nowadays, as I have already pointed out, such postures have become standard features of the public-relations programs of all men of power. So firm a part of the style of power-wielding have they become that

conservative writers readily misinterpret them as indicating a trend toward an 'amorphous power situation.'

But the 'power situation' of America today is less amorphous than is the perspective of those who see it as a romantic confusion. It is less a flat, momentary 'situation' than a graded, durable structure. And if those who occupy its top grades are not omnipotent, neither are they impotent. It is the form and the height of the gradation of power that we must examine if we would understand the degree of power held and exercised by the elite.

If the power to decide such national issues as are decided were shared in an absolutely equal way, there would be no power elite; in fact, there would be no *gradation* of power, but only a radical homogeneity. At the opposite extreme as well, if the power to decide issues were absolutely monopolized by one small group, there would be no gradation of power; there would simply be this small group in command, and below it, the undifferentiated, dominated masses. American society today represents neither the one nor the other of these extremes, but a conception of them is nonetheless useful: it makes us realize more clearly the question of the structure of power in the United States and the position of the power elite within it.

Within each of the most powerful institutional orders of modern society there is a gradation of power. The owner of a roadside fruit stand does not have as much power in any area of social or economic or political decision as the head of a multi-million-dollar fruit corporation; no lieutenant on the line is as powerful as the Chief of Staff in the Pentagon; no deputy sheriff carries as much authority as the President of the United States. Accordingly, the problem of defining the power elite concerns the level at which we wish to draw the line. By lowering the line, we could define the elite out of existence; by raising it, we could make the elite a very small circle indeed. In a preliminary and minimum way, we draw the line crudely, in charcoal as it were: By the power elite, we refer to those political, economic, and military circles which as an intricate set of overlapping cliques share decisions having at least national consequences. In so far as national events are decided, the power elite are those who decide them. . . .

6

It is not my thesis that for all epochs of human history and in all nations, a creative minority, a ruling class, an omnipotent elite, shape all historical events. Such statements, upon careful examination, usually turn out to be mere tautologies,[6] and even when they are not, they are so entirely general as to be useless in the attempt to understand the history of the present. The minimum definition of the power elite as those who decide whatever is decided of major consequence, does not imply that the members of this elite are always and necessarily the history-makers; neither does it imply that they never are. We must not confuse the conception of the elite, which we wish to define, with one theory about their role: that they are the history-makers of our time. To define the elite, for example, as 'those who rule America' is less to define a conception than to state one hypothesis about the role and power of that elite. No matter how we might define the elite, the extent of its members' power is subject to historical variation. If, in a dogmatic way, we try to include that variation in our generic definition, we foolishly limit the use of a needed conception. If we insist that the elite be defined as a strictly coordinated class that continually and absolutely rules, we are closing off from our view much to which the term more modestly defined might open to our observation. In short, our definition of the power elite cannot properly contain dogma concerning the degree and kind of power that ruling groups everywhere have. Much less should it permit us to smuggle into our discussion a theory of history.

During most of human history, historical change has not been visible to the people who were involved in it, or even to those enacting it. Ancient Egypt and Mesopotamia, for example, endured for some four hundred generations with but slight changes in their basic structure. That is six and a half times as long as the entire Christian era, which has only prevailed some sixty generations; it is about eighty times as long as the five generations of the United States' existence. But now the tempo of change is so rapid, and the means of observation so accessible, that the interplay of event and decision seems often to be quite historically visible, if we will only look carefully and from an adequate vantage point.

When knowledgeable journalists tell us that 'events, not men, shape the big decisions,' they are echoing the theory of history as Fortune, Chance, Fate, or the work of The Unseen Hand. For 'events' is merely a modern word for these older ideas, all of which separate men from history-making, because all of them lead us to believe that history goes on behind men's backs. History is drift with no mastery; within it there is action but no deed; history is mere happening and the event intended by no one.[7] The course of events in our time depends more on a series of human decisions than on any inevitable fate. The sociological meaning of 'fate' is simply this: that, when the decisions are innumerable and each one is of small consequence, all of them add up in a way no man intended—to history as fate. But not all epochs are equally fateful. As the circle of those who decide is narrowed, as the means of decision are centralized and the consequences of decisions become enormous, then the course of great events often rests upon the decisions of determinable circles. This does not necessarily mean that the same circle of men follow through from one event to another in such a way that all of history is merely their plot. The power of the elite does not necessarily mean that history is not also shaped by a series of small decisions, none of which are thought out. It does not mean that a hundred small arrangements and compromises and adaptations may not be built into the going policy and the living event. The idea of the power elite implies nothing about the process of decision-making as such: it is an attempt to delimit the social areas within which that process, whatever its character, goes on. It is a conception of who is involved in the process.

The degree of foresight and control of those who are involved in decisions that count may also vary. The idea of the power elite does not mean that the estimations and calculated risks upon which decisions are made are not often wrong and that the consequences are sometimes, indeed often, not those intended. Often those who make decisions are trapped by their own inadequacies and blinded by their own errors.

Yet in our time the pivotal moment does arise, and at that moment, small circles do decide or fail to decide. In either case, they are an elite of power. The dropping of the A-bombs over Japan was such a moment; the decision on Korea was such a moment; the confusion about Quemoy and Matsu, as well as before Dienbienphu were such moments; the sequence of maneuvers which involved the United States in World War II was such a 'moment.' Is it not true that much of the history of our times is composed of such moments? And is not that what is meant when it is said that we live in a time of big decisions, of decisively centralized power?

Most of us do not try to make sense of our age by believing in a Greek-like, eternal recurrence, nor by a Christian belief in a salvation to come, nor by any steady march of human progress. Even though we do not reflect upon such matters, the chances are we believe with Burckhardt that we live in a mere succession of events; that sheer continuity is the only principle of history. History is merely one thing after another; history is meaningless in that it is not the realization of any determinate plot. It is true, of course, that our sense of continuity, our feeling for the history of our time, is affected by crisis. But we seldom look beyond the immediate crisis or the crisis felt to be just ahead. We believe neither in fate nor providence; and we assume, without talking about it, that 'we'—as a nation—can decisively shape the future but that 'we' as individuals somehow cannot do so.

Any meaning history has, 'we' shall have to give to it by our actions. Yet the fact is that although we are all of us within history we do not all possess equal powers to make history. To pretend that we do is sociological nonsense and political irresponsibility. It is nonsense because any group or any individual is limited, first of all, by the technical and institutional means of power at its command; we do not all have equal access to the means of power that now exist, nor equal influence over their use. To pretend that 'we' are all history-makers is politically irresponsible because it obfuscates any attempt to locate responsibility for the consequential decisions of men who do have access to the means of power.

From even the most superficial examination of the history of the western society, we learn that the power of decision-makers is first of all limited by the level of technique, by the *means* of power and violence and organization that prevail in a given society. In this connection we also learn that there is a fairly straight line running upward through the history of the West; that the means of oppression and exploitation, of violence and destruction, as well as the means of production and reconstruction, have been progressively enlarged and increasingly centralized.

As the institutional means of power and the means of communications that tie them together have become steadily more efficient, those now in command of them have come into command of instruments of rule quite unsurpassed in the history of mankind. And we are not yet at the climax of their development. We can no longer lean upon or take soft comfort from the historical ups and downs of ruling groups of previous epochs. In that sense, Hegel is correct: we learn from history that we cannot learn from it.

NOTES

1. Jacob Burckhardt, *Force and Freedom* (New York: Pantheon Books, 1943), pp. 303 ff.

2. Cf. Hans Gerth and C. Wright Mills, *Character and Social Structure* (New York: Harcourt, Brace, 1953), pp. 457 ff.

3. The statistical idea of choosing some value and calling those who have the most of it an elite derives, in modern times, from the Italian economist, Pareto, who puts the central point in this way: 'Let us assume that in every branch of human activity each individual is given an index which stands as a sign of his capacity, very much the way grades are given in the various subjects in examinations in school. The highest type of lawyer, for instance, will be given 10. The man who does not get a client will be given 1—reserving zero for the man who is an out-and-out idiot. To the man who has made his millions—honestly or dishonestly as the case may be—we will give 10. To the man who has earned his thousands we will give 6; to such as just manage to keep out of the poor-house, 1, keeping zero for those who get in. . . . So let us make a class of people who have the highest indices in their branch of activity, and to that class give the name of *elite*.' Vilfredo Pareto, *The Mind and Society* (New York: Harcourt, Brace, 1935), par. 2027 and 2031. Those who follow this approach end up not with one elite, but with a number corresponding to the number of values they select. Like many rather abstract ways of reasoning, this one is useful because it forces us to think in a clear-cut way. For a skillful use of this approach, see the work of Harold D. Lasswell, in particular, *Politics: Who Gets What, When, How* (New York: McGraw-Hill, 1936); and for a more systematic use, H. D. Lasswell and Abraham Kaplan, *Power and Society* (New Haven: Yale University Press, 1950).

4. The conception of the elite as members of a top social stratum, is, of course, in line with the prevailing common-sense view of stratification. Technically, it is closer to 'status group' than to 'class,' and has been very well stated by Joseph A. Schumpeter, 'Social Classes in an Ethically Homogeneous Environment,' *Imperialism and Social Classes* (New York: Augustus M. Kelley, Inc., 1951), pp. 133 ff., especially pp. 137–47. Cf. also his *Capitalism, Socialism and Democracy*, 3rd ed. (New York: Harper, 1950), Part II. For the distinction between class and status groups, see *From Max Weber: Essays in Sociology*, trans. and ed. by Gerth and Mills (New York: Oxford University Press, 1946). For an analysis of Pareto's conception of the elite compared with Marx's conception of classes, as well as data on France, see Raymond Aron, 'Social Structure and Ruling Class,' *British Journal of Sociology*, vol. I, nos. 1 and 2 (1950).

5. The most popular essay in recent years which defines the elite and the mass in terms of a morally evaluated character-type is probably José Ortega y Gasset's, *The Revolt of the Masses*, 1932 (New York: New American Library, Mentor Edition, 1950), esp. pp. 91 ff.

6. As in the case, quite notably, of Gaetano Mosca, *The Ruling Class* (New York: McGraw-Hill, 1939). For a sharp analysis of Mosca, see Fritz Morstein Marx, 'The Bureaucratic State,' *Review of Politics,* vol. I, 1939, pp. 457 ff. Cf. also Mills, 'On Intellectual Craftsmanship,' April 1952, mimeographed, Columbia College, February 1955.

7. Cf. Karl Löwith, *Meaning in History* (Chicago: University of Chicago Press, 1949), pp. 125 ff. for concise and penetrating statements of several leading philosophies of history.

---

14. Alvin W. Gouldner*
The Future of Intellectuals and the Rise of the New Class

In all countries that have in the twentieth century become part of the emerging world socioeconomic order, a New Class composed of intellectuals and technical intelligentsia—not the same—enters into contention with the groups already in control of the society's economy, whether these are businessmen or party leaders. A new contest of classes and a new class system is slowly arising in the third world of developing nations, in the second world of the USSR and its client states, and in the first world of late capitalism of North America, Western Europe, and Japan.

The early historical evolution of the New Class in Western Europe, its emergence into the public sphere as a structurally differentiated and (relatively) autonomous social stratum, may be defined in terms of certain critical episodes. What follows is only a synoptic inventory of some episodes decisive in the formation of the New Class.

1. A process of secularization in which most intelligentsia are no longer trained by, living within, and subject to close supervision by a churchly organization, and thus separated from the everyday life of society.[1] Secularization is important because it desacralizes authority-claims and facilitates challenges to

*Adapted from THE FUTURE OF INTELLECTUALS AND THE RISE OF THE NEW CLASS by Alvin W. Gouldner (1982), from pp. 1-8, 18-20, 28-29, 83-85, 102-104, 106, 110, 112-113. By permission of Oxford University Press, USA. As published in *Social Stratification: Class, Race, and Gender in Sociological Perspective,* 3rd edition, by David Grusky, copyright © 2009. Reprinted by permission of Westview Press, an imprint of Perseus Books, LLC, a subsidiary of Hachette Book Group, Inc.

definitions of social reality made by traditional authorities linked to the church. Secularization is important also because it is an infrastructure on which there develops the modern grammar of rationality, or culture of critical discourse, with its characteristic stress on self-groundedness—in Martin Heidegger's sense of the "mathematical project."[2]

2. A second episode in the emergence of the New Class is the rise of diverse vernacular languages, the corresponding decline of Latin as the language of intellectuals, and especially of their scholarly production. Latin becomes a ritual, rather than a technical language. This development further dissolves the membrane between everyday life and the intellectuals—whether clerical or secular.

3. There is a breakdown of the feudal and old regime system of personalized *patronage* relations between the old hegemonic elite and individual members of the New Class as cultural producers; and:

4. A corresponding growth of an anonymous *market* for the products and services of the New Class, thus allowing them to make an independent living apart from close supervision and *personalized controls by patrons.* Along with secularization, this means that the residence and work of intellectuals are both now less closely supervised by others.

They may now more readily take personal initiatives in the public, political sphere, while also having a "private" life.

5. The character and development of the emerging New Class also depended importantly on the multi-national structure of European polities. That Europe was not a single empire with a central authority able to impose a single set of norms throughout its territory, but a system of competing and autonomous states with diverse cultures and religions, meant that dissenting intellectuals, scientists, and divines could and did protect their own intellectual innovations by migrating from their home country when conditions there grew insupportable and sojourning in foreign lands. Even the enforced travel of exiled intellectuals also enabled them to enter into a European-wide communication network. In an article (as yet unpublished), Robert Wuthnow has suggested that their often extensive travel led many intellectuals to share a cosmopolitan identity transcending national limits and enhancing their autonomy from local elites.

6. A sixth episode in the formation of the New Class is the waning of the extended, patriarchal family system and its replacement by the smaller, nuclear

family. As middle class women become educated and emancipated, they may increasingly challenge paternal authority and side with their children in resisting it. With declining paternal authority and growing maternal influence, the autonomy strivings of children are now more difficult to repress; hostility and rebellion against paternal authority can become more overt. There is, correspondingly, increasing difficulty experienced by paternal authority in imposing and reproducing its social values and political ideologies in their children.

7. Following the French Revolution, there is in many parts of Europe, especially France and Germany, a profound reformation and extension of *public, non*-church controlled, (relatively more) *multi-class* education, at the lower levels as well as at the college, polytechnical, and university levels. On the one hand, higher education in the public school becomes the institutional basis for the *mass* production of the New Class of intelligentsia and intellectuals. On the other hand, the expansion of primary and secondary public school teachers greatly increases the jobs available to the New Class.

As teachers, intellectuals come to be defined, and to define themselves, as responsible for and "representative" of society as a *whole*,[3] rather than as having allegiance to the class interests of their students or their parents. As teachers, they are not defined as having an *obligation* to reproduce parental values in their children. Public teachers supersede private tutors.

8. The new structurally differentiated educational system is increasingly insulated from the family system, becoming an important source of values among students divergent from those of their families. The socialization of the young by their families is now mediated by a *semi*-autonomous group of teachers.

9. While growing public education limits family influence on education, it also increases the influence of the state on education. The public educational system thus becomes a major *cosmopolitanizing* influence on its students, with a corresponding distancing from *localistic* interests and values.

10. Again, the new school system becomes a major setting for the intensive linguistic conversion of students from casual to reflexive speech, or (in Basil Bernstein's terms) from "restricted" linguistic codes to "elaborated" linguistic codes,[4] to a culture of discourse in which claims and assertions may *not* be justified by reference to the speaker's social status. This has the profound consequence of making all *authority-referring* claims potentially problematic.

11. This new culture of discourse often diverges from assumptions fundamental to everyday life, tending to put them into question even when they are linked to the upper classes. These school-inculcated modes of speech are, also, (relatively) situation-free language variants. Their situation-freeness is further heightened by the "communications revolution" in general, and by the development of printing technology, in particular. With the spread of printed materials, definitions of social reality available to intellectuals may now derive increasingly from *distant* persons, from groups geographically, culturally, and historically distant and even from dead persons, and may therefore diverge greatly from any local environment in which they are received. Definitions of social reality made by local elites may now be invidiously contrasted (by intellectuals) with definitions made in other places and times.

12. With the spread of public schools, literacy spreads; humanistic intellectuals lose their exclusiveness and privileged market position, and now experience a status disparity between their "high" culture, as they see it, and their lower deference, repute, income, and social power. The social position of humanistic intellectuals, *particularly in a technocratic and industrial society*, becomes more marginal and alienated than that of the technical intelligentsia. The New Class becomes internally differentiated.

13. Finally, a major episode in the emergence of the modern intelligentsia is the changing form of the revolutionary *organization*. Revolution itself becomes a technology to be pursued with "instrumental rationality." The revolutionary organization evolves from a ritualistic, oath-bound secret society into the modern "vanguard" party. When the *Communist Manifesto* remarks that Communists have nothing to hide,[5] it is exactly a proposed emergence into *public* life which is implied. The *Communist Manifesto* was written by Marx and Engels for the "League of Communists," which was born of the "League of the Just" which, in turn, was descended from the "League of Outlaws." This latter group of German emigrants in Paris had a pyramidal structure, made a sharp distinction between upper and lower members, blindfolded members during initiation ceremonies, used recognition signs and passwords, and bound members by an oath.[6] The vanguard organization, however, deritualizes participation and entails elements of both the "secret society" and of the public political party. In the vanguard

organization, public refers to the public availability of the *doctrine* rather than the availability of the organization or its membership to public scrutiny. Here, to be "public" entails the organization's rejection of "secret doctrines" known only to an elite in the organization—as, for instance, Bakunin's doctrine of an elite dictatorship of anarchists.[7] The *modern* vanguard structure is first clearly encoded in Lenin's *What Is to Be Done?* Here it is plainly held that the proletariat cannot develop a *socialist* consciousness by itself, but must secure this from a scientific theory developed by the intelligentsia.[8] The "vanguard" party expresses the *modernizing* and elite ambitions of the New Class as well as an effort to overcome its political limitations. Lenin's call for the development of "professional" revolutionaries, as the core of the vanguard, is a rhetoric carrying the tacit promise of a *career*-like life which invites young members of the New Class to "normalize" the revolutionary existence. . . .

There are several distinguishable conceptions of the New Class:

1. *New Class as Benign Technocrats:* Here the New Class is viewed as a new historical elite already entrenched in institutional influence which it uses in benign ways for society; it is more or less inevitable and trustworthy: e.g., Galbraith,[9] Bell,[10] Berle and Means.[11] (*Sed contra:* This obscures the manner in which the New Class egoistically pursues its own special vested interests. Moreover, the power of the New Class today is scarcely entrenched. This view also ignores the limits on the rationality of the New Class.)

2. *New Class as Master Class:* Here the New Class is seen as another moment in a long-continuing circulation of historical elites, as a socialist intelligentsia that brings little new to the world and continues to exploit the rest of society as the old class had, but now uses education rather than money to exploit others: Bakunin,[12] Machajski.[13] (*Sed contra:* The New Class is more historically unique and discontinuous than this seems; while protecting its own special interests, it is not bound by the same *limits* as the old class and, at least transiently, contributes to collective needs.)

3. *New Class as Old Class Ally:* The New Class is here seen as a benign group of dedicated "professionals" who will uplift the old (moneyed) class from a venal group to a collectivity-oriented elite and who, fusing with it, will forge a new, genteel elite continuous with but better than the past: Talcott Parsons.[14]

(*Sed contra:* Neither group is an especially morally bound agent; the old class is constrained to protect its profits, the New Class is cashing in on its education. Immersed in the present, this view misses the fact that each is ready to exploit the other, if need be, and shows little understanding of the profound [if different] limits imposed on the rationality and morality of each of these groups, and of the important tensions between them.)

4. *New Class as Servants of Power:* Here the New Class is viewed as subservient to the old (moneyed) class which is held to retain power much as it always did, and is simply using the New Class to maintain its domination of society: Noam Chomsky[15] and Maurice Zeitlin.[16] (*Sed contra:* This ignores the revolutionary history of the twentieth century in which radicalized elements of the New Class played a major leadership role in the key revolutions of our time. It greatly overemphasizes the common interests binding the New and old class, systematically missing the tensions between them; it ignores the fact that elimination of the old class is an historical option open to the New Class. This static conception underestimates the growth in the numbers and influence of the New Class. The view is also unexpectedly Marcusean in overstressing the prospects of old class continuity; it really sees the old class as having no effective opponents, either in the New Class or in the old adversary class, the proletariat. It thus ends as seeing even less social change in prospect than the Parsonian view [#3 above].)

5. *New Class as Flawed Universal Class (my own view):* The New Class is elitist and self-seeking and uses its special knowledge to advance its own interests and power, and to control its own work situation. Yet the New Class may also be the best card that history has presently given us to play. The power of the New Class is growing. It is substantially more powerful and independent than Chomsky suggests, while still much less powerful than is suggested by Galbraith who seems to conflate present reality with future possibility. The power of this morally ambiguous New Class is on the ascendent, and it holds a mortgage on at least *one* historical future.

In my own left Hegelian sociology, the New Class bearers of knowledge are seen as an embryonic new "universal class"—as the prefigured embodiment of such future as the working class still has. It is that part of the working class which will survive cybernation. At the same time, a left Hegelian sociology also insists that the New Class is profoundly flawed as a universal class. Moreover, the New Class is not some unified subject or a seamless whole; it, too, has its own internal contradictions. It is a class internally divided with tensions between (technical) intelligentsia and (humanistic) intellectuals. No celebration, mine is a critique of the New Class which does not view its growing power as inevitable, which sees it as morally ambivalent, embodying the collective interest but partially and transiently, while simultaneously cultivating its own guild advantage. . . .

The New Class as a Cultural Bourgeoisie

1. The New Class and the old class are at first undifferentiated; the New Class commonly originates in classes with property advantages, that is, in the old class, or is sponsored by them. The New Class of intellectuals and intelligentsia are the relatively more *educated* counterpart—often the brothers, sisters, or children—of the old moneyed class. Thus the New Class contest sometimes has the character of a *civil war within the upper classes.* It is the differentiation of the old class into contentious factions. To understand the New Class contest it is vital to understand how the *privileged* and advantaged, not simply the suffering, come to be alienated from the very system that privileges them.

2. The "non-negotiable" objectives of the old moneyed class are to reproduce their capital, at a minimum, but, preferably, to make it accumulate and to appropriate profit: M-C-M, as Marx said. This is done within a structure in which all of them must compete with one another. This unrelenting competition exerts pressure to rationalize their productive and administrative efforts and unceasingly to heighten efficiency. (Marx called it, "revolutionizing" production.) But this rationalization is dependent increasingly on the efforts of the New Class intelligentsia and its expert skills. It is inherent in its structural situation, then, that the old class must bring the New Class into existence.

3. Much of the New Class is at first trained under the direct control of the old class's firms or enterprises. Soon, however, the old class is separated from the reproduction of the New Class by the emergence and development of a public system of education whose costs are "socialized."[17]

4. The more that the New Class's reproduction derives from specialized systems of public education, the more the New Class develops an ideology that stresses its *autonomy,* its separation from and presumable independence of "business" or political interests. This autonomy is said to be grounded in the specialized knowledge or cultural capital transmitted by the educational system, along with an emphasis on the obligation of educated persons to attend to the welfare of the collectivity. In other words, the *ideology* of "professionalism" emerges.

5. Professionalism is one of the public *ideologies* of the New Class and is the genteel subversion of the old class by the new. Professionalism is a phase in the historical development of the "collective consciousness" of the New Class. While not overtly a critique of the old class, professionalism is a tacit claim by the New Class to *technical and moral superiority* over the old class, implying that the latter lack technical credentials and are guided by motives of commercial venality. Professionalism silently installs the New Class as the paradigm of virtuous and legitimate authority, performing with technical skill and with dedicated concern for the society-at-large. Professionalism makes a focal claim for the legitimacy of the New Class which tacitly de-authorizes the old class.

On the one side, this is a bid for prestige *within* the established society; on the other, it tacitly presents the New Class as an *alternative* to the old. In asserting its own claims to authority, professionalism in effect *devalues the authority of the old class.*

6. The special privileges and powers of the New Class are grounded in their *individual* control of special cultures, languages, techniques, and of the skills resulting from these. The New Class is a cultural bourgeoisie who appropriates privately the advantages of a historically and collectively produced cultural capital. Let us be clear, then: the New Class is not just *like* the old class; its special culture is not just *like* capital. No metaphor is intended. The special culture of the New Class *is* a stock of capital that generates a stream of income (some of) which it appropriates privately.

7. The fundamental objectives of the New Class are: to increase its own share of the national product; to produce and reproduce the special social conditions enabling them to appropriate privately larger shares of the incomes produced by the special cultures they possess; to control their work and their work settings; and to increase their political power partly in order to achieve the foregoing. The struggle of the New Class is, therefore, to *institutionalize a wage system,* i.e., a social system with a distinct

principle of distributive justice: "from each according to his ability, to each according to his work," which is also the norm of "socialism." Correspondingly, the New Class may oppose other social systems and their different systems of privilege, for example, systems that allocate privileges and incomes on the basis of controlling stocks of money (i.e., old capital). The New Class, then, is prepared to be egalitarian so far as the privileges of the *old* class are concerned. That is, under certain conditions it is prepared to remove or restrict the special incomes of the old class: profits, rents, interest. The New Class is anti-egalitarian, however, in that it seeks special guild advantages—political powers and incomes—on the basis of its possession of cultural capital. . . .

The New Class as a Speech Community

1. The culture of critical discourse (CCD)[18] is an historically evolved set of rules, a grammar of discourse, which (1) is concerned to *justify* its assertions, but (2) whose *mode* of justification does not proceed by invoking authorities, and (3) prefers to elicit the *voluntary* consent of those addressed solely on the basis of arguments adduced. CCD is centered on a specific speech act: justification. It is a culture of discourse in which there is nothing that speakers will on principle permanently refuse to discuss or make problematic; indeed, they are even willing to talk about the value of talk itself and its possible inferiority to silence or to practice. This grammar is the deep structure of the common ideology shared by the New Class. *The shared ideology of the intellectuals and intelligentsia is thus an ideology about discourse.* Apart from and underlying the various technical languages (or sociolects) spoken by specialized professions, intellectuals and intelligentsia are commonly committed to a culture of critical discourse (CCD). CCD is the latent but mobilizable infrastructure of modern "technical" languages.

2. The culture of critical discourse is characterized by speech that is *relatively* more *situation-free*, more context or field "independent." This speech culture thus values expressly legislated meanings and devalues tacit, context-limited meanings. Its ideal is: "one word, one meaning," for everyone and forever.

The New Class's special speech variant also stresses the importance of particular modes of *justification*, using especially explicit and articulate rules, rather than diffuse precedents or tacit features of the speech context. The culture of critical speech requires that the validity of claims be justified without reference to the speaker's *societal position or authority.* Here, good speech is speech that can make its own principles *explicit* and is oriented to conforming with them, rather than stressing context-sensitivity and context-variability. Good speech here thus has *theoreticity.*[19] Being pattern- and principle-oriented, CCD implies that that which is said may *not* be correct, and may be *wrong.* It recognizes that "What Is" may be mistaken or inadequate and is therefore open to alternatives. CCD is also relatively more *reflexive,* self-monitoring, capable of more metacommunication, that is, of talk about talk; it is able to make its own speech problematic, and to edit it with respect to its lexical and grammatical features, as well as making problematic the validity of its assertions. CCD thus requires considerable "expressive discipline," not to speak of "instinctual renunciation."

3. Most importantly, the culture of critical speech forbids reliance upon the speaker's person, authority, or status in society to justify his claims. As a result, CCD de-authorizes all speech grounded in traditional societal authority, while it authorizes itself, the elaborated speech variant of the culture of critical discourse, as the standard of *all* "serious" speech. From now on, persons and their social positions must not be visible in their speech. Speech becomes impersonal. Speakers hide behind their speech. Speech seems to be dis-embodied, de-contextualized and self-grounded. (This is especially so for the speech of intellectuals and somewhat less so for the technical intelligentsia who may not invoke CCD except when their paradigms break down.) The New Class becomes the guild masters of an invisible pedagogy.

4. The culture of critical discourse is the common ideology shared by the New Class, although technical intelligentsia sometimes keep it in latency. The skills and the social conditions required to reproduce it are among the common *interests* of the New Class. Correspondingly, it is in the common interest of the New Class to prevent or oppose all censorship of its speech variety and to install it as the standard of good speech. *The New Class thus has both a common ideology in CCD and common interests in its cultural capital.* . . .

The Flawed Universal Class

1. The New Class is the most progressive force in modern society and is a center of whatever human

emancipation is possible in the foreseeable future. It has no motives to curtail the forces of production and no wish to develop them solely in terms of their profitability. The New Class possesses the scientific knowledge and technical skills on which the future of modern forces of production depend. At the same time, members of the New Class also manifest increasing sensitivity to the ecological "side effects" or distant diseconomies of continuing technical development. The New Class, further, is a center of opposition to almost all forms of censorship, thus embodying a universal societal interest in a kind of rationality broader than that invested in technology. Although the New Class is at the center of nationalist movements throughout the world, after that phase is secured, the New Class is also the most internationalist and most universalist of all social strata; it is the most cosmopolitan of all elites. Its control over ordinary "foreign" languages, as well as of technical sociolects, enables it to communicate with other nationalities and it is often a member of a technical guild of international scope.

2. For all that, however, the New Class is hardly the end of domination. While its ultimate significance is the end of the old moneyed class's domination, the New Class is also the nucleus of a *new* hierarchy and the elite of a new form of cultural capital.

The historical limits of the New Class are inherent in both the nature of its own characteristic rationality and in its ambitions as a cultural bourgeoisie. Its culture of critical discourse fosters a purely "theoretical" attitude toward the world. Speakers are held competent to the degree that they know and can *say* the rules, rather than just happening to follow them. The culture of critical discourse thus values the very theoreticity that the "common sense" long suspected was characteristic of intellectuals.

Intellectuals have long believed that those who know the rule, who know the theory by which they act, are superior because they lead an "examined" life. They thus exalt theory over practice, and are concerned less with the success of a practice than that the practice should have submitted itself to a reasonable rule. Since intellectuals and intelligentsia are concerned with doing things in the right way and for the right reason—in other words, since they value doctrinal conformity for its own sake—they (we) have a native tendency toward ritualism and *sectarianism.*

3. The culture of the New Class exacts still other costs: since its discourse emphasizes the importance of carefully edited speech, this has the vices of its virtues: in its *virtuous* aspect, self-editing implies a commendable circumspection, carefulness, self-discipline and "seriousness." In its negative modality, however, self-editing also disposes toward an unhealthy self-consciousness, toward stilted convoluted speech, an inhibition of play, imagination and passion, and continual pressure for expressive discipline. The new rationality thus becomes the source of a new alienation.

Calling for watchfulness and self-discipline, CCD is productive of intellectual reflexivity *and* the loss of warmth and spontaneity. Moreover, that very reflexivity stresses the importance of adjusting action to some pattern of propriety. There is, therefore, a structured inflexibility when facing changing situations; there is a certain disregard of the differences in situations, and an insistence on hewing to the required rule.

This inflexibility and insensitivity to the force of differing contexts, this inclination to impose one set of rules on different cases also goes by the ancient name of "dogmatism." Set in the context of human relationships, the vulnerability of the New Class to dogmatism along with its very *task*-centeredness, imply a certain insensitivity to *persons,* to their feelings and reactions, and open the way to the disruption of human solidarity. Political brutality, then, finds a grounding in the culture of critical discourse; the new rationality may paradoxically allow a new darkness at noon.

4. The paradox of the New Class is that it is both emancipatory *and* elitist. It subverts all establishments, social limits, and privileges, including its own. The New Class bears a culture of critical and careful discourse which is an historically emancipatory rationality. The new discourse (CCD) is the grounding for a critique of established forms of domination and provides an escape from tradition, but it also bears the seeds of a new domination. Its discourse is a lumbering machinery of argumentation that can wither imagination, discourage play, and curb expressivity. The culture of discourse of the New Class seeks to *control* everything, its topic and itself, believing that such domination is the only road to truth. The New Class begins by monopolizing truth and by making itself its guardian. It thereby makes even the claims of the old class dependent on it. The New Class sets itself above others, holding that its speech is better than theirs; that the examined life

(*their* examination) is better than the unexamined life which, it says, is sleep and no better than death. Even as it subverts old inequities, the New Class silently inaugurates a new hierarchy of the knowing, the knowledgeable, the reflexive and insightful. Those who talk well, it is held, excel those who talk poorly or not at all. It is now no longer enough simply to be good. Now, one has to explain it. The New Class is the universal class in embryo, but badly flawed.

NOTES

1. It is not my intention to suggest that modern intellectuals are merely the secular counterpart of clericals. Indeed, my own stress (as distinct, say, from Edward Shils who does appear to view intellectuals as priests *manqués*) is on the discontinuity of the two.

2. For full development of this, see chapter 2, especially p. 42, of my *Dialectic of Ideology and Technology* (New York, 1976).

3. Doubtless some will insist this is a "false consciousness." But this misses the point. My concern here is with their own definitions of their social role, precisely because these influence the manner in which they perform their roles. As W. I. Thomas and Florian Znaniecki long ago (and correctly) insisted, a thing defined as real is real in its consequences. Moreover, the state who employs most of these teachers is itself interested in having teachers consolidate the tie between students and itself, rather than with the students' parents.

4. See Basil Bernstein, *Class, Codes and Control,* vol. 1, *Theoretical Studies Towards a Sociology of Language* (London, 1971), vol. 2, *Applied Studies Towards a Sociology of Language* (London, 1973), vol. 3, *Towards a Theory of Educational Transmission* (London, 1975). Bernstein's theory is used here in a critical appropriation facilitated by the work of Dell Hymes and William Labov. My own critique of Bernstein emerges, at least tacitly, in the discussion of [the "Flawed Universal Class"] in the text. It is developed explicitly in my *Dialectic of Ideology and Technology*. While Labov has sharply criticized Bernstein, he himself also stresses the general importance of self-monitored speech and of speech *reflexivity* in general (i.e., not only of careful pronunciation) thus converging with Bernstein's focus on reflexivity as characterizing the elaborated linguistic variant and distinguishing it from the restricted variant. See William Labov, *Sociolinguistic Patterns* (Philadelphia, 1972), p. 208.

5. For example: "The Communists disdain to conceal their views and aims. They openly declare . . . " (*Communist Manifesto* [Chicago, 1888], authorized English edition edited by Engels, p. 58).

6. See E. Hobsbawm, *Primitive Rebels* (Manchester, 1959), p. 167 ff.

7. A secret doctrine is one which, because it is reserved only for the organization elite, can be made known only after persons join organizations and reach a certain membership position in it. A secret doctrine thus is never one which can have been a *motive* for joining the organization in the first instance.

8. Lenin's *What Is to Be Done?* was originally published in 1902.

9. *The New Industrial State* (Boston, 1967).

10. *The Coming of Post-Industrial Society* (New York, 1973).

11. *The Modern Corporation and Private Property* (New York, 1932).

12. "It stands to reason that the one who knows more will dominate the one who knows less," M. Bakounine, *Oeuvres,* Vol. 5 (Paris, 1911), p. 106.

13. See V. F. Calverton, *The Making of Society* (New York, 1937).

14. Talcott Parsons, *The Social System* (Glencoe, 1951), chapter 10; *Essays in Sociological Theory* (Glencoe, 1954), chapter 18; "The Professions," *International Encyclopedia of Social Sciences* (New York, 1968).

15. While Chomsky's position is exhibited in various of his writings, I shall rely here on his most recent statement in his Huizinga lecture, "Intellectuals and the State," delivered at Leiden, 9 October 1977. Citations will be from the manuscript copy. Cf. N. Chomsky, *American Power and the New Mandarins* (New York, 1969).

16. Maurice Zeitlin, "Corporate Ownership and Control: The Large Corporations and the Capitalist Class," *American Journal of Sociology* (March 1974), pp. 1073–1119.

17. Cf. James O'Connor, *Corporations and the State* (New York, 1974), pp. 126–28 for the argument that government financing of R & D and advanced education constitute a socialization of part of the costs of production whose net surplus is privately appropriated.

18. This section is indebted to Basil Bernstein and is based on a critical appropriation of his "elaborated and restricted linguistic codes," which have gone through various re-workings. That controversial classic was published in J. J. Gumperz and D. Hymes, *Directions in Sociolinguistics* (New York, 1972). A recent re-working is to be found in Bernstein's "Social Class, Language, and Socialization," in T. A. Sebeok, ed., *Current Trends in Linguistics* (The Hague, 1974). For full bibliographic and other details see note 4 above.

19. Cf. Peter McHugh, "A Common-Sense Perception of Deviance," in H. P. Dreitzel, ed., *Recent Sociology,* Number 2 (London, 1970), pp. 165 ff. For good speech as "serious" speech see David Silverman, "Speaking Seriously," *Theory and Society* (Spring, 1974).

15. David Brooks*
Bobos in Paradise: The New Upper Class and How They Got There

I'm not sure I'd like to be one of the people featured on the *New York Times* wedding page, but I know I'd like to be the father of one of them. Imagine how happy Stanley J. Kogan must have been, for example, when his daughter Jamie was admitted to Yale. Then imagine his pride when Jamie made Phi Beta Kappa and graduated summa cum laude. Stanley himself is no slouch in the brains department: he's a pediatric urologist in Croton-on-Hudson, with teaching positions at the Cornell Medical Center and the New York Medical College. Still, he must have enjoyed a gloat or two when his daughter put on that cap and gown.

And things only got better. Jamie breezed through Stanford Law School. And then she met a man—Thomas Arena—who appeared to be exactly the sort of son-in-law that pediatric urologists dream about. He did his undergraduate work at Princeton, where he, too, made Phi Beta Kappa and graduated summa cum laude. And he, too, went to law school, at Yale. After school, they both went to work as assistant US attorneys for the mighty Southern District of New York.

These two awesome résumés collided at a wedding ceremony in Manhattan, and given all the school chums who must have attended, the combined tuition bills in that room must have been staggering. The rest of us got to read about it on the *New York Times* weddings page. The page is a weekly obsession for hundreds of thousands of *Times* readers and aspiring Balzacs. Unabashedly elitist, secretive, and totally honest, the "mergers and acquisitions page" (as some of its devotees call it) has always provided an accurate look at at least a chunk of the American ruling class. And over the years it has reflected the changing ingredients of elite status.

When America had a pedigreed elite, the page emphasized noble birth and breeding. But in America today, it's genius and geniality that enable you to join the elect. And when you look at the *Times* weddings page, you can almost feel the force of the mingling SAT scores. It's Dartmouth marries Berkeley, MBA weds Ph.D., Fulbright hitches Rhodes, Lazard Frères joins CBS, and summa cum laude embraces summa cum laude (you rarely see a summa settling for a magna—the tension in such a marriage would be too great). The *Times* emphasizes four things about a person—college degrees, graduate degrees, career path, and parents' profession—for these are the markers of upscale Americans today. . . .

The Fifties

The *Times* weddings page didn't always pulse with the accomplishments of the Résumé Gods. In the late 1950s, the page projected a calm and more stately ethos. The wedding accounts of that era didn't emphasize jobs or advanced degrees. The profession of the groom was only sometimes mentioned, while the profession of the bride was almost never listed (and on the rare occasions when the bride's profession was noted, it was in the past tense, as if the marriage would obviously end her career). Instead, the *Times* listed pedigree and connections. Ancestors were frequently mentioned. The ushers were listed, as were the bridesmaids. Prep schools were invariably mentioned, along with colleges. The *Times* was also careful to list the groom's clubs—the Union League, the Cosmopolitan Club. It also ran down the bride's debutante history, where she came out, and whatever women's clubs she might be a member of, such as the Junior League. In short, the page was a galaxy of restricted organizations. . . .

The section from the late fifties evokes an entire milieu that was then so powerful and is now so dated: the network of men's clubs, country clubs, white-shoe law firms, oak-paneled Wall Street firms, and WASP patriarchs. Everybody has his or her own mental images of the old Protestant Establishment: lockjaw accents, the Social Register, fraternity jocks passing through Ivy League schools, constant rounds of martinis and highballs, bankers' hours, starched old men like Averell Harriman, Dean Acheson, and John J. McCloy, the local bigwigs that appear in John Cheever and John O'Hara stories. . . .

It really was possible to talk about an aristocratic ruling class in the fifties and early sixties, a national elite populated by men who had gone to northeastern prep schools like Groton, Andover, Exeter, and St. Paul's and then ascended through old-line firms on Wall Street into the boardrooms of the Fortune 500 corporations and into the halls of Washington power. The WASPs didn't have total control of the country or anything like it, but they did have the hypnotic magic of prestige. As Richard Rovere wrote in a famous 1962 essay entitled "The American Establishment," "It has very nearly unchallenged power in deciding what is and what is not respectable opinion in this country." . . .

This was the last great age of socially acceptable boozing. It was still an era when fox hunting and polo didn't seem antiquarian. But the two characteristics of that world that strike us forcefully today are its unabashed elitism and its segregation. Though this elite was nowhere near as restrictive as earlier elites—World War II had exerted its leveling influence—the 1950s establishment was still based on casual anti-Semitism, racism, sexism, and a thousand other silent barriers that blocked entry for those without the correct pedigree. Wealthy Jewish and Protestant boys who had been playing together from childhood were forced to endure "The Great Division" at age 17, when Jewish and Gentile society parted into two entirely separate orbits, with separate debutante seasons, dance schools, and social secretaries. A Protestant business executive may have spent his professional hours working intimately with his Jewish colleague, but he never would have dreamed of putting him up for membership in his club. When Senator Barry Goldwater attempted to play golf at the restricted Chevy Chase Club, he was told the club was restricted. "I'm only half Jewish, so can't I play nine holes?" he is said to have replied.

The WASP elite was also genially anti-intellectual. Its members often spoke of "eggheads" and "highbrows" with polite disdain. Instead, their status, as F. Scott Fitzgerald had pointed out a few decades before, derived from "animal magnetism and money." By contrast with today's ruling class, they had relatively uncomplicated attitudes about their wealth. They knew it was vulgar to be gaudy, they tended toward thriftiness, but they seem not to have seen their own money as an affront to American principles of equality. On the contrary, most took their elite status for granted, assuming that such position was simply part of the natural and beneficent order of the universe. There was always going to be an aristocracy, and so for the people who happened to be born into it, the task was to accept the duties that came along with its privileges. . . .

The Hinge Years

Then came the change. By 1960 the average verbal SAT score for incoming freshmen at Harvard was 678, and the math score was 695—these are stratospheric scores. The average Harvard freshman in 1952 would have placed in the bottom 10 percent of the Harvard freshman class of 1960. Moreover, the 1960 class was drawn from a much wider socioeconomic pool. Smart kids from Queens or Iowa or California, who wouldn't have thought of applying to Harvard a decade earlier, were applying and getting accepted. Harvard had transformed itself from a school catering mostly to the northeastern social elite to a high-powered school reaching more of the brightest kids around the country. And this transformation was replicated in almost all elite schools. . . .

History, as Pareto once remarked, is the graveyard of aristocracies, and by the late fifties and early sixties the WASP Establishment had no faith in the code—and the social restrictions—that had sustained it. Maybe its members just lost the will to fight for their privileges. As the writer David Frum theorizes, it had been half a century since the last great age of fortune making. The great families were into at least their third genteel generation. Perhaps by then there wasn't much vigor left. Or perhaps it was the Holocaust that altered the landscape by discrediting the sort of racial restrictions that the Protestant Establishment was built on.

In any case, in 1964 Digby Baltzell astutely perceived the crucial trends. "What seems to be happening," he wrote in *The Protestant Establishment*, "is that a scholarly hierarchy of campus communities governed by the values of admissions committees is gradually supplanting the class hierarchies of local communities which are still governed by the values of parents. . . . Just as the hierarchy of the Church was the main avenue of advancement for the talented and ambitious youth from the lower orders during the medieval period, and just as the business enterprise was responsible for the nineteenth century rags-to-riches dream (when we were predominantly an Anglo-Saxon country), so the campus community has now become the principal guardian of our traditional opportunitarian ideals."

The campus gates were thus thrown open on the basis of brains rather than blood, and within a few short years the university landscape was transformed. Harvard, as we've seen, was changed from a school for the well-connected to a school for brainy strivers. The remaining top schools eliminated their Jewish quotas and eventually dropped their restrictions on women. Furthermore, the sheer numbers of educated Americans exploded. The portion of Americans going to college had been rising steadily throughout the 20th century, but between 1955 and 1974 the growth rate was off the charts. Many of the new students were women. Between 1950 and 1960, the number of female students increased by 47 percent. It then jumped by an additional 168 percent between 1960 and 1970. Over the following decades the student population kept growing and growing. In 1960 there were about 2,000 institutions of higher learning. By 1980 there were 3,200. In 1960 there were 235,000 professors in the United States. By 1980 there were 685,000. . . .

The Sixties

The educated-class rebellion we call "the sixties" was about many things, some of them important and related to the Civil Rights movement and Vietnam, some of them entirely silly, and others, like the sexual revolution, overblown (actual sexual behavior was affected far more by the world wars than by the Woodstock era). But at its core the cultural radicalism of the sixties was a challenge to conventional notions of success. It was not only a political effort to dislodge the establishment from the seats of power. It was a cultural effort by the rising members of the privileged classes to destroy whatever prestige still attached to the WASP lifestyle and the WASP moral code, and to replace the old order with a new social code that would celebrate spiritual and intellectual ideals. The sixties radicals rejected the prevailing definition of accomplishment, the desire to keep up with the Joneses, the prevailing idea of social respectability, the idea that a successful life could be measured by income, manners, and possessions. . . .

And Then Comes Money

The hardest of the hard-core sixties radicals believed the only honest way out was to reject the notion of success altogether: drop out of the rat race, retreat to small communities where real human relationships would flourish. But that sort of utopianism was never going to be very popular, especially among college grads. Members of the educated class prize

human relationships and social equality, but as for so many generations of Americans before them, achievement was really at the core of the sixties grads' value system. They were meritocrats, after all, and so tended to define themselves by their accomplishments. Most of them were never going to drop out or sit around in communes smelling flowers, raising pigs, and contemplating poetry. Moreover, as time went by, they discovered that the riches of the universe were lying at their feet.

The rewards for intellectual capital have increased while the rewards for physical capital have not. That means that even liberal arts majors can wake up one day and find themselves suddenly members of the top-income brackets. A full professor at Yale who renounced the capitalist rat race finds himself making, as of 1999, $113,100, while a professor at Rutgers pulls in $103,700 and superstar professors, who become the object of academic bidding wars, now can rake in more than $300,000 a year. Congressional and presidential staffers top out at $125,000 (before quintupling that when they enter the private sector), and the journalists at national publications can now count on six-figure salaries when they hit middle age, not including lecture fees. Philosophy and math majors head for Wall Street and can make tens of millions of dollars from their quantitative models. America has always had a lot of lawyers, and now the median income for that burgeoning group is $72,500, while income for the big-city legal grinds can reach seven figures. And super-students still flood into medicine—three-quarters of private practitioners net more than $100,000. Meanwhile, in Silicon Valley there are more millionaires than people. . . .

The Anxieties of Abundance

Those who want to win educated-class approval must confront the anxieties of abundance: how to show—not least to themselves—that even while climbing toward the top of the ladder they have not become all the things they still profess to hold in contempt; how to navigate the shoals between their affluence and their self-respect; and how to reconcile their success with their spirituality; and their elite status with their egalitarian ideals. Socially enlightened members of the educated elite tend to be disturbed by the widening gap between rich and poor, and are therefore made somewhat uncomfortable by the fact that their own family income now tops $80,000. Some of them dream of social justice yet went to a college where the tuition costs could feed an entire village in Rwanda for a year. Some once had "Question Authority" bumper stickers on their cars but now find themselves heading start-up software companies with 200 people reporting to them. The sociologists they read in college taught that consumerism is a disease, and yet now they find themselves shopping for $3,000 refrigerators. They took to heart the lessons of *Death of a Salesman,* yet now find themselves directing a sales force. They laughed at the plastics scene in *The Graduate,* but now they work for a company that manufactures . . . plastic.

When you are amidst the educated upscalers, you can never be sure if you're living in a world of hippies or stockbrokers. In reality, you have entered the hybrid world in which everybody is a little of both.

Marx told us that classes inevitably conflict, but sometimes they just blur. The values of the bourgeois mainstream culture and the values of the 1960s counterculture have merged. That culture war has ended, at least within the educated class. In its place that class has created a third culture, which is a reconciliation between the previous two. The educated elites didn't set out to create this reconciliation. It is the product of millions of individual efforts to have things both ways. But it is now the dominant tone of our age. In the resolution between the culture and the counterculture, it is impossible to tell who co-opted whom, because in reality the bohemians and the bourgeois co-opted each other. They emerge from this process as bourgeois bohemians, or "Bobos". . . .

The New Establishment

Today the *New York Times* weddings section is huge once again. In the early 1970s the young rebels didn't want to appear there, but now that their own kids are in college and getting married, they are proud to see their offspring in the Sunday paper. For a fee the *Times* will send you a reproduction of your listing, suitable for framing.

And the young people, the second-generation Bobos, are willing to see their nuptials recorded. Look at the newlyweds on any given Sunday morning, beaming out at you from the pages of the *Times.* Their smiles seem so genuine. They all look so nice and approachable, not dignified or fearsome, the way some of the brides on the 1950s pages did. Things are different but somehow similar. . . .

Today's establishment is structured differently. It is not a small conspiracy of well-bred men with interlocking family and school ties who have enormous influence on the levers of power. Instead, this establishment is a large, amorphous group of meritocrats who share a consciousness and who unselfconsciously reshape institutions to accord with their values. They are not confined to a few East Coast institutions. In 1962, Richard Rovere could write, "Nor has the Establishment ever made much headway in such fields as advertising, television or motion pictures." Today's establishment is everywhere. It exercises its power subtly, over ideas and concepts, and therefore pervasively. There are no sure-fire demographic markers to tell who is a member of this establishment. Members tend to have gone to competitive colleges, but not all have. They tend to live in upscale neighborhoods, such as Los Altos, California, and Bloomfield, Michigan, and Lincoln Park, Illinois, but not all do. What unites them is their shared commitment to the Bobo reconciliation. People gain entry into the establishment by performing a series of delicate cultural tasks: they are prosperous without seeming greedy; they have pleased their elders without seeming conformist; they have risen toward the top without too obviously looking down on those below; they have achieved success without committing certain socially sanctioned affronts to the ideal of social equality; they have constructed a prosperous lifestyle while avoiding the old clichés of conspicuous consumption (it's okay to hew to the new clichés).

Class Rank

This has got to be one of the most anxious social elites ever. We Bobos are not anxious because there is an angry mob outside the gates threatening to send us to the guillotine. There isn't. The educated elite is anxious because its members are torn between their drive to succeed and their fear of turning into sellouts. Furthermore, we are anxious because we do not award ourselves status sinecures. Previous establishments erected social institutions that would give their members security. In the first part of the 20th century, once your family made it into the upper echelons of society, it was relatively easy to stay there. You were invited on the basis of your connections to the right affairs. You were admitted, nearly automatically, to the right schools and considered appropriate for the right spouses. The pertinent question in those circles was not what do you do, but who are you. Once you were established as a Biddle or an Auchincloss or a Venderlip, your way was clear. But members of today's educated class can never be secure about their own future. A career crash could be just around the corner. In the educated class even social life is a series of aptitude tests; we all must perpetually perform in accordance with the shifting norms of propriety, ever advancing signals of cultivation. Reputations can be destroyed by a disgraceful sentence, a lewd act, a run of bad press, or a terrible speech at the financial summit at Davos.

And more importantly, members of the educated class can never be secure about their children's future. The kids have some domestic and educational advantages—all those tutors and developmental toys—but they still have to work through school and ace the SATs just to achieve the same social rank as their parents. Compared to past elites, little is guaranteed.

The irony is that all this status insecurity only makes the educated class stronger. Its members and their children must constantly be alert, working and achieving. Moreover, the educated class is in no danger of becoming a self-contained caste. Anybody with the right degree, job, and cultural competencies can join. Marx warned that "the more a ruling class is able to assimilate the most prominent men [or women] of the dominated classes, the more stable and dangerous its rule." And in truth it is hard to see how the rule of the meritocrats could ever come to an end. The WASP Establishment fell pretty easily in the 1960s; it surrendered almost without a shot. But the meritocratic Bobo class is rich with the spirit of self-criticism. It is flexible and amorphous enough to co-opt that which it does not already command. The Bobo meritocracy will not be easily toppled, even if some group of people were to rise up and conclude that it should be.

16. Shamus Khan*
Privilege: The Making of an Adolescent Elite

One of the curiosities in recent years is how our social institutions have opened to those they previously excluded, yet at the same time inequality has increased. We live in a world of democratic inequality,

*Reprinted from *Privilege: The Making of an Adolescent Elite at St. Paul's School*, by Shamus Rahman Khan, published by Princeton University Press. © 2011 by Shamus Raman Khan. Reprinted by permission.

by which I mean that our nation embraces the democratic principle of openness and access, yet as that embrace has increased so too have our levels of inequality. We often think of openness and equality as going hand in hand. And yet if we look at our experiences over the last fifty years, we can see that that is simply not the case.

This is most notable in elite colleges, where student bodies are increasingly racially diverse but simultaneously richer. In 1951, blacks made up approximately 0.8 percent of the students at elite colleges. Today, blacks make up about 8 percent of Ivy League students; the Columbia class of 2014 is 13 percent black—representative of the black population in our nation as a whole. A similar change could be shown for other races, and women today are outperforming men, creating a gender gap in college attendance in favor of women. Without question our elite educational institutions have become far more open racially and to women. This is a tremendous transformation, nothing short of a revolution. And it has happened not only in our schools but also in our political and economic life. . . .

Who is at elite schools seems to have shifted. The SAT is used to evaluate the "natural aptitude" of students and to move away from favoring wealth and lineage. . . . With "merit" we seem to have stripped individuals of the old baggage of social ties and status and replaced it with personal attributes—hard work, discipline, native intelligence, and other forms of human capital that can be evaluated separate from social life. . . . Though we tend to think of merit as those qualities that are abstract and ahistorical, in fact what counts as meritorious is highly contextual. . . . Rather than "rule by the best" (aristos) or "rule by the people" (demos), "meritocracy" would establish "rule by the cleverest people." We often think of the word as something admirable, but Michael Young invented it to damn what he saw as the cold scientization of ability and the bureaucratization of talent. . . .

The impact of the adoption of this approach has led to rather contradictory outcomes. It has undercut nepotism. It has been used to promote the opening of schools to talented members of society who previously were excluded. But it has also been used to . . . justify the increased wages of the already wealthy (as their skills are so valuable and irreplaceable). And most important for me, it has obscured how outcomes are not simply a product of individual traits. This meritocracy of hard work and achievement has naturalized socially constituted distinctions, making differences in outcomes appear a product of who people are rather than a product of the conditions of their making. It is through looking at the rise of the meritocracy that we can better understand the new elite and thereby some of the workings of our contemporary inequality. In exploring St. Paul's, I will show how the school produces "meritorious" traits of students. . . .

Returning to St. Paul's: Privilege and the New Elite

Before us stood two enormous closed doors. Heavily carved slabs of thick oak with large looping braided wrought iron handles, it was clear that opening them would be no easy task. Standing in a hallway outside, we could look out through the arched windows upon the immaculate lawns, ponds, buildings, and brick paths of the school that surrounded us. Behind those doors we could hear the muffled sounds of an organ and the murmurs of hundreds. Behind those doors . . . was our future.

As the doors opened, a quiet overcame everyone. A deep, steady voice began announcing names. With each name another one of us stepped into a dark silence beyond those doors. . . . I told myself I shouldn't be nervous. After all, I had been through this before, years earlier. But it was hard to suppress my nerves. . . . As I casually and slowly walked between the pews, I spotted faces I recognized and places I had occupied years ago as a student. I was the last new faculty member to enter; after me came a stream of incoming freshmen, sophomores, and juniors. . . . This was our first ceremony at the school, "taking one's place." Through this ritual new members were formally introduced to the school and shown where we belonged among the community. . . .

Stretched before me were girls and boys who had fought to gain entry to St. Paul's School. The pews were bursting with the weight and the promise of monumental success. The seniors closest to me knew that next year the college they were most likely to attend was Harvard—almost a third of them would be at the Ivy League, and nearly all of them at one of the top colleges in the nation. And college placement was merely the next step in their carefully cultivated lives. Just as this seating ceremony endowed them with a specific place at St. Paul's, so too would graduation from St. Paul's endow them with a place in an even more bountiful world. . . . The students around me, though fighting sleep and the hormonal haze of adolescence, knew that they were sitting in seats

once occupied by the men and women who had led American commerce, government, and culture for the last century and a half. For the boys and girls around me, their own challenge was no less daunting; they were the new elite. . . .

Today, the dominant role of the elite has become less straightforward. Looking at the faces before me I saw boys and girls from every part of the world. St. Paul's could never be mistaken for a public high school. It has an intentional diversity that few communities share or can afford. Sitting next to a poor Hispanic boy from the Bronx—who forty years ago would never have been admitted—is a frighteningly self-possessed girl from one of the richest WASP families in the world. St. Paul's is still a place for the already elite. Parents who visit often do so in a sea of Mercedes and BMWs, with the occasional chauffeured Rolls Royce; on sunny days, the campus seems to shimmer from the well-appointed jewelry that hangs carelessly from necks and wrists and fingers. But it is more. Today the school seeks to be a microcosm of our world. Rich and poor, black and white, boys and girls live in a community together. . . . Sitting there in my Chapel seat, I saw before me a showcase of the promise of the diverse twenty-first-century world. And I began to understand the new ways that St. Paul's instills in its members the privileges of belonging to an elite. . . .

The new elite are not an entitled group of boys who rely on family wealth and slide through trust-funded lives. The new elite feel their heritage is not sufficient to guarantee a seat at the top of the social hierarchy, nor should their lives require the exclusion of others. Instead, in certain fundamental ways, they are like the rest of twenty-first-century America: they firmly believe in the importance of the hard work required to achieve their position at a place like St. Paul's and the continued hard work it will take to maintain their advantaged position. Like new immigrants and middle-class Americans, they believe that anyone can achieve what they have, that upward mobility is a perpetual American possibility. . . .

[The Lessons] of St. Paul's

Whereas elites of the past were entitled—building their worlds around the "right" breeding, connections, and culture—new elites develop privilege: a sense of self and a mode of interaction that advantage them. The old entitled elites constituted a class that worked to construct moats and walls around the resources that advantaged them. The new elite think of themselves as far more individualized, supposing that their position is a product of what they have done. They deemphasize refined tastes and "who you know" and instead highlight how you act in and approach the world. . . . The story that the new elite tell is built on America's deeply held belief that merit and hard work will pay off. And it also harnesses a twenty-first-century global outlook, absorbing and extracting value from anything and everything, always savvy to what's happening at the present moment. Part of the way in which institutions like St. Paul's and the Ivy League tell their story is to look less and less like an exclusive yacht club and more and more like a microcosm of our diverse social world—albeit a microcosm with very particular social [lessons]. . . .

Lesson 1: Hierarchies Are Natural and They Can Be Treated Like Ladders, Not Ceilings

Students learn to emphasize hard work and talent when explaining their good fortune. This framing is reinforced by a commitment to an open society—for only in such a society can these qualities explain one's success. However, students also learn that the open society does not mean equality—far from it. A persistent lesson is the enduring, natural presence of hierarchy. Within the open society there are winners and losers. But unlike the past where these positions were ascribed through inheritance, today they are achieved. Hierarchies are not barriers that limit but ladders that allow for advancement. Learning to climb requires interacting with those above (and below) you in a very particular way: by creating intimacy without acting like you are an equal. This is a tricky interactive skill, pretending the hierarchy isn't there but all the while respecting it. Hierarchies are dangerous and unjustifiable when too fixed or present—when society is closed and work and talent don't matter. And so students learn a kind of interaction and sensibility where hierarchies are enabling rather than constraining—in short, where they are fair.

Lesson 2: Experiences Matter

Many St. Paul's students are from already privileged backgrounds, and it would not be unreasonable to think that they would have an easier time. . . . Yet adjusting to life at the school is difficult for everyone. The students who act as if they already hold the keys to success are rejected as entitled. In learning their place at the school, students rely not on their heritage but instead on experiences. There is a shift from the logic of the old elite—who you are—to that of the new elite—what you have done. Privilege is not something you are born with; it is something you learn to develop and cultivate.

Lesson 3: Privilege Means Being at Ease, No Matter What the Context

What students cultivate is a sense of how to carry themselves, and at its core this practice of privilege is ease: feeling comfortable in just about any social situation. In classrooms they are asked to think about both *Beowulf* and *Jaws*. Outside the classroom they listen to classical music and hip-hop. Rather than mobilizing what we might think of as "elite knowledge" to mark themselves as distinct— epic poetry, fine art and music, classical learning— the new elite learn these and everything else. Embracing the open society, they display a kind of radical egalitarianism in their tastes. Privilege is not an attempt to construct boundaries around knowledge and protect such knowledge as a resource. Instead, students display a kind of omnivorousness. Ironically, exclusivity marks the losers in the hierarchical, open society. From this perspective, inequality is explained not by the practices of the elite but instead by the character of the disadvantaged. Their limited knowledge, tastes, and dispositions mean they have not seized upon the fruits of our newly open world.

This elite ease is also an embodied interactional resource. In looking at seemingly mundane acts of everyday life—from eating meals to dancing and dating—privilege becomes inscribed upon the bodies of students, and students are able to display their privilege through their interactions. In being embodied, privilege is not seen as a product of differences in opportunities but instead as a skill, talent, capacity—"who you are." Students from St. Paul's appear to naturally have what it takes to be successful. This helps hide durable inequality by naturalizing socially produced distinctions.

Democratic Inequality

My return to St. Paul's was inspiring. I saw how even our most august institutions could rewrite the assumptions of previous generations and attempt to create a more inclusive world. And yet like all good tales, this one has another side. Students from St. Paul's are undoubtedly privileged. They accrue extraordinary advantages, and the disjuncture between the lives of these students and the lives of other American teenagers . . . can be shocking. The elite adoption of the American Dream, however well-intentioned, happens against a backdrop of increasing social inequality. . . .

Throughout the twentieth century the battles against inequality were battles of access: could women, blacks, and other excluded groups be integrated into the highest institutions and positions in our society? These battles were largely won. Yet the results have not been what we imagined. The promise of the open society was not just more access but more equality. This promise has proven to be a fiction. Twenty-first-century America is increasingly open yet relentlessly unequal. Our next great American project is to find a way out of this paradox.

PART IV

POVERTY AND THE UNDERCLASS

In Part IV of the reader, our attention turns to the bottom of the class structure, where again one finds a large body of high-quality social science research addressing the causes of poverty, the consequences of poverty, and the effects of various poverty-reducing interventions. It is useful to lay the groundwork for this research by describing two important myths about the causes of poverty and how it might be addressed.

The first such myth, which we call the "nothing-can-be-done" myth, misrepresents recent trends in poverty. This myth has it that poverty is immutable and timeless, that it has always been with us and always will be, and that nothing can accordingly be done to affect or reduce it. In justifying this view, the usual trope is to present the trend line in the official poverty measure, a trend line that shows that US poverty has not declined over the last half-century. Although this result makes it appear as if all of our efforts to reduce poverty have gone for naught, in fact such a conclusion would be misleading because the official poverty measure does not take into account the effects of key poverty-fighting programs, like the Earned Income Tax Credit (EITC), that rely on noncash transfers. When we instead use a measure, like the Supplemental Poverty Measure, that *does* take noncash credits into account, we find that poverty has declined in recent decades. The simple conclusion here is that the safety net is doing much poverty-reducing work. Although some might want it to do more such work, there is no denying that the country's apparatus of anti-poverty programs is having a real effect.

The second—and closely related—myth has it that poverty is a deeply complicated affair that has proven resistant to the best efforts of modern science to understand it. It is frequently argued that the science of poverty is a largely failed science and that the best one can do, therefore, is simply to maintain a holding pattern while funding more research and waiting for that elusive magic-bullet cure to be discovered. What is wrong with this view? It is misleading because it understates how much we have learned about poverty in recent decades. As the readings in this section demonstrate, in fact much is known about the causes of poverty, arguably more than enough to fashion powerful and effective anti-poverty programs.

How did we come to believe that poverty is such a deeply complicated and unfathomable affair? The simple answer: We have confused causes with consequences. The consequences of poverty are indeed multifarious and complicated, whereas the causes are relatively straightforward and have come to be well-understood through decades of high-quality research. These causes take the form of (a) economic factors (e.g., globalization) that have eliminated manufacturing jobs for low-skill workers; (b) the weakening of unions and the associated rise of precarious jobs; (c) the declining real value of the minimum wage; (d) relatively anemic redistributive programs in the US; (e) high rates of incarceration among children raised in poverty (especially black children); (f) the role of concentrated poverty in reducing access to jobs, good schools, and other neighborhood assets; (g) the lasting effects of early childhood stress on cognitive development; (h) the limited access to high-quality childcare and early schooling among poor children; and (i) the high costs of housing and the high rates of eviction among the poor. The readings in this and other sections introduce these results and speculate on their implications for mounting a major new initiative to reduce poverty in the U.S.

The implication of this research is clear: If we wanted to wage a second "War on Poverty," we have a good understanding of the many ways in which that war might be waged. It is equally important, of course, not to overclaim in this regard. Although we know a lot about the sources of poverty, it is a much harder task to sort out which interventions are optimizing, how these interventions would interact with other changes, and whether they might provoke a political counterreaction (much as affirmative action programs sometimes did). It follows that, if indeed a major new anti-poverty initiative were undertaken, we would do well to build in provisions for constant testing, retesting, and evidence-based reform.

The Everyday Life of the Poor

17. Barbara Ehrenreich*
Nickel and Dimed

At the beginning of June 1998 I leave behind everything that normally soothes the ego and sustains the body—home, career, companion, reputation, ATM card—for a plunge into the low-wage workforce. There, I become another, occupationally much diminished "Barbara Ehrenreich"—depicted on job-application forms as a divorced homemaker whose sole work experience consists of housekeeping in a few private homes. I am terrified, at the beginning, of being unmasked for what I am: a middle-class journalist setting out to explore the world that welfare mothers are entering, at the rate of approximately 50,000 a month, as welfare reform kicks in. Happily, though, my fears turn out to be entirely unwarranted: during a month of poverty and toil, my name goes unnoticed and for the most part unuttered. In this parallel universe where my father never got out of the mines and I never got through college, I am "baby," "honey," "blondie," and, most commonly, "girl."

My first task is to find a place to live. I figure that if I can earn $7 an hour—which, from the want ads, seems doable—I can afford to spend $500 on rent, or maybe, with severe economies, $600. In the Key West area, where I live, this pretty much confines me to flophouses and trailer homes—like the one, a pleasing fifteen-minute drive from town, that has no air-conditioning, no screens, no fans, no television, and, by way of diversion, only the challenge of

evading the landlord's Doberman pinscher. The big problem with this place, though, is the rent, which at $675 a month is well beyond my reach. . . .

So I decide to make the common trade-off between affordability and convenience, and go for a $500-a-month efficiency thirty miles up a two-lane highway from the employment opportunities of Key West, meaning forty-five minutes if there's no road construction and I don't get caught behind some sun-dazed Canadian tourists. . . .

I am not doing this for the anthropology. My aim is nothing so mistily subjective as to "experience poverty" or find out how it "really feels" to be a long-term low-wage worker. I've had enough unchosen encounters with poverty and the world of low-wage work to know it's not a place you want to visit for touristic purposes; it just smells too much like fear. And with all my real-life assets—bank account, IRA, health insurance, multiroom home—waiting indulgently in the background, I am, of course, thoroughly insulated from the terrors that afflict the genuinely poor.

No, this is a purely objective, scientific sort of mission. The humanitarian rationale for welfare reform—as opposed to the more punitive and stingy impulses that may actually have motivated it—is that work will lift poor women out of poverty while simultaneously inflating their self-esteem and hence their future value in the labor market. Thus, whatever the hassles involved in finding child care, transportation, etc., the transition from welfare to work will end happily, in greater prosperity for all. Now there are many problems with this comforting prediction, such as the fact that the economy will inevitably undergo a downturn, eliminating many jobs. Even without a downturn, the influx of a million former welfare recipients into the low-wage labor market could depress wages by as much as 11.9 percent, according to the Economic Policy Institute (EPI) in Washington, D.C.

But is it really possible to make a living on the kinds of jobs currently available to unskilled people?

Mathematically, the answer is no, as can be shown by taking $6 to $7 an hour, perhaps subtracting a dollar or two an hour for child care, multiplying by 160 hours a month, and comparing the result to the prevailing rents. According to the National Coalition for the Homeless, for example, in 1998 it took, on average nationwide, an hourly wage of $8.89 to afford a one-bedroom apartment, and the Preamble Center for Public Policy estimates that the odds against a typical welfare recipient's landing a job at such a "living wage" are about 97 to 1. If these numbers are right, low-wage work is not a solution to poverty and possibly not even to homelessness. . . .

On the morning of my first full day of job searching, I take a red pen to the want ads, which are auspiciously numerous. Everyone in Key West's booming "hospitality industry" seems to be looking for someone like me—trainable, flexible, and with suitably humble expectations as to pay. I know I possess certain traits that might be advantageous—I'm white and, I like to think, well-spoken and poised—but I decide on two rules: One, I cannot use any skills derived from my education or usual work—not that there are a lot of want ads for satirical essayists anyway. Two, I have to take the best-paid job that is offered me and of course do my best to hold it; no Marxist rants or sneaking off to read novels in the ladies' room. . . .

Most of the big hotels run ads almost continually, just to build a supply of applicants to replace the current workers as they drift away or are fired, so finding a job is just a matter of being at the right place at the right time and flexible enough to take whatever is being offered that day. This finally happens to me at one of the big discount hotel chains, where I go for housekeeping and am sent, instead, to try out as a waitress at the attached "family restaurant," a dismal spot with a counter and about thirty tables that looks out on a parking garage and features such tempting fare as "Pollish [sic] sausage and BBQ sauce" on 95-degree days. Phillip, the dapper young West Indian who introduces himself as the manager, interviews me with about as much enthusiasm as if he were a clerk processing me for Medicare, the principal questions being what shifts can I work and when can I start. I mutter something about being woefully out of practice as a waitress, but he's already on to the uniform: I'm to show up tomorrow wearing black slacks and black shoes; he'll provide the rust-colored polo shirt with Hearthside embroidered on it, though I might want to wear my own shirt to get to work, ha ha. At the word "tomorrow,"

something between fear and indignation rises in my chest. I want to say, "Thank you for your time, sir, but this is just an experiment, you know, not my actual life."

So begins my career at the Hearthside, I shall call it, one small profit center within a global discount hotel chain, where for two weeks I work from 2:00 till 10:00 p.m. for $2.43 an hour plus tips. In some futile bid for gentility, the management has barred employees from using the front door, so my first day I enter through the kitchen, where a red-faced man with shoulder-length blond hair is throwing frozen steaks against the wall and yelling, "Fuck this shit!" "That's just Jack," explains Gail, the wiry middle-aged waitress who is assigned to train me. "He's on the rag again"—a condition occasioned, in this instance, by the fact that the cook on the morning shift had forgotten to thaw out the steaks. For the next eight hours, I run after the agile Gail, absorbing bits of instruction along with fragments of personal tragedy. All food must be trayed, and the reason she's so tired today is that she woke up in a cold sweat thinking of her boyfriend, who killed himself recently in an upstate prison. No refills on lemonade. And the reason he was in prison is that a few DUIs caught up with him, that's all, could have happened to anyone. Carry the creamers to the table in a monkey bowl, never in your hand. And after he was gone, she spent several months living in her truck, peeing in a plastic pee bottle and reading by candlelight at night, but you can't live in a truck in the summer, since you need to have the windows down, which means anything can get in, from mosquitoes on up.

At least Gail puts to rest any fears I had of appearing overqualified. From the first day on, I find that of all the things I have left behind, such as home and identity, what I miss the most is competence. Not that I have ever felt utterly competent in the writing business, in which one day's success augurs nothing at all for the next. But in my writing life, I at least have some notion of procedure: do the research, make the outline, rough out a draft, etc. As a server, though, I am beset by requests like bees: more iced tea here, ketchup over there, a to-go box for table fourteen, and where are the high chairs, anyway? Of the twenty-seven tables, up to six are usually mine at any time, though on slow afternoons or if Gail is off, I sometimes have the whole place to myself. There is the touch-screen computer-ordering system to master, which is, I suppose, meant to minimize server-cook contact, but in practice requires constant verbal fine-tuning: "That's gravy on the mashed, okay? None on the meatloaf," and so forth—while the cook scowls as if I were inventing these refinements just to torment him. Plus, something I had forgotten in the years since I was eighteen: about a third of a server's job is "side work" that's invisible to customers—sweeping, scrubbing, slicing, refilling, and restocking. If it isn't all done, every little bit of it, you're going to face the 6:00 p.m. dinner rush defenseless and probably go down in flames. I screw up dozens of times at the beginning, sustained in my shame entirely by Gail's support—"It's okay, baby, everyone does that sometime"—because, to my total surprise and despite the scientific detachment I am doing my best to maintain, I care. . . .

Sometimes I play with the fantasy that I am a princess who, in penance for some tiny transgression, has undertaken to feed each of her subjects by hand. But the non-princesses working with me are just as indulgent, even when this means flouting management rules—concerning, for example, the number of croutons that can go on a salad (six). "Put on all you want," Gail whispers, "as long as Stu isn't looking." She dips into her own tip money to buy biscuits and gravy for an out-of-work mechanic who's used up all his money on dental surgery, inspiring me to pick up the tab for his milk and pie. . . .

Ten days into it, this is beginning to look like a livable lifestyle. I like Gail, who is "looking at fifty" but moves so fast she can alight in one place and then another without apparently being anywhere between them. I clown around with Lionel, the teenage Haitian busboy, and catch a few fragments of conversation with Joan, the svelte fortyish hostess and militant feminist who is the only one of us who dares to tell Jack to shut the fuck up. I even warm up to Jack when, on a slow night and to make up for a particularly unwarranted attack on my abilities, or so I imagine, he tells me about his glory days as a young man at "coronary school"—or do you say "culinary"?—in Brooklyn, where he dated a knock-out Puerto Rican chick and learned everything there is to know about food. I finish up at 10:00 or 10:30, depending on how much side work I've been able to get done during the shift, and cruise home to the tapes I snatched up at random when I left my real home—Marianne Faithfull, Tracy Chapman, Enigma, King Sunny Ade, the Violent Femmes— just drained enough for the music to set my cranium resonating but hardly dead. Midnight snack is Wheat Thins and Monterey Jack, accompanied by cheap white wine on ice and whatever AMC has to offer. To bed by 1:30 or 2:00, up at 9:00 or 10:00, read for an hour while my uniform whirls around in the landlord's washing machine, and then it's another eight hours spent following Mao's central instruction, as laid out in the Little Red Book, which was: Serve the people.

I could drift along like this, in some dreamy proletarian idyll, except for two things. One is management. If I have kept this subject on the margins thus far, it is because I still flinch to think that I spent all those weeks under the surveillance of men (and later women) whose job it was to monitor my behavior for signs of sloth, theft, drug abuse, or worse. Not that managers and especially "assistant managers" in low-wage settings like this are exactly the class enemy. In the restaurant business, they are mostly former cooks or servers, still capable of pinch-hitting in the kitchen or on the floor, just as in hotels they are likely to be former clerks, and paid a salary of only about $400 a week. But everyone knows they have crossed over to the other side, which is, crudely put, corporate as opposed to human. Cooks want to prepare tasty meals; servers want to serve them graciously; but managers are there for only one reason—to make sure that money is made for some theoretical entity that exists far away in Chicago or New York, if a corporation can be said to have a physical existence at all. . . .

Managers can sit—for hours at a time if they want—but it's their job to see that no one else ever does, even when there's nothing to do, and this is why, for servers, slow times can be as exhausting as rushes. You start dragging out each little chore, because if the manager on duty catches you in an idle moment, he will give you something far nastier to do. So I wipe, I clean, I consolidate ketchup bottles and recheck the cheesecake supply, even tour the tables to make sure the customer evaluation forms are all standing perkily in their places—wondering all the time how many calories I burn in these strictly theatrical exercises. When, on a particularly dead afternoon, Stu finds me glancing at a *USA Today* a customer has left behind, he assigns me to vacuum the entire floor with the broken vacuum cleaner that has a handle only two feet long, and the only way to do that without incurring orthopedic damage is to proceed from spot to spot on your knees. . . .

The other problem, in addition to the less-than-nurturing management style, is that this job shows no sign of being financially viable. You might imagine, from a comfortable distance, that people who live, year in and year out, on $6 to $10 an hour have discovered some survival stratagems unknown to the middle class. But no. It's not hard to get my co-workers to talk about their living situations, because housing, in almost every case, is the principal source of disruption in their lives, the first thing they fill you in on when they arrive for their shifts. After a week, I have compiled the following survey:

• Gail is sharing a room in a well-known downtown flophouse for which she and a roommate pay about $250 a week. Her roommate, a male friend, has begun hitting on her, driving her nuts, but the rent would be impossible alone.

• Claude, the Haitian cook, is desperate to get out of the two-room apartment he shares with his girlfriend and two other, unrelated, people. As far as I can determine, the other Haitian men (most of whom only speak Creole) live in similarly crowded situations.

• Annette, a twenty-year-old server who is six months pregnant and has been abandoned by her boyfriend, lives with her mother, a postal clerk.

• Marianne and her boyfriend are paying $170 a week for a one-person trailer.

• Jack, who is, at $10 an hour, the wealthiest of us, lives in the trailer he owns, paying only the $400-a-month lot fee.

• The other white cook, Andy, lives on his dry-docked boat, which, as far as I can tell from his loving descriptions, can't be more than twenty feet long. He offers to take me out on it, once it's repaired, but the offer comes with inquiries as to my marital status, so I do not follow up on it.

• Tina and her husband are paying $60 a night for a double room in a Days Inn. This is because they have no car and the Days Inn is within walking distance of the Hearthside. When Marianne, one of the breakfast servers, is tossed out of her trailer for subletting (which is against the trailer-park rules), she leaves her boyfriend and moves in with Tina and her husband.

• Joan, who had fooled me with her numerous and tasteful outfits (hostesses wear their own clothes), lives in a van she parks behind a shopping center at night and showers in Tina's motel room. The clothes are from thrift shops.

It strikes me, in my middle-class solipsism, that there is gross improvidence in some of these arrangements. When Gail and I are wrapping silverware in napkins—the only task for which we are permitted to sit—she tells me she is thinking of escaping from her roommate by moving into the Days Inn herself.

I am astounded: How can she even think of paying between $40 and $60 a day? But if I was afraid of sounding like a social worker, I come out just sounding like a fool. She squints at me in disbelief, "And where am I supposed to get a month's rent and a month's deposit for an apartment?" I'd been feeling pretty smug about my $500 efficiency, but of course it was made possible only by the $1,300 I had allotted myself for start-up costs when I began my low-wage life: $1,000 for the first month's rent and deposit, $100 for initial groceries and cash in my pocket, $200 stuffed away for emergencies. In poverty, as in certain propositions in physics, starting conditions are everything.

There are no secret economies that nourish the poor; on the contrary, there are a host of special costs. If you can't put up the two months' rent you need to secure an apartment, you end up paying through the nose for a room by the week. If you have only a room, with a hot plate at best, you can't save by cooking up huge lentil stews that can be frozen for the week ahead. You eat fast food, or the hot dogs and Styrofoam cups of soup that can be microwaved in a convenience store. If you have no money for health insurance—and the Hearthside's niggardly plan kicks in only after three months—you go without routine care or prescription drugs and end up paying the price. Gail, for example, was fine until she ran out of money for estrogen pills. She is supposed to be on the company plan by now, but they claim to have lost her application form and need to begin the paperwork all over again. So she spends $9 per migraine pill to control the headaches she wouldn't have, she insists, if her estrogen supplements were covered. Similarly, Marianne's boyfriend lost his job as a roofer because he missed so much time after getting a cut on his foot for which he couldn't afford the prescribed antibiotic.

My own situation, when I sit down to assess it after two weeks of work, would not be much better if this were my actual life. The seductive thing about waitressing is that you don't have to wait for payday to feel a few bills in your pocket, and my tips usually cover meals and gas, plus something left over to stuff into the kitchen drawer I use as a bank. But as the tourist business slows in the summer heat, I sometimes leave work with only $20 in tips (the gross is higher, but servers share about 15 percent of their tips with the busboys and bartenders). With wages included, this amounts to about the minimum wage of $5.15 an hour. Although the sum in the drawer is piling up, at the present rate of accumulation it will be more than a hundred dollars short of my rent when the end of the month comes around. Nor can I see any expenses to cut. True, I haven't gone the lentil-stew route yet, but that's because I don't have a large cooking pot, pot holders, or a ladle to stir with (which cost about $30 at Kmart, less at thrift stores), not to mention onions, carrots, and the indispensable bay leaf. I do make my lunch almost every day—usually some slow-burning, high-protein combo like frozen chicken patties with melted cheese on top and canned pinto beans on the side. Dinner is at the Hearthside, which offers its employees a choice of BLT, fish sandwich, or hamburger for only $2. The burger lasts longest, especially if it's heaped with gut-puckering jalapeños, but by midnight my stomach is growling again.

So unless I want to start using my car as a residence, I have to find a second, or alternative, job. I call all the hotels where I filled out housekeeping applications weeks ago—the Hyatt, Holiday Inn, Econo Lodge, HoJo's, Best Western, plus a half dozen or so locally run guesthouses. Nothing. Then I start making the rounds again, wasting whole mornings waiting for some assistant manager to show up, even dipping into places so creepy that the front-desk clerk greets you from behind bulletproof glass and sells pints of liquor over the counter. But either someone has exposed my real-life housekeeping habits—which are, shall we say, mellow—or I am at the wrong end of some infallible ethnic equation: most, but by no means all, of the working housekeepers I see on my job searches are African Americans, Spanish-speaking, or immigrants from the Central European post-Communist world, whereas servers are almost invariably white and monolingually English-speaking. When I finally get a positive response, I have been identified once again as server material. Jerry's, which is part of a well-known national family restaurant chain and physically attached here to another budget hotel chain, is ready to use me at once. The prospect is both exciting and terrifying, because, with about the same number of tables and counter seats, Jerry's attracts three or four times the volume of customers as the gloomy old Hearthside. . . .

I start out with the beautiful, heroic idea of handling the two jobs at once, and for two days I almost do it: the breakfast/lunch shift at Jerry's, which goes till 2:00, arriving at the Hearthside at 2:10, and attempting to hold out until 10:00. In the ten minutes between jobs, I pick up a spicy chicken sandwich at the Wendy's drive-through window, gobble it down in the car, and change from khaki slacks to black, from Hawaiian to rust polo. There is a problem, though. When during the 3:00 to 4:00 p.m. dead time I finally sit down to wrap silver, my flesh seems to bond to the seat. I try to refuel with a purloined cup of soup, as I've seen Gail and Joan do dozens of times, but a manager catches me and hisses "No eating!" though there's not a customer around to be offended by the sight of food making contact with a server's lips. So I tell Gail I'm going to quit, and she hugs me and says she might just follow me to Jerry's herself.

But the chances of this are minuscule. She has left the flophouse and her annoying roommate and is back to living in her beat-up old truck. But guess what? she reports to me excitedly later that evening: Phillip has given her permission to park overnight in the hotel parking lot, as long as she keeps out of sight, and the parking lot should be totally safe, since it's patrolled by a hotel security guard! With the Hearthside offering benefits like that, how could anyone think of leaving? . . .

Management at Jerry's is generally calmer and more "professional" than at the Hearthside, with two exceptions. One is Joy, a plump, blowsy woman in her early thirties, who once kindly devoted several minutes to instructing me in the correct one-handed method of carrying trays but whose moods change disconcertingly from shift to shift and even within one. Then there's B. J., a.k.a. B.J.-the-bitch, whose contribution is to stand by the kitchen counter and yell, "Nita, your order's up, move it!" or, "Barbara, didn't you see you've got another table out there? Come on, girl!" Among other things, she is hated for having replaced the whipped-cream squirt cans with big plastic whipped-cream-filled baggies that have to be squeezed with both hands—because, reportedly, she saw or thought she saw employees trying to inhale the propellant gas from the squirt cans, in the hope that it might be nitrous oxide. On my third night, she pulls me aside abruptly and brings her face so close that it looks as if she's planning to butt me with her forehead. But instead of saying, "You're fired," she says, "You're doing fine." The only trouble is I'm spending time chatting with customers: "That's how they're getting you." Furthermore I am letting them "run me," which means harassment by sequential demands: you bring the ketchup, and they decide they want extra Thousand Island; you bring that, and they announce they now need a side of fries; and so on into distraction. Finally she tells me not to take her wrong. She tries to say things in a nice way, but you get into a mode, you know, because everything has to move so fast. . . .

I make friends, over time, with the other "girls" who work my shift: Nita, the tattooed twenty-something who taunts us by going around saying brightly, "Have we started making money yet?" Ellen, whose teenage son cooks on the graveyard shift and who once managed a restaurant in Massachusetts but won't try out for management here because she prefers being a "common worker" and not "ordering people around." Easy-going fifty-ish Lucy, with the raucous laugh, who limps toward the end of the shift because of something that has gone wrong with her leg, the exact nature of which cannot be determined without health insurance. We talk about the usual girl things—men, children, and the sinister allure of Jerry's chocolate peanut-butter cream pie—though no one, I notice, ever brings up anything potentially expensive, like shopping or movies. As at the Hearthside, the only recreation ever referred to is partying, which requires little more than some beer, a joint, and a few close friends. Still, no one here is homeless, or cops to it anyway, thanks usually to a working husband or boyfriend. All in all, we form a reliable mutual-support group: If one of us is feeling sick or overwhelmed, another one will "bev" a table or even carry trays for her. If one of us is off sneaking a cigarette or a pee, the others will do their best to conceal her absence from the enforcers of corporate rationality. . . .

I make the decision to move closer to Key West. First, because of the drive. Second and third, also because of the drive: gas is eating up $4 to $5 a day, and although Jerry's is as high-volume as you can get, the tips average only 10 percent, and not just for a newbie like me. Between the base pay of $2.15 an hour and the obligation to share tips with the busboys and dishwashers, we're averaging only about $7.50 an hour. Then there is the $30 I had to spend on the regulation tan slacks worn by Jerry's servers—a setback that could take weeks to absorb. (I had combed the town's two downscale department stores hoping for something cheaper but decided in the end that these marked-down Dockers, originally $49, were more likely to survive a daily washing.) Of my fellow servers, everyone who lacks a working husband or boyfriend seems to have a second job: Nita does something at a computer eight hours a day; another welds. Without the

forty-five-minute commute, I can picture myself working two jobs and having the time to shower between them.

So I take the $500 deposit I have coming from my landlord, the $400 I have earned toward the next month's rent, plus the $200 reserved for emergencies, and use the $1,100 to pay the rent and deposit on trailer number 46 in the Overseas Trailer Park, a mile from the cluster of budget hotels that constitute Key West's version of an industrial park. Number 46 is about eight feet in width and shaped like a barbell inside, with a narrow region—because of the sink and the stove—separating the bedroom from what might optimistically be called the "living" area, with its two-person table and half-sized couch. The bathroom is so small my knees rub against the shower stall when I sit on the toilet, and you can't just leap out of the bed, you have to climb down to the foot of it in order to find a patch of floor space to stand on. Outside, I am within a few yards of a liquor store, a bar that advertises "free beer tomorrow," a convenience store, and a Burger King—but no supermarket or, alas, laundromat. By reputation, the Overseas park is a nest of crime and crack, and I am hoping at least for some vibrant, multicultural street life. But desolation rules night and day, except for a thin stream of pedestrian traffic heading for their jobs at the Sheraton or 7-Eleven. There are not exactly people here but what amounts to canned labor, being preserved from the heat between shifts. . . .

When my month-long plunge into poverty is almost over, I finally land my dream job—housekeeping. I do this by walking into the personnel office of the only place I figure I might have some credibility, the hotel attached to Jerry's, and confiding urgently that I have to have a second job if I am to pay my rent and, no, it couldn't be front-desk clerk. "All right," the personnel lady fairly spits, "So it's housekeeping," and she marches me back to meet Maria, the housekeeping manager, a tiny, frenetic Hispanic woman who greets me as "babe" and hands me a pamphlet emphasizing the need for a positive attitude. The hours are nine in the morning till whenever, the pay is $6.10 an hour, and there's one week of vacation a year. I don't have to ask about health insurance once I meet Carlotta, the middle-aged African-American woman who will be training me. Carla, as she tells me to call her, is missing all of her top front teeth.

On that first day of housekeeping and last day of my entire project—although I don't yet know it's the last—Carla is in a foul mood. We have been given nineteen rooms to clean, most of them "checkouts," as opposed to "stay-overs," that require the whole enchilada of bed-stripping, vacuuming, and bathroom-scrubbing. When one of the rooms that had been listed as a stay-over turns out to be a checkout, Carla calls Maria to complain, but of course to no avail. "So make up the motherfucker," Carla orders me, and I do the beds while she sloshes around the bathroom. For four hours without a break I strip and remake beds, taking about four and a half minutes per queen-sized bed, which I could get down to three if there were any reason to. We try to avoid vacuuming by picking up the larger specks by hand, but often there is nothing to do but drag the monstrous vacuum cleaner—it weighs about thirty pounds—off our cart and try to wrestle it around the floor. Sometimes Carla hands me the squirt bottle of "BAM" (an acronym for something that begins, ominously, with "butyric"; the rest has been worn off the label) and lets me do the bathrooms. No service ethic challenges me here to new heights of performance. I just concentrate on removing the pubic hairs from the bathtubs, or at least the dark ones that I can see. . . .

When I request permission to leave at about 3:30, another housekeeper warns me that no one has so far succeeded in combining housekeeping at the hotel with serving at Jerry's: "Some kid did it once for five days, and you're no kid." With that helpful information in mind, I rush back to number 46, down four Advils, shower, stooping to fit into the stall, and attempt to compose myself for the oncoming shift. So much for what Marx termed the "reproduction of labor power," meaning the things a worker has to do just so she'll be ready to work again. . . .

Then it comes, the perfect storm. Four of my tables fill up at once. Four tables is nothing for me now, but only so long as they are obligingly staggered. As I bev table 27, tables 25, 28, and 24 are watching enviously. As I bev 25, 24 glowers because their bevs haven't even been ordered. Twenty-eight is four yuppyish types, meaning everything on the side and agonizing instructions as to the chicken Caesars. Twenty-five is a middle-aged black couple, who complain, with some justice, that the iced tea isn't fresh and the tabletop is sticky. But table 24 is the meteorological event of the century: ten British tourists who seem to have made the decision to absorb the American experience entirely by mouth. Here everyone has at least two drinks—iced tea and milk shake, Michelob

and water (with lemon slice, please)—and a huge promiscuous orgy of breakfast specials, mozz sticks, chicken strips, quesadillas, burgers with cheese and without, sides of hash browns with cheddar, with onions, with gravy, seasoned fries, plain fries, banana splits. Poor Jesus (the cook)! Poor me! Because when I arrive with their first tray of food—after three prior trips just to refill bevs—Princess Di refuses to eat her chicken strips with her pancake-and-sausage special, since, as she now reveals, the strips were meant to be an appetizer. Maybe the others would have accepted their meals, but Di, who is deep into her third Michelob, insists that everything else go back while they work on their "starters." Meanwhile, the yuppies are waving me down for more decaf and the black couple looks ready to summon the NAACP.

Much of what happened next is lost in the fog of war. Jesus starts going under. The little printer on the counter in front of him is spewing out orders faster than he can rip them off, much less produce the meals. Even the invincible Ellen is ashen from stress. I bring table 24 their reheated main courses, which they immediately reject as either too cold or fossilized by the microwave. When I return to the kitchen with their trays (three trays in three trips), Joy confronts me with arms akimbo: "What is this?" She means the food—the plates of rejected pancakes, hash browns in assorted flavors, toasts, burgers, sausages, eggs. "Uh, scrambled with cheddar," I try, "and that's . . . " "NO," she screams in my face. "Is it a traditional, a super-scramble, an eye-opener?" I pretend to study my check for a clue, but entropy has been up to its tricks, not only on the plates but in my head, and I have to admit that the original order is beyond reconstruction. "You don't know an eye-opener from a traditional?" she demands in outrage. All I know, in fact, is that my legs have lost interest in the current venture and have announced their intention to fold. I am saved by a yuppie (mercifully not one of mine) who chooses this moment to charge into the kitchen to bellow that his food is twenty-five minutes late. Joy screams at him to get the hell out of her kitchen, please, and then turns on Jesus in a fury, hurling an empty tray across the room for emphasis.

I leave. I don't walk out, I just leave. I don't finish my side work or pick up my credit-card tips, if any, at the cash register or, of course, ask Joy's permission to go. And the surprising thing is that you *can* walk out without permission, that the door opens, that the thick tropical night air parts to let me pass, that my car is still parked where I left it. There is no vindication in this exit, no fuck-you surge of relief, just an overwhelming, dank sense of failure pressing down on me and the entire parking lot. I had gone into this venture in the spirit of science, to test a mathematical proposition, but somewhere along the line, in the tunnel vision imposed by long shifts and relentless concentration, it became a test of myself, and clearly I have failed. . . .

When I moved out of the trailer park, I gave the key to number 46 to Gail and arranged for my deposit to be transferred to her. She told me that Joan is still living in her van and that Stu had been fired from the Hearthside. . . .

In one month, I had earned approximately $1,040 and spent $517 on food, gas, toiletries, laundry, phone, and utilities. If I had remained in my $500 efficiency, I would have been able to pay the rent and have $22 left over (which is $78 less than the cash I had in my pocket at the start of the month). During this time I bought no clothing except for the required slacks and no prescription drugs or medical care (I did finally buy some vitamin B to compensate for the lack of vegetables in my diet). Perhaps I could have saved a little on food if I had gotten to a supermarket more often, instead of convenience stores, but it should be noted that I lost almost four pounds in four weeks, on a diet weighted heavily toward burgers and fries.

How former welfare recipients and single mothers will (and do) survive in the low-wage workforce, I cannot imagine. Maybe they will figure out how to condense their lives—including child-raising, laundry, romance, and meals—into the couple of hours between full-time jobs. Maybe they will take up residence in their vehicles, if they have one. All I know is that I couldn't hold two jobs and I couldn't make enough money to live on with one. And I had advantages unthinkable to many of the long-term poor—health, stamina, a working car, and no children to care for and support. . . .

The thinking behind welfare reform was that even the humblest jobs are morally uplifting and psychologically buoying. In reality they are likely to be fraught with insult and stress. But I did discover one redeeming feature of the most abject low-wage work—the camaraderie of people who are, in almost all cases, far too smart and funny and caring for the work they do and the wages they're paid. The hope, of course, is that someday these people will come to know what they're worth, and take appropriate action.

18. Kathryn Edin, Timothy Nelson, and Joanna Miranda Reed*
Low-Income Urban Fathers and the "Package Deal" of Family Life

Economically disadvantaged fathers are far less likely to marry before having children than middle-class fathers are, and they have them far earlier (Nock 2007). When they do marry, they are more likely to divorce (Martin 2004). In the absence of a marital tie, the government assigns them financial obligations, which most do not satisfy fully (U.S. Census Bureau 2007). Thus, such men's fathering behavior attracts a good deal of attention from both scholars and policymakers.

Little attention is paid, however, to these men's roles as romantic partners. Qualitative studies have been an exception to this trend (i.e., Drake and Cayton 1945; Liebow 1967; Nelson, Clampet-Lundquist, and Edin 2002; Furstenberg 2001). As these studies have repeatedly shown, economically disadvantaged men do engage in romantic relationships; this is the context into which most of their children are born (though some children are the product of non-relationships, i.e., one-night stands) (Augustine, Nelson, and Edin 2009). New survey research reveals that fully eight in ten nonmarital children now enter the world with a mother and father who describe themselves as "romantically involved"; up to half of those parents live together, and at least 70 percent of both mothers and fathers say there is at least a 50–50 chance they'll marry each other. Yet it is also true that fewer than a third of such couples are still together by the time the child turns five (Center for Research on Child Wellbeing 2007). Low-income couples who marry before having children are fragile as well—much more so than middle-class married couples are—but they still function as partners for a considerable period of time (Martin 2004; McLanahan 2004).

We offer the reader a portrait of the romantic partnerships of such men. [Our sample] is of a relatively large group of very economically disadvantaged white and black men (with earnings below the poverty line for a family of four in the formal

*From *Social Class and Changing Families in an Unequal America* by Marcia Carlson and Paula England, eds. Copyright © 2011 by the Board of Trustees of the Leland Stanford Jr. University. All rights reserved. Reprinted by permission of the publisher, Stanford University Press, sup.org.

economy over the prior year) who live in poor and struggling working-class neighborhoods throughout the Philadelphia metropolitan area and have biological children, most of them outside of marriage. All were fathers of at least one minor child outside of a marital tie when we interviewed them.

By exploring in depth the texture of their romantic lives and worldviews, we show that the function of the romantic tie for the father role departs radically from the traditional 1950s "package deal" conception of family life. Furstenberg and Cherlin (1991), and more recently Nicholas Townsend (2002), point to the family behaviors of men who came of age in an earlier generation, arguing that for these men fatherhood flowed through, and was contingent upon, men's relationship with the children's mother. Furstenberg and Cherlin coined the term "package deal" to explain the very low rates of father involvement among the divorced fathers they observed. In this view, the tie between the mother and father is central and serves to bind men to their obligations to their children—obligations they would otherwise ignore (e.g., in the case of divorce).

Two of us (Edin and Nelson) and a multiracial team of graduate students spent seven years observing and interviewing low-income fathers residing in high-poverty neighborhoods in Philadelphia and its poorest inner suburb, Camden, New Jersey.

For the men we have studied, the *father-child* relationship is typically what is viewed as central and is what binds men to couple relationships—relationships that might not have otherwise formed or been maintained (see also Edin et al. 2007; Reed 2007). This is not to say that such men are child-centric to the degree that mothers are (Edin and Kefalas 2005), only that in the realm of family relations, "Daddy, baby; momma, maybe" is a fair representation of the worldview of many of the fathers we studied.

The Philadelphia/Camden Fathers Study (PCFS): Method

We began the Philadelphia/Camden Fathers Study with two and a half years of participant observation in one of the eight low-income communities (census tract clusters where at least 20 percent of the population lived in poverty in 1990) selected for the study. Based on this fieldwork, which began in 1995, we constructed an interview guide that we administered in systematic, repeated, in-depth interviews with 110 white and African American men between 1997 and 2002. We sampled equal numbers of blacks and non-Hispanic whites. To offer more of a life-course view, roughly half of our fathers were under thirty and the rest were older. During the prior year, the earnings of all of them were below the poverty line for a family of four in the formal economy. In the course of our conversations with these men, we collected detailed life histories. Our data came from these life histories (e.g., "Tell me the whole story of your relationship from the time you first met until now"), and from their answers to questions formulated to capture their worldview (e.g., "What should fathers do for their children?" "In your view, what makes for a good father?").

Findings

In PCFS, we asked each father to tell us "the whole story" of how he got together with the mothers of each of his children and how these relationships developed over time. Typically, the pre-pregnancy narrative was noticeably succinct: the couple met, began to "affiliate," and then "came up pregnant." Men seldom even mentioned, much less discussed, any special qualities of their partners or any common tastes or values that drew the two together. Usually, the woman lived on his block, hung out on his corner, worked at the same job, was a friend of his sister, or the girlfriend of a friend, and she was simply willing to "affiliate" with him. Hanging out on the stoop, an occasional outing to a bar or a club, a window-shopping trip to a hot venue such as the downtown Gallery or the popular South Street strip, and fantasizing about shared children is what constituted romance (see also Townsend 2002: 42).

In the case of couples with a first birth together, the length of the courtship before conception was usually exceedingly brief—typically well under a year. Only rarely did such couples "fall in love," get engaged, or get married *before* conceiving a child together, though some did so later. Instead, they meet, they "associate," "affiliate," "communicate," begin to "kick it," "talk to each other," "get with each other," or "end up together." Then, "one thing leads to another." Planned pregnancies were rare, yet the contraceptive practices that couples usually engaged in initially seldom continued for long (see also Edin and Kefalas 2005; Edin et al. 2007; Augustine, Nelson, and Edin 2009). Then the inevitable occurred: the woman "comes up pregnant" (see also Davis, Gardner, and Gardner 1941: 127).

John, a twenty-four-year-old white father of one, described the sequencing of his relationship with his child's mother in this way: "Actually she was dating a friend of mine and somehow . . . she wanted me. . . . Eventually, I just got stuck with her for a little while." John didn't feel that he had found the ideal match—he "got stuck" with his baby's mother "for a little while." No language of love or even attraction (except her attraction to him) entered into this narrative, although there may well have been attraction involved. Nor does the phrase "a little while" indicate much commitment.

Thirty-nine-year-old Amin, a black father of two, described the development of his relationship with his youngest son's mother, a coworker in the dietary department of a local hospital, in this way: "She was attractive to me when I first saw her and I made my approach and we begin to socialize and communicate and then from there we began to affiliate at some point and we became intimate and our son was born." As Amin told it, attraction, affiliation, and intimacy quite naturally—and inevitably—led to a son being born.

Despite the vague and bureaucratic language often used to describe these relationships (e.g., "affiliation"), almost no father had much trouble pinpointing when his relationship with his baby's mother began; they knew the point at which they got "together" with their baby's mother (though a small number of pregnancies do occur outside of relationships). Being together generally means that the couple is spending regular time together and defines the relationship as something more than a casual encounter or a one-night stand.

The verbs "affiliate," "associate," and "get with" suggest a bond that is more than a casual liaison, but not exactly a boyfriend/girlfriend relationship. Few of these men were consciously "courting" or searching for a life partner. Indeed, there is little evidence that they were even attempting to discriminate much based on who would be a suitable mother for their child. Many recalled that they did very much want children and fairly soon, even if not right then. Yet, the partnering process was far more haphazard than discriminating.

Bruce was a white father of two-year-old twins. At forty-two, Bruce met a "new girl," Debbie. He didn't use protection because "Every time I had any kind of relationship there is no babies born so I didn't believe in safe sex. Next thing I knew, this girl Debbie, she was pregnant." Debbie made the announcement that she was seven weeks pregnant after the two had been together for only four months. Bruce told her, "'I am shooting blanks, you can't be pregnant! . . .' Then we went for a DNA test and that was when she found out that I was the father and she was the mother." Here a "family" was formed through a pregnancy brought to term in a relationship that was neither casual nor serious. Yet for Bruce, and most other men in our study, this was not viewed as a problem.

Children, while usually desired, were only rarely explicitly planned, according to the narratives of men in PCFS (see Augustine, Nelson, and Edin 2009). Yet contraception and other attempts to avoid pregnancy faded quickly as the couple began "affiliating." Once she became pregnant and decided to take the pregnancy to term (this decision is generally ceded to the woman), the bond between the two typically coalesced into more of a "relationship," though often in dramatic fits and starts (see also Edin and Kefalas 2005).

David, a black thirty-year-old, was the father of five children by three women. In the months just before conceiving his fifth child, he was both "with" Deborah and "seeing" Kathy on the side. He went to Kathy whenever he and Deborah argued (though Deborah didn't know about Kathy). Which woman he should choose became a dilemma. However, when Deborah ended up pregnant, he decided to "do what was right" and chose her:

[When I was first with Deborah] I had a girlfriend on the side too. Kathy. She's somebody that I met at an NA meeting. We got close and we were helping each other [with our addictions]. One thing led to another, and we got intimate. . . . Me and Deborah would get into an argument, she'd tell me to leave, I'd go stay with Kathy. (So how did you end it with Kathy?) Deborah got pregnant, and I had to do what was right, stand by Deborah.

For Jack, a thirty-three-year-old white father of two, his babies' mother was just one of several "girls" he met on a weekend home from college. She was already married to someone else, but left her husband for Jack that very day. Three months later she was pregnant, yet Jack saw nothing remarkable about the process by which he first became a father.

[After high school] I went to college. . . . My grades weren't great but I was getting through. I was going back home every other weekend. . . . Met some girls. In turn, met my [baby's mother]. Shortly afterwards, she became pregnant, so I quit school, got a job.

Kahlid, a twenty-eight-year-old black father of one, said that it was just a few months into the relationship with his child's mother that the pair conceived. Despite the fact that the outside observer might read his narrative as a classic example of putting the cart before the horse, Kahlid, like Jack, viewed the sequence of events leading up to the pregnancy as unexceptional:

(How long were you and your girlfriend together before she got pregnant?) Six, seven months. (What went through your mind?) I was happy! I came [over after] work and she said that she was getting symptoms and I was like, "What you talking about?" Morning sickness, throwing up, like this. So she went to the hospital. She took the test and she says she was pregnant . . . and I was excited. It was my first child. And she was going to keep the baby, and I was happy. I knew I had to keep a job and take care of my responsibilities.

The glories of the delivery room are the high point of many fathers' life histories in PCFS. But the arrival of a child introduces a sharp contradiction. On the one hand, fathers' narratives offer evidence that they are making some effort to sustain a relationship with their babies' mothers—often motivated by the desire to live with or be intensely involved with the children. But they also recognize, at least in part, that they are trying live out the dream of being part of a real "family unit" against almost impossible odds. Thus, while working to solidify these relationships, they are also often deeply fatalistic about their chances of staying together over the long term. This fatalism is fueled by men's fears about their ongoing ability to provide and their utter conviction that their babies' mothers will leave them if they fail, often rendered men's relational efforts half-hearted.

Most fathers [in our sample] emphatically said that their relationship with their children ought not be contingent on their relationship with their child's mother—they outright rejected the package deal. Yet they nonetheless realized that due to normative and legal practices governing the custody of nonmarital children, as well as their own limited economic prospects, their relationship to the mother was their conduit to the child.

Across the income distribution, most couples now stay together, at least in part, because they share common interests and values. Owing to the lightning speed of the courtship period, disadvantaged couples who bear children together often find they have little in common, as we show below. But childbirth offers a vital new shared interest—a child—and this often brings some measure of emotional closeness. Consider the story of thirty-eight-year-old Tony, father of one.

(How do you think the birth of Lyssa affected your relationship?) I think in the beginning it brought us a lot closer together. (Why would it bring you closer together?) It just—being with this little baby that's just a part of both of us—it was amazing.

Bucket, a black father of two children by the same woman, described how the birth of his first child made things even a "little better:"

(How'd you all get along during the rest of the pregnancy?) We had a good time man. While she was pregnant, I couldn't go *nowhere*. Shoot! She wanted me to do this, wanted me to do that. I was like a puppy anyway. I waited on her. I did certain things that she wanted me to do. I was *glad* man. (How did the birth of your child affect your relationship with her?) It didn't affect it at all. See like, when the baby was born and we had a *baby*, it seemed like things got a little better and stuff.

Yet men like Bucket have powerful reasons *not* to invest in the relationship as well. The ethnographic literature typically focuses on how much women mistrust men. What is less well known is how little men trust women (for exceptions, see Waller 2008; Hannertz 1969: 100–102; Liebow 1967: 137–60; Rainwater 1970: 209). The chief source of power (outside of physical violence) in these relationships is control over the child. In the context of a nonmarital birth, women have much greater power in this regard. Because men view children as their most precious resource (Nelson and Edin, forthcoming), they are, on the one hand, eager to hang on, and expect to be actively involved in parenting the child. Yet they are often very apprehensive about their ability to satisfy the economic demands they also know their children's mothers will place on them over time, and most are convinced that a woman's love for a man will come to an abrupt halt the minute he fails to provide (see Drake and Cayton 1945: 564–99; Rainwater 1970: 216; Furstenberg 2011).

Men on the economic edge, even those in multi-year partnerships with several children, often obsessed about the younger guy with the nicer car who had a better job and might turn their partner's head. Most were convinced that, for women, "there is no source of commitment in a relationship." Donald was certain that a woman would dump any man if he failed to provide. This black 37-year-old found himself always "feuding and fightin'" with his child's mother during their eight-year on-again-off-again relationship, which he blamed on the fact that she was too controlling, plus the fact that "I was not committed to really being with her" (see also Waller 2008). Reading between the lines of his narrative, we can assume that spotty employment and drug use were probably also a cause. After their breakup, Donald's ex-partner went on to have two additional children by two other men and had just married a third man, who was trying to play the role of father to his 14-year-old daughter while her mother was trying to push Donald out of their lives. Listen to the deep cynicism in Donald's view of women:

Yeah, their whole thing is, "What can you give me?" and "What can I get from you and how fast can I get it?" More or less money-wise. There is no commitment to a real relationship. Particularly in black women, their whole goal is let me see how much I can get for it and how good I can look and you know. . . . To be honest, yeah, I do [have a theory], a lot of them are caught up in, "I want to look good." "I want to be independent." "I don't want to be dependent upon you." "I want to be able to be with you, but not like that." There is no source of commitment in a relationship. [It is not] just men [that aren't committed], but anybody [nowadays]. In a relationship it is about, "We are in it 50–50 commitment," and so forth. They are not here. Their thing is, "When things go bad, I am out of here." To me, that was my experience and I am not taking it [anymore].

Amin was similarly convinced that money was necessary to sustain a relationship and that "situations"—such as unemployment—would almost certainly bring a relationship to an end. Because he lacked confidence that he could remain stably employed, Amin felt that he couldn't even contemplate marriage and worried he might not even be able to sustain a long-term relationship.

When a woman is a woman and she accepts a man for who he is and not necessarily what he does and doesn't have, then she will stand by a man regardless. But when a woman starts to allow the fact that he is not bringing as much money into the home affect her relationship and her attitude towards him then that is a problem. . . . And that is another reason why I have not considered marriage because . . . there is not too many women out there that is really ready themselves to honestly fulfill the covenant of the words that you recite when you are at the podium.

Jeff, a black forty-seven-year-old father of two, also believed a woman's love was contingent on money. He also saw this mercenary strain in his daughter.

[My daughter's mother taught me that] love is like running water. It turns off and on. I really believe that behind the fact that they can love you when you're doing, but when you don't do, they don't love. . . . My daughter had told me on numerous occasions that this [or that] individual does more for her than I do and I felt hurt. Regardless if this person is doing something for you or not, he can't fill my shoes. I'm still your father regardless. If I give you a million dollars or I give you a penny, I'm still your father.

Tom, a white father of three, believed that when a man is "down and out" a woman could easily be attracted away by a guy who was doing better or "has a nicer car." In his case, a slowdown at work while the mother of his younger two children was pregnant the second time led to unbearable conflict.

I was working every day and I was paying the bills. I did everything that I possibly could. I came home, I took care of the kids, I would put the kids to bed, just so we would have some (alone) time. . . . Her father had got me a job doing the roofing. . . . We saved money and we moved into the house and things were good and we were splitting the rent. Then I lost the job and I couldn't afford them payments anymore. . . . Yeah, it got real slow and the winter time came and there was just no work, so I didn't know what to do. I couldn't collect unemployment because I wasn't on the books. . . . She was already pregnant with the second baby and that is when I couldn't deal with her anymore and we couldn't get along.

Conclusions

Once mothers learned they were pregnant, sharing the news with the father-to-be and deciding what to do about it were important defining moments for the couple. The pregnancy often prompted many of the men [in our sample] to think of themselves as a couple for the first time, or to reconsider a partner who had fallen out of favor. The decision whether to have the baby was usually left to the mother, with fathers typically agreeing to "support what she wants to do."

Pregnancy is a challenging time for most fathers' romantic relationships. Economic pressures were great, such troubles were likely to break the couple up before the birth. Many couples' troubles momentarily disappeared after the "magic moment" of their child's birth, as the fact of a shared child brought some measure of cohesion. Fathers who were still romantically involved, even if things were rough during the pregnancy, saw the baby as sufficient reason to renew their efforts to stay together with the mother.

While entry into a "real relationship," sometimes symbolized by the move to cohabitation, may have indicated a growing level of commitment to the romantic partner, it also reflected a father's wish to be an involved parent. Usually, among fathers, the impulse to parent is at least as strong as, if not stronger than, the desire to remain partnered for the sake of the relationship. Work done by Edin and Kefalas (2005) on a companion sample of mothers in the PCFS communities shows that mothers share the desire for fathers to be involved, but view his involvement as a desirable, yet optional, complement to their mothering activities.

In sum, for this group of mostly disadvantaged men parenting children outside of marriage, multiple and serious problems such as infidelity, sexual mistrust, substance abuse, domestic violence, criminal activity, and incarceration abound in their narratives about their experiences as romantic partners. Despite their desire to form strong relationships with their children, men found that in the aftermath of the breakup, staying in regular contact with their progeny was surprisingly difficult.

What is evident from the narratives presented here is that the haphazard nature of the way that these families are formed places enormous pressure on already disadvantaged young people who don't know each other very well, but who nonetheless attempt to form "real" relationships, sometimes via cohabitation. Although pregnancy and birth do typically prompt relationship investment among men, their precarious economic situations and their mistrust of women prompt disinvestment. Men's behavior is usually the most proximate cause of a relationship's demise. Another significant factor is the ambiguous nature of the relationships themselves, where expectations are seldom revealed until they are violated. And though men may have believed they could have a direct relationship with their children with or without the mothers—"daddy baby, momma maybe"—accomplishing this feat is far more difficult than most had imagined.

REFERENCES

Augustine, Jennifer March, Timothy Nelson, and Kathryn Edin. 2009. "Why Do Poor Men Have Children?" *Annals of the American Academy of Political and Social Science* 624 (July): 99–117.

Center for Research on Child Wellbeing. 2007. "Parents' Relationship Status Five Years after a Non Marital Birth." Princeton, NJ: Center for research on Child Wellbeing, *Research Brief* 39 (August).

Davis, Allison, Burleigh B. Gardner, and Mary B. Gardner. 1941. *Deep South: A Social Anthropological Study of Caste and Class.* Chicago: University of Chicago Press.

Drake, St. Clair, and Horace R. Cayton. 1945. *Black Metropolis: A Study of Negro Life in a Northern City.* New York: Harcourt Brace.

Edin, Kathryn, Paula England, Emily Fitzsimmons Shafer, and Joanna Reed. 2007. "Forging Fragile Families: Are the Pregnancies Planned, Unplanned, or In-Between?" In *Unmarried Couples with Children: The Unfolding Lives of New Unmarried Urban Parents,* edited by Paula England and Kathryn Edin. New York: Russell Sage Foundation.

Edin, Kathryn, and Maria B. Kefalas. 2005. *Promises I Can Keep: Why Poor Women Put Motherhood before Marriage.* Berkeley: University of California Press.

Grail, Timothy S. 2007. "Custodial Mothers and Fathers and Their Child Support: 2005." *Current*

Population Reports P60–234. Washington, DC: U.S. Census Bureau.

———. 2011. "The Recent Transformation of the American Family: Witnessing and Exploring Social Change." In *Families in an Unequal Society*, edited by Marcia Carlson and Paula England. Palo Alto, CA: Stanford University Press.

Furstenberg, Frank F., Jr., and Andrew B. Cherlin. 1991. *Divided Families: What Happens to Children When Parents Part*. Cambridge, MA: Harvard University Press.

Furstenberg, Frank F., Jr. 2001. "The Fading Dream: Prospects for Marriage in the Inner City." In *Problem of the Century*, edited by Elijah Anderson and Douglas Massey, pp. 224–47. New York: Russell Sage Foundation.

Martin, Steven P. 2004. "Growing Evidence for a Divorce Divide? Education and Marital Dissolution Rates in the United States since the 1970's." New York, NY: *Russell Sage Foundation Working Papers: Series on Social Dimensions' of Inequality*.

McLanahan, Sara. 2004. "Diverging Destinies: How Children Fare under the Second Demographic Transition." *Demography* 41(4): 607–27.

Nelson, Timothy, and Kathryn Edin. Forthcoming. *Fragile Fatherhood: What Being a Daddy Means in the Lives of Low-Income Men*. New York: Russell Sage Foundation.

Nelson, Timothy J., Susan Clampet-Lundquist, and Kathryn Edin. 2002. "Sustaining Fragile Fatherhood: How Low-Income, Non-Custodial Fathers in Philadelphia Talk about Their Families." In *The Handbook of Father Involvement: Multidisciplinary Perspectives*, edited by Catherine Tamis-LeMonda and Natasha Cabrera, pp. 525–53. Mahwah, NJ: Lawrence Erlbaum Associates.

Nock, Stephen. 2007. "Marital and Unmarried Births to Men." Department of Health and Human Services Publication (PHS) 2006–1978. Hyattsville, MD: U.S. Department of Health and Human Services.

Reed, Joanna. 2007 "Anatomy of the Break-Up: How and Why Do Unmarried Parents Break Up?" In *Unmarried Couples with Children*, edited by Paula England and Kathryn Edin. New York: Russell Sage Foundation.

Townsend, Nicholas W. 2002. *The Package Deal: Marriage, Work and Fatherhood in Men's Lives*. Philadelphia: Temple University Press.

Waller, Maureen R. 2002. *My Baby's Father: Unmarried Parents and Paternal Responsibility*. Ithaca, NY: Cornell University Press.

———. 2008. "How Do Disadvantaged Parents View Tensions in Their Relationships? Insights for Relationship Longevity among At-Risk Couples." *Family Relations* 57(2): 128–43.

The Extent of Poverty in the U.S.

19. Sheldon Danziger and Christopher Wimer*
The War on Poverty[1]

What has happened since President Lyndon Johnson declared an unconditional War on Poverty in his January 8, 1964 State of the Union Address? There is no doubt that the United States has become a more affluent nation since that famous declaration: Real gross domestic product (GDP) per capita has in fact *doubled* over the past 50 years. Despite this growth, the official poverty rate for 2012 now stands at 15 percent, a full 4 percentage points higher than it was during the early 1970s. And the poverty rate is only 4 percentage points lower than the 19 percent rate of 1964.

*Danziger, Sheldon, and Christopher Wimer. 2014. "Poverty." *Pathways Magazine*, pp. 13-18.

This apparent lack of progress against poverty cannot be blamed on the economic devastation wrought by the Great Recession, although that certainly increased poverty over the last five years. Rather, the direct connection between economic growth and poverty reduction is now much weaker than in the past. Poverty remains high because many workers have not shared in the economic gains of the past 40 years; instead most of those gains have been captured by the economic elite.

Over these same decades, the official poverty measure has increasingly obscured some of the progress that *has* been made in reducing poverty because it fails to account for many government benefits the poor now receive, such as Food Stamps and the Earned Income Tax Credit. If these safety net benefits were counted as family income, today's official poverty rate would fall from 15 to about 11 percent.

The purpose of this brief is to lay out where we now stand on the war on poverty. We first describe long-term trends in poverty for the full population

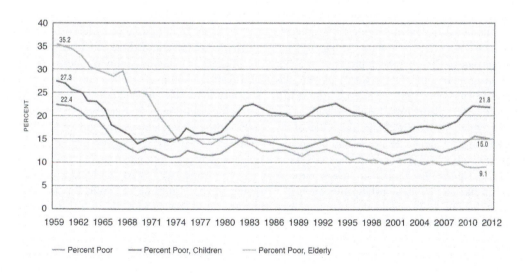

FIGURE 19.1 Trends in Official Poverty
Source: U.S. Census Bureau, Historical Poverty Tables

and for key subpopulations; we next examine why poverty has remained stubbornly high; we then discuss more appropriate ways to measure poverty that reveal how the modern safety net significantly reduces poverty. We conclude by discussing trends in extreme poverty and deep poverty. The theme throughout is that labor market failures—not safety net failure—is a main reason why progress against poverty has been so difficult.

Key Trends in Poverty

Figure 19.1 shows trends in the official poverty rate for all persons, the elderly, and children. In 1959, 22.4 percent of all persons were poor according to the official measure. This was cut in half by 1973 because of rapid economic growth and the expansion of safety net programs in the aftermath of the War on Poverty.[2]

But nothing much happened for the next four decades. The poverty rate has never fallen below the historic low of 11.1 percent reached in 1973, and only in the booming economy of the late 1990s did it come close to that mark. Instead, the trend over the past 40 years consists of ups during recessions and downs during economic recoveries, but no long-term progress. Most disturbing, the child poverty rate in 2012, 21.8 percent, was as high as it was in the mid-1960s.

Worse yet, some groups have experienced an increase in their poverty rates.[3] We examine the official poverty rate for adults classified by age cohort (Figure 19.2), educational attainment (Figure 19.3), and race or ethnicity (Figure 19.4). As shown in Figure 19.2, the poverty rate for 18-24 year olds increased by about 11 percentage points and the rate for 25-34 year olds by about 5 points since 1968.[4] Figure 19.3 shows that adults without a college degree have fared badly, with the poverty rate for those without a high school degree increasing by almost 20 percentage points and the rate for high school graduates by about 10 points since 1968. Figure 19.4 shows that poverty rates for both Hispanics and White non-Hispanics are higher in 2012 than in 1970, while the rate for Black non-Hispanics is slightly lower.[5]

Clearly, the goals of the war on poverty have not been achieved. Although there have been many important successes (as will be discussed subsequently), much remains to be done. In the next section, we ask what went wrong as well as what went right,

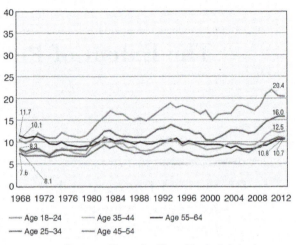

FIGURE 19.2 Poverty Rates for Nonelderly Adults by Age Cohort, 1968–2012

Source: Stanford Center on Poverty and Inequality using March CPS data downloaded from IPUMS

questions best addressed by taking an historical perspective.

What Went Wrong? And What Went right?

To understand recent trends in poverty, we begin with the economic situation in the quarter century after the end of World War II. Rapid economic growth at that time translated into more employment, higher earnings, and increasing family incomes for most Americans. Poverty fell as the living standards of the poor and the middle class increased as rapidly as they did for the rich.

Yet, many families were being left behind during this period of rapid growth, as careful observers such as Michael Harrington, John Kenneth Galbraith, and Robert Lampman pointed out. The paradox of "poverty amidst plenty" led President Johnson to declare "unconditional" war on poverty in his first State of the Union address on January 8, 1964. He emphasized that the fight against poverty could not rely solely on economic growth:

"Americans today enjoy the highest standard of living in the history of mankind. But for nearly a fifth of our fellow citizens, this is a hollow achievement. They often live without hope, below minimum standards of decency. ... We cannot and need not wait for the gradual growth of the economy to lift this forgotten fifth of our nation above the poverty line. We know what must be done, and this Nation of abundance can surely afford to do it. . . .

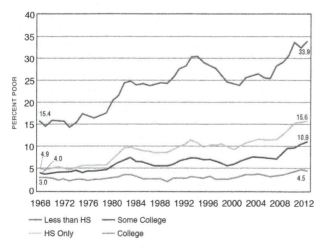

FIGURE 19.3 Poverty Rates by Educational Attainment, Persons Ages 25–64

Source: Stanford Center on Poverty and Inequality using March CPS data downloaded from IPUMS

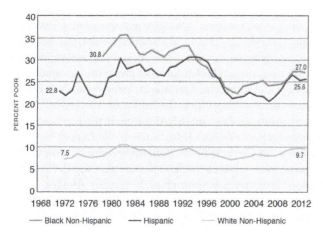

FIGURE 19.4 Poverty Rates by Race/Ethnicity, Persons Ages 18–64

Source: "White Non-Hispanic" and "Hispanic any race" are a combination of the Census Bureau's published poverty figures (Historical Poverty Tables— People, Table 3, http://www.census.gov/hhes/www/poverty/data/historical/ people.html) and estimates produced by the Stanf+I33ord Center on Poverty and Inequality using March CPS microdata from IPUMS. For "White Non-Hispanics," estimates for years 1974–2010 are from the Census Bureau, and estimates for 1970–1973 are produced by the Stanford Center on Poverty and Inequality For "Hispanic any race," estimates for years 1976–2010 are from the Census Bureau, and estimates for 1970–1975 are produced by the Stanford Center on Poverty and Inequality.

The poverty rate for Black Non-Hispanics is not available from the Census Bureau, and was produced by Stanford Center on Poverty and Inequality using March CPS data from IPUMS.

Today, as in the past, higher employment and speedier economic growth are the cornerstones of a

concerted attack on poverty. . . . But general prosperity and growth leave untouched many of the roots of human poverty."

The Johnson administration proposed many strategies for reducing poverty. The 1964 *Economic Report of the President* argued for maintaining high levels of employment, accelerating economic growth, fighting discrimination, improving labor markets, expanding educational opportunities, improving health, and assisting the aged and disabled. Indeed, these remain important antipoverty priorities.

This last goal, assisting the aged and disabled, is widely accepted as the greatest achievement of the War on Poverty. Elderly poverty has fallen dramatically, from 35.2 percent in 1959 to 9.1 percent in 2012 (see Figure 19.1). Medicare and Medicaid, introduced in 1965, greatly expanded access to medical care and improved the health of the elderly and disabled. An expanded safety net raised their incomes and insulated them from both recessions and inflation, through the expansion and indexation of social security benefits and the introduction of the Supplemental Security Income program. The poverty rate for the elderly has been lower than the rate for working-age adults for the past two decades.

But the Johnson administration's optimism that macroeconomic policies and an expanded social safety net could eliminate poverty for all persons had all but disappeared by the 1980s. Many observers focused on the limited progress that had been made in reducing poverty among the population as a whole. The War on Poverty programs came to be seen as the *cause* of the problem, to the point that in his 1988 State of the Union Address President Reagan declared:

"In 1964, the famous War on Poverty was declared. And a funny thing happened. Poverty, as measured by dependency, stopped shrinking and actually began to grow worse. I guess you could say 'Poverty won the War.' Poverty won, in part, because instead of helping the poor, government programs ruptured the bonds holding poor families together."

Was President Reagan right? Are safety net programs to blame for the stagnation in the official poverty rate since the early 1970s? The short answer: No. A careful analysis reveals that the lack of progress results from two opposing forces—an economy that has increasingly left more of the poor behind and a safety net that has successfully kept more of them afloat.

The primary reason that poverty remains high is that the benefits of economic growth are no longer shared by almost all workers, as they were in the quarter century after the end of World War II. In recent decades, it has been difficult for many workers, especially those with no more than a high school degree (see Figure 19.3), to earn enough to keep their families out of poverty.

This economic trend represents a sharp break with the past. Inflation-adjusted median earnings of full-time year-round male workers grew 42 percent from 1960 to 1973. But, four decades later, median earnings were $49,398 in 2012, 4 percent lower than the inflation-adjusted 1973 value, $51,670.[6] Men with no more than a high school degree fared even worse.

Further, men are less likely to be working today than in the past. The annual unemployment rate for men over the age of twenty was below 5 percent in 92 percent of the years between 1950 and 1974, but in only 37 percent of the years since.

Stagnant earnings for the typical worker and higher unemployment represent a failure of the economy, not a failure of antipoverty policies. Most economists agree that several factors have contributed to wage stagnation and increasing earnings inequality. These include labor-saving technological changes, the globalization of labor and product markets, immigration of less-educated workers, the declining real value of the minimum wage, and declining unionization.

This evidence refutes President Reagan's view that poverty remains high because the safety net provided too much aid for the poor and thus encouraged dysfunctional behaviors. Studies do show that poverty would be somewhat lower if fewer low-skilled men had withdrawn from the labor market, if marriage rates had not declined so much, and if there had been less immigration of workers with little education. But these effects are small compared to the role of turbulent labor markets, slower growth, and rising inequality.

(Mis)measuring Poverty

The poverty-fighting role of the safety net can only be revealed by using a more accurate poverty measure. The official poverty rate is so high in part because it does not actually *count* many of the benefits now provided to the poor, especially noncash benefits and refundable tax credits.

One reason that Reagan's critique of the safety net resonates with the public is that the official poverty measure, the main statistical tool to gauge progress against poverty, understates the effects of government programs. The official measure was adopted in the late-1960s to represent the income necessary to provide a minimally decent standard of living. The poverty line varies with family size. For example, in 2012, it was $11,011 for an elderly person and $23,283 for a married couple with two children.

Each year, this official statistic provides the main message to policymakers and the public about trends in poverty, even though many have questioned whether a minimally decent standard of living can mean the same thing today as in the mid-1960s.[7] Yet, the measure has not been updated for almost fifty years.

Wherever the poverty line is set, however, the poverty rate should be based on a full accounting of family resources. Families are considered poor under the official measure if their *money income* from all sources and all family members falls below the line. Money income includes wages and salaries, interest, dividends, rents, cash transfers from the government, such as social security and unemployment insurance, and other forms of pretax cash income.

The official measure excludes noncash benefits such as those from the Supplemental Nutrition Assistance Program (SNAP, formerly food stamps) and refundable tax credits, such as the Earned Income Tax Credit (EITC). Noncash benefits were not common when the official poverty line was developed, but they have grown rapidly in recent decades.

The Census Bureau has developed a "Supplemental Poverty Measure"–or SPM–in response to the recommendations of a National Academy of Sciences panel on how to better measure poverty.[8] The SPM has been released for each year since 2009.[9] It does count *all* the resources we channel toward ameliorating poverty, such as SNAP and the EITC. According to the SPM, poverty has increased slightly from 15.1 in 2009 to 16.0 in 2012.

Recently, researchers at Columbia University estimated the SPM for every year from 1967 to 2012. They document the importance of counting all benefits the poor receive.[10] They estimate what the poverty rate would have been in the absence of (1) the cash safety net programs that *are* counted in the official measure (OPM); and (2) all the safety net programs, including near cash benefits and refundable tax credits.

In Figure 19.5, we show the percentage of all persons removed from poverty by safety net pro-

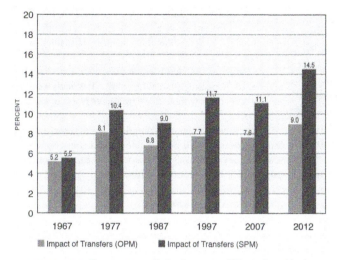

FIGURE 19.5 Percentage Point Impact of Transfers Under OPM and SPM, 1967–2012

Source: The poverty rates for people living in families with a female householder (no husband present) and unrelated individuals are from the Census Bureau Historical Poverty Tables, http://www.census.gov/hhes/www/poverty/data/historical/people.html, Table 2.

The rates for people living in married-couple families are produced by the Stanford Center on Poverty and Inequality using March CPS data downloaded from IPUMS.

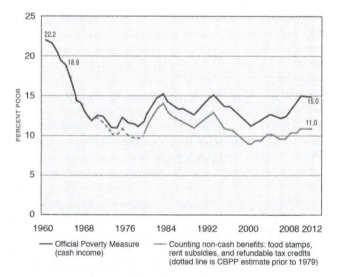

FIGURE 19.6 Poverty Rate Shows Greater Improvements Since 1960s When Non-Cash Benefits Are Counted

Source: The percentage of people living in working families comes from the Census Bureau Detailed Poverty Tables, http://www.census.gov/hhes/www/cpstables/032011/pov/toc.htm.

grams according to each measure. In the left-hand bar, we show the percentage point difference in poverty between the actual OPM and what it would have been if all cash benefits had been "zeroed out;"

in the right-hand bar, the analogous difference for the SPM.

In 1967, when most safety net benefits were cash transfers (e.g., social security benefits, unemployment insurance, cash welfare), moving from the OPM to the SPM made little difference, as the safety net reduced poverty by about 5 percentage points using either measure.

But during subsequent decades, noncash benefits and refundable tax credits grew more rapidly than cash benefits, with the result that the OPM increasingly understates the "antipoverty impact" of safety net programs. By 2012, according to the OPM, the safety net reduced poverty by 9 percentage points; but the SPM shows that the *full* safety net reduced poverty by 14.5 percentage points. Thus, the official measure fails to account for about a third of the antipoverty impact of safety net programs.[11]

To be consistent with the priorities of the War on Poverty planners, Figure 19.6 maintains the official poverty lines but counts all resources, including noncash benefits and refundable tax credits. According to Arloc Sherman,[12] counting these resources reduces the official poverty rate to 10.9 percent in 2011 from 15.0 percent (the difference between the top and bottom lines). This means that the poverty rate would have fallen by 8 percentage points, not 4 points, since 1965.

Beneath the Poverty Line: Extreme Poverty and Deep Poverty

We now consider measures of extreme and deep poverty. The OPM and SPM focus on a single point in the income distribution. For instance, if the poverty line for a given family is $23,000, the OPM or SPM simply document whether a family falls above or below that line. Over recent decades, however, there have also been substantial income changes among those below the poverty line.

In a recent paper, H. Luke Shaefer and Kathryn Edin examine trends in "extreme poverty," which they define as living on less than $2 a day, the World Bank metric of global poverty.[13]

They find that, for households with children, extreme poverty based on money income has rapidly increased from 1.7 percent in 1996 to 4.3 percent in 2011. If noncash benefits and refundable tax credits are counted as income, extreme poverty rises by much less, from 1.1 to 1.6 percent over these years. Thus, even though extreme poverty has increased, the situation would have been much worse without additional resources provided by safety net programs.

A similar result holds for "deep poverty," defined as income less than 50 percent of the poverty line. According to the Columbia study, deep poverty for children would have risen to over 20 percent in some years without government benefits.[14] When all safety benefits are counted, however, deep child poverty is around 5-6 percent in almost all years since 1967.

Taken together, these studies suggest that safety net programs raise the living standards of millions of people even though they are not always large enough to raise them out of poverty.

Where do We Go from Here?

Poverty remains high because, since the early 1970s, unemployment rates have been high and economic growth has been less effective in reducing poverty than it was in the quarter century following World War II. Although the economy has largely failed the poor, safety net programs that were introduced or expanded in response to the War on Poverty take more people out of poverty today than was the case in the early 1970s. This increased antipoverty impact is obscured because the official poverty measure does not value the poverty-reducing effects of noncash benefits and refundable tax credits.

President Johnson's vision and policy priorities of 1964 remain relevant today. If poverty is to be significantly reduced, we must find ways to ensure that the benefits of economic growth are more widely distributed than they have been in recent decades. The best way to do this is to adopt policies to increase the employment and earnings of the poor. Even with such a renewed focus on raising the market incomes of the poor, we must also continue to strengthen the safety net programs to prevent even more families from falling through the cracks.

NOTES

1. Miles Corak, David Haproff, H. Luke Shaefer, and Jane Waldfogel provided thoughtful feedback on a previous draft.
2. See Danziger and Gottschalk, 1995, and Bailey and Danziger, 2013.

3. These analyses begin in 1968 given limitations in the available data for earlier years. The chart on race/ethnicity begins in 1970 as it is difficult to identify Hispanics in prior years.
4. As the population has become more educated, dropouts are an increasingly smaller group. The long-term trend for all persons without a college degree is also toward greater poverty.
5. Over time, immigrants comprise a larger share of all Hispanics, causing their poverty rate to rise because recent immigrants are more likely to be poor than the native-born.
6. See U.S. Bureau of the Census, 2013.
7. See Citro and Michael, 1995.
8. See Citro and Michael, 1995.
9. See Short, 2012.
10. See Fox, Garfinkel, Kaushal, Waldfogel, and Wimer, 2013.
11. The SPM addresses the effects of having public health insurance, such as Medicaid and Medicare, by subtracting medical out-of-pocket expenses from income. Sommers and Oellerich (2013) estimate the extent to which Medicaid reduces out-of-pocket medical expenses of the poor and conclude that, without Medicaid, an additional 2.6 million persons would have been poor in 2010 according to the SPM.
12. See Sherman, 2013.
13. See Shaefer and Edin 2013.
14. See Fox, Garfinkel, Kaushal, Waldfogel, and Wimer, 2013.

20. H. Luke Shaefer and Kathryn Edin*
The Rise of Extreme Poverty in the United States

The number of adults on welfare has dropped dramatically since its reform in 1996. As of 2011, a little over 1 million adults remained on the welfare rolls in a typical month, down from about 4.6 million at the program's peak in the early 1990s. As these numbers plummeted, the number of single mothers joining the workforce or returning to it grew at rates that were largely unexpected. For these reasons, welfare reform has been touted as a success.

At the same time, in the years since 1996, a new group of American poor has emerged: families with children who are living on virtually no income—$2

* Shaefer, H. Luke and Kathryn Edin. 2014. "The Rise of Extreme Poverty in the United States." *Pathways Magazine: Jobs & Joblessness,* 28–32.

or less per person per day in a given month. These are America's "extreme poor." The U.S. official poverty line for a family of three would equate to roughly $17 per person per day. What scholars call "deep poverty"—incomes at less than half the poverty line—is about $8.50 per person per day, over four times higher than our cutoff. This new group of American poor, the extreme poor, are likely experiencing a level of destitution not captured in prior poverty measures, one that few of us knew even existed in such a rich country.

The purpose of this chapter is to expose the rise of extreme poverty and to examine how the safety net is—or is not—addressing it. We cannot fully address *why* extreme poverty is on the rise, but it may well be related to the landmark 1996 welfare reform. After 1996, it became far more difficult to get any cash assistance from the government if you didn't have a job, even if you were raising young children and had no other sources of income.

Measuring Extreme Poverty

To examine trends in the prevalence of extreme poverty in the United States over the past fifteen years, we use a unique data source, the Survey of Income and Program Participation (SIPP), collected by the U.S. Census Bureau. While not perfect, this is the best available source of information in the United States about (a) participation in public programs, and (b) family incomes among the poor. We begin in 1996, which is before states were required to implement welfare reform and before the national unemployment rate fell to a low of 4 percent in 2000. The period ends with the most recent SIPP data available at the time of analysis, from the middle of 2011, when the national unemployment rate was roughly 9 percent. We include only households with children under eighteen and with household heads under sixty-five. We adjust income values to 2011 dollars using the Consumer Price Index for urban customers and use household-level sample weights to produce nationally representative estimates. We derive three estimates of extreme poverty from these data, using three different definitions of household income. These estimates differ in the extent to which they take into account noncash benefits, ranging from the "baseline" measure that excludes all such benefits to the "full safety net measures" that include them.

Baseline estimates: Our baseline estimates, which most closely align to the official US poverty line and the deep poverty measure described above, use monthly pretax cash income values (which include cash assistance) and take family size into account. . . .

SNAP estimates: The second measure adds benefits from the Supplemental Nutrition Assistance Program (SNAP), treating them as if they were cash, even though they can be used only at certified vendors for the purchase of food. This allows us to examine how effective the SNAP program has been in addressing the needs of the extreme poor.

Full safety net estimates: The third measure not only treats SNAP as cash, but also adds in the estimated average monthly value of the household's net refundable tax credits, specifically the Earned Income Tax Credit (EITC) and the Child Tax Credit (CT), plus government housing subsidies (Housing Choice Vouchers, known as "Section 8" and public housing), which serve about a quarter of the eligible population. This third measure allows us to judge just how successful the US social safety net is, even in this post-welfare era, in addressing the needs of the poorest Americans.

Trends in Extreme Poverty

Are more people in extreme poverty now than fifteen years ago? No matter which of the three measures we use, the answer is *yes*.

Figure 20.1 plots estimates from our baseline measure in solid black. It plots the number of households with non-elderly heads and minor children living in extreme poverty between 1996 and 2011. The breaks in the lines represent breaks between SIPP panels. The baseline estimates show that the number of households living on $2 or less in cash income per person per day in a given month increased from about 636,000 in 1996 to about 1.65 million in mid-2011, a growth of 159.1 percent. In mid-2011 about 3.55 million children lived in extreme poverty in a given month (see Table 20.2).

This rise in extreme poverty is reduced—but not eliminated—when we count SNAP as cash (dashed line). By that measure, the number of extreme-poor households increases by 80.4 percent, from roughly 475,000 to 857,000. When tax credits and housing subsidies are included as well (light gray line), thus generating our most conservative measure of extreme poverty, the increase is still about 50 percent, from 409,000 to 613,000 households. It follows that 1.17 million children were in extreme poverty

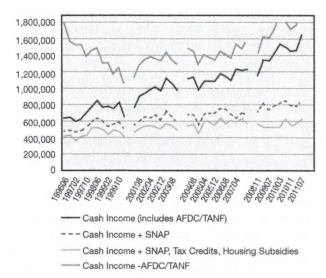

Cash Income (includes AFDC/TANF)

- - - Cash Income + SNAP

Cash Income + SNAP, Tax Credits, Housing Subsidies

Cash Income -AFDC/TANF

FIGURE 20.1 Households with Children in Extreme Poverty in the United States (≤$2 per person, per day)

Source: Authors' analyses of the 1996 through 2008 panels of the SIPP. The horizontal axis represents approximate years and months of SIPP fourth reference month estimates. The vertical axis represents the number of non-elderly households with children. Breaks in the trend lines represent breaks in the SIPP panels.

in mid-2011 under our most conservative measure (see Table 20.2).

The bottom line is that extreme poverty has grown sharply since welfare reform. And though means-tested public programs have done much to stem the tide, growth in extreme poverty is still substantial even after accounting for major federal means-tested transfers. The beneficial effects of these programs are especially evident after the passage of the American Recovery and Reinvestment Act (ARRA), which expanded both SNAP and refundable tax credits. As Figure 20.1 demonstrates, "baseline" extreme poverty, measured using only cash income (including TANF, but excluding SNAP, housing subsidies, and tax credits), increased by about 35 percent between late 2007 and early 2011. But when SNAP, tax credits, and housing subsidies are added, the rise in extreme poverty was less than 10 percent over this period. In fact, it fell slightly in some months.

The dark gray trend line presented in Figure 20.1 reveals how much extreme poverty there would likely have been in the absence of AFDC or TANF (and assuming no behavioral response). . . . By comparing this line with the "cash only" line, we can examine how effective cash assistance has been in lifting households out of extreme poverty.

The results show a stark decline in the role of cash assistance in reducing extreme poverty. In 1996, cash assistance had a substantial effect, bringing the incomes of 1.15 million households above the extreme poverty threshold. But throughout the 1990s, the impact of cash assistance in reducing

extreme poverty declined substantially and flattened out in the early 2000s. By mid-2011, cash assistance was lifting only about 300,000 families out of extreme poverty. Indeed, when cash assistance is subtracted from household income, extreme poverty in 1996 and 2011 would have been about the same.

The exposure of children to extreme poverty has grown dramatically even when longer, rather than shorter, spells are considered. In Table 20.1, the starting and ending points for the monthly estimates reported in Figure 20.1 are provided, as well as alternative estimates using quarterly income. Compared with the baseline monthly measure, we find that, for a calendar quarter, fewer households experience extreme poverty. When comparing the *growth* in extreme poverty, however, the results based on quarterly income are consistent with the monthly estimates. After adding in the estimated cash value of all means-tested programs, and using our monthly measure, the growth in the number of households experiencing extreme poverty was 49.9 percent. In contrast, using quarterly income, that figure was 97.4 percent. Although these higher growth rates are a function of lower starting values in 1996, it is clear that, even when using quarterly income, there is reason for concern.

The bottom row of Table 20.1 reports a final specification for our baseline definition—the measure that uses cash income only. The number of households with children who reported at least one month of extreme poverty over a calendar quarter increased from about 1.30 million in 1996 to 2.41 million households in mid-2011. This represents 6.3 percent of all households with children in mid-2011.

TABLE 20.1 Alternative Estimates of Extreme Poverty of Households with Children

	Number of Households with Children (Rounded in Thousands)			Percent of Households with Children		
	1996	*2011*	*% Growth*	*1996*	*2011*	*% Growth*
Monthly estimates (based on Figure 1)						
Pretax cash only	636,000	1,648,000	159.1%	1.7%	4.3%	151.8%
Add SNAP	475,000	857,000	80.4%	1.3%	2.2%	69.2%
Add SNAP, tax credits, housing subsidies	409,000	613,000	49.9%	1.1%	1.6%	45.5%
Quarterly estimates						
Pretax cash only	307,000	1,039,000	238.4%	0.8%	2.7%	237.5%
Add SNAP	209,000	478,000	128.7%	0.6%	1.2%	100.0%
Add SNAP, tax credits, housing subsidies	189,000	373,000	97.4%	0.5%	1.0%	100.0%
1 or more months per quarter (cash only)	1,295,000	2,407,000	85.9%	3.5%	6.3%	80.0%

Source: Authors' analyses of the 1996 and 2008 panels of the SIPP. For the full tables, see Shaefer & Edin, 2013

TABLE 20.2 Characteristics of Households with Children in Extreme Poverty

Number in Extreme Poverty, Monthly	Cash Only			Adding in SNAP, Tax Credits, and Housing Subsidies		
	1996	*2011*	*% Growth*	*1996*	*2011*	*% Growth*
Total households	**636,000**	**1,648,000**	**159.1%**	**409,000**	**613,000**	**49.9%**
Married Households	323,000	602,000	86.4%	255,000	330,000	29.4%
Single female households	254,000	838,000	229.9%	112,000	188,000	67.9%
Race of household head						
White, Non-Hispanic	334,000	782,000	134.1%	243,000	375,000	54.3%
African American & Hispanic	265,000	758,000	186.0%	130,000	182,000	40.0%
Children	1,383,000	3,547,000	156.5%	788,000	1,166,000	48.0%

Source: Authors' analyses of the 1996 and 2008 panels of the SIPP. For the full tables, see Shaefer & Edin, 2013

Which Groups Are Most Vulnerable?

It is important to consider whether the risk of extreme poverty is borne by groups that, in the United States, have historically been disadvantaged. In Table 20.2, we report the characteristics of the households living in extreme poverty, first using the baseline cash-income-only measure, and then adding in the estimated cash value of other means-tested programs. Because different groups may vary in the extent to which they underreport on program participation and income, these particular estimates should be treated with caution. . . .

We begin with the association between marital status and extreme poverty. Using the baseline measure for 2011, about 37 percent of the households in extreme poverty were headed by a married couple, and 51 percent were headed by a single female. After adding in SNAP, tax credits, and housing subsidies, just over half of the extreme poverty households are married, and less than one-third are single female–

headed, reflecting greater reliance on public programs among households headed by single mothers than by married couples.

What about the association between race and ethnicity and extreme poverty? In mid-2011, the baseline measure shows that about 47 percent of households in extreme poverty were headed by white non-Hispanics, while 46 percent were headed by African Americans or Hispanics (reported together because of small sample sizes). After adding in the other programs, the proportion headed by white non-Hispanics increases to about 61 percent.

The takeaway from these estimates is that extreme poverty is not limited to households headed by single mothers or disadvantaged minorities. But it is also clear that the percentage growth in extreme poverty over the fifteen-year study period was greatest among these more vulnerable groups, those who were most likely to have been impacted by the 1996 welfare reform. . . .

Why the Rise of Extreme Poverty Matters

The prevalence of extreme poverty in the United States may shock many. As of mid-2011, our analyses show that about 1.65 million households with about 3.55 million children were surviving on $2 or less in cash income per person per day in a given month. These estimates account for income received from TANF and other direct cash income transfer programs, plus contributions from family and friends and income from odd jobs, among other things. Households in extreme poverty constituted 4.3 percent of all non-elderly households with children. Worse yet, the prevalence of extreme poverty rose sharply between 1996 and 2011, with the highest growth rates found among groups most affected by the 1996 welfare reform. . . .

The safety net is succeeding in reducing the most extreme forms of deprivation. Yet by no means does it eliminate extreme poverty. When we recalculate the mid-2011 figures after treating SNAP benefits as equivalent to cash, this reduces the number of extremely poor households with children by about half (48 percent), and when refundable tax credits and housing subsidies are subsequently added, the number falls by 63 percent. We estimate that these major means-tested aid programs currently save roughly 2.38 million children from extreme poverty each month, but they leave 1.17 million children behind.

The simple but important conclusion is that a growing population of children experience spells with virtually no income. . . . Although our results are troubling by most any calculus, we ought not overlook the silver lining. It is clear that, especially in the aftermath of the Great Recession, our current major safety-net programs are blunting some of the hardship that the very-bottom households would otherwise face. However, it would be wrong to conclude that the US safety net is strong or even adequate, as the number and proportion of households with children surviving on less than $2 per day has risen so dramatically over the past fifteen years, even after accounting for all sources of income, plus means-tested transfers.

RESOURCES

Ben-Shalom, Y., Moffit, R., & Scholz, J. K. (in press). An assessment of the effectiveness of anti-poverty programs in the United States. In P. Jefferson (Ed.), *Oxford Handbook of Economics of Poverty*. New York: Oxford University Press. Currently available as NBER working paper No. w17042, http://www.nber.org/papers/w17042.

Czajka, J. L., & Denmead, G. (2008). Income data for policy analysis: a comparative assessment of eight surveys. Final Report. Report by Mathematica Policy Research, Inc. under contract to the Department of Health and Human Services, ASPE. http://www.mathema-tica-mpr.com/publications/PDFs/incomedata. pdf.

Edin, K. & Lein, L. (1997). *Making ends meet*. New York: Russell Sage Foundation.

Loprest, P. J. (November 2011). Disconnected families and TANF. Urban Institute, OPRE research brief, #02.

Meyer, B. D., Mok, W. K. C., & Sullivan, J. X. (2009). *The under-reporting of transfers in house-hold surveys: Its nature and consequences* (NBER working paper 15181). http://www.nber.org/ papers/w15181.

Ravallion, M., Chen, S., & Sangraula, P. (2008). Dollar a day revisited. The World Bank Development Research Group Policy Research Working Paper 4620. http:// www-wds.world-bank.org/external/default/WDSContentServer/ IW3P/IB/2008/09/02/000158349_20080 902 095754/Rendered/PDF/wps4620.pdf.

Shaefer, H.L. & Edin, K. (2013). "Rising Extreme Poverty in the United States and the Response of Federal Means-Tested Transfers." *Social Service Review*, 87(2), 250–268.

Sherman, A., Greenstein, R., & Ruffing, K. (2012). Contrary to "entitlement society" rhe-toric, over nine-tenths of entitlement benefits go to elderly, disabled, or working households. Report by the Center on Budget and Policy Priorities. http://www.cbpp.org/files/2-10-12pov.pdf.

NOTES

1. This article draws heavily on Shaefer & Edin, 2013.

2. Ideally, we would also report annual estimates. Unfortunately, to produce annual estimates, the SIPP requires the use of calendar year weights, which, at the time of analysis, had not yet been made available for the final year of our study period, nor are they available for other years in the study period because of breaks between SIPP panels. The virtue of monthly estimates is that they better protect against biasing from non-random attrition throughout the SIPP panels. Still, this is an important limitation of our analysis, as it is possible that households could experience a month or even a calendar quarter in extreme poverty, but have larger incomes over a full year.

3. A second figure, which appears in Shaefer & Edin (2013), examines the proportion of all non-elderly households with children in extreme poverty. The results in that figure are consistent with those presented here.

4. Readers should note that all estimates come from a household survey and thus fluctuate somewhat from month to month, as is shown in Figures 20.1 and 20.2. Therefore, the exact point estimates should be treated with caution. Of more interest are the trends over time, which are quite clear, substantial, and robust to numerous sensitivity tests.

5. Virtually all of the difference between the SNAP-only trend line and the final trend line is attributable to refundable tax credits.

Why Is There So Much Poverty?

21. Jack Shonkoff*
Poverty and Child Development

Science tells us that early childhood is a time of both great opportunity and considerable risk. For better or worse, its influence can extend over a lifetime. A strong foundation in early childhood lays the groundwork for responsible citizenship, economic prosperity, healthy communities, and successful parenting of the next generation. A weak foundation can seriously undermine the social and economic vitality of the nation.

Dramatic advances in neuroscience, molecular biology, genomics, and the behavioral and social sciences are deepening our understanding of how healthy development happens, how it can be derailed, and what societies can do to keep it on track. We now know, for example, that:

• Genes provide the initial blueprint for building brain architecture;

• Environmental influences affect how the neural circuitry actually gets wired;

• Reciprocal interactions among genetic predispositions and early experiences affect the extent to which the foundations of learning, behavior, and both physical and mental health will be strong or weak. . . .

The foundations of healthy development and the origins of many physical and cognitive impairments are increasingly likely to be found in the biological "memories" that are created by gene-environment interactions in the early years of life, in some cases as early as during the prenatal period. The science explaining these phenomena is grounded in the basic biological principle that the immature organism "reads" salient environmental characteristics in the service of developing its capacity to adapt to the environment in which it "expects" it will live. For example, inadequate maternal nutrition during pregnancy prepares biological systems for a life of scarcity after birth—a life in which the baby must make the most of limited nutrients. This healthy adaptation becomes a liability when the post-natal environment in fact offers plenty of high-caloric nutrition. Hence the result of poor prenatal nutrition can be increased likelihood of obesity in childhood and adulthood, as well as later hypertension and heart disease.

Similarly, when early experiences are nurturing, contingent, stable, and predictable, healthy brain development is promoted and other organ regulatory systems are facilitated. When early experiences are fraught with threat, uncertainty, neglect, or abuse, stress management systems are over-activated. The consequences can include disruptions of developing brain circuitry, as well as the establishment of a short fuse for subsequent stress response activation, which leads to greater vulnerability to a host of physical diseases. As a result of these biological adaptations, stable, responsive, nurturing caregiving early in life is associated with better physical and mental health, fewer behavioral problems, higher educational achievement, more productive employment, and less involvement with social services in adulthood. For the one in seven US children who experience some form of maltreatment, such as chronic neglect or physical, sexual, or emotional abuse, biological adaptations can lead to increased risk of a compromised immune system, hypertension and heart disease, obesity, substance abuse, and mental illness.

A Roadmap for Childhood Policy

[This] scientific evidence . . . points to the particular importance of addressing the needs of our most disadvantaged children at the earliest ages. [We can develop] a roadmap for a new, science-driven era in early childhood policy, starting with three promising

* Shonkoff, Jack. 2011. "Building A Foundation for Prosperity on the Science of Early Childhood Development." *Pathways Magazine: The Effects of Deprivation*, 10–15.

targets for innovative intervention strategies, beginning as early as the prenatal period. . . .

Target #1: Healthy, stable relationships. The first target area—the environment of relationships in which a young child develops—requires attention to a continuum from providing more nurturing, responsive caregiving to protecting children from neglectful or abusive interactions. These relationships include those with family and non-family members, as both are important sources of stable and growth-promoting experiences. Moreover, these relationships can provide critical buffers against potential threats to healthy development.

Target #2: Physical environments. The second target area—the physical, chemical, and built environments in which the child and family live—requires protection from neurotoxic exposures such as lead, mercury, and organophosphate insecticides; safeguards against injury such as the use of infant seat restraints in automobiles and safe play spaces; and the availability of safe neighborhoods and their associated social capital, both of which improve the prospects of families with young children. When communities provide children with safer and less toxic environments, the architecture of their brains and bodies is more likely to develop in healthy ways, leading to more success and productivity further on down the road.

Target #3: Appropriate nutrition. The third target area for intervention—appropriate versus poor nutrition—requires attention to the availability and affordability of nutritious food; parent knowledge about age-appropriate meal planning for young children; and effective controls against the growing problem of excess caloric consumption and early obesity. . . . The foundation for healthy nutrition starts as early as the prenatal period, when scarcity and proper maternal nutrition literally lay the groundwork for later health and nutritional status throughout the life course.

Together, experiences in each of these target areas trigger a variety of physiological responses. In some cases, specific adverse events or experiences that occur during sensitive periods in the development of the brain or other organ systems may leave physiological "markers" whose effects are seen later. Lifelong cognitive deficits and physical impairments associated with first-trimester rubella infection or significant prenatal alcohol exposure are two prominent examples. In other circumstances, physiological changes may reflect the cumulative damage or biological "wear and tear" caused by recurrent abuse or chronic neglect over time. This breakdown of the physiological "steady state" is believed to be due to chronic activation of the stress response system. And this breakdown, in turn, gives a much greater sense of urgency to the disproportionate exposure of low-income children to ongoing environmental stressors, traumatic experiences, and family chaos. When early influences are positive, physiological systems are typically healthy and adaptive. When influences are negative, systems may become dysfunctional. In both cases, genetic predisposition affects whether a child is more or less sensitive to environmental influences. The identification and measurement of both types of physiological "footprints" offer considerable promise for understanding both resilience and vulnerability in the face of adversity.

Physiological responses to early experiences affect adult outcomes such as educational achievement and economic productivity; health-related behaviors like diet, exercise, smoking, alcohol and substance abuse, antisocial behavior, and violent crime; and both the preservation of physical health and the avoidance of disease and disorder. . . . Children who, early in life, experience adverse conditions such as deep, sustained poverty, profound neglect or abuse, exposure to violence, and parental mental illness or substance abuse tend to drop out of school earlier, earn less, depend more on social supports, adopt a range of unhealthy behaviors, and die at a younger age. And this winds up costing us all more in the end than if we had addressed these problems early on.

Learning how to cope with adversity is an important part of healthy child development. When we are threatened, our bodies activate a variety of physiological responses to stress. Scientists now know that chronic, unrelenting stress in early childhood, in the absence of supportive relationships with adults, can be toxic to the developing brain. Toxic stress disrupts brain architecture, adversely affects other organs, and leads to stress-management systems that establish relatively lower thresholds for responsiveness that persist throughout life, thereby increasing the risk of stress-related disease or disorder as well as cognitive impairment well into the adult years.

From Science to Policy

There is sufficient evidence right now to make the scientific and economic case for investing in innovative, relationship-based interventions for young children burdened by the stresses of child maltreatment, parental mental health impairments, or family violence. Another candidate for intervention is the disruptive impact of emotional and behavioral problems in early learning. . . . All available information points to the same conclusion—intervention in the early years can make an important difference, but the magnitude of policy and program impacts must be increased.

The field of early childhood intervention currently stands at an important crossroads. One path leads toward the vital task of closing the gap between what we know and what we do right now. This road's directions are clear—it requires enhanced staff development, increased quality improvement, appropriate measures of accountability, and expanded funding to serve more children and families. The second path heads into less charted territory, yet its purpose is deeply compelling—to create the building blocks for a new mindset that promotes innovation, invites experimentation, and leverages the frontiers of both the biological and social sciences into transformational changes in policy and practice. The first path will bring state-of-the-art services to greater numbers of children and families. The second views current best practices as a promising starting point, not a final destination. . . .

An exciting new era in early childhood policy, practice, and research lies at the convergence of these two agendas—an era driven by science, creativity, and pragmatic problem-solving in the service of building a more humane present and more promising future for all young children and their families.

22. William Julius Wilson*
Being Poor, Black, and American

Through the second half of the 1990s and in to the early years of the 21st century, public attention to the plight of poor black Americans seemed to wane. There was scant media attention to the problem of

*William Julius Wilson. "Being Poor, Black, and American," *American Educator* (Spring 2011), pp. 10–23, 46. Reprinted with permission from the Spring 2011 issue of *American Educator*, the quarterly journal of the American Federation of Teachers, AFL-CIO. Includes adapted material from Wilson, W.J. *Race and Social Problems* (2009) 1: 3. doi:10.1007/s12552-009-9004-4 © Springer Science+Business Media, LLC 2009, and from *Political Science Quarterly*, Vol. 123, No. 4.

concentrated urban poverty (neighborhoods that fall beneath the federally designated poverty line), little or no discussion of inner-city challenges by mainstream political leaders, and even an apparent quiescence on the part of ghetto residents themselves. This was dramatically different from the 1960s, when the transition from legal segregation to a more racially open society was punctuated by social unrest that sometimes expressed itself in violent terms, as seen in the riots that followed the assassination of Dr. Martin Luther King, Jr.

But in 2005, Hurricane Katrina exposed concentrated poverty in New Orleans. When television cameras focused on the flooding, the people trapped in houses and apartments, and the vast devastation, many Americans were shocked to see the squalid living conditions of the poor. Of course, the devastation of Katrina was broadly visited upon the residents of New Orleans, black and white, rich and poor, property owner and public housing tenant alike. But while many residents were able to flee, the very poor, lacking automobiles or money for transportation and lodging, stayed to wait out the storm with tragic results. And through Katrina, the nation's attention became riveted on these poor, urban neighborhoods.

If television cameras had focused on the urban poor in New Orleans, or in any inner-city ghetto, before Katrina, I believe the initial reaction to descriptions of poverty and poverty concentration would have been unsympathetic. Public opinion polls in the United States routinely reflect the notion that people are poor and jobless because of their own shortcomings or inadequacies; in other words, few people would have reflected on how the larger forces in society—including segregation, discrimination, a lack of economic opportunity, and failing public schools—adversely affect the inner-city poor. However, because Katrina was clearly a natural disaster that was beyond the control of the inner-city poor, Americans were much more sympathetic. In a sense, Katrina turned out to be something of a cruel natural experiment, wherein better-off Americans could readily see the effects of racial isolation and chronic economic subordination.

Despite the lack of national public awareness of the problems of the urban poor prior to Katrina, social scientists have rightly devoted considerable attention to concentrated poverty, because it magnifies the problems associated with poverty in general: joblessness, crime, delinquency, drug trafficking, broken families, and dysfunctional schools. Neighborhoods of highly concentrated poverty are seen as dangerous, and therefore they become isolated, socially and economically, as people go out of their way to avoid them.[1] In this chapter, I provide a political, economic, and cultural framework for understanding the emergence and persistence of concentrated urban poverty. I pay particular attention to poor inner-city black neighborhoods, which have the highest levels of concentrated poverty. I conclude this article by suggesting a new agenda for America's ghetto poor, based on the analysis I put forth in the following sections.

Political Forces

Since 1934, with the establishment of the Federal Housing Administration (FHA), a program necessitated by the massive mortgage foreclosures during the Great Depression, the US government has sought to enable citizens to become homeowners by underwriting mortgages. In the years following World War II, however, the federal government contributed to the early decay of inner-city neighborhoods by withholding mortgage capital and making it difficult for these areas to retain or attract families who were able to purchase their own homes. The FHA selectively administered the mortgage program by formalizing a process that excluded certain urban neighborhoods using empirical data that suggested a probable loss of investment in these areas. "Redlining," as it came to be known, was assessed largely on racial composition.

Although many neighborhoods with a considerable number of European immigrants were redlined, virtually all black neighborhoods were excluded. Homebuyers hoping to purchase a home in a redlined neighborhood were universally denied mortgages, regardless of their financial qualifications. This severely restricted opportunities for building or even maintaining quality housing in the inner city, which in many ways set the stage for the urban blight that many Americans now associate with black neighborhoods. This action was clearly motivated by racial bias, and it was not until the 1960s that the FHA discontinued mortgage restrictions based on the racial composition of the neighborhood.[2] Subsequent policy decisions worked to trap blacks in these increasingly unattractive inner cities. Beginning in the 1950s, the suburbanization of the middle class, already under way with government-subsidized loans to veterans, was aided further by federal transportation and highway policies that included the building

of freeway networks through the hearts of many cities, which had a devastating impact on the neighborhoods of black Americans. These developments not only spurred relocation from the cities to the suburbs among better-off residents, the freeways themselves also "created barriers between the sections of the cities, walling off poor and minority neighborhoods from central business districts."[3] For instance, a number of studies have revealed how Richard J. Daley, the former mayor of Chicago, used the Interstate Highway Act of 1956 to route expressways through impoverished African American neighborhoods, resulting in even greater segregation and isolation.[4] A lasting legacy of that policy is the 14-lane Dan Ryan Expressway, which created a barrier between black and white neighborhoods.[5] At the same time, government policies such as mortgages for veterans and mortgage interest tax exemptions for developers enabled the quick, cheap production of massive amounts of tract housing[6] and drew middle-class whites into the suburbs.[7] The homes in these neighborhoods were manufactured on a large scale, using an assembly line model of production, and were arranged in carefully engineered suburban neighborhoods that included many public amenities, such as shopping centers and space for public schools. These neighborhoods represented an ideal alternative for people who were seeking to escape cramped city apartments, and were often touted as "utopian communities" that enabled people to live out the "suburban dream."

Explicit racial policies in the suburbs reinforced this segregation by allowing suburbs to separate their financial resources and municipal budgets from those of the cities. In the 19th and early 20th centuries, strong municipal services in cities were very attractive to residents of small towns and suburbs; as a result, cities tended to annex suburbs and surrounding areas. But the relations between cities and suburbs in the United States began to change following the Great Depression; the century-long influx of poor migrants who required expensive services and paid relatively little in taxes could no longer be profitably absorbed into the city economy. Annexation largely ended in the mid-20th century as suburbs began to successfully resist incorporation. Suburban communities also drew tighter boundaries through the use of zoning laws, discriminatory land-use controls, and site selection practices that made it difficult for inner-city racial minorities to access these areas because these practices were effectively used to screen out residents on the basis of race.

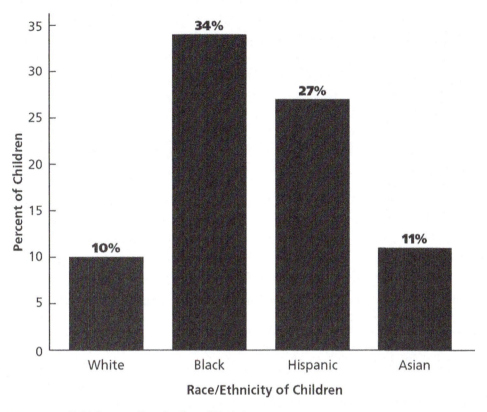

FIGURE 22.1 Child Poverty Rate by Race/Ethnicity

Source: A Call for Change, Figure 1.9 (Data from Kidscount; Population Reference Bureau, Analysis of Data from the U.S. Census Bureau, 2008 American Community Survey).

As separate political jurisdictions, suburbs also exercised a great deal of autonomy through covenants and deed restrictions. In the face of mounting pressure for integration in the 1960s, "suburbs chose to diversify by race rather than class. They retained zoning and other restrictions that allowed only affluent blacks (and in some instances Jews) to enter, thereby intensifying the concentration and isolation of the urban poor."[8] Although these policies clearly had racial connotations, they also reflected class bias and helped reinforce the exodus of white working-class and middle-class families from urban neighborhoods and the growing segregation of low-income blacks in inner-city neighborhoods.

Federal public housing policy contributed to the gradual growth of segregated black ghettos as well. The federal public housing program's policies evolved in two stages that represented two distinct styles. The Wagner-Steagall Housing Act of 1937 initiated the first stage. Concerned that the construction of public housing might depress private rent levels, groups such as the US Building and Loan

League and the National Association of Real Estate Boards successfully lobbied Congress to require, by law, that for each new unit of public housing erected, one "unsafe or unsanitary" unit of public housing must be destroyed.

The early years of the public housing program produced positive results. Initially, the program mainly served intact families temporarily displaced by the Depression or in need of housing after the end of World War II. For many of these families, public housing was the first step on the road toward economic recovery. Their stays in the projects were relatively brief because they were able to accumulate sufficient economic resources to move on to private housing.

The passage of the Housing Act of 1949 marked the beginning of the second policy stage. It instituted and funded the urban renewal program, designed to eradicate urban slums, and therefore was seemingly nonracial. However, the public housing that it created "was now meant to collect the ghetto residents left homeless by the urban renewal bulldozers."[9] A

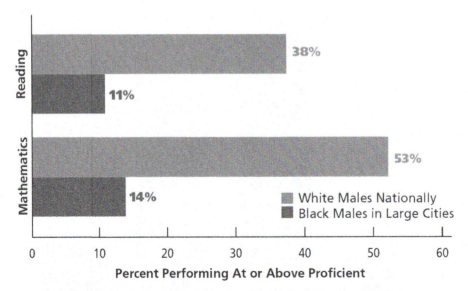

FIGURE 22.2 Gaps in Mathematics and Reading Among Forth Graders (2009)

Note: Large cities data include students from all cities in the nation with populations of 250,000 or more. National data include students attending public schools across the nation.

Source: A Call for Change, Figures 2.5 and 2.23 (Data from the U.S. Department of Education, National Assessment of Educational Progress 2009, Reading and Mathematics Assessments).

new, lower income ceiling for public housing residency was established by the Federal Public Housing Authority, and families with incomes above that ceiling were evicted, thereby restricting access to public housing to only the most economically disadvantaged segments of the population.

This change in federal housing policy coincided with the Second Great Migration of African Americans from the rural South to the cities of the Northeast and Midwest, which lasted thirty years—from 1940 to 1970. As the black urban population in the North grew, pressure mounted in white communities to keep blacks out. Suburban communities, with their restrictive covenants and special zoning laws, refused to permit the construction of public housing. And the federal government acquiesced to opposition to the construction of public housing in the neighborhoods of organized white groups in the city. Thus, units were overwhelmingly concentrated in the over-crowded and deteriorating inner-city ghettos—the poorest and least-powerful sections of cities and metropolitan areas. In short, public housing became a federally funded institution that isolated families by race and class, resulting in high concentrations of poor black families in inner-city ghettos.[10] In the last quarter of the 20th century, one of the most significant changes in

these neighborhoods was the outmigration of middle-income blacks. Before the 1970s, African American families faced extremely strong barriers when they considered moving into white neighborhoods. Not only did many experience overt discrimination in the housing market, some were violently attacked. Although even today fair-housing audits continue to reveal the existence of discrimination in the housing market, fair-housing legislation has reduced the strength of these barriers. At the same time, middle-income African Americans have increased their efforts to move from areas with concentrated black poverty to more desirable neighborhoods throughout metropolitan areas, including white neighborhoods.[11] In addition, beginning in 1980, when Ronald Reagan became president, sharp spending cuts in direct aid to cities dramatically reduced budgets for general revenue sharing (unrestricted funds that can be used for any purpose), urban mass transit, economic development assistance, urban development action grants, social service block grants, local public works, compensatory education, public service jobs, and job training. Many of these programs were designed to help disadvantaged individuals gain some traction in attaining financial security.[12] It is telling that the federal contribution was 17.5

percent of the total city budgets in 1977, but only 5.4 percent by 2000.[13] These cuts were particularly acute for older cities in the East and Midwest that largely depended on federal and state aid to fund social services for their poor population and to maintain aging infrastructure.

The decline in federal support for cities since 1980 coincided with an increase in the immigration of people from poorer countries—mainly low-skilled workers from Mexico—and whites steadily moving to the suburbs. With minorities displacing whites as a growing share of the population, the implications for the urban tax base were profound. . . .

This financial crisis left many cities ill-equipped to handle three devastating public health problems that emerged in the 1980s and disproportionately affected areas of concentrated poverty: first, the prevalence of drug trafficking and associated violent crime; second, the acquired immunodeficiency syndrome (AIDS) epidemic and its escalating public health costs; and third, the rise in the homeless population, including not only individuals, but entire families as well.[14] A number of fiscally strapped cities have watched helplessly as these problems—aggravated by the reduction of citywide social services as well as high levels of neighborhood joblessness—have reinforced the perception that cities are dangerous places to live and have perpetuated the exodus of working- and middle-class residents. Thus, while poverty and joblessness, and the social problems they generate, remain prominent in ghetto neighborhoods, many cities have fewer and fewer resources with which to combat them.

Finally, policymakers have indirectly contributed to concentrated poverty in inner-city neighborhoods with decisions that have decreased the attractiveness of low-paying jobs and accelerated the relative decline in the wages of low-income workers. In particular, in the absence of an effective labor market policy, policymakers have tolerated industry practices that undermine worker security—including the erosion of benefits and the rise of involuntary part-time employment.

In sum, federal government policies, even those that are not explicitly racial, have had a profound impact on inner-city neighborhoods. These impacts have been felt in many cities across the country, but they perhaps have been felt more in the older central cities of the Midwest and Northeast—the traditional Rust Belt—where depopulated, high-poverty areas have experienced even greater problems.

Economic Forces

Older urban areas were once the hubs of economic growth and activity, and were therefore major destinations for people in search of economic opportunity. However, the economies of many of these cities have since been eroded by complex economic transformations and shifting patterns in metropolitan development. These economic forces are typically considered non-racial—in the sense that their origins are not the direct result of actions, processes, or ideologies that explicitly reflect racial bias. Nevertheless, they have accelerated neighborhood decline in the inner city and widened gaps in race and income between cities and suburbs.[15] Since the mid-20th century, the mode of production in the United States has shifted dramatically from manufacturing to one increasingly fueled by finance, services, and technology. This shift has accompanied the technological revolution, which has transformed traditional industries and brought about changes that range from streamlined information technology to biomedical engineering.[16] In the last several decades, almost all improvements in productivity have been associated with technology and human capital, thereby drastically reducing the importance of physical capital.[17] With the increased globalization of economic activity, firms have spread their operations around the world, often relocating their production facilities to developing nations that have dramatically lower labor costs.[18] These global economic transformations have adversely affected the competitive position of many US Rust Belt cities. For example, Baltimore, Cleveland, Detroit, Philadelphia, and Pittsburgh perform poorly on employment growth, an important traditional measure of economic performance. Nationally, employment increased by 25 percent between 1991 and 2001, yet job growth in these older central cities did not exceed 3 percent.[19] With the decline in manufacturing employment in many of the nation's central cities, most of the jobs for lower-skilled workers are now in retail and service industries (for example, store cashiers, customer service representatives, fast-food servers, and custodial work). Whereas jobs in manufacturing industries typically were unionized, relatively stable, and carried higher wages, those for workers with low to modest levels of education in the retail and service industries tend to provide lower wages, be unstable, and lack the benefits and worker protections—such as workers' health insurance, medical leave, retirement benefits, and paid vacations—typically offered

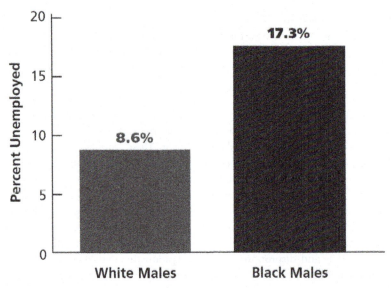

FIGURE 22.3 Unemployment Rate for White and Black Males Age 20 and Older (2nd Quarter 2010)

Source: *A Call for Change*, Figure 6.2 (Data from the U.S. Department of Labor, U.S. Bureau of Labor Statistics).

through unionization. This means that workers relegated to low-wage service and retail firms are more likely to experience hardships as they struggle to make ends meet. In addition, the local economy suffers when residents have fewer dollars to spend in their neighborhoods.[20] Beginning in the mid-1970s, the employment balance between central cities and suburbs shifted markedly to the suburbs. Since 1980, over two-thirds of employment growth has occurred outside the central city: manufacturing is now over 70 percent suburban, and wholesale and retail trade is just under 70 percent.[21] The suburbs of many central cities, developed originally as bedroom localities for commuters to the central business and manufacturing districts, have become employment centers in themselves. For example, in Baltimore, Detroit, and Philadelphia, less than 20 percent of the jobs are now located within three miles of the city center.[22] Accompanying the rise of suburban and exurban economies has been a change in commuting patterns. Increasingly, workers completely bypass the central city by commuting from one suburb to another. As Radhika Fox and Sarah Treuhaft conclude, "less than one-third of workers commute to a job in the central city and over half (55 percent) begin and end in the suburbs."[23] Sprawl and economic stagnation reduce inner-city residents' access to meaningful economic opportunities and thereby fuel the economic decline of their neighborhoods. For example, in Cleveland, although entry-level workers are concentrated in inner-city neighborhoods, 80 percent of the entry-level jobs are located in the suburbs,[24] and there is little public transportation between these neighborhoods and jobs.

In addition to the challenges in learning about and reaching jobs, there is persistent racial discrimination in hiring practices, especially for younger and less-experienced minority workers.[25] This racial factor affects black males especially seriously. Today, most of the new jobs for workers with limited education and experience are in the service sector, which includes jobs that tend to be held by women, such as waitstaff, sales clerks, and nurse's aides. Indeed, "employment rates of young black women now exceed those of young black men, even though many of these women must also care for children."[26] The shift to service jobs has resulted in a greater demand for workers who can effectively serve and relate to the consumer. In an extensive study in Chicago that my colleagues and I conducted, many employers indicated they felt that, unlike women and immigrants (who have recently expanded the labor pool for service-sector jobs), inner-city black males lack these qualities.[27] Instead, low-skilled black males are perceived as dangerous or threatening. In the past, all black men had to demonstrate was a strong back and muscles for heavy lifting and physical labor in a factory, at a construction site, or on an assembly line.

They did not have to interact with customers. Today, they have to search for work in the service sector, and employers are less likely to hire them because they have to come into contact with the public. Consequently, black male job-seekers face rising rates of rejection. This may well account for the higher dropout rate and lower academic achievement of black males in comparison with black females. Black males are far less likely than black females to see a strong relationship between their schooling and postschool employment.

With the departure of higher-income families, the least upwardly mobile in society—mainly low-income people of color—are left behind in neighborhoods with high concentrations of poverty and deteriorating physical conditions. These neighborhoods offer few jobs and typically lack basic services and amenities, such as banks, grocery stores and other retail establishments, parks, and quality transit.[28] Typically, these communities also suffer from substandard schools, many with run-down physical plants. Two of the most visible indicators of neighborhood decline are abandoned buildings and vacant lots. According to one recent report, there are 60,000 abandoned and vacant properties in Philadelphia, 40,000 in Detroit, and 26,000 in Baltimore.[29]

Cultural Forces

In addition to racial and nonracial political and economic forces, cultural forces may also contribute to or reinforce racial inequality. Two types of cultural forces are in play: (1) national views and beliefs on race, and (2) cultural traits—shared outlooks, modes of behavior, traditions, belief systems, worldviews, values, skills, preferences, styles of self-presentation, etiquette, and linguistic patterns—that emerge from patterns of intragroup interaction in settings created by discrimination and segregation and that reflect collective experiences within those settings.

Racism has historically been one of the most prominent American cultural frames and has played a major role in determining how whites perceive and act toward blacks. At its core, racism is an ideology of racial domination with two key features: (1) beliefs that one race is either biologically or culturally inferior to another, and (2) the use of such beliefs to rationalize or prescribe the way members of the "inferior" race should be treated as well as to explain their social position as a group and their collective accomplishments. Today, there is no question

that the more categorical forms of racist ideology—in particular, those that assert the biogenetic inferiority of blacks—have declined significantly, even though they still may be embedded in institutional norms and practices. For example, school tracking, the practice of grouping students of similar capability for instruction, not only tends to segregate African American students but often results in placing some black students in lower-level classes, even though they have the cultural capital—requisite skills for learning—to compete with students in higher-level classes.[30] However, there has emerged a form of what some scholars refer to as "laissez faire racism," a perception that blacks are responsible for their own economic predicament and therefore are undeserving of special government support.[31] The idea that the federal government "has a special obligation to help improve the living standards of blacks" because they "have been discriminated against for so long" was supported by only one in five whites in 2001, and has not exceeded support by more than one in four since 1975. Significantly, the lack of white support for this idea is not related to background factors such as level of education or age.

The vast majority of social scientists agree that as a national cultural frame, racism, in its various forms, has had harmful effects on African Americans as a group. Indeed, considerable research has been devoted to the effects of racism in American society. Distinct cultural frames in the inner city have not only been shaped by race and poverty, but in turn often shape responses to poverty, including responses that may contribute to the perpetuation of poverty.

I have researched how several factors determine the extent to which communities, as areas bounded by place, differ in outlook and behavior.[32] These factors include the degree to which the community is socially isolated from the broader society; the material assets or resources controlled by members of the community; the benefits and privileges the community members derive from these resources; their accumulated cultural experiences from current as well as historical, political, and economic arrangements; and the influence members of the community wield because of these arrangements.

Culture is closely intertwined with social relations in the sense of providing tools (skills, habits, and styles) and creating constraints (restrictions on behavior or outlooks) in patterns of social interaction.[33] These constraints include cultural frames (shared visions of human behavior) developed over time through the processes of ingroup meaning making (shared views on how the world works) and decision making (choices that reflect shared definitions of how the world works)—for example, in the inner-city ghetto cultural frames define issues of trust/street smarts and "acting black" or "acting white"—that lead to observable group characteristics.

One of the effects of living in racially segregated neighborhoods is exposure to group-specific cultural traits (cultural frames, orientations, habits, and worldviews as well as styles of behavior and particular skills) that emerged from patterns of racial exclusion and that may not be conducive to social mobility. For example, research has found that some groups in the inner city put a high value on "street smarts," the behaviors and actions that keep them safe in areas of high crime.[34] Street smarts may be an adaptation to living in unsafe neighborhoods. In this environment, it is wise to avoid eye contact with strangers and keep to yourself. This mindset may also lead someone to approach new situations with a certain level of skepticism or mistrust. Although such an approach is logical and smart in an unsafe neighborhood, the same behavior can be interpreted as antisocial in another setting. Moreover, this street-smart behavior may, in some cases, prevent individuals from performing well on a job interview, creating a perception that they are not desirable job candidates.

Elijah Anderson finds that for some young men, the draw of the street is so powerful that they cannot avail themselves of legitimate employment opportunities when they become available. Likewise, Sudhir Venkatesh maintains that adherence to the code of shady dealings impedes social mobility.[35] The "underground economy enables people to survive but can lead to alienation from the wider world," he states.[36] For example, none of the work experience accrued in the informal economy can be listed on a resume for job searches in the formal labor market, and time invested in underground work reduces time devoted to accumulating skills or contacts for legitimate employment.

For those committed to fighting inequality, especially those involved in multiracial coalition politics, the lesson from this discussion of key social, political, economic, and cultural forces is to fashion a new agenda that gives more scrutiny to both racial and nonracial policies. Given our devastating recent recession and slow, jobless recovery, it is especially important to scrutinize fiscal, monetary, and trade policies that may have long-term consequences for our national and regional economies.

We must ameliorate the primary problem feeding concentrated poverty: inner-city joblessness. The ideal solution would be economic policies that produce a tight labor market—that is, one in which there are ample jobs for all applicants. More than any other group, low-skilled workers depend upon a strong economy, particularly a sustained tight labor market.

This new agenda should also include an even sharper focus on traditional efforts to fight poverty, to ensure that the benefits from any economic upturn are widely shared among the poor and that they become less vulnerable to downward swings in the economy. I refer especially to the following:

• combating racial discrimination in employment, which is especially devastating during slack labor markets;

• revitalizing poor urban neighborhoods, including eliminating abandoned buildings and vacant lots to make them more attractive for economic investment that would help improve the quality of life and create jobs in the neighborhood;

• promoting job training programs to enhance employment opportunities for ghetto residents;

• improving public education to prepare inner-city youngsters for higher-paying and stable jobs in the new economy; and

• strengthening unions to provide the higher wages, worker protections, and benefits typically absent from low-skilled jobs in retail and service industries.

• In short, this new agenda would reflect a multipronged approach that attacks inner-city poverty on various levels, an approach that recognizes the complex array of factors that have contributed to the crystallization of concentrated urban poverty and limited the life chances of so many inner-city residents.

NOTES

1. Paul A. Jargowsky, "Ghetto Poverty among Blacks in the 1980s," *Journal of Policy Analysis and Management* 13, no. 2 (Spring 1994): 288–310.

2. Michael B. Katz, "Reframing the 'Underclass' Debate," in *The "Underclass" Debate: Views from History*, ed. Michael B. Katz (Princeton, NJ: Princeton University Press, 1993), 440–478; David W. Bartelt, "Housing the 'Underclass,'" in *The "Underclass" Debate: Views from History*, ed. Michael B. Katz (Princeton, NJ: Princeton University Press, 1993), 118–157; Thomas J. Sugrue, "The Structure of Urban Poverty: The Reorganization of Space and Work in Three Periods of American History," in *The*

"Underclass" Debate: Views from History, ed. Michael B. Katz (Princeton, NJ: Princeton University Press, 1993), 85–117; and Robin D. G. Kelley, "The Black Poor and the Politics of Opposition in a New South City, 1929–1970," in *The "Underclass" Debate: Views from History,* ed. Michael B. Katz (Princeton, NJ: Princeton University Press, 1993), 293–333.

3. Katz, "Reframing the 'Underclass' Debate," 462. Also see Bartelt, "Housing the 'Underclass'"; Sugrue, "The Structure of Urban Poverty"; and Martin Anderson, *The Federal Bulldozer: A Critical Analysis of Urban Renewal, 1949–1962* (Cambridge, MA: MIT Press, 1964).

4. Raymond A. Mohl, "Planned Destruction: The Interstates and Central City Housing," in *From Tenements to the Taylor Homes: In Search of an Urban Housing Policy in Twentieth-Century America,* ed. John F. Bauman, Roger Biles, and Kristin M. Szylvian (University Park, PA: Pennsylvania State University Press, 2000), 226–245; Adam Cohen and Elizabeth Taylor, *American Pharaoh: Mayor Richard J. Daley; His Battle for Chicago and the Nation* (Boston: Little, Brown, 2000); and Arnold R. Hirsch, *Making the Second Ghetto: Race and Housing in Chicago, 1940–1960* (Cambridge, MA: Cambridge University Press, 1983).

5. Cohen and Taylor, *American Pharaoh.*

6. Robert J. Sampson and William Julius Wilson, "Toward a Theory of Race, Crime, and Urban Inequality," in *Crime and Inequality,* ed. John Hagan and Ruth D. Peterson (Stanford, CA: Stanford University Press, 1995), 37–54.

7. Katz, "Reframing the 'Underclass' Debate."

8. Katz, "Reframing the 'Underclass' Debate," 461–462. On the history of suburbs in America, see Kenneth T. Jackson, *Crabgrass Frontier: The Suburbanization of the United States* (New York: Oxford University Press, 1985). For a good discussion of the effects of housing discrimination on the living conditions, education, and employment of urban minorities, see John Yinger, *Closed Doors, Opportunities Lost: The Continuing Costs of Housing Discrimination* (New York: Russell Sage Foundation, 1995).

9. Mark Condon, "Public Housing, Crime and the Urban Labor Market: A Study of Black Youth in Chicago," Working Paper Series (Cambridge, MA: Malcolm Wiener Center, John F. Kennedy School of Government, Harvard University, 1991), 4.

10. Sampson and Wilson, "Toward a Theory of Race." Also see Bartelt, "Housing the 'Underclass'"; Kelley, "The Black Poor and the Politics of Opposition"; Sugrue, "The Structure of Urban Poverty"; Hirsch, *Making the Second Ghetto*; and John F. Bauman, Norman P. Hummon, and Edward K. Muller, "Public Housing, Isolation, and the Urban Underclass," *Journal of Urban History* 17, no. 3 (May 1991): 264–292.

11. Lincoln Quillian, "Migration Patterns and the Growth of High-Poverty Neighborhoods, 1970–1990," *American Journal of Sociology* 105, no. 1 (July 1999): 1–37.

12. See Demetrios Caraley, "Washington Abandons the Cities," *Political Science Quarterly* 107, no. 1 (Spring 1992): 1–30.

13. Bruce A. Wallin, *Budgeting for Basics: The Changing Landscape of City Finances* (Washington, DC: Brookings Institution Metropolitan Policy Program, August 2005).

14. Caraley, "Washington Abandons the Cities."

15. Radhika K. Fox and Sarah Treuhaft, *Shared Prosperity, Stronger Regions: An Agenda for Rebuilding America's Older Core Cities* (Oakland, CA: PolicyLink, 2006).

16. Fox and Treuhaft, *Shared Prosperity*; and Bill Joy, "Why the Future Doesn't Need Us," *Wired* (April 2000): 238–262.

17. William Julius Wilson, *When Work Disappears: The World of the New Urban Poor* (New York: Alfred A. Knopf, 1996).

18. Fox and Treuhaft, *Shared Prosperity.*

19. Fox and Treuhaft, *Shared Prosperity.*

20. Fox and Treuhaft, *Shared Prosperity*; and Wilson, *When Work Disappears.*

21. U.S. Department of Housing and Urban Development, *The State of the Cities.*

22. Fox and Treuhaft, *Shared Prosperity.*

23. Fox and Treuhaft, *Shared Prosperity,* 32.

24. Fox and Treuhaft, *Shared Prosperity.*

25. See, for example, Wilson, *When Work Disappears*; Joleen Kirschenman and Kathryn M. Neckerman, "'We'd Love to Hire Them, But . . . ': The Meaning of Race for Employers," in *The Urban Underclass,* ed. Christopher Jencks and Paul E. Peterson (Washington, DC: Brookings Institution, 1991), 203–234; Kathryn M. Neckerman and Joleen Kirschenman, "Hiring Strategies, Racial Bias, and Inner-City Workers," *Social Problems* 38, no. 4 (November 1991): 433–447; and Harry J. Holzer, *What Employers Want: Job Prospects for Less-Educated Workers* (New York: Russell Sage, 1995).

26. Harry J. Holzer, Paul Offner, and Elaine Sorensen, "What Explains the Continuing Decline in Labor Force Activity among Young Black Men?" (paper presented for Color Lines Conference, Harvard University, August 30, 2003).

27. Wilson, *When Work Disappears.*

28. William Julius Wilson, *The Truly Disadvantaged: The Inner City, the Underclass, and Public Policy* (Chicago: University of Chicago Press, 1990); Wilson, *When Work Disappears*; and Fox and Treuhaft, *Shared Prosperity.*

29. Fox and Treuhaft, *Shared Prosperity.*

30. For a review of the literature on school tracking, see Janese Free, "Race and School Tracking: From a Social Psychological Perspective" (paper presented at the annual meeting of the American Sociological Association, San Francisco, CA, August 14, 2004).

31. Lawrence Bobo, James R. Kluegel, and Ryan A. Smith, "Laissez-Faire Racism: The Crystallization of a Kinder, Gentler, Antiblack Ideology," in *Racial Attitudes in the 1990s: Continuity and Change,* ed. Steven A. Tuch and Jack K. Martin (Westport, CT: Praeger, 1997), 15–44.

32. Wilson, *When Work Disappears.*

33. Charles Tilly, *Durable Inequality* (Berkeley, CA: University of California Press, 1998).

34. Elijah Anderson, *Code of the Street: Decency, Violence, and the Moral Life of the Inner City* (New York: W. W. Norton, 1999).

35. Anderson, *Code of the Street*; and Sudhir Alladi Venkatesh, *Off the Books: The Underground Economy of the Urban Poor* (Cambridge, MA: Harvard University Press, 2006).

36. Venkatesh, *Off the Books*, 385. For another excellent study of how activities in the underground economy can adversely affect inner-city residents, see Loïc Wacquant, "Inside the Zone: The Art of the Hustler in the Black American Ghetto," *Theory, Culture, and Society* 15, no. 2 (1998): 1–36.

23. Douglas S. Massey and Nancy A. Denton*

American Apartheid: Segregation and the Making of the Underclass

It is quite simple. As soon as there is a group area then all your uncertainties are removed and that is, after all, the primary purpose of this bill [requiring racial segregation in housing].

—Minister of the Interior, Union of
South Africa legislative debate on the
Group Areas Act of 1950

During the 1970s and 1980s a word disappeared from the American vocabulary.[1] It was not in the speeches of politicians decrying the multiple ills besetting American cities. It was not spoken by government officials responsible for administering the nation's social programs. It was not mentioned by journalists reporting on the rising tide of homelessness, drugs, and violence in urban America. It was not discussed by foundation executives and think-tank experts proposing new programs for unemployed parents and unwed mothers. It was not articulated by civil rights leaders speaking out against

the persistence of racial inequality; and it was nowhere to be found in the thousands of pages written by social scientists on the urban underclass. The word was segregation.

Most Americans vaguely realize that urban America is still a residentially segregated society, but few appreciate the depth of black segregation or the degree to which it is maintained by ongoing institutional arrangements and contemporary individual actions. They view segregation as an unfortunate holdover from a racist past, one that is fading progressively over time. If racial residential segregation persists, they reason, it is only because civil rights laws passed during the 1960s have not had enough time to work or because many blacks still prefer to live in black neighborhoods. The residential segregation of blacks is viewed charitably as a "natural" outcome of impersonal social and economic forces, the same forces that produced Italian and Polish neighborhoods in the past and that yield Mexican and Korean areas today.

But black segregation is not comparable to the limited and transient segregation experienced by other racial and ethnic groups, now or in the past. No group in the history of the United States has ever experienced the sustained high level of residential segregation that has been imposed on blacks in large American cities for the past fifty years. This extreme racial isolation did not just happen; it was manufactured by whites through a series of self-conscious actions and purposeful institutional arrangements that continue today. Not only is the depth of black segregation unprecedented and utterly unique compared with that of other groups, but it shows little sign of change with the passage of time or improvements in socioeconomic status.

If policymakers, scholars, and the public have been reluctant to acknowledge segregation's persistence, they have likewise been blind to its consequences for American blacks. Residential segregation is not a neutral fact; it systematically undermines the social and economic well-being of blacks in the United States. Because of racial segregation, a significant share of black America is condemned to experience a social environment where poverty and joblessness are the norm, where a majority of children are born out of wedlock, where most families are on welfare, where educational failure prevails, and where social and physical deterioration abound. Through prolonged exposure to such an environment, black chances for social and economic success are drastically reduced.

Deleterious neighborhood conditions are built into the structure of the black community. They occur because segregation concentrates poverty to build a set of mutually reinforcing and self-feeding spirals of decline into black neighborhoods. When economic dislocations deprive a segregated group of employment and increase its rate of poverty, socio-economic deprivation inevitably becomes more concentrated in neighborhoods where that group lives. The damaging social consequences that follow from increased poverty are spatially concentrated as well, creating uniquely disadvantaged environments that become progressively isolated—geographically, socially, and economically—from the rest of society.

The effect of segregation on black well-being is structural, not individual. Residential segregation lies beyond the ability of any individual to change; it constrains black life chances irrespective of personal traits, individual motivations, or private achievements. For the past twenty years, this fundamental fact has been swept under the rug by policymakers, scholars, and theorists of the urban underclass. Segregation is the missing link in prior attempts to understand the plight of the urban poor. As long as blacks continue to be segregated in American cities, the United States cannot be called a race-blind society.

The Forgotten Factor

The present myopia regarding segregation is all the more startling because it once figured prominently in theories of racial inequality. Indeed, the ghetto was once seen as central to black subjugation in the United States. In 1944 Gunnar Myrdal wrote in *An American Dilemma* that residential segregation "is basic in a mechanical sense. It exerts its influence in an indirect and impersonal way: because Negro people do not live near white people, they cannot . . . associate with each other in the many activities founded on common neighborhood. Residential segregation . . . becomes reflected in uni-racial schools, hospitals, and other institutions" and creates "an artificial city . . . that permits any prejudice on the part of public officials to be freely vented on Negroes without hurting whites."[2] Kenneth B. Clark, who worked with Gunnar Myrdal as a student and later applied his research skills in the landmark *Brown v. Topeka* school integration case, placed residential segregation at the heart of the US system of racial oppression. In *Dark Ghetto,* written in 1965, he argued that "the dark ghetto's invisible walls have been erected by the white society, by those who have power, both to confine those who have *no* power and to perpetuate their powerlessness. The dark ghettos are social, political, educational, and—above all—economic colonies. Their inhabitants are subject peoples, victims of the greed, cruelty, insensitivity, guilt, and fear of their masters."[3] Public recognition of segregation's role in perpetuating racial inequality was galvanized in the late 1960s by the riots that erupted in the nation's ghettos. In their aftermath, President Lyndon B. Johnson appointed a commission chaired by Governor Otto Kerner of Illinois to identify the causes of the violence and to propose policies to prevent its recurrence. The Kerner Commission released its report in March 1968 with the shocking admonition that the United States was "moving toward two societies, one black, one white—separate and unequal."[4] Prominent among the causes that the commission identified for this growing racial inequality was residential segregation.

In stark, blunt language, the Kerner Commission informed white Americans that "discrimination and segregation have long permeated much of American life; they now threaten the future of every American."[5] "Segregation and poverty have created in the racial ghetto a destructive environment totally unknown to most white Americans. What white Americans have never fully understood—but what the Negro can never forget—is that white society is deeply implicated in the ghetto. White institutions created it, white institutions maintain it, and white society condones it."[6] The report argued that to continue present policies was "to make permanent the division of our country into two societies; one, largely Negro and poor, located in the central cities; the other, predominantly white and affluent, located in the suburbs."[7] Commission members rejected a strategy of ghetto enrichment coupled with abandonment of efforts to integrate, an approach they saw "as another way of choosing a permanently divided country."[8] Rather, they insisted that the only reasonable choice for America was "a policy which combines ghetto enrichment with programs designed to encourage integration of substantial numbers of Negroes into the society outside the ghetto."[9] America chose differently. Following the passage of the Fair Housing Act in 1968, the problem of housing discrimination was declared solved, and residential segregation dropped off the national agenda. Civil rights leaders stopped pressing for the enforcement of open housing, political leaders increasingly debated employment and educational policies rather than housing integration, and academicians focused their theoretical scrutiny on everything from culture to family structure, to institutional racism, to federal welfare systems. Few people spoke of racial segregation as a problem or acknowledged its persisting consequences. By the end of the 1970s, residential segregation became the forgotten factor in American race relations.[10] While public discourse on race and poverty became more acrimonious and more focused on divisive issues such as school busing, racial quotas, welfare, and affirmative action, conditions in the nation's ghettos steadily deteriorated.[11] By the end of the 1970s, the image of poor minority families mired in an endless cycle of unemployment, unwed childbearing, illiteracy, and dependency had coalesced into a compelling and powerful concept: the urban underclass.[12] In the view of many middle-class whites, inner cities had come to house a large population of poorly educated single mothers and jobless men—mostly black and Puerto Rican—who were unlikely to exit poverty and become self-sufficient. In the ensuing national debate on the causes for this persistent poverty, four theoretical explanations gradually emerged: culture, racism, economics, and welfare.

Cultural explanations for the underclass can be traced to the work of Oscar Lewis, who identified a "culture of poverty" that he felt promoted patterns of behavior inconsistent with socioeconomic advancement.[13] According to Lewis, this culture originated in endemic unemployment and chronic social immobility, and provided an ideology that allowed poor people to cope with feelings of hopelessness and despair that arose because their chances for socioeconomic success were remote. In individuals, this culture was typified by a lack of impulse control, a strong present-time orientation, and little ability to defer gratification. Among families, it yielded an absence of childhood, an early initiation into sex, a prevalence of free marital unions, and a high incidence of abandonment of mothers and children.

Although Lewis explicitly connected the emergence of these cultural patterns to structural conditions in society, he argued that once the culture of poverty was established, it became an independent cause of persistent poverty. This idea was further elaborated in 1965 by the Harvard sociologist and then Assistant Secretary of Labor Daniel Patrick Moynihan, who in a confidential report to the President focused on the relationship between male unemployment, family instability, and the intergenerational transmission of poverty, a process he labeled a "tangle of pathology."[14] He warned that because of the structural absence of employment in the ghetto, the black family was disintegrating in a way that threatened the fabric of community life.

When these ideas were transmitted through the press, both popular and scholarly, the connection between culture and economic structure was somehow lost, and the argument was popularly perceived to be that "people were poor because they had a defective culture." This position was later explicitly adopted by the conservative theorist Edward Banfield, who argued that lower-class culture—with its limited time horizon, impulsive need for gratification, and psychological self-doubt—was primarily responsible for persistent urban poverty.[15] He believed that these cultural traits were largely imported, arising primarily because cities attracted lower-class migrants.

The culture-of-poverty argument was strongly criticized by liberal theorists as a self-serving ideology that "blamed the victim."[16] In the ensuing wave of reaction, black families were viewed not as weak but, on the contrary, as resilient and well-adapted survivors in an oppressive and racially prejudiced society.[17] Black disadvantages were attributed not to a defective culture but to the persistence of institutional racism in the United States. According to theorists of the underclass such as Douglas Glasgow and Alphonso Pinkney, the black urban underclass came about because deeply imbedded racist practices within American institutions—particularly schools and the economy—effectively kept blacks poor and dependent.[18] As the debate on culture versus racism ground to a halt during the late 1970s, conservative theorists increasingly captured public attention by focusing on a third possible cause of poverty: government welfare policy. According to Charles Murray, the creation of the underclass was rooted in the liberal welfare state.[19] Federal antipoverty programs altered the incentives governing the behavior of poor men and women, reducing the desirability of marriage, increasing the benefits of unwed childbearing, lowering the attractiveness of menial labor, and ultimately resulted in greater poverty.

A slightly different attack on the welfare state was launched by Lawrence Mead, who argued that it was not the generosity but the permissiveness of the US welfare system that was at fault.[20] Jobless men and unwed mothers should be required to display "good citizenship" before being supported by the state. By not requiring anything of the poor, Mead argued, the welfare state undermined their independence and competence, thereby perpetuating their poverty.

This conservative reasoning was subsequently attacked by liberal social scientists, led principally by the sociologist William Julius Wilson, who had long been arguing for the increasing importance of class over race in understanding the social and economic problems facing blacks.[21] In his 1987 book *The Truly Disadvantaged*, Wilson argued that persistent urban poverty stemmed primarily from the structural transformation of the inner-city economy.[22] The decline of manufacturing, the suburbanization of employment, and the rise of a low-wage service sector dramatically reduced the number of city jobs that paid wages sufficient to support a family, which led to high rates of joblessness among minorities and a shrinking pool of "marriageable" men (those financially able to support a family). Marriage thus became less attractive to poor women, unwed childbearing increased, and female-headed families proliferated. Blacks suffered disproportionately from these trends because, owing to past discrimination, they were concentrated in locations and occupations particularly affected by economic restructuring.

Wilson argued that these economic changes were accompanied by an increase in the spatial concentration of poverty within black neighborhoods. This new geography of poverty, he felt, was enabled by the civil rights revolution of the 1960s, which provided middle-class blacks with new opportunities outside the ghetto.[23] The out-migration of middle-class families from ghetto areas left behind a destitute community lacking the institutions, resources, and values necessary for success in post-industrial society. The urban underclass thus arose from a complex interplay of civil rights policy, economic restructuring, and a historical legacy of discrimination.

Theoretical concepts such as the culture of poverty, institutional racism, welfare disincentives, and structural economic change have all been widely debated. None of these explanations, however, considers residential segregation to be an important contributing cause of urban poverty and the underclass. In their principal works, Murray and Mead do not mention segregation at all;[24] and Wilson refers to racial segregation only as a historical legacy from the past, not as an outcome that is institutionally supported and actively created today.[25] Although Lewis mentions segregation sporadically in his writings, it is not assigned a central role in the set of structural factors responsible for the culture of poverty, and Banfield ignores it entirely. Glasgow, Pinkney, and

other theorists of institutional racism mention the ghetto frequently, but generally call not for residential desegregation but for race-specific policies to combat the effects of discrimination in the schools and labor markets. In general, then, contemporary theorists of urban poverty do not see high levels of black-white segregation as particularly relevant to understanding the underclass or alleviating urban poverty.[26] The purpose of this book is to redirect the focus of public debate back to issues of race and racial segregation, and to suggest that they should be fundamental to thinking about the status of black Americans and the origins of the urban underclass. Our quarrel is less with any of the prevailing theories of urban poverty than with their systematic failure to consider the important role that segregation has played in mediating, exacerbating, and ultimately amplifying the harmful social and economic processes they treat.

We join earlier scholars in rejecting the view that poor urban blacks have an autonomous "culture of poverty" that explains their failure to achieve socioeconomic success in American society. We argue instead that residential segregation has been instrumental in creating a structural niche within which a deleterious set of attitudes and behaviors—a culture of segregation—has arisen and flourished. Segregation created the structural conditions for the emergence of an oppositional culture that devalues work, schooling, and marriage and that stresses attitudes and behaviors that are antithetical and often hostile to success in the larger economy. Although poor black neighborhoods still contain many people who lead conventional, productive lives, their example has been overshadowed in recent years by a growing concentration of poor, welfare-dependent families that is an inevitable result of residential segregation.

We readily agree with Douglas, Pinkney, and others that racial discrimination is widespread and may even be institutionalized within large sectors of American society, including the labor market, the educational system, and the welfare bureaucracy. We argue, however, that this view of black subjugation is incomplete without understanding the special role that residential segregation plays in enabling all other forms of racial oppression. Residential segregation is the institutional apparatus that supports other racially discriminatory processes and binds them together into a coherent and uniquely effective system of racial subordination. Until the black ghetto is dismantled as a basic institution of American urban life, progress ameliorating racial inequality in other arenas will be slow, fitful, and incomplete.

We also agree with William Wilson's basic argument that the structural transformation of the urban economy undermined economic supports for the black community during the 1970s and 1980s.[27] We argue, however, that in the absence of segregation, these structural changes would not have produced the disastrous social and economic outcomes observed in inner cities during these decades. Although rates of black poverty were driven up by the economic dislocations Wilson identifies, it was segregation that confined the increased deprivation to a small number of densely settled, tightly packed, and geographically isolated areas.

Wilson also argues that concentrated poverty arose because the civil rights revolution allowed middle-class blacks to move out of the ghetto. Although we remain open to the possibility that class-selective migration did occur,[28] we argue that concentrated poverty would have happened during the 1970s with or without black middle-class migration. Our principal objection to Wilson's focus on middle-class out-migration is not that it did not occur, but that it is misdirected: focusing on the flight of the black middle class deflects attention from the real issue, which is the limitation of black residential options through segregation.

Middle-class households—whether they are black, Mexican, Italian, Jewish, or Polish—always try to escape the poor. But only blacks must attempt their escape within a highly segregated, racially segmented housing market. Because of segregation, middle-class blacks are less able to escape than other groups, and as a result are exposed to more poverty. At the same time, because of segregation, no one will move into a poor black neighborhood except other poor blacks. Thus both middle-class blacks and poor blacks lose compared with the poor and middle class of other groups: poor blacks live under unrivaled concentrations of poverty and affluent blacks live in neighborhoods that are far less advantageous than those experienced by the middle class of other groups.

Finally, we concede Murray's general point that federal welfare policies are linked to the rise of the urban underclass, but we disagree with his specific hypothesis that generous welfare payments, by themselves, discouraged employment, encouraged unwed childbearing, undermined the strength of the family, and thereby caused persistent poverty.[29] We argue instead that welfare payments were only harmful to the socioeconomic well-being of groups that were residentially segregated. As poverty rates rose among blacks in response to the economic dislocations of the 1970s and 1980s, so did the use of welfare programs. Because of racial segregation, however, the higher levels of welfare receipt were confined to a small number of isolated, all-black neighborhoods. By promoting the spatial concentration of welfare use, therefore, segregation created a residential environment within which welfare dependency was the norm, leading to the intergenerational transmission and broader perpetuation of urban poverty.

Coming to Terms with American Apartheid

Our fundamental argument is that racial segregation—and its characteristic institutional form, the black ghetto—are the key structural factors responsible for the perpetuation of black poverty in the United States. Residential segregation is the principal organizational feature of American society that is responsible for the creation of the urban underclass. . . . It can be shown that any increase in the poverty rate of a residentially segregated group leads to an immediate and automatic increase in the geographic concentration of poverty. When the rate of minority poverty is increased under conditions of high segregation, all of the increase is absorbed by a small number of neighborhoods. When the same increase in poverty occurs in an integrated group, the added poverty is spread evenly throughout the urban area, and the neighborhood environment that group members face does not change much.

During the 1970s and 1980s, therefore, when urban economic restructuring and inflation drove up rates of black and Hispanic poverty in many urban areas, underclass communities were created only where increased minority poverty coincided with a high degree of segregation—principally in older metropolitan areas of the northeast and the midwest. Among Hispanics, only Puerto Ricans developed underclass communities, because only they were highly segregated; and this high degree of segregation is directly attributable to the fact that a large proportion of Puerto Ricans are of African origin.

The interaction of intense segregation and high poverty leaves black neighborhoods extremely vulnerable to fluctuations in the urban economy, because any dislocation that causes an upward shift in black poverty rates will also produce a rapid change in the concentration of poverty and, hence, a dramatic shift in the social and economic composition of black neighborhoods. The concentration of poverty, for example, is associated with the wholesale withdrawal of commercial institutions and the deterioration or elimination of goods and services distributed through the market.

Neighborhoods, of course, are dynamic and constantly changing, and given the high rates of residential turnover characteristic of contemporary American cities, their well-being depends to a great extent on the characteristics and actions of their residents. Decisions taken by one actor affect the subsequent decisions of others in the neighborhood. In this way isolated actions affect the well-being of the community and alter the stability of the neighborhood.

Because of this feedback between individual and collective behavior, neighborhood stability is characterized by a series of thresholds, beyond which various self-perpetuating processes of decay take hold. Above these thresholds, each actor who makes a decision that undermines neighborhood well-being makes it increasingly likely that other actors will do the same. Each property owner who decides not to invest in upkeep and maintenance, for example, lowers the incentive for others to maintain their properties. Likewise, each new crime promotes psychological and physical withdrawal from public life, which reduces vigilance within the neighborhood and undermines the capacity for collective organization, making additional criminal activity more likely.

Segregation increases the susceptibility of neighborhoods to these spirals of decline. During periods of economic dislocation, a rising concentration of black poverty is associated with the simultaneous concentration of other negative social and economic conditions. Given the high levels of racial segregation characteristic of American urban areas, increases in black poverty, such as those observed during the 1970s, can only lead to a concentration of housing abandonment, crime, and social disorder, pushing poor black neighborhoods beyond the threshold of stability.

By building physical decay, crime, and social disorder into the residential structure of black communities, segregation creates a harsh and extremely disadvantaged environment to which ghetto blacks must adapt. In concentrating poverty, moreover, segregation also concentrates conditions such as drug use, joblessness, welfare dependency, teenage childbearing, and unwed parenthood, producing a social context where these conditions are not only common but the norm. By adapting to this social environment, ghetto dwellers evolve a set of behaviors, attitudes, and expectations that are sharply at variance with those common in the rest of American society.

As a direct result of the high degree of racial and class isolation created by segregation, for example, Black English has become progressively more distant from Standard American English, and its speakers are at a clear disadvantage in US schools and labor markets. Moreover, the isolation and intense poverty of the ghetto provides a supportive structural niche for the emergence of an "oppositional culture" that inverts the values of middle-class society. Anthropologists have found that young people in the ghetto experience strong peer pressure not to succeed in school, which severely limits their prospects for social mobility in the larger society. Quantitative research shows that growing up in a ghetto neighborhood increases the likelihood of dropping out of high school, reduces the probability of attending college, lowers the likelihood of employment, reduces income earned as an adult, and increases the risk of teenage childbearing and unwed pregnancy.

Segregation also has profound political consequences for blacks, because it so isolates them geographically that they are the only ones who benefit from public expenditures in their neighborhoods. The relative integration of most ethnic groups means that jobs or services allocated to them will generally benefit several other groups at the same time. Integration thus creates a basis for political coalitions and pluralist politics, and most ethnic groups that seek public resources are able to find coalition partners because other groups can anticipate sharing the benefits. That blacks are the only ones to benefit from resources allocated to the ghetto—and are the only ones harmed when resources are removed—makes it difficult for them to find partners for political coalitions. Although segregation paradoxically makes it easier for blacks to elect representatives, it limits their political influence and marginalizes them within the American polity. Segregation prevents blacks from participating in pluralist politics based on mutual self-interest.

Because of the close connection between social and spatial mobility, segregation also perpetuates poverty. One of the primary means by which individuals improve their life chances—and those of their children—is by moving to neighborhoods with higher home values, safer streets, higher-quality schools, and better services. As groups move up the socioeconomic ladder, they typically move up the residential hierarchy as well, and in doing so they not only improve their standard of living but also enhance their chances for future success. Barriers to spatial mobility are barriers to social mobility, and by confining blacks to a small set of relatively disadvantaged neighborhoods, segregation constitutes a very powerful impediment to black socioeconomic progress.

Despite the obvious deleterious consequences of black spatial isolation, policymakers have not paid much attention to segregation as a contributing cause of urban poverty and have not taken effective steps to dismantle the ghetto. Indeed, for most of the past two decades, public policies tolerated and even supported the perpetuation of segregation in American urban areas. Although many political initiatives were launched to combat discrimination and prejudice in the housing and banking industries, each legislative or judicial act was fought tenaciously by a powerful array of people who believed in or benefited from the status quo.

Although a comprehensive open housing bill finally passed Congress under unusual circumstances in 1968, it was stripped of its enforcement provisions as its price of enactment, yielding a Fair Housing Act that was structurally flawed and all but doomed to fail. As documentation of the law's defects accumulated in multiple congressional hearings, government reports, and scholarly studies, little was done to repair the situation until 1988, when a series of scandals and political errors by the Reagan administration finally enabled a significant strengthening of federal antidiscrimination law.

Yet even more must be done to prevent the permanent bifurcation of the United States into black and white societies that are separate and unequal. As of 1990, levels of racial segregation were still extraordinarily high in the nation's large urban areas, particularly those of the north. Segregation has remained high because fair housing enforcement relies too heavily on the private efforts of individual victims of discrimination. Whereas the processes that perpetuate segregation are entrenched and institutionalized, fair housing enforcement is individual, sporadic, and confined to a small number of isolated cases.

As long as the Fair Housing Act is enforced individually rather than systemically, it is unlikely to be effective in overcoming the structural arrangements that support segregation and sustain the ghetto. Until the government throws its considerable institutional weight behind efforts to dismantle the ghetto, racial segregation will persist. . . .

Ultimately, however, dismantling the ghetto and ending the long reign of racial segregation will require more than specific bureaucratic reforms; it requires a moral commitment that white America has historically lacked. The segregation of American blacks was no historical accident; it was brought about by actions and practices that had the passive acceptance, if not the active support, of most whites in the United States. Although America's apartheid may not be rooted in the legal strictures of its South African relative, it is no less effective in perpetuating racial inequality, and whites are no less culpable for the socioeconomic deprivation that results.

As in South Africa, residential segregation in the United States provides a firm basis for a broader system of racial injustice. The geographic isolation of Africans within a narrowly circumscribed portion of the urban environment—whether African townships or American ghettos—forces blacks to live under extraordinarily harsh conditions and to endure a social world where poverty is endemic, infrastructure is inadequate, education is lacking, families are fragmented, and crime and violence are rampant.[30] Moreover, segregation confines these unpleasant by-products of racial oppression to an isolated portion of the urban geography far removed from the experience of most whites. Resting on a foundation of segregation, apartheid not only denies blacks their rights as citizens but forces them to bear the social costs of their own victimization.

Although Americans have been quick to criticize the apartheid system of South Africa, they have been reluctant to acknowledge the consequences of their own institutionalized system of racial separation. The topic of segregation has virtually disappeared from public policy debates; it has vanished from the list of issues on the civil rights agenda; and it has been ignored by social scientists spinning endless theories of the underclass. Residential segregation has become the forgotten factor of American race relations, a minor footnote in the ongoing debate on the urban underclass. Until policymakers, social scientists, and private citizens recognize the crucial role of America's own apartheid in perpetuating urban poverty and racial injustice, the United States will remain a deeply divided and very troubled society.[31]

NOTES

1. Epigraph from Edgar H. Brookes, *Apartheid: A Documentary Study of Modern South Africa* (London: Routledge and Kegan Paul, 1968), p. 142.

2. Gunnar Myrdal, *An American Dilemma,* vol. 1 (New York: Harper and Brothers, 1944), p. 618; see also Walter A. Jackson, *Gunnar Myrdal and America's Conscience* (Chapel Hill: University of North Carolina Press, 1990), pp. 88–271.

3. Kenneth B. Clark, *Dark Ghetto: Dilemmas of Social Power* (New York: Harper and Row, 1965), p. 11.

4. U.S. National Advisory Commission on Civil Disorders, *The Kerner Report* (New York: Pantheon Books, 1988), p. 1.

5. Ibid.

6. Ibid., p. 2.

7. Ibid., p. 22.

8. Ibid.

9. Ibid.

10. A few scholars attempted to keep the Kerner Commission's call for desegregation alive, but their voices have largely been unheeded in the ongoing debate. Thomas Pettigrew has continued to assert the central importance of residential segregation, calling it the "linchpin" of American race relations; see "Racial Change and Social Policy," *Annals of the American Academy of Political and Social Science* 441 (1979):114–31. Gary Orfield has repeatedly pointed out segregation's deleterious effects on black prospects for education, employment, and socioeconomic mobility; see "Separate Societies: Have the Kerner Warnings Come True?" in Fred R. Harris and Roger W. Wilkins, eds., *Quiet Riots: Race and Poverty in the United States* (New York: Pantheon Books, 1988), pp. 100–122; and "Ghettoization and Its Alternatives," in Paul E. Peterson, ed., *The New Urban Reality* (Washington, D.C.: Brookings Institution, 1985), pp. 161–96.

11. See Thomas B. Edsall and Mary D. Edsall, *Chain Reaction: The Impact of Race, Rights, and Taxes on American Politics* (New York: Norton, 1991).

12. For an informative history of the evolution of the concept of the underclass, see Michael B. Katz, *The Undeserving Poor: From the War on Poverty to the War on Welfare* (New York: Pantheon, 1989), pp. 185–235.

13. Oscar Lewis, *La Vida: A Puerto Rican Family in the Culture of Poverty—San Juan and New York* (New York: Random House, 1965); "The Culture of Poverty," *Scientific American* 215 (1966): 19–25; "The Culture of Poverty," in Daniel P. Moynihan, ed., *On Understanding Poverty: Perspectives from the Social Sciences* (New York: Basic Books, 1968), pp. 187–220.

14. The complete text of this report is reprinted in Lee Rainwater and William L. Yancey, *The Moynihan Report and the Politics of Controversy* (Cambridge: MIT Press, 1967), pp. 39–125.

15. Edward C. Banfield, *The Unheavenly City* (Boston: Little, Brown, 1970).

16. William Ryan, *Blaming the Victim* (New York: Random House, 1971).

17. Carol Stack, *All Our Kin: Strategies of Survival in a Black Community* (New York: Harper and Row, 1974).

18. Douglas C. Glasgow, *The Black Underclass: Poverty, Unemployment, and Entrapment of Ghetto Youth* (New York: Vintage, 1981), p. 11; Alphonso Pinkney, *The Myth of Black Progress* (Cambridge: Cambridge University Press, 1984), pp. 78–80.

19. Charles Murray, *Losing Ground: American Social Policy, 1950–1980* (New York: Basic Books, 1984).

20. Lawrence M. Mead, *Beyond Entitlement: The Social Obligations of Citizenship* (New York: Free Press, 1986).

21. William Julius Wilson, *The Declining Significance of Race: Blacks and Changing American Institutions* (Chicago: University of Chicago Press, 1978).

22. William Julius Wilson, *The Truly Disadvantaged: The Inner City, the Underclass, and Public Policy* (Chicago: University of Chicago Press, 1987), pp. 1–108.

23. Ibid., pp. 49–62.

24. The subject indices of *Losing Ground* and *Beyond Entitlement* contain no references at all to residential segregation.

25. The subject index of *The Truly Disadvantaged* contains two references to pre-1960s Jim Crow segregation.

26. Again with the exception of Thomas Pettigrew and Gary Orfield.

27. We have published several studies documenting how the decline of manufacturing, the suburbanization of jobs, and the rise of low-wage service employment eliminated high-paying jobs for manual workers, drove up rates of black male unemployment, and reduced the attractiveness of marriage to black women, thereby contributing to a proliferation of female-headed families and persistent poverty. See Mitchell L. Eggers and Douglas S. Massey, "The Structural Determinants of Urban Poverty," *Social Science Research* 20 (1991): 217–55; Mitchell L. Eggers and Douglas S. Massey, "A Longitudinal Analysis of Urban Poverty: Blacks in U.S. Metropolitan Areas between 1970 and 1980," *Social Science Research* 21 (1992): 175–203.

28. The evidence on the extent of middle-class out-migration from ghetto areas is inconclusive. Because racial segregation does not decline with rising socioeconomic status, out-movement from poor black neighborhoods certainly has not been to white areas. When Kathryn P. Nelson measured rates of black out-migration from local "zones" within forty metropolitan areas, however, she found higher rates of out-movement for middle- and upper-class blacks compared with poor blacks; but her "zones" contained more than 100,000 inhabitants, making them considerably larger than neighborhoods (see "Racial Segregation, Mobility, and Poverty Concentration," paper presented at the annual meetings of the Population Association of America, Washington, D.C., March 19–23, 1991). In contrast, Edward Gramlich and Deborah Laren found that poor and middle-class blacks displayed about the same likelihood of out-migration from poor census tracts (see "Geographic Mobility and Persistent Poverty," Department of Economics, University of Michigan, Ann Arbor, 1990).

29. See Eggers and Massey, "A Longitudinal Analysis of Urban Poverty."

30. See International Defense and Aid Fund for Southern Africa, *Apartheid: The Facts* (London: United Nations Centre against Apartheid, 1983), pp. 15–26.

31. We are not the first to notice the striking parallel between the institutionalized system of racial segregation in U.S. cities and the organized, state-sponsored system of racial repression in South Africa. See John H. Denton, *Apartheid American Style* (Berkeley, Calif.: Diablo Press, 1967); James A. Kushner, "Apartheid in America: An Historical and Legal Analysis of Contemporary Racial Residential Segregation in the United States," *Howard Law Journal* 22 (1979):547–60.

24. Ann Owens and Robert J. Sampson*
Community Well-Being and the Great Recession

The effects of the Great Recession on individuals and workers are well-studied. Many reports document how and why individuals became more likely to be unemployed, to be in poverty, or to face foreclosure. But how have neighborhoods fared during the Great Recession? Although most research has focused on individual-level outcomes, many of the conventional narratives about the Great Recession are in fact neighborhood-level narratives. In discussing the housing crisis, for example, we don't just focus on individuals facing foreclosure, but on entire neighborhoods that were hard hit and with house after house on the same street all in foreclosure. Likewise, the unemployment crisis is often understood to be spatially clustered, with areas that depend disproportionately on construction, manufacturing, and other heavily-affected industries especially hard hit.

These narratives suggest a country increasingly divided into advantaged and disadvantaged neighborhoods. It matters that neighborhood-level inequality may be increasing because social science research has shown that aggregate neighborhood characteristics—beyond the traits of individuals themselves—influence the well-being and future life chances of residents. Declining neighborhood contexts could thus be a key channel through which the

*Owens, Ann and Robert J. Sampson. 2013. "Community Well-Being and the Great Recession." *Pathways Magazine* (Spring), pp. 3–7.

Great Recession has affected individuals and families and will continue to affect them into the future. If poor children are now growing up in increasingly disadvantaged neighborhoods with more unemployment, poverty, and abandoned houses, the recession may have quite profound long-term negative effects.

But we simply don't know if the Great Recession has indeed had this inequality increasing effect at the neighborhood level. This article thus poses these neighborhood-level questions: To what extent have the impacts of the recession been spatially concentrated? Has this been a recession in which all communities have suffered roughly equally? Or has the pain been especially borne by some communities? In answering these questions, we pay particular attention to how communities that were disadvantaged before the recession fared, asking whether historically poor communities were especially hard hit.

Monitoring the Rise of Neighborhood Inequality

These questions can be addressed by comparing the same neighborhoods before and after the recession on key indicators. It's useful to distinguish between three possible scenarios of how the pain of the recession is (or is not) equally shared, all illustrated in Figure 24.1.

Equal-sharing outcome: In the first scenario (bottom line), the equal-sharing outcome, rates of unemployment, poverty, or housing vacancy, increase by the same amount in each community. For example, if the recession affected community-level unemployment rates equally, unemployment would increase by roughly the same amount, say one point, in each community. Figure 1 shows that a community with 1% pre-recession unemployment (x-axis) has a post-recession unemployment rate of 2% (y-axis). A neighborhood with 5% pre-recession unemployment has a post-recession unemployment rate of 6%. Therefore, while the most-disadvantaged communities remain so, the absolute differences between the most- and least-disadvantaged communities remain the same before and after the recession (here, 4 percentage points). This type of recession effect does not reduce inequality but preserves the inter-community differences that prevailed before the recession.

Moderate inequality-increasing: The second scenario (middle line) operates multiplicatively. Neighborhoods with higher initial rates of, for example,

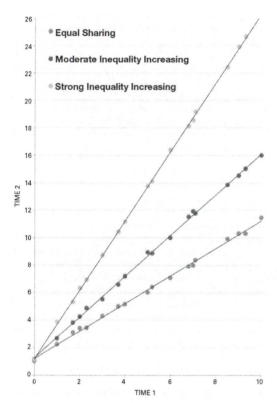

FIGURE 24.1 Three Ideal-Typical Ways of Reproducing Spatial Inequality

unemployment, experience larger increases in the unemployment rate. Figure 1 presents a scenario in which the unemployment rate increases by a factor of 1.5 (with an additive increase of 1 point, so y=1+1.5x). For example, a neighborhood with 1% unemployment pre-recession would have a post-recession unemployment rate of 2.5% while a neighborhood with 5% unemployment pre-recession would have a post-recession unemployment rate of 8.5%. Therefore, the absolute difference between high- and low-unemployment communities would grow (here, from 4 to 6 points), and inequality would increase. . .

Strong inequality-increasing: The final scenario in Figure 24.1 (top line) differs from the previous one only due to its larger multiplicative factor (the slope is 2 rather than 1.5). When the multiplicative factor is very large, there's an especially large penalty borne by communities with high baseline rates.

In this article, we investigate how strongly a community's initial level of disadvantage determines the recession's impact. In Figure 24.1, each dot representing a neighborhood is very close to the fitted line, representing scenarios in which a neighbor-

hood's initial level of disadvantage strongly dictates its outcome during the recession. If the relationship between initial conditions and the impact of the recession is not as strong ([and hence] the dots along the line [are] scattered more widely), it suggests that other variables influence which communities suffered most during the recession.

We examine how communities fared both in terms of the magnitude of the relationship between pre- and post-recession conditions (the slope of the line) and how precisely pre-recession conditions predict the impact of the recession (the degree of scatter around the line). The magnitude of the relationship reveals the extent to which the recession is inequality-increasing, with a slope over 1 indicating that poor communities bear more of the brunt than rich communities.[1] . . .

Our analyses are constrained by how the government collects census data. Past research often defines neighborhoods using the census tract, an administratively defined unit of about 4,000 residents on average. The most recent census data on tract-level economic characteristics come from the American Community Survey (ACS) aggregated across the five-year period from 2007-2011. This is a problem for studying the recession because the available data combine years before and after the recession began.

Because we wish to explore the effects of the Great Recession, we must therefore define neighborhoods in a different way. Our solution is to examine another census-defined statistical area—Public Use Microdata Areas (PUMAs). PUMAs are geographically contiguous areas with at least 100,000 residents. Although PUMAs are clearly larger than the census tracts or zip codes (average population of 30,000) used in past research, they delineate all places in the US into smaller geographic areas that are proxies for local communities. We compare three-year estimates from the ACS that aggregate data from 2005 to 2007 (defined as pre-recession) with the latest three-year ACS estimates currently available, from 2009 to 2011 (defined as post-recession). . . .

Community-Level Patterns

We begin with simple descriptive maps (see Figure 24.2) of the spatial distribution of changes in community well-being and then turn to a more formal discussion of the trends in inequality (see Figure 24.3). Figure 24.2 presents changes in poverty, unemployment, and vacancy rates for all PUMAs in the U.S. from 2005-07 to 2009-11.[2] Given the role of the foreclosure crisis in this recession, the vacancy rate provides an important indicator of community well-being in terms of the physical and social state of the neighborhood. High vacancy rates are associated with increased crime rates and decreased rates of neighborhood cohesion and residential stability, which influence individual well-being and community-level economic and social changes. When we compare the pre-recession and post-recession periods, we find that the poverty rate (top) increased in 84% of PUMAs, the vacancy rate (middle) increased in 74% of PUMAs, and the unemployment rate (bottom) increased in 97% of PUMAs. On average, the changes were modest— about a 2 percentage point increase for poverty rates, 1 percentage point for vacancy rates and, perhaps most troubling, nearly 4 percentage points for unemployment. The simple conclusion: In most communities, community-level economic well-being has clearly declined alongside families' and individuals' economic hardships, all in a relatively short time.

That the maps display recession-induced decline is hardly surprising. We are more interested in the spatial distribution of that decline. Were there any protected pockets? PUMAs in the middle of the country, from Texas to North Dakota, typically fared better, evidenced by the relative prevalence of areas shaded dark gray (indicating declines). Communities in Michigan, Florida, and several Western states fared particularly poorly in the recession, and these are areas where foreclosures were concentrated as well (though sparsely populated states have few PUMAs, masking declines within them). When it comes to unemployment, however, there's less dark gray in the "protected" midsection of the country, suggesting that labor market problems were widely shared and came closer to being a true across-the-board experience.

These maps tell us about the regional distribution of the recession's effects. We turn next to the question of whether disadvantaged PUMAs were hardest hit and thus became even more disadvantaged relative to advantaged PUMAs. Figure 24.2 presents scatterplots comparing poverty, vacancy, and unemployment rates in 2005-07 (on the x-axis) and in 2009-11 (on the y-axis). The first and very

Change in Poverty Rate, 2005–07 to 2009–11

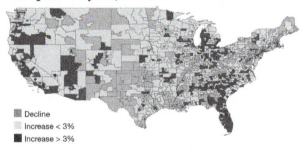

- ■ Decline
- Increase < 3%
- ■ Increase > 3%

Change in Vacancy Rate, 2005–07 to 2009–11

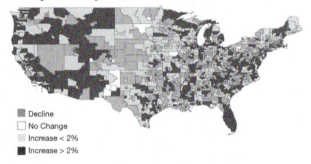

- ■ Decline
- ☐ No Change
- Increase < 2%
- ■ Increase > 2%

Change in Unemployment Rate, 2005–07 to 2009–11

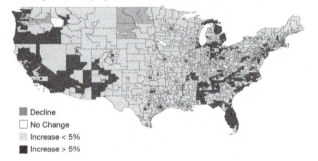

- ■ Decline
- ☐ No Change
- Increase < 5%
- ■ Increase > 5%

FIGURE 24.2 Poverty, Vacancy, and Unemployment Rates Before and After the Great Recession

important conclusion: These plots reveal striking persistence in community-level inequality throughout the recession—PUMAs with the lowest economic profiles in 2005-07 remain at the bottom in 2009-11, while the well-off communities remain at the top.

But has inequality increased? The reference line in each scatterplot has a slope of 1, representing the "equal sharing" scenario of Figure 24.1. Departures from this line reveal if recession effects have increased inequality. . . .

We find that poverty rates increased by a multiplicative factor of 1.004.[3] Therefore, poverty rate increases are borne fairly equally across communities

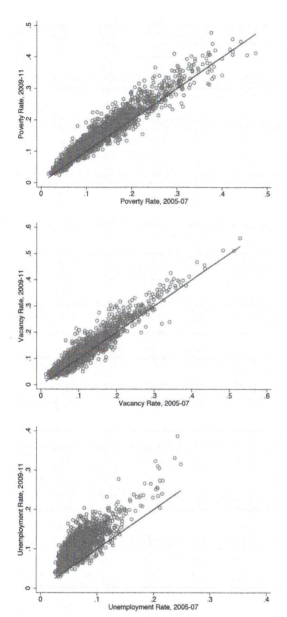

FIGURE 24.3 PUMA-level Poverty, Vacancy, and Unemployment Rates in 2005-07 and 2009-11

during the recession, though they increased slightly more in neighborhoods with higher pre-recession poverty rates. Vacancy rates increased multiplicatively by a factor of 1.04, indicating a slight inequality-increasing effect of the recession.

The unemployment scatterplot departs most strikingly from the reference line, indicating the stronger inequality-increasing effects of the recession. Unemployment increased by a factor of 1.10 during the recession. While Figure 24.2 showed

widespread increases in unemployment across the US, the magnitude of the increases was higher in places that initially had high unemployment rates, increasing inequality. Neighborhoods with 1% unemployment pre-recession have 1.1% unemployment post-recession, while neighborhoods with 10% unemployment pre-recession have 11% unemployment post-recession, increasing the absolute difference between the two neighborhoods by nearly 1 point. The inequality-increasing impact on unemployment likely arises because industries that were especially hard hit by the Great Recession, such as manufacturing, were typically industries that were already in trouble. In effect, the Great Recession accelerated a deindustrialization process that was already underway, and manufacturing-intensive PUMAs, which had preexisting high unemployment rates, experienced disproportionate increases in unemployment.

As is evident in Figure 24.3, there is some scatter around these lines, suggesting that factors besides initial poverty, vacancy, and unemployment rates shaped the recession's effect on these characteristics. What were these other factors? In exploratory analyses, we found that (a) increases in poverty, vacancy, and unemployment rates from 2005-07 to 2009-11 were higher in communities with higher initial proportions of Hispanic and black residents, and (b) unemployment rates increased more in communities with higher initial proportions of immigrants.[4] These results imply that the scatter in Figure 24.3 arises in part because communities with Hispanics, blacks, or immigrants suffered disproportionately even when those communities didn't have especially high initial poverty, vacancy, or unemployment rates.

Overall, we conclude that the recession did increase inequality among neighborhoods, particularly with respect to unemployment. PUMAs with especially high poverty, unemployment, and housing vacancy rates before the recession pulled away during the recession and became even more disadvantaged in absolute terms. That minority and immigrant communities were particularly affected demonstrates that the recession has exacerbated long-standing economic and racial inequalities. . . .

Communities, Inequality, and the Great Recession

The story of the Great Recession has largely been told in individual terms. Important research documents the burgeoning numbers of long-term unemployed, the rising poverty rate, and the growing number of homeowners facing foreclosures. The purpose of this article has been to turn our attention to how neighborhoods fared. To what extent has the Great Recession hit already-disadvantaged neighborhoods especially hard and thus increased neighborhood-level inequality? Our analyses show that communities, like families and individuals, have suffered economic hardships during the Great Recession and that these hardships were distributed unequally. Many of the nation's most vulnerable communities have borne the brunt of the economic crisis, as poverty, vacancy rates, and particularly unemployment rates increased more in disadvantaged and minority neighborhoods. The simple result is a growing divide between the have and have-not communities.

NOTES

1. A slope less than one suggests that the recession is reducing spatial inequality.

2. The maps are shaded to indicate decline, no change, moderate increase, and large increase (distinguished by the 75th percentile of each change indicator).

3. Excluding the poorest 5% of PUMAs, the slope for poverty is 1.03, suggesting poverty increased multiplicatively in most communities but not the very poorest.

4. Regression models predicted changes in poverty, unemployment, and vacancy rates from 2005-07 to 2009-11 from poverty rate, unemployment rate, vacancy rate, percent non-Hispanic black, percent Hispanic, and percent foreign-born in 2005-07.

---

25. Patrick Sharkey and Felix Elwert*

The Legacy of Multigenerational Disadvantage

Research on the relationship between neighborhoods and child development has frequently overlooked a

*The ideas, issues, and theories considered in this brief commissioned piece are examined in greater depth in the following publication: Patrick Sharkey and Felix Elwert, "The Legacy of Disadvantage: Multigenerational Neighborhood Effects on Cognitive Ability," *American Journal of Sociology* 116:6 (March 2011), pp. 1934–1981, published by the University of Chicago Press. The article printed here was originally prepared by Patrick Sharkey and Felix Elwert for the fourth edition of *Social Stratification: Class, Race, and Gender in Sociological Perspective*, edited by David B. Grusky. Copyright © 2014 by Westview Press.

crucial dimension of neighborhood stratification: *time.* Whereas much research on the impact of neighborhoods implicitly treats the environment as a static feature of a child's life and assumes that the neighborhood has instantaneous effects on children, a life course perspective on neighborhood inequality shifts attention toward continuity and change in the environment over time and across generations and considers the role that neighborhoods play in altering or structuring individuals' or families' trajectories.

Recent research demonstrates the complex relationships between exposure to disadvantaged neighborhood environments and child developmental outcomes (Sampson, Sharkey, and Raudenbush 2008; Wheaton and Clarke 2003). But what if the child's caregivers were also raised in similarly disadvantaged environments? Could a parent's childhood neighborhood environment have an influence on the next generation? In this study, we add to the recent line of research that incorporates time into the literature on neighborhood inequality, but we reach further back in time than other studies and ask how the neighborhood environment, experienced over multiple generations of a family, influences children's cognitive abilities.

Our focus on multigenerational disadvantage is motivated by recent research on the persistence of neighborhood economic status across generations, which demonstrates that neighborhood inequality in one generation is commonly transmitted to the next. For example, more than 70 percent of African American children who grow up in the poorest quarter of American neighborhoods remain in the poorest quarter of neighborhoods as adults (Sharkey 2008). The persistence of neighborhood disadvantage across generations adds considerable complexity to how researchers approach the relationship between neighborhoods and child development, because it forces one to consider direct and indirect pathways by which neighborhood exposures in both the parents' and children's generations may influence children's trajectories. A child's own neighborhood may influence her cognitive ability through, for example, the quality of her schooling experience or the influence of her peers. But there also may be pathways by which a parent's childhood neighborhood, experienced a generation earlier, continues to exert a lingering influence on his child's cognitive ability. It is plausible that the parent's childhood neighborhood may influence his own schooling experience, his experiences in the labor market, and even his mental health. All of these aspects of a parent's life may, in turn, influence the resources available to him for childrearing—including the quality of the home environment, the resources available for the child, and the neighborhood in which he raises his child.

Illuminating the relationships that link parents' and children's residential environments to children's cognitive outcomes is not only a theoretical problem, but also poses considerable methodological challenges. Virtually all previous observational studies of neighborhood effects used regression techniques (or some variant, such as propensity score matching), in which a set of family background measures is controlled. The same techniques are not appropriate for investigating multigenerational effects if the dimensions of family background that influence neighborhood location in the second generation are influenced by neighborhood conditions in the first generation. In essence, controlling for family background would block the indirect pathways by which first-generation neighborhood characteristics may influence developmental outcomes a generation later, thus underestimating the importance of parents' neighborhoods for children's outcomes.

The theoretical problem of multigenerational relationships thus becomes a methodological problem, arising in any scenario in which confounders are potentially endogenous to treatments experienced at an earlier point in time—or in an earlier generation. Instead of conventional regression models, we draw on newly developed methods designed to generate unbiased treatment effects in such situations, under assumptions that we specify in the following discussion. In a series of articles introducing marginal structural models and the method of inverse probability of treatment weighting, Robins and colleagues (Robins 1998, 1999b; Hernán, Brumback, and Robins 2000; Robins, Hernán, and Brumback 2000) show that treatment effect bias can be addressed by using a model that weights each subject by the inverse of the predicted probability that the subject receives a given treatment at a given point conditional on prior treatment history and prior confounders (both time-varying and time-invariant). Here we adapt this method for treatments received across generations to estimate multigenerational neighborhood effects on children's cognitive abilities.

Intergenerational Pathways of Influence

The theory underlying a multigenerational perspective argues that there are numerous possible pathways, observed and unobserved, by which the neighborhood environment in one generation may be linked with a child's cognitive ability in the next generation. If childhood neighborhoods affect any dimension of adult social or economic status, health, or family life, then disadvantages experienced during childhood in one generation may linger and affect cognitive ability in the next. The fact that several studies have found strong childhood neighborhood effects on specific aspects of adult attainment, such as education and mental health (Harding 2003; Kaufman and Rosenbaum 1992; Wheaton and Clarke 2003), lends credence to the hypothesis that neighborhood effects may extend across generations. The presence of neighborhood effects in studies examining various additional dimensions of adult life strengthens this hypothesis considerably, even if these studies produce inconsistent results.

For such indirect effects to exist, however, we must make the additional assumption that aspects of family background and the social environments in which children spend their childhoods have an influence on their cognitive development. This assumption taps into a long-standing debate on the malleability of cognitive ability (Heckman 1995; Herrnstein and Murray 1994; Jacoby and Glauberman 1995; Neisser et al. 1996). Although there is little doubt that cognitive ability—whether conceived as intelligence, IQ, or simply performance on tests of cognitive skills—has a genetic component, there is also near consensus that development is sensitive to the family, school, and social environment. Empirically, children's cognitive development has been linked with parents' education, alcohol use, mental health, social and economic status, and parenting practices, as well as various aspects of the home environment (Guo and Harris 2000; Shonkoff and Phillips 2000). These same characteristics of parents may also affect the schooling experiences of children, which influence their cognitive development (Alexander, Entwisle, and Olson 2007; Downey, von Hippel, and Broh 2004; Winship and Korenman 1997). This literature provides a sense of the multiple ways in which different aspects of the home or family environment may be linked with children's cognitive development. The presence of numerous possible pathways linking parents' own childhood environments to their children's development a generation later provides the theoretical basis for a multigenerational analysis.

Data

To assess the multigenerational effects of neighborhood poverty on cognitive ability, we draw on data from the Panel Study of Income Dynamics (PSID) (Hill and Morgan 1992), a nationally representative survey that began with a sample of roughly five thousand families in 1968 and has followed the members of these families over time. We match families to their census tract of residence through the PSID restricted-use geocode file, which contains tract identifiers for sample families from 1968 through 2003. Finally, we utilize data on cognitive ability from the 2002 Child Development Supplement (CDS) (Hofferth et al. 1997; Mainieri 2004), a follow-up survey of a sample of PSID parents with children ages five to eighteen who were originally assessed in the 1997 CDS at ages zero to twelve. The CDS was designed to supplement the core PSID interview with information on child development and details about the home, school, and neighborhood environments, as well as familial and social relationships. The final sample comprises 1,556 parent-child pairs, including 730 African American pairs, 792 white pairs, and 34 pairs of all other racial and ethnic groups.

The outcomes under study represent two dimensions of child and adolescent cognitive ability measured using the Woodcock-Johnson Psycho-Educational Battery-Revised (WJ-R) (Woodcock and Johnson 1989): broad reading scores and applied problems scores. The broad reading score measures reading ability and combines results from two subscales, the letter-word assessment and the passage comprehension assessment. To measure ability in math, we use the applied problems score. Raw results from each subtest are normalized to reflect the child's abilities relative to the national average for the child's age (Mainieri 2004).

The treatment is defined as living in a high-poverty neighborhood during childhood; it is measured for children in the three survey years prior to the CDS and for their parents when they were ages fifteen to seventeen. Specifically, we define high-poverty neighborhoods as those where the poverty rate is at least 20 percent. However, mindful of severe racial discrepancies in exposure to high-poverty neighborhoods, Sharkey and Elwert (2011) conduct an additional set of race-specific analyses in which the definition of the treatment is allowed to vary by race. In these analyses, they use a 40 percent poverty threshold to define high-poverty neighborhoods for blacks and a 10 percent threshold for whites. Parental neighborhood poverty is measured as the average poverty rate in the census tracts where parents lived during the three survey years from ages fifteen to

seventeen. Child neighborhood poverty is measured as the average poverty rate in children's neighborhoods in the three survey years prior to the 2002 CDS: 1997, 1999, and 2001. All models include extensive control variables from each generation, including demographic characteristics of the head of household and the child (age, gender); various dimensions of family background (family income, occupational status, educational attainment); employment characteristics of the head of the household or family (disability status, welfare receipt, annual hours worked); and other measured attitudes and characteristics of the family, such as home ownership and attitudes about the future.

Defining Multigenerational Effects of Neighborhood Disadvantage

The primary objective of this study is to estimate the joint multigenerational effects of parents' and children's exposure to neighborhood poverty on child cognitive ability, in order to capture the effect of enduring disadvantage. Formally, A is the child's observed cognitive ability, and the potential outcome A^N is the child's cognitive ability that would be observed if her family had experienced the multigenerational neighborhood regime $N = \{N^p, N^o\}$, consisting of the neighborhood environments in the parent generation, N^p, and the neighborhood environment in the child's generation, N^o. The difference between the two potential outcomes, $\partial_i = A^N - A^{N*}$, defines the causal effect of experiencing the multigenerational residential history N rather than some other residential history, $N*$. In each generation, we classify neighborhoods as either poor or nonpoor, yielding four possible multigenerational regimes: $N \in \{$(poor, poor), (poor, nonpoor), (nonpoor, poor), (nonpoor, nonpoor)$\}$. We are primarily interested in two causal contrasts: (1) $E[A^{N=\{poor,poor\}}] - E[A^{N=\{nonpoor,nonpoor\}}]$, which defines the average causal effect if both parents and children had grown up in poor rather than nonpoor neighborhoods, which we term the *joint*, or *multigenerational*, *causal effect*; and (2) $E[A^{N=\{poor,fix\}}] - E[A^{N=\{nonpoor,fix\}}]$, which defines the average causal effect if the parents had grown up in a poor rather than a nonpoor neighborhood and their children had grown up in a neighborhood of fixed type (either poor or nonpoor), which we term the *direct causal effect* of parents' exposure on children's cognitive abilities. Note that this direct effect captures the portion of parental exposure that does not operate through influencing

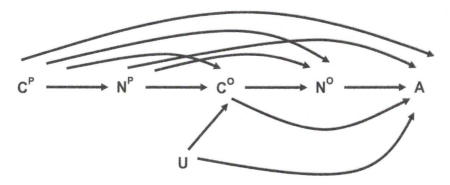

FIGURE 25.1 Directed Acyclic Graph Displaying Possible Direct and Indirect Causal Pathways Linking Neighborhood Exposure (N) and Confounding Variables (C), Which Determine Neighborhood of Residence in the Parent (P) and Child (O) Generations, to Child Cognitive Outcomes (A). The Vector U Represents Unobserved Factors

the children's own neighborhood of residence; instead, it may operate via parents' education, income, parenting style, or other characteristics of the parents or the home environment that are influenced by the parents' childhood neighborhood context.

Two Difficulties of Estimating Multigenerational Causal Effects

The causal effect of multigenerational neighborhood poverty on children's cognitive abilities, A, can be identified from observational data if neighborhood of residence in each generation, N^P and N^O, is statistically independent of the potential outcomes, A^N, given observed covariates and previous treatments. This assumption is known in the technical literature as sequential ignorability or unconfoundedness of treatment assignment (Robins 1986, 1999b). It implies that there are no unobserved variables that jointly affect the treatment (N^P or N^O) and the outcome.

Even under this assumption, however, traditional regression (as well as conventional propensity score) methods generally cannot estimate the multigenerational effect of neighborhood disadvantage, because neighborhood disadvantage in the second generation is endogenous to neighborhood disadvantage in the first generation in two distinct ways.

Figure 25.1 illustrates these two endogeneity problems. The figure shows a directed acyclic graph (Pearl 1995, 2000) representing the causal relationships among neighborhood poverty, child cognitive outcomes, and other variables. All arrows between the temporally ordered variables represent direct causal effects, and the absence of an arrow indicates the absence of a direct causal effect. The variables in

Figure 25.1 are defined as indicated, with U representing unmeasured variables causing both C^O and A. For expositional clarity, we assume without loss of generality that Figure 25.1 contains all variables in the system. We note that treatments in Figure 25.1 are sequentially ignorable, because there are no arrows from any unobserved variables into N^P or N^O. Therefore, the multigenerational effect of N on A is identifiable from the observed data.

Simply conditioning on the measured cofounders C^P and C^O in a conventional regression model, such as ordinary least squares (OLS), however, will not provide an unbiased estimate for the multigenerational effect of N on A. To understand why, we consider how the confounding variable C^O should best be handled. On the one hand, C^O must be controlled to avoid bias from confounding, as C^O causes both N^O and A. On the other hand, conditioning on C^O creates two endogeneity problems. First, note that C^O is on the causal pathway from N^P to A. Controlling for C^O may thus "control away" part of the effect of parental neighborhood poverty on the child's cognitive outcome and consequently produce bias. Second, even if N^P had no direct or indirect causal effect on A (i.e., if there are no pathways to be "controlled away"), conditioning on C^O will induce a noncausal association between N^P and A because of the unobserved variable U—conditioning on C^O will induce an association between N^P and U (because conditioning on the common effect of two variables always does; Pearl 1995) and thus between N^P and A, inducing endogenous selection bias that would make it impossible to reject the causal null hypothesis of no direct causal effect of N^P on A, even if the null hypothesis were true (Elwert and Winship, forthcoming). In sum, the analyst is thus obliged to simultaneously condition on C^o to control for confounding of N^o and not to condition on C^o to avoid controlling away part of the effect of N^p on A and inducing endogenous selection bias. Conventional regression models, however, cannot simultaneously control and not control for the same variable. But so-called marginal structural models (MSMs) can.

Marginal Structural Models for Multigenerational Neighborhood Effects

We use MSMs with inverse probability of treatment (IPT) weighting to estimate the multigenerational effects of neighborhood disadvantage on children's cognitive outcomes. The models are well-suited for the task because they are more powerful than conventional regression models in at least two senses. First, they are designed to resolve the core endogeneity problems of time-varying (here, multigenerational) exposure (Robins 1998, 1999a, 1999b; Robins et al. 2000; Hernán et al. 2000), and second, they can do so making *fewer* assumptions than traditional regression models do.[1]

The MSMs have two steps. In the first step, every family is weighted by the inverse of the estimated probability of experiencing the sequence of neighborhood conditions that they did in fact experience. This weighting removes all confounding by observed variables C^p and C^o. In the second step, the weighted data are analyzed with a (weighted) regression model. With observed confounders taken care of by weighting, there is no longer any need to control for observed confounders on the causal pathway in the outcomes equation, which therefore does not "control away" part of the effect of interest. The outcomes equation is

$$E_{weighted}[A| N_p, N_o] = a + N_p b_1 + N_o b_2 \quad (1)$$

Under the assumption of no sequential ignorability, the parameters in Equation (1) have a causal interpretation. The model intercept, a, estimates the child's mean cognitive ability if all parents and children had grown up in advantaged neighborhoods, and the sum of $a + b_1 + b_2$ estimates the child's mean cognitive ability if all parents and children had grown up in disadvantaged neighborhoods. The sum of the two slopes $b_1 + b_2$ thus gives the *joint causal effect* of multigenerational neighborhood disadvantage on children's cognitive outcomes. The slope b_1 by itself gives the *direct causal effect* of parental neighborhood disadvantage.

Results from Regression and Marginal Structural Models

Table 25.1 shows estimates for the causal effects of multigenerational neighborhood poverty on children's cognitive abilities from three models: one unadjusted for any covariates, a conventional regression-adjusted model, and an IPT-weighted MSM. Prior to accounting for nonrandom selection into neighborhoods, neighborhood poverty in each generation is strongly and negatively associated with children's broad reading scores (column 1). Standard regression adjustments reduce the apparent direct effect of parental and child neighborhood poverty substantially; however, the conventional regression model includes all of the parents' covariates, including their educational attainment, income, and so forth. If the influence of parents' childhood neighborhoods is mediated by these or other aspects of parents' adult lives, then the regression estimates will "control away" all of these indirect pathways of influence and hence underestimate the true effect.

Column 3 presents estimates from an MSM, which accounts for observed selection into treatment status in both generations through IPT weighting (which, unlike conventional regression models, does not "control away" mediated effects). The multigenerational effect of coming from a family residing in poor neighborhoods in two successive generations rather than from a family living in nonpoor neighborhoods is a reduction of 9.27 points in a child's broad reading scores. This multigenerational effect of neighborhood disadvantage on reading scores is substantively large (more than half a standard deviation in broad reading scores) and statistically significant at the (p-value < 0.05). Results for applied problem-solving scores are similar to results for broad reading scores. For this outcome, the joint causal effect of multigenerational exposure to neighborhood poverty is substantively large and statistically significant, reducing children's applied problem scores by 8.36 points, more than half a standard deviation (p-value < 0.01). A formal sensitivity analysis (not shown) in Sharkey and Elwert (2011) demonstrates that these results are quite robust to possible unobserved selection bias.

Discussion

The evidence presented here suggests that a multigenerational perspective is crucial to understanding

TABLE 25.1 Estimated Effects of Multigenerational Exposure to Neighborhood Poverty on Children's Cognitive Ability

	Neighborhood poverty: >=20% poor					
	Broad reading score			Applied problems score		
	Unadjusted estimates	Regression adjusted	Marginal struct. model	Unadjusted estimates	Regression adjusted	Marginal struct. model
Parent neighborhood poverty only, β1	-8.83*** (1.16)	-2.85** (1.21)	-5.07** (2.38)	-9.68*** (0.97)	-2.40** (1.12)	-5.97*** (1.85)
Child neighborhood poverty only, β2	-5.98*** (1.23)	-1.73 (1.10)	-4.20** (2.00)	-5.66*** (1.00)	-0.84 (1.02)	-2.39 (1.79)
Multigenerational exposure, β1+β2	- -	- -	-9.27*** (1.68)	- -	- -	-8.36*** (1.69)

Notes: *** = significant at p < .01; ** = significant at p < .05; * = significant at p < .10
Standard errors account for clustering at the family level.

the relationship between neighborhood environments and cognitive ability. A family's exposure to neighborhood poverty over two consecutive generations is found to reduce the average child's cognitive ability by more than half a standard deviation. This empirical result points to a revised, broader conceptualization of how the neighborhood environment influences cognitive ability, and furthermore suggests a revised theoretical and empirical perspective on the influence of social contexts on child development. We argue that this revised perspective should inform interpretations of experimental and quasi-experimental research assessing the impact of neighborhood change arising from residential mobility, as well as observational research on social contexts and child development.

First we consider the experimental and quasi-experimental evidence available from residential mobility programs, including the Gautreaux program in Chicago, the Moving to Opportunity experiment, and other similar programs (Briggs 1997). In all such programs, participants (typically low-income families living in public housing) are given the chance to move to less disadvantaged environments, frequently in the same city or within the metropolitan area. Research based on these programs exploits exogenous variation in the destinations of participants in the programs to estimate how a change in the neighborhood environment impacts children's and adults' social outcomes. Although this type of study provides sound evidence on the causal effect of *contemporary* neighborhood exposure due to a change in the neighborhood environment arising from a residential move, by design these studies do not capture the *lagged or cumulative* effects of previous neighborhood environments.

This focus on contemporary neighborhood circumstances has been questioned in recent research on youth in Chicago, which shows that the impact of living in severely disadvantaged neighborhoods continues to be felt years later (Sampson et al. 2008). The challenge is strengthened considerably when one considers the possibility of generation-lagged effects or cumulative, multigenerational effects. A change in a family's neighborhood may bring about an abrupt and radical change in the social environment surrounding children, but this change may be a short-term departure from a familial history of life in disadvantaged environments. The shift in context may improve the opportunities available to adults and children, the child's peers and school environment, and the parent's mental health, but it may not undo the lingering influence of the parent's childhood environment. In short, a temporary change of scenery may not disrupt the effects of a family history of disadvantage.

This assessment should not be taken as a criticism of the residential mobility literature, but as a lens with which to interpret it. Evaluations of residential mobility programs provide powerful evidence for policy makers interested in designing programs to move families into areas that may improve adults' mental health or children's life chances. But these programs tell us little about the cumulative disadvantages facing a family living in America's poorest neighborhoods over long periods of time.

Next we consider the extensive literature on neighborhood effects based on observational data. The most common analytical approach in this literature involves estimating neighborhood effects while controlling for a set of family background measures. A common claim made in reviews of these studies is that the family environment is more important for child development than the neighborhood environment (Ellen and Turner 1997; Leventhal and Brooks-Gunn 2000). A multigenerational perspective suggests that such a conclusion is misleading. Aspects of family background that are linked with child developmental outcomes, such as parental income or education, may be endogenous to neighborhood conditions in the prior generation. Parents' educational attainment, economic position, and health are better thought of as partial outcomes of their own earlier residential circumstances. In this sense, individuals and families inseparably *embody* neighborhood histories, and it is therefore a mistake to think of the family and the neighborhood as competing developmental contexts.

Our theory and results indicate that the family and the neighborhood environments are closely intertwined, combining to influence the developmental trajectories of individuals in ways that extend across generations. As we have shown, a multigenerational perspective is essential to understanding inequality in cognitive ability. Our findings support other studies showing a link between the neighborhood environment and children's cognitive ability, but we extend this literature by calling attention to the history of social environments occupied by family members over generations. This approach reflects the broader implication of this chapter, which is that to understand inequality in cognitive ability and other developmental domains, it is not sufficient to focus on a single point in a child's life, or even on a single generation of a family. Instead, we must understand the history of disadvantages experienced by generations of family members.

REFERENCES

Alexander, Karl L., Doris R. Entwisle, and Linda Steffel Olson. 2007. "Lasting Consequences of the Summer Learning Gap." American Sociological Review 72: 167–180.

Briggs, Xavier de Souza. 1997. "Moving Up Versus Moving Out: Neighborhood Effects in Housing Mobility Programs." Housing Policy Debate 8: 195–234.

Downey, Douglas B., Paul T. von Hippel, and Beckett A. Broh. 2004. "Are Schools the Great Equalizer? Cognitive Inequality During the Summer Months and the School Year." American Sociological Review 69: 613–635.

Ellen, Ingrid Gould, and Margery Austin Turner. 1997. "Does Neighborhood Matter? Assessing Recent Evidence." Housing Policy Debate 8: 833–866.

Elwert, Felix, and Christopher Winship. Forthcoming. "Endogenous Selection Bias." In Annual Review of Sociology.

Guo, Guang, and Kathleen Mullan Harris. 2000. "The Mechanisms Mediating the Effects of Poverty on Children's Intellectual Development." Demography 37: 431–447.

Harding, David. 2003. "Counterfactual Models of Neighborhood Effects: The Effect of Neighborhood Poverty on Dropping Out and Teenage Pregnancy." American Journal of Sociology 109: 676–719.

Heckman, James J. 1995. "Lessons from the Bell Curve." The Journal of Political Economy 103: 1091–1120.

Hernán, Miguel Ángel, Babette Brumback, and James M. Robins. 2000. "Marginal Structural Models to Estimate the Causal Effect of Zidovudine on the Survival of HIV-Positive Men." Epidemiology 11: 561–570.

Herrnstein, Richard, and Charles Murray. 1994. The Bell Curve: Intelligence and Class Structure in American Life. New York: Free Press.

Hill, Martha S., and James N. Morgan. 1992. The Panel Study of Income Dynamics: A User's Guide. Newbury Park, CA: Sage Publications.

Hofferth, Sandra, Pamela E. Davis-Kean, Jean Davis, and Jonathan Finkelstein. 1997. The Child Development Supplement to the Panel Study of Income Dynamics: 1997 User Guide. Ann Arbor, MI: Institute for Social Research.

Jacoby, Russess, and Naomi Glauberman, eds. 1995. The Bell Curve Debate: History, Documents, Opinions. New York: Random House.

Kaufman, Julie E., and James Rosenbaum. 1992. "The Education and Employment of Low-Income Black Youth in White Suburbs." Educational Evaluation & Policy Analysis 14: 229–240.

Leventhal, Tama, and Jeanne Brooks-Gunn. 2000. "The Neighborhoods They Live in: The Effects of Neighborhood Residence on Child and Adolescent Outcomes." Psychological Bulletin 126: 309–337.

Mainieri, Tina. 2004. The Panel Study of Income Dynamics Child Development Supplement: User Guide for CDS-II. Ann Arbor, MI: Institute for Social Research.

Neisser, Ulric, Gwyneth Boodoo, Thomas J. Bouchard Jr., A. Wade Boykin, Nathan Brody, Stephen J. Ceci, Diane F. Halpern, John C. Loehlin, Robert Perloff, Robert J. Sternberg, and Susana Urbina. 1996. "Intelligence: Knowns and Unknowns." American Psychologist 51: 77–101.

Pearl, Judea. 1995. "Causal Diagrams for Empirical Research." Biometrika 82: 669–710.

———. 2009. Causality: Models, Reasoning, and Inference. Cambridge, UK: Cambridge University Press.

Robins, James M. 1986. "A New Approach to Causal Inference in Mortality Studies with Sustained Exposure Periods—Application to Control of the Healthy

Worker Survivor Effect." Mathematical Modelling 7: 1393–1512.

———. 1998. "Marginal Structural Models." 1997 Proceedings of the American Statistical Association, Section on Bayesian Statistical Science.

———. 1999a. "Association, Causation, and Marginal Structural Models." Synthese 121: 151–179.

———. 1999b. "Marginal Structural Models versus Structural Nested Models as Tools for Causal Inference." In Statistical Models in Epidemiology, edited by E. Halloran, 95–134. New York: Springer-Verlag.

Robins, James M., Miguel Hernán, and Babette Brumback. 2000. "Marginal Structural Models and Causal Inference in Epidemiology." Epidemiology 11: 550–560.

Sampson, Robert J., Patrick Sharkey, and Stephen W. Raudenbush. 2008. "Durable Effects of Concentrated Disadvantage on Verbal Ability among African-American Children." Proceedings of the National Academy of Sciences 105 (3): 845–853.

Sharkey, Patrick. 2008. "The Intergenerational Transmission of Context." American Journal of Sociology 113: 931–969.

Shonkoff, Jack P., and Deborah A. Phillips, eds. 2000. From Neurons to Neighborhoods: The Science of Early Childhood Development. Washington, DC: National Academy Press.

Wheaton, Blair, and Philippa Clarke. 2003. "Space Meets Time: Integrating Temporal and Contextual Influences on Mental Health in Early Adulthood." American Sociological Review 68: 680–706.

Winship, Christopher, and Sanders Korenman. 1997. "Does Staying in School Make You Smarter?" In Intelligence, Genes, and Success: Scientists Respond to the Bell Curve, edited by B. Devlin, S. E. Fienberg, D. P. Resnick and K. Roeder, 215–234. New York: Springer-Verlag.

Woodcock, Richard W., and M. Bonner Johnson. 1989. Tests of Achievement, Standard Battery (Form B). Chicago: Riverside Publishing.

NOTES

1. MSMs make fewer assumptions than conventional regression models in that MSMs can handle (as illustrated in Figure 25.1) unobserved variables U that affect the confounders C of treatment N, whereas conventional regression cannot handle the presence of U.

26. Matthew Desmond*
Eviction and the Reproduction of Urban Poverty

Jori and his cousin were cutting up, tossing snowballs at passing cars. From Jori's street corner on Milwaukee's near South Side, cars driving on Sixth Street passed squat duplexes with porch steps ending at a sidewalk edged in dandelions. Those heading north approached the Basilica of St. Josaphat, whose crowning dome looked to Jori like a giant overturned plunger. It was January of 2008, and the city was experiencing the snowiest winter on record. Every so often, a car turned off Sixth Street to navigate Arthur Avenue, hemmed in by the snow, and that's when the boys would take aim. Jori packed a tight one and let it fly. The car jerked to a stop, and a man jumped out. The boys ran inside and locked the door to the apartment where Jori lived with his mother, Arleen, and younger brother, Jafaris. The lock was cheap, and the man broke down the door with a few hard-heeled kicks. He left before anything else happened. When the landlord found out about the door, she decided to evict Arleen and her boys. They had been there eight months.

The day Arleen and her boys had to be out was cold. But if she waited any longer, the landlord would summon the sheriff, who would arrive with a gun, a team of boot-footed movers, and a folded judge's order saying that her house was no longer hers. She would be given two options: truck or curb. "Truck" would mean that her things would be loaded into an eighteen-footer and later checked into bonded storage. She could get everything back after paying $350. Arleen didn't have $350, so she would have opted for "curb," which would mean watching the movers pile everything onto the sidewalk. Her mattresses. A floor-model television. Her copy of *Don't Be Afraid to Discipline*. Her nice glass dining table and the lace tablecloth that fit just-so. Silk plants. Bibles. The meat cuts in the freezer. The shower curtain. Jafaris's asthma machine.

Arleen took her sons—Joni was thirteen, Jafaris was five—to a homeless shelter, which everyone called the Lodge so you could tell your kids, "We're staying at the Lodge tonight," like it was a motel. The two-story stucco building could have passed for one, except for all the Salvation Army signs. Arleen stayed in the 120-bed shelter until April, when she found a house on Nineteenth and Hampton, in the predominantly black inner city, on Milwaukee's North Side, not far from her childhood home. It had thick trim around the windows and doors and was once Kendal green, but the paint had faded and chipped so much over the years that the bare wood siding was now exposed, making the house look camouflaged. At one point someone had started repainting the house plain white but had given up mid-brushstroke, leaving more than half unfinished. There was often no water in the house, and Jori had to bucket out what was in the toilet. But Arleen loved that it was spacious and set apart from other houses. "It was quiet," she remembered. "And five-twenty-five for a whole house, two bedrooms upstairs and two bedrooms downstairs. It was my favorite place."

After a few weeks, the city found Arleen's favorite place "unfit for human habitation," removed her, nailed green boards over the windows and doors, and issued a fine to her landlord. Arleen moved Jori and Jafaris into a drab apartment complex deeper into the inner city, on Atkinson Avenue, which she soon learned was a haven for drug dealers. She feared for her boys, especially Jori—slack-shouldered, with pecan-brown skin and a beautiful smile—who would talk to anyone.

Arleen endured four summer months on Atkinson before moving into a bottom duplex unit on Thirteenth Street and Keefe, a mile away. She and the boys walked their things over. Arleen held her breath and tried the lights, smiling with relief when they came on. She could live off someone else's electricity bill for a while. There was a fist-sized hole in a living-room window, the front door had to be locked with an ugly wooden plank dropped into metal brackets, and the carpet was filthy and ground-in. But the kitchen was spacious and the living room well-lit. Arleen stuffed a piece of clothing into the window hole and hung ivory curtains.

The rent was $550 a month, utilities not included, the going rate in 2008 for a two-bedroom unit in one of the worst neighborhoods in America's fourth-poorest city. Arleen couldn't find a cheaper place, at least not one fit for human habitation, and most landlords wouldn't rent her a smaller one on account of her boys. The rent would take 88 percent of Arleen's $628-a-month welfare check.

Maybe she could make it work. Maybe they could at least stay through winter, until crocuses and tulips stabbed through the thawed ground of spring, Arleen's favorite season....

Even in the most desolate areas of American cities, evictions used to be rare. They used to draw crowds. Eviction riots erupted during the Depression, even though the number of poor families who faced eviction each year was a fraction of what it is today. A *New York Times* account of community resistance to the eviction of three Bronx families in February 1932 observed, "Probably because of the cold, the crowd numbered only 1,000."[1] Sometimes neighbors confronted the marshals directly, sitting on the evicted family's furniture to prevent its removal or moving the family back in despite the judge's orders. The marshals themselves were ambivalent about carrying out evictions. It wasn't why they carried a badge and a gun.

These days, there are sheriff squads whose full-time job is to carry out eviction and foreclosure orders. There are moving companies specializing in evictions, their crews working all day, every weekday. There are hundreds of data-mining companies that sell landlords tenant screening reports listing past evictions and court filings.[2] These days, housing courts swell, forcing commissioners to settle cases in hallways or makeshift offices crammed with old desks and broken file cabinets—and most tenants don't even show up. Low-income families have grown used to the rumble of moving trucks, the early-morning knocks at the door, the belongings lining the curb.

Families have watched their incomes stagnate, or even fall, while their housing costs have soared. Today, the majority of poor renting families in America spend over half of their income on housing, and at least one in four dedicates over 70 percent to paying the rent and keeping the lights on.[3] Millions of Americans are evicted every year because they can't make rent. In Milwaukee, a city of fewer than 105,000 renter households, landlords evict roughly 16,000 adults and children each year. That's sixteen families evicted through the court system daily. But there are other ways, cheaper and quicker ways, for landlords to remove a family than through court order. Some landlords pay tenants a couple hundred dollars to leave by the end of the week. Some take off the front door. Nearly half of all forced moves experienced by renting families in Milwaukee are "informal evictions" that take place in the shadow of the law. If you count all forms of involuntary displacement—formal and informal evictions, landlord foreclosures, building condemnations—you discover that between 2009 and 2011, more than one in eight Milwaukee renters experienced a forced move.[4]

There is nothing special about Milwaukee when it comes to eviction. The numbers are similar in Kansas City, Cleveland, Chicago, and other cities. In 2013, one in eight poor renting families nationwide were unable to pay all of their rent, and a similar number thought it was likely they would be evicted soon.[5]...

Eviction's fallout is severe. Losing a home sends families to shelters, abandoned houses, and the street. It invites depression and illness, compels families to move into degrading housing in dangerous neighborhoods, uproots communities, and harms children. Eviction reveals people's vulnerability and desperation, as well as their ingenuity and guts.

Fewer and fewer families can afford a roof over their head. This is among the most urgent and pressing issues facing America today, and acknowledging the breadth and depth of the problem changes the way we look at poverty. For decades, we've focused mainly on jobs, public assistance, parenting, and mass incarceration. No one can deny the importance of these issues, but something fundamental is missing. We have failed to fully appreciate how deeply housing is implicated in the creation of poverty. Not everyone living in a distressed neighborhood is associated with gang members, parole officers, employers, social workers, or pastors. But nearly all of them have a landlord.

NOTES

1. Frances Fox Piven and Richard Cloward, *Poor People's Movements: Why They Succeed, How They Fail* (New York: Vintage, 1979), 53-55; St. Clair Drake and Horace Cayton, *Black Metropolis: A Study of Negro Life in a Northern City* (New York: Harcourt, Brace, and World, 1945), 85-86; Beryl Satter, *Family Properties: How the Struggle over Race and Real Estate Transformed Chicago and Urban America* (New York: Metropolitan Books, 2009). Although nationally representative historical data on eviction do not exist, these historical accounts of the first half of the twentieth century depict evictions as rare and shocking events. Some local studies from the second half of the twentieth centry, however, document nontrivial rates of involuntary displacement in American cities. See Peter Rossi, *Why Families Move*, 2nd ed. (Beverly Hills, Sage, 1980 [1955]); H. Lawrence Ross, "Reasons for Moves to and from a Central City Area," *Social Forces* 40 (1962): 261-63.

2. Rudy Kleysteuber, "Tenant Screening Thirty Years Later: A Statutory Proposal to Protect Public Records," *Yale Law Journal* 116 (2006): 1344-88.

3. These estimates draw on the American Housing Survey (AHS), 1991-2013. They are conservative, since they exclude renter households reporting no cash income as well as those reporting zero or negative income. The AHS records renting households that reported housing costs in excess of 100 percent of family income. For some households, this scenario reflects response error. For others, including those living off savings and those whose rent and utility bill actually is larger than their income, it does not. Analyses that have examined renter households reporting a housing cost burden in excess of 100 percent of their family income have found that only a minority of these households report receiving some assistance with rent (11 percent) or utilities (5 percent)—assistance which may be ongoing or take place on a single occasion. If you include households reporting a housing cost burden in excess of 100 percent of family income, you find that in 2013, 70 percent of poor renting families were dedicating half of their income to housing costs, and 53 percent were dedicating 70 percent or more of their income. If you exclude those households, you find that 51 percent of poor renting families were dedicating at least half of their income to housing costs, and almost one-quarter were dedicating over 70 percent of their income to it. The right number rests somewhere in the middle of those two point estimates, meaning that in 2013 between 50 and 70 percent of poor renting families spent half of their income on housing and between 25 and 50 percent spent at least 70 percent on it....

4. Milwaukee County Eviction Records, 2003-2007, and GeoLytics Population Estimates, 2003-2007; Milwaukee Area Renters Study, 2009-2011.

5. The national estimates about the proportion of poor renting families being unable to pay all of their rent and believing they soon would be evicted come from the American Housing Survey, 2013, Table S-08-RO, which also reported that over 2.8 million renting households in the US believed it was "very likely" or "somewhat likely" that they would be evicted within the next two months. Chester Hartman and David Robinson ("Evictions: The Hidden Housing Problem," Housing Policy Debate 14 [2003]: 461-501, 461) estimate that the number of Americans evicted every year "is likely in the many millions." See also Kathryn Edin and Laura Lein, *Making Ends Meet: How Single Mothers Survive Welfare and Low-Wage Work* (New York: Russell Sage Foundation, 1997), 53. With respect to statewide eviction estimates, The Neighborhood Law Clinic at the University of Wisconsin Law School has begun to record state-level eviction filings....

27. Bruce Western and Becky Pettit*

Incarceration and Social Inequality

In the last few decades, the institutional contours of American social inequality have been transformed by the rapid growth in the prison and jail population.[1] America's prisons and jails have produced a new social group, a group of social outcasts who are joined by the shared experience of incarceration, crime, poverty, racial minority, and low education. As an outcast group, the men and women in our penal institutions have little access to the social mobility available to the mainstream. Social and economic disadvantage, crystallizing in penal confinement, is sustained over the life course and transmitted from one generation to the next. This is a profound institutionalized inequality that has renewed race and class disadvantage. Yet the scale and empirical details tell a story that is largely unknown.

Though the rate of incarceration is historically high, perhaps the most important social fact is the inequality in penal confinement. This inequality produces extraordinary rates of incarceration among young African American men with no more than a high school education. For these young men, born since the mid-1970s, serving time in prison has become a normal life event.

The influence of the penal system on social and economic disadvantage can be seen in the economic and family lives of the formerly incarcerated. The social inequality produced by mass incarceration is sizable and enduring for three main reasons: it is invisible, it is cumulative, and it is intergenerational. The inequality is invisible in the sense that institutionalized populations commonly lie outside our official accounts of economic well-being. Prisoners, though drawn from the lowest rungs in society, appear in no measures of poverty or unemployment. As a result, the full extent of the disadvantage of groups with high incarceration rates is underestimated. The inequality is cumulative because the social and economic penalties that flow from incarceration are accrued by those who already have the weakest economic opportunities. Mass incarceration thus deepens disadvantage and forecloses mobility for the most marginal in society. Finally, carceral inequalities are intergenerational,

affecting not just those who go to prison and jail, but their families and children, too.

The scale of incarceration is measured by a rate that records the fraction of the population in prison or jail on an average day. From 1980 to 2008, the US incarceration rate climbed from 221 to 762 per 100,000. In the previous five decades, from the 1920s through the mid-1970s, the scale of punishment in America had been stable at around 100 per 100,000. Though the incarceration rate is now nearly eight times its historic average, the scale of punishment today gains its social force from its unequal distribution.

Like criminal activity, prisons and jails are overwhelmingly a male affair. Men account for 90 percent of the prison population and a similar proportion of those in local jails. The social impact of mass incarceration lies in the gross asymmetry of community and family attachment. Women remain in their communities raising children while men confront the possibility of separation through incarceration.[2] Age intensifies these effects: incarceration rates are highest for those in their twenties and early thirties. These are key years in the life course, when most men are establishing a pathway through adulthood by leaving school, getting a job, and starting a family. These years are important not just for a man's life trajectory, but also for the family and children that he helps support.

The profound race and class disparities in incarceration produce the new class of social outsiders. African Americans have always been incarcerated at higher rates than whites, at least since statistics were available from the late nineteenth century. The extent of racial disparity, however, has varied greatly over the past century, following a roughly inverse relationship to the slow incorporation of African Americans as full citizens in American society. In the late nineteenth century, US Census data show that the incarceration rate among African Americans was roughly twice that of whites. The demographic erosion of Jim Crow through the migration of Southern African Americans to the North increased racial disparity in incarceration through the first half of the twentieth century. (Racial disparities in incarceration have always been higher in the North than the South.) By the late 1960s, at the zenith of civil rights activism, the racial disparity had climbed to its contemporary level, leaving African Americans seven times more likely to be in prison or jail than whites.

Class inequalities in incarceration are reflected in the very low educational level of those in prison and jail. The legitimate labor market opportunities for

*Bruce Western and Becky Pettit, 'Incarceration & Social Inequality', Daedalus, 139:3 (Summer, 2010), pp. 8-19. © 2010 by the American Academy of Arts and Sciences.

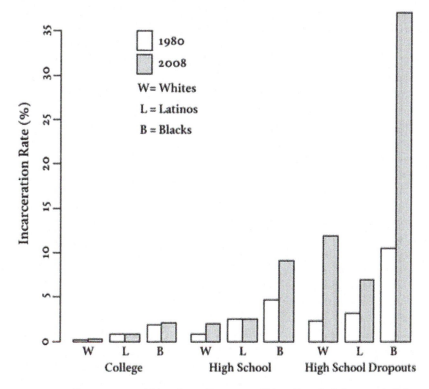

FIGURE 27.1 Percentage of Men Aged Twenty to Thirty-Four in Prison or Jail, by Race/Ethnicity and Education, 1980 and 2008

Source: Becky Pettit, Bryan Sykes, and Bruce Western, "Technical Report on Revised Population Estimates and NLSY79 Analysis Tables for the Pew Public Safety and Mobility Project" (Harvard University, 2009).

men with no more than a high school education have deteriorated as the prison population has grown, and prisoners themselves are drawn overwhelmingly from the least educated. State prisoners average just a tenth grade education, and about 70 percent have no high school diploma.[3] Disparities of race, class, gender, and age have produced extraordinary rates of incarceration among young African American men with little schooling. Figure 27.1 shows prison and jail incarceration rates for men under age thirty-five in 1980, at the beginning of the prison boom, and in 2008, after three decades of rising incarceration rates. The figure reports incarceration separately for whites, Latinos, and African Americans, and separately for three levels of education. Looking at men with a college education, we see that incarceration rates today have barely increased since 1980. Incarceration rates have increased among African Americans and whites who have completed high school. Among young African American men with high school diplomas, about one in ten is in prison or jail.

Most of the growth in incarceration rates is concentrated at the very bottom, among young men with very low levels of education. In 1980, around 10 percent of young African American men who dropped out of high school were in prison or jail. By 2008, this incarceration rate had climbed to 37 percent, an astonishing level of institutionalization given that the average incarceration rate in the general population was 0.76 of 1 percent. Even among young white dropouts, the incarceration rate had grown remarkably, with around one in eight behind bars by 2008. The significant growth of incarceration rates among the least educated reflects increasing class inequality in incarceration through the period of the prison boom.

These incarceration rates provide only a snapshot at a point in time. We can also examine the lifetime chance of incarceration—that is, the chance that someone will go to prison at some point in his or her life. This cumulative risk of incarceration is important if serving time in prison confers an enduring status that affects life chances after returning to free society. The lifetime risk of imprisonment describes how many people are at risk of these diminished life chances.

We calculated the cumulative chance of imprisonment for two birth cohorts, one born just after World War II, from 1945 to 1949, and another born from 1975 to 1979 (Table 27.1). For each cohort, we calculated the chances of imprisonment, not jail incarceration. Prisons are the deep end of the criminal justice system, now incarcerating people for an average of twenty-eight months for a felony conviction. While there are about ten million admissions to local jails each year—for those awaiting trial or serving short sentences—around seven hundred thousand prisoners are now admitted annually to state and federal facilities.

These cumulative chances of imprisonment are calculated up to age thirty-four. For most of the population, this represents the lifetime likelihood of serving prison time. For the older post-war cohort who reached their mid-thirties at the end of the 1970s, about one in ten African American men served time in prison. For the younger cohort born from 1975 to 1979, the lifetime risk of imprisonment for African American men had increased to one in four. Prison time has become a normal life event for African American men who have dropped out of high school. Fully 68 percent of these men born since the mid-1970s have prison records. The high rate of incarceration has redrawn the pathway through young adulthood. The main sources of upward mobility for African American men—namely, military service and a college degree—are significantly less common than a prison record. For the first generations growing up in the post–civil rights era, the prison now looms as a significant institutional influence on life chances.

The ubiquity of penal confinement in the lives of young African American men with little schooling is historically novel, emerging only in the last decade. However, this new reality is only half the story of understanding the significance of mass incarceration in America. The other half of the story concerns the effects of incarceration on social and economic inequality. Because the characteristic inequalities produced by the American prison boom are invisible, cumulative, and intergenerational, they are extremely enduring, sustained over lifetimes and passed through families.

Invisible Inequality. The inequality created by incarceration is often invisible to the mainstream of society because incarceration is concentrated and segregative. We have seen that steep racial and class disparities in incarceration have produced a generation of social outliers whose collective experience is

TABLE 27.1 Cumulative Risk of Imprisonment by Age Thirty to Thirty-Four for Men Born from 1945 to 1949 and 1975 to 1979, by Educational Attainment and Race/Ethnicity

	All	High School Dropouts	High School/ GED*	College
1945–1949 COHORT				
White	1.4	3.8	1.5	0.4
Black	10.4	14.7	11.0	5.3
Latino	2.8	4.1	2.9	1.1
1975–1979 COHORT				
White	5.4	28.0	6.2	1.2
Black	26.8	68.0	21.4	6.6
Latino	12.2	19.6	9.2	3.4

*Denotes completed high school or equivalency.

Source: Becky Pettit, Bryan Sykes, and Bruce Western, "Technical Report on revised Population Estimates and NLSY79 Analysis Tables for the Pew Public Safety and Mobility Project" (Harvard University, 2009).

wholly different from the rest of American society. The extreme concentration of incarceration rates is compounded by the obviously segregative function of the penal system, which often relocates people to far-flung facilities distant from their communities and families. As a result, people in prison and jail are disconnected from the basic institutions—households and the labor market—that dominate our common understanding and measurement of the population. The segregation and social concentration of incarceration thus help conceal its effects. This fact is particularly important for public policy because in assessing the social and economic well-being of the population, the incarcerated fraction is frequently overlooked, and inequality is underestimated as a result.

The idea of invisible inequality is illustrated by considering employment rates as they are conventionally measured by the Current Population Survey, the large monthly labor force survey conducted by the Census Bureau. For groups that are weakly attached to the labor market, like young men with little education, economic status is often measured by the employment-to-population ratio. This figure, more expansive than the unemployment rate, counts as jobless those who have dropped out of the labor market altogether. The Current Population Survey is drawn on a sample of households, so those who are institutionalized are not included in the survey-based description of the population.

Figure 27.2 shows the employment-to-population ratio for African American men under age

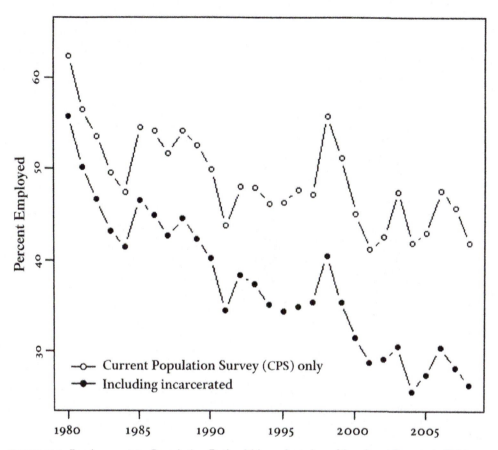

FIGURE 27.2 Employment-to-Population Ratio, African American Men Aged Twenty to Thirty-Four with Less than Twelve Years of Schooling, 1980 to 2008

Source: Becky Pettit, Bryan Sykes, and Bruce Western, "Technical Report on Revised Population Estimates and NLSY79 Analysis Tables for the Pew Public Safety and Mobility Project" (Harvard University, 2009).

thirty-five who have not completed high school. Conventional estimates of the employment rate show that by 2008, around 40 percent of African American male dropouts were employed. These estimates, based on the household survey, fail to count that part of the population in prison or jail. Once prison and jail inmates are included in the population count (and among the jobless), we see that employment among young African American men with little schooling fell to around 25 percent by 2008. Indeed, by 2008, these men were more likely to be locked up than employed.

Cumulative Inequality. Serving time in prison or jail diminishes social and economic opportunities. As we have seen, these diminished opportunities are found among those already most socioeconomically disadvantaged. A burgeoning research literature examining the economic effects of incarceration finds that incarceration is associated with reduced earn-

ings and employment.[4] We analyzed panel data from the National Longitudinal Survey of Youth (NLSY), one of the few surveys that follows respondents over a long period of time and interviews incarcerated respondents in prison. The NLSY began in 1979, when its panel of respondents was aged fourteen to twenty-one; it completed its latest round of interviews in 2006. Matching our population estimates of incarceration, one in five African American male respondents in the NLSY has been interviewed at some point between 1979 and 2006 while incarcerated, compared to 5 percent of whites and 12 percent of Latino respondents. Analysis of the NLSY showed that serving time in prison was associated with a 40 percent reduction in earnings and with reduced job tenure, reduced hourly wages, and higher unemployment.

The negative effects of incarceration, even among men with very poor economic opportunities to

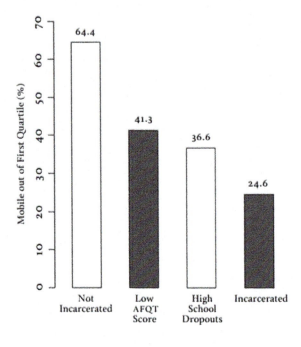

FIGURE 27.3 Twenty-Year Earnings Mobility Among Men in the Bottom Quintile of Earnings Distribution in 1986, National Longitudinal Survey of Youth (NLSY) Men

AFQT stands for Armed Forces Qualifying Test.

Source: Becky Pettit, Bryan Sykes, and Bruce Western, "Technical Report on Revised Population Estimates and NLSY79 Analysis Tables for the Pew Public Safety and Mobility Project" (Harvard University, 2009).

begin with, are related to the strong negative perceptions employers have of job seekers with criminal records. Devah Pager's experimental research has studied these employer perceptions by sending pairs of fake job seekers to apply for real jobs.[5] In each pair, one of the job applicants was randomly assigned a resume indicating a criminal record (a parole officer is listed as a reference), and the "criminal" applicant was instructed to check the box on the job application indicating he had a criminal record. A criminal record was found to reduce callbacks from prospective employers by around 50 percent, an effect that was larger for African Americans than for whites.

Incarceration may reduce economic opportunities in several ways. The conditions of imprisonment may promote habits and behaviors that are poorly suited to the routines of regular work. Time in prison means time out of the labor force, depleting the work experience of the incarcerated compared to their nonincarcerated counterparts. The stigma of a criminal conviction may also repel employers who prefer job applicants with clean records. Pager's audit study offers clear evidence for the negative effects of criminal stigma. Employers, fearing legal liability or even just unreliability, are extremely reluctant to hire workers with criminal convictions.

A simple picture of the poor economic opportunities of the formerly incarcerated is given by the earnings mobility of men going to prison compared to other disadvantaged groups. The NLSY data can be used to study earnings mobility over several decades. We calculated the chances that a poor man in the lowest fifth of the earnings distribution in 1986 would move up and out of the lowest fifth by 2006. Among low-income men who are not incarcerated, nearly two-thirds are upwardly mobile by 2006 (Figure 27.3). Another group in the NLSY has very low levels of cognitive ability, scoring in the bottom quintile of the Armed Forces Qualifying Test, the standardized test used for military service. Among low-income men with low scores on the test, only 41 percent are upwardly mobile. Upward mobility is even less common among low-income high school dropouts. Still, we observe the least mobility of all among men who were incarcerated at some point between 1986 and 2006. For these men, only one in four rises out of the bottom quintile of the earnings distribution.

Intergenerational Inequality. Finally, the effects of the prison boom extend also to the families of those who are incarcerated. Through the prism of research on poverty, scholars find that the family life of the disadvantaged has become dramatically more complex and unstable over the last few decades. Divorce and nonmarital births have contributed significantly to rising rates of single parenthood, and these changes in American family structure are concentrated among low-income mothers. As a consequence, poor children regularly grow up, at least for a time, with a single mother and, at different times, with a variety of adult males in their households.

High rates of parental incarceration likely add to the instability of family life among poor children. Over half of all prisoners have children under the age of eighteen, and about 45 percent of those parents were living with their children at the time they were sent to prison. About two-thirds of prisoners stay in regular contact with their children either by phone, mail, or visitation.[6] Ethnographer Megan Comfort paints a vivid picture of the effects of men's incarceration on the women and families in their lives. She quotes a prisoner at San Quentin State Prison in California:

> Nine times out of ten it's the woman [maintaining contact with prisoners]. Why? Because your homeboys, or your friends, if you're in that lifestyle, most the time they're gonna be sittin' right next to your ass in prison . . . The males, they don't really participate like a lot of females in the lives of the incarcerated . . . They don't deal with it, like first of all they don't like to bring to reality that you're in prison; they don't wanna think about that . . . Or some of 'em just don't care. So the male's kinda like wiped out of there, so that *puts all the burden on the woman.*[7]

Partly because of the burdens of incarceration on women who are left to raise families in free society, incarceration is strongly associated with divorce and separation. In addition to the forced separation of incarceration, the post-release effects on economic opportunities leave formerly incarcerated parents less equipped to provide financially for their children. New research also shows that the children of incarcerated parents, particularly the boys, are at greater risk of developmental delays and behavioral problems.[8] Against this evidence for the negative effects of incarceration, we should weigh the gains to public safety obtained by separating violent or otherwise antisocial men from their children and partners. Domestic violence is much more common among the formerly incarcerated compared to other disadvantaged men. Survey data indicate that formerly incarcerated men are about four times more likely to assault their domestic partners than men who have never been incarcerated. Though the relative risk is very high, around 90 percent of the partners of formerly incarcerated report no domestic violence at all.

The scale of the effects of parental incarceration on children can be revealed simply by statistics showing the number of children with a parent in prison or jail. Among white children in 1980, only 0.4 of 1 percent had an incarcerated parent; by 2008 this figure had increased to 1.75 percent. Rates of parental incarceration are roughly double among Latino children, with 3.5 percent of children having a parent locked up by 2008. Among African American children, 1.2 million, or about 11 percent, had a parent incarcerated by 2008 (Figure 27.4).

The spectacular growth in the American penal system over the last three decades was concentrated in a small segment of the population, among young minority men with very low levels of education. By the early 2000s, prison time was a common life event for this group, and today more than two-thirds of African American male dropouts are expected to serve time in state or federal prison. These demographic contours of mass imprisonment have created a new class of social outsiders whose relationship to the state and society is wholly different from the rest of the population.

Social marginality is deepened by the inequalities produced by incarceration. Workers with prison records experience significant declines in earnings and employment. Parents in prison are likely to divorce or separate, and through the contagious effects of the institution, their children are in some degree "prisonized," exposed to the routines of prison life through visitation and the parole supervision of their parents. Yet much of this reality remains hidden from view. In social life, for all but those whose incarceration rates are highest, prisons are exotic institutions unknown to the social mainstream. Our national data systems, and the social facts they produce, are structured around normative domestic and economic life, systematically excluding prison inmates.

Thus we define carceral inequalities as invisible, cumulative, and intergenerational. Because they are so deeply concentrated in a small disadvantaged fraction of the population, the social and economic effects of incarceration create a discrete social group whose collective experience is so distinctive yet unknown that their disadvantage remains largely beyond the apprehension of public policy or public conversation. The redrawing of American social inequality by mass incarceration amounts to a contraction of citizenship—a contraction of that population

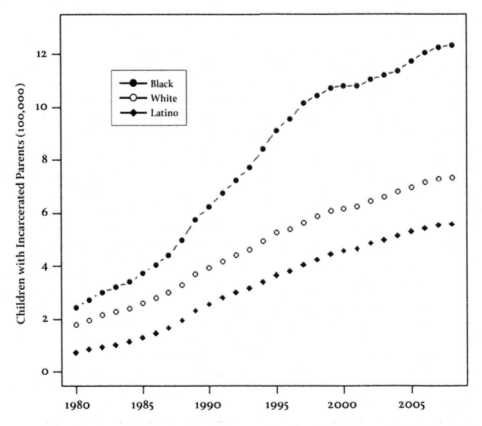

FIGURE 27.4 Number of Children under Eighteen with a Parent in Prison or Jail, 1980 to 2008

Source: Becky Pettit, Bryan Sykes, and Bruce Western, "Technical Report on Revised Population Estimates and NLSY79 Analysis Tables for the Pew Public Safety and Mobility Project" (Harvard University, 2009).

that enjoys, in T. H. Marshall's words, "full membership in society."[9] Inequality of this kind threatens to be self-sustaining. Socioeconomic disadvantage, crime, and incarceration in the current generation undermine the stability of family life and material support for children. As adults, these children will be at greater risk of diminished life chances and criminal involvement, and at greater risk of incarceration as a result.

Skeptics will respond that these are false issues of social justice: the prison boom substantially reduced crime, and criminals should forfeit their societal membership in any case. The crime-reducing effects of incarceration are hotly debated, however. Empirical estimates of the effects of incarceration on crime vary widely, and often they turn on assumptions that are difficult to test directly. Researchers have focused on the sharp decline in US crime rates through the 1990s, studying the influence of rising prison populations. Conservative estimates attribute about one-tenth of the 1990s crime decline to the growth in

imprisonment rates.[10] Though the precise impact of incarceration on crime is uncertain, there is broad agreement that additional imprisonment at high rates of incarceration does little to reduce crime. The possibility of improved public safety through increased incarceration is by now exhausted.

Studies of the effects of incarceration on crime also focus only on the short term. Indeed, because of the negative effects of incarceration on economic opportunities and family life, incarceration contributes to crime in the long run by adding to idleness and family breakdown among released prisoners. Scale matters, too. If the negative effects of incarceration were scattered among a small number of serious criminal offenders, these effects may well be overwhelmed by reduction in crime through incapacitation.

Today, however, clear majorities of the young men in poor communities are going to prison and returning home less employable and more detached from their families. In this situation, the institutions charged with public safety have become vitally implicated in the unemployment and the fragile family structure characteristic of high-crime communities. For poorly educated young men in high-incarceration communities, a prison record now carries little stigma; incentives to commit to the labor market and family life have been seriously weakened.

To say that prison reduces crime (perhaps only in the short run) is a spectacularly modest claim for a system that now costs $70 billion annually. Claims to the crime-reducing effects of prison, by themselves, provide little guidance for policy because other approaches may be cheaper. Measures to reduce school dropout, increase human capital, and generally increase employment among young men seem especially promising alternatives. Results for programs for very young children are particularly striking. Evaluations of early childhood educational programs show some of their largest benefits decades later in reduced delinquency and crime.[11] For adult men now coming out of prison, new evaluations show that jobs programs reduce recidivism and increase employment and earnings.[12] The demographic concentration of incarceration accompanies spatial concentration. If some portion of that $70 billion in correctional expenditures were spent on improving skills and reducing unemployment in poor neighborhoods, a sustainable and socially integrative public safety may be produced.

Much of the political debate about crime policy ignores the contemporary scale of criminal punishment, its unequal distribution, and its negative social and economic effects. Our analysis of the penal system as an institution of social stratification, rather than crime control, highlights all these neglected outcomes and leaves us pessimistic that widespread incarceration can sustainably reduce crime. The current system is expensive, and it exacerbates the social problems it is charged with controlling. Our perspective, focused on the social and economic inequalities of American life, suggests that social policy improving opportunity and employment, for young men in particular, holds special promise as an instrument for public safety.

Our perspective on inequality points to a broader view of public safety that is not produced by punishment alone. Robust public safety grows when people have order and predictability in their daily lives. Crime is just one danger, joining unemployment, poor health, and family instability along a spectrum of threats to an orderly life. Public safety is built as much on the everyday routines of work and family as it is on police and prisons. Any retrenchment of the penal system therefore must recognize how deeply the prison boom is embedded in the structure of American social inequality. Ameliorating these inequalities will be necessary to set us on a path away from mass incarceration and toward a robust, socially integrative public safety.

NOTES

1. We gratefully acknowledge Bryan Sykes, Deirdre Bloome, and Chris Muller, who helped conduct the research reported in this paper. This research was supported in part by a gift from The Elfenworks Foundation.

2. In her essay for this issue, Candace Kruttschnitt shows that women's incarceration has pronounced effects by separating mothers from their children. The continued growth of women's incarceration rates threatens to have large effects on family life.

3. Bruce Western, *Punishment and Inequality in America* (New York: Russell Sage Foundation, 2006); Caroline Wolf Harlow, *Education and Correctional Populations* (Washington, D.C.: Bureau of Justice Statistics, 2003).

4. Marry J. Holzer, "Collateral Costs: Effects of Incarceration on Employment and Earnings Among Young Workers," in *Do Prisons Make Us Safer?* ed. Steven Raphael and Michael A. Stoll (New York: Russell Sage Foundation, 2009).

5. Devah Pager, *Marked: Race, Crime, and Finding Work in an Era of Mass Incarceration* (Chicago: University of Chicago Press, 2007).

6. Christopher Murnola, "Incarcerated Parents and Their Children" (Washington, D.C.: Bureau of Justice Statistics, 2000).

7. Megan Comfort, "In the Tube at San Quentin: The 'Secondary Prisonization' of Women Visiting Inmates," *Journal of Contemporary Ethnography* 32 (1) (2003): 82; emphasis original.

8. Christopher Wildeman, "Paternal Incarceration and Children's Physically Aggressive Behaviors: Evidence from the Fragile Families and Child Wellbeing Study." Working paper 2008-02-FF (Fragile Families and Child Wellbeing, 2008).

9. T. H. Marshall, *Citizenship and Social Class* (Concord. Mass.: Pluto Press, 1992).

10. Western, *Punishment and Inequality in America*, chap. 7.

11. Pedro Carneiro and James J. Heckman, "Human Capital Policy," in James J. Heckman and Alan B. Krueger, *Inequality in America: What Role for Human Capital Policies?* (Cambridge, Mass.: MIT Press, 2005).

12. Cindy Redcross, Dan Bloom, and Gilda Azurdia, "Transitional Jobs for Ex-prisoners: Implementation, Two-Year Impacts, and Costs of the Center for Employment Opportunities (CEO) Prisoner Reentry Program" (MDRC, 2009).

PART V

MOBILITY AND THE AMERICAN DREAM

The importance of social science research on social mobility is well-illustrated with the parable of the stork. The stork's job, as we all know, is to deliver the newborn baby to her new home. We might imagine one of these hard-working storks, a mile-high in the sky with a baby dangling from his bill, saying to his charge, "little girl, you seem really sweet, and I'd like to help you ... shall I drop you into a really rich family?" The newborn girl, having just read a Horatio Alger novel, might well respond, "No, no, that's America down there—the land of opportunity—so anywhere is just fine."

If indeed this were her response, our suspicion is that the little girl had been reading too many Horatio Alger novels and not enough social science research. The latter research suggests that, insofar as the little girl wants a decent job and income when she grows up, her odds of securing them would in fact be much improved were she dropped into a well-off family.

Why should we care about this research? We should care because Americans make a sharp distinction between the distribution of social rewards (e.g., the income distribution) and the distribution of opportunities for securing these rewards. It is the latter distribution that governs popular judgments about the legitimacy of inequality: The typical American, for example, is quite willing to tolerate substantial inequalities in power, wealth, or prestige provided that the opportunities for securing these rewards are distributed equally. If the competition has been fairly run, most Americans are willing to reward the winners and punish the losers.

This sensibility has in turn led to much research assessing to what extent the country's commitment to equal opportunity has indeed been upheld. The purpose of Part V of the reader is to introduce readers to the best of this research. We will introduce the country's first comprehensive analyses of mobility using administrative tax records; we will introduce sophisticated models of mobility; and we will introduce the best evidence and research on the mechanisms by which mobility can be achieved.

The latter line of research is especially well-developed. There is a long tradition of research, for example, on (a) the extent to which children raised in high-income families have better school outcomes (e.g., test scores) even at very early ages (see Reardon, Ch. 28); (b) the extent to which educational achievement is a key mediating variable between origins and destinations (see Torche, Ch. 34); (c) the role of social psychological variables, such as aspirations and expectations, in affecting whether a child "gets ahead" (see Morgan, Ch. 31; MacLeod, Ch. 36); (d) the effects of contacts, networks, and "who you know" on income and occupational outcomes (see Granovetter, Ch. 38; Fernandez and Fernandez-Mateo, Ch. 39); and (e) the extent to which partying and other non-academic activities affect the likelihood of mobility (see Armstrong, Ch. 35). We have also devoted an entire subsection to examining how educational opportunities are allocated and how educational investments are rewarded.

The backdrop to this research is of course the growing concern that opportunities for getting ahead may be growing more unequal. This "rigidification hypothesis" was prominent during the Depression years, the postwar period, and has now surfaced again. Although these concerns about declining opportunity have not been borne out in the past, the recent takeoff in income inequality has revived them. Why might the takeoff matter for class mobility? The argument is simple: As income inequality grows, interclass differences in family income will become greater, and children born into privileged classes will have comparatively more resources that then advantage them in the competition to get ahead. These extra resources at the top might be used to buy high-quality child care and preschool, educational toys and books, after-school training and preparation, elite preparatory schools, and elite colleges.

It is considerations of this sort that have motivated many politicians, scholars, and the general public to worry that opportunities in the US may be declining. It is difficult to assess whether these worries are on the mark because the US does not have a high-quality time series on long-term trends in mobility. The available evidence on this question, although clearly incomplete, is addressed to the extent possible in several of the readings in this section.

The Race for Education

28. Sean F. Reardon*

The Widening Academic Achievement Gap Between the Rich and the Poor

Introduction

The socioeconomic status of a child's parents has always been one of the strongest predictors of the child's academic achievement and educational attainment. The relationship between family socioeconomic characteristics and student achievement is one of the most robust patterns in educational scholarship, yet the causes and mechanisms of this relationship have been the subject of considerable disagreement and debate (see, for example, Bowles and Gintis 1976, 2002; Brooks-Gunn and Duncan 1997; Duncan and Brooks-Gunn 1997; Duncan, Brooks-Gunn, and Klebanov 1994; Herrnstein and Murray 1994; Jacoby and Glauberman 1995; Lareau 1989, 2003).

Trends in socioeconomic achievement gaps—the achievement disparities between children from high- and low-income families or between children from families with high or low levels of parental educational attainment—have received [surprisingly little] attention.

The question is whether and how that relationship between family socioeconomic characteristics and academic achievement has changed during the last fifty years. In particular, I investigate the extent to which the rising income inequality of the last four decades has been paralleled by a similar increase in the income achievement gradient. As the income gap between high- and low-income families has widened, has the achievement gap between children in high- and low-income families also widened?

Data

Assembling information on trends in the relationship between socioeconomic status and academic achievement requires examination of multiple sources of data. I use data from nineteen nationally representative studies, including studies conducted by the National Center for Education Statistics (NCES), the Long-Term Trend and Main National Assessment of Educational Progress (NAEP) studies, US components of international studies, and other studies. Although these studies vary in a number of ways, each of them provides data on the math or reading skills, or both, of nationally representative samples of students, together with some data on students' family socioeconomic characteristics, such as family income, parental education, and parental occupation.[1]

Measuring Achievement Gaps

To compare the size of the achievement gap across studies, I report test-score differences between groups in standard-deviation units, adjusted for the estimated reliability of each test. This is standard practice when comparing achievement gaps measured with different tests (see, for example, Clotfelter, Ladd, and Vigdor 2006; Fryer and Levitt 2004, 2006.) So long as the true variance of achievement remains constant over time, this allows valid comparisons in the size of the gaps across different studies using different tests (see online appendix section for technical details).

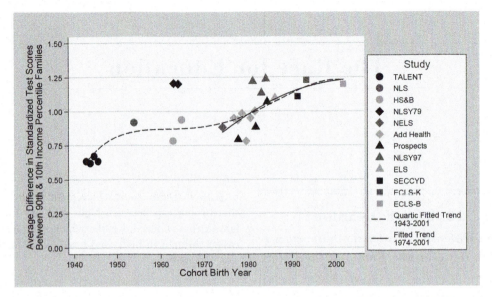

FIGURE 28.1 Trend in 90/10 Income Achievement Gap in Reading, by Birth Cohort (1943 to 2001 Cohorts)

Source: Author's compilation based on data from Project Talent (Flanagan et al. n.d.); NLS, HS&B, NELS, ELS, ECLS-K, ECLS-B (U.S. Department of Education, Center for Education Statistics 1999, 2000, 2001, 2004, 2009, 2010); Prospects (U.S. Department of Education 1995); NLSY79, NLSY97 (U.S. Bureau of Labor Statistics 1980, 1999); SECCYD (National Institute of Child Health and Human Development 2010); and Add Health (Harris 2009, reading only).

Note: See note 4 and online appendix for further details.

Measures of Socioeconomic Status

I rely on two key measures of socioeconomic status: family income and parental educational attainment. Each of the nineteen studies used includes information on parental educational attainment; twelve of the studies include information on family income. Nine of the studies include parent-reported family income, [and . . .] three include student-reported income.[2] In all studies, I adjust the estimated associations between family income and achievement for measurement error in family income.

Although each of the nineteen studies includes a measure of parental educational attainment, in some studies this is reported by students, while in others it is reported by parents. Because reports of their parents' education are particularly unreliable for younger students, I include studies with student-reported parental education only if the students were in high school themselves when reporting their parents' educational attainment. As a measure of parental educational attainment, I use the maximum of the mother's and father's attainment (or the attainment of the single parent in the home if both are not present).

Trends in Socioeconomic Status–Achievement Gradients

To begin with, consider the difference in achievement between children from high- and low-income families. One way to measure this difference is to compare the average math and reading skills of children from families with incomes at the 90th percentile of the family income distribution (about $160,000 in 2008) to those in families with incomes at the 10th percentile of the family income distribution (about $17,500 in 2008).[3]

Figures 28.1 and 28.2 present the estimated 90/10 income achievement gap for cohorts of students born from the mid-1940s through 2001.[4] These estimates are derived from the twelve nationally representative studies available that include family income as well as reading and/or math scores for school-age children.

Although the tests used are not exactly comparable across all the studies included, both figures show a clear trend of increasing income achievement gaps across cohorts born over a nearly sixty-year period. The estimated income achievement gaps among children born in 2001 are roughly 75

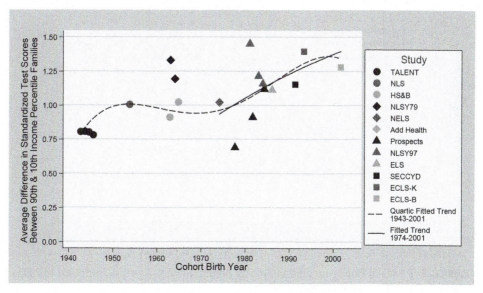

FIGURE 28.2 Trend in 90/10 Income Achievement Gap in Math, by Birth Cohort (1943 to 2001 Cohorts)

Source: Author's compilation based on data from Project Talent (Flanagan et al. n.d.); NLS, HS&B, NELS, ELS, ECLS-K, ECLS-B (U.S. Department of Education, Center for Education Statistics 1999, 2000, 2001, 2004, 2009, 2010); Prospects (U.S. Department of Education 1995); NLSY79, NLSY97 (U.S. Bureau of Labor Statistics 1980, 1999); and SECCYD (National Institute of Child Health and Human Development 2010).

Note: See online appendix for further details.

percent larger than the estimated gaps among children born in the early 1940s. The gap appears to have grown among cohorts born in the 1940s and early 1950s, stabilized for cohorts born from the 1950s through the mid-1970s, and then grown steadily since the mid-1970s.

There are, however, several reasons to suspect that the trend in the estimated gaps for the earliest cohorts, those born before 1970, is not as accurately estimated as the later trend. For one thing, the quality of the achievement tests used in the early studies may not have been as good as those used in the more recent studies. In addition, as I have noted, family income was reported by students rather than by a parent in three of the early studies. Furthermore, [these studies] exclude [high school] dropouts, who are disproportionately low-income and low-achieving students. Each of these factors might lead the gaps to be underestimated in the early cohorts relative to later cohorts.

Although the trend in achievement gaps prior to 1970 is somewhat unclear, the trend from the mid-1970s to 2001 appears relatively clear. Figures 28.1 and 28.2 include fitted trend lines from 1974 to

2001 (the solid lines); these indicate that the income achievement gap has grown by roughly 40 to 50 percent within twenty-five years, a very sizable increase.

How Large Are These Gaps?

Figures 28.1 and 28.2 report income gaps in standard-deviation units. Although this is a metric familiar to researchers and one that is useful for comparing the size of gaps across studies using different tests, it may not be immediately obvious how large these gaps are in substantive terms. One way to get a sense of the size of the gaps is to compare them to the amount that an average student learns during the course of a year. Data from the NAEP indicate that the average student gains 1.2 to 1.5 standard deviations in math and reading between fourth and eighth grade, and between 0.6 and 0.7 standard deviations in math and reading between eighth and twelfth grade.[5] Thus, a gap of 1 standard deviation is substantively very large, corresponding to roughly 3 to 6 years of learning in middle or high school. . . .

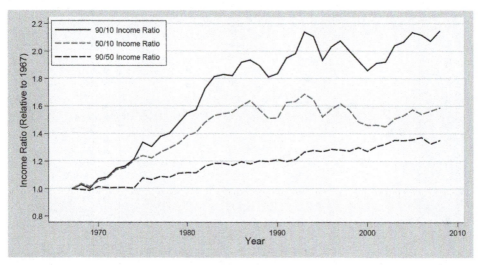

FIGURE 28.3 Trends in Family-Income Inequality Among School-Age Children, 1967 to 2008 (Weighted by Number of School-Age Children)

Source: Author's calculations, based on U.S. Bureau of the Census (King et al. 2010).

Note: Each line shows the trends in the ratio of household incomes at two percentiles of the income distribution. All trends are divided by their value in 1967 in order to put the trends on a common scale.

Why Has the Income Achievement Gap Grown?

The evidence thus far indicates that the relationship between a family's position in the income distribution and their children's academic achievement has grown substantially stronger during the last half-century. In the following section I discuss four broad possible explanations for this increase: (1) income inequality has grown during the last forty years, meaning that the income difference between families at the 90th and 10th percentiles of the income distribution has grown; (2) family investment patterns have changed differentially during the last half-century, so that high-income families now invest relatively more time and resources in their children's cognitive development than do lower-income families; (3) income has grown more strongly correlated with other socioeconomic characteristics of families, meaning that high-income families increasingly have greater socioeconomic and social resources that may benefit their children; and (4) increasing income segregation has led to greater differentiation in school quality and schooling opportunities between the rich and the poor.

Rising Income Inequality

Income inequality in the United States has grown substantially in the last four decades and as of 2007

was at a level similar to the levels in 1925 to 1940, when US income inequality was at its twentieth-century peak (Burkhauser et al. 2009; Piketty and Saez 2003, 2008).[6] If rising income inequality is responsible for the growth in the income achievement gap, we would expect to see that gap grow in a pattern similar to the growth in income inequality. To investigate this, consider the trends in measures of family income inequality illustrated in Figure 28.3, which shows the changes in the 90/10 family income ratio (the ratio of the family income of the child at the 90th percentile of the family income distribution to that of the child at the 10th percentile), the 90/50 family income ratio, and the 50/10 family income ratio among school-age children from 1967 to 2008.[7] Several key trends are evident in Figure 28.3. First, the 90/10 family income ratio grew rapidly from 1967 to the early 1990s, more than doubling in twenty-five years. In 1967, the family income of the child at the 90th percentile of the family income distribution was 4.6 times greater than that of the child at the 10th percentile; in 1993 this 90/10 ratio was 9.9. After 1993, the 90/10 ratio declined to 8.6 in 2000 before climbing again to 9.9 by 2005. Second, the growth in the ratio of the incomes in the 90th to those in the 10th percentiles from 1967 to 1993 was driven largely by a rapid increase in the 50/10 family income ratio, which grew from 2.5 in 1967 to 4.1 in 1987, a 64 percent increase in twenty years. After the late 1980s, however, the 50/10 family

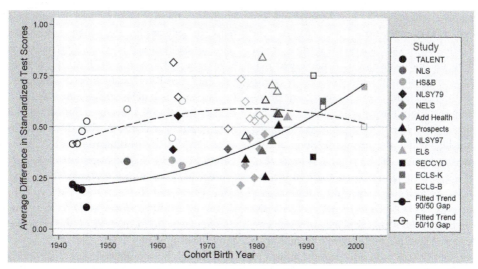

FIGURE 28.4 Trend in 90/50 and 50/10 Income Achievement Gap, Reading, by Birth Year (1943 to 2001 Cohorts)

Source: Author's compilation based on data from Project Talent (Flanagan et al. n.d.); NLS, HS&.B, NELS, ELS, ECIS-K, ECLS-B (U.S. Department of Education, Center for Education Statistics 1999, 2000, 2001, 2004, 2009, 2010); Prospects (U.S. Department of Education 1995); NLSY79, NLSY97 (U.S. Bureau of Labor Statistics 1980, 1999); SECCYD (National Institute of Child Health and Human Development 2010); and Add Health (Harris 2009, reading only).

Note: Solid symbols represent 90/50 income achievement gaps; hollow symbols represent 50/10 income achievement gaps.

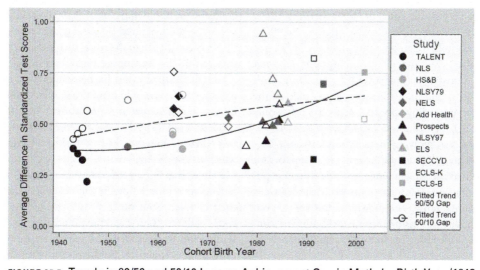

FIGURE 28.5 Trends in 90/50 and 50/10 Income Achievement Gap in Math, by Birth Year (1943 to 2001 Cohorts)

Source: Author's compilation based on data from Project Talent (Flanagan et al. n.d.); NLS, HS&B, NELS, ELS, ECLS-K, ECLS-B (U.S. Department of Education, Center for Education Statistics 1999, 2000, 2001, 2004, 2009, 2010); Prospects (U.S. Department of Education 1995); NLSY79, NLSY97 (U.S. Bureau of Labor Statistics 1980, 1999); and SECCYD (National Institute of Child Health and Human Development 2010).

Note: Solid symbols represent 90/50 income achievement gaps; hollow symbols represent 50/10 income achievement gaps.

income ratio leveled off and then declined to 3.6 by 2002. Third, the ratio between the 90th and the 50th family income percentiles grew steadily from the early 1970s through 2008, increasing from 1.8 in 1974 to 2.5 in 2005, an increase of 36 percent. Thus, from the late 1960s through the late 1980s, the increase in lower-tail family income inequality was largely responsible for the increase in the ratio between the incomes of the 90th and 10th percentiles. After the late 1980s, however, increasing upper-tail inequality and decreasing lower-tail inequality largely offset one another for the next twenty years.

If the increasing income achievement gap is driven by increasing income inequality, we would expect that gap to grow most sharply between students at the 50th and 10th percentiles of the family income distribution from the 1960s through the 1980s (or for cohorts born in these years), and then to grow among those at the high end of the income distribution after that. Moreover, because the 50/10 ratio is larger than the 90/50 ratio, we might expect the 50/10 income achievement gap to be larger than the 90/50 income achievement gap as well.[8] Figures 28.4 and 28.5 display the estimated 90/50 and 50/10 income achievement gaps for each of the studies with income data.

Figures 28.4 and 28.5 do not exactly conform to what we would expect if the growing income achievement gap were simply due to rising income inequality among families with school-age children. Although the 50/10 income achievement gap in reading is generally larger than the 90/50 income achievement gap for cohorts born before 1990, the gaps are roughly similar in size in math, and the 90/50 gap is actually equal or larger than the 50/10 gap in the most recent cohorts. Moreover, the 90/50 gap appears to have grown faster than the 50/10 gap during the 1970s and 1980s, the opposite of what we would predict on the basis of the rates of growth of the 90/50 and 50/10 income ratios (indeed, the 50/10 gap in reading appears to have been basically flat through this time period, when the 50/10 income ratio was growing most rapidly). In sum, Figures 28.4 and 28.5 do not provide much support for the idea that the growing income achievement gap is attributable to rising income inequality, at least not in any simple sense. Nor, however, do they rule out the possibility that rising income inequality has contributed to the rising income achievement gap.

Differential Investments in Children's Cognitive Development

Families may be changing how they invest in their children's cognitive development. If so, this may explain some of the rising income achievement gap. Sociologists and historians of the family have argued that parents, particularly those in the middle class, have become increasingly focused on children's cognitive development during the last fifty years (Lareau 1989; Schaub 2010; Wrigley 1989).

Another factor that may contribute to parents' increasing focus on their children's cognitive development is the rise of test-based accountability systems in education. Although some forms of standardized testing, including IQ tests and the SAT, have been prevalent for much of the twentieth century (Lemann 1999), standardized achievement testing has become much more common with the rise of the accountability movement following the 1983 publication of *A Nation at Risk* (National Commission on Excellence in Education 1983). The combination of the increasing importance of educational success in determining earnings (Levy and Murnane 1992) and the increasing importance of test scores in defining educational success may have caused parents to focus more on their children's cognitive development.

Although both middle-class and low-income parents may have become increasingly aware of the intellectual development of their children, Annette Lareau (1989, 2003) argues that middle- and upper-class parents engage much more commonly in what she calls "concerted cultivation"—the deliberate organization of childhood around intellectual and socioemotional development. If this concerted cultivation is effective at improving children's intellectual skills—at least, those measured by standardized tests—then this may contribute to the rising income achievement gap. If middle- and upper-income families are increasingly likely to invest in their children's cognitive development, we would expect to see evidence of this in the trends in parental investment in children's child care, education, and education-related activities. There is, however, little available evidence with which to test this hypothesis. Studies of parental time use show that highly educated and higher-income parents spend more time in child-care activities with their children than do less-educated and lower-income children (Guryan, Hurst, and Kearney 2008; Ramey and Ramey 2010). Moreover, the amount of time parents spend in child-care activities (broadly defined) has increased from 1965 to 2008, and has increased more for college-educated parents than for less-educated parents (Bianchi 2000; Ramey and Ramey 2010). In addition, in a recent paper using data from the Consumer Expenditure Survey, Sabino Kornrich and Frank Furstenburg (2010) find that families' spending on children increased substantially from 1972 to 2007, particularly among high-income and college-educated families. Spending increases were particularly sharp among families with preschool-age children. Consistent with this is evidence that the relationship between family income and preschool enrollment among three- and four-year-old

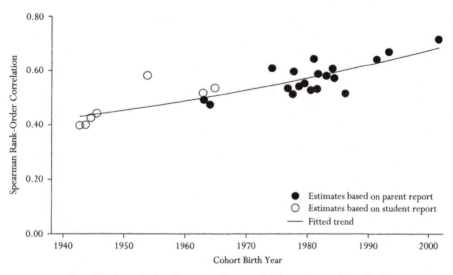

FIGURE 28.6 Trend in Correlation Between Parental Education and Family Income (1943 to 2001 Cohorts)

Source: Author's compilation based on data from Project Talent (Flanagan et al. n.d.); NLS, HS&B, NELS, ELS, ECLS-K, ECLS-B (U.S. Department of Education, Center for Education Statistics 1999, 2000, 2001, 2004, 2009, 2010); Prospects (U.S. Department of Education 1995); NLSY79, NLSY97 (U.S. Bureau of Labor Statistics 1980, 1999); SECCYD (National Institute of Child Health and Human Development 2010); and Add Health (Harris 2009, reading only).

children grew from the late 1960s to the late 1980s (Bainbridge et al. 2005). These patterns are broadly consistent with the hypothesis that the rising income achievement gap is at least partly driven by the increasing investment of upper-income families in their children's cognitive development, particularly during the preschool years, though the evidence is far from conclusive on this point.

Changes in the Relationships among Family Income, Family Socioeconomic Characteristics, and Children's Achievement

Another possible explanation for the rising income achievement gap is that high-income families not only have more income than low-income families but also have access to a range of other family and social resources. On average, families with higher incomes tend to be those in which the parent(s) are highly educated. This has long been true, though the link between parental educational attainment and family income has grown stronger in recent decades, as the wage returns to educational attainment have increased since 1979 (Levy and Murnane 1992). Because highly educated parents are more able and more likely than less-educated parents to provide resources and opportunities for their children to develop cognitive and academic

skills in both the preschool years and the school-age years (Lareau 1989), children of parents with college degrees may have higher academic achievement, on average, than children of parents with lower levels of education, all else being equal. Thus, the income achievement gap may be partly a result of the effects of parental educational attainment.

This argument suggests two possible explanations for the rising income achievement gap. First, the trend may result from an increase in the correlation between parental educational attainment and family income—which would mean that high- and low-income families are increasingly differentiated by education levels, leading to larger differences in children's achievement. Second, the trend may derive from an increase in the achievement returns to parental education, net of income. This would mean that children of highly educated parents benefit more from their parents' educational attainment than they did in the past.

The trend in the correlation between family income and parental education is illustrated in Figure 28.6, which shows a relatively unambiguous trend of increasing correlation between parental education and family income across cohorts.[9] There are several possible explanations for this trend. First, as Frank Levy and Richard Murnane (1992) point out, changes in the structure of the economy and the composition of the labor force during the 1970s and

1980s, along with declines in the real minimum wage and the weakening of unions, resulted in a decline in the real wages of those with only a high-school degree and an increase in the wage premium for a college degree. These changes would be reflected in the studies of cohorts born in the 1950s through the 1970s because these students and their parents were surveyed in the 1970s and 1980s. It is not clear, however, whether this explanation can account for the continued increase in the correlation between income and education for studies conducted after the 1980s.

A second possible reason for increasing correlation between parental education and income is the increasing polarization of families. Sara McLanahan (2004) argues that trends since 1960 in family structure and composition have led to an increasingly polarized distribution of family contexts for children—mothers with low levels of education are increasingly likely to be young, unemployed, and single or divorced; mothers with high levels of education are, conversely, increasingly likely to be older, employed, and married. As a result, the correlation of parental education and income among families with children is likely to increase with time. Moreover, McLanahan argues, this polarization in family structure implies a corresponding polarization in key resources (income, parental time) available for children, which may have important implications for the distribution of children's academic achievement.

Related to this argument is the fact that marital homogamy (the tendency for individuals to marry those with similar levels of educational attainment) has increased substantially since 1960 (Schwartz and Mare 2005). As a result, in two-parent families, the educational attainment of the higher-educated parent is increasingly predictive of the educational attainment of the less educated spouse. This trend, coupled with the increasing disparity in single parenthood and employment between mothers with high and low levels of education described by McLanahan, and the increasing wage premium to education described by Levy and Murnane, implies that children with one highly educated parent are increasingly likely to have two highly educated, married parents and a high family income, while children with one less-educated parent are increasingly likely to live either with a single mother or with two parents, both with low levels of education and low wages.

Because income and parental education are correlated, and increasingly so with time, as shown in Figure 28.6, I conduct a set of analyses to determine

whether the growth in the income achievement gap is due to increases in the association between income and achievement or parental education and achievement. For each study with measures of both family income and parental education, I estimate the association between income and achievement, controlling for parental education, and the association between parental education and achievement, controlling for family income. These partial associations are shown in Figures 28.7 and 28.8.

The key result evident in Figures 28.7 and 28.8 is that the income coefficient grew steeply for cohorts born from the 1940s to 2000. The income coefficient for reading increased fourfold during this period, and it more than doubled for math. At the same time, the parental-education coefficient has been generally unchanged during the six decades of cohorts in the studies. Even if we focus only on the cohorts born since the mid-1970s, the income coefficient has increased substantially, more than doubling in reading and increasing more than 50 percent in math. In this same time period, the coefficient on educational attainment appears to have grown as well, albeit at a slower rate.

It is instructive to compare the trends in Figures 28.7 and 28.8 with those in Figures 28.1 and 28.2. Parental education accounts for a large proportion of the association between income and achievement in the early cohorts, but that proportion declines across cohorts. In reading, for example, parental education accounts for roughly 60 to 80 percent of the income achievement gap in the studies of cohorts born in the 1940s, 1950s, and 1960s. But among cohorts born between 1980 and 2001, parental education and race explain only 40 to 60 percent of the income gap. This pattern is at odds with the explanation that the growing income gap is due to the increasing correlation of income and parental education: all else being equal, we would expect the increasing correlation between the two to mean that education should explain more of the income gap over time, not less.

A second lesson evident in Figures 28.7 and 28.8 is that the association between parental education and children's academic achievement, controlling for family income and race, remains larger than the association between family income and achievement, controlling for parental education and race. That is, although the association between income and achievement has grown rapidly during the last fifty years, parental educational attainment is still a more powerful predictor of student achievement than is family income.[10]

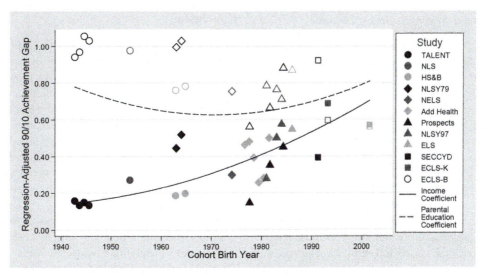

FIGURE 28.7 Estimated Partial Associations Between Reading Test Scores and Both Income and Parental Education, by Birth Cohort (1943 to 2001 Cohorts)

Source: Author's compilation based on data from Project Talent (Flanagan et al. n.d.); NLS, HS&B, NELS, ELS, ECLS-K, ECLS-B (U.S. Department of Education, Center for Education Statistics 1999, 2000, 2001, 2004, 2009, 2010; Prospects (U.S. Department of Education 1995); NLSY79, NLSY97 (U.S. Bureau of Labor Statistics 1980,1999); and SECCYD (National Institute of Child Health and Human Development 2010).

Note: Solid symbols represent regression-adjusted 90/10 income coeffi cients; hollow symbols represent regression-adjusted parental education coeffi cients.

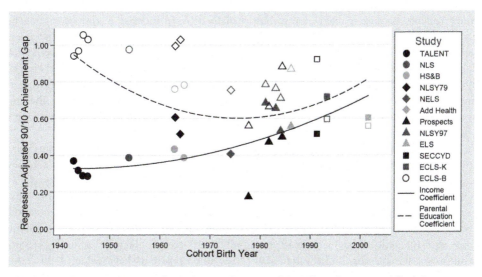

FIGURE 28.8 Estimated Partial Associations Between Math Test Scores and Both Income and Parental Education, by Birth Cohort (1943 to 2001 Cohorts)

Source: Author's compilation based on data from Project Talent (Flanagan et al. n.d.); NLS, HS&B, NELS, ELS, ECLS-K, ECLS-B (U.S. Department of Education, Center for Education Statistics 1999, 2000, 2001, 2004, 2009, 2010; Prospects (U.S. Department of Education 1995; NLSY79, NLSY97 (U.S. Bureau of Labor Statistics 1980, 1999); and SECCYD (National Institute of Child Health and Human Development 2010).

Note: Solid symbols represent regression-adjusted 90/10 income coefficients; hollow symbols represent regression-adjusted parental education coefficients.

Increased Segregation by Income

A final possible explanation for the rising income achievement gap is the pattern of increasing income segregation during the last forty years. Several recent studies have found that residential segregation by income increased from 1970 to 2000, partly as a result of rising income inequality and likely partly as a result of low-income housing policy (Jargowsky 1996; Reardon and Bischoff 2011; Watson 2009). In particular, rising income inequality has led to the increasing segregation of high-income families from middle- and low-income families; high-income families increasingly live spatially far from the middle class (Reardon and Bischoff 2011). Because residential patterns are closely linked to school-attendance patterns, the rise of residential income segregation has likely led to a concurrent rise in school segregation by income, though there is little empirical evidence on this.[11] Because the growth in income segregation has been largely a result of increasing segregation of the affluent, this might explain the pattern of the rising association between income and achievement among higher-income families.

Greater residential income segregation may affect the school-quality differential between high- and low-income students, because high-income parents are better able to garner resources for their schools. Likewise, increased income segregation may lead to less variance of test scores within schools and more variance of test scores between schools, given that higher-income students generally have higher scores than lower-income students.[12]

It is not clear, however, that these factors would lead to increases in the income achievement gap. The evidence on the effects of school socioeconomic composition is somewhat weak, though a new study taking advantage of quasi-random variation in school poverty rates experienced by low-income students in Montgomery County, Maryland, finds evidence that low-income students perform better on math tests after moving to low-poverty schools (Schwartz 2010). Likewise, some studies of peer effects find evidence that the academic-achievement level of one's classmates may impact one's own achievement (for recent evidence, see Lavy, Silma, and Weinhardt 2009). Nonetheless, the evidence is far from clear if, how, and how much differences among schools in peers and school quality may affect achievement. As a result, there is little evidence to answer the question of whether rising income segregation has played a role in the increasing income achievement gap.

Conclusion

Most of the evidence presented in this chapter suggests that the achievement gap between children from high- and low-income families has grown substantially in recent decades. The income achievement gap is now considerably larger than the black-white gap, a reversal of the pattern fifty years ago. At the same time, income inequality in the United States began to grow sharply in the 1970s, a trend that continues to the present. The gap between the rich and the poor has widened significantly, particularly among families with children.

Many of the other patterns in this chapter are not fully consistent with the simple explanation that income inequality has driven these trends. First, the analyses described in the chapter show that the income achievement gaps do not grow in the ways that would be predicted by the changes in income inequality. Although income inequality grew sharply for families with below-median incomes during the 1970s and 1980s, the income achievement gap among children from these families was largely unchanged. The achievement gap did grow among children from above-median-income families, but this appears to be better explained by an increase in the association between income and achievement, not by increases in income inequality. Evidence from other studies suggests that parental investment in their children's cognitive development has grown during the last half-century, particularly for higher-income families, a pattern that may explain the growing returns to income during this time period.

There are a number of other possible explanations for the evident trends in the income achievement gap. Education policy increasingly focuses on standardized test scores as outcome measures for schools; as these scores become more important, families may be increasingly likely to invest in improving their children's scores. Likewise, cultural perceptions of the role of parents have changed throughout the twentieth century to focus increasingly on early-childhood cognitive and psychological development, which may lead parents with resources to invest more in their young children's development.

In sum, the forces at work behind the rising income achievement gap are likely complex and interconnected. At the same time that family income has become more predictive of children's academic achievement, so have educational attainment and cognitive skills become more predictive of adults' earnings. The combination of these trends creates a feedback mechanism that may decrease intergenerational mobility. As the children of the rich do better in school, and those who do better in school are more likely to become rich, we risk producing an even more unequal and economically polarized society.

REFERENCES

Bainbridge, J., M. K. Meyers, S. Tanaka, and Jane Waldfogel. 2005. "Who Gets an Early Education? Family Income and the Enrollment of Three- to Five-Year-Olds from 1968 to 2000." *Social Science Quarterly* 86(3): 724–45.

Bianchi, Susan. 2000. "Maternal Employment and Time with Children: Dramatic Change or Surprising Continuity?" *Demography* 37(4): 401–14.

Bowles, S., and H. Gintis. 1976. *Schooling in Capitalist America: Educational Reform and the Contradictions of Economic Life.* New York: Basic Books.

———. 2002. "The Inheritance of Inequality." *Journal of Economic Perspectives* 16(3): 3–30.

Brooks-Gunn, Jeanne, and Greg Duncan. 1997. "The Effects of Poverty on Children." *Future of Children* 7(2): 55–71.

Burkhauser, R. V., A. Feng, S. P. Jenkins, and J. Larrimore. 2009. "Recent Trends in Top Income Shares in the USA: Reconciling Estimates from March CPS and IRS Tax Return Data." NBER Working Paper No. 15320. Cambridge, Mass.: National Bureau of Economic Research.

Clotfelter, C. T., H. F. Ladd, and J. L. Vigdor. 2006. "The Academic Achievement Gap in Grades Three to Eight." NBER Working Paper No. 12207. Cambridge, Mass.: National Bureau of Economic Research.

Duncan, Greg J., and Jeanne Brooks-Gunn. 1997. "Income Effects Across the Life-Span: Integration and Interpretation." In *Consequences of Growing Up Poor*, edited by Greg J. Duncan and Jeanne Brooks-Gunn. New York: Russell Sage Foundation.

Duncan, Greg J., Jeanne Brooks-Gunn, and P. K. Klebanov. 1994. "Economic Deprivation and Early Childhood Development." *Child Development* 65(2): 296–318.

Dupriez, V., and X. Dumay. 2006. "Inequalities in School Systems: Effect of School Structure or of Society Structure? *Comparative Education* 42(2): 243–60.

Dura-Bellat, M., and B. Suchaut. 2005. "Organisation and Context, Efficiency and Equity of Educational Systems: What PISA Tells Us." *European Educational Research Journal* 4(3): 181–94.

Flanagan, John C., David V. Tiedeman, William V. Clemans, and Lauress L. Wise. n.d. Project Talent Public Use File, 1960–1976 [Computer file]. ICPSR07823-v1. Ann Arbor, Mich.: Interuniversity Consortium for Political and Social Research [distributor]. Ordering information available at http://www.projecttalent.org/contact (accessed June 24, 2011).

Fryer, R. G., and S. D. Levitt. 2004. "Understanding the Black-White Test Score Gap in the First Two Years of School." *Review of Economics and Statistics* 86(2): 447–64.

———. 2006. "The Black-White Test Score Gap Through Third Grade." *American Law and Economics Review* 8(2): 249–81.

Guryan, E. Hurst, and M. Kearney. 2008. "Parental Education and Parental Time with Children." *Journal of Economic Perspectives* 22(3): 23–46.

Harris, Kathleen Mullan. 2009. The National Longitudinal Study of Adolescent Health (Add Health), Waves I & II, 1994–1996; Wave III, 2001–2002; Wave IV, 2007–2009 [machine-readable data file and documentation]. Chapel Hill, N.C.: Carolina Population Center, University of North Carolina at Chapel Hill. Ordering information available at http://www.cpc.unc.edu/projects/addhealth/data/restricteduse (accessed June 24, 2011).

Herrnstein, R. J., and C. Murray. 1994. *The Bell Curve: Intelligence and Class Structure in American Life.* New York: Free Press.

Huang, M.-H., and R. M. Hauser. 2001. "Convergent Trends in Black-White Verbal Test-Score Differentials in the U.S.: Period and Cohort Perspectives." *EurAmerica* 31(2): 185–230.

Jacoby, R., and N. Glauberman, eds. 1995. *The Bell Curve Debate: History Documents Opinions.* New York: Random House.

Jargowsky, P. A. 1996. "Take the Money and Run: Economic Segregation in U.S. Metropolitan Areas." *American Sociological Review* 61(6): 984–98.

Kagan, J. 2002. "Empowerment and Education: Civil Rights, Expert-Advocates, and Parent Politics in Head Start, 1964–1980." *Teachers College Record* 104(3): 516–62.

King, Miriam, Steven Ruggles, J. Trent Alexander, Sarah Flood, Katie Genadek, Matthew B. Schroeder, Brandon Trampe, and Rebecca Vick. 2010. Integrated Public Use Microdata Series, Current Population Survey: Version 3.0 [Machine-readable database]. Minneapolis: University of Minnesota.

Kornrich, Sabino, and Frank Furstenberg. 2010. "Investing in Children: Changes in Parental Spending on Children, 1972 to 2007." Unpublished manuscript.

Lareau, Annette. 1989. *Home Advantage: Social Class and Parental Intervention in Elementary Education.* London: Falmer Press.

———. 2003. *Unequal Childhoods: Class Race and Family Life.* Berkeley: University of California Press.

Lavy, V., O. Silma, and F. Weinhardt. 2009. "The Good, the Bad, and the Average: Evidence on the Scale and Nature of Peer Effects in Schools." NBER Working Paper No. 15600. Cambridge, Mass.: National Bureau of Economic Research.

Lemann, N. 1999. *The Big Test: The Secret History of The American Meritocracy.* New York: Farrar, Straus and Giroux.

Levy, Frank, and Richard J. Murnane. 1992. "U.S. Earnings Levels and Earnings Inequality: A Review of Recent Trends and Proposed Explanations." *Journal of Economic Literature* 30(3): 1333–81.

Marks, G. N. 2005. "Cross-National Differences and Accounting for Social Class Inequalities in Education." *International Sociology* 20(4): 483–505.

McLanahan, Sara. 2004. "Diverging Destinies: How Children Are Faring Under the Second Demographic Transition." *Demography* 41(4): 607–27.

Miller, Jon. 1994. Longitudinal Survey of American Youth [dataset]. Ordering information available at: http://www.lsay.org (accessed June 24, 2011).

Murray, C. 2007. "The Magnitude and Components of Change in the Black-White IQ Difference from 1920 to 1991: A Birth Cohort Analysis of the Woodcock-Johnson Standardizations." *Intelligence* 35(4): 305–18.

National Commission on Excellence in Education. 1983. *A Nation at Risk: The Imperative for Educational Reform.* Washington, D.C.: National Commission on Excellence in Education.

National Institute of Child Health and Human Development. 2010. Study of Early Child Care and Youth Development [dataset]. Received 2010. Ordering information available at: http://www.nichd.nih.gov/research/supported/seccyd/datasets.cfm (accessed June 24, 2011).

Phillips, M., Jeanne Brooks-Gunn, Greg J. Duncan, P. Klebanov, and J. Crane. 1998. "Family Background, Parenting Practices, and the Black-White Test Score Gap." In *The Black-White Test Score Gap*, edited by C. Jencks and M. Phillips. Washington, D.C.: Brookings Institution Press.

Piketty, T., and E. Saez. 2003. "Income Inequality in the United States, 1913–1998." *Quarterly Journal of Economics* 118(1): 1–39.

———. 2008. "Income Inequality in the United States, 1913–1998; Tables and Figures Updated to 2006." Available at: http://www.econ.berkeley.edu/~saez/TabFig2006.xls (accessed September 2, 2009).

Ramey, G., and V. A. Ramey. 2010. "The Rug Rat Race." Unpublished paper.

Reardon, Sean F., and K. Bischoff. 2011. "Income Inequality and Income Segregation." *American Journal of Sociology* 116(4): 1092–153.

Reardon, Sean F., and C. Galindo. 2009. "The Hispanic-White Achievement Gap in Math and Reading in the Elementary Grades." *American Educational Research Journal* 46(3): 853–91.

Schaub, M. 2010. "Parenting for Cognitive Development from 1950 to 2000: The Institutionalization of Mass Education and the Social Construction of Parenting in the United States." *Sociology of Education* 83(1): 46–66.

Schwartz, C. R., and R. D. Mare. 2005. "Trends in Educational Assortative Marriage from 1940–2003." *Demography* 42(4): 621–46.

Schwartz, H. 2010. *Housing Policy Is School Policy: Economically Integrative Housing Promotes Academic Success in Montgomery County, Maryland.* New York: Century Foundation.

U.S. Bureau of Labor Statistics. 1980. National Longitudinal Survey of Youth, 1979 [dataset]. Available at: http://www.bls.gov/nls/nlsy79.htm (accessed June 24, 2011).

———. 1999. National Longitudinal Survey of Youth, 1997 [dataset]. Available at: http://www.bls.gov/nls/nlsy97.htm (accessed June 24, 2011).

U.S. Department of Education. 1995. Prospects: The Congressionally Mandated Study of Educational Growth and Opportunity [dataset]. Ordering information available at: http://www.ed.gov/pubs/Prospects/index.html (accessed June 24, 2011).

U.S. Department of Education, Center for Education Statistics, n.d. National Assessment of Educational Progress-Main [dataset]. Ordering information available at: http://nces.ed.gov/nationsreportcard/researchcenter/datatools.asp (accessed June 24, 2011).

———. 1999. National Longitudinal Study of the Class of 1972 [Computer file]. ICPSR version. Chicago, Ill: National Opinion Research Center [producer], 1992. Ann Arbor, Mich.: Interuniversity Consortium for Political and Social Research [distributor] doi:10.3886/ICPSR08085.

———. 2000. Early Childhood Longitudinal Survey-Kindergarten (Base Year) [dataset]. Ordering information available at: http://nces.ed.gov/ecls/kinderdatainformation.asp (accessed June 24, 2011) [Computer file]. 2nd ICPSR version. Chicago, Ill.: National Opinion Research Center [producer], 1980. Ann Arbor, Mich.: Interuniversity Consortium for Political and Social Research [distributor]. doi:10.3886/ICPSR07896.

———. 2004. National Education Longitudinal Study: Base Year Through Fourth Follow-Up, 1988–2000 [Computer file], ICPSR version. Washington, D.C.: U.S. Department of Education, National Center for Education Statistics [producer], 2002. Ann Arbor, Mich: Inter-university Consortium for Political and Social Research [distributor].

———. 2005. National Assessment of Educational Progress-Long Term Trend [dataset]. Ordering information available at: http://nces.ed.gov/nationsreportcard/researchcenter/datatools.asp (accessed June 24, 2011).

———. 2009. Early Childhood Longitudinal Survey-Birth Cohort (9 Month-Kindergarten) [dataset]. Ordering information available at: http://nces.ed.gov/ecls/birthdatainformation.asp (accessed June 24, 2011).

———. 2010. Education Longitudinal Study: Base Year Through Second Follow-Up, 2002–2006 [dataset]. Washington, D.C.: U.S. Department of Education, National Center for Education Statistics [producer], 2010. Available at: http://nces.ed.gov/surveys/els2002/orderingcds.asp (accessed June 24, 2011).

Watson, T. 2009. "Inequality and the Measurement of Residential Segregation by Income." *Review of Income and Wealth* 55(3): 820–44.

Wrigley, Julia. 1989. "Do Young Children Need Intellectual Stimulation? Experts' Advice to Parents, 1900–1985." *History of Education Quarterly* 29(1): 41–75.

Zigler, E., and S. Muenchow. 1992. *Head Start: The Inside Story of America's Most Successful Educational Experiment*. New York: Basic Books.

NOTES

1. Online appendix available at: http://www.russellsage.org/duncan_murnane_online_appendix.pdf.

The included NCES studies are the National Longitudinal Study (NLS), High School and Beyond (HS&B), the National Education Longitudinal Study (NELS), the Education Longitudinal Study (ELS), the Early Childhood Longitudinal Study, Kindergarten Cohort (ECLS-K), and the Early Childhood Longitudinal Study, Birth Cohort (ECLS-B). The included international studies are the Third International Mathematics and Science Study (TIMSS), the Program of International Assessment (PISA), and the Progress in International Reading Study (PIRLS). The additional included studies are the National Longitudinal Survey of Youth: 1979 (NLSY79), the National Longitudinal Survey of Youth: 1997 (NLSY97), Prospects: The Congressionally Mandated Study of Educational Growth and Opportunity (Prospects), the National Longitudinal Study of Adolescent Health (Add Health), the Longitudinal Survey of American Youth (LSAY), the NICHD Study of Early Child Care and Youth Development (SECCYD), the Equality of Educational Opportunity study (EEO), and Project Talent. For further information about each study, see http://russlesage.org/duncan_murnane-online-appendix.pdf.

2. The names of these studies are provided in full in note 1. Although HS&B includes parent's reported family income for a subsample of roughly 15 percent of the full sample, the measure of family income appears highly unreliable (see online appendix 5.A2 for detail). I rely instead on the student-reported family income measure for HS&B, as described in online appendix 5.A2. NLSY79 includes parent-reported income for subjects who live with their parents; I use only the sample of sixteen- to eighteen-year-olds from NLSY79 for this reason.

3. My calculations, based on 2009 Current Population Survey data. See online appendix section 5.A3 for details.

4. Figures 28.1 and 28.2 display estimated 90/10 income achievement gaps from all available nationally representative studies that include reading- or math-achievement test scores for school-age children and family income. Labels indicate the modal grade in which students were tested in a given sample. For most of the longitudinal studies (HS&B, NELS, Prospects, ELS, and ECLS-K), only estimates from the initial wave of the study are included. ECLS-B estimates come from wave 4, when children were five years old and tested on school readiness; SECCYD come from wave 5, when children were in third grade and were first administered a broad academic achievement test.

The quartic fitted regression line is weighted by the inverse of the sampling variance of each estimate. Included studies are Project Talent, NLS, HS&B, NLSY79, NELS, Add Health (reading only), Prospects, NLSY97, ELS, SECCYD, ECLS-K, and ECLS-B. Family income is student-reported in Project Talent, NLS, and HS&B. See online appendix for details on computation of 90/10 gaps.

5. My calculations, based on Main NAEP math and reading scores. See National Center for Education Statistics website, available at: http://nces.ed.gov/nationsreportcard/naepdata/dataset.aspx (accessed March 7, 2011).

6. Figure 5.A12 in the online appendix displays the trend in U.S. income inequality throughout the last century.

7. My calculations, based on Current Population Survey, 1968–2009. See appendix section 5.A3 for details.

8. We would expect this if we thought the relationship between achievement and log income was linear, which may not be the case. See online appendix section 5.A6 for discussion.

9. The same trend is evident if the correlations are plotted against the year of the study rather than against birth year.

10. The income coefficients displayed in Figures 28.6 and 28.7 are roughly 20 to 40 percent the size of the parental-education coefficients in the earliest cohorts, but they are 60 to 90 percent the size of the parental-education coefficients in the later cohorts. The income coefficients here are adjusted for the estimated reliability of family income, so these differences in the magnitudes of the income and education coefficients are likely not substantially biased by the less reliable measurement of family income. Figure 28.6 shows the Spearman rank-order correlation between parental educational attainment (coded as the maximum level of educational attainment of both parents, if two are present in the home) and family income. Because both income and parental education are measured by ordered categories in most studies (parental education is measured in four to eight categories; income in five to fifteen categories), I compute the rank-order correlation between income and parental education for each of the twelve studies with measures of both income and parental education. Correlations are disattenuated for estimated measurement error in both family income and parental educational attainment. Note that because these are rank-order correlations, they are not directly comparable to standard (Pearson) correlation coefficients.

11. Because of the relatively small within-school samples in many of the studies that include measures of family income, it is difficult to assess the trends in school income segregation using the data available.

12. An examination (not shown) of the intracluster correlations of test scores from the school-based studies included in this chapter provides some evidence that the intracluster correlation has grown with time, but these estimates are very noisy because of the small sample sizes within each school in most of the studies.

29. Richard Breen, Ruud Luijkx, Walter Müller, and Reinhard Pollak*

Nonpersistent Inequality in Educational Attainment

In their seminal study on the development of inequality in educational attainment in the 20th century, Shavit and Blossfeld (1993) summarize the results under the guiding title *Persistent Inequality*. In spite of dramatic educational expansion during the 20th century, of the thirteen countries studied in their project, all but two, Sweden and the Netherlands, "exhibit stability of socio-economic inequalities of educational opportunities. Thus, whereas the proportions of all social classes attending all educational levels have increased, the relative advantage associated with privileged origins persists in all but two of the thirteen societies" (p. 22). This conclusion is based on a meta-analysis of individual country studies, all of which adopt two different approaches to assess socioeconomic inequalities of educational opportunities: one is to use ordinary least squares to regress years of education achieved by sons and daughters on parents' education and occupational prestige; the other is to regress, using binary logistic regression, a set of successive educational transitions on the same social background variables (the "Mare model"; Mare 1980, 1981). Change or persistence in inequalities of educational opportunities is diagnosed depending on whether or not significant variation over birth cohorts is found in the regression coefficients linking social background to years of education attained and the educational transitions considered. While the two analyses address different empirical phenomena—of which Shavit and Blossfeld are well aware—the results of both suggest

essentially the same conclusion, which the authors then summarize as "stability of socio-economic inequalities of educational opportunities." In the scientific community, in particular in sociology and in the education sciences, the results have been viewed as evidence of a persistently high degree of class inequality of educational attainment that can change only under rather exceptional conditions.

Shavit and Blossfeld's result echoed earlier findings from some single-country studies, but subsequently several analyses have contested this finding. They have shown that equalization also took place in Germany (Müller and Haun 1994; Henz and Maas 1995; Jonsson, Mills, and Müller 1996), France (Vallet 2004), Italy (Shavit and Westerbeek 1998), and the United States (Kuo and Hauser 1995). Rijken's (1999) comparative analysis comes to the same conclusion. In other studies, Breen and Whelan (1993) and Whelan and Layte (2002) confirm persistent inequality for Ireland, whereas for Soviet Russia, Gerber and Hout (1995) find mixed results (declining inequality in secondary education and increasing inequality in transitions to university). For the post-socialist period in various countries of Eastern Europe, the origin-education association is regularly found to be very high and is likely higher than in the socialist period (Gerber [2000] for Russia; Iannelli [2003] for Hungary, Romania, and Slovakia).

The aim of this article is to reassess the empirical evidence concerning the conclusion of *Persistent Inequality* using more recent data and larger samples from a selection of European countries. In contrast to Shavit and Blossfeld, we base our conclusions on analyses using ordered logit models of educational attainment rather than on educational transition models. The reason is that we are interested in inequalities related to social origin in completed education, which constitutes the major starting condition for unequal opportunities in the life course. Another reason for not using educational transition models is that we lack data on individuals' complete educational histories. Indeed, there are no cross-nationally comparable large data sets that contain complete education histories and also cover long historical periods.

Reasons to Suppose That Educational Inequality Was Not Persistent

Differences between students from different social classes in how they fare in the educational system

*The ideas, issues, and theories considered in this brief commissioned piece are examined in greater depth in the following publication: Richard Breen, Ruud Luijkx, Walter Müller, and Reinhard Pollak, "Nonpersistent Inequality in Educational Attainment," *American Journal of Sociology* 114:5 (2009), pp. 1475–1521, published by the University of Chicago Press. The article printed here was originally prepared by Richard Breen, Ruud Luijkx, Walter Müller, and Reinhard Pollak for *The Inequality Reader: Contemporary and Foundational Readings in Race, Class, and Gender*, Second Edition, edited by David B. Grusky and Szonja Szelényi, pp. 455–468. Copyright © 2011. Reprinted by permission of Westview Press, an imprint of Perseus Books, LLC, a subsidiary of Hachette Book Group, Inc.

can, in simple terms, be seen to derive from differences in how they perform in the educational system (which Boudon [1974] called "primary effects") and differences in the educational choices they make, even given the same level of performance ("secondary effects"). In both areas, developments in the course of the 20th century would lead us to expect declining class differences.

As far as primary effects are concerned, children raised in families in the more advantaged classes encounter better conditions in their home environments that help them to do better in school. They get more intellectual stimulation that strengthens their cognitive abilities, and their parents are more highly motivated and supportive of schoolwork than parents of working-class children. Different performance at school may also derive from different nutrition and health in different classes, whereas genetic differences between individuals from different class backgrounds may play a role as well as class differences in sibship sizes (see Erikson and Jonsson 1996a). Yet, as Erikson and Jonsson (1996b, p. 81) suggest, the general improvement in conditions of living should have made working-class children less disadvantaged in terms of health and nutrition. With economic development and welfare-state protection, the minimum standards of living have improved and average family size has declined. Such changes should have been more relevant for families in the less-advantaged classes, such as the working classes and the small-farmer class, who have been able to move out of absolute economic misery. Some decline in primary class effects should thus have occurred over the long-term and particularly during the substantial improvement of general living conditions in the decades of economic growth and welfare-state expansion following World War II. This should have been reinforced by changes within educational institutions, such as the growth in public provision of early child care and preschool education; the development of full-day rather than part-time schooling; increased school support to counteract performance gaps of pupils; and differences in the timing, extent, and manner of tracking, all of which may reduce class differences in school performance.

As far as secondary effects are concerned, one factor that should have brought about a major reduction is the declining costs of education. Direct costs, especially in secondary education, have become smaller; school fees have been largely abolished; the number of schools has increased, even in rural areas,

so schools can be reached more easily; and traveling conditions have improved. In many countries, educational support programs for less wealthy families have been set up, albeit of rather different kinds and levels of generosity. Real average family income has increased, and that should make it easier to bear the costs of education. While at least in the first half of the last century working-class children were urged to contribute to the family income as early as possible, such pressures have declined. In most countries, economic growth and the reduction in family size have led to an increase in disposable incomes beyond what is required for basic needs. In practically all countries, the length of compulsory schooling has expanded, thus reducing the number of additional school years beyond compulsory education needed to reach full secondary education. Countries certainly differ in the specifics of institutional reforms, and these probably have different implications; but the lengthening of compulsory education should everywhere have contributed to a decline in the additional costs of post-compulsory education.

Countries also differ in their welfare-state and social security arrangements and in their ability to prevent unemployment among students' parents. In countries such as Sweden, in which serious income equalization policies have been pursued successfully, the equalization of conditions is believed to have had an additional impact on reducing the class differential in the ability to bear the costs of education. The recurrence of high levels of unemployment in many countries since the 1980s, especially for the unskilled working class, and the increase in income inequality observed in some countries in recent years (Alderson and Nielsen 2002) are probably the most important changes that may have counteracted a long-term trend toward lowering the impact of costs in producing class inequalities in educational participation, but these developments are mostly too recent to be evident in our data. In sum, both primary and secondary effects changed in ways such that declining disparities between classes in educational attainment can be expected; in particular, it is the children of working-class and farm families who should have most markedly improved their relative position.

Data

Our data come from nine European countries—Germany, France, Italy, Ireland, Britain, Sweden, Poland, Hungary, and the Netherlands—and they were originally assembled for a comparative analysis

TABLE 29.1 Sources of Data

Country	No. of Tables	Sources of Data	Years for Which Data Are Included
Germany	30	Zumabus	1976–77, 1979 (2), 1980, 1982
		ALLBUS	1980, 1982, 1984, 1986, 1988, 1990–92, 1994, 1996, 1998, 2000, 2002
		Politik in der BRD	1978, 1980
		Wohlfahrtssurvey	1978
		German Life History Study	1981–83 (I), 1985–88 (II), 1988–89 (III)
		German Socio-economic Panel	1986, 1999, 2000
France	4	Formation-qualification professionnelle INSEE surveys	1970, 1977, 1985, 1993
Italy	2	National Survey on Social Mobility	1985
		Italian Household Longitudinal Survey	1997
Ireland	3	Survey of the Determinants of Occupational Status and Mobility	1973
		Survey of Income Distribution and Poverty	1987
		Living in Ireland Survey	1994
Great Britain	15	General Household Survey	1973, 1975–76, 1979–84, 1987–92
Sweden	24	Annual Surveys of Living Conditions (ULF)	1976–99
Poland	3	Zagórski (1976)	1972
		Slomczynski et al. (1989)	1988
		Social Stratification in Eastern Europe after 1989	1994
Hungary	4	Social Mobility and Life History Survey	1973, 1983, 1992
		Way of Life and Time Use Survey (Hungarian Central Statistical Office)	2000
Netherlands	35	Parliamentiary Election Study	1970, 1971, 1977, 1981, 1982, 1986, 1994, 1998
		Political Action Survey I	1974, 1979
		Justice of Income Survey	1976
		CBS Life Situation Survey	1977, 1986
		National Labour Market Survey	1982
		National Prestige and Mobility Survey	1982
		Strategic Labour Market Survey	1985, 1988, 1990, 1992, 1994, 1996, 1998
		Cultural Changes (ISSP)	1987
		Justice of Income Survey	1987
		Primary and Social Relationships	1987
		Social and Cultural Trends	1990
		Justice of Income Survey (ISJP)	1991
		Family Survey I, 1992–93	1992
		Households in the Netherlands pilot	1994
		Households in the Netherlands	1995
		Social Inequality in the Netherlands	1996
		National Crime Study	1996
		Social and Economic Attitudes	1998
		Netherlands Family Survey II	1998
		Use of Information Technology	1999

of social mobility in Europe (Breen 2004). That project sought to bring together all the high-quality data sets collected between 1970 and 2000 in eleven European countries that could be used for the analysis of social mobility. The data used here are identical to those employed in that project except that the German data have been augmented by six surveys. These six surveys contain the first three German Life History Surveys for West Germany (fielded between 1981 and 1989) as well as the 2000 sample for West Germany from the German Socio-economic Panel and the ALLBUS Surveys for 2000 and 2002. The Hungarian data are excluded from the final analysis, as will be described later. The data sets that we use are listed in Table 29.1. In total we use 120 surveys collected between 1970 and 2002, but each country provides rather different numbers of surveys (up to a maximum of 35 from the Netherlands). In Sweden, for example, there is a survey for every year from 1976 to 1999, whereas the analysis for Italy is based on only two surveys and those for Ireland and Poland on only three surveys each.

We use data on men ages 30–69 (30–59 in Great Britain, except for the years 1979–88, when the age range is 30–49). We adopt thirty as the lower age limit to ensure that everyone in the samples will have attained his highest level of education, and we take 60 as an upper limit in order to minimize any effects of differential mortality. We confine our analysis to men because the inclusion of both sexes, and comparisons between them, would have made a long article excessively so. We intend to analyze educational inequality among women, and compare it with the results reported here, in a further paper.

Variables

We use four variables in our analysis. *Cohort* (*C*) defines five birth cohorts: 1908–24, 1925–34, 1935–44, 1945–54, and 1955–64. Thus we have information on cohorts born throughout the first two-thirds of the 20th century. *Survey period* (*S*) defines the five-year interval in which the data were collected: 1970–74, 1975–79, 1980–84, 1985–89, 1990–94, 1995–99, and 2000–2004.

Highest level of educational attainment (*E*) is measured using the CASMIN educational schema (Comparative Analysis of Social Mobility in Industrial Nations; see Table 29.2; Braun and Müller 1997). We have amalgamated categories 1a, 1b, and 1c and also 2a and 2b, giving us five educational categories:

TABLE 29.2 CASMIN Educational Categories

Category	Definition
1a	Inadequately completed elementary education
1b	Completed (compulsory) elementary education
1c	(Compulsory) elementary education and basic vocational qualification
2a	Secondary: intermediate vocational qualification or intermediate general qualification and vocational training
2b	Secondary: intermediate general qualification
2c_gen	Full general maturity qualification
2c_voc	Full vocational maturity certificate or general maturity certificate and vocational qualification
3a	Lower-tertiary education
3b	Higher-tertiary education

1abc.—Compulsory education with or without elementary vocational education

2ab.—Secondary intermediate education, vocational or general

2c.—Full secondary education

3a.—Lower tertiary education

3b.—Higher tertiary education

We have only four educational categories in the Hungarian data, where 2ab is missing, and in the Italian and the Irish data, where no distinction has been made between 3a and 3b. The CASMIN educational schema seeks to capture distinctions not only in the level of education but also in the type, and one consequence of this is that the five levels we identify cannot be considered to be sequentially ordered in any simple way. For example, in some countries lower tertiary education can be accessed directly from secondary intermediate education, whereas in most countries, higher tertiary is not usually entered after lower tertiary.

Class origins (*O*) are categorized using the Erikson-Goldthorpe-Portocarero (EGP) class schema (see Table 29.3; also Erikson and Goldthorpe 1992, chap. 2). We identify seven classes:

I.—Upper service

II.—Lower service

IIIa.—Higher-grade routine nonmanual

IVab.—Self-employed and small employers

IVc.—Farmers

V + VI.—Skilled manual workers, technicians, and supervisors

VIIab + IIIb.—Semi- and unskilled manual, agricultural, and lower-grade routine nonmanual workers

TABLE 29.3 EGP Class Categories

Category	Definition
I	Higher-grade professionals, administrators, and officials; managers in large industrial establishments; large proprietors
II	Lower-grade professionals, administrators, and officials; higher-grade technicians; managers in small industrial establishments; supervisors of nonmanual employees
IIIa	Routine nonmanual employees, higher grade (administration and commerce)
IVa	Small proprietors, artisans, etc. with employees
IVb	Small proprietors, artisans, etc. without employees
IVc	Farmers and smallholders; other self-employed workers in primary production
V	Lower-grade technicians; supervisors of manual workers
VI	Skilled manual workers
VIIa	Semi- and unskilled manual workers (not in agriculture, etc.)
VIIb	Agricultural and other workers in primary production
IIIb	Routine nonmanual employees, lower grade (sales and services)

In Britain and Poland the data allow us to identify only six class origins. In both countries, we cannot distinguish classes I and II, whereas in Britain, members of IVa are included in I + II (see Goldthorpe and Mills 2004). Furthermore, in Poland, we cannot split the class III, so here IIIb is included with IIIa rather than with VIIab. In Ireland we also combine I and II because of very small numbers in class I in some cohorts.

The resulting four-way table of class origins (*O*) by educational attainment (*E*) by cohort (*C*) by survey period (*S*) is of maximum dimensions 7 × 5 × 5 × 7 = 1,225, though this number includes many structural zeros in those combinations of cohort and survey that are not observed. Furthermore, we omitted all those observations of cohort by survey in which the table of origins by education would have been extremely sparse. All the cells in such a table were treated as structural zeros.

Table 29.4 shows the resulting sample sizes for all the countries by cohort. These vary quite considerably, and this will obviously affect our ability to detect statistically significant trends. The sample sizes for Italy and Ireland are particularly small, and one consequence of this is that we have very few observations of the oldest cohort in Italy, so we omit it from our analyses.

Changes in Educational Attainment and Class Origins

Perhaps the single most striking thing that differentiates the older from the younger cohorts in our data is the massive increase in educational attainment that has occurred. Figure 29.1 shows the proportions in each cohort in each country that have attained at least upper-secondary (2c) education, and Figure 29.2 shows the proportions having attained tertiary (3a and 3b) education.[1] The upward trends in both are obvious and are similar across countries.

It is not only the educational distributions that have shifted, however. During the course of the 20th century, the class structures of European nations underwent major change, with a move away from farming and unskilled occupations and toward skilled jobs and white-collar jobs. Some aspects of this are shown in Figure 29.3, which reports the share of the service class (I and II), intermediate class (IIIa and IVab), the

TABLE 29.4 Sample Sizes for Cohorts by Country

Country	Cohort 1908–24	1925–34	1935–44	1945–54	1955–64	Total
Germany	2,323	3,110	4,852	4,007	2,832	17,124
France	11,283	14,169	13,126	10,517	2,610	51,705
Italy		742	1,182	1,286	827	4,037
Ireland	744	1,176	1,509	1,289	863	5,581
Great Britain	6,473	9,112	24,481	20,971	5,437	66,474
Sweden	8,032	8,209	10,875	10,145	4,093	41,354
Poland	7,729	9,248	8,851	1,002	784	27,614
Hungary	5,698	6,829	7,175	5,643	2,583	27,928
Netherlands	2,385	3,507	4,736	5,612	3,511	19,751
Total	44,667	56,102	76,787	60,472	23,540	261,568

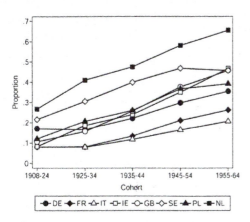

FIGURE 29.1 Proportion of Men Reaching at Least Upper-Secondary Education, by Country and Cohort

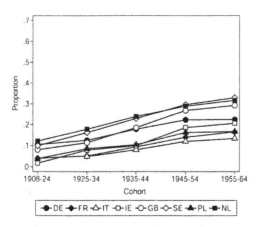

FIGURE 29.2 Proportion of Men Reaching Tertiary Education, by Country and Cohort

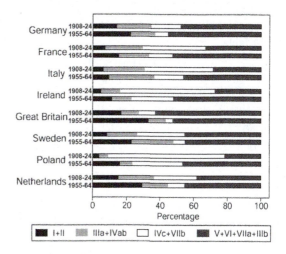

FIGURE 29.3 Proportions of Men in Various Class Origins for First and Last Cohort by Country (Marginal Distributions)

In Great Britain, class IVa is included in classes I + II; in Poland, class IIIb is included in classes IIIa + IVab.

Analyses

farm classes (IVc and VIIb), and working class (V + VI, VIIa + IIIb) in the origins of the oldest and youngest cohorts in each country. The decline of the farm class and growth of the service class are evident everywhere, and the working class has grown or remained stable everywhere except Britain.

Analyses

We focus on modeling the joint distribution of class origins and highest level of education using the ordered logit model. Letting Y be the random variable measuring educational attainment, we can write the probability that Y is less than a particular level of education, j, given background variables X, as $\gamma_j(x)$. There exists a family of statistical models that sets

$g[\gamma_j(x)] = t_j - \beta x$ (McCullagh 1980), where g is a link function (such as the logit, the inverse normal, or the complementary log-log) that maps the (0, 1) interval into $(-\infty,\infty)$. The logit link, which yields the ordered logit model, sets $g[\gamma_j(x)] = \ln [\gamma_j(x)]/[1 - \gamma_j(x)]$ and for any two observations with covariate values x and x' we get

$$g[\gamma(x)] - g[\gamma(x')] = \ln \frac{\gamma(x)}{1-\gamma(x)} - \ln \frac{\gamma(x')}{1-\gamma(x')}$$
$$= \beta(x'-x),$$

and so the log odds ratio of exceeding, or failing to exceed, any particular threshold is independent of the thresholds themselves and depends only on the betas.

The ordered logit model has two attractive properties: it is more parsimonious than the multinomial logit or the Mare model, and provided that the ordered logit is the correct model for the data, the estimates of the β parameters are unaffected by collapsing adjacent categories of Y. This invariance means that if the educational system makes finer distinctions than have been captured in the variable Y, the β's are unaffected by our having measured education less precisely. It also implies that when making comparisons, provided that the same stochastic ordering of categories is used in all samples, we do not require the categories to be defined in exactly the

TABLE 29.5 Model Fits for Ordered Logit Models, by Country, Survey, and Cohort: Chi-Squared Summary Measure of Change of OE Effects Across Cohorts for SCOE Data Table (Controlling for SOE) and COE Data Table

Country	Data from SCOE Table, Controlling for SOE			Data from COE Table (Collapsed over S)		
	Change COE (1)	No OE Change (2)	$\triangle G^2$ (3)	Change COE (4)	No OE Change (5)	$\triangle G^2$ (6)
Germany	557.0	642.0	84.9	134.4	234.6	100.2
	(468)	(492)	(24)	(90)	(114)	(24)
France	515.0	629.3	114.3	283.5	459.5	176
	(312)	(336)	(24)	(90)	(114)	(24)
Italy	90.1*	111.0*	20.8*	43.7*	67*	23.3*
	(96)	(114)	(18)	(48)	(66)	(18)
Ireland	189.2	221.1	31.8	101.8	155.3	53.4
	(130)	(150)	(20)	(50)	(70)	(20)
Great Britain	709.9	780.0	70.1	502.7	604.4	101.7
	(275)	(295)	(20)	(75)	(95)	(20)
Sweden	624.1	723.4	99.3	286.2	413.2	126.9
	(450)	(474)	(24)	(90)	(114)	(24)
Poland	191.5	318.8	127.3	192.5	351.3	158.8
	(115)	(135)	(20)	(50)	(70)	(20)
Netherlands	613.5	694.3	80.8	154.1	266.5	112.4
	(516)	(540)	(24)	(90)	(114)	(24)

Note: Numbers in parentheses are degrees of freedom.

* Not significant at P<.05.

same way. This facilitates both temporal and cross-national comparisons. This property is not shared by the educational transition model or by multinomial logit models, whose estimates are tied to particular categorizations of educational attainment. But the advantages of the ordered logit come at a price: the model assumes that class inequalities are identical at each level of education. This is sometimes called the parallel slopes or proportional odds assumption and is frequently found not to hold. We address this problem in our analyses.

In Table 29.5 we report the goodness of fit of the ordered logit models in which we control for survey (cols. 1–3) and in which we do not (cols. 4–6). In all models the thresholds, t_j, are allowed to vary over cohort: in the models in columns 1 and 4, class origin effects are allowed to vary over cohorts, whereas in columns 2 and 5 they are held constant. The final column in each case shows the deviance comparing the model of change against the model of constancy in class effects. This shows significant change everywhere except Italy (although the Irish data barely reach significance when we control for survey period). The deviance associated with this change is

lesser when we control for survey effects compared with when we do not, so our conclusions about change are unaffected, though the magnitude of that change is a little smaller.

One can also see, however, that with the .05 level of significance, the ordered logit model fails to fit the data in almost all countries, suggesting that the parallel slopes assumption does not hold. Elsewhere, we discuss the departures from proportionality in our data, and we find that they are not consequential, so for the most part we base our findings on the results of the models whose goodness of fit is reported in column 1 of Table 29.5 and whose parameter estimates are shown in Figure 29.4 (see Breen et al. 2009).

In Figure 29.4 each line refers to a class origin and shows how the coefficients for that class evolve over cohorts, with class I always acting as the reference category (classes I + II in Ireland and Poland and I + II + IVa in Britain) and having a coefficient of zero. The overall impression is of a decline in class inequalities everywhere (even in Italy, where the change is not statistically significant), but Figure 29.4 also allows us to see how the relative posi-

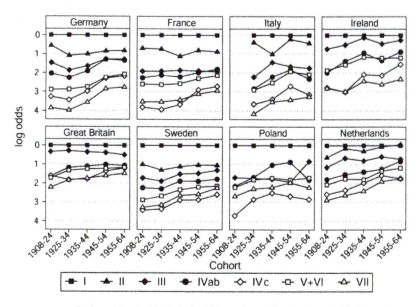

FIGURE 29.4 Ordered Logit Models for Educational Attainment in Eight Countries for Men

Note: Class origin effects over cohorts, controlled for survey effects. Class I is classes I + II in Ireland and Poland and classes I + II + IVa in Britain; educational levels 3a and 3b are merged in Italy and Ireland.

tions of the various classes have shifted. In Germany there was a general narrowing of class differentials in educational attainment following the 1925–34 birth cohort and continuing until the 1945–54 cohort. Little change is evident between the latter and the youngest cohort. In France, equalization started later, with the 1935–44 cohort, and continued longer, persisting into the 1955–64 cohort. It was slightly more differentiated by class origins than in Germany because men from class III showed no change in their position relative to men from class I, whereas men of farm origins (class IVc) experienced a particularly marked improvement in their relative position. In Sweden all classes have improved their position relative to class I, as in Germany, and the decline in inequality largely took place throughout the whole observation period. The Dutch case too shows a general tendency toward a narrowing of class differentials; this occurs over all cohorts, for the most part, and classes IVab, IVc, V + VI, and VII have made the greatest gains. In contrast with these four countries, the British picture is more complicated. Although all classes except III are less differentiated from class I in the youngest cohort than they were in the oldest, almost all the improvement for classes IVb and V + VI occurred between the 1908–24 and 1925–34

cohorts, whereas for class VII there has been a more prolonged improvement and for class IVc an improvement from the 1935–44 cohort onward. In Poland, there has been a steady improvement in the relative positions of classes IVc, V + VI, and VII until the middle cohort, at which point the position of IVc worsens, followed by a worsening of the positions of IVab and VII in the youngest cohort. In Italy, we find a modest decrease in class inequalities until the 1945–54 cohort, after which class inequalities tended to reassert themselves. Class VII is an exception because its position continues to improve, albeit slightly. Finally, in the Irish case, over the five cohorts the distance between class I and all other classes was reduced, and the positions of the petty bourgeoisie (IVab) and farmers (IVc) have improved noticeably.

Overall it seems to be the most disadvantaged classes that experienced the greatest improvement in their position over the first two-thirds of the 20th century. Whereas the position of class II, relative to that of class I, tends to show little change and classes III and IVab show improvements in some countries and in some cohorts but not in others, classes IVc, V + VI, and, particularly, VII show general and widespread improvement in their position vis-à-vis the other classes. As to the more precise timing of the change, we can note that we observe a trend of declining inequality in all countries for the cohorts born between 1935 and 1954, in particular for the least advantaged classes. These are the cohorts that made the crucial educational transitions in the first three post–World War II decades up to about 1975, during which there were significant improvements in living conditions during a period of strong economic growth in most European countries.

Conclusions

Even given that the weight of evidence now supports the thesis of a declining association between class origins and educational attainment, it may be argued that to interpret this trend as demonstrating an increase in equality is mistaken because education is a positional good. In this case, the value of an educational qualification diminishes in proportion to the number of people who acquire it. But for this argument to have any force, it is not enough to show that, over time, the value of some qualification declines; rather, it must be demonstrated that differences between the returns to educational levels diminish. The issue is not whether the returns to a tertiary qualification are less in one cohort than in an older one, but whether, for example, the gap in returns between a tertiary and an upper-secondary qualification has narrowed. As far as we know, there is no such evidence, and indeed, there are good grounds for supposing that, as the number of graduates increases, young people with only an upper-secondary qualification will be forced to take less attractive jobs than their counterparts in older cohorts.

A potentially more telling objection to the argument that declining association implies declining class inequality is that there may be distinctions within the broad CASMIN educational categories that are consequential for life chances. For example, it is commonly the case that differences exist between classes in their choice of particular subjects of study or field of education (Lucas 2001; Van de Werfhorst 2001; Kim and Kim 2003). If these differences have become stronger as inequalities in level of education have declined, then a focus solely on educational level will overestimate the extent to which inequalities have declined. Nevertheless, it is difficult to believe that inequalities stemming from differences in field of study within a given level of education will be as important for variations in life

chances as differences between the levels of education attained.

The data that we have used are uniquely suited to the purpose of describing long-term trends in educational inequality and comparing these trends across countries. But this breadth of coverage in time and space comes at a cost: we lack many items of information that would be needed if we were to explain the trends. As a consequence, our article has been primarily empirical, descriptive, and methodological. But it is clear that our findings present a challenge to theory because much recent theorizing on educational differentials, such as Breen and Goldthorpe's (1997) relative risk aversion theory and Raftery and Hout's (1993) maximally maintained inequality hypothesis, has taken as its starting point the need to explain the supposed regularity exemplified by *Persistent Inequality*. Our results show that the focus needs to shift not only from the explanation of stability to the explanation of change, but from accounts based on the assumption of widespread commonality to those that encompass the differences between countries in the magnitude of class inequalities in educational attainment and in the timing of their decline.

REFERENCES

Alderson, Arthur S., and François Nielsen. 2002. "Globalization and the Great U-turn: Income Inequality Trends in 16 OECD Countries." *American Journal of Sociology* 107:1244–99.

Boudon, Raymond. 1974. *Education, Opportunity, and Social Inequality: Changing Prospects in Western Society*. New York: Wiley.

Braun, Michael, and Walter Müller. 1997. "Measurement of Education in Comparative Research." *Comparative Social Research* 16:163–201.

Breen, Richard, ed. 2004. *Social Mobility in Europe*. Oxford: Oxford University Press.

———. 2007. "Statistical Models of Educational Careers." Manuscript. Yale University, CIQLE.

Breen, Richard, and John H. Goldthorpe. 1997. "Explaining Educational Differentials: Towards a Formal Rational Action Theory." *Rationality and Society* 9:275–305.

Breen, Richard, Ruud Luijkx, Walter Müller, and Reinhard Pollak. 2009. "Nonpersistent Inequality in Educational Attainment: Evidence from Eight European Countries." *American Journal of Sociology* 114: 1475–1521.

Breen, Richard, and Christopher T. Whelan. 1993. "From Ascription to Achievement? Origins, Education and Entry to the Labour Force in the Republic of Ireland during the Twentieth Century." *Acta Sociologica* 36:3–18.

Erikson, Robert, and John H. Goldthorpe. 1992. *The Constant Flux: A Study of Class Mobility in Industrial Societies.* Oxford: Clarendon.

Erikson, Robert, and Jan O. Jonsson, eds. 1996a. "Explaining Class Inequality in Education: The Swedish Test Case." Pp. 1–64 in *Can Education Be Equalized? The Swedish Case in Comparative Perspective*, edited by Robert Erikson and Jan O. Jonsson. Boulder, Colo.: Westview.

———. 1996b. "The Swedish Context: Educational Reform and Long-Term Change in Educational Inequality." Pp. 65–93 in *Can Education Be Equalized? The Swedish Case in Comparative Perspective*, edited by Robert Erikson and Jan O. Jonsson. Boulder, Colo.: Westview.

Gerber, Theodore P. 2000. "Educational Stratification in Russia during the Soviet Period." *American Journal of Sociology* 101:611–60.

Gerber, Theodore P, and Michael Hout. 1995. "Educational Stratification in Russia During the Soviet Period." *American Journal of Sociology*, 101:611–660.

Goldthorpe, John H., and Colin Mills. 2004. "Trends in Intergenerational Class Mobility in Britain in the Late Twentieth Century." Pp. 195–224 in *Social Mobility in Europe*, edited by Richard Breen. Oxford: Oxford University Press.

Henz, Ursula, and Ineke Maas. 1995. "Chancengleichheit durch die Bildungs-expansion." *Kölner Zeitschrift fur Soziologie und Sozialpsychologie* 47:605–33.

Iannelli, Cristina. 2003. "Parental Education and Young People's Educational and Labour Market Outcomes: A Comparison across Europe." Pp. 27–53 in *School-to-Work Transitions in Europe: Analyses of the EU LFS 2000 Ad Hoc Module*, edited by Irena Kogan and Walter Müller. Mannheim: Mannheimer Zentrum für Europäische Sozialforschung.

Jonsson, Jan O., Colin Mills, and Walter Müller. 1996. "Half a Century of Increasing Educational Openness? Social Class, Gender and Educational Attainment in Sweden, Germany and Britain." Pp. 183–206 in *Can Education Be Equalized? The Swedish Case in Comparative Perspective*, edited by Robert Erikson and Jan O. Jonsson. Boulder, Colo.: Westview.

Kim, Anna, and Ki-Wan Kim. 2003. "Returns to Tertiary Education in Germany and the UK: Effects of Fields of Study and Gender." Working paper no. 62. Mannheimer Zentrum für Europäische Sozialforschung, Mannheim.

Kuo, Hsiang-Hui Daphne, and Robert M. Hauser. 1995. "Trends in Family Effects on the Education of Black and White Brothers." *Sociology of Education* 68:136–60.

Lucas, Samuel R. 2001. "Effectively Maintained Inequality: Education Transitions, Track Mobility, and Social Background Effects." *American Journal of Sociology* 106:1642–90.

Mare, Robert D. 1980. "Social Background and School Continuation Decisions." *Journal of the American Statistical Association* 75:295–305.

———. 1981. "Change and Stability in Educational Stratification." *American Sociological Review* 46:72–87.

McCullagh, Peter. 1980. "Regression Models for Ordinal Data." *Journal of the Royal Statistical Society*, ser. B, 42:109–42.

Müller, Walter, and Dietmar Haun. 1994. "Bildungsungleichheit im sozialen Wandel." *Kölner Zeitschrift fur Soziologie und Sozialpsychologie* 46:1–42.

Müller, Walter, and Wolfgang Karle. 1993. "Social Selection in Educational Systems in Europe." *European Sociological Review* 9:1–23.

Raftery, Adrian E., and Michael Hout. 1993. "Maximally Maintained Inequality: Educational Stratification in Ireland." *Sociology of Education* 65:41–62.

Rijken, Susanne. 1999. Educational Expansion and Status Attainment: A Cross-National and Over-Time Comparison. Amsterdam: Thela Thesis (ICS Dissertation).

Shavit, Yossi, and Hans-Peter Blossfeld, eds. 1993. *Persistent Inequality: Changing Educational Attainment in Thirteen Countries.* Boulder, Colo.: Westview.

Shavit, Yossi, and Karin Westerbeek. 1998. "Educational Stratification in Italy: Reforms, Expansion, and Equality of Opportunity." *European Sociological Review* 14:33–47.

Slomczynski, Kazimierz M., Ireneusz Bialecki, Henryk Domanski, et al. 1989. *Struktura spoleczna: Schemat teoretyczny i warsztat badawczy.* Warsaw: Polish Academy of Sciences.

Vallet, Louis-André. 2004. "The Dynamics of Inequality of Educational Opportunity in France: Change in the Association between Social Background and Education in Thirteen Five-Year Birth Cohorts (1908–1972)." Paper prepared for the meeting of the ISA Research Committee on Social Stratification and Mobility, Neuchâtel, May 6–8.

Van de Werfhorst, Herman. 2001. Field of Study and Social Inequality: Four Types of Educational Resources in the Process of Stratification in the Netherlands. Nijmegen: ICS Dissertation.

Whelan, Christopher T., and Richard Layte. 2002. "Late Industrialisation and the Increased Merit Selection Hypothesis: Ireland as a Test Case." *European Sociological Review* 18:35–50.

Zagórski, Krzysztof. 1976. *Zmiany struktury i ruchliwość społeczno-zawadowa w Polsce.* Warsaw: GUS.

NOTES

1. At this point we omit Hungary from our comparison.

30. Michael Hout*
Rationing College Opportunity

Americans put great stock in the promise of a college education. Most adults see a degree as important for personal success, and they are right. Social and economic data confirm that individuals benefit from college. Communities gain, too. College graduates are more likely to stay employed, buy houses, marry, pay taxes, avoid welfare, commit fewer crimes, volunteer for socially useful causes, vote, be happier and healthier, and live longer.

Thus it comes as quite a surprise to learn that the current college attainment rate is about what it was in the 1970s. Today, 32 percent of young people earn a college degree, compared to 31 percent back in the early 1970s. Between 1965 and 1974, college attainment increased from 23 percent to 31 percent, continuing an upward trend that started in the 1920s. Between the high point in 1974 and the low point in 1984, college attainment slumped back to 27 percent before rebounding to 32 percent by 1994. Since then, higher education in the US has settled into a steady state, at about 32 percent college attainment, one that is too low for the good of young people or the nation. . . .

Historically, public universities have been the inexpensive avenue of upward mobility for the children of the non-affluent. But the era of state investment in affordable higher education is over. Cutbacks replaced expansion in the late 1970s. Each subsequent recession required another cost-cutting round as legislatures withdrew support.

State universities adapted to less funding in ways that helped them maintain quality for those in attendance but that ended up leaving too many qualified and motivated students out. [They] . . . adapted to the new funding limits by increasing tuition, especially at the most prestigious "flagship" public universities. Less prestigious state universities typically reduced the amount spent on instruction. One consequence was a sharper distinction between the flagship public universities and the rest. Another was a shift in instructional costs to students and parents.

A system that once thrived on almost four state dollars to every parent's or student's dollar now asks families to match the state contribution dollar for dollar, or more. In some state systems, public funding now provides as little as 8 percent of costs. Consequently, public university tuition and fees have risen at exactly the same pace as soaring private tuition, according to data from the National Center for Education Statistics. . . .

The flagship public universities have dramatically lower freshman admission rates than they used to. Berkeley is illustrative. In 2007, Berkeley accepted 23 percent of its applicants and denied 77 percent. Thirty years earlier, in 1977, the figures were the opposite: Berkeley admitted 67 percent and denied only 33 percent that year. . . .

Berkeley actually admits more freshmen than it used to, but it gets 49,000 applications a year now compared to 12,000 in 1984. Applications raced ahead of admissions mainly because more of California's young people aspired to attend college. (Some of this statistical shift reflects multiple applications. Lower acceptance rates prompt students to submit more applications.) In short, America's colleges and universities are too selective. Too many aspiring applicants end up with too few options.

Could community colleges fill the gap? More students take community college courses every year. But few community colleges receive the public funding they need to serve as an academic pipeline to a four-year degree. Among community college students who aspire to bachelor's degrees, only one in seven succeeds, because legislators think of community colleges as places to grant terminal associate degrees and ignore the fact that community college students need guidance and support services to make the transition to a university.

To be competitive in the high-tech global economy of the next twenty years, the United States must reverse the downward trend and increase admissions at four-year institutions. That will be very hard to do. Even if funding were not an issue, academic culture seldom questions the wisdom of being selective. However, Berkeley's excellence was unquestioned when it admitted 67 percent of applicants. In 2007, 23 percent of freshman applicants were admitted not out of a conviction that only the selected applicants can succeed, but out of a practical concern that the campus space and facilities can accommodate only about 4,000 freshmen. . . .

What if, by some miracle or practical intervention, state universities were to reverse themselves and become less selective? Is there evidence that the rejected applicants could succeed if some university gave them a chance? It turns out that far more students could flourish at universities and that the admission process is not very good at predicting who deserves a chance. . . .

In the mid-1990s, William Bown and Derek Bok evaluated affirmative-action programs from a sample of America's most selective private and public colleges and universities. From the universities, they acquired the academic records of nearly all the students who entered in 1951, 1976, and 1989. They linked the college records to data on test scores and family characteristics. Finally, they interviewed the students themselves about their post-college experiences. These data revealed that students admitted under affirmative-action programs graduated and proceeded to earn advanced degrees at the same rate as a reference group of other students. They also had the same post-degree earnings. . . .

In the second natural experiment, the City University of New York (CUNY) in 1970 went from having a highly selective admissions process to open enrollments almost overnight. Sociologists Paul Attewell and David E. Lavin tracked down a sample of women from the first three years of open enrollment. They compared the women admitted under the open admissions policy at CUNY with women nationwide who underwent a more selective admissions process. In *Passing the Torch*, they report that the open-enrollment women did slightly better in the areas of graduating, continuing to advanced degrees and earnings than did the comparison group who underwent selective admissions processes. In further comparisons with a national sample of comparable women, Attewell and Lavin showed that open enrollment substantially increased the probability of attending college as well as completing college. . . .

[Another] piece of evidence is the most general. Sociologists Jennie E. Brand and Yu Xie examined three large cohorts of students—two nationally representative cohorts and one of Wisconsin high school graduates. For each cohort they calculated the probability that representative students would have attended college, based on the kinds of things admissions officers know: high school grades, gender, race, and family characteristics. They found that the students who were least likely to get in and go to college benefited more from their degree than did the students who usually attend college.

This is just a sampling of [the evidence]. In all fifteen [of the available] tests, the unlikely college students . . . outperformed or equaled a matched set of students on an important criterion—graduating, getting an advanced degree, or earning a high salary.

This is very important. It means that if we could get out of the current political and fiscal corner, expanding college enrollments and college graduations would pay off at rates comparable to and probably exceeding the rates that pertain today. Far from wasting young peoples' time and universities' resources, expanding admissions would increase college attainment and American workers' productivity.

Improving individual lives is reason enough to expand college enrollments and college graduation rates. [But there is] . . . a broader benefit as well: For young people who graduate from college, family background has no effect on adult occupations and earnings. A college education is the great equalizer.

31. Stephen L. Morgan*
A New Social Psychological Model of Educational Attainment

The decision of whether or not to enter college is vexing for a substantial proportion of high school students. The alternative choices are clearly in view from early adolescence onward, but there is no simple normative guide for behavior. As a result, everyday commitment to preparation for college instruction varies across high school students, affecting resulting enrollment decisions and the potential gains from college instruction.

Consider two students, Max and Vinny, who have been raised in similar families. Their parents have identical educational and occupational profiles and value hard work to the same degree. By the end of middle school, Max and Vinny have equivalent academic records, and they both have access to equally strong opportunities in their respective high schools. In fact, at this point in their lives, Max and Vinny differ substantially in only one way: the amount of information that is available in their communities about the likelihood of graduating from college if enrolled and the typical life outcomes that college graduates and college dropouts receive.

In particular, Max attends a high school in which the majority of students carry on to college after

* This original article first appeared in *Social Stratification: Class, Race, and Gender in Sociological Perspective*, 3rd Edition by David B. Grusky, pp. 542–549, copyright © 2009. Reprinted by permission of Westview Press, an imprint of Perseus Books, LLC, a subsidiary of Hachette Book Group, Inc.

high school graduation, and about half of whom then graduate from college. In contrast, Vinny attends a high school in which very few students per year enter college after high school graduation, even though they are also about equally likely to graduate from college after enrolling. As a result of this dearth of information, Vinny sometimes wonders whether a college education is worth the investment of time and money. And, in fact, every once in a while when thinking through the attractiveness of college, he comes to the conclusion that a college education may not be worthwhile. In these moments, his attention to schoolwork wanes. Max, in contrast, remains diligent all the while. The abundant information that is available to him keeps him focused on ensuring that he is adequately prepared for the next phase of his educational career.

Now suppose that, in addition to differences in the amount of available information, Max's parents have college degrees while Vinny's parents have only high school degrees. In this case, status socialization theory (see Sewell, Haller, and Portes 1969) predicts that Max will have more ambitious college plans, because in general students' own expectations of future behavior are shaped by the expectations that their parents, teachers, and peers have of them. Even if Max and Vinny receive the same amount of encouragement from their parents, it is likely that Max's teachers, who know his parents from parent-teacher conferences, are more likely to communicate to Max that they expect he will attend college just like his parents did.

Stepping back from the case of Max and Vinny, how important are differences in the amount of available information, on which students form their own expectations of future behavior, relative to social influence processes that shape expectations as well? And how do teachers and peers form their expectations? Do they transmit accurate information about a student's likely success in the educational system? Or do they systematically mislead students so that some students who could succeed in college are discouraged while others who would likely fail are encouraged?

The stochastic decision tree model of commitment that I develop here is designed to enable the explicit modeling of questions such as these, based on a belief formation framework that gives separable influence to the accuracy and amount of information available to students. Before laying out the primary features of the model, I first adopt a specific conception of commitment that generates everyday behavioral preparation. I then introduce a standard decision tree model of educational choice, which is then modified for use in the stochastic decision tree model of commitment, as justified by the literature on cognitive constraints and bounded rationality.

Commitment and Preparation

The stochastic decision tree model of commitment is grounded on the specific assumption that in the period leading up to the college entry decision:

A1. Everyday courses of behavior are self-regulated by commitments toward alternative future courses of behavior.

For example, the strength of a high school student's commitment to the future course of behavior, "Go to college immediately following high school," is the ease with which he or she is able to envision entering and ultimately graduating from a college degree program.

For modeling educational attainment, there are three types of commitment toward alternative futures: purposive, normative, and imitative. For the nonrepeatable decision "Go to college" versus "Do not go to college," these three types of commitment are set in response to three forward-looking prediction rules: "I will go to college if I perceive it to be in my best interest to do so," "I will go to college if my significant others perceive it to be in my best interest to do so," and "I will go to college if I expect other students similar to me will also go to college." These three generative dimensions are roughly analogous to the self-reflection, adoption, and imitation mechanisms of status socialization theory (see Morgan 1998).

Although all three dimensions of commitment are important, purposive commitment has the most power to subsume the other two. I will therefore focus development of the stochastic decision tree model here on the construction of purposive commitment (see Morgan 2005, Chapters 5 and 6, for proposals for how to then introduce reinforcing and destabilizing normative and imitative sources of commitment into the model). Thus, I motivate the development of the stochastic decision tree model by assuming that:

A2. Individuals use a decision tree to identify and commit to the future course of behavior that they believe is in their best interest.

Having defined commitment as a cognitive attachment to a future course of behavior, the course of everyday behavior that positions an individual to realize their commitment can then be labeled preparatory commitment, or even more simply as just preparation. I assume that:

A3. An individual's level of preparation for a future course of behavior is a direct function of the strength of their commitment to that course of behavior.

Accordingly, a student with maximal commitment toward the future course of action "I will enroll in college" will enact all possible behavior that prepares the student for enrolling in college and then successfully obtaining a college degree. While in high school, such students will take college preparatory classes, complete their homework diligently, focus their attention when taking tests, sign up early for college entrance examinations, and investigate their range of realistic college alternatives. And, because the payoff to college instruction is a function of the ability to benefit from opportunities for learning, commitment and preparation determine final levels of well-being, above and beyond simply pushing students over a decision threshold to enroll in college.

A Decision Tree Model of Educational Choice

Figure 31.1 presents a standard decision tree for choice under uncertainty. This specific tree is isomorphic with the set of equations used to model students' enrollment decisions by Manski (1989). For this model, a prospective college student must contemplate whether it is in their best interest to choose the course of action "Go to college" or "Do not go to college."

Assume that students consider two possible abstract life outcomes—a very good position in life denoted by "High" and a not very good position in life denoted by "Low." High school students must decide which among three alternative paths through the educational system will put them in the best possible position to obtain the life position High rather than Low: (1) go to college and graduate with a degree; (2) go to college but fail to graduate; or (3) forego college and enter the labor market immediately. For rational choice models of educational attainment, students are presumed to think of these paths as alternative lotteries that are

controlled by success parameters π, α, β, and γ that are probabilities between 0 and 1.

In particular, each student's decision tree has a parameter π that represents each student's subjective belief about the probability of completing college if initially enrolled. Similarly, students maintain a set of beliefs about the relative likelihood of attaining High versus Low after traversing each of the three possible paths through the educational system. They expect that if they complete college, they will attain High with probability α and Low with probability $(1-\alpha)$. If they attempt but do not complete college, then they expect that they will attain High with probability β and Low with probability $(1-\beta)$. And finally, if they choose to forego college, they expect that they will attain High with probability γ and Low with probability $(1-\gamma)$.

Rational choice theory offers the prediction that, under specific assumptions about optimization and consistency of choice, prospective college students will choose to go to college if:

$$\pi\alpha[u(\text{High}_1)-u(\text{Low}_1)]+(1-\pi)\beta[u(\text{High}_2)-u(\text{Low}_2)] > \gamma[u(\text{High}_3)-u(\text{Low}_3)]$$

$$(1a)$$

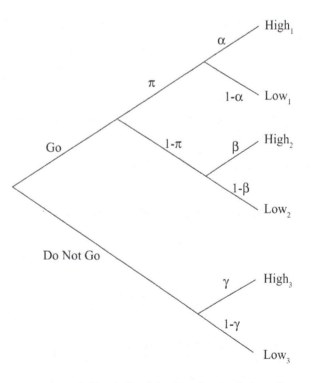

FIGURE 31.1 A Simple Decision Tree for the College Entry Decision

where $u(.)$ is a utility function that, in its most general sense, assigns subjective value to the alternative payoffs High and Low. If an individual's utility function is process-independent so that $u(\text{High}_1) = u(\text{High}_2) = u(\text{High}_3)$ and $u(\text{Low}_1) = u(\text{Low}_2) = u(\text{Low}_3)$, then both sides of Equation (1a) can be divided by a common utility difference, $u(\text{High})-u(\text{Low})$, in order to obtain the simplified decision rule:

$$\pi\alpha+(1-\pi)\beta > \gamma \qquad (1b)$$

The left hand sides of Equations (1a) and (1b) represent the expected utility of enrolling in college, and the right-hand sides represent the expected utility of not enrolling in college. If the expected utility of enrolling is greater than the expected utility of not enrolling, rational choice theory assumes that a high school student will choose to enroll in college.

After students choose either the upper or lower branch of the tree—and thus either enroll in college or enter the labor force—they are subject to a set of real-life lotteries. The probability of reaching High instead of Low is a function of more than simply a student's decision. Each lottery has a "true" probability, denoted respectively as $\tilde{\pi}$, $\tilde{\alpha}$, $\tilde{\beta}$, and $\tilde{\gamma}$. Actual outcomes are therefore determined in large part by exogenous factors that structure these probabilities. For researchers, claims about the relative sizes of $\tilde{\pi}$, $\tilde{\alpha}$, $\tilde{\beta}$, and $\tilde{\gamma}$ are usually based on assumptions about institutional constraints on educational attainment and the distribution of High versus Low outcomes in society. It is generally assumed that there are positive returns to schooling so that $\tilde{\alpha} \geq \tilde{\beta}$ and $\tilde{\beta} > \tilde{\gamma}$. However, Manski (1989:307) argues that "analysis is trivial" unless, in the notation used here, for at least some students $\tilde{\beta} < \tilde{\gamma}$ and $\beta < \gamma$. If that were not the case, all students would choose to enter college.

When contemplating college entry decisions, do students maintain reasonable beliefs about the lotteries that they face? In other words, for each individual and for a decision tree such as the one depicted in Figure 31.1, is there a close correspondence between π, α, β, and γ and $\tilde{\pi}$, $\tilde{\alpha}$, $\tilde{\beta}$, and $\tilde{\gamma}$? The traditional assumption among rational choice researchers is that individuals, on average, have correct beliefs about $\tilde{\pi}$, $\tilde{\alpha}$, $\tilde{\beta}$, and $\tilde{\gamma}$. Accordingly, the values of π, α, β, and γ that students rely on when making college entry decisions are assumed to equal the true probabilities that students will face in their futures.

The model I develop in the next section provides a foundation for a more comprehensive approach.

The model is based in part on rational choice theory but also embraces the core claim of the Wisconsin model of Sewell, Haller, and Portes (1969) that one's current behavior is conditioned by socially structured beliefs about one's future.

A Stochastic Decision Tree Model of Commitment

The action "Go to college" can be thought of as a compound outcome of a series of underlying decisions, many of which must be enacted long before the first college tuition bill is due. Moreover, the payoff to obtaining a college degree is a function not just of having enrolled in college but of how seriously one has prepared to master the college curriculum before being exposed to it.

Decision Tree Structure

For the college entry decision, I assume that:

A4. The decision tree that individuals use to commit to a future course of behavior is more simple in structure than that which would be required to explicitly model all underlying decisions that are consequential for the college entry decision.

Equivalently, I assume that preparation cannot be modeled as a long series of fully conscious, forward-looking decisions. For the numerical demonstration of the framework that I offer in Morgan (2005), I use the simple decision tree in Figure 31.1, and hence, when referring to the college choice example, adopt the position of Manski (1989) that for enrollment decisions potential enrollees consider four basic lotteries. Trees with alternative and slightly more elaborate structures are permissible, but I stipulate with Assumption A4 that these must remain simple.

For example, if a student were contemplating a high school course enrollment decision, the decision tree in Figure 31.1 could be expanded to model this decision explicitly. In this case, the decision tree in Figure 31.1 could be specified as two alternative subtrees for the pressing current decision: "Enroll in trigonometry" or "Do not enroll in trigonometry." A more comprehensive tree of this form would be justified if beliefs such as p or the utility evaluations of High and Low depend on whether or not one enrolls in the trigonometry class.

Even though some very consequential short-run decisions may be approached in this sophisticated way, I presume that students have no desire to use a finely specified decision tree for every consequential underlying decision they must make, such as whether to study hard for an upcoming test or whether to do their homework on any given night. Were this the case, the large number of preparatory commitment decisions that adolescents must navigate in middle school and high school would render any such comprehensive decision trees massive and ever-changing as each intermediate decision is considered and then enacted.

Belief Distributions

Instead of requiring high school students to construct comprehensive decision trees for all intermediate decisions, I allow the complexity of the everyday decisions that constitute preparation to be modeled as uncertainty about the parameters of a simple decision tree for a future course of behavior. Thus, I assume that:

A5. The parameters of the decision tree that students use to commit to a future course of behavior are fundamentally stochastic.

This assumption is the major departure from standard practice in rational choice modeling of educational attainment. For the stochastic decision tree model of commitment, students recognize that the decision tree they are consulting is simply a rough approximation to the complex set of real-life lotteries to which they will ultimately be subjected. Thus, students forecast their futures as if any ostensibly true parameters such as and have distributions. Accordingly, Assumption A5 stipulates that students maintain entire belief distributions for the parameters of a decision tree, such as π, α, β, and γ in Figure 31.1.

How are belief distributions constructed and revised? I address this question in substantial detail in Morgan (2005), but here I simply assume for brevity that individuals store belief distributions in memory based on observations of individuals whom they regard as payoff models. Furthermore, I assume that individuals with sparse information at their disposal will have uncertain belief distributions with large variances, and individuals with abundant information will have precise belief distributions with small variances. For example, consider two high school students contemplating the decision tree presented in Figure 31.1 when forecasting their own future decision of whether to enter college immediately. Student A observes twenty college graduates and ten college dropouts. In contrast, Student B observes

only two college graduates and one college dropout. The framework I will adopt stipulates that Student A will have more confidence than Student B in eliminating extreme values from his or her belief distributions about the subjective probability of graduating from college if enrolled. Student A would consider values such as .66 much more likely than values such as .96 or .36. Student B would likewise consider .66 more likely than either .96 or .36 but would be less willing than Student A to discount the plausibility of .96 or .36. This position is consistent with the dominant literature on belief distributions, which for Bayesian decision theory (see Pratt, Raiffa, and Schlaifer 1995) and information-integration theory in psychology (see Davidson 1995) similarly allows uncertainty and imprecision of beliefs to be a function of the amount of available information.

Decision Tree Evaluation

How do students evaluate their stochastic decision trees? By principles of statistical decision theory, the traditional answer would be that they calculate the means of their belief distributions, declare them as their best estimates of their point-value beliefs, and use them to solve a decision rule such as Equation (1a). Instead, I accept the position from the bounded rationality literature that individuals are subject to substantial cognitive constraints. Accordingly, they cannot numerically evaluate density functions in order to quickly recover arbitrarily exact estimates of the means of their belief distributions. Rather, individuals must rely on "fast and frugal" strategies to evaluate their decision trees (see Gigerenzer and Selten 2001). Based on this position, I assume that:

A6. Students evaluate their stochastic decision trees by solving a decision rule with parameter values that are simple averages of a few randomly sampled candidate values drawn from their belief distributions.

In the numerical simulations of the framework offered in Morgan (2005), I allow students to randomly draw only a few candidate parameter values for a decision tree of the structure presented in Figure 31.1 and then average over these values to form a set of candidate point-value beliefs $\{\pi', \alpha', \beta', \gamma'\}$. Assuming that utility evaluations are equivalent across paths and scaled to values of 1 for High and 0 for Low, an individual will set a dichotomous variable E equal to 1 if:

$$\pi'\alpha' + (1-\pi')\beta' > \gamma' \qquad (1c)$$

Otherwise, E will be set equal to 0. E signifies an instantaneous commitment to the future affirmative decision "Go to college" (for example, the choice "Go" in Figure 31.1).

Over a set of J evaluations of the same stochastic decision tree with stable belief distributions, the average level of commitment to future college attendance is then:

$$\Pr(E{=}1){=}\frac{1}{J}\sum_{j=1,..,J}E_1 \quad (2)$$

$\Pr(E{=}1)$ is therefore equal in expectation to the probability that E will be evaluated as 1 for a given set of beliefs and prespecified total number of candidate parameter draws selected for decision tree evaluation. Thus, whereas the binary orientation E represents the instantaneous commitment that guides each preparation decision, $\Pr(E = 1)$ represents the average level of commitment that is consistent with a set of stable beliefs and a procedure to analyze those beliefs in the process of constructing forward-looking commitment. The distinction implies that for two students who at a specific point in time both set E equal to 1, the student whose beliefs imply a lower value for $\Pr(E = 1)$ will be less likely to set E equal to 1 when contemplating subsequent preparation decisions. $\Pr(E = 1)$ is therefore the more fundamental quantity of interest.

Why would students use this form of decision evaluation? I assume that students generally wish to orient their current behavior to a long-run plan that is in their best interest, but doing so in a way that is as rigorous as stipulated by statistical decision theory is too costly, especially since students themselves must recognize that they cannot form comprehensive decision trees to capture all consequential intermediate decisions. Thus, students seek to avoid short-run mistakes in judgment by adopting a relatively frugal process of planning for their futures.

The simulations and the analytic results in Chapter 4 of Morgan (2005) demonstrate that when the uncertainty of beliefs is allowed to explicitly enter a decision evaluation, preparation for a future course of behavior such as college entry is sensitive to the amount and type of uncertainty in one's beliefs as well as the effort expended to analyze those beliefs. Thus, even in a world where the returns on investments in higher education are massive, if beliefs are the least bit uncertain, and if students have limited information processing and analysis capacities, some

high school students some of the time will perceive it to be in their future best interest to forego a college education. In these episodic and contrarian instances, they will adjust their current behavior accordingly, failing to enact preparation decisions that their beliefs nonetheless imply are genuinely in their best interest.

Conclusions

To construct the stochastic decision tree model of commitment, I have borrowed and then extended the strongest pieces of both status socialization and rational choice models of educational attainment. The key innovation of the framework is the specification of a simple decision tree with fundamentally stochastic parameters. When a simple, boundedly rational decision rule is invoked to specify the way in which individuals draw forecasts of future behavior from their stochastic decision trees, commitment and preparation can be shown to be functions of the accuracy and precision of beliefs about future courses of behavior. If, as assumed by status socialization theory, current behavior is a function of beliefs about the future, then everyday forecasts of future behavior operate as self-fulfilling prophecies by regulating preparation for the course of behavior that is thought to be in one's best interest.

The conception of educational attainment that I have developed here can be read as a strategic evasion of the question that is the title of Diego Gambetta's 1987 book, *Were They Pushed or Did They Jump? Individual Decision Mechanisms in Education*. From the perspective developed here, students wander through a series of daily decisions, adjusting current behavior to anticipation of future behavior. If belief formation has its own inertia, is easily contaminated through social influence, and regulates current behavior, then it would seem best not to conceive of students as if they are standing on the edge of a cliff, contemplating whether to jump. It should suffice to see students as if they are on the edge of commitment to alternative futures. Although less dramatic, this metaphor is sufficient to motivate the new generation of theoretically guided empirical analysis that is now needed.

REFERENCES

Davidson, Andrew R. 1995. "From Attitudes to Actions to Attitude Change: The Effects of Amount and Accuracy of Information." In *Attitude Strength: Antecedents and*

Consequences, edited by R. E. Petty and J. A. Krosnick. Mahwah, NJ: Erlbaum.

Gambetta, Diego. 1987. *Were They Pushed or Did They Jump? Individual Decision Mechanisms in Education*. Cambridge: Cambridge University Press.

Gigerenzer, Gerd, and Reinhard Selten, eds. 2001. *Bounded Rationality: The Adaptive Toolbox*. Cambridge, MA: MIT Press.

Manski, Charles F. 1989. "Schooling as Experimentation: A Reappraisal of the Postsecondary Dropout Phenomenon." *Economics of Education Review* 8: 305–312.

Morgan, Stephen L. 1998. "Adolescent Educational Expectations: Rationalized, Fantasized, or Both?" *Rationality and Society* 10: 131–162.

———. 2005. *On the Edge of Commitment: Educational Attainment and Race in the United States*. Stanford, CA: Stanford University Press.

Pratt, John W., Howard Raiffa, and Robert Schlaifer. 1995. *Introduction to Statistical Decision Theory*. Cambridge, MA: MIT Press.

Sewell, William H., Archibald O. Haller, and Alejandro Portes. 1969. "The Educational and Early Occupational Attainment Process." *American Sociological Review* 34:89–92.

32. Josipa Roksa and Richard Arum*

Academically Adrift

How much are students learning in college? That question begs another one: What should students be learning in college? In *Our Underachieving Colleges*, former president of Harvard, Derek Bok, proposed a range of goals, from learning to communicate to developing character and learning to live in a diverse and global society. He also pointed out that while faculty rarely agree on the purposes of higher education and tend to shy away from discussions of values and morals, they overwhelmingly agree that their students should learn how to think critically. Indeed, a recent study by the Higher Education Research Institute noted that virtually all faculty report that developing students' ability to think critically is a very important or essential goal of undergraduate education, as is promoting students' ability to write effectively.

But even if faculty concur that students should develop critical thinking and writing skills (among

many others) during college, the question remains of how those skills should be assessed. . . .[The Collegiate Learning Assessment (CLA)] focuses on general skills such as critical thinking, analytical reasoning, and written communication. It consists of three components: a performance task and two analytical writing exercises (make an argument and break an argument). The performance task is the CLA's most innovative component. Students have ninety minutes to respond to a writing prompt representing a "real-world" scenario, in which they are presented with a task or a dilemma and need to use a range of background documents (from memos and newspaper articles to reports, journal articles, and graphic representations) to solve it. The testing materials, including the background documents, are accessed through a computer. . . .

Over 2,300 students across twenty-four four-year institutions took the CLA in fall 2005, at the beginning of their freshman year, and again in spring 2007, at the end of their sophomore year. The colleges and universities were representative of four-year institutions across the country based on demographics (gender and race/ethnicity) and academic preparation (as measured by the SAT/ACT scores of entering freshmen).

It is important to note that we focused on traditional-age students. Assessing the learning of non-traditional students, such as those who enter college years after high school graduation or who typically attend community colleges, presents a unique set of challenges which were beyond the scope of our study.

So, how much are students learning? Based on our analysis of the CLA, the answer for many undergraduates is: not much. In the first two years of college, students on average improve their critical thinking, analytical reasoning, and writing skills by only 0.18 standard deviations. This translates into a 7 percentile point gain, meaning that freshmen who entered higher education at the 50th percentile would reach a level equivalent to the 57th percentile of the incoming freshman class by the end of their sophomore year.

Since standard deviations and percentiles are not the most intuitive ways of describing learning, we also put it this way: how many students show no statistically significant gains in learning over the first two years of college? Answer: 45 percent. A high proportion of students are progressing through higher education today without measurable gains in critical thinking, analytical reasoning, and writing skills as assessed by the CLA.

While this overall portrayal of learning is not encouraging, there is much variation among students. By asking students about their college experiences during their sophomore year, we were able to explore how different factors are related to student learning, as measured by improvement in CLA scores over the first two years of college.

We find a positive association between hours spent studying and gains on the CLA: Not surprisingly, the more time students spend studying, the more they learn. As much educational research has argued, time on task matters. But college students today do not spend much time on task.

Students in our sample reported studying on average only twelve hours a week during their sophomore year. Even more alarming, over 40 percent reported preparing for their courses for less than ten hours per week, and almost 40 percent dedicated less than five hours per week to studying alone. Students also went to classes and labs for an average of fifteen hours a week. Taken together, this means that students on average spent less than one fifth (16 percent) of their seven-day week in academic pursuits.

This is not an anomaly of our sample or a "sophomore slump." Findings from the National Survey of Student Engagement show that almost half (44 percent) of students from freshmen to seniors spend ten or fewer hours per week studying. And for those who are tempted to suggest that students never spent much time studying, recent work by labor economists Philip Babcock and Mindy Marks indicates that the precipitous drop in study time occurred after the 1960s. In the first half of the 20th century, students spent twice as much time studying as they do today.

If they are not studying, what are students doing with their time? Some of it is spent working, volunteering, and participating in clubs and other organized college activities. However, on average, students in four-year institutions spend most of their "free time" (i.e., time outside of class) socializing and recreating. A recent study of University of California undergraduates by sociologist Steven Brint reported that while students there spent thirteen hours a week studying, they also spent twelve hours socializing with friends, eleven using computers for fun, six watching television, six exercising, five on hobbies, and three on other forms of entertainment. Students were thus spending on average forty-three hours per week outside of the classroom on these activities – i.e., over three times more than the time they spent studying. . . .

When faculty have high expectations, students learn more. Students who reported that faculty had high expectations developed their critical thinking, analytical reasoning, and writing skills during the first two years of college more than those who reported that their professors had low expectations. These findings align with an established sociological model of educational attainment, which has highlighted how expectations of significant others, including teachers, are important for spurring students' educational success. . . .

Our findings regarding academic rigor corroborate results from previous research. The distinctiveness of our study is the ability to relate what students do in college to changes in an objective measure of student learning over time, and to do so for a large number of students across two dozen four-year institutions. The simple answer is that in order for students to learn more, we need to increase our demands and expectations of them. . . .

While faculty spend a sizable proportion of their time teaching and preparing for classes, reward structures generally do not focus on these activities. Research is increasingly the key requirement for tenure in four-year colleges and universities of whatever type. The current system seems to produce what George Kuh has termed a "disengagement compact" in which faculty do not require much of students and in return are not bothered by them. Perhaps even more problematically, graduate students, the future professoriate, are trained primarily to do research. . . .

Similarly, administrators are rewarded for leading "successful" institutions. This tends to imply increasing the selectivity of the student body, since college-ranking systems place a disproportionate weight on the characteristics of the entering student body and pay no attention to whether and how much students are learning. Increasing one's position in the prestige hierarchy thus becomes equivalent to restricting access and not improving learning. Building the endowment (or in general securing financial resources, whether from private donors, state governments, granting agencies, or other sources) is another priority for administrators.

Having an academically prepared student body and an abundance of resources are obviously desirable characteristics. But they are not a reality for many institutions of higher education, and in chasing them, leaders can be diverted from pursuing what should be regarded as the core mission of colleges and universities: learning.

Economic and Occupation Mobility

**Raj Chetty, Nathaniel Hendren,
Patrick Kline, and
Emmanuel Saez***

Economic Mobility

The United States is often hailed as the "land of opportunity," a society in which a child's chances of success depend little on her family background. Is this reputation warranted? And is it especially warranted in some states, regions, or areas of the United States? . . .

In two recent papers, we address these questions by compiling statistics from millions of anonymous income records.[1] These data have less measurement error and much larger sample sizes than previous survey-based studies and thus yield more precise estimates of intergenerational mobility across cities and states over time. Our core sample consists of all children in the United States born between 1980–1982, whose income we measure in 2011–2012, when they are approximately 30 years old. We divide our analysis into two parts: an analysis of time trends and an analysis of geographical variation in mobility across areas of the United States.

Time Trends

We find that the most robust way to measure intergenerational mobility is by ranking parents by parental income (at the time the child was growing up in the family) and by ranking children by their

income when they are adults. For each percentile of parent's income, we compute the average rank of the income of the children when adults. As shown in Figure 1, we find that this rank-rank relationship is almost perfectly linear, with a slope of 0.34.

Contrary to popular perception, we find that such percentile rank-based measures of intergenerational mobility have remained extremely stable for the 1971-1993 birth cohorts. For example, the probability that a child reaches the top fifth of the income distribution given parents in the bottom fifth is 8.4 percent for children born in 1971, compared with 9.0 percent for those born in 1986. . . .

Figure 33.2 illustrates the stability of intergenerational mobility for children born between 1971 and 1993. The y-axis, "intergenerational persistence," is a measure of the gap in average income percentiles for

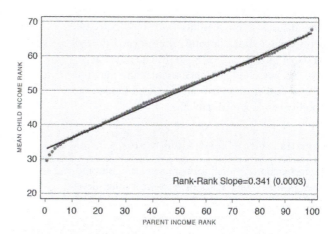

Note: The figure presents a non-parametric binned scatter plot of the relationship between child and parent income ranks. Both figures are based on a population sample of the 1980–1982 birth cohorts and baseline family income definitions for parents and children. Child income is the mean of 2011–2012 family income (when the child was around 30), while parent income is mean family income from 1996–2000. We define a child's rank as her family income percentile rank relative to other children in her birth cohort and his parents' rank as their family income percentile rank relative to other parents of children in the core sample. The slopes and best-fit lines are estimated using an OLS regression on the micro data. Standard errors are reported in parentheses.

FIGURE 33.1 Trends in Intergenerational Mobility in the United States

Source: Chetty et al., 2014a.

* Chetty, Raj, Nathaniel Hendren, Patrick Kline, and Emmanuel Saez. 2015. "Economic Mobility." *Pathways Magazine: State of the States*, Special Issue, 55-60. Print.

FIGURE 33.2
Intergenerational
Mobility by State
Source: Chetty et al., 2014b.

children born in the poorest versus richest families. On average, children with parents in the bottom 1 percent of the income distribution grow up to earn an income approximately 30 percentiles lower than their peers with parents in the top 1 percent of the income distribution. This difference has remained relatively steady across the birth cohorts we studied.

Although rank-based measures of mobility remained stable, income inequality increased substantially over the period we study. Hence, the consequences of the "birth lottery"—the parents to whom a child is born—are larger today than in the past. A useful visual analogy is to envision the income distribution as a ladder, with each percentile representing a different rung. The rungs of the ladder have grown farther apart (inequality has increased), but children's chances of climbing from lower to higher rungs have not changed (rank-based mobility has remained stable). . . .

Variation within the United States

Intergenerational mobility, on average, is significantly lower in the United States than in most other developed countries.[2] However, mobility varies widely within the United States, and we now turn to examine this regional and state variability. We begin by constructing measures of relative and absolute mobility for 741 "commuting zones" (CZs) in the United States. Commuting zones are geographical aggregations of counties that are similar to metro areas but also cover rural areas. Children are assigned to a CZ based on their location at age sixteen (no matter where they live as adults), so that their location represents where they grew up. When analyzing local area variation, we rank both children and parents based on

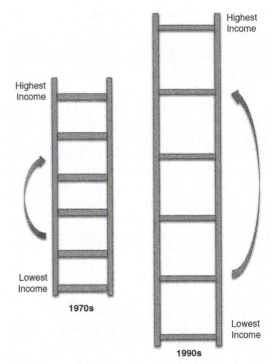

The rungs of the income ladder have grown farther apart (income inequality has increased)

...but children's chances of climbing from lower to higher rungs have not changed.

FIGURE 33.3 Changes in the Income Ladder in the United States

their positions in the national income distribution. Hence, our statistics measure how well children fare relative to those in the nation as a whole rather than to those in their own particular community. . . .

In Figure 33.4, the . . . variation between regions is notable. Poor children in western states have the

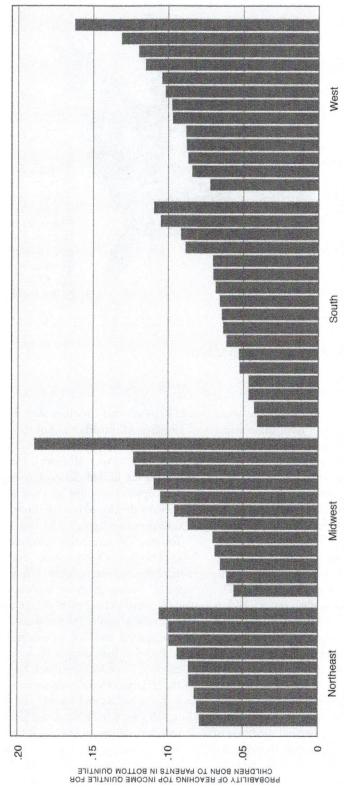

FIGURE 33.4 Intergenerational Mobility by State

Note: This figure plots the state average (weighted by children in 1980–1982 cohorts) of the commuting zone mobility measure presented in Figure 33.5. Multistate commuting zones are assigned to the state with the largest city in the CZ. This figure is constructed using data from Online Data Table V of Chetty et al., 2014a.

Source: Chetty et al., 2014a.

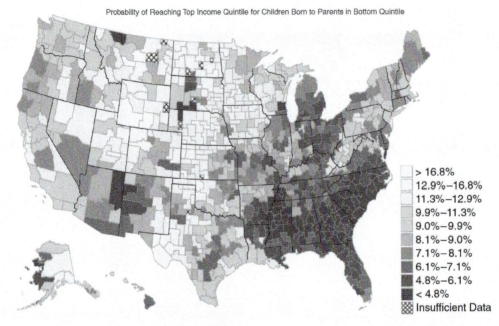

Probability of Reaching Top Income Quintile for Children Born to Parents in Bottom Quintile

> 16.8%
12.9%–16.8%
11.3%–12.9%
9.9%–11.3%
9.0%–9.9%
8.1%–9.0%
7.1%–8.1%
6.1%–7.1%
4.8%–6.1%
< 4.8%
Insufficient Data

Note: This figure presents a heat map of the probability that a child reaches the top quintile of the national family income distribution for children conditional on having parents in the bottom quintile of the family income distribution for parents. Children are assigned to commuting zones based on the location of their parents (when the child was claimed a dependent), irrespective of where they live as adults. This figure is constructed using data from Online Data Table V of Chetty et al., 2014a.

FIGURE 33.5 The Geography of Intergenerational Mobility
Source: Chetty et al., 2014a.

best chances of making it to the top quintile, while their counterparts in the South have the bleakest odds. There is also evidence of variation within regions. Rust Belt and southeastern states have markedly lower mobility than other midwestern and southern states. There is, by contrast, no sharp subregional variability in the Northeast, while the West is notable for its two outlier states: Arizona (very low mobility) and Wyoming (very high mobility).

There is also much variation across states that are in close geographic proximity and have similar sociodemographic characteristics. For example, North Dakota has the highest mobility in the country (children in the bottom fifth have an 18.9 percent chance of reaching the top fifth), whereas South Dakota has much less mobility (a corresponding statistic of 12.2 percent). Likewise, neighboring states like Texas and Arkansas or New Mexico and Arizona also offer very different opportunities for children born into them.

If we next drop down to the level of CZs themselves (see Figure 33.5), we again find that rates of mobility vary by where one grows up. In areas with the highest rates of mobility (denoted by the lightest color on the map), children growing up in the bottom fifth have more than a 16.8 percent chance of reaching the top fifth. That number is higher

than in most other countries with the highest rates of mobility. At the other end of the spectrum, that is, the darkest-colored areas, children have less than a 4.8 percent chance of moving from the bottom fifth to the top fifth of the income distribution. The rates of upward mobility in these areas are lower than in any developed country for which data have been analyzed to date. . . .

This map also reveals that urban areas tend to have lower rates of social mobility than rural areas. The successful children growing up in rural areas do not just "move up" but also generally "move out." That is, they typically move to large metropolitan areas, often out of their state of birth. There is also substantial variation in upward mobility across cities, even among large cities that have comparable economies and demographics. Table 33.1 lists upward mobility statistics for the 50 largest metro areas, focusing on the 10 cities with the highest and lowest levels of upward mobility. Salt Lake City, Boston, and San Jose have rates of mobility similar to the most upwardly mobile countries in the world, while other cities—such as Charlotte, Atlanta, and Milwaukee—offer children very limited prospects of escaping poverty. The odds of moving from the bottom to the top are two to three times larger for those growing up in Salt Lake City or

TABLE 33.1 Upward Mobility in the 50 Largest Metro Areas: The Top 10 and Bottom 10

Rank	Commuting Zone	Odds of Reaching Top Fifth from Bottom Fifth	Rank	Commuting Zone	Odds of Reaching Top Fifth from Bottom Fifth
1	San Jose, CA	12.9%	41	Cleveland, OH	5.1%
2	San Francisco, CA	12.2%	42	St. Louis, MO	5.1%
3	Washington, D.C.	11.0%	43	Raleigh, NC	5.0%
4	Seattle, WA	10.9%	44	Jacksonville, FL	4.9%
5	Salt Lake City, UT	10.8%	45	Columbus, OH	4.9%
6	New York, NY	10.5%	46	Indianapolis, IN	4.9%
7	Boston, MA	10.5%	47	Dayton, OH	4.9%
8	San Diego, CA	10.4%	48	Atlanta, GA	4.5%
9	Newark, NJ	10.2%	49	Milwaukee, WI	4.5%
10	Manchester, NH	10.0%	50	Charlotte, NC	4.4%

Note: This table reports selected statistics from a sample of the 50 largest commuting zones (CZs) according to their populations in the 2000 Census. The columns report the percentage of children whose family income is in the top quintile of the national distribution of child family income conditional on having parent family income in the bottom quintile of the parental national income distribution—these probabilities are taken from Online Data Table VI of Chetty et al., 2014a.

Source: Chetty et al., 2014a.

San Jose as compared with those growing up in Milwaukee or Atlanta.

In ongoing work, Chetty and Hendren find that if a child moves from a city with low upward mobility (such as Milwaukee) to a city with high upward mobility (such as Salt Lake City), her own income in adulthood rises in proportion to the time she is exposed to the better environment.[3] This finding suggests that much of the variation in upward mobility across areas may be driven by a causal effect of the local environment rather than differences in the characteristics of the people who live in different cities. Hence it may be effective to tackle social mobility at the community level. If we can make every city in America have mobility rates like San Jose or Salt Lake City, the United States would become one of the most upwardly mobile countries in the world.

Correlates of Spatial Variation

What drives the variation in social mobility across areas? To answer this question, we begin by noting that the spatial pattern in gradients of college attendance and teenage birth rates with respect to parent income is very similar to the spatial pattern in intergenerational income mobility. The fact that much of the spatial variation in children's outcomes emerges before they enter the labor market suggests that the differences in mobility are driven by factors that affect children while they are growing up. . . .

We begin by showing that upward income mobility is significantly lower in areas with larger African-American populations. However, white individuals in areas with large African-American populations also have lower rates of upward mobility, implying that racial shares matter at the community (rather than individual) level. One mechanism for such a community-level effect of race is segregation. Areas with larger black populations tend to be more segregated by income and race, which could affect both white and black low-income individuals adversely. Indeed, we find a strong, negative correlation between standard measures of racial and income segregation and upward mobility. . . . These findings lead us to identify segregation as the first of five major factors that are strongly correlated with mobility.

The second factor we explore is income inequality. CZs with larger Gini coefficients have less upward mobility, consistent with the "Great Gatsby curve" documented across countries. In contrast, top 1 percent income shares are not highly correlated with intergenerational mobility both across CZs within the United States and across countries. Although one cannot draw definitive conclusions from such correlations, they suggest that the factors that erode the middle class hamper intergenerational mobility more than the factors that lead to income growth in the upper tail. Third, proxies for the quality of the K–12 school system are also correlated with mobility. Areas with higher test scores (controlling for income levels), lower dropout rates, and smaller class sizes have higher rates of upward mobility. In addition, areas with higher local tax rates, which are predominantly used to finance public schools, have higher rates of mobility.

Fourth, social capital indices[4]—which are proxies for the strength of social networks and community involvement in an area—are very strongly correlated with mobility. For instance, areas of high upward mobility tend to have higher fraction of religious individuals and greater participation in local civic organizations. Finally, the strongest predictors of upward mobility are measures of family structure, such as the fraction of single parents in the area. As with race, parents' marital status does not matter purely through its effects at the individual level. Children of married parents also have higher rates of upward mobility if they live in communities with fewer single parents.

We find modest correlations between upward mobility and local tax and government expenditure policies, and no systematic correlation between mobility and local labor market conditions, rates of migration, or access to higher education.

We caution that all of the findings in this study are correlational and cannot be interpreted as causal effects. For instance, areas with high rates of segregation may also have other characteristics that could be the root cause driving the differences in children's outcomes. What is clear from this research is that there is substantial variation in the United States in the prospects for escaping poverty. Understanding the properties of the highest-mobility areas—and how we can improve mobility in areas that currently have lower rates of mobility—is an important question for future research that we and other social scientists are exploring.

NOTES

1. Chetty, Raj, Nathan Hendren, Patrick Kline, and Emmanuel Saez. 2014a. "Where is the Land of Opportunity? The Geography of Intergenerational Mobility in the United States." Quarterly Journal of Economics, 129(4), 15531623; Chetty, Raj, Nathan Hendren, Patrick Kline, Emmanuel Saez, and Nicholas Turner. 2014b. "Is the United States Still a Land of Opportunity? Recent Trends in Intergenerational Mobility." American Economic Review: Papers and Proceedings, 104(5), 141-147. This article also draws on two earlier summaries of our research: Chetty, Raj, Nathan Hendren, Patrick Kline, and Emmanuel Saez. 2014c. "Where is the Land of Opportunity? Intergenerational Mobility in the U.S." Vox. Centre for Economic Policy Research. Available at http://www.voxeu.org/article/where-land-opportunityintergenerational-mobility-us; Chetty, Raj. 2015. "Socio-Economic Mobility in the United States: New Evidence and Policy Lessons," forthcoming in Building Shared Prosperity in America's Communities (working title), to be published by the University of Pennsylvania Press, edited by Susan Wachter and Lei Ding.

2. Corak, Miles. 2013. "Income Inequality, Equality of Opportunity, and Intergenerational Mobility." Journal of Economic Perspectives, 27(3), 79-102.

3. Chetty, Raj, and Nathan Hendren. 2015. "The Effects of Neighborhoods on Children's Long-Term Outcomes: Quasi-Experimental Estimates for the United States." Unpublished Working Paper.

4. Putnam, Robert D. 1995. "Bowling Alone: America's Declining Social Capital." Journal of Democracy, 6(1), 65-78.

---

34. Florencia Torche[*]
Does College Still Have Equalizing Effects?

A college degree yields substantial economic returns. By the early twenty-first century, college graduates' earnings were about 90 percent higher than those of their high school graduate counterparts, a premium that has increased over the last quarter century (Autor, Katz, and Kearney 2008). College attainment is also related to better health, longevity, happiness, and a host of extra-economic outcomes (Ross and Mirowsky 1999; Pallas 2000; Rowley and Hurtado 2003; Attewell and Lavin 2007; Stevens, Armstrong, and Arum 2008).

But college attainment is related to more than economic and extra-economic well-being. An important finding of stratification research is that the direct influence of parental resources on the economic position of adult children is much weaker among college graduates than among those with less schooling (Hout 1984, 1988). That influence decreases to almost zero among college graduates.

It does not of course follow that all social inequality has been eliminated. Access to college is strongly dependent on parental resources (Ellwood and Kane

*The ideas, issues, and theories considered in this brief commissioned piece are examined in greater depth in the following publication: Florencia Torche, "Is a College Degree Still the Great Equalizer? Intergenerational Mobility Across Levels of Schooling in the United States," *American Journal of Sociology* 117:3 (November 2011), pp. 763–807, published by the University of Chicago Press. The article printed here was originally prepared by Florencia Torche for the fourth edition of *Social Stratification: Class, Race, and Gender in Sociological Perspective*, edited by David B. Grusky. Copyright © 2014 by Westview Press.

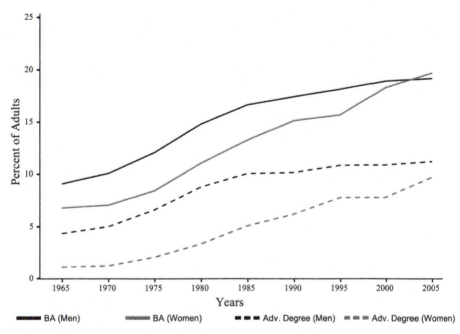

FIGURE 34.1 Percentage of Adults 30–60 with a Bachelor's Degree and an Advanced Degree by Gender and Year, United States 1965–2005

Source: Current Population Survey, 1965–2005, March annual demographic file data. (Note: This table appears in Torche [2011].)

2000; Haveman and Smeeding 2006), and the socioeconomic gap in access appears to have increased over time (Kane 2004; Belley and Lochner 2007). The finding mentioned previously, however, means that for those who receive a college degree, their socioeconomic attainment is independent of their socioeconomic origins. In other words, a college degree fulfills the promise of meritocracy: it offers equal opportunity for economic success regardless of the advantages of birth.

This finding is not a US anomaly. Researchers have shown a weaker intergenerational association at higher levels of schooling in other industrialized countries such as France, Sweden, and Germany (Vallet 2004; Breen and Jonsson 2007; Breen and Luijkx 2007). However, the US case is the clearest one in which the intergenerational socioeconomic association fully disappears among college graduates, providing "a new answer to the old question about overcoming disadvantaged origins: A college degree can do it" (Hout 1988, 1391).

A New Landscape for the Meritocratic Power of a College Degree?

These findings come largely from the 1970s. Many things have changed since then. College expansion

and differentiation and the increase in post-baccalaureate advanced degrees define a new educational landscape that may have altered mobility patterns of college graduates.

A notable change over the last quarter century has been an increase in the proportion of adult Americans with a college degree. According to the Current Population Survey (CPS), the percentage of men ages thirty to sixty with a college degree grew from 13 percent in 1965 to 30 percent in 2005, and for women there is an even more impressive increase, from 8 to 29 percent.

To date, stratification research has treated college graduates as a single, homogeneous category. However, this group comprises two distinct levels of attainment: bachelor's degree and advanced degree. As Figure 34.1 shows, in 1970 only 5 percent of adult men and 1 percent of women held a degree beyond a bachelor's, including master's, first-professional, and doctoral degrees. By 2005 these numbers had reached 11 percent for men and 10 percent for women. The substantial increase in the proportion of advanced degree holders renders them an important group that should be studied separately from those with just a bachelor's degree.

In parallel with its expansion, postsecondary education has undergone differentiation in institutional characteristics and college experience (Gerber and Cheung 2008). Differentiation matters for the intergenerational reproduction of inequality if the *type* of college education received depends on socioeconomic origins and in turn shapes the economic outcomes of college graduates, a phenomenon called "horizontal stratification."

College differentiation involves diverse domains, but the literature has highlighted two: institutional selectivity and field of study. Studies show an association between advantaged social origins and college selectivity (Davies and Guppy 1997, Karen 2002), an association that appears to have increased over time (Astin and Oseguera 2004). Evidence about field of study is limited and less conclusive. Although the association between social origins and a lucrative major appears to be weak (Davies and Guppy 1997), an indirect influence is likely to exist. Upper-class students are more likely to major in the arts and sciences, which in turn increases their chances of pursuing an advanced degree (Goyette and Mullen 2006).

The association between social origins and college differentiation shapes inequality to the extent that college locations accessed by the upper class yield higher economic returns. Evidence consistently suggests that graduates of more selective institutions earn more (Brewer and Ehrenberg 1996; Thomas and Zhang 2005), although the "selective college" effect may be at least partially driven by academic performance and ability of recruits (Loury and Garman 1995; Monks 2000; Dale and Krueger 2002). As for field of study, research shows substantial variation in returns across fields, with business-related, math, engineering, and health majors receiving higher earnings, and education-related fields receiving lower returns (Berger 1988; Grogger and Eide 1995; Carnevale et al. 2011).

To date, virtually no study has examined differentiation at the advanced-degree level, but there is a sharp earning gradient across programs—with professional degrees such as medicine and law at the top, followed by doctoral degrees, and master's degrees a distant third (Day and Newburger 2002; College Board 2005). This pattern suggests that differential access by social origins to a particular type of advanced degree program may provide an avenue for the intergenerational reproduction of advantage.

The findings about the "meritocratic power" of a college degree discussed at the outset of this chapter referred specifically to intergenerational class mobility. Recent developments in mobility research show that measures such as class, occupational status, earnings, and family income capture different dimensions of economic well-being and suggest that mobility findings may be contingent on the measure used. Given these findings, this study examines various measures of socioeconomic advantage. I pay particular attention to family income. Measures such as social class, occupational status, and earnings are based on labor market participation, but total family income includes extra-occupational components, such as financial assets and public and private transfers. These resources are central at either extreme of the economic distribution, among the "underclass" poorly attached to the labor market (Grusky and Weeden 2008) and among the "overclass," whose income largely depends on returns to capital. By using family income, I am able to assess the economic well-being of those not in the labor force and include occupational and extra-occupational sources of well-being. Furthermore, this measure accounts for family-level dynamics, such as spousal selection (assortative mating), shown to play a crucial role in the transmission of advantage across generations (Chadwick and Solon 2002; Ermisch, Francesconi, and Siedler 2006).

Results: Is a College Degree Still the Great Equalizer?

Figure 34.2 presents the main findings of this analysis. It displays the level of intergenerational income mobility for men with different levels of schooling—less than high school, high school graduate, some college, college graduate, and advanced degree.[1] The measure of mobility used is the intergenerational income elasticity, which captures the association between parents' income and adult children's income. Elasticity measures range from zero to one.

An elasticity of zero represents "perfect mobility," in which the incomes of parents and children are completely unrelated. An elasticity of one represents "perfect immobility," in which the income advantage of parents is mirrored in their children's generation. An elasticity of 0.4, for example, means that a 10 percent difference in two families' incomes is associated with a 4 percent difference in their sons' incomes.

A striking U-shaped pattern of association across levels of schooling emerges from the analysis. The intergenerational elasticity is substantial for those with less than a college degree, but it declines to a value not significantly different from zero for those who graduated from college. As in the past, a college degree erases the impact of socioeconomic origins on economic success. However, the influence of social

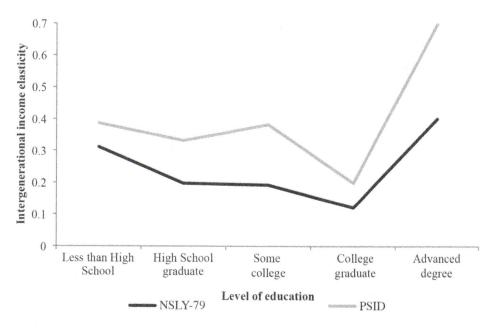

FIGURE 34.2 Intergenerational Family Income Elasticity among Men Born 1957–1961 (NLSY) and 1951–1966 (PSID)

Source: National Longitudinal Survey of Youth 1979 and Panel Study of Income Dynamics.

origins reemerges for those with a graduate degree. For graduate degree holders, a 100 percent increase in parents' income results in a more than 40 percent increase in their own incomes, an even larger magnitude than for those with less than a high school diploma. The U-shaped pattern is not idiosyncratic to family income, but rather emerges—although more weakly—for other indicators of socioeconomic advantage, including class, occupational status, and earnings (Torche 2011).

The sharply different levels of intergenerational mobility of BA holders vis-à-vis advanced degree holders begs the question about mechanisms. Two competing hypotheses account for these findings: dynamic selectivity and labor market meritocracy. The *dynamic selectivity* hypothesis posits that as students advance in their educational careers, the association between social origins and unobserved determinants of socioeconomic attainment, such as cognitive ability or motivation, declines (Mare 1980). In other words, given the substantial economic and cultural barriers that lower-class students face in obtaining a college degree, those who "make it" to college are positively selected on unobserved attributes—they are "the best and the brightest." To the extent that these attributes are rewarded in the labor market, lower-class college graduates will be economically successful regardless of

their humble origins. This hypothesis claims that such selectivity accounts for the high level of mobility among BA holders.

In contrast, the *labor market meritocracy* hypothesis suggests that college graduates tend to work in sectors and firms where meritocratic selection is more prevalent and origin characteristics count for less, insofar as higher qualifications are a powerful signal for employers, leaving little leeway for social network effects (Breen and Jonsson 2007: 1778). Highly bureaucratized contexts in which college graduates are likely to be employed operate as "great levelers" (Baron et al. 2007) because their formal practices reduce subjectivity in personnel decisions, ensuring that opportunity and rewards reflect role-specific qualifications and performance (Tomaskovic-Devey 1993; Bielby 2000; Reskin 2000; Elvira and Graham 2002).

The evidence emerging from this analysis is not consistent with the selectivity hypothesis. First, the role of selectivity in accounting for intergenerational mobility at a particular educational level should decrease as that level expands and the relative number of credential holders grows. In the extreme, when an educational level becomes universal, selectivity is by definition null (Raftery and Hout 1993). However, as I have shown, mobility among BA holders did not decrease as this level expanded over the last quarter century, questioning a negative effect of declining selectivity.

Second, the intergenerational association is stronger among advanced degree holders than among BA holders. But several factors suggest that, if unobserved selectivity accounted for mobility, mobility should be higher, not lower, among advanced degree holders. Research shows that the association between social origins and enrollment in a graduate program conditional on college graduation is weaker than at earlier educational levels (Mare 1980) and virtually null for at least some programs, such as master's degrees and MBAs (Stolzenberg 1994; Mullen, Goyette, and Soares 2003). As a result, lower-class individuals who remain in the educational system after completing a BA may be exceptionally selected on attributes such as motivation and ability. In addition, attending graduate school involves spending additional time in the educational system, undergoing not only formal training but also professional socialization, as well as building social connections. This extended exposure may contribute to the development of networks of professional referral among lower-background students, providing expanded opportunities to detach themselves from their disadvantaged origins. Furthermore, advanced degrees typically provide more specific and technically sophisticated skills than those acquired through a BA, which could rule out the use of cultural capital based on social origins or social networks as determinants of occupational placement and rewards (Jackson 2007).

If selectivity does not explain the findings, does labor market meritocracy do so? To test this hypothesis, I focus on three processes potentially leading to differences in opportunity based on social origins: *horizontal differentiation* in postsecondary education, *allocative inequality*, and *within-occupation differences in economic rewards* (Treiman and Hartmann 1981; England 1992; Petersen and Morgan 1995; Padavic and Reskin 2002). As discussed, horizontal differentiation matters for mobility if individuals with lower-class origins attain a degree in low-prestige institutions and less lucrative fields of study. *Allocative inequality* refers to differences in occupational placement after completing education, so that lower-class individuals are concentrated in relatively low-paying occupations. *Within-occupation rewards inequality* emerges when individuals with disadvantaged origins receive lower economic returns than their advantaged peers even if they are employed in the same occupation. A meritocratic labor market would mean, then, that college graduates of lower-class origins have the same chances as their upper-class peers to access prestigious universities and

lucrative fields of study and to engage in profitable occupations, and that they receive similar earnings conditional on their occupations.

I evaluate the meritocracy hypothesis by examining the type of college education attained and the type of occupation held by male college graduates from different social origins. To measure social origins, I divide parental income into three groups—the poorest third, the middle third, and the wealthiest third—and evaluate the educational and occupational outcomes of BA holders coming from each third. The results are presented in the top left graph of Figure 34.3. Analysis of institutional selectivity of the college attended shows that BA holders with origins in the wealthiest income third are more likely to attend selective institutions: 30 percent versus 12 percent of those in the bottom income third. However, the differences in field of study across social origins are relatively minor. Upper-class BA holders are somewhat more likely to major in the social sciences and less likely to major in education, but these differences do not extend to other majors.

The bottom left graph in the figure examines whether BA holders from different social origins display unequal occupational outcomes. I distinguish five occupational groups: managers; professionals in computer sciences, engineering, and math (CSEM); other professionals; workers in sales and administration; and craft workers and operatives. Although a more finely grained occupational classification would be preferable, the limited sample sizes constrain further disaggregation.

Allocation into occupational groups is remarkably even across social origins. The main source of difference is that college graduates coming from the lower income third are less likely to hold managerial jobs: 36 percent versus 44 percent of their wealthier counterparts. This is compensated for by a higher proportion of lower-background individuals in craft/operatives occupations. These differences are small, and they pale when compared, for example, with occupational gaps across gender. The same is the case with within-occupation earnings: the gradient across social origins is discernible but not prominent (Torche 2011).

The right-hand graphs in Figure 34.3 repeat this exercise for advanced degree holders. As with BA holders, advanced degree holders with origins in the top income third are more likely to have attended selective institutions: 47 percent versus 31 percent among lower-class graduates. But differences in social origins are not restricted to institutional selectivity. Rather, they extend to field of study and type of program.

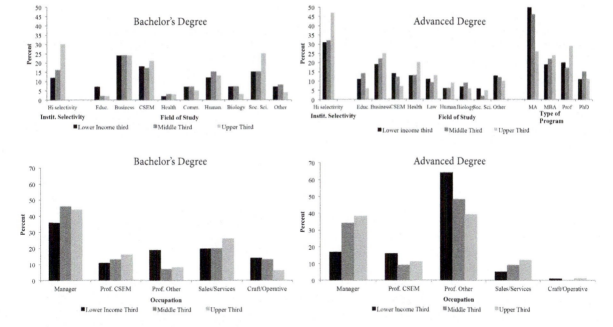

FIGURE 34.3 Institutional Selectivity, Field of Study, Type of Program, and Occupation among Male Bachelor's Degree Holders and Advanced Degree Holders

Source: Baccalaureate and Beyond 1993–2003 and National Longitudinal Survey of Youth 1979.

Advanced degree holders with origins in the top income third are also more likely to earn degrees in professional fields such as business, health, and law. They are also much more likely to obtain lucrative first-professional degrees (about 90 percent of which are in medicine, dentistry, and law) and MBAs, rather than MAs. The differences based on social origins are magnified in the labor market. The bottom right-hand graph shows that whereas about 38 percent of upper-class advanced degree holders attain a lucrative managerial occupation, only 17 percent of their lower-class peers do so. Lower-class graduates are much more likely to engage in a professional occupation that is not in the CSEM field. These occupational and educational differences are compounded by within-occupation earnings gaps. On average, a professional with an advanced degree and origins in the lower income third receives earnings that are only about 60 percent of those of his upper-class counterparts—a gap substantially higher than among BA holders. This pattern is not restricted to men; rather, it is even more pronounced among women (Torche 2011).

Conclusions

The findings from this analysis are clear. The intergenerational socioeconomic association is substantial

among those without a college degree, but it virtually disappears among those with only a bachelor's degree. Intergenerational mobility among BA holders supports the hypothesis that labor markets for college graduates operate on the basis of meritocratic criteria.

However, a second finding from this study questions this interpretation: a strong intergenerational association reemerges among advanced degree holders, reaching levels comparable to those with low levels of schooling. This is an unexpected result. Given that the human capital attained by advanced degree holders is more technically specialized than that of college graduates, that it requires spending more time in educational institutions undergoing socialization that may erase the direct influence of social origins, and that it is probably associated with positive unobserved selectivity, one might expect weaker rather than stronger intergenerational association vis-à-vis BA holders. To explain both intergenerational mobility of BA holders and intergenerational persistence of advanced degree holders, I examine *horizontal differentiation* in postsecondary education, and *occupational inequality* for these groups. I found that these factors account for both the substantial intergenerational mobility among BA holders and strong intergenerational reproduction among advanced degree holders. Among men who attain an advanced degree, their social origins are strongly correlated with the type of graduate education they obtain, in terms of institutional selectivity, field of study, and type of program attended. Social origin is also strongly correlated with the type of job attained and the economic rewards received.

The evidence is not consistent with unobserved selectivity as the cause of high mobility among college graduates. There is, however, an alternative way in which unobserved selectivity may affect observed mobility. As graduate education expands, the undergraduate level may serve an increasingly important sorting function into graduate school, differentially allocating individuals according to social background and unobserved characteristics. As highlighted by Goyette and Mullen (2006), upper-background students may opt to maximize their chances of attending graduate school by choosing specific fields and, probably, specific postsecondary institutions and trajectories. In contrast, lower-background individuals may favor locations in the system that would maximize the returns of a bachelor's degree, reducing the risk of downward mobility (Breen and Goldthorpe 1997).

It is plausible, then, that upper-background students who fail to advance to graduate school have miscalculated, choosing suboptimal college fields, institutions, or trajectories. This miscalculation may result in downward mobility among advantaged students, whereas the optimal investment of lower-background individuals in a BA but no subsequent degrees would account for upward mobility. The overall result of this process would be a weak intergenerational association among those with a bachelor's degree only, but reduced mobility among advanced degree holders. More analysis of colleges as "sorting machines" could shed further light on this process. The findings from this analysis strongly question the unqualified interpretation of increasing meritocracy among higher levels of education and indicate that mobility opportunity is embedded in educational and labor market processes, including, but not reduced to, horizontal educational stratification and the patterning of occupational allocation and economic rewards by social origins.

NOTES

1. The analysis presented here is restricted to men. The reader is referred to Torche (2011) for a complete analysis by gender, using all measures of socioeconomic well-being.

REFERENCES

Astin, Alexander, and Leticia Oseguera. 2004. "The Declining 'Equity' of American Higher Education." *Review of Higher Education* 27: 321–341.

Attewell, Paul, and David Lavin. 2007. *Passing the Torch.* New York: Sage.

Autor, David, Lawrence Katz, and Melissa Kearney. 2008. "Trends in U.S. Wage Inequality: Revising the Revisionists." *Review of Economics and Statistics* 90 (2): 300–323.

Baron, James, Michael Hannan, Greta Hsu, and Özgecan Koçak. 2007. "In the Company of Women: Gender Inequality and the Logic of Bureaucracy in Start-Up Firms." *Work and Occupations* 34: 35–66.

Belley, Philippe, and Lance Lochner. 2007. "The Changing Role of Family Income and Ability in Determining Educational Achievement." *Journal of Human Capital* 1: 37–89.

Berger, Mark. 1988. "Predicted Future Earnings and Choice of College Major." *Industrial and Labor Relations Review* 41: 418–429.

Bielby, William. 2000. "Minimizing Workplace Gender and Racial Bias." *Contemporary Sociology* 29: 120–129.

Breen, Richard, and John Goldthorpe. 1997. "Explaining Educational Differentials: Towards a Formal Rational Action Theory." *Rationality and Society* 9: 275–305.

Breen, Richard, and Jan Jonsson. 2007. "Explaining Change in Social Fluidity: Educational Equalization and Educational Expansion in Twentieth-Century Sweden." *American Journal of Sociology* 112 (6): 1775–1810.

Breen, Richard, and Ruud Luijkx. 2007. "Social Mobility and Education: A Comparative Analysis of Period and Cohort Trends in Britain and Germany." In *From Origin to Destination*, edited by Stefani Scherer, Reinhard Pollak, Gunnar Otte, and Markus Gangl, 102–124. New York: Campus.

Brewer, Dominic, and Ronald Ehrenberg. 1996. "Does It Pay to Attend an Elite Private College? Evidence from the Senior High School Class of 1980." *Research in Labor Economics* 15: 239–271.

Carnevale, Anthony, Stephen Rose, and Ban Cheah. 2011. "The College Payoff: Education, Occupations, and Lifetime Earnings." Working paper, The Georgetown University Center on Education and the Workforce.

Chadwick, Laura, and Gary Solon. 2002. "Intergenerational Income Mobility among Daughters." *American Economic Review* 92 (1): 335–344.

College Board. 2005. Education Pays Update. Trends in Higher Education Series. Washington, DC: College Board.

Dale, Stacy, and Alan Krueger. 2002. "Estimating the Payoff to Attending a More Selective College: An Application of Selection on Observables and Unobservables." *Quarterly Journal of Economics* 117: 1491–1527.

Davies, Scott, and Neil Guppy. 1997. "Fields of Study, College Selectivity and Student Inequalities in Higher Education." *Social Forces* 75 (4): 1417–1438.

Day, Jennifer C., and Eric Newburger. 2002. "The Big Payoff: Educational Attainment and Synthetic Estimates of Work-Life Earnings." Current Population Reports (P23-210): 1–13.

Ellwood, David, and Thomas Kane. 2000. "Who Is Getting a College Education? Family Background and the Growing Gaps in Enrollment." In *Securing the Future*, edited by Sheldon Danziger and Jane Waldfogel, 283–324. New York: Russell Sage Foundation.

Elvira, Marta, and Mary Graham. 2002. "Not Just a Formality: Pay System Formalization and Sex-Related Earnings Effects." *Organization Science* 13 (6): 601–618.

England, Paula. 1992. *Comparable Worth: Theories and Evidence*. New York: Walter de Gruyter.

Ermisch, John, Marco Francesconi, and Thomas Siedler. 2006. "Intergenerational Mobility and Marital Sorting." *Economic Journal* 116: 659–679.

Gerber, Theodore, and Sin Yi Cheung. 2008. "Horizontal Stratification in Postsecondary Education: Forms, Explanations, and Implications." *Annual Review of Sociology* 34: 299–318.

Goyette, Kimberly, and Ann Mullen. 2006. "Who Studies the Arts and Sciences? Social Background and the Choice and Consequences of Undergraduate Field of Study." *Journal of Higher Education* 77 (3): 488–538.

Grogger, Jeff, and Eric Eide. 1995. "Changes in College Skills and the Rise in the College Wage Premium." *Journal of Human Resources* 30: 280–310.

Grusky, David, and Kim Weeden. 2008. "Are There Social Classes? A Framework for Testing Sociology's Favorite Concept." In *Social Class: How Does It Work?*, edited by Annette Lareau and Dalton Conley, ch. 2. New York: Russell Sage.

Haveman, Robert, and Timothy Smeeding. 2006. "The Role of Higher Education in Social Mobility." *Future of Children* 16 (2): 125–150.

Hout, Michael. 1984. "Status, Autonomy, and Training in Occupational Mobility." *American Journal of Sociology* 89 (6): 1397–1409.

———. 1988. "More Universalism, Less Structural Mobility: The American Occupational Structure in the 1980s." *American Sociological Review* 93 (6): 1358–1400.

Jackson, Michelle. 2007. "How Far Merit Selection? Social Stratification and the Labour Market." *British Journal of Sociology* 58 (3): 367–390.

Kane, Thomas. 2004. "College-Going and Inequality." In *Social Inequality*, edited by Kathryn M. Neckerman, ch. 8. New York: Russell Sage.

Karen, David. 2002. "Changes in Access to Higher Education in the United States: 1980–1992." *Sociology of Education* 75: 191–210.

Loury, Linda, and David Garman. 1995. "College Selectivity and Earnings." *Journal of Labor Economics* 13 (2): 289–308.

Mare, Robert. 1980. "Social Background and School Continuation Decisions." *Journal of the American Statistical Association* 75: 295–305.

Monks, James. 2000. "The Returns to Individual and College Characteristics: Evidence from the National Longitudinal Survey of Youth." *Economics of Education Review* 19: 279–289.

Mullen, Ann, Kimberly Goyette, and Joseph Soares. 2003. "Who Goes to Graduate School? Social and Academic Correlates of Educational Continuation after College." *Sociology of Education* 76 (2): 143–169.

Padavic, Irene, and Barbara Reskin. 2002. *Women and Men at Work*. Thousand Oaks, CA: Pine Forge Press.

Pallas, Aaron. 2000. "The Effects of Schooling on Individual Lives." In *Handbook of the Sociology of Education*, edited by Maureen Hallinan, 499–525. New York: Kluwer Academic.

Petersen, Trond, and Laurie Morgan. 1995. "Separate and Unequal: Occupation-Establishment Sex Segregation and the Gender Wage Gap." *American Journal of Sociology* 101 (2): 329–365.

Raftery, Adrian, and Michael Hout. 1993. "Maximally Maintained Inequality: Expansion, Reform and Opportunity in Irish Education, 1921–1975." *Sociology of Education* 66 (1): 41–62.

Reskin, Barbara. 2000. "The Proximate Causes of Employment Discrimination." *Contemporary Sociology* 29 (2): 319–328.

Ross, Catherine, and John Mirowsky. 1999. "Refining the Association between Education and Health: The Effects of Quantity, Credential, and Selectivity." *Demography* 36: 445–460.

Rowley, Larry, and Sylvia Hurtado. 2003. "Non-Monetary Benefits of Undergraduate Education." In *The Public Research University: Serving the Public Good in New Times*, edited by Darrell Lewis and James Hearn. Lanham, MD: University Press of America.

Stevens, Mitchell, Elizabeth Armstrong, and Richard Arum. 2008. "Sieve, Incubator, Temple, Hub: Empirical and Theoretical Advances in the Sociology of Higher Education." *Annual Review of Sociology* 34: 127–151.

Stolzenberg, Ross. 1994. "Educational Continuation by College Graduates." *American Journal of Sociology* 99 (4): 1042–1077.

Thomas, Scott, and Liang Zhang. 2005. "Post-baccalaureate Wage Growth within Four Years of Graduation: The Effects of College Quality and College Major." *Research in Higher Education* 46: 437–459.

Tomaskovic-Devey, Donald. 1993. *Gender and Racial Inequality at Work: The Sources and Consequences of Job Segregation*. Ithaca, NY: ILR Press.

Torche, Florencia. 2011. "Is a College Degree Still the Great Equalizer? Intergenerational Mobility across Levels of Schooling in the United States." *American Journal of Sociology* 117: 763–807.

Treiman, Donald, and Heidi Hartmann. 1981. *Women, Work, and Wages: Equal Pay for Jobs of Equal Value.* Washington, DC: National Academy Press.

Vallet, Louis-Andre. 2004. "Change in Intergenerational Class Mobility in France from the 1970s to the 1990s and Its Explanation: An Analysis Following the CASMIN Approach." In *Social Mobility in Europe,* edited by Richard Breen, 115–147. Oxford: Oxford University Press.

35. Laura Hamilton and Elizabeth A. Armstrong*
Paying for the Party

Monica grew up in a small, struggling Midwestern community, population 3,000, that was once a booming factory town.

She was from a working-class family and paid for most of her education at Midwest U, a "moderately selective" residential university, herself. She worked two jobs, sometimes over forty hours a week, to afford in-state tuition. Going out-of-state, or to a pricey private school, was simply out of the question without a large scholarship. Attending MU was even a stretch; one year there cost as much as four years at the regional campus near her hometown.

Karen grew up in the same small town as Monica, but in a solidly middle-class family. Her college-educated parents could afford to provide more financial assistance. But even though MU was only three hours away, her father "wasn't too thrilled" about her going so far from home. He had attended a small religious school that was only ten minutes away.

Neither Karen nor Monica was academically well-prepared for college. Both had good, but not stellar, grades and passable SAT scores, which made admission to a more selective school unlikely. Given the lower cost, ease of admission, and opportunity to commute from home, they might have started at the regional campus. However, MU offered, as Monica's

*Adapted from Hamilton, Laura and Elizabeth A. Armstrong (2012). "The (Mis)Education of Monica and Karen." *Contexts* Vol. 11 (4) pp. 22-27. Copyright © 2012 by American Sociological Association. Reprinted by permission of SAGE Publications, Inc.

mother put it, a chance to "go away and experience college life." Karen refused to look at any other school because she wanted to leave home. As she noted, "I really don't think I'm a small town girl." Monica's family was betting on MU as the best place for her to launch her dream career as a doctor.

Karen and Monica's stories offer us a glimpse into the college experiences of average, in-state students at large, mid-tier public universities. Though they struggled to gain entrance to the flagship campus, they soon found that the structure of social and academic life there served them poorly — and had deleterious effects.

The Great Mismatch

Most four-year residential colleges and universities in the United States are designed to serve well-funded students, who have minimal (if any) caretaking responsibilities, and who attend college full-time after they graduate from high school.

Yet only a minority of individuals who pursue postsecondary education in the United States fit this profile. There is a great gap between what the vast majority of Americans need and what four-year institutions offer them.

This mismatch is acutely visible at Midwest U, where Karen and Monica started their college careers. Almost half of those attending four-year colleges find themselves at schools like this one. Students from modest backgrounds who have above average, but not exceptional, academic profiles attend state flagship universities because they believe such schools offer a surefire route to economic security.

Public universities were founded to enable mobility, especially among in-state populations of students—which contributes to their legitimacy in the eyes of the public. In an era of declining state funding, schools like Midwest U have raised tuition and recruited more out-of-state students. They especially covet academically accomplished, ambitious children of affluent families.

As sociologist Mitchell Stevens describes in *Creating a Class,* elite institutions also pursue such students. While observing a small, private school, Stevens overheard an admissions officer describe an ideal applicant: "He's got great SATs [and] he's free [not requiring any financial aid].... He helps us in every way that's quantifiable." Once private colleges skim off affluent, high-performing students, large, middle-tier, public universities are left to compete for the tuition dollars of less studious students from wealthy families.

How, we wondered, do in-state students fare in this context? To find out, for over five years we followed a dormitory floor of female students through their college careers and into the workforce, conducted an ethnography of the floor, and interviewed the women and their parents. What we found is that schools like MU only serve a segment of their student body well—affluent, socially-oriented, state students—to the detriment of typical in-state students like Karen and Monica.

"I'm Supposed to Get Drunk"

Monica and Karen approached the housing application process with little information, and were unprepared for what they encountered when they were assigned to a room in a "party dorm." At MU, over a third of the freshman class is housed in such dorms. Though minimal partying actually took place in the heavily policed residence halls, many residents partied off-site, typically at fraternities, returning in the wee hours drunk and loud. Affluent students — both in and out-of-state — often requested rooms in party dorms, based on the recommendations of their similarly social siblings and friends.

Party dorms are a pipeline to the Greek system, which dominates campus life. Less than 20 percent of the student body at MU is involved in a fraternity or sorority, but these predominately white organizations enjoy a great deal of power. They own space in central campus areas, across from academic buildings and sports arenas. They monopolize the social life of first-year students, offering underage drinkers massive, free supplies of alcohol, with virtual legal impunity. They even enjoy special ties to administrators, with officers sitting on a special advisory board to the dean of students.

Over 40 percent of Monica and Karen's floor joined sororities their first year. The pressure to rush was so intense that one roommate pair who opted out posted a disclaimer on their door, asking people to stop bugging them about it. The entire campus — including academic functions — often revolved around the schedule of Greek life. When a math test for a large, required class conflicted with women's rush, rather than excusing a group of women from a few rush events, the test itself was rescheduled.

Monica, like most economically disadvantaged students, chose not to rush a sorority, discouraged by the mandatory $60 t-shirt, as well as by the costly membership fees. Karen, who was middle class, had just enough funds to make rushing possible. However, she came to realize that Greek houses implicitly screen for social class. She pulled out her boots — practical rain boots that pegged her as a small town, in-state girl instead of an affluent, out-of-state student with money and the right taste in clothing. They were a "dead give-away," she said. She soon dropped out of rush.

Like all but a few students on the fifty-three-person floor, Monica and Karen chose to participate in the party scene. Neither drank much in high school. Nor did they arrive armed with shot glasses or party-themed posters, as some students did. They partied because, as a woman from a similar background put it, "I'm supposed to get drunk every weekend. I'm supposed to go to parties every weekend." With little party experience, and few contacts in the Greek system, Monica and Karen were easy targets for fraternity men's sexual disrespect. Heavy alcohol consumption helped to put them at ease in otherwise uncomfortable situations. "I pretty much became an alcoholic," said Monica. "I was craving alcohol all the time."

Their forced attempts to participate in the party scene showed how poorly it suited their needs. "I tried so hard to fit in with what everybody else was doing here," Monica explained. "I think one morning I just woke up and realized that this isn't me at all; I don't like the way I am right now." She felt it forced her to become more immature. "Growing up to me isn't going out and getting smashed and sleeping around," she lamented. Partying is particularly costly for students of lesser means, who need to grow up sooner, cannot afford to be financially irresponsible, and need the credentials and skills that college offers.

Academic Struggles and "Exotic" Majors

Partying also takes its toll on academic performance, and Monica's poor grades quickly squelched her pre-med dreams. Karen, who hoped to become a teacher, also found it hard to keep up. "I did really bad in that math class, the first elementary ed math class," one of three that were required. Rather than retake the class, Karen changed her major to one that was popular among affluent, socially-oriented students on the floor: sports broadcasting.

She explained, "I'm from a really small town, and it's just all I ever really knew was jobs that were around me, and most of those are teachers." A woman on her floor was majoring in sports broadcasting, which Karen had never considered. "I would have never thought about that. And so I saw hers, and I was like, that's something that I really like. One of my interests is sports, watching them, playing them," she reasoned. "I could be a sportscaster on ESPN if I really wanted to." . . .

Karen's experience shows the seductive appeal of certain "easy majors." These are occupational and professional programs that are often housed in their own schools and colleges. They are associated with a higher overall GPA, and as sociologists Richard Arum and Josipa Roksa report in *Academically Adrift*, lower levels of learning than majors in the more challenging sciences and humanities housed in colleges of arts and sciences.

In many easy majors, career success also depends on personal characteristics (such as appearance, personality, and aesthetic taste) that are developed outside of the classroom— often prior to entering college. Socially-oriented students flock to fields like communications, fashion, tourism, recreation, fitness, and numerous "business-lite" options, which are often linked to sports or the arts, rather than the competitive business school. About a third of the student body majored in business, management, marketing, communications, journalism, and related subfields.

Karen's switch to sports broadcasting gave her more time to socialize. But education is a more practical major that translates directly into a career; hiring rests largely on the credential. In contrast, success in sports broadcasting is dependent on class-based characteristics — such as family social ties to industry insiders. Several of Karen's wealthier peers secured plum internships in big cities because their parents made phone calls for them; Karen could not even land an unpaid internship with the Triple-A baseball team located twenty-five minutes from her house.

No one Karen encountered on campus helped her to assess the practicality of a career in this field. Her parents were frustrated that she had been persuaded not to graduate with a recognizable marketable skill. As her mother explained, "She gets down there and you start hearing all these exotic sounding majors…. I'm not sure quite what jobs they're going to end up with." Her mother was frustrated that

Karen "went to see the advisor to make plans for her sophomore year, and they're going, 'Well, what's your passion?'" Her mother was not impressed. "How many people do their passion? To me, that's more what you do for a hobby…. I mean most people, that's not what their job is."

Halfway through college, when Karen realized she could not get an internship, much less a job, in sports broadcasting, her parents told her to switch back to education. The switch was costly: it was going to take her two more years to complete. As her mother complained, "When you're going through the orientation…they're going, 'oh, most people change their major five times.' And they make it sound like it's no big deal. But yeah, they're making big bucks by kids changing."

Leaving Midwest U Behind

Monica left MU after her first year. "I was afraid if I continued down there that I would just go crazy and either not finish school, or get myself in trouble," she explained. "And I just didn't want to do that." She immediately enrolled in a beauty school near her home. Dissatisfied with the income she earned as a hairstylist, she later entered a community college to complete an associate degree in nursing. She paid for her nursing classes as she studied, but had $10,000 in student loan debt from her time at MU. Still, her debt burden was substantially smaller than if she had stayed there; some of her MU peers had amassed over $50,000 in loans by graduation. . . .

Because her GPA was too low to return to elementary education at MU, Karen transferred to a regional college during her fourth year. Since the classes she took for sports broadcasting did not fulfill any requirements, it took her six years to graduate. Karen's parents, who reported that they spent the first ten years of their married life paying off their own loans, took out loans to cover most of the cost, and anticipated spending even longer to finance their daughter's education.

Monica and Karen were not the only ones on their dormitory floor to leave MU. Nine other in-state women, the majority of whom were from working-class or lower-middle-class backgrounds, did as well. The only out-of-state student who transferred left for a higher-ranked institution. While we were concerned that the in-state leavers, most of whom were moving down the ladder of prestige to regional campuses, would suffer, they actually did better than in-state women from less privileged families who stayed at MU. Their GPAs improved, they selected majors with a more direct payoff, and they were happier overall.

The institutions to which women moved played a large role in this transformation. As one leaver described the regional campus to which she transferred, it "doesn't have any fraternities or sororities. It only has, like, ten buildings." But, she said, "I just really love it." One of the things she loved was that nobody cared about partying. "They're there just to graduate and get through." It prioritized the needs of a different type of student: "Kids who have lower social economic status, who work for their school."

Without the social pressures of MU, it was possible to, as Karen put it, "get away from going out all the time, and refocus on what my goal was for this part of my life." Few majors like sports broadcasting and fashion merchandising were available, reducing the possible ways to go astray academically. Those who attended regional or community colleges trained to become accountants, teachers, social workers, nurses, or other health professionals. At the conclusion of our study, they had better employment prospects than those from similar backgrounds who stayed at MU.

The Importance of Institutional Context

It is tempting to assume that academic success is determined, in large part, by what students bring with them—different ability levels, resources, and orientations to college life. But Monica and Karen's stories demonstrate that what students get out of college is also organizationally produced. Students who were far more academically gifted than Monica or Karen sometimes floundered at MU, while others who were considerably less motivated breezed through college. The best predictor of success was whether there was a good fit between a given student's resources and agendas, and the structure of the university.

Monica and Karen's struggles at MU can be attributed, in part, to the dominance of a "party pathway" at that institution. These organizational arrangements—a robust, university-supported Greek system, and an array of easy majors—are designed to attract and serve affluent, socially-oriented students. The party pathway is not a hard sell; the idea that college is about fun and partying is celebrated in popular culture and actively promoted by leisure and alcohol industries. The problem is that this pathway often appeals to students for whom it is ill-suited.

Regardless of what they might want, students from different class backgrounds require different things. What Monica and Karen needed was a "mobility pathway." When resources are limited, mistakes—whether a semester of grades lost to partying, or courses that do not count toward a credential—can be very costly. Monica and Karen needed every course to move them toward a degree that would translate directly into a job.

They also needed more financial aid than they received— grants, not loans—and much better advising. A skilled advisor who understood Karen's background and her abilities might have helped her realize that changing majors was a bad idea. But while most public universities provide such advising support for disadvantaged students, these programs are often small, and admit only the best and brightest of the disadvantaged—not run-of-the-mill students like Monica and Karen.

Monica, Karen, and others like them did not find a mobility pathway at MU. Since university resources are finite, catering to one population of students often comes at a cost to others, especially if their needs are at odds with one another. When a party pathway is the most accessible avenue through a university, it is easy to stumble upon, hard to avoid, and it crowds out other pathways. . . .

Collectively, the priorities of public universities and other higher education institutions that support "party pathways" should be challenged. Reducing the number of easy majors, pulling university support from the Greek system, and expanding academic advising for less privileged students would help. At federal and state levels, greater commitment to the funding of higher education is necessary. If public universities are forced to rely on tuition and donations for funding, they will continue to appeal to those who can pay full freight. Without these changes, the mismatch between what universities offer and what most postsecondary students need is likely to continue.

36. Jay MacLeod*

Ain't No Makin' It: Leveled Aspirations in a Low-Income Neighborhood

"Any child can grow up to be president." So maintains the dominant ideology in the United States. This perspective characterizes American society as an open one in which barriers to success are mainly personal rather than social. In this meritocratic view, education ensures equality of opportunity for all individuals, and economic inequalities result from differences in natural qualities and in one's motivation and will to work. Success is based on achievement rather than ascription. Individuals do not inherit their social status—they attain it on their own. Because schooling mitigates gender, class, and racial barriers to success, the ladder of social mobility is there for all to climb. A favorite Hollywood theme, the rags-to-riches story resonates in the psyche of the American people. We never tire of hearing about Andrew Carnegie, for his experience validates much that we hold dear about America, the land of opportunity. Horatio Alger's accounts of the spectacular mobility achieved by men of humble origins through their own unremitting efforts occupy a treasured place in our national folklore. The American Dream is held out as a genuine prospect for anyone with the drive to achieve it.

"I ain't goin' to college. Who wants to go to college? I'd just end up gettin' a shitty job anyway." So says Freddie Piniella,[1] an intelligent eleven-year-old boy from Clarendon Heights, a low-income housing development in a northeastern city. This statement, pronounced with certitude and feeling, completely contradicts our achievement ideology. Freddie is pessimistic about his prospects for social mobility and disputes schooling's capacity to "deliver the goods." Such a view offends our sensibilities and seems a rationalization. But Freddie has a point. What of Carnegie's grammar school class-

*Jay MacLeod. *Ain't No Makin' It: Leveled Aspirations in a Low-Income Neighborhood* (Boulder: Westview Press, 1987), pp. 1–2, 4–5, 8, 60–63, 69–75, 78–79, 81, 137–141, 162. Copyright © 1987. Reprinted by permission of Westview Press, an imprint of Perseus Books, LLC, a subsidiary of Hachette Book Group, Inc. The postscript to this selection is taken from *Ain't No Makin' It: Leveled Aspirations in a Low-Income Neighborhood* (Boulder: Westview Press, 1995), pp. 155, 169–170, 196, 240–241. Copyright © 1995. Reprinted by permission of Westview Press, an imprint of Perseus Books, LLC, a subsidiary of Hachette Book Group, Inc.

mates, the great bulk of whom no doubt were left behind to occupy positions in the class structure not much different from those held by their parents? What about the static, nearly permanent element in the working class, whose members consider the chances for mobility remote and thus despair of all hope? These people are shunned, hidden, forgotten—and for good reason—because just as the self-made man is a testament to certain American ideals, so the very existence of an "underclass" in American society is a living contradiction to those ideals.

Utter hopelessness is the most striking aspect of Freddie's outlook. Erik H. Erikson writes that hope is the basic ingredient of all vitality;[2] stripped of hope, there is little left to lose. How is it that in contemporary America a boy of eleven can feel bereft of a future worth embracing? This is not what the United States is supposed to be. The United States is the nation of hopes and dreams and opportunity. As Ronald Reagan remarked in his 1985 State of the Union Address, citing the accomplishments of a young Vietnamese immigrant, "Anything is possible in America if we have the faith, the will, and the heart."[3] But to Freddie Piniella and many other Clarendon Heights young people who grow up in households where their parents and older siblings are unemployed, undereducated, or imprisoned, Reagan's words ring hollow. For them the American Dream, far from being a genuine prospect, is not even a dream. It is a hallucination.

I first met Freddie Piniella in the summer of 1981, when as a student at a nearby university, I worked as a counselor in a youth enrichment program in Clarendon Heights. For ten weeks I lived a few blocks from the housing project and worked intensively with nine boys, aged eleven to thirteen. While engaging them in recreational and educational activities, I was surprised by the modesty of their aspirations. The world of middle-class work was entirely alien to them; they spoke about employment in construction, factories, the armed forces, or, predictably, professional athletics. In an ostensibly open society, they were a group of boys whose occupational aspirations did not even cut across class lines.

The male teenage world of Clarendon Heights is populated by two divergent peer groups. The first group, dubbed the Hallway Hangers because of the group's propensity for "hanging" in a particular hallway in the project [i.e., outside doorway #13], consists predominantly of white boys. Their characteristics and attitudes stand in marked contrast to the second group, which is composed almost exclusively of black youths who call themselves the Brothers. Surprisingly, the Brothers speak with relative optimism about their futures, while the Hallway Hangers are despondent about their prospects for social mobility.

Before describing the boys' orientation toward work [in more detail], I would like to make an analytical distinction between aspirations and expectations. Both involve assessments of one's desires, abilities, and the character of the opportunity structure. In articulating one's aspirations, an individual weighs his or her preferences more heavily; expectations are tempered by perceived capabilities and available opportunities. Aspirations are one's preferences relatively unsullied by anticipated constraints; expectations take these constraints squarely into account.[4]

The Hallway Hangers: Keeping a Lid on Hope

Conventional, middle-class orientations toward employment are inadequate to describe the Hallway Hangers' approach to work. The notion of a career, a set of jobs that are connected to one another in a logical progression, has little relevance to these boys. They are hesitant when asked about their aspirations and expectations. This hesitancy is not the result of indecision; rather it stems from the fact that these boys see little choice involved in getting a job. No matter how hard I pressed him, for instance, Jinks refused to articulate his aspirations: "I think you're kiddin' yourself to have any. We're just gonna take whatever we can get." Jinks is a perceptive boy, and his answer seems to be an accurate depiction of the situation. Beggars cannot be choosers, and these boys have nothing other than unskilled labor to offer on a credential-based job market.

It is difficult to gauge the aspirations of most of the Hallway Hangers. Perhaps at a younger age they had dreams for their futures. At ages sixteen, seventeen, and eighteen, however, their own job experiences as well as those of family members have contributed to a deeply entrenched cynicism about their futures. What is perceived as the cold, hard reality of the job market weighs very heavily on the Hallway Hangers; they believe their preferences will have almost no bearing on the work they actually will do. Their expectations are not merely tempered by perceptions of the opportunity structure; even their aspirations are crushed by their estimation of the job market. These generalizations may seem bold and rather extreme, but they do not lack ethnographic support.

The pessimism and uncertainty with which the Hallway Hangers view their futures emerge clearly when the boys are asked to speculate on what their lives will be like in twenty years.

(all in separate interviews)

STONEY: Hard to say. I could be dead tomorrow. Around here, you gotta take life day by day.

BOO-BOO: I dunno. I don't want to think about it. I'll think about it when it comes.

FRANKIE: I don't fucking know. Twenty years. I may be fucking dead. I live a day at a time. I'll probably be in the fucking pen.

SHORTY: Twenty years? I'm gonna be in jail.

These responses are striking not only for the insecurity and despondency they reveal, but also because they do not include any mention of work. It is not that work is unimportant—for people as strapped for money as the Hallway Hangers are, work is crucial. Rather, these boys are indifferent to the issue of future employment. Work is a given; they all hope to hold jobs of one kind or another in order to support themselves and their families. But the Hallway Hangers believe the character of work, at least all work in which they are likely to be involved, is essentially the same: boring, undifferentiated, and unrewarding. Thinking about their future jobs is a useless activity for the Hallway Hangers. What is there to think about?

For Steve and Jinks, although they do see themselves employed in twenty years, work is still of tangential importance.

JM: If you had to guess, what do you think you'll be doing twenty years from now?

(in separate interviews)

STEVE: I don't fucking know. Working probably. Have my own pad, my own house. Bitches, kids. Fucking fridge full of brewskies. Fine wife, likes to get laid.

JINKS: Twenty years from now? Probably kicked back in my own apartment doing the same shit I'm doing now—getting high. I'll have a job, if I'm not in the service, if war don't break out, if I'm not dead. I just take one day at a time.

Although the Hallway Hangers expect to spend a good portion of their waking hours on the job, work is important to them not as an end in itself, but solely as a means to an end—money.

In probing the occupational aspirations and expectations of the Hallway Hangers, I finally was able to elicit from them some specific hopes. Although Shorty never mentions his expectations, the rest of the Hallway Hangers have responded to my prodding with some definite answers. The range of answers as well as how they change over time are as significant as the particular hopes each boy expresses.

Boo-Boo's orientation toward work is typical of the Hallway Hangers. He has held a number of jobs in the past, most of them in the summer. During his freshman year in high school, Boo-Boo worked as a security guard at school for $2.50 an hour in order to make restitution for a stolen car he damaged. Boo-Boo also has worked on small-scale construction projects through a summer youth employment program called Just-A-Start, at a pipe manufacturing site, and as a clerk in a gift shop. Boo-Boo wants to be an automobile mechanic. Upon graduating from high school, he studied auto mechanics at a technical school on a scholarship. The only black student in his class, Boo-Boo was expelled early in his first term after racial antagonism erupted into a fight. Boo-Boo was not altogether disappointed, for he already was unhappy with what he considered the program's overly theoretical orientation. (Howard London found this kind of impatience typical of working-class students in the community college he studied.[5]) Boo-Boo wanted hands-on training, but "all's they were doing was telling me about how it's made, stuff like that." Boo-Boo currently is unemployed, but he recently had a chance for a job as a cook's helper. Although he was not hired, the event is significant nevertheless because prior to the job interview, Boo-Boo claimed that his ambition now was to work in a restaurant. Here we have an example of the primacy of the opportunity structure in determining the aspirations of the Hallway Hangers. One job opening in another field was so significant that the opening prompted Boo-Boo to redefine totally his aspirations.

In contrast to the rest of the Hallway Hangers who are already on the job market, Steve wants to stay in school for the two years required to get his diploma. Yet he has a similar attitude toward his future work as do the other youths. He quit his summer job with the Just-A-Start program and has no concrete occupational aspirations. As for expectations, he believes he might enlist in the Air Force after graduation but adds, "I dunno. I might just go up and see my uncle, do some fuckin' construction or something."

Many of these boys expect to enter military service. Jinks and Frankie mention it as an option; Stoney has tried to enlist, but without success. Although Jinks refuses to think in terms of aspirations, he will say what he expects to do after he finishes school.

JM: What are you gonna do when you get out?

JINKS: Go into the service, like everybody else. The Navy.

JM: What about after that?

JINKS: After that, just get a job, live around here.

JM: Do you have any idea what job you wanna get?

JINKS: No. No particular job. Whatever I can get.

Jinks subsequently quit school. He had been working twenty hours a week making clothes-racks in a factory with his brother. He left school with the understanding that he would be employed full-time, and he was mildly content with his situation: "I got a job. It ain't a good job, but other things will come along." Two weeks later, he was laid off. For the past three months he has been unemployed, hanging full-time in doorway #13.

Shorty has worked construction in the past and has held odd jobs such as shoveling snow. Shorty, an alcoholic, has trouble holding down a steady job, as he freely admits. He was enrolled in school until recently. Ordered by the court to a detoxification center, Shorty apparently managed to convince the judge that he had attended enough Alcoholics Anonymous meetings in the meantime to satisfy the court. He has not returned to school since, nor has he landed a job. Given that Shorty is often on the run from the police, he is too preoccupied with pressing everyday problems to give serious thought to his long-term future. It is not surprising that my ill-timed query about his occupational aspirations met with only an impatient glare.

The definitions of aspirations and expectations given [earlier] suggest that an assessment of the opportunity structure and of one's capabilities impinge on one's preferences for the future. However, the portrait of the Hallway Hangers painted in these pages makes clear that "impinge" is not a strong enough word. But are the leveled aspirations and pessimistic expectations of the Hallway Hangers a result of strong negative assessments of their capabilities or of the opportunity structure?

This is not an easy question to answer. Doubtless, both factors come into play, but in the case of the Hallway Hangers, evaluation of the opportunity structure has the dominant role. Although in a discussion of why they do not succeed in school, the Hallway Hangers point to personal inadequacy ("We're all just fucking burnouts"; "We never did good anyways"), they look to outside forces as well. In general, they are confident of their own abilities.

(*In a group interview*)

JM: If you've got five kids up the high school with all A's, now are you gonna be able to say that any of them are smarter than any of you?

SLICK: (*immediately*) No.

JM: So how'd that happen?

SLICK: Because they're smarter in some areas just like we're smarter in some areas. You put them out here, right? And you put us up where they're living—they won't be able to survive out here.

SHORTY: But we'd be able to survive up there.

FRANKIE: See, what it is—they're smarter more academically because they're taught by teachers that teach academics.

JM: Not even streetwise, just academically, do you think you could be up where they are?

FRANKIE: Yeah.

CHRIS: Yeah.

SHORTY: Yeah.

JM: When it comes down to it, you're just as smart?

FRANKIE: Yeah.

SLICK: (*matter-of-factly*) We could be smarter.

FRANKIE: Definitely.

CHRIS: On the street, like.

FRANKIE: We're smart, we're smart, but we're just smart [inaudible]. It's fucking, y'know, we're just out to make money, man. I know if I ever went to fucking high school and college in a business course. . . .

SLICK: And concentrated on studying. . . .

FRANKIE: I know I could make it. I am a businessman.

JM: So all of you are sure that if you put out in school. . . .

FRANKIE: Yeah! If I went into business, I would, yeah. If I had the fucking money to start out with like some of these fucking rich kids, I'd be a millionaire. Fucking right I would be.

Although these comments were influenced by the dynamics of the group interview, they jibe with the general sense of self-confidence the Hallway Hangers radiate and indicate that they do not have low perceptions of their own abilities.

If their assessments of their own abilities do not account for the low aspirations of the Hallway Hangers, we are left, by way of explanation, with their perceptions of the job opportunity structure. The dominant view in the United States is that American society is an open one that values and differentially rewards individuals on the basis of their merits. The Hallway Hangers question this view, for it runs against the grain of their neighbors' experiences, their families' experiences, and their own encounters with the labor market.

The Clarendon Heights community, as a public housing development, is by definition made up of individuals who do not hold even modestly remunerative jobs. A large majority are on additional forms of public assistance; many are unemployed. Like most old housing projects, Clarendon Heights tends to be a cloistered, insular neighborhood, isolated from the surrounding community. Although younger residents certainly have external points of reference, their horizons are nevertheless very narrow. Their immediate world is composed almost entirely of people who have not "made it." To look around at a great variety of people—some lazy, some alcoholics, some energetic, some dedicated, some clever, some resourceful—and to realize all of them have been unsuccessful on the job market is powerful testimony against what is billed as an open society.

The second and much more intimate contact these boys have with the job market is through their families, whose occupational histories only can be viewed as sad and disillusioning by the Hallway Hangers. These are not people who are slothful or slow-witted; rather, they are generally industrious, intelligent, and very willing to work. With members of their families holding low-paying, unstable jobs or unable to find work at all, the Hallway Hangers are unlikely to view the job opportunity structure as an open one.

The third level of experience on which the Hallway Hangers draw is their own. These boys are not newcomers to the job market. As we have seen, all have held a variety of jobs. All except Steve are now on the job market year-round, but only Stoney has a steady job. With the exceptions of Chris, who presently is satisfied with his success peddling drugs, and Steve, who is still in school, the Hallway Hangers are actively in search of decent work. Although they always seem to be following up on some promising lead, they are all unemployed. Furthermore, some who were counting on prospective employment have had their hopes dashed when it fell through. The work they have been able to secure typically has been in menial, dead-end jobs paying minimum wage.

Thus, their personal experience on the job market and the experiences of their family members and their neighbors have taught the Hallway Hangers that the job market does not necessarily reward talent or effort. Neither they nor their parents, older siblings, and friends have shared in the "spoils" of economic success. In short, the Hallway Hangers are under no illusions about the openness of the job opportunity structure. They are conscious, albeit vaguely, of a number of class-based obstacles to economic and social advancement. Slick, the most perceptive and articulate of the Hallway Hangers, points out particular barriers they must face.

SLICK: Out here, there's not the opportunity to make money. That's how you get into stealin' and all that shit.

(*in a separate interview*)

SLICK: That's why I went into the army—cuz there's no jobs out here right now for people that, y'know, live out here. You have to know somebody, right?

In discussing the problems of getting a job, both Slick and Shorty are vocal.

SLICK: All right, to get a job, first of all, this is a handicap, out here. If you say you're from the projects or anywhere in this area, that can hurt you. Right off the bat: reputation.

SHORTY: Is this dude gonna rip me off, is he. . . .

SLICK: Is he gonna stab me?

SHORTY: Will he rip me off? Is he gonna set up the place to do a score or somethin'? I tried to get a couple of my buddies jobs at a place where I was working construction, but the guy says, "I don't want 'em if they're from there. I know you; you ain't a thief or nothing."

Frankie also points out the reservations prospective employers have about hiring people who live in Clarendon Heights. "A rich kid would have a better chance of getting a job than me, yeah. Me, from where I live, y'know, a high crime area, I was prob'ly crime-breaking myself, which they think your nice honest rich kid from a very respected family would never do."

Frankie also feels that he is discriminated against because of the reputation that attaches to him because of his brothers' illegal exploits. "Especially me, like I've had a few opportunities for a job, y'know. I didn't get it cuz of my name, because of my brothers, y'know. So I was deprived right there, bang. Y'know they said, 'No, no, no, we ain't havin' no Dougherty work for us.'" In a separate discussion, Frankie again

makes this point. Arguing that he would have almost no chance to be hired as a fireman, despite ostensibly meritocratic hiring procedures, even if he scored very highly on the test, Frankie concludes, "Just cuz fuckin' where I'm from and what my name is."

The Hallway Hangers' belief that the opportunity structure is not open also emerges when we consider their responses to the question of whether they have the same chance as a middle- or upper-class boy to get a good job. The Hallway Hangers generally respond in the negative. When pushed to explain why, Jinks and Steve made these responses, which are typical.

(*in separate interviews*)

JINKS: Their parents got pull and shit.

STEVE: Their fucking parents know people.

Considering the boys' employment experiences and those of their families, it is not surprising that the Hallway Hangers' view of the job market does not conform to the dominant belief in the openness of the opportunity structure. They see a job market where rewards are based not on meritocratic criteria, but on "who you know." If "connections" are the keys to success, the Hallway Hangers know that they are in trouble.

Aside from their assessment of the job opportunity structure, the Hallway Hangers are aware of other forces weighing on their futures. A general feeling of despondency pervades the group. As Slick puts it, "The younger kids have nothing to hope for." The Hallway Hangers often draw attention to specific incidents that support their general and vague feelings of hopelessness and of the futility of nurturing aspirations or high expectations. Tales of police brutality, of uncaring probation officers and callous judges, and of the "pull and hook-ups of the rich kids" all have a common theme, which Chris summarizes, "We don't get a fair shake and shit." Although they sometimes internalize the blame for their plight (Boo-Boo: "I just screwed up"; Chris: "I guess I just don't have what it takes"; Frankie: "We've just fucked up"), the Hallway Hangers also see, albeit in a vague and imprecise manner, a number of hurdles in their path to success with which others from higher social strata do not have to contend.

Insofar as contemporary conditions under capitalism can be conceptualized as a race by the many for relatively few positions of wealth and prestige, the low aspirations of the Hallway Hangers, more than anything else, seem to be a decision, conscious or unconscious, to withdraw from the running. The competition, they reason, is not a fair one when some people have an unobstructed lane. As Frankie maintains, the Hallway Hangers face numerous barriers: "It's a steeplechase, man. It's a motherfucking steeplechase." The Hallway Hangers respond in a way that suggests only a "sucker" would compete seriously under such conditions.

Chris's perspective seems a poignant, accurate description of the situation in which the Hallway Hangers find themselves.

CHRIS: I gotta get a job, any fucking job. Just a job. Make some decent money. If I could make a hundred bucks a week, I'd work. I just wanna get my mother out of the projects, that's all. But I'm fucking up in school. It ain't easy, Jay. I hang out there [in doorway #13] 'til about one o'clock every night. I never want to go to school. I'd much rather hang out and get high again. It's not that I'm dumb. You gimme thirty bucks today, and I'll give you one hundred tomorrow. I dunno. It's like I'm in a hole I can't get out of. I guess I could get out, but it's hard as hell. It's fucked up.

The Brothers: Ready at the Starting Line

Just as the pessimism and uncertainty with which the Hallway Hangers view their futures emerges when we consider what they perceive their lives will be like in twenty years, so do the Brothers' long-term visions serve as a valuable backdrop to our discussion of their aspirations. The ethos of the Brothers' peer group is a positive one; they are not resigned to a bleak future but are hoping for a bright one. Nowhere does this optimism surface more clearly than in the Brothers' responses to the question of what they will be doing in twenty years. Note the centrality of work in their views of the future.

(*all in separate interviews*)

SUPER: I'll have a house, a nice car, no one bothering me. Won't have to take no hard time from no one. Yeah, I'll have a good job, too.

JUAN: I'll have a regular house, y'know, with a yard and everything. I'll have a steady job, a good job. I'll be living the good life, the easy life.

MIKE: I might have a wife, some kids. I might be holding down a regular business job like an old guy. I hope I'll be able to do a lot of skiing and stuff like that when I'm old.

CRAIG: I'll probably be having a good job on my hands, I think. Working in an office as an architect, y'know, with my own drawing board, doing my own stuff, or at least close to there.

James takes a comic look into his future without being prompted to do so. "The ones who work hard in school, eventually it's gonna pay off for them and everything, and they're gonna have a good job and a family and all that. Not me though! I'm gonna have *myself.* I'm gonna have some money. And a different girl every day. And a different car. And be like this (*poses with one arm around an imaginary girl and the other on a steering wheel*)."

The Brothers do not hesitate to name their occupational goals. Although some of the Brothers are unsure of their occupational aspirations, none seems to feel that nurturing an aspiration is a futile exercise. The Brothers have not resigned themselves to taking whatever they can get. Rather, they articulate specific occupational aspirations (although these often are subject to change and revision).

Like all the Brothers, Super has not had extensive experience on the job market; he only has worked at summer jobs. For the past three summers, he has worked for the city doing maintenance work in parks and school buildings through a CETA-sponsored summer youth employment program. During the last year, Super's occupational aspirations have fluctuated widely. His initial desire to become a doctor was met with laughter from his friends. Deterred by their mocking and by a realization of the schooling required to be a doctor, Super immediately decided that he would rather go into business: "Maybe I can own my own shop and shit." This aspiration, however, also was ridiculed. "Yeah, right," commented Mokey, "Super'll be pimping the girls, that kinda business." In private, however, Super still clings to the hope of becoming a doctor, although he cites work in the computer field as a more realistic hope. "Really, I don't know what I should do now. I'm kinda confused. First I said I wanna go into computers, right? Take up that or a doctor." The vagueness of Super's aspirations is important; once again, we get a glimpse of how little is known about the world of middle-class work, even for somebody who clearly aspires to it. Of one thing Super is certain: "I just know I wanna get a good job."

Although Super does not distinguish between what constitutes a good job and what does not, he does allude to criteria by which the quality of a job can be judged. First, a good job must not demand that one "work on your feet," a distinction, apparently, between white and blue-collar work. Second, a good job implies at least some authority in one's workplace, a point Super makes clearly, if in a disjointed manner. "Bosses—if you don't come on time, they yell at you and stuff like that. They want you to do work and not sit down and relax and stuff like that, y'know. I want to try and be a boss, y'know, tell people what to do. See, I don't always want people telling me what to do, y'know—the low rank. I wanna try to be with people in the high rank." Although Super does not know what occupation he would like to enter, he is certain that he wants a job that is relatively high up in a vaguely defined occupational hierarchy. . . .

The Brothers display none of the cockiness about their own capabilities that the Hallway Hangers exhibit. Instead, they attribute lack of success on the job market exclusively to personal inadequacy. This is particularly true when the Brothers speculate about the future jobs the Hallway Hangers and their own friends will have. According to the Brothers, the Hallway Hangers (in Super's words) "ain't gonna get nowhere," not because of the harshness of the job market but because they are personally lacking. The rest of the Brothers share this view.

JM: Some of those guys who hang with Frankie, they're actually pretty smart. They just don't channel that intelligence into school, it seems to me.

CRAIG: I call that stupid, man. That's what they are.

JM: I dunno.

CRAIG: Lazy.

(in a separate interview)

SUPER: They think they're so tough they don't have to do work. That don't make sense, really. You ain't gonna get nowhere; all's you gonna do is be back in the projects like your mother. Depend on your mother to give you money every week. You ain't gonna get a good job. As you get older, you'll think about that, y'know. It'll come to your mind. "Wow, I can't believe, I should've just went to school and got my education."

(in a separate interview)

MOKEY: They all got attitude problems. They just don't got their shit together. Like Steve. They have to improve themselves.

In the eyes of the Brothers, the Hallway Hangers have attitude problems, are incapable of considering their long-term future, and are lazy or stupid.

Because this evidence is tainted (no love is lost between the two peer groups), it is significant that the Brothers apply the same criteria in judging each other's chances to gain meaningful employment. James thinks Mokey is headed for a dead-end job because he is immature and undisciplined. He also blames Juan for currently being out of work. "Juan's outta school, and Juan does *not* have a job (*said with contempt*). Now that's some kind of a senior. When

I'm a senior, I'm gonna have a job already. I can see if you're gonna go to college right when you get out of school; but Juan's not doin' nothin'. He's just stayin' home." Juan, in turn, thinks that Mokey and Super will have difficulty finding valuable work because of their attitudes. He predicts that Derek and Craig will be successful for the same reason.

These viewpoints are consistent with the dominant ideology in America; barriers to success are seen as personal rather than social. By attributing failure to personal inadequacy, the Brothers exonerate the opportunity structure. Indeed, it is amazing how often they affirm the openness of American society.

(all in separate interviews)

DEREK: If you put your mind to it, if you want to make a future for yourself, there's no reason why you can't. It's a question of attitude.

SUPER: It's easy to do anything, as long as you set your mind to it, if you wanna do it. If you really want to do it, if you really want to be something. If you don't want to do it . . . you ain't gonna make it. I gotta get that through my mind: I wanna do it. I wanna be somethin'. I don't wanna be livin' in the projects the rest of my life.

MOKEY: It's not like if they're rich they get picked [for a job]; it's just mattered by the knowledge of their mind.

CRAIG: If you work hard, it'll pay off in the end.

MIKE: If you work hard, really put your mind to it, you can do it. You can make it.

This view of the opportunity structure as an essentially open one that rewards intelligence, effort, and ingenuity is shared by all the Brothers. Asked whether their chances of securing a remunerative job are as good as those of an upper-class boy from a wealthy district of the city, they all responded affirmatively. Not a single member of the Hallway Hangers, in contrast, affirms the openness of American society. . . .

Reproduction Theory Reconsidered

This basic finding—that two substantially different paths are followed within the general framework of social reproduction—is a major challenge to economically determinist theories. Two groups of boys from the same social stratum who live in the same housing project and attend the same school nevertheless experience the process of social reproduction in fundamentally different ways. This simple fact alone calls into question many of the theoretical formulations of Bowles and Gintis.[6] If, as they argue, social class is the overriding determinant in social reproduction, what accounts for the variance in the process between the Brothers and Hallway Hangers? Bowles and Gintis, in considering a single school, maintain that social reproduction takes place primarily through educational tracking. Differential socialization through educational tracking prepares working-class students for working-class jobs and middle-class students for middle-class jobs. But the Hallway Hangers and the Brothers, who are from the same social class background and exposed to the curricular structure of the school in the same manner, undergo the process of social reproduction in substantially different manners. The theory of Bowles and Gintis cannot explain this difference.

Bourdieu's notion of habitus, however, can be used to differentiate the Hallway Hangers and the Brothers.[7] The habitus, as defined by Giroux, is "the subjective dispositions which reflect a class-based social grammar of taste, knowledge, and behavior inscribed in . . . each developing person."[8] According to Bourdieu, the habitus is primarily a function of social class. Bourdieu does not give an adequate sense of the internal structure of the habitus, but there is some precedent in his work for incorporating other factors into constructions of the habitus; for example, he differentiates people not only by gender and class, but also by whether they come from Paris or not. Although Bourdieu sometimes gives the impression of a homogeneity of habitus within the boundaries of social class, I understand habitus to be constituted at the level of the family and thus can include, as constitutive of the habitus, factors such as ethnicity, educational histories, peer associations, and demographic characteristics (e.g., geographical mobility, duration of tenancy in public housing, sibling order, and family size) as these shape individual action. Although Bourdieu never really develops the notion along these lines, he does allude to the complexity and interplay of mediations within the habitus. "The habitus acquired in the family underlies the structuring of school experiences, and the habitus transformed by schooling, itself diversified, in turn underlies the structuring of all subsequent experiences (e.g. the reception and assimilation of the messages of the culture industry or work experiences), and so on, from restructuring to restructuring."[9] When understood along the lines I have indicated, the concept of habitus becomes flexible enough to accommodate the interactions among ethnicity, family, schooling, work experiences, and peer associations that have been documented [here].

Although we may accept the notion of habitus as a useful explanatory tool, we must reject the inevitability of its *function* in Bourdieu's theoretical scheme. According to Bourdieu, the habitus functions discreetly to integrate individuals into a social world geared to the interests of the ruling classes; habitus engenders attitudes and conduct that are compatible with the reproduction of class inequality. The outstanding example of this process is the development by working-class individuals of depressed aspirations that mirror their actual chances for social advancement.

The circular relationship Bourdieu posits between objective opportunities and subjective hopes is incompatible with the findings [presented here]. The Brothers, whose objective life chances probably were lower originally than those available to the Hallway Hangers because of racial barriers to success, nevertheless nurture higher aspirations than do the Hallway Hangers. By emphasizing structural determinants at the expense of mediating factors that influence subjective renderings of objective probabilities, Bourdieu presumes too mechanistic and simplistic a relationship between aspiration and opportunity. This component of his theory fails to fathom how a number of factors lie between and mediate the influence of social class on individuals; Bourdieu cannot explain, for instance, how ethnicity intervenes in the process of aspiration formation and social reproduction.

Thus, the theoretical formulations of Bowles and Gintis and the deterministic elements of Bourdieu's theory, although elegant and intuitively plausible, are incapable of accounting for the processes of social reproduction as they have been observed and documented in Clarendon Heights. These theories give an excellent account of the hidden structural and ideological determinants that constrain members of the working class and limit the options of Clarendon Heights teenagers. What the Hallway Hangers and the Brothers demonstrate quite clearly, however, is that the way in which individuals and groups respond to structures of domination is open-ended. Although there is no way to avoid class-based constraints, the outcomes are not predefined. Bowles and Gintis and Bourdieu pay too little attention to the active, creative role of individual and group praxis. As Giroux maintains, what is missing from such theories "is not only the issue of resistance, but also any attempt to delineate the complex ways in which working-class subjectivities are constituted."[10]

From Ethnography to Theory

Once we descend into the world of actual human lives, we must take our theoretical bearings to make some sense of the social landscape, but in doing so we invariably find that the theories are incapable of accounting for much of what we see. The lives of the Hallway Hangers and the Brothers cannot be reduced to structural influences or causes; although structural forces weigh upon the individuals involved, it is necessary, in the words of Willis, "to give the social agents involved some meaningful scope for viewing, inhabiting, and constructing their own world in a way which is recognizably human and not theoretically reductive."[11] We must appreciate both the importance and the relative autonomy of the cultural level at which individuals, alone or in concert with others, wrest meaning out of the flux of their lives.

The possibilities open to these boys as lower-class teenagers are limited structurally from the outset. That they internalize the objective probabilities for social advancement to some degree is beyond question. The process by which this takes place, however, is influenced by a whole series of intermediate factors. Because gender is constant in the study discussed in these pages, race is the principal variable affecting the way in which these youths view their situation. Ethnicity introduces new structurally determined constraints on social mobility, but it also serves as a mediation through which the limitations of class are refracted and thus apprehended and understood differently by different racial groups. The Brothers comprehend and react to their situation in a manner entirely different from the response the Hallway Hangers make to a similar situation; ethnicity introduces a new dynamic that makes the Brothers more receptive to the achievement ideology. Their acceptance of this ideology affects their aspirations but also influences, in tandem with parental encouragement, their approach to school and the character of their peer group, factors that in turn bear upon their aspirations.

If we modify the habitus by changing the ethnicity variable and altering a few details of family occupational and educational histories and duration of tenancy in public housing, we would have the Hallway Hangers. As white lower-class youths, the Hallway Hangers view and interpret their situation in a different light, one that induces them to reject the achievement ideology and to develop aspirations and expectations quite apart from those the ideology attempts to generate. The resultant perspective, which is eventually reinforced by the Hallway Hangers' contact with the job market, informs the boys' approach to school and helps us understand the distinctive attributes of this peer group. Thus, although social class is of primary importance, there are intermediate factors at work that, as constitutive of the habitus, shape the subjective responses of the two groups of boys and produce quite different expectations and actions.

Having grown up in an environment where success is not common, the Hallway Hangers see that the connection between effort and reward is not as clear-cut as the achievement ideology would have them believe. Because it runs counter to the evidence in their lives and because it represents a forceful assault on their self-esteem, the Hallway Hangers repudiate the achievement ideology. Given that their parents are inclined to see the ideology in the same light, they do not counter their sons' rejection of the American Dream.

A number of important ramifications follow from the Hallway Hangers' denial of the dominant ideology: the establishment of a peer group that provides alternative means of generating self-esteem, the rejection of school and antagonism toward teachers, and, of course, the leveling of aspirations. In schematizing the role of the peer group, it is difficult not to appear tautological, for the group does wield a reciprocal influence on the boys: It attracts those who are apt to reject school and the achievement ideology and those with low aspirations and then deepens these individuals' initial proclivities and further shapes them to fit the group. But at the same time, the peer subculture itself, handed down from older to younger boys, is the product of the particular factors that structure the lives of white teenagers in Clarendon Heights.

In addition to the peer group, the curricular structure of the school solidifies the low aspirations of the Hallway Hangers by channeling them into programs that prepare students for manual labor jobs. Low aspirations, in turn, make the Hallway Hangers more likely to dismiss school as irrelevant. Once on the job market, the Hallway Hangers' inability to secure even mediocre jobs further dampens their occupational hopes. Thus although each individual ultimately retains autonomy in the subjective interpretation of his situation, the leveled aspirations of the Hallway Hangers are, to a large degree, a response to the limitations of social class as they are manifest in the Hallway Hangers' social world.

The Brothers' social class origins are only marginally different from those of the Hallway Hangers. Being black, the Brothers also must cope with racially rooted barriers to success that, affirmative action measures notwithstanding, structurally inhibit the probabilities for social advancement, although to a lesser degree than do shared class limitations. What appears to be a comparable objective situation to that of the Hallway Hangers, however, is apprehended in a very different manner by the Brothers.

As black teenagers, the Brothers interpret their families' occupational and educational records in a much different light than do the Hallway Hangers. Judging by the Brothers' constant affirmation of equality of opportunity, the boys believe that racial injustice has been curbed in the United States in the last twenty years. Whereas in their parents' time the link between effort and reward was very tenuous for blacks, the Brothers, in keeping with the achievement ideology, see the connection today as very strong: "If you work hard, it'll pay off in the end" (Craig). Hence, the achievement ideology is more compatible with the Brothers' attitudes than with those of the Hallway Hangers, for whom it cannot succeed against overwhelming contrary evidence. The ideology is not as emotionally painful for the Brothers to accept because past racial discrimination can help account for their families' poverty, whereas the Hallway Hangers, if the ideology stands, are afforded no explanation outside of laziness and stupidity for their parents' failures. The optimism that acceptance of the achievement ideology brings for the Brothers is encouraged and reinforced by their parents. Thus, we see how in the modified habitus ethnicity affects the Brothers' interpretation of their social circumstances and leads to acceptance of the achievement ideology, with all the concomitant results.

Postscript: The Hallway Hangers and Brothers Eight Years Later

"Hey, Jay, what the fuck brings you back to the Ponderosa?" Greeted by Steve in July 1991, I surveyed a Clarendon Heights that had changed considerably since 1983. Steve jerked his thumb over his shoulder at a group of African American teenagers lounging in the area outside doorway #13, previously the preserve of the Hallway Hangers. "How do you like all the new niggers we got here? Motherfuckers've taken over, man." I asked Steve about Frankie, Slick, and the other Hallway Hangers. "I'm the only one holding down the fort," he answered. "Me and Jinks—he lives in the back. The rest of 'em pretty much cut loose, man."

In their mid-twenties, the seven Hallway Hangers should be in the labor force full-time. Most of them aren't: They are unemployed or imprisoned, or are working sporadically either for firms "under the table" or for themselves in the drug economy. . . . The Hallway Hangers have been trapped in what economists call the secondary labor market—the subordinate segment of the job structure where the market is severely skewed against workers. Jobs in the primary labor markets provide wages that can support families and an internal career structure, but the rules of the game are different in the secondary labor market. Wages are lower, raises are infrequent, training is minimal, advancement is rare, and turnover is high.

When the legitimate job market fails them, the Hallway Hangers can turn to the underground economy. Since 1984, almost all of the Hallway Hangers have at least supplemented their income from earnings in the burgeoning, multibillion-dollar drug market. The street economy promises better money than does conventional employment. It also provides a work site that does not demean the Hallway Hangers or drain their dignity. As workers in the underground economy, they won't have to take orders from a boss's arrogant son, nor will they have to gossip with office colleagues and strain to camouflage their street identities. . . .

Although they have certainly fared better than the Hallway Hangers, the Brothers have themselves stumbled economically in the transition to adulthood. Even more so than the Hallway Hangers, the Brothers have been employed in the service sector of the economy. They have bagged groceries, stocked shelves, flipped hamburgers, delivered pizzas, repaired cars, serviced airplanes, cleaned buildings, moved furniture, driven tow trucks, pumped gas, delivered auto parts, and washed dishes. They have also worked as mail carriers, cooks, clerks, computer operators, bank tellers, busboys, models, office photocopiers, laborers, soldiers, baggage handlers, security guards, and customer service agents. Only Mike, as a postal service employee, holds a unionized position. Although their experiences on the labor market have been varied, many of the Brothers have failed to move out of the secondary labor market. Instead, like the Hallway Hangers, they have been stuck in low-wage, high-turnover jobs. . . .

These results are depressing. The experiences of the Hallway Hangers since 1984 show that opting out of the contest—neither playing the game nor accepting its rules—is not a viable option. Incarceration and other less explicit social penalties are applied by society when the contest is taken on one's own terms. There is no escape: The Hallway Hangers must still generate income, build relationships, and establish households. Trapped inside the game, the Hallway Hangers now question their youthful resistance to schooling and social norms. Granted the opportunity to do it over again, the Hallway Hangers say they would have tried harder to succeed.

But the Brothers *have* always tried, which is why their experiences between 1984 and 1991 are as disheartening as the Hallway Hangers'. If the Hangers show that opting out of the contest is not a viable option, the Brothers show that dutifully playing by the rules hardly guarantees success either. Conservative and liberal commentators alike often contend that if the poor would only apply themselves, behave responsibly, and adopt bourgeois values, then they will propel themselves into the middle class. The Brothers followed the recipe quite closely, but the outcomes are disappointing. They illustrate how rigid and durable the class structure is. Aspiration, application, and intelligence often fail to cut through the firm figurations of structural inequality. Though not impenetrable, structural constraints on opportunity, embedded in both schools and job markets, turn out to be much more debilitating than the Brothers anticipated. Their dreams of comfortable suburban bliss currently are dreams deferred, and are likely to end up as dreams denied.

NOTES

1. All names of neighborhoods and individuals have been changed to protect the anonymity of the study's subjects.

2. Erik H. Erikson, *Gandhi's Truth* (New York: Norton, 1969), p. 154.

3. Ronald Reagan, "State of the Union Address to Congress," *New York Times*, 6 February 1985, p. 17.

4. Kenneth I. Spenner and David L. Featherman, "Achievement Ambitions," *Annual Review of Sociology* 4 (1978):376–378.

5. Howard B. London, *The Culture of a Community College* (New York: Praeger, 1978).

6. Samuel Bowles and Herbert Gintis, *Schooling in Capitalist America* (New York: Basic Books, 1976).

7. See Pierre Bourdieu, *Outline of a Theory of Practice* (Cambridge: Cambridge University Press, 1977).

8. Henry A. Giroux, *Theory & Resistance in Education* (London: Heinemann Educational Books, 1983), p. 89.

9. Bourdieu, *Outline of a Theory of Practice*, p. 87.

10. Giroux, *Theory & Resistance*, p. 85.

11. Paul E. Willis, *Learning to Labor* (Aldershot: Gower, 1977), p. 172.

37. Jan O. Jonsson, David B. Grusky, Matthew Di Carlo, and Reinhard Pollak*

It's a Decent Bet That Our Children Will Be Professors Too

Are children born into privilege very likely to end up privileged themselves? Are children born into less-privileged families likewise fated to remain in their social class of origin? We care about such questions for many reasons but perhaps primarily because they speak to whether the competition for money, power, and prestige is fairly run. For many people, the brute facts of extreme poverty or inequality are not in themselves problematic or objectionable, and what really matters is simply whether the competition for riches is a fair one in which everyone, no matter how advantaged or disadvantaged their parents may be, has an equal chance to win. This commitment to a fair competition motivates a quite extensive research literature on how much mobility there is, whether some countries have more of it than others, and whether opportunities for mobility are withering away.

The purpose of this chapter is to ask whether conventional methods of monitoring mobility are adequate for the task. We're concerned that they're not and that, in particular, such methods may overlook some of the most important forms and sources of rigidity. The long-standing convention in the field, and one that we regard as problematic, has been to assume that intergenerational reproduction takes

*The ideas, issues, and theories considered in this brief commissioned piece are examined in greater depth in materials appearing in: Jonsson et al. 2009, Grusky et al. 2008, and Jonsson et al. 2011. The article printed here was originally prepared by Jan O. Jonsson, David B. Grusky, Matthew Di Carlo, and Reinhard Pollak, in *The Inequality Reader: Contemporary and Foundational Readings in Race, Class, and Gender*, Second Edition, edited by David B. Grusky pp. 499–516. Copyright © 2011. Reprinted by permission of Westview Press, an imprint of Perseus Books, LLC, a subsidiary of Hachette Book Group, Inc.

one of two forms, either a categorical form that has parents passing on a big-class position (e.g., manager, professional, craft worker) to their children or a gradational form that has parents passing on their socioeconomic standing to their children. We argue here that these standard approaches ignore the important role that detailed occupations play in reproducing inequality.

The conventional wisdom about how to measure mobility was codified a half century ago. The study of mobility bifurcated at that time into one camp that represented social structure in gradational terms (e.g., Svalastoga 1959) and another that represented it in big-class terms (e.g., Carlsson 1958; Glass 1954). These competing representations of social structure were subsequently attached to competing understandings of how inequality is reproduced: The class scholar assumed that parents pass on their social class to children, while the gradational scholar assumed that parents pass on their occupational prestige or socioeconomic standing to their children. Under both approaches, detailed occupations were usually treated as the appropriate starting point in representing the underlying structure of inequality, but they were transformed either by aggregating them into big social classes (i.e., the class approach) or by scaling them in terms of their socioeconomic status or prestige (i.e., the gradational approach). The study of mobility has in this sense been reduced to the study of either class or socioeconomic mobility, yet quite strikingly these simplifying assumptions have come to be adopted with little in the way of evidence that they adequately characterize the structure of opportunity.

Is it possible that both class and gradational representations are incomplete and obscure important rigidities in the mobility regime? We suggest that indeed these simplifying representations provide only partial accounts and that the structure of inequality is best revealed by supplementing them with a third representation that treats detailed occupations as fundamental conduits of reproduction. Because the social, cultural, and economic resources conveyed to children depend so fundamentally on the detailed occupations of their parents, one might expect such occupations to play a featured role in intergenerational reproduction, but in fact this role has gone largely unexplored in most mobility analyses.

It's not just that detailed occupations serve as a main conduit for reproduction. In addition, they index the main communities and identities of workers, and as such they should be understood as a powerful omnibus indicator of the social world within which individuals are located. At a dinner party, we tend to ask a new acquaintance, "What do you do?" because the response, almost invariably conveyed in the form of a detailed occupation, provides at once evidence about life chances and capacities (skills and credentials, earnings capacity, networks), honor and esteem (prestige, socioeconomic status), and the social and cultural world within which interactions occur (consumption practices, politics, and attitudes). We care, in other words, about occupations because they are pregnant with information on the life chances, social standing, and social world of their incumbents (see Weeden and Grusky 2005). The (largely untested) bias in this regard is that occupation is far more strongly correlated with these many variables than is income. If we tend to avoid asking acquaintances about their income, it's not just because doing so is viewed as too intrusive and personal, but also because we suspect that querying about occupation will yield more in the way of useful information.

Mechanisms of Reproduction

If our main argument, therefore, is that occupations are an important conduit for reproduction, this is obviously not to suggest that inequality is reproduced *exclusively* through occupations. Rather, there's good reason to believe that, while much reproduction occurs through occupations, the more frequently studied big-class and socioeconomic mechanisms are also doing important reproductive work. We suggest below that a comprehensive mobility model should examine at once reproduction at the socioeconomic, big-class, and microclass levels. In most mobility analyses, the three levels are confounded, and conclusions about the structure of mobility may conceal possible differences in how these forms of reproduction play out. We develop this argument below by reviewing each of these three mechanisms of reproduction in turn.[1]

Gradational regime: The gradational (or socioeconomic) approach to studying mobility has inequality taking on a simple unidimensional form in which families are arrayed in terms of either income or occupational status. The life chances of children growing up within such systems are a function, then, of their standing within this unidimensional queue of families. When children are born high in the queue, they tend to secure high-status and highly rewarded occupations by virtue of (1) their privileged access to the economic resources (e.g., wealth, income) needed either to purchase training for the best occupations (e.g., an elite education) or to "purchase" the jobs themselves (e.g., a proprietorship), (2) their privileged access to social networks providing information about and entrée to the best occupations, and (3) their privileged access to cultural resources (e.g., socialization) that motivate them to acquire the best jobs and provide them with the cognitive and interactional skills (e.g., culture of critical discourse) to succeed in them. Under the gradational model, it is the total *amount* of resources that matters, and children born into privileged circumstances are privileged because they have access to so many resources (e.g., Hout and Hauser 1992). The imagery here is accordingly that of two unidimensional hierarchies, one for each generation, smoothly joined together through the mediating mechanism of total resources (economic, social, or cultural). In Figure 37.1a, an ideal-typical gradational regime is depicted by projecting a detailed cross-classification of occupational origins and destinations onto a third dimension, one that represents the densities of mobility and immobility. This graph, which orders origin and destination occupations by socioeconomic score, shows the characteristic falloff in mobility chances as the distance between origin and destination scores increases.

Big-class regime: The big-class regime, by contrast, has inequality taking the form of mutually exclusive and exhaustive classes. These classes are often assumed to convey a package of conditions (e.g., employment relations), a resulting social environment that structures behavior and decision making, and a culture that may be understood as an adaptation (or maladaptation) to this environment. For our purposes, the relevant feature of this formulation is that all children born into the same class will have largely the same mobility chances, even though their parents may hold different occupations with different working conditions and socioeconomic standing. The logic of the class situation is assumed, then, to be overriding and to determine the life chances of the children born into it. Obversely, two big classes of similar status will not necessarily convey to their incumbents identical mobility chances, as they may differ on various non-status dimensions that have implications for mobility. For example, even though proprietors and routine nonmanuals are roughly similar in socioeconomic status, the children of proprietors will tend to become proprietors and the children of routine nonmanuals will tend to become routine nonmanuals. This pattern arises because tastes and aspirations develop in class-specific ways (e.g., the children of proprietors de-

velop tastes for autonomy, and the children of routine nonmanuals develop tastes for stability); because human capital is cultivated and developed in class-specific ways (e.g., the children of proprietors develop entrepreneurial skills, and the children of routine nonmanuals develop bureaucratic skills); because social capital is distributed in class-specific ways (e.g., the children of proprietors are apprised of entrepreneurial opportunities, and the children of routine nonmanuals are apprised of routine nonmanual opportunities); and because the tangible physical capital (e.g., a shop, business) passed on to children of proprietors motivates them to remain proprietors. By virtue of these processes, children do not have generic access to all occupations of comparable standing (as gradationalists would have it), but instead are especially well-positioned to assume occupations that align with the culture, training, contacts, and capital that their class origins entail. We represent an ideal-typical class regime of this sort in Figure 37.1b. Because we are focusing on reproduction, we have assumed here (and in Figure 37.1c) that all off-diagonal cells have the same density, save for random noise.

Microclass regime: The occupational, or "microclass," approach shares with the big-class model the presumption that contemporary labor markets are balkanized into discrete categories, but such balkanization is assumed to take principally the form of institutionalized occupations (e.g., doctor, plumber, postal clerk) rather than institutionalized big classes (e.g., routine nonmanuals). By implication, the occupations constituting big classes will have differing propensities for mobility and immobility, a heterogeneity that obtains because the distinctive occupational worlds into which children are born have consequences for the aspirations they develop, the skills they value and to which they have access, and the networks upon which they can draw (see Table 37.1). The children of carpenters, for example, may be especially likely to become carpenters because they are exposed to carpentry skills at home, socialized in ways that render them especially appreciative of carpentry as a vocation, and embedded in social networks that provide them with information about how to become carpenters and how to secure jobs in carpentry. Although a microclass regime again assumes a lumpy class form, the lumpiness is much finer than big-class analysts would allow (see Figure 37.1c). The strong big-class reproduction that we long thought was revealed in mobility tables may instead be artifactual and express little more than the tendency for reproduction at the detailed occupational level.

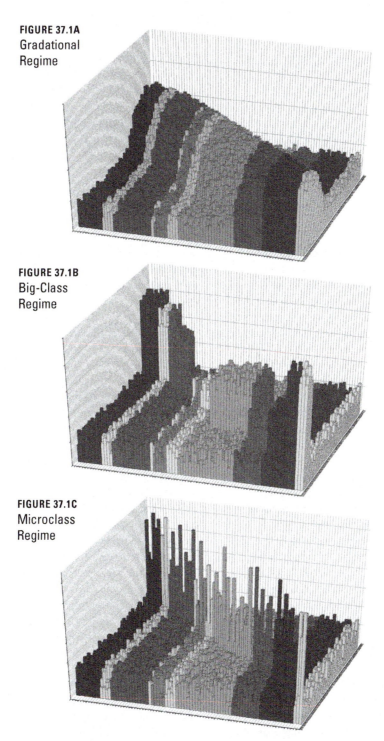

FIGURE 37.1A
Gradational
Regime

FIGURE 37.1B
Big-Class
Regime

FIGURE 37.1C
Microclass
Regime

Note: The base of each figure indexes occupational origin and destination, while
the vertical dimension indexes densities of mobility and immobility for each possible
combination of origin and destination.

TABLE 37.1 Mechanisms of Intergenerational Reproduction

Type of resources	Type of reproduction	
	Big-class	*Micro-class*
Human capital	General or abstract skills (e.g., cognitive or verbal abilities)	Occupation-specific skills (e.g., acting skills, carpentry skills)
Cultural capital	Abstract culture and tastes (e.g., "culture of critical discourse")	Occupation-specific culture and tastes (e.g., aspirations to become a medical doctor)
Social networks	Classwide networks (typically developed through neighborhood- or job-related interactions)	Occupation-specific networks (typically developed through on-the-job interactions)
Economic resources	Liquid resources (e.g., stocks, bonds, income)	Fixed resources (e.g., business, farm)

We have referred above to the occupational skills, culture, and networks that parents transmit to their children. The transmission of skills should, however, be particularly stressed and may well be especially important in understanding why occupations are passed on. The conventional view would have it that the ongoing separation of home and workplace has made it more difficult for parents to transmit such occupational human capital. We agree that its transmission may now be weakened, but this obviously does not mean that it's altogether precluded. The sociologist, for example, may well talk shop with her or his children at the dinner table, litter the home with books and magazines that betray a sociological orientation, and in all other ways inculcate a sociological perspective in the natural course of everyday child rearing. The engineer, by contrast, may bring home toys that involve building things, focus conversation and inquiry on the world of things, and impart a special interest in understanding "how things work." In the aftermath of the World Trade Center collapse, we can imagine the engineer's family talked mainly about why the building failed structurally, whereas the sociologist's family talked mainly about why there is terrorism.

The transmission of occupation-specific human capital is likely to occur outside the professional sector as well. The mechanic is especially likely to spend time at home engaging in repairs, may take her or his children into the repair shop, and may otherwise encourage an interest in taking things apart and fixing them (i.e., a "practical" engineer). Likewise, the seamstress may talk frequently about fashion at home, take her or his children to fashion shows, and train them in sewing and designing clothes. These examples make the simple point that the occupa-

tional commitments of parents can affect what they discuss or practice at home, how they spend time with their children, and hence the skills that they impart to their children.

It would be possible to presume that reproduction takes on an exclusively gradational, big-class, or microclass form and build a mobility model that then capitalizes on the imagery underlying that particular form. The field has indeed often proceeded in just that way: That is, big-class analysts have often insisted on building purist big-class models, while gradationalists have in turn insisted on building purist gradational models. The model that we develop will, by contrast, combine all three forms (big class, microclass, gradational) and thereby make it possible to tease out the net contribution of each. We apply this approach to ask (1) whether the mobility regime contains pockets of extreme microclass rigidity that are concealed when microclasses are aggregated into big classes, and (2) whether such microclass reproduction is the main mechanism through which big classes are reproduced. If the answer to these questions is in the affirmative, it will follow that there is more microclass rigidity than is consistent with the practice of ignoring it and less big-class rigidity than is consistent with the practice of building our analyses exclusively around it.

We suspect that a microclass foundation to reproduction is a generic feature of late industrialism rather than something idiosyncratic to the United States. The mechanisms that we've laid out are, after all, in play to a greater or lesser extent in all countries (see Table 37.1). The relative strength of big-class or microclass reproduction in any given society will be affected by the prevailing mix of institutional forms, some supporting big-class structuration (e.g., trade unions) and others supporting microclass structuration (e.g., state-supported occupational closure). We have chosen to analyze four countries (Germany, the United States, Sweden, and Japan) that, by virtue of this different mix of institutional forms, have mobility regimes that support reproduction of different types.

How might mobility vary by country? Whereas Germany and the United States are often understood as the home ground of occupationalization, Sweden has a long tradition of big-class organization, and Japan is typically assumed to be stratified more by family and firm than by big class or occupation. We have sought in this fashion to explore the reach of microclass mechanisms into labor markets, like those of Sweden and Japan, that have not historically been regarded as taking a microclass form. If a microclass mechanism nonetheless emerges as fundamental in Sweden or Japan, the case for building that mechanism more systematically into our models is strengthened. This design allows us to assess the strong claim, as recently advanced by Goldthorpe, that "a reliance on occupationally specific factors, which are likely themselves to be quite variable over time and space, would seem especially inadequate" in explaining class reproduction (2007, 144).

In the present analysis, we will not be exploring the structure of cross-national variation in reproduction, and instead we'll be presenting the shared features that hold in approximate form in all countries. We refer the reader elsewhere (Jonsson et al. 2009, 2011) for a discussion of cross-national variability in microclass mobility.

The Structure of Contemporary Mobility

The analyses presented here will be carried out with data sets that provide information on the father's occupation, the child's occupation and age, and other variables that aid in occupational and big-class coding (e.g., employment status, branch of industry). Because our analyses are pitched at the occupational level, our father-by-son mobility tables will have many cells, and large data sets for each country are needed. We meet this requirement by drawing on multiple surveys in all countries save Sweden. For Sweden, the occupational data for the children come from the 1990 Census, and the occupational data for the parents are recovered by linking to the 1960 and 1970 Censuses (Erikson and Jonsson 1993). The data from the remaining countries come from the

sources listed in Table 37.2. For this chapter, we're forced to focus on the mobility of men, as we've found that women experience more complicated mobility processes that are not as readily summarized in such a short treatment. We have discussed the mobility of women in Jonsson et al. (2009).

We have worked hard to render the data as comparable as possible. Given our need for large data sets, some compromises nonetheless had to be made, most notably pertaining to the period covered and the age of the respondents. The data from the United States, for example, are drawn disproportionately from earlier time periods, although more recent data from the United States are used as well (see Table 37.3 for details). Additionally, the Swedish data set covers only respondents between thirty and forty-seven years old, whereas all other data sets cover respondents between thirty and sixty-four years old. We have elsewhere shown that such differences in coverage don't affect our results much (Jonsson et al. 2009).

The starting point for all of our analyses is the detailed microclass coding scheme represented in Table 37.2. The microclass category may be defined as "a grouping of technically similar jobs that is institutionalized in the labor market through such means as (a) an association or union, (b) licensing or certification requirements, or (c) widely diffused understandings . . . regarding efficient or otherwise preferred ways of organizing production and dividing labor" (Grusky 2005, 66). The scheme used here includes eighty-two microclasses and captures many of the boundaries in the division of labor that are socially recognized and defended. These microclasses were then scaled in terms of the international socioeconomic scale (Ganzeboom, de Graaf, and Treiman 1992). We have applied this scheme to model an 82 × 82 mobility table formed by cross-classifying the father's and offspring's occupation in data pooled from the United States, Sweden, Germany, and Japan (for details, see Jonsson et al. 2009). The distinctive feature of the resulting analysis is that microclass effects, represented on the main diagonal of Figure 37.2, are layered over more conventional big-class effects.

Given our suspicion that net big-class effects may be weak, it is clearly important to adopt a big-class scheme that fully captures such big-class effects as can be found, as otherwise any possible shortfall in big-class explanatory power might be attributed to poor operationalization. We have accordingly

TABLE 37.2 Micro-Classes Nested in Manual-Nonmanual Classes, Macro Classes, and Meso Classes

1. NONMANUAL CLASS			2. MANUAL CLASS	
1. Professional-managerial	*2. Proprietors*	*3. Routine nonmanual*	*4. Manual*	*5. Primary*
1. Classical professions	1. Proprietors	**1. Sales**	**1. Craft**	1. Fishermen
1. Jurists		1. Real estate agents	1. Craftsmen, n.e.c.	2. Farmers
2. Health professionals		2. Agents, n.e.c.	2. Foremen	3. Farm laborers
3. Professors and instructors		3. Insurance agents	3. Electronics service and repair	
4. Natural scientists		4. Cashiers	4. Printers and related workers	
5. Statistical and social scientists		5. Sales workers	5. Locomotive operators	
6. Architects		**2. Clerical**	6. Electricians	
7. Accountants		1. Telephone operators	7. Tailors and related workers	
8. Authors and journalists		2. Bookkeepers	8. Vehicle mechanics	
9. Engineers		3. Office workers	9. Blacksmiths and machinists	
2. Managers and officials			10. Jewelers	
1. Officials, government and non-profit organizations			11. Other mechanics	
2. Other managers			12. Plumbers and pipe-fitters	
3. Commercial managers			13. Cabinetmakers	
4. Building managers and proprietors			14. Bakers	
3. Other professions			15. Welders	
1. Systems analysts and programmers			16. Painters	
2. Aircraft pilots and navigators			17. Butchers	
3. Personnel and labor relations workers			18. Stationary engine operators	
4. Elementary and secondary teachers			19. Bricklayers and carpenters	
5. Librarians			20. Heavy machine operators	
6. Creative artists			**2. Lower manual**	
7. Ship officers			1. Truck drivers	
8. Professional and technical, n.e.c.			2. Chemical processors	
9. Social and welfare workers			3. Miners and related workers	
10. Workers in religion			4. Longshoremen	
11. Nonmedical technicians			5. Food processing workers	
12. Health semiprofessionals			6. Textile workers	
13. Hospital attendants			7. Sawyers	
14. Nursery school teachers and aides			8. Metal processors	
			9. Operatives and kindred, n.e.c.	
			10. Forestry workers	
			3. Service workers	
			1. Protective service workers	
			2. Transport conductors	
			3. Guards and watchmen	
			4. Food service workers	
			5. Mass transportation operators	
			6. Service workers, n.e.c.	
			7. Hairdressers	
			8. Newsboys and deliverymen	
			9. Launderers	
			10. Housekeeping workers	
			11. Janitors and cleaners	
			12. Gardeners	

TABLE 37.3 Surveys for Intergenerational Mobility Analysis

Survey Sample Size	Period	Ages	Birth Cohorts	Occup.[1]	Sample Size
Occupational Changes in a Generation I (OCG I)	1962	30–64	1898–1932	1960 SOC	17,544
Occupational Changes in a Generation II (OCG II)	1973	30-64	1909–1943	1960–70 SOC	18,856
General Social Survey (GSS)	1972–2003	30–64	1908–1970	1970–80 SOC	9,685
Survey of Social Stratification & Mobility (SSM)	1955–1995	30–64	1891–1970	Japanese SCO	6,703
Japan General Social Survey (JGSS)	2000–2002	30–64	1936–1972	Japanese SCO	1,917
German Social Survey[2] (ALLBUS)	1980–2002	30–64	1916–1972	ISCO-68, ISCO-88	5,647
German Socioeconomic Panel (GSOEP)	1986, 1999, 2000	30–64	1922–1970	ISCO-68, ISCO-88	2,886
German Life History Study LV I-III	1981–1989	30–64	1921–1959	ISCO-68	1,234
ZUMA-Standarddemographie Survey	1976–1982	30–64	1912–1952	ISCO-68	2,929
1990 Swedish Census (linked to 1960 and 1970 Censuses)	1990	30–47	1943–1960	NYK80	184,451

1. SOC = Standard Occupational Classification; SCO = Standard Classification of Occupations; ISCO = International Standard Classification of Occupations; NYK = Nordiskyrkesklassificering.

2. German data exclude respondents from East Germany (GDR). If a respondent was not gainfully employed at the time of the survey, his last occupation was used.

proceeded by fitting a set of nested big-class contrasts that capture the many and varied big-class distinctions that scholars have identified. As shown in Table 37.2, we begin by distinguishing the manual and nonmanual classes, a big-class distinction so important that early class scholars often focused on it alone. We next identify three "macroclasses" in the nonmanual category (i.e., professional-managerial, proprietor, routine nonmanual) and another two macroclasses in the manual category (i.e., manual, primary). Within three of these macroclasses, we then allow further "mesoclass" distinctions to emerge: the professional-managerial class is divided into classical professions, managers and officials, and other professions; the routine nonmanual class is divided into sales workers and clerks; and the manual class is divided into craft, lower manual, and service workers. The resulting scheme, which embodies three layers of big-class distinctions (i.e., manual-nonmanual, macroclass, and mesoclass), may be understood as a nondenominational hybrid of conventional schemes that assembles in one scheme many of the contrasts that have historically been emphasized by big-class scholars.

These distinctions are introduced in our mobility models as a nested set of contrasts (see Jonsson et al.

2009). This approach not only allows us to tease out the net residue of reproduction at the mesoclass, macroclass, and manual-nonmanual levels, but also allows for patterns of exchange that are more complicated than those conventionally allowed. The stylized parent-to-child mobility table in Figure 37.2 depicts these three sets of overlapping big-class parameters and shows how they capture quite complicated affinities off the microclass diagonal, off the mesoclass diagonal, and even off the macroclass diagonal. If we had instead proceeded by fitting mesoclass effects alone (as is conventional), we could absorb excess densities in the dark-gray regions of Figure 37.2 but not the surrounding light-gray regions. The cells in the white zones of Figure 37.2 are in fact the only ones that index mobility with respect to *all* class levels. Moreover, even the cells in these zones will be modeled with a gradational term, a parameter that allows us to estimate the extent to which short-distance moves occur more frequently than long-distance ones.

This gradational term captures the tendency of children to assume occupations that are socioeconomically close to their origins. If the apparent clustering at the microclass, mesoclass, macroclass, or manual-nonmanual levels reflects nothing more than

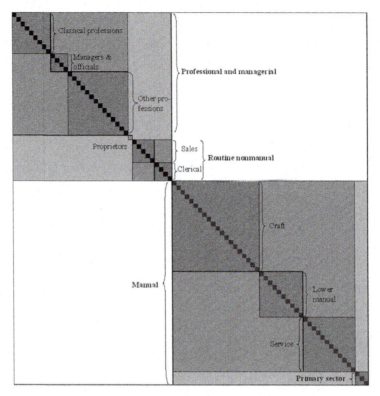

FIGURE 37.2 Overlapping Inheritance Terms in Mobility Model

Note: The Y axis pertains to occupational origins and the X axis to occupational destinations. The unlabeled microdiagonal squares represent occupational immobility. The size of each big-class category represents the number of microclass categories it encompasses (not the number of workers within the class).

this gradational tendency, then the inheritance parameters represented in Figure 37.2 will become insignificant when the gradational parameter is included. The big-class and microclass parameters, taken together, thus speak to the extent to which the mobility regime is lumpy rather than gradational, while the relative size of these parameters speaks to whether conventional big-class analyses have correctly represented the main type of lumpiness. The following model is therefore yielded:

$$m_{ij} = \alpha\beta_i\gamma_j\varphi^{\mu_i\mu_j}\delta_{ij}^A\delta_{ij}^B\delta_{ij}^C\delta_{ij}^M$$

where i indexes origins, j indexes destinations, m_{ij} refers to the expected value in the ij^{th} cell, α refers to the main effect, β_i and γ_j refer to row and column marginal effects, φ refers to the socioeconomic effect, μ_i (origin) and μ_j (destination) are socioeconomic scale values assigned to each of the eighty-two microclasses, and δ^A, δ^B, δ^C, and δ^M refer to manual-nonmanual, macroclass, mesoclass, and microclass

immobility effects, respectively. The latter parameters are fitted simultaneously and therefore capture net effects. The manual-nonmanual parameter, for example, indexes the average density across those cells pertaining to manual or nonmanual inheritance after purging the additional residue of inheritance that may obtain at the macroclass, mesoclass, and microclass levels.

The Structure of Mobility

When this model is applied to our pooled four-nation sample, the microclass and big-class parameters take on the form represented in Figure 37.3. Although cross-national variations of interest have emerged in our analyses (see Jonsson et al. 2009), Figure 37.3 is based on pooled data that smooth out such variation and thus represent the cross-nationally shared features of mobility.

The most striking feature of this figure is the microdiagonal clustering that appears as a palisade

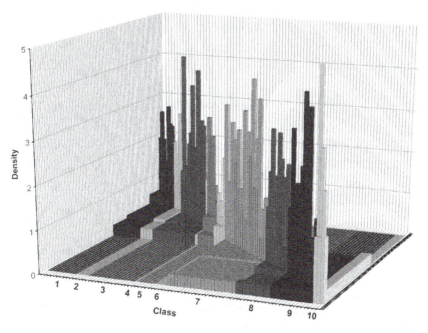

FIGURE 37.3 The Contours of Class Reproduction for Men

Note: The base indexes occupational origins and destinations, while the vertical dimension indexes densities of mobility and immobility (for each possible combination of origin and destination). 1 = classical professions; 2 = managers and offi cials; 3 = other professions; 4 = proprietors; 5 = sales; 6 = clerical; 7 = craft; 8 = lower manual; 9 = service; 10 = primary sector.

protecting occupational positions from intruders. This palisade bespeaks very substantial departures from equality of opportunity. For example, children born into the classical professions are, on average, 4.2 times more likely to remain in their microclass of origin than to move elsewhere within their meso-class, while the corresponding coefficients for children born into managerial, craft, and service occupations are 4.6, 7.9, and 5.6, respectively. Although the interior regions of the class structure are typically represented as zones of fluidity (e.g., Feather-erman and Hauser 1978), we find here substantial microclass reproduction throughout the class struc-ture, even among the "middle classes."

How do the microclass and big-class coefficients compare? Of the fourteen big-class coefficients, the two largest are for proprietors and primary-sector workers, but even these two are smaller than all but the very smallest microclass coefficients. It also bears noting that both of these big classes are big classes in name only. That is, because the proprietor class com-prises only shopkeepers, it is not the usual amalgam of many occupations, and there is accordingly good reason to regard proprietors as effectively a micro-

class. Likewise, the primary sector is not much of an amalgam, dominated as it is by farmers (see Table 37.2). The remaining twelve big-class effects, all of which pertain to true amalgams, are comparatively weak. The strongest of these effects, those for classi-cal professions, sales work, clerical work, and the manual-nonmanual strata, range in size from 1.3 to 1.4 (in multiplicative form).

Is Big-Class Reproduction a Myth?

The foregoing results raise the possibility that the big-class inheritance showing up in generations of mobility studies is largely microclass inheritance in disguise. Have conventional mobility studies in-deed created the false impression that big-class re-production is the dominant form of reproduction? We can address this question by examining whether the big-class effects that appear in conventional mobility analyses are much reduced in size when microclass effects are overlaid on them. It's useful to proceed by re-estimating our model after omitting the microclass inheritance terms. The relevant esti-mates from this trimmed model, which represents a

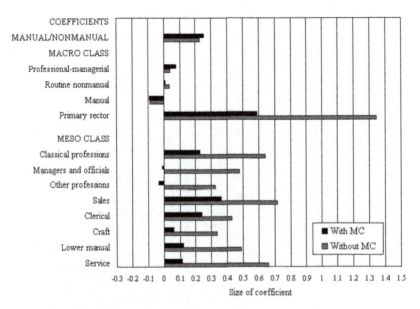

FIGURE 37.4 Immobility Coefficients With and Without Microclass Controls

Note: For convenience in presentation, the two primary-sector coeffi cients are each divided by two.

conventional big-class analysis, are shown in Figure 37.4.

We begin by noting that the mesoclass effects under this trimmed model are indeed strong and consistent with the effects secured in conventional mobility analyses. The coefficient for managers, for example, implies that children born into the managerial class are 1.62 times more likely to remain in that class than to exit it (i.e., $e^{.48} = 1.62$). The corresponding inheritance coefficients for craft workers, lower manual workers, and service workers are 1.40, 1.63, and 1.93, respectively. It is coefficients such as these, all of which are net of gradational effects, that have motivated generations of mobility scholars to regard big-class reproduction as a powerful force.

The results from our full model nonetheless imply that this conclusion is somewhat misleading. When microclass effects are allowed, some of the big-class effects are greatly reduced in strength (i.e., classical professions, sales, clerical), while others disappear altogether or become quite small (i.e., managers and officials, other professionals, craft workers, service workers, lower manual workers). It follows that conventional big-class analyses have generated the appearance of big-class reproduction because it is confounded with microclass reproduction. This is not to suggest that all big-class reproduction is just microclass reproduction in disguise. Clearly, some big-class reproduction persists even in the presence

of microclass controls, a result that was also revealed in Figure 37.3.

We may conclude on the basis of these results that the big-class reproduction appearing in conventional analyses is largely generated by the tendency for children to inherit their microclass. The practical implication of this result is that big-class reproduction may not be easily reduced without interventions that take on inheritance at the occupational level. We return to this issue in the concluding discussion.

Conclusion

The main intellectual backdrop to this analysis is the ongoing sociological debate about the types of social groupings that have taken hold in contemporary industrialism. Throughout much of the twentieth century, sociologists were fascinated, arguably obsessed, with theorizing about the conditions under which big classes might form, an understandable fascination insofar as individual life chances and even collective outcomes (e.g., revolutions) were believed to depend on class processes. At the same time, class analysts viewed occupations as mere technical positions in the division of labor (rather than meaningful social groups), while scholars in the occupations and professions of literature focused narrowly on individual occupations and how they developed under conditions of professionalization or proletarianization.

The occupational form was not understood within either of these traditions as a critical source of inequality and social reproduction (see Grusky 2005). At best, occupations were described as the "backbone" of the inequality system (e.g., Parkin 1971), but such a characterization served principally as an impetus for then reducing occupations to gradational scores (e.g., Hauser and Warren 1997; Ganzeboom, de Graaf, and Treiman 1992) or using them as aggregates in constructing big classes (e.g., Erikson and Goldthorpe 1992).

These characteristic representations of the form of mobility have been treated as assumptions rather than amenable to evidence. The main objective of our research has been to consider whether, when treated as empirical matters, these conventional representations of the structure of mobility are incomplete. We have found that occupations are an important conduit for reproduction and that incorporating this conduit into mobility models can improve our understanding of the mobility process.

There are two main ways in which conventional models misrepresent the structure of opportunity: (1) The most extreme pockets of rigidity are concealed when analysis is carried out exclusively at the big-class level, and (2) the main rigidities in the big-class mobility table have been taken as evidence of big-class reproduction when in fact occupational reproduction is the principal underlying mechanism. These results suggest that the big-class mobility table, long a fixture in the discipline, obscures important mechanisms behind intergenerational reproduction.

Why are occupations such an important conduit for social reproduction? In all countries, parents accumulate much occupation-specific capital, identify with their occupation, and accordingly "bring home" their occupation in ways, both direct and indirect, that then make it salient to their children and lead them to invest in it. It follows that children develop a taste for occupational reproduction, are trained by their parents in occupation-specific skills, have access to occupational networks that facilitate occupational reproduction, and use those skills and networks to acquire more occupation-specific training outside the home. If children are risk averse and oriented principally to avoiding downward mobility, the safest path to realizing this objective may well be to use their occupation-specific resources on behalf of occupational reproduction. Indeed, even in the absence of any intrinsic interest in occupational reproduction, children may still pursue it

because it is the best route to big-class reproduction (Erikson and Jonsson 1996). The son of an embalmer, for example, may not have any particular interest in becoming an embalmer but may decide it's foolhardy to fail to exploit the in-house training that is available to him.

It might be tempting to take the position that the extreme microclass inequalities uncovered here are not all that objectionable. Should we really care, for example, that the child of the truck driver has a special propensity to become a truck driver while the child of a gardener has a special propensity to become a gardener? Must we truly commit ourselves to equal access to truck driving and gardening? If pressed, we would argue that all ascriptive constraints on choice, even those pertaining to purely horizontal inequalities, are inconsistent with a commitment to an open society. By this logic, *all* types of origin-by-destination association are problematic because they imply that human choice has been circumscribed, a circumscription that is wholly determined by the accident of birth. We care, in other words, that the truck driver is fated to become a truck driver at birth because that amounts to a stripping away of choice, and most of us would embrace an open society in which choices are expanded, not stripped away. Although our illustrative nonchoice (i.e., being a truck driver versus being a gardener) may not have implications for total rewards (of the sort that are *consensually* valued), it is nonetheless a fateful nonchoice that determines the texture and content of a human life. It is this commitment to an open society, sometimes left quite implicit, that underlies the discipline's long-standing interest in monitoring marital homogamy, occupational sex segregation, and many other forms of ascription that are hybrids of vertical and horizontal processes.

It bears emphasizing, however, that such an argument need not be pursued in the present case, given that the horizontal inequalities uncovered here contribute directly to the perpetuation of vertical ones. That is, we should care about the immobility of truck drivers and gardeners not just because truck driving and gardening imply different styles of life (i.e., "horizontal" inequality), but also because microclass immobility of this sort is the principal mechanism ensuring that the working class reproduces itself. The results from our models make it clear that big-class reproduction arises largely because children frequently remain within their microclass of origin.

We are left with the conclusion that, insofar as microclass reproduction could be eliminated, real declines in big-class reproduction would be observed. It is troubling in this regard that microclass reproduction is deeply rooted in family dynamics and may require unacceptably intrusive policy to root it out. Although our results provide some insight, then, into why contemporary efforts to equalize opportunity have underperformed, they do not necessarily lead us to any wholesale rethinking of those efforts.

REFERENCES

Carlsson, G. 1958. *Social Mobility and Class Structure.* Lund: Gleerups.

Erikson, Robert, and John H. Goldthorpe. 1992. *The Constant Flux: A Study of Class Mobility in Industrial Societies.* Oxford: Clarendon Press.

Erikson, Robert, and Jan O. Jonsson. 1993. *Ursprung och utbildning.* SOU 1993:85. Stockholm: Fritzes.

———. 1996. "Explaining Class Inequality in Education: The Swedish Test Case." In *Can Education Be Equalized?* edited by Robert Erikson and Jan O. Jonsson, 1–64. Boulder: Westview.

Featherman, David L., and Robert M. Hauser. 1978. *Opportunity and Change.* New York: Academic Press.

Ganzeboom, Harry B. G., Paul de Graaf, and Donald J. Treiman. 1992. "A Standard International Socio-Economic Index of Occupational Status." *Social Science Research* 21: 1–56.

Glass, D. V. 1954. *Social Mobility in Britain.* London: Routledge and Kegan Paul.

Goldthorpe, John H. 2007. *On Sociology.* Stanford: Stanford University Press.

Grusky, David B. 2005. "Foundations of a Neo-Durkheimian Class Analysis." In *Approaches to Class Analysis,* edited by Erik Olin Wright, 51–81. Cambridge: Cambridge University Press.

Grusky, David B., Yoshimichi Sato, Jan O. Jonsson, Satoshi Miwa, Matthew Di Carlo, Reinhard Pollak, and Mary C. Brinton. 2008. "Social Mobility in Japan: A New Approach to Modeling Trend in Mobility." In *Intergenerational Mobility and Intragenerational Mobility,* edited by Tsutomu Watanabe, 3:1–25. Sendai, Japan: SSM Research Project Series.

Hauser, Robert M., and John R. Warren. 1997. "Socioeconomic Indexes for Occupations: A Review, Update, and Critique." *Sociological Methods* 27: 177–298.

Hout, Michael, and Robert M. Hauser. 1992. "Hierarchy and Symmetry in Occupational Mobility." *European Sociological Review* 8 (December): 239–266.

Jonsson, Jan O., David B. Grusky, Matthew Di Carlo, Reinhard Pollak, and Mary C. Brinton. 2009. "Micro-Class Mobility: Social Reproduction in Four Countries." *American Journal of Sociology* (January).

Jonsson, Jan O., David B. Grusky, Reinhard Pollak, and Matthew Di Carlo. 2011. "Occupations and Social Mobility: Gradational, Big Class, and Micro-Class Reproduction in Comparative Perspective." In *Persistence, Privilege, and Parenting,* edited by Robert Erikson, Markus Jannti, and Timothy Smeeding. New York: Russell Sage Foundation.

Parkin, Frank. 1971. *Class Inequality and Political Order: Social Stratification in Capitalist and Communist Societies.* New York: Praeger.

Svalastoga, Kaare. 1959. *Prestige, Class, and Mobility.* Copenhagen: Gyldendal.

Weeden, Kim A., and David B. Grusky. 2005. "The Case for a New Class Map." *American Journal of Sociology* 111: 141–212.

NOTES

1. We will often refer to occupations as "microclasses" because they have many of the features and characteristics that are often attributed to big classes.

Who Do You Know?

38. Mark S. Granovetter*
The Strength of Weak Ties

Most intuitive notions of the "strength" of an interpersonal tie should be satisfied by the following definition: the strength of a tie is a (probably linear) combination of the amount of time, the emotional intensity, the intimacy (mutual confiding), and the reciprocal services which characterize the tie. Each of these is somewhat independent of the other, though the set is obviously highly intracorrelated. Discussion of operational measures of and weights attaching to each of the four elements is postponed to future empirical studies. It is sufficient for the present purpose if most of us can agree, on a rough intuitive basis, whether a given tie is strong, weak, or absent.

Consider, now, any two arbitrarily selected individuals—call them A and B—and the set, $S = C, D, E, \ldots$, of all persons with ties to either *or* both of them. The hypothesis which enables us to relate dyadic ties to larger structures is: the stronger the tie between A and B, the larger the proportion of individuals in S to whom they will *both* be tied, that is, connected by a weak or strong tie. This overlap in their friendship circles is predicted to be least when their tie is absent, most when it is strong, and intermediate when it is weak.

The proposed relationship results, first, from the tendency (by definition) of stronger ties to involve larger time commitments. If A-B and A-C ties exist,

* Mark S. Granovetter. "The Strength of Weak Ties," *American Journal of Sociology* 78:6 (May 1973), pp. 1361–1366, 1371–1373, 1378–1380. Copyright © 1973 by The University of Chicago. Used by permission of the University of Chicago Press and the author. All rights reserved. As published in *Social Stratification: Class, Race, and Gender in Sociological Perspective*, 3rd edition, by David Grusky, copyright © 2009. Reprinted by permission of Westview Press, an imprint of Perseus Books, LLC, a subsidiary of Hachette Book Group, Inc.

then the amount of time C spends with B depends (in part) on the amount A spends with B and C, respectively. (If the events "A is with B" and "A is with C" were independent, then the event "C is with A and B" would have probability equal to the product of their probabilities. For example, if A and B are together 60% of the time, and A and C 40%, then C, A, and B would be together 24% of the time. Such independence would be less likely after than before B and C became acquainted.) If C and B have no relationship, common strong ties to A will probably bring them into interaction and generate one. Implicit here is Homans's idea that "the more frequently persons interact with one another, the stronger their sentiments of friendship for one another are apt to be" (1950, p. 133).

The hypothesis is made plausible also by empirical evidence that the stronger the tie connecting two individuals, the more similar they are in various ways (Berscheid and Walster 1969, pp. 69–91; Bramel 1969, pp. 9–16; Brown 1965, pp. 71–90; Laumann 1968; Newcomb 1961, chap. 5; Precker 1952). Thus, if strong ties connect A to B and A to C, both C and B, being similar to A, are probably similar to one another, increasing the likelihood of a friendship once they have met. Applied in reverse, these two factors—time and similarity—indicate why weaker A-B and A-C ties make a C-B tie less likely than strong ones: C and B are less likely to interact and less likely to be compatible if they do. . . .

To derive implications for large networks of relations, it is necessary to frame the basic hypothesis more precisely. This can be done by investigating the possible triads consisting of strong, weak, or absent ties among A, B, and any arbitrarily chosen friend of either or both (i.e., some member of the set S, described above). A thorough mathematical model would do this in some detail, suggesting probabilities for various types. This analysis becomes rather involved, however, and it is sufficient for my purpose in this paper to say that the triad which is most unlikely to occur, under the hypothesis stated above, is that in which *A* and *B* are strongly linked, *A* has a strong tie to some friend *C*, but the tie between *C* and *B* is absent. This triad is shown in Figure 38.1. To see the consequences of this assertion, I will exaggerate it in what follows by supposing that the triad shown never occurs—that is, that the *B–C* tie is always present (whether weak or strong), given the other two strong ties. Whatever results are inferred from this supposition should tend to occur in the degree that the triad in question tends to be absent.

Some evidence exists for this absence. Analyzing 651 sociograms, Davis (1970, p. 845) found that in 90% of the triads consisting of two mutual choices and one nonchoice occurred less than the expected random number of times. If we assume that mutual choice indicates a strong tie, this is strong evidence in the direction of my argument. Newcomb (1961, pp. 160–65) reports that in triads consisting of dyads expressing mutual "high attraction," the configuration of three strong ties became increasingly frequent as people knew one another longer and better; the frequency of the triad pictured in Figure 38.1 is not analyzed, but it is implied that processes of cognitive balance tended to eliminate it.

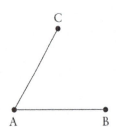

FIGURE 38.1 Forbidden Triad

The significance of this triad's absence can be shown by using the concept of a "bridge"; this is a line in a network which provides the *only* path between two points (Harary, Norman, and Cartwright 1965, p. 198). Since, in general, each person has a great many contacts, a bridge between *A* and *B* provides the only route along which information or influence can flow from any contact of *A* to any contact of *B*, and, consequently, from anyone connected *indirectly* to *A* to anyone connected indirectly to *B*. Thus, in the study of diffusion, we can expect bridges to assume an important role.

Now, if the stipulated triad is absent, it follows that, except under unlikely conditions, *no strong tie is a bridge.* Consider the strong tie *A–B*: if *A* has another strong tie to *C*, then forbidding the triad of

Figure 38.1 implies that a tie exists between *C* and *B*, so that the path *A–C–B* exists between *A* and *B*; hence, *A–B* is not a bridge. A strong tie can be a bridge, therefore, *only if* neither party to it has any *other* strong ties, unlikely in a social network of any size (though possible in a small group). Weak ties suffer no such restriction, though they are certainly not automatically bridges. What is important, rather, is that all bridges are weak ties.

In large networks, it probably happens only rarely, in practice, that a specific tie provides the *only* path between two points. The bridging function may nevertheless be served *locally*. In Figure 38.2a, for example, the tie *A–B* is not strictly a bridge, since one can construct the path *A–E–I–B* (and others). Yet, *A–B* *is* the shortest route to *B* for *F, D,* and *C*. This function is clearer in Figure 38.2b. Here, *A–B* is, for *C, D,* and others, not only a local bridge to *B*, but, in most real instances of diffusion, a much more likely and efficient path. Harary et al. point out that "there may be a distance [length of path] beyond which it is not feasible for *u* to communicate with *v* because of costs or distortions entailed in each act of transmission. If *v* does not lie within this critical distance, then he will not receive messages originating with *u*" (1965, p. 159). I will refer to a tie as a "local bridge of degree *n*" if *n* represents the shortest path between its two points (other than itself), and *n* > 2. In Figure 38.2a, *A–B* is a local bridge of degree 3, in 38.2b, of degree 13. As with bridges in a highway system, a local bridge in a social network will be more significant as a connection between two sectors to the extent that it is the only alternative for many people—that is, as its degree increases. A bridge in the absolute sense is a local one of infinite degree. By the same logic used above, only weak ties may be local bridges.

Suppose, now, that we adopt Davis's suggestion that "in interpersonal flows of most any sort the probability that 'whatever it is' will flow from person *i* to person *j* is (*a*) directly proportional to the number of all-positive (friendship) paths connecting *i* and *j*; and (*b*) inversely proportional to the length of such paths" (1969, p. 549). The significance of weak ties, then, would be that those which are local bridges create more, and shorter, paths. Any given tie may, hypothetically, be removed from a network; the number of paths broken and the changes in average path length resulting between arbitrary pairs of points (with some limitation on length of path considered) can then be computed. The contention here is that removal of the average weak tie would do

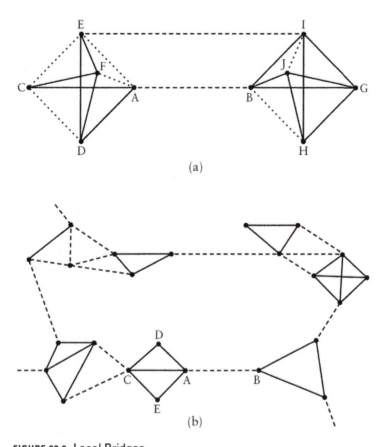

FIGURE 38.2 Local Bridges

(a) Degree 3; (b) Degree 13. Straight line = strong tie; dotted line = weak tie.

more "damage" to transmission probabilities than would that of the average strong one.

Intuitively speaking, this means that whatever is to be diffused can reach a larger number of people, and traverse greater social distance (i.e., path length), when passed through weak ties rather than strong. If one tells a rumor to all his close friends, and they do likewise, many will hear the rumor a second and third time, since those linked by strong ties tend to share friends. If the motivation to spread the rumor is dampened a bit on each wave of retelling, then the rumor moving through strong ties is much more likely to be limited to a few cliques than that going via weak ones; bridges will not be crossed. . . .

I will develop this point empirically by citing some results from a labor-market study I have recently completed. Labor economists have long been aware that American blue-collar workers find out about new jobs more through personal contacts than by any other method. (Many studies are reviewed by Parnes 1954, chap. 5.) Recent studies

suggest that this is also true for those in professional, technical, and managerial positions (Shapero, Howell, and Tombaugh 1965; Brown 1967; Granovetter 1970). My study of this question laid special emphasis on the nature of the *tie* between the job changer and the contact person who provided the necessary information.

In a random sample of recent professional, technical, and managerial job changers living in a Boston suburb, I asked those who found a new job through contacts how often they *saw* the contact around the time that he passed on job information to them. I will use this as a measure of tie strength. A natural a priori idea is that those with whom one has strong ties are more motivated to help with job information. Opposed to this greater motivation are the structural arguments I have been making: those to whom we are weakly tied are more likely to move in circles different from our own and will thus have access to information different from that which we receive.

I have used the following categories for frequency of contact: often—at least twice a week; occasionally—more than once a year but less than twice a week; rarely—once a year or less. Of those finding a job through contacts, 16.7% reported that they saw their contact often at the time, 55.6% said occasionally, and 27.8% rarely ($N = 54$). The skew is clearly to the weak end of the continuum, suggesting the primacy of structure over motivation.

In many cases, the contact was someone only marginally included in the current network of contacts, such as an old college friend or a former workmate or employer, with whom sporadic contact had been maintained (Granovetter 1970, pp. 76–80). Usually such ties had not even been very strong when first forged. For work-related ties, respondents almost invariably said that they never saw the person in a non-work context. Chance meetings or mutual friends operated to reactivate such ties. It is remarkable that people receive crucial information from individuals whose very existence they have forgotten. . . .

From the individual's point of view, then, weak ties are an important resource in making possible mobility opportunity. Seen from a more macroscopic vantage, weak ties play a role in effecting social cohesion. When a man changes jobs, he is not only moving from one network of ties to another, but also establishing a link between these. Such a link is often of the same kind which facilitated his own movement. Especially within professional and technical specialties which are well-defined and limited in size, this mobility sets up elaborate structures of bridging weak ties between the more coherent clusters that constitute operative networks in particular locations.

REFERENCES

Berscheid, E., and E. Walster. 1969. *Interpersonal Attraction.* Reading, Mass.: Addison-Wesley.

Bramel, D. 1969. "Interpersonal Attraction, Hostility and Perception." In *Experimental Social Psychology*, edited by Judson Mills. New York: Macmillan.

Brown, David. 1967. *The Mobile Professors.* Washington, D.C.: American Council on Education.

Brown, Roger. 1965. *Social Psychology.* New York: Free Press.

Davis, James A. 1969. "Social Structures and Cognitive Structures." In R. P. Abelson et al., *Theories of Cognitive Consistency.* Chicago: Rand McNally.

———. 1970. "Clustering and Hierarchy in Interpersonal Relations." *American Sociological Review* 35 (October): 843–52.

Granovetter, M. S. 1970. "Changing Jobs: Channels of Mobility Information in a Suburban Community." Doctoral dissertation, Harvard University.

Harary, F., R. Norman, and D. Cartwright. 1965. *Structural Models.* New York: Wiley.

Homans, George. 1950. *The Human Group.* New York: Harcourt, Brace & World.

Laumann, Edward. 1968. "Interlocking and Radial Friendship Networks: A Cross-sectional Analysis." *Mimeographed.* Ann Arbor: University of Michigan.

Newcomb, T. M. 1961. *The Acquaintance Process.* New York: Holt, Rinehart & Winston.

Parnes, Herbert. 1954. *Research on Labor Mobility.* New York: Social Science Research Council.

Precker, Joseph. 1952. "Similarity of Valuings as a Factor in Selection of Peers and Near-Authority Figures." *Journal of Abnormal and Social Psychology* 47, suppl. (April): 406–14.

Shapero, Albert, Richard Howell, and James Tombaugh. 1965. *The Structure and Dynamics of the Defense R & D Industry.* Menlo Park, Calif.: Stanford Research Institute.

39. Roberto M. Fernandez and Isabel Fernandez-Mateo*
Networks, Race, and Hiring

It is common for scholars interested in race and poverty to invoke a lack of access to job networks as a reason why minorities face difficulties in the labor market (e.g., Royster 2003; Wilson 1996). Previous studies on this issue, however, have produced mixed results. Minorities have been found to be *more* likely to have obtained their job through networks than nonminorities (e.g., Elliott 1999). Yet, these jobs pay *less* than jobs obtained by other means (e.g., Falcon 1995). Rather than exclusion from white networks (e.g., Royster 2003), the emphasis in the literature has shifted to minorities' over-reliance on ethnic networks. Thus, the imagery that emerges from these

*The ideas, issues, and theories considered in this brief article are examined in greater depth in the following publication: Roberto M. Fernandez and Isabel Fernandez-Mateo, "Networks, Race, and Hiring," *American Sociological Review* 71 (2006), pp. 42–71. The article as printed here was originally prepared by Roberto M. Fernandez and Isabel Fernandez-Mateo in *Social Stratification: Class, Race, and Gender in Sociological Perspective*, 3rd Edition by David B. Grusky, pp. 587–595. Copyright © 2009. Reprinted by permission of Westview Press, an imprint of Perseus Books, LLC, a subsidiary of Hachette Book Group, Inc.

studies is that minorities are stuck in the "wrong networks," that is, those that lead to low-wage jobs.

There is something slippery about the way these network arguments are currently being used, however. Because "wrong network" is defined in terms of the eventual outcome (a network is "good" if it leads to a good outcome, otherwise, it is a "wrong network"), such explanations run the danger of circular reasoning. To give network accounts of minority underperformance analytical bite, we need to specify the mechanisms by which minorities are "excluded" from productive networks or "stuck" in unproductive ethnic networks.

We argue that being "stuck" in the "wrong network" can be produced by minority underrepresentation in *any* of a number of steps in the recruitment and hiring process. Using unique data from one employer, we illustrate the mechanisms by which minorities can be isolated from good job opportunities. To avoid circular reasoning, we form proper baselines of comparison using data on both networked and nonnetworked minorities and nonminorities at each stage of the hiring pipeline and identify the specific points in the process where network factors could lead minorities to have less access to these desirable jobs than nonminorities.

Race and Networks in the Labor Market

A common argument in sociology is that jobs found through networks pay better and are of higher status than those found through formal channels (Lin 2002). Evidence on this issue, however, is mixed, especially for minority groups. Reingold (1999) suggests that social networks lead to racial insularity and contribute to the economic marginalization of minorities. However, since many of these studies analyze samples of job incumbents, they often suffer from causal ambiguity (do ties to higher status people cause superior labor market outcomes, or is it that people with superior labor market outcomes gain access to high-status people?). In order to avoid the causal ambiguity problem, a number of studies use samples of job seekers and examine the chances of obtaining employment for various search methods (e.g., Elliott 1999). Employer surveys (e.g., Holzer 1996) are an alternative way of studying this issue, by fleshing out the employer side of the hiring process.

Neither of these approaches, however, examines actual hiring processes and their role in social

isolation from good jobs. Without baseline information on the presence or absence of social ties for the pool of competing applicants, some of whom are hired and others are not, it is impossible to identify the effect of social contacts on hiring per se. In order to address this issue, some authors have used single-firm screening studies (e.g., Fernandez, Castilla, and Moore 2000; Fernandez and Sosa 2005), but most of this research has not analyzed the role of race in hiring due to lack of appropriate data (a prominent exception is Petersen, Saporta, and Seidel 2000).

"Wrong Networks"

A key component of understanding whether minorities are cut off from employment opportunities is to understand why they may be underrepresented in networks that lead to *good* jobs. That is, in order to attribute logically the exclusion of minorities to the absence of network ties to good jobs, we would need to feel confident that minorities might plausibly have been hired except for the lack of the contact. It is critical to define the various processes whereby network factors could limit minorities' access to desirable jobs. In our conceptualization, the "wrong network" account is consistent with underrepresentation of minorities in any of a number of stages in the recruitment and hiring process. Figure 39.1 represents a conceptual map of the ways in which networks might affect the various stages. These are separated into two sets of processes: referring and screening.

The referral process may contribute to minorities' isolation either if there are no minority employees available to refer in the pool of workers (as in Kasinitz and Rosenberg's [1996] account), or if these employees are reluctant to pass on information about good jobs (see Smith 2005). Even if there are potential referrers who are willing to refer someone, minorities could still be cut off if these referrers were not to refer minority applicants (step 1c.). This could happen if job referral networks are less than perfectly homophilous by race (see Rubineau and Fernandez 2005). If all these conditions are met (steps 1a.–1c.), there will be a set of networked minority candidates in the applicant pool. At this point the screening stage on the demand side of the hiring interface begins.

The effect of screening processes on minorities' access to desirable jobs depends on the employer's attitude towards referrals. If firms prefer to recruit

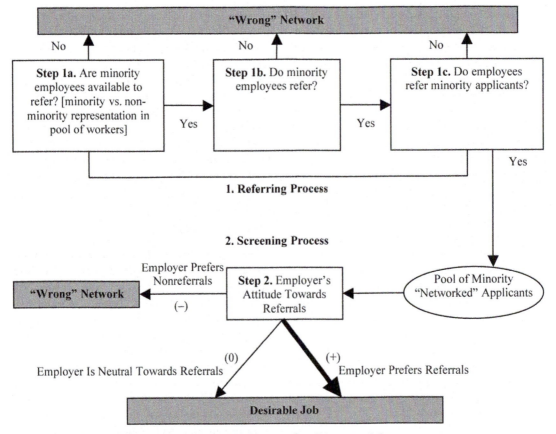

FIGURE 39.1 Steps in Network Processes that Connect Candidates to Jobs

employee referrals (Fernandez, Castilla, and Moore 2000), they will tend to hire minority workers in proportion to their representation in the *networked* pool of applicants. In this case, minorities would thus be cut off from good jobs only if they are underrepresented in the networked applicant pool. However, if employers avoid hiring through networks (see Ullman 1966), being well-represented in the pool of referred applicants is bad news for minorities. Finally, if the employer is neutral toward hiring referrals, access to desirable jobs for minorities will be provided in step 2 (screening) in proportion to the *overall applicant pool*, as opposed to the networked applicant pool. In such case the employers' preferences would have no effect in cutting off minorities from desirable jobs.

Analyses

We illustrate these processes using unique data on employees working at one company site and trace their networks of job contacts to applicants for desirable entry-level jobs. Minorities account for 50 percent of employees at this site, with Asian Americans and Hispanics being the largest groups. We collected all 2,065 paper applications to the plant's entry-level production jobs from September 1997 to November 30, 2000. We coded data on applicants' education, work history, and other human capital characteristics and geocoded candidates to the addresses they listed on the application form. Most importantly, and unusually, we have data on the applicants' race. All applicants must turn in their form in person, and when they do so, the receptionist at the company (who is the same one for the whole period) records the applicant's apparent race and gender. Race is thus not self-identified as in most surveys and is well-suited to our purposes of understanding the role of race in the screening process.

As mentioned above, in order to ensure that we are not misattributing the effect of networks to the effect of human capital factors, we must show that the candidates for these jobs might plausibly have been hired even without network ties. In this setting, it is clear that these entry-level jobs are within reach for people with modest education and labor force experience. The median years of education and experience for the people hired into these jobs are 12 and 7.9, respectively. Moreover, the local labor market was experiencing high rates of unemployment during the period (between 6.76 and 14.1 percent). Data from the local labor market (see Table 39.1) show that the wages offered by the firm were attractive—particularly for females and minorities. Starting wages were $7.75/hour for the first eight months of the study, and $8.05 afterwards. These wages fell in the 25th and 27th percentiles of the overall wage distribution for males in the area (35th and 36th percentiles for females). For whites, these starting wages fell in the 18th and 19th percentiles of the male wage distribution, while they were more attractive for minority males (27th and 28th percentiles for African Americans; 35th and 36th for Hispanics; 32nd and 35th for Asian Americans). The pattern is similar for females, although for them the wages are even more attractive than for males in every case. Furthermore, most hires receive pay raises after a 90-day probation period (to $8.50, $10.05, or $10.35), which makes wages even more attractive. In fact, the top wage approaches the median of the wage distribution for white and African American women in the area and well exceeds the median for Hispanic and Asian American females.

Are Minority Employees Available to Refer?

In order to study the role of job-referral networks in the application process, we distinguish networked candidates using data from the original application forms. Employee referrals made up 30.2 percent of the applications for which we could identify recruitment source (2,556 out of 2,605). Using the company's employee database, we have been able to link referrers with their referral for 83.7 percent of the "employee referral" applications. For studying who among company employees produces referrals, we use the firm's personnel records. Five hundred fifty-seven workers were employed at the focal plant at any point over the study period, and for these we coded their self-identified race and gender.

We address step 1a in Figure 39.1 by studying the race and gender distribution of employees who could have produced referral applications during the period. For both genders, over half the workers are minorities (this percentage increases to over 60 percent for entry-level employees). Relatively large percentages of Asian Americans and Hispanics, but more modest percentages of African Americans, are represented. Women make up 69.4 percent of entry-level workers, and they are overrepresented irrespective of race.

We also compare these race and gender distributions of workers with the composition of persons employed in the local area (Table 39.2). We find that white workers are underrepresented in this factory compared to their proportion in the area. Asian Americans, however, are extremely overrepresented. While they make up 6.1 percent of employed males in the local labor market, they account for 26.8 percent of male employees. Hispanics are slightly underrepresented (24.9 percent of employees, 35.3 percent in the area), while the percentages of African Americans employed at the factory are quite similar to their proportion in the area (5.9 versus 4.0 percent for males). In sum, minorities are definitely available to refer in this setting.

Do Minority Employees Refer?

Of the 557 employees, 200 of them originated a total of 580 applications. Asian Americans refer the most (50.9 percent of male Asian Americans originated at least one referral applicant). Interestingly, whites show the lowest rates of producing referrals (27.7 percent for females and 18.8 percent for males). To determine whether background factors might account for the observed race differences in referral behavior, we estimate a set of negative binomial regressions (see Fernandez and Fernandez-Mateo 2006, Table 5). These models show that there are no significant gender differences in the counts of referrals originated by employees at the company. There are race differences, however, as minorities generate more referrals than whites (with Asian Americans producing the most). These effects remain even when adding the extensive controls for individual background mentioned above. Thus, at step 1b in Figure 39.1, we have no evidence that minorities are less likely than whites to produce referral applicants.

TABLE 39.1 Percentile Ranks of Company Offered Wages in Wage Distribution of All Non-College Population in Local Metro Area by Racial Group

	All Racial Groups		Non-Hispanic White		African American	
	Male	*Female*	*Male*	*Female*	*Male*	*Female*
Starting Wages (N = 192)						
Hired 9/97–4/98						
8.3% ($7.75)	25	35	18	30	27	37
Hired 5/98–11/00						
91.7% ($8.05)	27	36	19	31	28	38
Wages after 90-Day Probation (N = 109)						
15.6% ($8.05)	27	36	19	31	28	38
62.4% ($8.50)	29	40	21	34	32	41
21.1% ($10.05)	37	51	27	45	40	48
0.1% ($10.35)	38	52	28	46	41	48
	Hispanic		Asian American		All Minorities	
	Male	*Female*	*Male*	*Female*	*Male*	*Female*
Starting Wages (N = 192)						
Hired 9/97–4/98						
8.3% ($7.75)	35	43	32	39	33	41
Hired 5/98–11/00						
91.7% ($8.05)	36	44	35	41	35	42
Wages after 90-Day Probation (N = 109)						
15.6% ($8.05)	36	44	35	41	35	42
62.4% ($8.50)	39	49	37	45	37	46
21.1% ($10.05)	49	61	43	55	46	58
0.1% ($10.35)	50	62	45	57	48	59

Source: Persons in the U.S. Census Bureau's 5 percent 2000 Public Use Micro Sample for the local metro area who are at least 15 years of age and have fewer than 16 years of education with positive wage and salary income in 1999. Data are weighted to reflect the population.

Do Minority Employees Refer Minority Applicants?

The simplest criterion to assess if this is a point of disconnection for minorities is whether there are any minorities at all produced by the referral process, irrespective of the race of the referrer. We analyze the race distribution of applicants produced by referrers of different racial backgrounds. We find that there is a strong relationship between the race of the referrer and the race of the referral applicant (for both genders). Most importantly, 61.8 percent of male and 57.2 percent of female referred applicants are minorities. Clearly, by this first criterion, minorities are not cut off at step 1c.

A more stringent criterion would be to assess whether the referral process is reproducing the racial distribution of the referring population (the 200 employees identified above). We find that whites are the most insular of the groups in referring (76.9 percent

of the referrals produced by white employees are white). The percentage of African Americans and Asian Americans in the referral pool matches the percentage of the referring population quite closely (5.6 vs. 4.0 percent for African Americans; 34.6 vs. 32.5 percent for Asian Americans). Hispanics, however, constitute a third of referrers, but only 19 percent of referrals. Hispanics, therefore, seem to be somehow cut off, in relative terms, from the networks leading to these jobs.

A final criterion depends on whether minorities refer minority applicants less than they refer white applicants. We find, however, that irrespective of which minority group one considers, the percentage referring whites is lower than the percentage referring minorities. By this final criterion, we find no evidence that a lack of racial homophily in minorities' referring patterns is weakening their access to this company. In sum, there is little evidence that

TABLE 39.2 Racial and Gender Distributions of Workers Employed During Hiring Window (September 1997–November 2000), and Persons Employed in the Metropolitan Area

	All Plant Employees[1]		Entry Level Employees Only		2000 PUMS[2]	
	Female	*Male*	*Female*	*Male*	*Female*	*Male*
Non-Hispanic White	44.0	41.5	38.5	28.6	54.3	50.4
African American	3.1	5.9	3.1	5.6	5.0	4.0
Hispanic	28.7	24.9	30.1	28.6	29.8	35.3
Asian American	23.3	26.8	27.6	35.7	6.5	6.1
Native American	0.9	1.0	0.7	1.6	0.9	0.7
Other, Multirace	—	—	—	—	—	—
Total	100.0	100.0	100.0	100.0	100.0	100.0
Total N	352	205	286	126	174838	208174

1. Each person is counted equally if they were employed at any time during the hiring window (September 1, 1997–November 30, 2000).

2. Persons in the 5 percent 2000 PUMS who are at least 15 years of age and less than 16 years of education with positive wage and salary income in 1999. Data are weighted to reflect the population.

minorities in this setting are cut off from the job networks that lead to employment at this company due to the behavior of the originators of referral networks (the "referring" process).

Hiring Interface

Even if networked minorities are well-represented in the application pool, this does not necessarily mean that they will be similarly represented at subsequent stages of the screening process. This step depends on the employer's racial biases and attitudes towards referrals ("screening process" in Figure 39.1). Our fieldwork and interviews with HR managers at this site suggest that the employer has neither a strong preference nor distaste for referred applicants. We assembled data on all applicants for entry-level jobs and tracked their progress through the hiring pipeline (from application, to interview, to offer, to hire).

For females (see Figure 39.2a), there is little evidence of a preference for networked candidates (33.9 percent of female applicants and 35.3 percent of female hires were referrals). Also, the race distribution did not change much across stages. Similarly for males (Figure 39.2b), the percentage of networked applicants does not increase across the various stages of the screening process. If anything, it decreases (networked candidates constitute 35.3 percent of the overall male applicant pool and 28.6 percent of hires).

We also performed multivariate (probit) analyses of who is hired versus not hired in order to introduce controls into the analysis. For female applicants, both recruitment source and race do not significantly influence the probability of hire. This does not change

when human capital and controls are added to the model (although some of these controls such as "years of experience" are significant). There is thus no evidence of a preference for networked candidates among females, and the race distribution of hires is not different from the distribution of applicants. For males, the results show that all minority racial groups are more likely to be hired than whites—irrespective of whether the person was a referral or not. The only significant pattern is that Asian American nonnetworked males are 8.5 percent more prevalent among hires than among applicants, even after everything else is controlled for.

In sum, the regression results show that there is little evidence of an employer's preference either for, or against, candidates who were referred to the company at the hiring interface. The one exception is the case of Asian American males, where nonnetworked candidates are more likely to be hired compared with networked applicants. We can only speculate whether this reflects a conscious effort to limit the number of Asian Americans—who are overrepresented in the application pool relative to the population in the local labor market. The hiring interface is thus a point of disconnection for Asian American males (i.e., the arrow labeled "(–)" in step 2 of Figure 39.1), but this employer is otherwise neutral with respect to networked candidates (i.e., the arrow labeled "0" in step 2 of Figure 39.1).

Summary and Conclusion

This paper makes a number of theoretical contributions to the study of racial inequality and networks.

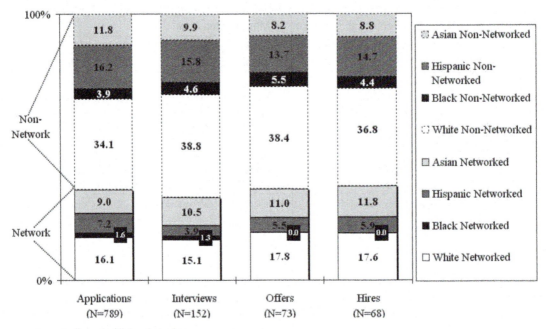

FIGURE 39.2A Female Hiring Interface

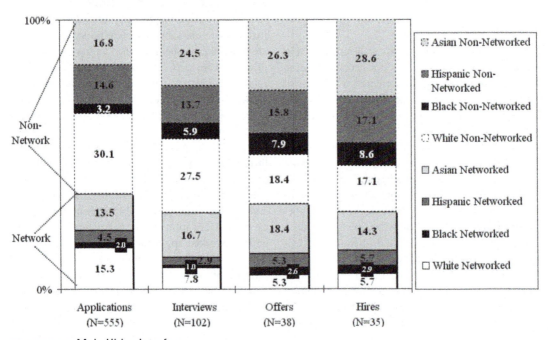

FIGURE 39.2B Male Hiring Interface

First, it contributes to specifying the mechanisms operating in network accounts of racial inequality in the labor market. Past accounts in this area often run the danger of circular reasoning because "wrong network" is defined in terms of the eventual outcome. We argue that much more analytical precision is needed to specify what it means to be "stuck" in the "wrong network," as these stories are consistent with minority underrepresentation in *any* of a number of steps in the recruitment and hiring process. Indeed, this study is the first to analyze comprehensively the racial implications of *both* the referring process and the screening mechanisms at the point of hire. We found that network factors operate at several stages of the recruitment process, but we found scant evidence that these factors serve to cut off minorities from employment at this company.

This study also has significant implications for policy. Since policies are often designed to target distinct steps in the recruitment process (National Research Council 2004), understanding each of these steps is crucial for crafting effective policy interventions. Affirmative action, for example, is focused on affecting the behavior of labor market screeners (Reskin 1998). Assessing the effect of these policies will be very difficult without data on both hires and non-hires. Other policy prescriptions recommend that companies open up their recruitment practices by broad advertising and use of formal recruitment systems, on the theory that informal, referral-based recruitment is inherently exclusionary (LoPresto 1986). The results presented here, however, suggest that this heuristic is too simple. Relying on referrals can help reproduce the distribution of the referring population. Therefore, in settings where the current workforce is racially diverse—as is the case in this setting—the referral processes can actually help *perpetuate* diversity (see Rubineau and Fernandez 2005).

Although the "wrong network" account does not fit the facts in this setting, this is not to say that in another, less diverse setting, where referrals may be preferred by screeners, the empirical results would not be markedly different. While we can make no claims of empirical generalizability, however, this study has important methodological implications. Its value is apparent in the light it sheds on mechanisms that are normally hidden from view. We suggest that the fine-grained processes that we have uncovered here need to be addressed to render the "wrong network" hypothesis testable in other settings. Moreover, it is important to realize that the race and network effects that are often reported in analyses of highly aggregated survey data are likely conflating the effects of the multiple mechanisms that we have delineated. Distinguishing among these steps should be a high priority in future research at the intersection of networks and race in the labor market.

REFERENCES

Elliott, James R. 1999. "Social Isolation and Labor Market Insulation: Network and Neighborhood Effects on Less-Educated Urban Workers." *Sociological Quarterly* 40: 199–216.

Falcon, Luis M. 1995. "Social Networks and Employment for Latinos, Blacks, and Whites." *New England Journal of Public Policy* 11: 17–28.

Fernandez, Roberto M., Emilio J. Castilla, and Paul Moore. 2000. "Social Capital at Work: Networks and Employment at a Phone Center." *American Journal of Sociology* 105: 1288–1356.

Fernandez, Roberto M., and Isabel Fernandez-Mateo. 2006. "Networks, Race and Hiring." *American Sociological Review* 71: 42–71.

Fernandez, Roberto M., and M. Lourdes Sosa. 2005. "Gendering the Job: Networks and Recruitment at a Call Center." *American Journal of Sociology* 111: 859–904.

Holzer, Harry J. 1996. *What Employers Want: Job Prospects for Less-Educated Workers*. New York: Russell Sage Foundation.

Kasinitz, Philip, and Jan Rosenberg. 1996. "Missing the Connection: Social Isolation and Employment on the Brooklyn Waterfront." *Social Problems* 43: 180–93.

Lin, Nan. 2002. *Social Capital: A Theory of Social Structure and Action*. New York: Cambridge University Press.

LoPresto, Robert. 1986. "Recruitment Sources and Techniques." Pp. 13-1 to 13-26 in *Handbook of Human Resource Administration*, 2nd ed., edited by J. J. Famularo. New York: McGraw-Hill.

National Research Council. 2004. *Measuring Racial Discrimination. Panel on Methods for Assessing Discrimination*, edited by Rebecca M. Blank, Marilyn Dabady, and Constance F. Citro. *Committee on National Statistics, Division of Behavioral and Social Sciences and Education*. Washington, DC: National Academies Press.

Petersen, Trond, Ishak Saporta, and Marc-David Seidel. 2000. "Offering a Job: Meritocracy and Social Networks." *American Journal of Sociology* 106: 763–816.

Reingold, David A. 1999. "Social Networks and the Employment Problem of the Urban Poor." *Urban Studies* 36: 1907–32.

Reskin, Barbara F. 1998. *The Realities of Affirmative Action*. Washington, DC: American Sociological Association.

Royster, Deirdre A. 2003. *Race and the Invisible Hand: How White Networks Exclude Black Men from Blue-Collar Jobs*. Berkeley: University of California Press.

Rubineau, Brian, and Roberto M. Fernandez. 2005. "Missing Links: Referral Processes and Job Segregation." MIT Sloan School of Management, Massachusetts Institute of Technology, Cambridge, MA. Unpublished manuscript.

Smith, Sandra. 2005. "'Don't Put My Name on It': Social Capital Activation and Job-Finding Assistance Among the Black Urban Poor." *American Journal of Sociology* 111: 1–57.

Ullman, Joseph C. 1966. "Employee Referrals: A Prime Tool for Recruiting Workers." *Personnel* 43: 30–35.

Wilson, William Julius. 1996. *When Work Disappears: The World of the New Urban Poor*. New York: Alfred A. Knopf.

Work and Mobility

40. Jacob Hacker*
The Great Risk Shift

Economic risk is a lot like a hurricane. Hurricanes strike powerfully and suddenly. They rip apart what they touch: property, landscape, and lives. They are common enough to affect many, yet rare enough still to shock. And although they can be prepared for, they cannot be prevented. Some people will inevitably suffer and require help; others will be spared. Recovery is inevitably traumatic and slow. And so it is with families whose lives have been touched by economic risk. What happens in an instant may change a life forever.

The comparison is not just metaphorical: For more than half a century, Americans responded to economic risk as if it were a natural disaster largely beyond the control or responsibility of those it struck. In the wake of the Great Depression in the 1930s, which left a "third of the nation," in FDR's famous telling, "ill-housed, ill-clad, ill-nourished," political and business leaders put in place new institutions designed to spread broadly the burden of key economic risks, including the risk of poverty in retirement, the risk of unemployment and disability, and the risk of widowhood due to the premature death of a breadwinner. These public and private institutions did not let the individual off the hook; they required contributions and work and proof of eligibility. But they were based on an ideal known as "social insurance"—the notion that certain risks can be effectively dealt with only through institutions that spread their costs across rich and poor, healthy and sick, able-bodied and disabled, young and old.

Today, however, the social fabric that bound us together in good times and bad is unraveling. Over

the last generation, we have witnessed a massive transfer of economic risk from broad structures of insurance, including those sponsored by the corporate sector as well as by government, onto the fragile balance sheets of American families. This transformation, which I call the "Great Risk Shift," is the defining feature of the contemporary American economy—as important as the shift from agriculture to industry a century ago. It has fundamentally reshaped Americans' relationships to their government, their employers, and each other. . . .

One crucial point must be understood from the start: This dramatic transformation isn't a natural occurrence—a financial hurricane beyond human control. Sweeping changes in the global and domestic economy have helped propel it, but America's corporate and political leaders could have responded to these powerful forces by reinforcing the floodwalls that protect families from economic risk. Instead, in the name of personal responsibility, many of these leaders are busy tearing the floodwalls down. Proponents of these changes speak of a nirvana of individual economic management—a society of empowered "owners," in which Americans are free to choose. What these advocates are helping to create, however, is very different: a harsh new world of economic insecurity, in which far too many Americans are free to lose.

Economic insecurity isn't just a problem of the poor and uneducated, as most of us assume. Increasingly, it affects . . . educated, upper-middle-class Americans—men and women who thought that by staying in school, by buying a home, by investing in their 401(k)s, they had bought the ticket to upward mobility and economic stability. Insecurity today reaches across the income spectrum, across the racial divide, across lines of geography and gender. It speaks to the common "us" rather than to the insular, marginalized "them."

To understand the change, we must first understand what is changing. America's distinctive framework of economic protection grew out of specific

*THE GREAT RISK SHIFT by Jacob Hacker (2006): 1,403 words (from pp. 1–9). © 2006 by Jacob Hacker. By permission of Oxford University Press USA.

political struggles and a unique set of values and beliefs. Less expansive than some hoped and more expansive than others desired, it was a curious and sometimes contradictory amalgam of goals and institutions. By the early 1970s, it worked tolerably well in insulating most middle-class Americans from the major financial risks of a dynamic capitalist economy. Today, however, it is falling apart under the weight of political attack and economic change . . . .

It is common to say that the United States does little to provide economic security compared with other rich capitalist democracies. Whether because of a deeply embedded mistrust of government, a constitutional structure that makes big policy reforms hard to achieve, the weakness of the American labor movement, or the depth of American ethnic divisions, the United States has provided infertile soil for the comprehensive welfare states that now dominate the economic landscape of most affluent countries. This is true, but it is only half the story. The United States does spend less on government benefits as a share of its economy, but it also relies more—far more—on private workplace benefits, such as health care and retirement pensions. Indeed, when these private benefits are factored into the mix, the U.S. framework of economic security is not smaller than the average system in other rich democracies; it is actually slightly larger. With the help of hundreds of billions in tax breaks, American employers serve as the United States' unique mini-welfare states—the first line of defense for millions of workers buffeted by the winds of economic change.

The problem is that these mini-welfare states are coming undone, and in the process, risk is shifting back onto workers and their families. Employers want out of the social contract that forged the more stable economy of the past. And because they do not need to answer to the broader public, employers are getting what they want. . . .

As private and public support erodes, workers and their families must bear a greater burden. This is the essence of the Great Risk Shift. Through the cutback and restructuring of workplace benefits, employers are seeking to offload more and more of the risk once pooled under their auspices. Facing fiscal constraints and political opposition, public social programs have eroded even as the demands on them have risen. And if critics have their way, these programs will erode even further. The next frontier in the Great Risk Shift is the transformation of existing

programs—Social Security chief among them—from guaranteed benefits defined by law to individualized private accounts that leave workers and families shouldering more and more of the risks that these programs once covered.

The Great Risk Shift might be less worrisome if work and family were stable sources of security themselves. Unfortunately, they are not. Beneath the rosy economic talk, the job market has grown markedly more uncertain and unstable, especially for those who were once best protected from its vagaries. The family, once a refuge from economic risk, is creating new risks of its own. With families needing two earners to maintain a middle-class standard of living, families' economic calculus has changed in ways that accentuate many of the risks they face. At the same time, families are making greater, and more risky, investments in their futures—in buying a home, in gaining new skills, in raising well-educated children—and they are paying the price when those investments fail. . . .

One of its overarching causes [is] what I call "The Personal Responsibility Crusade"— a political drive to shift a growing amount of economic risk from government and the corporate sector onto ordinary Americans in the name of enhanced individual responsibility and control. Thanks in part to this crusade, even middle-class families are facing greater insecurity in the workplace, in the balancing of work and family, in planning for retirement, and in obtaining and paying for health care. . . .

Work, family, and public and private benefits have all grown more risky at roughly the same time, which is one reason why the weakening of these traditional sources of security has proved so sweeping and so difficult to address. . . . These deep and worsening problems call for bold solutions. What we need are new ways of allowing families to save and insure against some of the most potent risks to their income, coupled with new ideas for revitalizing American social insurance and providing economic opportunity to all. An "insurance and opportunity society" would emphasize work and responsibility, but it would also provide real protection when families fall from the ladder of economic advancement, encouraging families to look to the future rather than fear the present. The old canard that ensuring security always hurts the economy turns out to be cruelly false. Economic security is vital to economic opportunity, and economic insecurity is one of the greatest barriers between American families and the American Dream.

41. Jake Rosenfeld*

Little Labor: How Union Decline Is Changing the American Landscape

A recent *Wall Street Journal* editorial decrying the role of Big Labor in shaping the Obama administration's domestic policy expressed worry that unions' outsize clout would force higher taxes on investment income. Such articles are typical fare for a newspaper long critical of the labor movement's role in American life. But what's strange is the continued use of "Big Labor" as a shorthand moniker for trade unions in the contemporary United States. If organized labor remains big today, then back in its post–World War II peak, it was positively enormous. Fully one-third of the private sector workforce belonged to a labor union during the 1950s, and millions more resided in households reliant on a union wage. During the heyday of collective bargaining in this country, unions helped pattern pay and benefit packages among nonunion workers, as employers matched union contracts to forestall organizing drives and maintain a competitive workforce. Politicians, Democrats especially, depended on organized labor's support during elections and consulted closely with labor leaders when devising policy in office. Big Labor, then, was once quite big indeed.

The only thing that remains big about labor unions today is their problems. Figure 41.1 tracks unionization rates for private and public sector workers between 1973 and 2009. By the early 1970s, organized labor had already begun its decades-long decline, but still nearly a quarter of all private-sector employees belonged to a labor union at this time. The late 1970s and 1980s proved especially brutal for organized labor, with unionization rates halving during the period. The nation's intellectuals and journalists covered this phenomenon extensively, linking union decline to a new post-industrial economy increasingly open to global trade. Recent trends have garnered less attention, yet private-sector unionization rates *nearly halved again* between 1990 and 2009. The story for public sector unions has been a bit brighter. Rates of organization among government workers increased steadily

during the 1970s, settling at slightly over one-third of all public sector workers, where they have remained relatively consistent up to the present. Three decades of stasis in public-sector organization rates suggests that the earlier expansion may have reached its limit. And over four-fifths of the US workforce is employed in the private sector. Moreover, recent research has demonstrated that the benefits of union membership are much smaller in the public sector, due to the relative transparency and standardization that govern many public-sector contracts. Organized labor, then, is disappearing in the sector where historically it has had the greatest impact on people's livelihoods.

But even less understood than the overall decline in unions' *prevalence* is the concomitant decline in unions' *activity*. Academics have long debated whether high levels of unionization are a net good when it comes to global competitiveness or overall economic performance. But fewer dispute that unions have been a historically positive force in bolstering the economic prospects of union members themselves. Unions bolster workers' clout in confrontations with employers, historically winning them higher wages, better benefits, and greater workplace protections than might be offered otherwise. Strikes represent unions' most potent weapon in confrontations with employers, and this weapon used to be a regular feature of America's industrial landscape, affecting millions of workers each year. But this has changed. Figure 41.2 presents two series: the first shows the number of large strikes (involving 1,000 or more workers) over the last forty-five years. The number of strikes involving 1,000 or more workers peaked at over 400 in 1974. In 2009, there were five. While the sheer precipitousness of this decline is staggering, we know that strikes of such magnitude are often unrepresentative of more typical work stoppages. But to date, no public data has been available to document strikes of all sizes in recent decades. Because of this, I filed a Freedom of Information Act (FOIA) request to obtain information on all strikes for the years in which data were collected. Figure 41.2 presents this data, and the trend mirrors what's been happening with large strikes. As late as the mid-1980s, nearly 1,000 walkouts occurred in a single year. By the dawn of the 21st century, that number had fallen to just over 200, a decline of nearly 80 percent in less than 20 years. What we've seen, then, is a rise in what might be called "union dormancy," whereby

* Rosenfeld, Jake. "Little Labor: How Union Decline Is Changing the American Landscape," *Pathways* (Summer 2010), pp. 3–6. Used by permission of the Center on Poverty and Inequality, Stanford University.

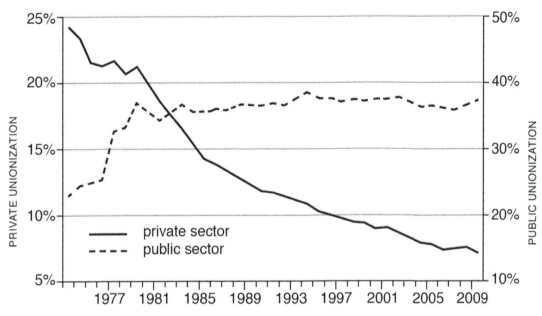

FIGURE 41.1 Unionization Rates by Sector, 1973–2009

Data are provided by Barry T. Hirsch and David A. McPherson's www.unionstats.com database (2010), and are based on Current Population Survey (CPS) data. Unionization data for 1982 are unavailable; I generate 1982 estimates by averaging 1981 and 1983 rates.

unions are no longer routinely agitating on behalf of their membership, at least not in the traditional form of the labor strike.

So what happened to Big Labor? Organized labor's penetration was especially deep in core manufacturing industries. The transformation to a post-industrial economy hit union workers in these industries hard, as jobs became increasingly vulnerable to outsourcing, deskilling, and technological innovations rendering many positions redundant. The process accelerated throughout the 1970s and 1980s, as traditionally protected industries, like auto manufacturing, opened up to competition from abroad, pushing domestic manufacturers to search for less labor-friendly jurisdictions. Yet private sector deunionization was not limited to the manufacturing sector; across all major industries with some union presence, membership rates remain lower today than in the past. This is true even in those industries not threatened by cheaper labor overseas, such as transportation and retail. The wave of deregulation that began in the Carter administration opened up some of these sectors to cutthroat competition, pressuring employers to shed expensive contracts and the unions that bargained for them. Partly as a response to deindustrialization and deregulation,

there arose a concerted, broad-based effort by employers to shift bargaining power away from labor unions. By the early 1980s, innovative tactics adopted by management and used against organizing drives and existing unions shattered the relative detente between business and labor that had predominated for decades. These sophisticated strategies took full advantage of existing policies governing labor-management relations and proved incredibly effective at pushing back at what employers felt was overreach by unions.

A New Landscape

While the causes of organized labor's decades-long decline in the private sector are well-known, the broad consequences are not. Existing research tends to focus on deunionization's consequences for the earnings of male, blue-collar workers. But the removal of organized labor from much of the private sector also affects the economic assimilation of recent immigrants and their offspring, widens black-white wage inequality among female workers, redistributes political power, and redefines the nature of strikes in modern America. I touch on each of these consequences below.

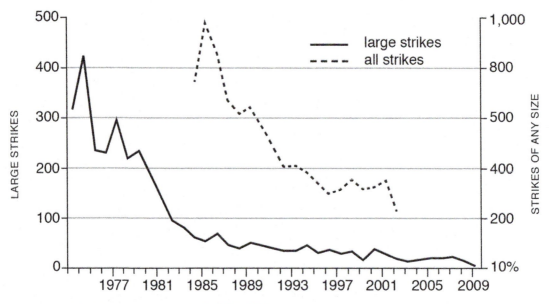

FIGURE 41.2 Work Stoppages in the U.S., 1973–2009

Data for large strikes provided by the Bureau of labor Statistics (BLS) Historical Work Stoppage Database (http://www.bls.gov/wsp/data.htm). The BLS defines large strikes as those including 1,000 or more workers. Data for strikes of any size provided to the author by the Federal Mediation and Conciliation Service (FMCS).

The Disappearing Economic Ladder for Hispanic Immigrants

Unionization has always been unevenly spread across demographic groups. The labor movement's great upsurge between the Great Depression and World War II relied heavily on European immigrants and their children, with many arrivals assuming top leadership posts in the nation's fastest growing unions. During the labor movement's peak, unions helped provide a firm economic foundation for these otherwise disadvantaged populations, propelling millions into the middle class. Some have argued that labor's future is brightening once again, given the influx of Hispanic immigration since the 1960s. That is, if labor can organize recent immigrants, unions might once again reclaim a powerful position in the economic landscape. This optimism is driven by events like the labor movement's success in organizing largely Hispanic janitors in Southern California, many of them recent immigrants.

But how is organized labor actually interacting with this new wave of immigration? Despite the historical role immigrants played in building the US labor movement, in more recent decades top unions have eyed immigrant workers warily. Many assumed immigrants were largely unorganizable, due to the precarious legal status of some recent arrivals, the lower labor standards immigrants were accustomed to in their home countries, and the resulting worry that employers would use immigrant labor to undercut existing wages and benefits of native-born workers. The "Justice for Janitors" campaign in Southern California helped counter such claims and helped galvanize organizers across the nation, who sought to capitalize on the class-based solidarity exhibited by many Hispanic immigrants. And indeed, certain Hispanic subgroups, including immigrants who have lived in the United States for a number of years and immigrants who are citizens, are joining unions at higher rates than native-born Whites. Figure 41.3 displays the odds of joining a union over a one-year period for various Hispanic subgroups compared to US-born Whites. Odds ratios above 1 indicate that the Hispanic subgroup is more likely to join a union than a White nonimmigrant. US-born Hispanics have over 40 percent higher odds of joining a union compared to US-born whites, echoing the historical pattern of immigrant groups and their children seeking unionized employment to assimilate upward into the middle class. Hispanic immigrant citizens and Hispanic immigrants who have lived in the United States for many years are also joining unions at higher rates than native-born Whites.

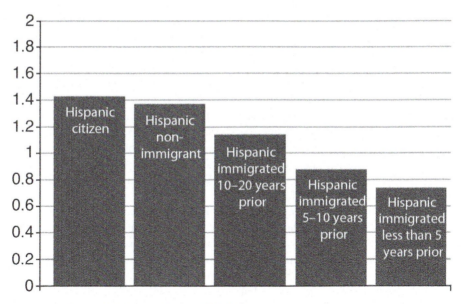

FIGURE 41.3 Odds of Joining a Union, 1973–2009

Odds ratios refer to the relative odds of joining a union over a one-year period where the reference category is non-immigrant whites. Data come from matched files of the Current Population Survey (CPS), and estimates adjust for a range of factors infl uencing unionization. For more on the estimation procedure, see Rosenfeld, Jake, and Meredith Kleykamp. 2009. "Hispanics and Organized Labor in the United States, 1973 to 2007." *American Sociological Review* 74:916–37.

But there are limits to such trends. Despite the highly publicized organizing drives of the "Justice for Janitors" campaign, the percentage of Hispanic janitors in labor unions has actually declined since 1990, as has the fraction of all janitors who claim union membership. Unlike the Southern and Eastern European migrants who once swelled the ranks of the union workforce, recent arrivals face an economic context largely hostile to trade unions. In those remaining parts of the private sector where unions remain active, Hispanics' and Hispanic subgroups' *relative* unionization rates are high, but their *overall* unionization rates are low—along with nearly everyone else's. Thus, contemporary immigrants and their offspring enter labor markets that increasingly lack an established unionized pathway to the middle class, a pathway that past immigrant populations relied upon extensively.

The Declining Significance of Unions for Black Females

Aside from limiting mobility for low-skilled immigrant populations, the decline of organized labor exacerbates economic inequality between African Americans and Whites. Unionization rates for African Americans have exceeded those of Hispanics and Whites for decades now. As the labor movement began integrating its ranks, African-American workers, eager to escape discriminatory treatment institutionalized in US labor markets, sought out organized labor as a partial refuge against economic inequity. This is especially true for females. Despite the stereotypical image of the blue-collar male union worker, unionization rates for African-American females rose dramatically during the 1960s and 1970s, with nearly one in four Black women in the private sector belonging to a union by the end of the 1970s. In the heavily industrialized Midwest, rates of unionization for African-American females working in the private sector peaked at 40 percent. Past work by economists John Bound and Richard Freeman has found that union decline widened wage gaps between young Black and White males, especially in the Midwest. But the ramifications of deunionization for racial wage inequality are actually larger for *females,* given that differences in private sector unionization rates between Black and White females far exceed differences between Black and White males. Indeed, had unionization rates remained at their peak levels, Black–White wage differences among private sector females would be nearly 30 percent smaller than where they stand today.

A Political Force Diminished

As unions vanish from the economic landscape, their presence in the political realm is reduced as well. Historically, the labor movement has channeled and organized the political energies of the working class, helping to counter the robust, positive connection between civic participation and socioeconomic status. Indeed, trade unions have historically stood as one of the few institutions equalizing political participation across income and educational divides. Nowhere was this role more pronounced than in the private sector, where voting rates run comparatively low, especially among those lacking a college education. This is not true in the public sector. The combined effects of unionization and public-sector employment are not simply additive: public-sector employment bolsters political participation, but being in a public-sector union results in only a slight increase in the propensity to vote. Figure 41.4 presents predicted probabilities of voting for public- and private-sector union members and nonmembers. The difference in voting turnout among public sector members and nonmembers is only 2.5 percentage points. The effect of union membership on voting in the private sector is nearly three times as large.

Today, the number of public sector union members equals the number of private sector union members, marking a dramatic break from when private sector union rolls dwarfed those of government employees. This shift has important political consequences. The already high voter turnout rates—and education levels—among government workers, union and nonunion alike, leave little room for unions to raise turnout in the public sector. Meanwhile, in the private sector, union status remains a significant indicator of whether an *individual* will vote or not. However, given the reduced fraction of private-sector workers in labor unions, the *aggregate* effect of unionization on voting turnout is now quite small, and shrinking union rolls reduce the ability of unions to drive up turnout among nonunion citizens.

The consequences of union decline described above largely focus on nonunion workers—those who in the past would have benefited from union membership but who no longer will, whether they be an immigrant employee who once would have been organized, a female African-American worker no longer able to rely on a union wage to reduce pay gaps with her white counterpart, or a less-educated worker lacking the training, resources, and knowledge to participate in politics. But union decline affects remaining union workers as well. Research by economists John DiNardo and David S. Lee suggests that the union wage benefits for newly organized manufacturing firms are negligible. This may be due, in part, to the dramatic decline in strikes described earlier. In decades past, unions often authorized a walkout during contract negotiations, pressuring employers to raise wages and benefits. These pressure tactics worked; union members who had participated in a strike had higher wages, on average, than non-striking members. This no longer seems true today. While we lack direct measures of strikes' impacts on an individual striker's pay, the Federal Mediation and Conciliation Service data presented in Figure 41.2 allow for comparisons between pay scales in industries and regions in which strike activity remains relatively high and those in which strikes have disappeared. I find that the positive wage-strike relationship has been severed; workers in high-strike locales see no wage gains compared to workers in relatively quiescent sectors. Strikes now are often last-ditch attempts to hold the line on wages and benefits, as union leaders simply refrain from striking except in the most desperate situations. Thus, unions are not only failing to bolster the fortunes of those who once would have been organized, they are also struggling to protect the fortunes of those still in their ranks.

Where from Here?

It is difficult indeed to counter the self-perpetuating dynamic behind the foregoing trends. As union ranks shrink, so too does the constituency directly mobilized to press for change, and with it, labor's leverage in convincing lawmakers to risk the political consequences of business opposition. The present economic climate further dampens enthusiasm for worker activism, as employees cling to their positions, while millions of others less fortunate scramble to find work.

Organized labor's signature legislative effort is the Employee Free Choice Act (EFCA). In its most robust form, the proposed legislation would radically recast how union elections are held in the United States, bypassing the traditional election campaign in favor of a "card check" policy whereby a union is recognized after over half of workers sign up in support of collective bargaining. A compromise version of the bill would retain the "secret ballot" election procedure but would reduce election times, grant organizers greater access to employees on the worksite, and institute binding arbitration if a contract has not

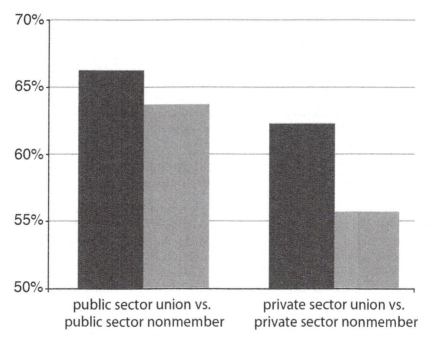

FIGURE 41.4 Predicted Probabilities of Voting for Union Members and Nonmembers, 1984–2006

Probabilities generated from voter turnout models that adjust for a range of demographic, economic, and geographic factors found to influence voting. Sample is restricted to employed citizens only, age 18 and over. Data come from the November series of the Current Population Survey (CPS). For more on the estimation procedure, see Rosenfeld, Jake, 2010. "Economic Determinants of Voting in an Era of Union Decline." *Social Science Quarterly* 91:379–96.

been agreed upon after a specified period of time. Passage of either version would shift some of the power in organizing drives to labor, although it would not address the broader economic challenges labor faces, such as the continuing decline of manufacturing employment, the pressures of international competition among remaining manufacturing firms, and aggressive competition in many deregulated domestic industries.

There are other institutional changes that, if implemented, might alter the balance of power somewhat. The Obama administration has, for example, floated a proposal to revamp the way the government allocates federal contracts to companies. The proposal would prioritize firms that offer high wages while penalizing those that had committed labor violations, thereby giving an edge to unionized companies and benefiting millions of nonunion workers by providing an incentive to nonunion firms to raise wages and improve treatment of workers. An estimated one in four workers is employed by a company that contracts with the government, so the scale of the regulatory change could be enormous.

Importantly, the administration is exploring ways to change regulations through executive order, thus avoiding difficulties in generating a filibuster-proof majority in the Senate.

Any policy effort to help organized labor faces formidable political opposition, although we can't rule out the possibility that the administration will creatively short-circuit the full legislative process. For many employers, the costs of unionization are substantial, and thus the benefits of continuing inaction are clear. Unions often reduce flexibility in hiring and firing decisions, may slow managers' abilities to shift resources and capital as soon as opportunities arise, and substantially reduce managerial discretion in setting pay, all the while increasing wage and benefit bills. Strong employer opposition has helped push unionization down to levels unseen since before the Great Depression. Because such declines are self-perpetuating, at this point, it will take decisive legal and institutional action to reverse or even halt the trend—action that, if not taken soon, won't have much of a constituency behind it any longer. The simple fact: Big Labor cannot get much smaller.

42. Ann Huff Stevens*

Labor Market Shocks: Are There Lessons for Anti-Poverty Policy?

The Great Recession and its aftermath brought hardship to many American families; its full toll will likely not be realized or documented for many years to come. More than eight million workers lost their jobs during the recession, experiencing dramatically reduced income, increased stress, and a variety of other negative outcomes for themselves and their families. These effects are important to document and understand in their own right, but they also offer important lessons in how low or variable income may affect the well-being of children and adults in a more general sense—lessons with important implications for anti-poverty policy. What are the effects of job loss, and what does that tell us about the lasting effects of low income more generally?

The research on the broad question of the effects of limited income has developed and advanced in recent years in ways that have not been fully appreciated by politicians, policymakers, and the public. Here, I will focus on the effects of job loss on future earnings and a host of other outcomes. Because jobs of course provide earnings, one can gain some leverage on whether money matters for later life outcomes by asking how much the loss of a job matters. The Great Recession provides an important experiment in this respect because—unfortunately—it delivered much in the way of job loss. It reminds us yet again that even those faring well in the labor market in one year can see fortunes change when the economy weakens. The seemingly random shock of a recession-induced job loss can go a long way toward identifying the true effect of losing a job and the income it provides.

The profoundly negative effects of job loss on individuals and families are quite well-documented in academic work. I will review evidence accumulated by social scientists over the past two decades that makes clear that the negative income "surprises" that come from permanent job loss have large and persistent effects. This result suggests that long-term exposure to low and uncertain income may have similar negative effects. As mentioned above, the persistence and breadth of these effects have not

been well-appreciated by policymakers, nor perhaps by citizens who have not themselves been through the unfortunate experience of losing a job. By studying these effects, we can not only better understand how recession and job loss affect current and future generations, but we can also speak to critical policy questions concerning how low or uncertain income affects the well-being of adults and children.

Longitudinal Analysis as the Key Breakthrough

What accounts for the recent growth of knowledge about the effects of job and income loss? The rise of longitudinal analysis is one of the key breakthroughs in this regard.

Although the effects of job loss on income have been studied for decades, in the 1990s longitudinal data became more widely available, enabling analysts to carefully document the persistence of reduced earnings and income that follow job loss over the long haul. Earnings fall steeply when people lose jobs, but even once new jobs are found, average earnings remain below—and sometimes far below—what they were before the initial losses. As time moves on, earnings and family income will recover somewhat, but the research shows that even in the sixth year following a job loss, average earnings are at least 10 percent lower than their starting point.[1] During a deep recession, when a great number of people experience job loss, long-term reductions in earnings may be as high as 25 percent. Although spouses' earnings and other income sources may increase to compensate for the reduced earnings of affected family members, these offsetting increases end up being relatively small contributions to total family income. In Figure 42.1, I have charted the steep income loss among fathers experiencing a firm closure (and hence job loss) in the early 1980s in Canada, a time when both the Canadian and U.S. economies were undergoing severe recessions.

Recessions Provide More Information on Effects

That job loss frequently leads to sizable and permanent changes in the family income of those affected may not be all that surprising. But job losses also indirectly affect other long-term outcomes, including health outcomes, like mortality. I will discuss these indirect effects in more detail shortly, but first I discuss how recessions, in conjunction with

*Stevens, Ann H. 2014. "Labor Market Shocks: Are There Lessons for Anti-Poverty Policy?" *Pathways Magazine: Jobs & Joblessness*, 19–22.

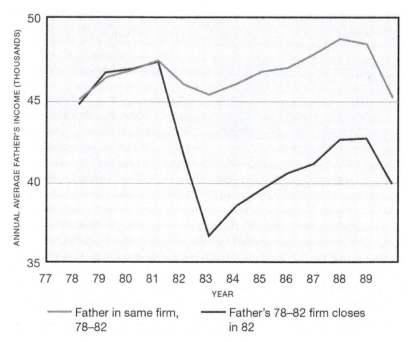

FIGURE 42.1 Effects of Job Loss on Income

longitudinal analysis, have provided much help in identifying the true causal effect of jobs and income. Although recessions may have little redeeming value in general, I will argue that they do at least provide some analytic leverage on the question of the effects of job and income loss.

If we want to understand how income or material resources affect families and children, job loss provides one important vehicle to do so, as families and children will typically experience dramatic change in income when a job is lost. But does an empirically observed job loss tell us much about its true causal effects? Typically, economists and other social scientists are careful to distinguish between correlation and causation. It is generally difficult to claim, for example, that the low income of parents *causes* any possible academic troubles among their children, because the background characteristics that led to their low income may have also caused academic difficulties. . . . However, studies of job loss provide a potential way around this problem, because we can observe families prior to job loss (when they have higher income) and can then study how the *change* in income, presumably driven by forces outside the family, leads to changes in other outcomes, such as children's achievement.

The obvious caveat: This causal inference will be warranted only if the job loss itself is not associated with individual characteristics that might also lead to

worse outcomes for parents or kids. For example, a working parent may suffer a major health problem, such as depression, that leads to job loss. And while this parent's income does drop, it may be the deterioration in parental health that leads to negative outcomes for children, rather than the drop in income per se.

This is precisely why recessions are so useful for purposes of research. In particular, studying job losses that occur as part of broad economic downturns, firm closings, and mass layoffs makes it less likely that individual workers have been selected for dismissal for reasons that might also account for the outcomes of interest (e.g., children's academic achievement). In addition, we can often measure outcomes for the same individuals both before and after a job loss, sometimes even accounting for typical trends in those outcomes and, in this way, track the change in income to the change in outcomes. These approaches have helped establish that the long-term reductions in earnings are caused by job loss, and the same approaches can help tie the associated earnings reductions to changes in health, education, and other outcomes. . . .

The Wide Span of Consequences

With the preceding detour into methods of research that help establish causality, we are now in a position to lay out the wide span of consequences of job and income loss. And the span of consequences is indeed wide.

First, there is strong evidence that job losses lead to substantive changes in health outcomes for affected workers. Job losses from mass layoff events result in increases in mortality among laid-off workers over the next several decades. Important work by economists has followed workers who lost jobs as part of mass layoffs in the recessionary periods of 1980s Pennsylvania.[2] Among workers who lost jobs, the risk of death increased by 10 to 15 percent per year over the next twenty years. What leads to these increases in mortality? Here we know less, but there is evidence that the greater the income loss and the greater the variability of income after a job loss, the larger the increase in mortality.

Other studies have examined health after a job loss, but over a shorter time frame. Among the best of such studies, there is evidence that many conditions that are likely related to higher stress, including both physical and mental health problems, increase substantially in the years following a job loss.[3]

The effects of job loss extend beyond the person directly affected. Income losses, after all, are shared with the entire family. In this sense, the effects of economic shocks on children may shed some light on why low incomes might have causal effects that extend well into the next generation. For example, we know that kids whose parents have lost jobs are more likely to experience difficulties in school, such as being expelled or needing to repeat a grade.[4] At the aggregate level, researchers have shown that local firm closings can lead to reductions in school-level test scores, presumably reflecting the cumulative effects of many parents located in a single district experiencing economic stress.[5]

We also have evidence that effects of job losses on kids are extremely persistent. A study of Canadian parents who lost jobs in the 1980s found that their children had substantially reduced earnings when they were tracked down in young adulthood, with earnings roughly 9 percent below that of comparable kids whose parents had not experienced a job loss.[6] Such research suggests that labor market shocks can haunt the children of affected parents even into their own adult lives. It also seems, though, that families in precarious financial situations *before* a job loss may be those most likely to be harmed when a job loss occurs. . . . Job losses among families that begin with relatively high incomes are often found to have

smaller effects than those occurring among those closer to the bottom of the income distribution. . . .

What Does It Mean for Policy?

The evidence that job and income loss matter for many outcomes is compelling. . . . The simple conclusion here: The loss of income and material resources does cause harm and suggests that income support and stability can play a role in reducing the long-term consequences of poverty.

Can we make more specific policy recommendations on the basis of such evidence? The instinct of course is to target policy precisely to causes. If, in other words, the loss of money is causing bad outcomes, then it might be argued that income assistance is the only or best type of intervention needed to improve the fortunes of poor families.

The latter conclusion, attractive though it may seem, ought not be reached unthinkingly. Better education policies, for example, may still be a more efficient and effective remedy to poor children's long-term disadvantages. What we can conclude, however, is that we need to undertake policies that—either directly or indirectly—address the key role that the lack of money plays in producing all sorts of bad outcomes.

The next step is to assess whether direct or indirect approaches to raising income are more likely to have payoff. All else equal, most would probably prefer approaches that provide a human capital foundation for raising income, as these will have enduring effects. It has to be appreciated, however, that policies promoting the development of human capital are sometimes just not enough. However much we ramp up human capital and make people more employable, we will still have far too much poverty, in part because market economies are intrinsically cyclical and have frequent periods of "creative destruction" in which many workers will lose their jobs. In the contemporary US economy, less-skilled workers also face ongoing downward pressure on their wages because of global competition, skill-biased technical change, and other broad economic changes.

The long-term effects of job loss are really a combination of relatively short-term disruptions in employment and much longer-term reductions in wage levels even after workers are re-employed. It follows that policies to increase human capital are not the full answer for either displaced workers or the poor in general. We must also have policies that provide short-term assistance to individuals facing short-term difficulties for a variety of reasons. We know that income loss and stress associated with job loss have real consequences for individuals and their families. While those in chronic poverty may well have additional challenges, including the need to build their underlying skills or stock of human capital, what we have learned about the effects of job loss make it difficult to argue that effective income support policies should play no role in improving the lives of the poor.

NOTES

1. Jacobson, L S., LaLonde, R. J., Sullivan, D. G. (1993). "Earnings losses of displaced workers." *The American Economic Review*, 685–709.

2. Couch, K. A., Placzek, D. W. (2010). "Earnings losses of displaced workers revisited." *The American Economic Review*, 1oo(1), 572–589.

3. Stevens, A. H. (1997). "Persistent effects of job displacement: The importance of multiple job losses." *Journal of Labor Economics*, 165–188.

4. Jacobson, L. S., LaLonde, R. J., Sullivan, D. G. (1993). "Earnings losses of displaced workers." *The American Economic Review*, 685–709.

5. Gallo, W. T., Bradley, E. H., Siegel, M., Kasl, S. V. (2000). "Health effects of involuntary job loss among older workers: Findings from the health and retirement survey." The *Journals of Gerontology Series B: Psychological Sciences and Social Sciences*, 55(3), S131—S14o.

6. Browning, M., & Heinesen, E. (2012). "Effect of job loss due to plant closure on mortality and hospitalization." *Journal of Health Economics*.

7. Salm, M. (2009). "Does job loss cause ill health?" *Health Economics*, 18(9), 1075-1089.

8. Strully, K. W. (2009). "Job loss and health in the US labor market." *Demography*, 46(2), 221-246.

9. Stevens, A. H., Schaller, J. (2011). "Short-run effects of parental job loss on children's academic achievement." *Economics of Education Review*, 30(2), 289-299.

10. Kalil, A., Ziol-Guest, K. (2008). "Parental job loss and children's academic progress in two-parent families." *Social Science Research*, 37, 500-515.

11. Ananat, E. 0., Gassman-Pines, A., Francis, D. V. Gibson-Davis, C. M., "Children left behind: The effects of statewide job loss on student achievement." National Bureau of Economic Research Working Paper No. 17104, June 2011.

12. Oreopoulos, P., Page, M., Stevens, A. H. (2008). "The intergenerational effects of worker displacement." *Journal of Labor Economics*, 26(3), 455-483.

13. Rege, M., Telle, K., Votruba, M. (2011). "Parental job loss and children's school performance." *The Review of Economic Studies*, 78(4), 1462-1489.

RACE, ETHNICITY, AND INEQUALITY

In Part VI, our attention shifts to racial and ethnic inequalities, which are arguably the most profound forms of ascription in the US case (and in many other countries). The obvious starting point in studying race and ethnicity is to understand how the classification schemes themselves (e.g., "black," "white," "Asian") come to be constructed and reconstructed over time. We thus lead off Part VI with an article on the institutional processes by which such schemes come into being (Omi and Winant, Ch. 43) as well as a study revealing how individuals are sorted (and sort themselves) into such schemes as are already in place (Saperstein and Penner, Ch. 44).

The next set of readings examine how newly entering groups, not just particular individuals, are sorted into the racial and ethnic system within the host country. The articles within this subsection explore whether such groups are assimilating in an uninterrupted "straight-line" fashion, whether the constant replenishment of the Hispanic population interrupts such straight-line assimilation, and whether ethnic enclaves work to hinder or impede the incorporation process (see Portes and Zhou, Ch. 45; Jiménez, Ch. 46). We then turn to the role of discrimination in perpetuating racial and ethnic disadvantage. Although statistical analyses of discrimination have been carried out for some time, they have been less influential than recent experimental studies in documenting the extent of discriminatory processes (see Bertrand and Mullainathan, Ch. 47; Pager, Ch. 48) and showing how discrimination and stereotyping can affect behavior in self-fulfilling ways (Steele, Ch. 49).

The final subsection of Part VI explores the forces making for change and stability in racial and ethnic inequality. Because our various institutions have all been profoundly racialized, there are accordingly many institutional arenas in which change might occur, a point that Wilson (Ch. 50) nicely makes. We have also included new research on the mechanisms through which Latino immigrants to the US are upsetting our binary understanding of race (see Frank, Akresh, Lu, Ch. 51), the mechanisms through which profound residential segregation affects the black middle class (Patillo, Ch. 52), and the ongoing construction and reconstruction of the Asian "model minority" stereotype (Lee, Ch. 53).

We close by noting the obvious: In the US, race and ethnicity play an especially central role in the stratification system, which is why some of the most talented scholars in the country study the dynamics of race and ethnicity. As a result, we have made great headway in understanding why the black-white binary, which modernization theorists very optimistically imagined would wither away, continues to so profoundly structure our neighborhoods, families, educational systems, criminal justice systems, political systems, and so much more. The pressing question of our time is whether the US—and other countries throughout the world—can control the most virulent forms of racism and nativism that rear up as rising income inequality impels those who are "losing" to look for answers in deeply problematic ways.

Race as a Social Construct

43. Michael Omi and Howard Winant*

Racial Formation in the United States

Race is a way of "making up people."[1] The very act of defining racial groups is a process fraught with confusion, contradiction, and unintended consequences. Concepts of race prove to be unreliable as supposed boundaries shift, slippages occur, realignments become evident, and new collectivities emerge. State-imposed classifications of race, for example, face continuing challenges by individuals and groups who seek to assert distinctive racial categories and identities. Historical shifts in scientific knowledge, in fields ranging from physical anthropology to the genomic sciences, fuel continuing debates about what race may or may not mean as an indicator of human variation. While such debates and reformulations regarding the concept of race initially occur in specific institutional arenas, public spaces, or academic fields, their consequences are often dramatic and reverberate broadly throughout society.

Race-making can also be understood as a process of "othering." Defining groups of people as "other" is obviously not restricted to distinctions based on race. Gender, class, sexuality, religion, culture, language, nationality, and age, among other perceived distinctions, are frequently evoked to justify structures of inequality, differential treatment, subordinate status, and in some cases, violent conflict and war. Classifying people as other, and making use of various perceived attributes in order to do so, is a universal phenomenon that also classifies (and works to amalgamate and homogenize) those who do the classifying (Blumer 1958). "Making up people" is both basic and ubiquitous. As social beings, we must categorize people so as to be able to

"navigate" in the world—to discern quickly who may be friend or foe, to position and situate ourselves within prevailing social hierarchies, and to provide clues that guide our social interactions with the individuals and groups we encounter.

But while the act of categorizing people and assigning different attributes to such categories may be universal, the categories themselves are subject to enormous variation over historical time and space. The definitions, meanings, and overall coherence of prevailing social categories are always subject to multiple interpretations. No social category rises to the level of being understood as a fixed, objective, social fact.

One might imagine, for example, that the category of a person's "age" (as measured in years) is an objective social category. But even this familiar concept's meaning varies across time and space. In many societies where the elderly are venerated and highly valued as leaders and living repositories of wisdom, individuals tend to overstate their age in years. By contrast, people in the youth-oriented United States tend to understate how old they are. Processes of classification, including self-classification, are reflective of specific social structures, cultural meanings and practices, and of broader power relations as well.

The definitions of specific categories are framed and contested from "above" and "below." The social identities of marginalized and subordinate groups, for example, are both imposed from above by dominant social groups and/or state institutions, and constituted from below by these groups themselves as expressions of self-identification and resistance to dominant forms of categorization. In any given historical moment, one can understand a social category's prevailing meaning, but such understandings can also be erroneous or transitory. They are often no more than the unstable and tentative result of the dynamic engagement between "elite" and "street" definitions and meanings.

Race as a Master Category

It is now widely accepted in most scholarly fields that race is a *social construction*. Simply stating that race is socially constructed, however, begs a number of important questions. How is race constructed? How and why do racial definitions and meanings change over time and place? And perhaps most importantly, what role does race play within the broader social system in which it is embedded?

With respect to this last question, we advance what may seem an audacious claim. We assert that in the United States, race is a master category—a fundamental concept that has profoundly shaped, and continues to shape, the history, polity, economic structure, and culture of the United States. Obviously, some clarification is in order. We are not suggesting that race is a transcendent category—something that stands above or apart from class, gender, or other axes of inequality and difference. The literature on intersectionality has clearly demonstrated the mutual determination and co-constitution of the categories of race, class, gender, and sexual orientation. It is not possible to understand the (il)logic of any form of social stratification, any practice of cultural marginalization, or any type of inequality or human variation, without appreciating the deep, complex, comingling, interpenetration of race, class, gender, and sexuality. In the cauldron of social life, these categories come together; they are profoundly transformed in the process.

We hold these truths of intersectional analysis to be self-evident. But we also believe that race has played a unique role in the formation and historical development of the United States. Since the historical encounter of the hemispheres and the onset of transatlantic enslavement were the fundamental acts of racemaking, and since they launched a global and world-historical process of "making up people" that constituted the modern world, race has become the template of both difference and inequality....

Racialization

Race is often seen as a social category that is either objective or illusory. When viewed as an objective matter, race is usually understood as rooted in biological differences, ranging from such familiar phenomic markers as skin color, hair texture, or eye shape, to more obscure human variations occurring at the genetic or genomic levels. When viewed as an illusion, race is usually understood as an ideological construct, something that masks a more fundamental material distinction or axis of identity: our three paradigms of ethnicity, class, and nation typify such approaches. Thus race is often treated as a metonym or epiphenomenon of culture (in the ethnicity paradigm), inequality and stratification (in the class paradigm), or primordial peoplehood (in the nation paradigm).

On the "objective" side, race is often regarded as an *essence*, as something fixed and concrete. The three main racial classifications of humans once posed (and now largely rejected) by physical anthropology—Negroid, Caucasoid, and Mongoloid—are examples of such an essentialist perspective. Another example is "mixed-race" identity: To consider an individual or group as "multiracial," or mixed race, presupposes the existence of clear, discernible, and discrete races that have subsequently been combined to create a hybrid, or perhaps mongrel, identity. Here, race is functioning as a metonym for "species," although that connection is generally not admitted in the present day.

While race is still popularly understood as essence, it has also been viewed as a mere *illusion*, especially in more recent accounts. As a purely ideological construct, race is considered to be unreal, a product of "false consciousness." Both orthodox (neoclassical) economics and orthodox Marxism viewed race this way. For the former, it was an irrational distraction from pure, market-based considerations of value in exchange; for the latter it was an ideological tool that capitalists (or sometimes privileged white workers) deployed to prevent the emergence of a unified working-class movement. In the current period, colorblind ideology—expressed, for example, in affirmative action debates—argues that any form of racial classification is itself inherently racist since race is not "real."

We are critical of both positions: race as essence and race as illusion. Race is not something rooted in nature, something that reflects clear and discrete variations in human identity. But race is also not an illusion. While it may not be "real" in a biological sense, race is indeed real as a social category with definite social consequences. The family, as a social concept, provides an intriguing analogy to grasp the "reality" of race:

> We know that families take many forms ... Some family categories correspond to biological categories; others do not. Moreover,

boundaries of family membership vary, depending on individual and institutional factors. Yet regardless of whether families correspond to biological definitions, social scientists study families and use membership in family categories in their study of other phenomena, such as well-being. Similarly, racial statuses, although not representing biological differences, are of sociological interest in their form, their changes, and their consequences (American Sociological Association 2003, 5).

We cannot dismiss race as a legitimate category of social analysis by simply stating that race is not real. With respect to race, the Thomases's sociological dictum is still in force: "It is not important whether or not the interpretation is correct—if men [sic] define situations as real, they are real in their consequences" (Thomas and Thomas 1928, pp. 571-572).

One of our aims here is to disrupt and reorganize the rigid and antinomic framework of essence-versus-illusion in which race is theorized and debated. We understand race as an unstable and "decentered" complex of social meanings constantly being transformed by political struggle. With this in mind, we advance the following definition: *Race is a concept that signifies and symbolizes social conflicts and interests by referring to different types of human bodies.* Although the concept of race invokes seemingly biologically based human characteristics (so-called phenotypes), selection of these particular human features for purposes of racial signification is always and necessarily a social and historical process. Indeed, the categories employed to differentiate among human beings along racial lines reveal themselves, upon serious examination, to be at best imprecise, and at worst completely arbitrary. They may be arbitrary, but they are not meaningless. Race is strategic; race does ideological and political work.

Despite the problematic nature of racial categorization, it should be apparent that there is a crucial and non-reducible *visual dimension* to the definition and understanding of racial categories. Bodies are visually read and narrated in ways that draw upon an ensemble of symbolic meanings and associations. Corporeal distinctions are common; they become essentialized. Perceived differences in skin color, physical build, hair texture, the structure of cheek bones, the shape of the nose, or the presence/absence of an epicanthic fold are understood as the manifestations of more profound differences that are situated *within* racially identified persons: differences in

such qualities as intelligence, athletic ability, temperament, and sexuality, among other traits.

Through a complex process of selection, human physical characteristics ("real" or imagined) become the basis to justify or reinforce social differentiation. Conscious or unconscious, deeply ingrained or reinvented, the making of race, the "othering" of social groups by means of the invocation of physical distinctions, is a key component of modern societies. "Making up people," once again. This process of selection, of imparting social and symbolic meaning to perceived phenotypical differences, is the core, constitutive element of what we term "racialization."

We define racialization as *the extension of racial meaning to a previously racially unclassified relationship, social practice, or group.* Racialization occurs in large-scale and small-scale ways, macro- and micro-socially. In large-scale, even world-historical settings, racialization can be observed in the foundation and consolidation of the modern world-system: The conquest and settlement of the western hemisphere, the development of African slavery, and the rise of abolitionism, all involved profuse and profound extension of racial meanings into new social terrain. In smaller-scale settings as well, "making up people" or racial interpellation [a concept drawn from Althusser 2001 (1971)] also operates as a quotidian form of racialization: Racial profiling for example, may be understood as a form of racialization. Racial categories, and the meanings attached to them, are often constructed from pre-existing conceptual or discursive elements that have crystallized through the genealogies of competing religious, scientific, and political ideologies and projects. These are so to speak the raw materials of racialization.

To summarize thus far: Race is a concept, a representation or signification of identity that refers to different types of human bodies, to the perceived corporeal and phenotypic markers of difference and the meanings and social practices that are ascribed to these differences.

It is important to emphasize that once specific concepts of race are widely circulated and accepted as a social reality, racial difference is not dependent on visual observation alone. Legal scholar Osagie Obasogie makes the intriguing point that iterative social practices give rise to "visual" understandings of race, even among those who cannot see. The respondents in his study, blind since birth, "see" race through interpersonal and institutional socializations and practices that shape their perceptions of what race is (Obasogie 2013). Thus race is neither self-evident nor obvious as an ocular phenomenon. Instead racialization depends on meanings and associations that permit phenotypic distinction among human bodies.

Some may argue that if the concept of race is so nebulous, so indeterminate, so flexible, and so susceptible to strategic manipulation by a range of political projects, why don't we simply dispense with it? Can we not get "beyond" race? Can we not see it as an illusory thing? Don't we see how much mischief has occurred in its name? These questions have been posed with tremendous frequency in both popular and academic discourse. An affirmative answer would of course present obvious practical difficulties: It is rather difficult to jettison widely held beliefs, beliefs which moreover are central to everyone's identity and understanding of the social world. So the attempt to banish the concept as an archaism is at best counterintuitive. But a deeper difficulty, we believe, is inherent in the very formulation of this schema, in its way of posing race as a *problem,* a misconception left over from the past, a concept no longer relevant to a "post-racial" society.

A more effective starting point is the recognition that despite its uncertainties and contradictions, the concept of race continues to play a fundamental role in structuring and representing the social world. The task for theory is to capture this situation and avoid both the utopian framework that sees race as an illusion we can somehow "get beyond," as well as the essentialist formulation that sees race as something objective and fixed, a biological given. We should think of race as an element of social structure rather than as an irregularity within it; we should see race as a dimension of human representation rather than an illusion. Such a perspective informs what we mean by racial formation....

Racial Projects

Race is a "crossroads" where social structure and cultural representation meet. Too often, the attempt is made to understand race simply or primarily in terms of only one of these two analytical dimensions. For example, efforts to explain racial inequality as a purely social structural phenomenon either neglect or are unable to account for the origins, patterning, and transformation of racial meanings, representations, and social identities. Conversely, many examinations of race as a system of signification, identity, or cultural attribution fail adequately to articulate

these phenomena with evolving social structures (such as segregation or stratification) and institutions (such as prisons, schools, or the labor market).

Race can never be merely a concept or idea, a representation or signification alone. Indeed race cannot be discussed, cannot even be *noticed,* without reference—however explicit or implicit— to social structure. To identify an individual or group racially is to locate them within a socially and historically demarcated set of demographic and cultural boundaries, state activities, "life-chances," and tropes of identity/difference/(in)equality. Race is both a social/historical structure and a set of accumulated signifiers that suffuse individual and collective identities, inform social practices, shape institutions and communities, demarcate social boundaries, and organize the distribution of resources. We cannot understand how racial representations set up patterns of residential segregation, for example, without considering how segregation reciprocally shapes and reinforces the meaning of race itself.

We conceive of racial formation processes as occurring through a linkage between structure and signification. *Racial projects* do both the ideological and the practical "work" of making these links and articulating the connection between them. *A racial project is simultaneously an interpretation, representation, or explanation of racial identities and meanings, and an effort to organize and distribute resources (economic, political, cultural) along particular racial lines.* Racial projects connect what race *means* in a particular discursive or ideological practice and the ways in which both social structures and everyday experiences are racially *organized,* based upon that meaning. Racial projects are attempts both to shape the ways in which social structures are racially signified and the ways that racial meanings are embedded in social structures.

Racial projects occur at varying scales, both large and small. Projects take shape not only at the macro-level of racial policy-making, state activity, and collective action, but also at the level of everyday experience and personal interaction. Both dominant and subordinate groups and individual actors, both institutions and persons, carry out racial projects. The imposition of restrictive state voting rights laws, organizing work for immigrants', prisoners', and community health rights in the ghetto or barrio are all examples of racial projects. Individuals' practices may be seen as racial projects as well: The cop who "stops and frisks" a young pedestrian, the student who joins a memorial march for the slain teenager Trayvon Martin, even the decision to wear dreadlocks, can all be understood as racial projects. Such projects should not, however, be simply regarded and analyzed as discrete, separate, and autonomous ideas and actions. Every racial project is both a reflection of and response to the broader patterning of race in the overall social system. In turn, every racial project attempts to reproduce, extend, subvert, or directly challenge that system.

Racial projects are not necessarily confined to particular domains. They can, for example, "jump" scale in their impact and significance. Projects framed at the local level, for example, can end up influencing national policies and initiatives. Correspondingly, projects at the national or even global level can be creatively and strategically recast at regional and local levels. Projects "travel" as well. Consider how migration recasts concepts of race, racial meaning, and racial identity: Immigrants' notions of race are often shaped in reference to, and in dialogue with, concepts of race in both their countries of origin and settlement. Thus migrants can maintain, adopt, and strategically utilize different concepts of race in transnational space (Kim 2008; Roth 2012).

At any given historical moment, racial projects compete and overlap, evincing varying capacity either to maintain or to challenge the prevailing racial system. A good example is the current debate over the relevance of "colorblind" ideology, policy, and practice; this provides a study of overlapping and competing racial projects. We discuss the hegemony of colorblindness in the concluding section of this book.

Racial projects link signification and structure not only in order to shape policy or exercise political influence, but also to organize our understandings of race as everyday "common sense." To see racial projects operating at the level of everyday life, we have only to examine the many ways in which we "notice" race, often unconsciously.

One of the first things we notice about people when we meet them (along with their sex) is their race. We utilize race to provide clues about who a person is. This fact is made painfully obvious when we encounter someone whom we cannot conveniently racially categorize— someone who is, for example, racially "mixed" or of an ethnic/racial group with which we are not familiar. Such an encounter becomes a source of discomfort and momentarily a crisis of racial meaning.

Our ability to interpret racial meanings depends on preconceived notions of a racialized social structure. Comments such as "Funny, you don't look black" betray an underlying image of what black should look like. We expect people to act out their apparent racial identities. Phenotype and performativity should match up. Indeed we become disoriented and anxious when they do not. Encounters with the black person who can't dance, the Asian American not proficient in math and science, or the Latin American who can't speak Spanish all momentarily confound our racial reading of the social world and how we navigate within it. The whole gamut of racial stereotypes testifies to the way a racialized social structure shapes racial experience and socializes racial meanings. Analysis of prevailing stereotypes reveals the always present, already active link between our view of the social structure—its demography, its laws, its customs, its threats—and our conception of what race means.

Conversely, the way we interpret our experience in racial terms shapes and reflects our relations to the institutions and organizations through which we are embedded in the social structure. Thus we expect racially coded human characteristics to explain social differences. "Making up people" once again. Temperament, sexuality, intelligence, athletic ability, aesthetic preferences are presumed to be fixed and discernible from the palpable mark of race. Such diverse questions as our confidence and trust in others (for example, salespeople, teachers, media figures, and neighbors), our sexual preferences and romantic images, our tastes in music, films, dance, or sports, and our very ways of talking, walking, eating, and dreaming become racially coded simply because we live in a society where racial awareness is so pervasive.

To summarize the argument so far: The theory of racial formation suggests that society is suffused with racial projects, large and small, to which all are subjected. This racial "subjection" is quintessentially ideological. Everybody learns some combination, some version, of the rules of racial classification, and of their own racial identity, often without obvious teaching or conscious inculcation. Thus are we inserted in a comprehensively racialized social structure. Race becomes "common sense"—a way of comprehending, explaining, and acting in the world. A vast web of racial projects mediates between the discursive or representational means in which race is identified and signified on the one hand, and the institutional and organizational forms in which it is routinized and standardized on the other. The interaction and accumulation of these projects are the heart of the racial formation process.

Because of the pervasion of society by race, because of its operation over the *longue durée* as a master category of difference and inequality, it is not possible to represent race discursively without simultaneously locating it, explicitly or implicitly, in a social structural (and historical) context. Nor is it possible to organize, maintain, or transform social structures without simultaneously engaging, once more either explicitly or implicitly, in racial significa-tion. Racial formation, therefore, is *a synthesis, a con-stantly reiterated outcome,* of the interaction of racial projects on a society-wide level. These projects are, of course, vastly different in scope and effect. They in-clude large-scale public action, state activities, and interpretations of racial conditions in political, artis-tic, journalistic, or academic fora, as well as the seemingly infinite number of racial judgments and practices, conscious and unconscious, that we carry out as part of our individual experience.

The concept of racial projects can be understood and applied across historical time to identify patterns in the *longue durée* of racial formation, both nationally and the entire modern world. At any particular histor-ical moment, one racial project can be hegemonic while others are subservient, marginal, or oppositional to it. White supremacy is the obvious example of this: an evolving hegemonic racial project that has taken different forms from the colonial era to the present.

With the foregoing account of racial formation in mind, we must turn our attention to the problem of *racism*. Racial politics are necessarily deeply bound up with this topic. But race and racism are not the same thing. What is the relationship between them?

Racism

Magnus Hirschfeld, a German physician and sexol-ogist of the Weimar era who was an early advocate of gay and transgender rights, initially gave currency to the term "racism." Published posthumously, Hirschfeld's book *Rassismus* (*Racism*; 1938) provided a history, analysis, and critical refutation of Nazi racial doctrines. Since the 1930s, the concept of racism has undergone significant changes in scope, meaning, and application. As historian George Fredrickson ob-serves, "Although commonly used, 'racism' has be-come a loaded and ambiguous term" (2002, 151). While ideological notions of race have been directly tied to practices ranging from social segregation, ex-clusion from political participation, restrictive access to economic opportunities and resources, and geno-cide, the precise definition and significance of *racism* has been subject to enormous debate.

Robert Miles (1989) has argued that the term "racism" has been conceptually "inflated" to the point where it has lost its precision. While the problem of conceptual inflation and its political implications are evident in an era of colorblindness, the term "racism" is also subject to conceptual *de* flation. That is, what is considered racist is often defined very narrowly, in ways that obscure rather than reveal the pervasiveness and persistence of racial inequality in the United States. For example, racism has been popularly and narrowly conceived as racial *hate*. The category of "hate crimes" has been introduced in many states as a specific offense with enhanced sentencing conse-quence, and many colleges and universities have in-stituted "hate speech" codes to regulate expression and behavior both inside and outside of the class-room. Dramatic acts of racial violence are given con-siderable play in the mass media and are the subject of extensive condemnation by political elites. But as critical race scholar David Theo Goldberg (1997) has pointed out, the conceptual and political reduction of racism to hate both limits our understanding of racism and of the ways to challenge it. Racist acts are seen as "crimes of passion"—abnormal, unusual, and irrational deeds that we popularly consider offensive. Missing from such a narrow interpretation of racism are the ideologies, policies, and practices in a variety of institutional arenas that normalize and reproduce racial inequality and domination.

How should we understand racism today? We have argued that race has no fixed meaning, that it is con-structed and transformed sociohistorically through the cumulative convergence and conflict of racial projects that reciprocally structure and signify race. Our emphasis on racial projects allows us to advance a definition of racism as well. A racial project can be defined as racist if it *creates or reproduces structures of domination based on racial significations and identities.*

NOTES

1. Ian Hacking (2006; 1999) has given us the phrase "making up people" to explain how the human sciences operate, but Hacking doesn't stop there: he discusses med-icine, education, ideology, law, art, and state institutions as they do this work. Hacking, Ian. "Making Up People." *London Review of Books*, Vol. 28, no. 16 (August 17, 2006).

REFERENCES

Althusser, Louis. 1971 (2001). *Lenin and Philosophy, and Other Essays*. New York: Monthly Review Press.
American Sociologist Association. 2003. "The Importance of Collecting Data and Doing Social Scientific Research on Race." http://www.asanet.org/sites/default/files/savvy

/images/asa/docs/pdf/Task%20Force%20on%20State
ment%20on%20Race.pdf

Blumer, Herbert. 1958. "Race Prejudice as a Sense of Group Position." *The Pacific Sociological Review* (Spring, 1958), pp. 3-7.

Fredrickson, George M. 2002. *Racism: A Short History.* Princeton: Princeton University Press.

Goldberg, David Theo. 1997. *The Racial State.* New York: Blackwell.

Kim, Nadia Y. 2008. *Imperial Citizens: Koreans and Race from Seoul to LA.* Stanford: Stanford University Press.

Miles, Robert. 1989. *Racism.* New York: Routledge.

Obasogie, Osagie K. 2013. *Blinded by Sight.* Stanford: Stanford University Press.

Roth, Wendy. 2012. *Race Migrations: Latinos and the Cultural Transformation of Race.* Stanford: Stanford University Press.

Thomas, W.I., and D.S. Thomas. 1928. *The Child in America: Behavior Problems and Programs.* New York: Knopf.

44. Aliya Saperstein and Andrew M. Penner*
The Dynamics of Racial Fluidity and Inequality

Race is generally treated as an input in the American stratification system. People are assumed to be identifiable as members of distinct racial populations and subject to differential treatment based on this presumed membership. Those belonging to valued populations receive greater access to the resources and rewards of society, on average, than do those from devalued populations (Massey 2007). Because membership in these populations is assigned partly by ancestry and/or is based on readily observable and heritable physical features, the hierarchy of social positions can be passed on generation after generation, resulting in relatively low levels of mobility (Tilly 1998). Indeed, despite several decades of attempts to ameliorate racial inequality in the United States, large gaps in social, physical, mental, and material

*The ideas, issues, and theories considered in this brief commissioned piece are examined in greater depth in the following publication: Aliya Saperstein and Andrew M. Penner, "Racial Fluidity and Inequality in the United States," *American Journal of Sociology* 118:3 (2012), pp. 676–727, published by University of Chicago Press. The article printed here was originally prepared by Aliya Saperstein and Andrew M. Penner for the fourth edition of *Social Stratification: Class, Race, and Gender in Sociological Perspective*, edited by David B. Grusky. Copyright © 2014 by Westview Press.

well-being remain, particularly between Americans of African origin and everyone else (Fischer and Hout 2006).

We seek to extend the standard sociological account of US racial inequality by incorporating recent research from the fields of race and ethnicity and social psychology. We argue that instead of taking an individual's race as a given and examining how it affects that person's life chances, sociologists should be asking who is perceived, or identifies, as a particular race when, and why? This implies a reversal of the typical relationship between race and stratification, in which inequality also reinforces racial distinctions. Drawing on more than two decades of longitudinal data from a national survey, we demonstrate that treating race as a fixed characteristic not only oversimplifies the relationship between race and social status, it also obscures the role that the racial fluidity of individuals plays in stabilizing the "social invention" (ASA 2003) that is race in the United States.

Fixing Race

Despite the sociological consensus that race is a social construction that varies by context, standard practice in quantitative research assumes one's race is set at birth and predates one's life chances (Zuberi 2000). Racial fluidity, to the extent that it is acknowledged at all, is generally believed to be limited to three circumstances: 1) a small minority of present-day Americans with widely recognized mixed ancestries, such as Latinos, American Indians, and the children of the post-1960s "biracial baby boom"; 2) changes in the US racial hierarchy in particular historical epochs, such as the early 20th century "whitening" of southern and eastern Europeans; or 3) places with a high degree of racial mixing, such as Brazil.

However, if race is a categorical distinction imposed on otherwise continuous human variation (Ossorio and Duster 2005), and racial categorization is a fundamentally social process, even from a cognitive perspective (Freeman et al. 2011), then in many cases it is inappropriate to treat an individual's race as a constant. The analyses that follow, along with a growing literature documenting the fluidity and complexity of racial self-identification in the United States (e.g., Harris and Sim 2002; Doyle and Kao 2007; Craemer 2010; Khanna and Johnson 2010), cast further doubt on the common assumption that although race might be "socially constructed" in a macrolevel, sociohistorical sense, it is nevertheless a fixed attribute in the life of any given American.

Fluidity and Inequality

Theories of social boundary maintenance describe a number of ways that racial hierarchies and individual racial categorizations can change over time (see Wimmer 2008 for a review). Sometimes racial boundaries *shift* to incorporate large groups of people, such as when Puerto Rico's "white" population grew dramatically between censuses (Loveman and Muniz 2007), or when southern and eastern European immigrants were socially "whitened" in the early twentieth century (Jacobson 1999). Individuals can also *cross* existing racial boundaries as a result of changes in their personal characteristics. A typical example is known as passing, such as when the late Anatole Broyard, a book critic for the *New York Times,* severed ties with his Louisiana Creole family of origin in order to "pass" from black to white (Gates 1997).

For stratification scholars, such racial fluidity matters when it is related to patterns of social inequality. For most of his adult life, Anatole Broyard's income, wealth, and occupational prestige would have been counted among those of "whites" rather than "blacks." In Latin America the phrase "money whitens" describes a related form of boundary crossing, in which: people with Afrocentric features can be racially reclassified, seemingly out of courtesy, after they manage to climb the social ladder (Loveman and Muniz 2007). Thus, in some sense both passing and "whitening" result in an overestimate of racial inequality.

However, the language of over- or underestimates implies that there is a correct racial category in which all people should be placed. We argue that status-driven racial change is not a misunderstanding of the individual's "true" race and the extent of racial inequality at a given point in time; rather, it is indicative of how racial fluidity and social mobility interact to maintain inequality over time. For example, one of the reasons the racial hierarchy in the United States has remained relatively stable could be that upward mobility leads to reclassification: white people appear to be more successful in part because successful people become white, through self-identification, external classification, or both. Theoretically, the relationship also works in reverse. Downward mobility could be hidden, as well: black people may appear to be more criminal, unemployable, and so forth, in part because criminals and the unemployed are more likely to be seen as black (or less likely to be seen as white). Either

way, individual-level racial fluidity would serve to maintain existing group boundaries and the hierarchy of social positions they imply.

Stereotypes and Categorization

Research on stereotypes and cognitive racial categorization supports this perspective. Americans generally associate whites with positive traits, such as "smart" and "rich," and blacks with negative traits, such as "corrupt" and "poor" (Allen 1996); these associations have been shown to be at least partly nonconscious and active even in individuals who are otherwise racially egalitarian (see, e.g., Greenwald, McGhee, and Schwartz 1998). Indeed, research has demonstrated that negative beliefs about blacks can be activated without mentioning race at all, through the use of racially coded words such as "inner city" (Hurwitz and Peffley 2005) and "welfare" (Gilens 1995).

Social psychological research also shows that the racial categorization process itself is influenced by stereotypes and value judgments about the individual in question. For example, Richeson and Trawalter (2005) find that people take longer to racially categorize photographs of admired blacks (e.g., Martin Luther King Jr.) and disliked whites (e.g., Jeffrey Dahmer), and they are more likely to make "mistakes" than when categorizing either disliked blacks or admired whites. These stereotypical associations also can be bidirectional: not only does seeing black people make Americans think about crime, but thinking about crime makes Americans pay more attention to black people (Eberhardt et al. 2004). Thus, we expect to find that people who better fit the stereotypes of a particular racial group will be more likely to be classified as such.

Analytic Approach

To test this relationship, we examine whether racial classifications shift over time for the same individuals and whether such shifts are related to changes in social position. We focus on aspects of social status for which racial differences in outcomes are well known and linked to group stereotypes, such as incarceration, unemployment, and unmarried parenthood, and we ask whether changes along these status dimensions also shape racial perceptions—by influencing the way individuals are perceived racially by others.

We begin with descriptive comparisons using sample restrictions to demonstrate that changes in racial classification are related to changes in social position. We construct our outcomes as dichotomous variables to explore which characteristics move individuals either toward or away from the traditional poles of privilege and stigma in the United States: whiteness and blackness. For example, among people who were previously classified as white and had never been unemployed, we report how differences in current employment status are related to differences in the percentage of respondents who are classified as white in a given year. We then present predicted probabilities from a multivariate logistic regression model examining whether respondents are classified as white (vs. nonwhite) in a given year, controlling for how they were classified previously.

Data

Our data come from the 1979 cohort of the National Longitudinal Survey of Youth, a representative sample of 12,686 US men and women who were fourteen to twenty-two years of age when first surveyed in 1979. We use observations from 1979 to 1998, the most recent year in which interviewers were asked to racially classify respondents.

Measures of Race

Interviewers were instructed to classify respondents as "black," "white," or "other" at the end of the interview. Thus, we do not have a measure of the interviewers' first impressions of the respondents' race; rather, we have a classification colored by the respondents' answers during the survey interviews. This is ideal for the purposes of assessing the effects of social status on racial classification, because the interviewers heard a range of status information about the respondents prior to recording the respondents' race. Of the observations for which respondents have racial classifications in consecutive survey years, 6 percent are described by a different race than in the previous person-year, and 20 percent of the individuals in the sample experienced at least one change in how they were racially classified between 1979 and 1998.

Respondents were also asked to self-identify their "origin or descent" in 1979 and their "race or races" in 2002. We distinguish these as different dimensions of race: racial identification, naming oneself as a member of a racial group (as on a survey); and racial classification, the categorization of others as members of particular racial populations. Each dimension has consequences for both an individual's life chances and how researchers understand the dynamics of racial

TABLE 44.1 Comparison of Interviewers' Racial Classification of Respondents Between Two Interviews

| Race in Previous Year | Race in Current Year | | | |
	White	Black	Other	Total
White	95.8	0.5	3.7	100
N	103,690	554	4,036	108,280
Black	1.3	98.3	0.5	100
N	553	42,550	199	43,302
Other	45.1	2.3	52.6	100
N	4,041	205	4,708	8,954
Total	67.5	27.0	5.6	100
N	108,284	43,309	8,943	160,536

Note: N is given in person-years. Percentages and Ns sum across the rows, but may not add up to 100 due to rounding. Table includes all observations in which respondents had nonmissing racial classifications in two consecutive surveys.

Source: National Longitudinal Survey of Youth (NLSY) 1979.

inequality (Saperstein 2006). The analyses below focus on racial classification because it is directly linked to discrimination and stereotypical expectations, and because we have up to seventeen years of classification data, compared to just two for racial identification. Where possible, we used information on racial identification to conduct similar analyses and confirm that our results can be extended to how people describe themselves (see Saperstein and Penner 2012 for more details).

Social Status and Other Variables

In the logistic regression analysis, our primary independent variables are repeated measures of the respondent's social position, including long-term unemployment, poverty, incarceration, and marital and parental status. We also control for other respondent characteristics, including country of birth, region of residence, gender, age, and whether the respondent identified as multiracial or of Hispanic origin, as well as the interviewer's race, gender, education, and age. We include year fixed effects to account for societal changes in the definition of race, along with other year-to-year changes in survey design, question wording, or interviewer training.

Results

We begin by establishing the extent of fluidity in individuals' racial classification in the United States. Table 44.1 reports year-to-year changes in racial

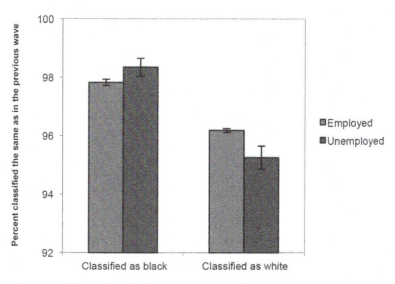

FIGURE 44.1 Changes in Social Status and Racial Classification

Notes: The percentage of people who were classified as black or white in the current survey (1980–1998), by whether they became unemployed for the first time. Restricted to those classified as black or white, respectively, in the previous survey and who were never previously unemployed. Unemployed indicates whether the respondent was unemployed for more than 4 months in the calendar year prior to the current survey. Error bars are ± 1SE.
Source: NLSY 1979.

classification in percentage terms. Each row displays the racial classification of respondents in the previous year by whether they were classified as white, black, or other by the interviewer in the current year. If race did not change over time, all of the observations would fall in the three cells representing consistent classification. Observations in the other cells indicate inconsistent classification, for example, 3.7 percent of respondents classified as white in the previous year are currently perceived as "other." Overall, this array suggests that the racial classification of Americans is more flexible than is commonly accounted for in models of racial inequality.

We next demonstrate how social status influences racial classification. Figure 44.1 illustrates how long-term unemployment leads to changes in respondents' racial classification; other status factors provide similar results. The figure includes two comparisons, depicting the percentage of respondents classified as either black or white in the current year. The observations are limited to people who were classified as black or white, respectively, in the previous year. To capture changes in employment status, we limit observations to respondents who as of the previous year had never been long-term unemployed. These sample restrictions allow us to compare the current racial classifications of

respondents who experienced a change in their employment status in the intervening year with the classifications of respondents who previously were classified the same way, but did not experience a change in social position.

Both comparisons in Figure 44.1 reveal classification differences in the expected directions: A higher percentage of unemployed respondents are classified as black and a lower percentage are classified as white, even if they were classified as such in the previous year. Although the differences are relatively small—for example, 96 percent of continuously employed respondents were again classified as white the following year, compared to 95 percent of respondents who lost their jobs in the interim—these represent year-to-year changes, and the differences for both black and white classification are statistically significant ($p < .05$). To the extent that status changes accumulate, even these small effects can play an important role in shaping racial classification over the life course, as we illustrate in the following figure.

Figure 44.2 depicts the cumulative effects of multiple status changes, drawing on the predicted probabilities from a logistic regression model estimating a person's odds of being classified as white.[1] We start with the probability that a hypothetical man who

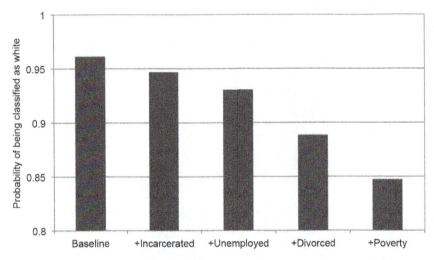

FIGURE 44.2 Cumulative Effect of Multiple Status Changes on Racial Classification

Note: The baseline category represents the predicted probability that a 29-year-old married father with a high school education, who lives in a nonsouthern inner city, does not identify as Hispanic or multiracial, and was classified as white in the previous year, was seen as white in 1990.
Source: NLSY 1979.

was classified as white in the previous year and had never been incarcerated, long-term unemployed, or in poverty would be classified as white again. Each subsequent bar in the figure makes one additional change to his status-related characteristics, so that the final bar illustrates the probability of being classified as white in the current year for a man who is now unmarried, has been incarcerated, has been unemployed for more than four months, and whose annual income is below the federal poverty line. This accumulation of negative status results in a decreased likelihood of being classified as white, from 96 percent at baseline to 85 percent.

To further explore this relationship, we also estimated four types of supplemental models.[2] First, we estimated multinomial logistic regression models that allow for changes among all three racial categories available to survey interviewers (black, white, and "other"); these models confirm that social status shapes changes among all three categories (and not only changes from white to other, or other to black). Second, we estimated models restricted to only non-multiracial, non-Hispanic, non-American Indian respondents to rule out the possibility that our findings were driven by the small minority of respondents for whom racial perceptions were already believed to be fluid and complex. Third, we estimated models with person-fixed effects, which show that our results are not fully explained by unmeasured respondent characteristics that are relatively

stable over time, such as family ancestry or skin tone. Finally, we estimated models that include racial classifications and status factors from each of the five previous years to confirm that the status factors still help to explain a person's current racial classification above and beyond knowing his or her recent history of racial classification. Though each of our modeling strategies has its strengths and weaknesses, we argue that in combination they provide consistent evidence of the reciprocal relationship between racial fluidity and inequality in the United States.

Discussion

Our results clearly demonstrate that racial classifications change over time, and they do so in response to changes in social position. However, such changes in an individual's race should not be thought of as permanent. Table 44.2 presents illustrative cases of respondents who have experienced long-term unemployment. These racial classification histories underscore that though respondents are more likely to be seen as black post-unemployment than they were pre-unemployment, they are not now always seen as black (Panel A). Similarly, people are more likely to be seen as nonwhite post-unemployment than they were before losing their jobs, but this does not mean that they are never again seen as white (Panel B). What seems to have changed is the per-

TABLE 44.2 Illustrative Racial Classification Histories Pre- and Post-unemployment

Panel A. Classified as Black

Person ID	Pre-unemployment	Post-unemployment	% Black Pre-unemployment	% Black Post-unemployment
343	OBO	BBBBBBBBBBBBBB	33	100
9266	W.OWW	BOBOWOBBOBO.	0	45
9372	OOO	BBBBBBBBBBBOBB	0	93

Panel B. Classified as White

Person ID	Pre-unemployment	Post-unemployment	% White Pre-unemployment	% White Post-unemployment
8857	WOOWWWW	WOOOOOOWOO	71	20
9282	WWWWWWWWOW	OWWOOOO	90	29
9969	WWWWWWWWWWWW	WWOOOO	100	33

Note: B denotes classification as black, W as white, and O as other, and a period denotes missing classification data. Percentages reflect the number of years the respondent was classified as the given race relative to all years with nonmissing classifications. Unemployment indicates whether the respondent was unemployed for more than 4 months in the previous calendar year.

Source: NLSY 1979.

son's likelihood of being seen as black or white in any given encounter.

These findings support defining race as a flexible propensity that changes over time and across contexts, rather than as a characteristic that is ascribed at birth and fixed. Race does not simply affect a person's social status; a loss or gain in status can alter both how people identify and how others perceive them. Americans who lose their jobs are more likely to be classified and identify as black, whereas people who get married are more likely to be classified and identify as white, regardless of how they were perceived or identified previously. These effects are only strengthened when one change in social position triggers, or is accompanied by, others—such as when marriage increases household income or unemployment follows incarceration.

Of course not every change in a person's social position results in racial fluidity. Changes in status that are stereotype inconsistent drive racial fluidity, whereas stereotype consistent shifts in status reinforce racial stability. Also, to trigger an observed change, the propensity to be classified as a particular race presumably must cross a certain threshold. People can be thought of as having different starting propensities to be classified as a given race: some will have relatively high baseline propensities to be racially classified in a variety of ways, whereas others will have relatively low, near-zero baseline propensities to be classified in more than one category. Nevertheless, our results suggest that a stint in prison or falling into poverty will increase everyone's odds of being seen as black and decrease everyone's odds of being seen as white in future encounters.

Conclusion

Demonstrations of the complexity and social construction of race are often met with calls for abandoning racial categorization because it is unnecessarily divisive and creates boundaries that would not otherwise exist (e.g., Connerly 2001). However, we do not believe that the idea that race is fluid at the individual level should be interpreted as evidence that racial divisions are only imagined. Race remains real because it has important consequences for people's life chances. Our results show that racial divisions, like other aspects of social structure, do not simply happen to people; racial inequality is actively (if sometimes unintentionally) reproduced in everyday interactions.

This process has implications for understanding racial discrimination. Like most research on racial inequality, studies typically assume that a person's race is fixed and self-evident. Our results are an important reminder that racial perceptions are central to the process of discrimination, and that an act of discrimination first requires classifying an individual as belonging in a particular racial category.

Finally, we suggest that thinking about race as fluid, ironically, helps explain the rigidity of racial hierarchy in the United States. If some Americans who experience an increase in status are "whitened" as a result of their upward mobility, and some who experience downward mobility are "darkened," these changes serve to reinforce both racial inequality and existing stereotypes. That is, race implies—and is defined in part by—a set of expectations by which people are continually judged in everyday interactions (see also Gross 1998). When a white person is someone who does what a white person is supposed to do, and a black person is someone who does what a black person is supposed to do, then race is not just an input into the stratification system; it is an output, as well.

REFERENCES

Allen, B. P. 1996. "African Americans' and European Americans' Mutual Attributions: Adjective Generation Technique Stereotyping." *Journal of Applied Social Psychology* 26: 884–912.

American Sociological Association (ASA). 2003. *The Importance of Collecting Data and Doing Social Scientific Research on Race*. Washington, DC: American Sociological Association.

Connerly, Ward. 2001. "The Irrelevance of Race." *San Francisco Chronicle*, July 8, C8.

Craemer, Thomas. 2010. "Ancestral Ambivalence and Racial Self-Classification Change." *Social Science Journal* 47: 307–325.

Doyle, Jamie M., and Grace Kao. 2007. "Are Racial Identities of Multiracials Stable? Changing Self-Identification among Single and Multiple Race Individuals." *Social Psychology Quarterly* 70 (4): 405–423.

Eberhardt, Jennifer L., Phillip Atiba Goff, Valeria J. Purdie, and Paul G. Davies. 2004. "Seeing Black: Race, Crime and Visual Processing." *Journal of Personality and Social Psychology* 87 (6): 876–893.

Fischer, Claude S., and Michael Hout. 2006. *Century of Difference: How America Changed in the Last One Hundred Years*. New York: Russell Sage.

Freeman, Jonathan B., Andrew M. Penner, Aliya Saperstein, Matthias Scheutz, and Nalini Ambady. 2011. "Looking the Part: Social Status Cues Shape Race Perception." PLoS One 6 (9): e25107.

Gates, Henry Louis, Jr. 1997. "The Passing of Anatole Broyard." In *Thirteen Ways of Looking at a Black Man*, 180–214. New York: Random House.

Gilens, Martin. 1995. "Racial-Attitudes and Opposition to Welfare." Journal of Politics 57: 994–1014.

Greenwald, Anthony G., Debbie E. McGhee, and Jordan L. K. Schwartz. 1998. "Measuring Individual Differences in Implicit Cognition: The Implicit Association Test." *Journal of Personality and Social Psychology* 74 (6): 1464–1480.

Gross, Ariela J. 1998. "Litigating Whiteness: Trials of Racial Determination in the Nineteenth Century U.S. South." *Yale Law Journal* 108 (1): 109–188.

Harris, David R., and Jeremiah Joseph Sim. 2002. "Who Is Multiracial? Assessing the Complexity of Lived Race." *American Sociological Review* 67: 614–627.

Hurwitz, J., and M. Peffley. 2005. "Playing the Race Card in the Post-Willie Horton Era—The Impact of Racialized Code Words on Support for Punitive Crime Policy." *Public Opinion Quarterly* 69: 99–112.

Jacobson, Matthew Frye. 1999. *Whiteness of a Different Color: European Immigrants and the Alchemy of Race*. Cambridge, MA: Harvard University Press.

Khanna, Nikki, and Cathryn Johnson. 2010. "Passing as Black: Racial Identity Work Among Biracial Americans." *Social Psychology Quarterly* 73 (4): 380–397.

Loveman, Mara, and Jeronimo O. Muniz. 2007. "How Puerto Rico Became White: Boundary Dynamics and Intercensus Racial Reclassification." *American Sociological Review* 72 (6): 915–939.

Massey, Douglas. 2007. *Categorically Unequal: The American Stratification System*. New York: Russell Sage Foundation.

Ossorio, Pilar, and Troy Duster. 2005. "Race and Genetics—Controversies in Biomedical, Behavioral and Forensic Sciences." *American Psychologist* 60 (1): 115–128.

Richeson, Jennifer A., and Sophie Trawalter. 2005. "On the Categorization of Admired and Disliked Exemplars of Admired and Disliked Racial Groups." *Journal of Personality and Social Psychology* 89 (4): 517–530.

Saperstein, Aliya. 2006. "Double-checking the Race Box: Examining Inconsistency between Survey Measures of Observed and Self-Reported Race." *Social Forces* 85 (1): 57–74.

Saperstein, Aliya, and Andrew M. Penner. 2012. "Racial Fluidity and Inequality in the United States." *American Journal of Sociology* 113 (3): 676–727.

Tilly, Charles. 1998. *Durable Inequalities*. Berkeley: University of California Press.

Wimmer, Andreas. 2008. "The Making and Unmaking of Ethnic Boundaries: A Multilevel Process Theory." *American Journal of Sociology* 113 (4): 970–1022.

Zuberi, Tukufu. 2000. "Deracializing Social Statistics: Problems in the Quantification of Race." *Annals of the American Academy of Political and Social Science* 568: 172–185.

NOTES

1 As noted previously, this model includes all measures of social position simultaneously, along with an indicator of whether the respondent was classified as white in the previous year, and controls for other respondent characteristics, interviewer characteristics, and year fixed effects. See Saperstein and Penner (2012) for more details.

2 See Saperstein and Penner (2012) for these results.

Immigration

45. Alejandro Portes and Min Zhou*

The New Second Generation: Segmented Assimilation and Its Variants

My name is Herb
and I'm not poor;
I'm the Herbie that you're looking for,
like Pepsi,
a new generation
of Haitian determination—
I'm the Herbie that you're looking for.

A beat tapped with bare hands, a few dance steps, and the Haitian kid was rapping. His song, titled "Straight Out of Haiti," was being performed at Edison High, a school that sits astride Little Haiti and Liberty City, the largest black area of Miami. The lyrics captured well the distinct outlook of his immigrant community. The panorama of Little Haiti contrasts sharply with the bleak inner city. In Miami's Little Haiti, the storefronts leap out at the passersby. Bright blues, reds, and oranges vibrate to Haitian merengue blaring from sidewalk speakers.[1] Yet, behind the gay Caribbean exteriors, a struggle goes on that will define the future of this community. As we will see later on, it involves the second generation—children like Herbie—subject to conflicting pressure from parents and peers and to pervasive outside discrimination.

Growing up in an immigrant family has always been difficult, as individuals are torn by conflicting social and cultural demands while they face the

*Alejandro Portes and Min Zhou. "The New Second Generation: Segmented Assimilation and Its Variants," *The Annals of the American Academy of Political and Social Science* 530 (November 1993), pp. 75–77, 81–92, 96. National American Woman Suffrage Association Collection. Copyright © 1993 by Sage Publications, Inc. Reprinted by permission of Sage Publications, Inc.

challenge of entry into an unfamiliar and frequently hostile world. And yet the difficulties are not always the same. The process of growing up American oscillates between smooth acceptance and traumatic confrontation depending on the characteristics that immigrants and their children bring along and the social context that receives them. In this article, we explore some of these factors and their bearing on the process of social adaptation of the immigrant second generation. We propose a conceptual framework for understanding this process and illustrate it with selected ethnographic material and survey data from a recent survey of children of immigrants.

Research on the new immigration—that which arose after the passage of the 1965 Immigration Act—has been focused almost exclusively on the first generation, that is, on adult men and women coming to the United States in search of work or to escape political persecution. Little noticed until recently is the fact that the foreign-born inflow has been rapidly evolving from single adult individuals to entire family groups, including infant children and those born to immigrants in the United States. By 1980, 10 percent of dependent children in households counted by the census were second-generation immigrants.[2] In the late 1980s, another study put the number of students in kindergarten through twelfth grade in American schools who spoke a language other than English at home at 3 to 5 million.[3] The great deal of research and theorizing on post-1965 immigration offers only tentative guidance on the prospects and paths of adaptation of the second generation because the outlook of this group can be very different from that of their immigrant parents. For example, it is generally accepted among immigration theorists that entry-level menial jobs are performed without hesitation by newly arrived immigrants but are commonly shunned by their US-reared offspring. This disjuncture gives rise to a race between the social and economic progress of first-generation immigrants and the material conditions and career prospects that their American children grow to expect.[4] Nor does the existing literature on second-generation adaptation, based as it is on the experience of descendants of pre-World War I immigrants, offer much guidance for the understanding of contemporary events. The last sociological study of children of immigrants was Irving Child's *Italian or American? The Second Generation in Conflict,* published fifty years ago.[5] Conditions at the time were quite different from those confronting settled immigrant groups today. Two such differences deserve special mention. First, descendants of European immigrants who confronted the dilemmas of conflicting cultures were uniformly white. Even if of a somewhat darker hue than the natives, their skin color reduced a major barrier to entry into the American mainstream. For this reason, the process of assimilation depended largely on individual decisions to leave the immigrant culture behind and embrace American ways. Such an advantage obviously does not exist for the black, Asian, and mestizo children of today's immigrants.

Second, the structure of economic opportunities has also changed. Fifty years ago, the United States was the premier industrial power in the world, and its diversified industrial labor requirements offered to the second generation the opportunity to move up gradually through better-paid occupations while remaining part of the working class. Such opportunities have increasingly disappeared in recent years following a rapid process of national deindustrialization and global industrial restructuring. This process has left entrants to the American labor force confronting a widening gap between the minimally paid menial jobs that immigrants commonly accept and the high-tech and professional occupations requiring college degrees that native elites occupy.[6] The gradual disappearance of intermediate opportunities also bears directly on the race between first-generation economic progress and second-generation expectations, noted previously. . . .

Assimilation as a Problem

The Haitian immigrant community of Miami is composed of some 75,000 legal and clandestine immigrants, many of whom sold everything they owned in order to buy passage to America. First-generation Haitians are strongly oriented toward preserving a strong national identity, which they associate both with community solidarity and with social networks promoting individual success.[7] In trying to instill national pride and an achievement orientation in their children, they clash, however, with the youngsters' everyday experiences in school. Little Haiti is adjacent to Liberty City, the main black inner-city area of Miami, and Haitian adolescents attend predominantly inner-city schools. Native-born youths stereotype Haitians as too docile and too subservient to whites and they make fun of French and Creole and of the Haitians' accent. As a result, second-generation Haitian children find themselves torn between conflicting ideas and values: to remain Haitian they would have to face social ostracism and continuing attacks in school; to become American—black American in this case—they would have to forgo their parents' dreams of making it in America on the basis of ethnic solidarity and preservation of traditional values.[8] An adversarial stance toward the white mainstream is common among inner-city minority youths who, while attacking the newcomers' ways, instill in them a consciousness of American-style discrimination. A common message is the devaluation of education as a vehicle for advancement of all black youths, a message that directly contradicts the immigrant parents' expectations. Academically outstanding Haitian American students, "Herbie" among them, have consciously attempted to retain their ethnic identity by cloaking it in black American cultural forms, such as rap music. Many others, however, have followed the path of least effort and become thoroughly assimilated. Assimilation in this instance is not into mainstream culture but into the values and norms of the inner city. In the process, the resources of solidarity and mutual support within the immigrant community are dissipated.

An emerging paradox in the study of today's second generation is the peculiar forms that assimilation has adopted for its members. As the Haitian example illustrates, adopting the outlooks and cultural ways of the native-born does not represent, as in the past, the first step toward social and economic mobility, but may lead to the exact opposite. At the other end, immigrant youths who remain firmly ensconced in their respective ethnic communities may, by virtue of this fact, have a better chance for educational and economic mobility through use of the material and social capital that their communities make available.[9] This situation stands the cultural blueprint for advancement of immigrant groups in American society on its head. As presented in innumerable academic and journalistic writings, the expectation is that the foreign-born and their offspring will first acculturate and then seek entry and acceptance among the native-born as a prerequisite for their social and economic advancement. Otherwise, they remain confined to the ranks of the ethnic lower and lower-middle classes.[10] This portrayal of the requirements for mobility, so deeply embedded in the national consciousness, stands contradicted today by a growing number of empirical experiences.

A closer look at these experiences indicates, however, that the expected consequences of assimilation have not entirely reversed signs, but that the process has become segmented. In other words, the question is into what sector of American society a particular immigrant group assimilates. Instead of a relatively uniform mainstream whose mores and prejudices dictate a common path of integration, we observe today several distinct forms of adaptation. One of them replicates the time-honored portrayal of growing acculturation and parallel integration into the white middle-class; a second leads straight in the opposite direction to permanent poverty and assimilation into the underclass; still a third associates rapid economic advancement with deliberate preservation of the immigrant community's values and tight solidarity. This pattern of segmented assimilation immediately raises the question of what makes some immigrant groups become susceptible to the downward route and what resources allow others to avoid this course. In the ultimate analysis, the same general process helps explain both outcomes. We advance next our hypotheses as to how this process takes place and how the contrasting outcomes of assimilation can be explained. This explanation is then illustrated with recent empirical material in the final section.

Vulnerability and Resources

Along with individual and family variables, the context that immigrants find upon arrival in their new country plays a decisive role in the course that their offspring's lives will follow. This context includes such broad variables as political relations between sending and receiving countries and the state of the economy in the latter and such specific ones as the size and structure of preexisting coethnic communities. The concept of modes of incorporation provides a useful theoretical tool to understand this diversity. As developed in prior publications, modes of incorporation consist of the complex formed by the policies of the host government; the values and prejudices of the receiving society; and the characteristics of the coethnic community. These factors can be arranged

in a tree of contextual situations, illustrated by Figure 45.1. This figure provides a first approximation to our problem.[11] To explain second-generation outcomes and their segmented character, however, we need to go into greater detail into the meaning of these various modes of incorporation from the standpoint of immigrant youths. There are three features of the social contexts encountered by today's newcomers that create vulnerability to downward assimilation. The first is color, the second is location, and the third is the absence of mobility ladders. As noted previously, the majority of contemporary immigrants are nonwhite. Although this feature may appear at first glance as an individual characteristic, in reality it is a trait belonging to the host society. Prejudice is not intrinsic to a particular skin color or racial type, and, indeed, many immigrants never experienced it in their native lands. It is by virtue of moving into a new social environment, marked by different values and prejudices, that physical features become redefined as a handicap.

The concentration of immigrant households in cities and particularly in central cities, as documented previously, gives rise to a second source of vulnerability because it puts new arrivals in close contact with concentrations of native-born minorities. This leads to the identification of the condition of both groups—immigrants and the native poor—as the same in the eyes of the majority. More important, it exposes second-generation children to the adversarial subculture developed by marginalized native youths to cope with their own difficult situation.[12] This process of socialization may take place even when first-generation parents are moving ahead economically and, hence, their children have no objective reasons for embracing a counter-cultural message. If successful, the process can effectively block parental plans for intergenerational mobility.

The third contextual source of vulnerability has to do with changes in the host economy that have led to the evaporation of occupational ladders for intergenerational mobility. As noted previously, new immigrants may form the backbone of what remains of labor-intensive manufacturing in the cities as well as in their growing personal services sector, but these are niches that seldom offer channels for upward mobility. The new hourglass economy, created by economic restructuring, means that children of immigrants must cross a narrow bottleneck to occupations requiring advanced training if their careers are to keep pace with their US-acquired aspirations. This race against a narrowing middle demands that immigrant parents accumulate sufficient resources to allow their children to effect the passage and to simultaneously prove to them the viability of aspirations for upward mobility. Otherwise, assimilation may not be into mainstream values and expectations but into the adversarial stance of impoverished groups confined to the bottom of the new economic hourglass.

The picture is painted in such stark terms here for the sake of clarity, although in reality things have not yet become so polarized. Middle-level occupations requiring relatively modest educational achievements have not completely vanished. By 1980, skilled blue-collar jobs—classified by the US census as "precision production, craft, and repair occupations"—had declined by 1.1 percent relative to a decade earlier but still represented 13 percent of the experienced civilian labor force, or 13.6 million workers. Mostly clerical administrative support occupations added another 16.9 percent, or 17.5 million jobs. In 1980, occupations requiring a college degree had increased by 6 percent in comparison with 1970, but they still employed less than a fifth—18.2 percent—of the American labor force.[13] Even in the largest cities, occupations requiring only a high school diploma were common by the late 1980s. In New York City, for example, persons with twelve years or less of schooling held just over one half of the jobs in 1987. Clerical, service, and skilled blue-collar jobs not requiring a college degree represented 46 percent.[14] Despite these figures, there is little doubt that the trend toward occupational segmentation has increasingly reduced opportunities for incremental upward mobility through well-paid blue-collar positions. The trend forces immigrants today to bridge in only one generation the gap between entry-level jobs and professional positions that earlier groups took two or three generations to travel.

Different modes of incorporation also make available, however, three types of resources to confront the challenges of contemporary assimilation. First, certain groups, notably political refugees, are eligible for a variety of government programs including educational loans for their children. The Cuban Loan Program, implemented by the Kennedy administration in connection with its plan to resettle Cuban refugees away from South Florida, gave many impoverished first- and second-generation Cuban youths a chance to attend college. The high proportion of professionals and executives among Cuban American workers today, a figure on a par with that for native white workers, can be traced, at least in part, to the success of that program.[15] Passage of the 1980 Refugee Act gave to subsequent groups of refugees, in particular Southeast Asians and Eastern Europeans, access to a similarly generous benefits package.[16] Second, certain foreign groups have been exempted from the traditional prejudice endured by most immigrants, thereby facilitating a smoother process of adaptation. Some political refugees, such as the early waves of exiles from Castro's Cuba, Hungarians and Czechs escaping the invasions of their respective countries, and Soviet Jews escaping religious persecution, provide examples. In other cases, it is the cultural and phenotypical affinity of newcomers to ample segments of the host population that ensures a welcome reception. The Irish coming to Boston during the 1980s are a case in point. Although many were illegal aliens, they came into an environment where generations of Irish Americans had established a secure foothold. Public sympathy effectively neutralized governmental hostility in this case, culminating in a change of the immigration law directly benefiting the newcomers.[17] Third, and most importantly, are the resources made available through networks in the coethnic community. Immigrants who join well-established and diversified ethnic groups have access from the start to a range of moral and material resources well beyond those available through official assistance programs. Educational help for second-generation youths may include not only access to college grants and loans but also the existence of a private school system geared to the immigrant community's values. Attendance at these private ethnic schools insulates children from contact with native minority youths, while reinforcing the authority of parental views and plans.

In addition, the economic diversification of several immigrant communities creates niches of opportunity that members of the second generation can occupy, often without a need for an advanced education. Small-business apprenticeships, access to skilled building trades, and well-paid jobs in local government bureaucracies are some of the ethnic niches documented in the recent literature.[18] In 1987, average sales per firm of the smaller Chinese, East Indian, Korean, and Cuban enterprises exceeded $100,000 per year and they jointly employed over 200,000 workers. These figures omit medium-sized and large ethnic firms, whose sales and work forces are much larger.[19] Fieldwork in these communities indicates that up to half of recently arrived immigrants are employed by coethnic firms and that self-employment offers a prime avenue for

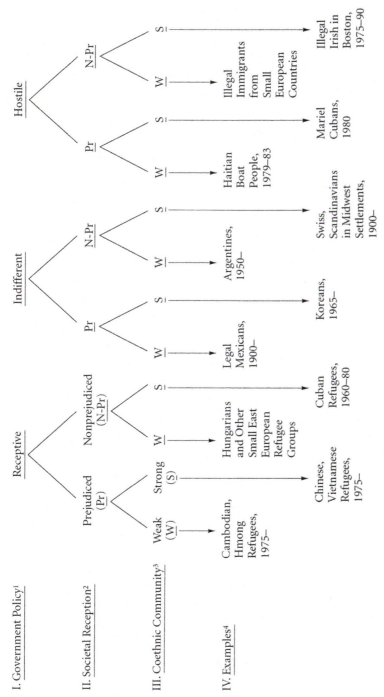

FIGURE 45.1 Models of Incorporation: A Typology

Source: Adapted from Alajandro Portes and Rubén G. Rumbaut, *Immigrant America: A Portrait* (Berkeley: University of California Press, 1990), p. 91. Copyright © 1990 by the Regents of the University of California.

1. Receptive Policy is defined as legal entry with resettlement assistance, indifferent as legal entry without resettlement assistance, hostile as active opposition to a group's entry or permanence in the country; 2. Prejudiced reception is defined as that accorded to nonphenotypically white groups; nonprejudiced is that accorded to European and European-origin whites; 3. Weak coethnic communities are either small in numbers or composed primarily of manual workers; strong communities feature sizable numerical concentrations and a diversified occupational structure including entrepreneurs and professionals; 4. Examples include immigrant groups arriving from the start of the century to the present. Dates of migration are approximate. Groups reflect broadly but not perfectly the characteristics of each ideal type.

mobility to second-generation youths.[20] Such community-mediated opportunities provide a solution to the race between material resources and second-generation aspirations not available through competition in the open labor market. Through creation of a capitalism of their own, some immigrant groups have thus been able to circumvent outside discrimination and the threat of vanishing mobility ladders.

In contrast to these favorable conditions are those foreign minorities who either lack a community already in place or whose coethnics are too poor to render assistance. The condition of Haitians in South Florida, cited earlier, provides an illustration of one of the most handicapped modes of incorporation encountered by contemporary immigrants, combining official hostility and widespread social prejudice with the absence of a strong receiving community.[21] From the standpoint of second-generation outcomes, the existence of a large but downtrodden coethnic community may be even less desirable than no community at all. This is because newly arrived youths enter into ready contact with the reactive subculture developed by earlier generations. Its influence is all the more powerful because it comes from individuals of the same national origin, "people like us" who can more effectively define the proper stance and attitudes of the newcomers. To the extent that they do so, the first-generation model of upward mobility through school achievement and attainment of professional occupations will be blocked.

Three Examples

Mexicans and Mexican Americans

Field High School (the name is fictitious) is located in a small coastal community of central California whose economy has long been tied to agricultural production and immigrant farm labor. About 57 percent of the student population is of Mexican descent. An intensive ethnographic study of the class of 1985 at Field High began with school records that showed that the majority of US-born Spanish-surname students who had entered the school in 1981 had dropped out by their senior year. However, only 35 percent of the Spanish-surname students who had been originally classified by the school as limited English proficient (LEP) had dropped out. The figure was even lower than the corresponding one for native white students, 40

percent. LEP status is commonly assigned to recently arrived Mexican immigrants.[22] Intensive ethnographic fieldwork at the school identified several distinct categories in which the Mexican-origin population could be classified. Recent Mexican immigrants were at one extreme. They dressed differently and unstylishly. They claimed an identity as Mexican and considered Mexico their permanent home. The most academically successful of this group were those most proficient in Spanish, reflecting their prior levels of education in Mexico. Almost all were described by teachers and staff as courteous, serious about their schoolwork, respectful, and eager to please as well as naive and unsophisticated. They were commonly classified as LEP.

The next category comprised Mexican-oriented students. They spoke Spanish at home and were generally classified as fluent English proficient (FEP). They had strong bicultural ties with both Mexico and the United States, reflecting the fact that most were born in Mexico but had lived in the United States for more than five years. They were proud of their Mexican heritage but saw themselves as different from the first group, the *recién llegados* (recently arrived), as well as from the native-born Chicanos and Cholos, who were derided as people who had lost their Mexican roots. Students from this group were active in soccer and the Sociedad Bilingue and in celebrations of May 5th, the anniversary of the Mexican defeat of French occupying forces. Virtually all of the Mexican-descent students who graduated in the top 10 percent of their class in 1981 were identified as members of this group.

Chicanos were by far the largest Mexican-descent group at Field High. They were mostly US-born second- and third-generation students whose primary loyalty was to their in-group, seen as locked in conflict with white society. Chicanos referred derisively to successful Mexican students as "schoolboys" and "schoolgirls" or as "wannabes." According to M. G. Matute-Bianchi,

> To be a Chicano meant in practice to hang out by the science wing . . . *not* eating lunch in the quad where all the "gringos" and "schoolboys" hang out . . . cutting classes by faking a call slip so you can be with your friends at the 7-11 . . . sitting in the back of classes and not participating . . . *not* carrying your books to class . . . *not* taking the difficult classes . . . doing the minimum to get by.[23]

Chicanos merge imperceptibly into the last category, the Cholos, who were commonly seen as "low riders" and gang members. They were also native-born Mexican Americans, easily identifiable by their deliberate manner of dress, walk, speech, and other cultural symbols. Chicanos and Cholos were generally regarded by teachers as "irresponsible," "disrespectful," "mistrusting," "sullen," "apathetic," and "less motivated," and their poor school performance was attributed to these traits.[24] According to Matute-Bianchi, Chicanos and Cholos were faced with what they saw as a forced-choice dilemma between doing well in school or being a Chicano. To act white was regarded as disloyalty to one's group.

The situation of these last two groups exemplifies losing the race between first-generation achievements and later generations' expectations. Seeing their parents and grandparents confined to humble menial jobs and increasingly aware of discrimination against them by the white mainstream, US-born children of earlier Mexican immigrants readily join a reactive subculture as a means of protecting their sense of self-worth. Participation in this subculture then leads to serious barriers to their chances of upward mobility because school achievement is defined as antithetical to ethnic solidarity. Like Haitian students at Edison High, newly arrived Mexican students are at risk of being socialized into the same reactive stance, with the aggravating factor that it is other Mexicans, not native-born strangers, who convey the message. The principal protection of *mexicanos* against this type of assimilation lies in their strong identification with home-country language and values, which brings them closer to their parents' cultural stance.

Punjabi Sikhs in California

Valleyside (a fictitious name) is a northern California community where the primary economic activity is orchard farming. Farm laborers in this area come often from India; they are mainly rural Sikhs from the Punjab. By the early 1980s, second-generation Punjabi students already accounted for 11 percent of the student body at Valleyside High. Their parents were no longer only farm laborers, since about a third had become orchard owners themselves and another third worked in factories in the nearby San Francisco area. An ethnographic study of Valleyside High School in 1980–82 revealed a very difficult process of assimilation for Punjabi Sikh students. According to its author, M.

A. Gibson, Valleyside is "redneck country," and white residents are extremely hostile to immigrants who look different and speak a different language: "Punjabi teenagers are told they stink . . . told to go back to India . . . physically abused by majority students who spit at them, refuse to sit by them in class or in buses, throw food at them or worse."[25] Despite these attacks and some evidence of discrimination by school staff, Punjabi students performed better academically than majority Anglo students. About 90 percent of the immigrant youths completed high school, compared to 70–75 percent of native whites. Punjabi boys surpassed the average grade point average, were more likely to take advanced science and math classes, and expressed aspirations for careers in science and engineering. Girls, on the other hand, tended to enroll in business classes, but they paid less attention to immediate career plans, reflecting parental wishes that they should marry first. This gender difference is indicative of the continuing strong influence exercised by the immigrant community over its second generation. According to Gibson, Punjabi parents pressured their children against too much contact with white peers who may "dishonor" the immigrants' families, and defined "becoming Americanized" as forgetting one's roots and adopting the most disparaged traits of the majority, such as leaving home at age eighteen, making decisions without parental consent, dating, and dancing. At the same time, parents urged children to abide by school rules, ignore racist remarks and avoid fights, and learn useful skills, including full proficiency in English.[26] The overall success of this strategy of selective assimilation to American society is remarkable because Punjabi immigrants were generally poor on their arrival in the United States and confronted widespread discrimination from whites without the benefit of either governmental assistance or a well-established coethnic community. In terms of our typology of vulnerability and resources, the Punjabi Sikh second generation was very much at risk except for two crucial factors. First, immigrant parents did not settle in the inner city or in close proximity to any native-born minority whose offspring could provide an alternative model of adaptation to white-majority discrimination. In particular, the absence of a downtrodden Indian American community composed of children of previous immigrants allowed first-generation parents to influence decisively the outlook of their offspring, including their ways of fighting white prejudice. There was no equivalent of a Cholo-like reactive subculture to offer an alternative blueprint of the stance that "people like us" should take.

Second, Punjabi immigrants managed to make considerable economic progress, as attested by the number who had become farm owners, while maintaining a tightly knit ethnic community. The material and social capital created by this first-generation community compensated for the absence of an older coethnic group and had decisive effects on second-generation outlooks. Punjabi teenagers were shown that their parents' ways paid off economically, and this fact, plus their community's cohesiveness, endowed them with a source of pride to counteract outside discrimination. Through this strategy of selective assimilation, Punjabi Sikhs appeared to be winning the race against the inevitable acculturation of their children to American-style aspirations.

Caribbean Youths in South Florida

Miami is arguably the American city that has been most thoroughly transformed by post-1960 immigration. The Cuban Revolution had much to do with this transformation, as it sent the entire Cuban upper class out of the country, followed by thousands of refugees of more modest backgrounds. Over time, Cubans created a highly diversified and prosperous ethnic community that provided resources for the adaptation process of its second generation. Reflecting this situation are average Cuban family incomes that, by 1989, approximated those of the native-born population; the existence in 1987 of more than 30,000 Cuban-owned small businesses that formed the core of the Miami ethnic enclave; and the parallel rise of a private school system oriented toward the values and political outlook of this community.[27] In terms of the typology of vulnerability and resources, well-sheltered Cuban American teenagers lack any extensive exposure to outside discrimination, they have little contact with youths from disadvantaged minorities, and the development of an enclave creates economic opportunities beyond the narrowing industrial and tourist sectors on which most other immigrant groups in the area depend. Across town, Haitian American teenagers face exactly the opposite set of conditions, as has been shown.

Among the other immigrant groups that form Miami's ethnic mosaic, two deserve mention because they represent intermediate situations between those of the Cubans and Haitians. One comprises Nicaraguans escaping the Sandinista regime during the

1980s. They were not as welcomed in the United States as were the Cuban exiles, nor were they able to develop a large and diversified community. Yet they shared with Cubans their language and culture, as well as a militant anti-Communist discourse. This common political outlook led the Cuban American community to extend its resources in support of their Nicaraguan brethren, smoothing their process of adaptation.[28] For second-generation Nicaraguans, this means that the preexisting ethnic community that provides a model for their own assimilation is not a downtrodden group but rather one that has managed to establish a firm and positive presence in the city's economy and politics.

The second group comprises West Indians coming from Jamaica, Trinidad, and other English-speaking Caribbean republics. They generally arrive in Miami as legal immigrants, and many bring along professional and business credentials as well as the advantage of fluency in English. These individual advantages are discounted, however, by a context of reception in which these mostly black immigrants are put in the same category as native-born blacks and discriminated against accordingly. The recency of West Indian migration and its small size have prevented the development of a diversified ethnic community in South Florida. Hence new arrivals experience the full force of white discrimination without the protection of a large coethnic group and with constant exposure to the situation and attitudes of the inner-city population. Despite considerable individual resources, these disadvantages put the West Indian second generation at risk of bypassing white or even native black middle-class models to assimilate into the culture of the underclass. . . .

Conclusion

Fifty years ago, the dilemma of Italian American youngsters studied by Irving Child consisted of assimilating into the American mainstream, sacrificing in the process their parents' cultural heritage in contrast to taking refuge in the ethnic community from the challenges of the outside world. In the contemporary context of segmented assimilation, the options have become less clear. Children of nonwhite immigrants may not even have the opportunity of gaining access to middle-class white society, no matter how acculturated they become. Joining those native circles to which they do have access may prove a ticket to permanent subordination and disadvantage. Remaining securely ensconced in their coethnic community, under these circumstances, may be not a symptom of escapism but the best strategy for capitalizing on otherwise unavailable material and moral resources. As the experiences of Punjabi Sikh and Cuban American students suggest, a strategy of paced, selective assimilation may prove the best course for immigrant minorities. But the extent to which this strategy is possible also depends on the history of each group and its specific profile of vulnerabilities and resources. The present analysis represents a preliminary step toward understanding these realities.

NOTES

1. Alejandro Portes and Alex Stepick, *City on the Edge: The Transformation of Miami* (Berkeley: University of California Press, 1993), chap. 8.

2. Defined as native-born children with at least one foreign-born parent or children born abroad who came to the United States before age twelve.

3. Joan N. First and John W. Carrera, *New Voices: Immigrant Students in U.S. Public Schools* (Boston: National Coalition of Advocates for Students, 1988).

4. Michael Piore, *Birds of Passage* (New York: Cambridge University Press, 1979); Herbert Gans, "Second-Generation Decline: Scenarios for the Economic and Ethnic Futures of the Post-1965 American Immigrants," *Ethnic and Racial Studies* 15:173–92 (Apr. 1992).

5. Irving L. Child, *Italian or American? The Second Generation in Conflict* (New Haven, CT: Yale University Press, 1943).

6. See, for example, Saskia Sassen, "Changing Composition and Labor Market Location of Hispanic Immigrants in New York City, 1960–1980," in *Hispanics in the U.S. Economy*, ed. George J. Borjas and Marta Tienda (New York: Academic Press, 1985), pp. 299–322.

7. See Alex Stepick, "Haitian Refugees in the U.S." (Report no. 52, Minority Rights Group, London, 1982); Alex Stepick and Alejandro Portes, "Flight into Despair: A Profile of Recent Haitian Refugees in South Florida," *International Migration Review*, 20:329–50 (Summer 1986).

8. This account is based on fieldwork in Miami conducted in preparation for a survey of immigrant youths in public schools.

9. On the issue of social capital, see James S. Coleman, "Social Capital in the Creation of Human Capital," *American Journal of Sociology*, supplement, 94:S95–121 (1988); Alejandro Portes and Min Zhou, "Gaining the Upper Hand: Economic Mobility among Immigrant and Domestic Minorities," *Ethnic and Racial Studies*, 15:491–522 (Oct. 1992). On ethnic entrepreneurship, see Ivan H. Light, *Ethnic Enterprise in America: Business and Welfare among Chinese, Japanese, and Blacks* (Berkeley: University of California Press, 1972); Kenneth Wilson and W. Allen Martin, "Ethnic Enclaves: A Comparison of the Cuban

and Black Economies in Miami," *American Journal of Sociology*, 88:135–60 (1982).

10. See W. Lloyd Warner and Leo Srole, *The Social Systems of American Ethnic Groups* (New Haven, CT: Yale University Press, 1945); Thomas Sowell, *Ethnic America: A History* (New York: Basic Books, 1981).

11. See Alejandro Portes and Rubén G. Rumbaut, *Immigrant America: A Portrait* (Berkeley: University of California Press, 1990), chap. 3.

12. See Mercer L. Sullivan, *"Getting Paid": Youth, Crime, and Work in the Inner City* (Ithaca, NY: Cornell University Press, 1989), chaps. 1, 5.

13. U.S. Department of Commerce, Bureau of the Census, *Census of Population and Housing, 1980: Public Use Microdata Samples A (MRDF)* (Washington, DC: Department of Commerce, 1983).

14. Thomas Bailey and Roger Waldinger, "Primary, Secondary, and Enclave Labor Markets: A Training System Approach," *American Sociological Review*, 56:432–45 (1991).

15. Professionals and executives represented 25.9 percent of Cuban-origin males aged 16 years and over in 1989; the figure for the total adult male population was 26 percent. See Jesus M. García and Patricia A. Montgomery, *The Hispanic Population of the United States: March 1990*, Current Population Reports, ser. P-20, no. 449 (Washington, DC: Department of Commerce, 1991).

16. Portes and Rumbaut, *Immigrant America*, pp. 23–25; Robert L. Bach et al., "The Economic Adjustment of Southeast Asian Refugees in the United States," in *World Refugee Survey, 1983* (Geneva: United Nations High Commission for Refugees, 1984), pp. 51–55.

17. The 1990 Immigration Act contains tailor-made provisions to facilitate the legalization of Irish immigrants. Those taking advantage of the provisions are popularly dubbed "Kennedy Irish" in honor of the Massachusetts Senator who coauthored the act. On the 1990 act, see Michael Fix and Jeffrey S. Passel, "The Door Remains Open: Recent Immigration to the United States and a Preliminary Analysis of the Immigration Act of 1990" (Working paper, Urban Institute and RAND Corporation, 1991). On the Irish in Boston, see Karen Tumulty, "When Irish Eyes Are Hiding . . . ," *Los Angeles Times*, 29 Jan. 1989.

18. Bailey and Waldinger, "Primary, Secondary, and Enclave Labor Markets"; Min Zhou, *New York's Chinatown: The Socioeconomic Potential of an Urban Enclave* (Philadelphia: Temple University Press, 1992); Wilson and Martin, "Ethnic Enclaves"; Suzanne Model, "The Ethnic Economy: Cubans and Chinese Reconsidered" (Manuscript, University of Massachusetts at Amherst, 1990).

19. U.S. Department of Commerce, Bureau of the Census, *Survey of Minority-Owned Business Enterprises, 1987*, MB-2 and MB-3 (Washington, DC: Department of Commerce, 1991).

20. Alejandro Portes and Alex Stepick, "Unwelcome Immigrants: The Labor Market Experiences of 1980 (Mariel) Cuban and Haitian Refugees in South Florida,"

American Sociological Review, 50:493–514 (Aug. 1985); Zhou, *New York's Chinatown;* Luis E. Guarnizo, "One Country in Two: Dominican-Owned Firms in New York and the Dominican Republic" (Ph.D. diss. Johns Hopkins University, 1992); Bailey and Waldinger, "Primary, Secondary, and Enclave Labor Markets."

21. Stepick, "Haitian Refugees in the U.S."; Jake C. Miller, *The Plight of Haitian Refugees* (New York: Praeger, 1984).

22. M. G. Matute-Bianchi, "Ethnic Identities and Patterns of School Success and Failure among Mexican-Descent and Japanese-American Students in a California High School," *American Journal of Education,* 95:233–55 (Nov. 1986). This study is summarized in Rubén G. Rumbaut, "Immigrant Students in California Public Schools: A Summary of Current Knowledge" (Report no. 11, Center for Research on Effective Schooling for Disadvantaged Children, Johns Hopkins University, Aug. 1990).

23. Matute-Bianchi, "Ethnic Identities and Patterns," p. 253.

24. Rumbaut, "Immigrant Students," p. 25.

25. M. A. Gibson, *Accommodation without Assimilation: Sikh Immigrants in an American High School* (Ithaca, NY: Cornell University Press, 1989), p. 268.

26. Gibson, *Accommodation without Assimilation.* The study is summarized in Rumbaut, "Immigrant Students," pp. 22–23.

27. García and Montgomery, *Hispanic Population;* U.S. Department of Commerce, Bureau of the Census, *Survey of Minority-Owned Business Enterprises,* MB-2.

28. Portes and Stepick, *City on the Edge,* chap. 7.

---

46. Tomás R. Jiménez*

Why Replenishment Strengthens Racial and Ethnic Boundaries

Introduction

It has long been argued that ethnic boundaries will fade and ethnic identities will become symbolic and optional as intermarriage increases and differences in socioeconomic status, residential location, and

*The ideas, issues, and theories considered in this brief commissioned piece are examined in greater depth in the following publication: Tomás R. Jiménez, "Mexican Immigrant Replenishment and the Continuing Significance of Ethnicity and Race," *American Journal of Sociology* 113:6 (May 2008), pp. 1527–1567, published by the University of Chicago Press. The article printed here was originally prepared by Tomás R. Jiménez for the fourth edition of *Social Stratification: Class, Race, and Gender in Sociological Perspective,* edited by David B. Grusky. Copyright © 2014 by Westview Press.

language abilities decrease (Alba 1990; Gans 1979; Gordon 1964; Waters 1990; Waters and Jiménez 2005). But the canonical account falls short by not adequately addressing the role that *immigration patterns* play in formation of ethnic identity. This is probably because the symbolic and optional ethnic identity of white ethnics today was formed against a backdrop of radically reduced levels of immigration. World War I, restrictive immigration laws passed in the 1920s, the Great Depression of the 1930s, and World War II combined to slow European immigration to a trickle. This near cessation meant that each generation born in the United States came of age in an American society that was decidedly less immigrant in character. These US-born ethnics thus had less contact with individuals for whom ethnicity played a more central role in daily life. Yet the literature on assimilation is silent in explaining *how* the halt of immigration contributed to the racial and ethnic identity formation of white ethnics. If ethnicity takes a symbolic, optional form after immigration ceases, what form does it take when the immigrant population is replenished with new waves of immigrants, such as the Mexican-origin population?

Mexican migration to the United States is distinct from that of other immigrant groups in many respects, but perhaps most especially in its long history. As Figure 46.1 shows, Mexican immigration continued to rise after European immigration declined. The diverging patterns are particularly prominent in the period after 1970, when the foreign-born Mexican population spiked, while the number of immigrants from European countries continued its downward path. Later-generation Mexican Americans who descend from early waves of Mexican immigrants thus live in a US society where migration from their ancestral homeland remains prominent. In sharp contrast, European-origin immigrants are mostly absent from the ethnic landscape that later-generation white ethnics negotiate. This continuous influx of immigrants means that the Mexican-origin population is both large and generationally diverse. Although a majority of Mexicans in the United States are either first- or second-generation (immigrants or children of immigrants), roughly three in ten are third- or later-generation (grandchildren and beyond).

Methods, Research Setting, and Respondents

The analysis in this chapter draws on 123 in-depth interviews with later-generation Mexican Americans

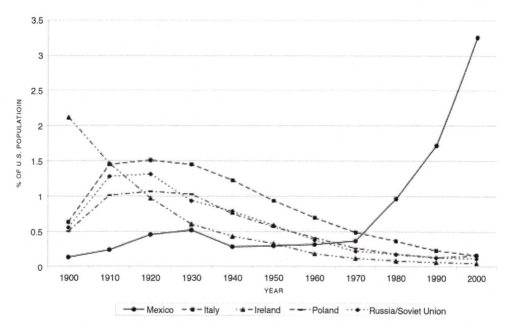

FIGURE 46.1 Number of Foreign-Born People from Mexico and Selected European Countries as a Percent of Total US Population, 1900–2000
Source: U.S. Census.

and participant observation in Garden City, Kansas, and Santa Maria, California. I interviewed respondents whose ancestors have been in the United States since 1940 or before, who are of Mexican descent on both their mother's and father's side of the family, and who have lived in their respective cities for most of their lives.

Garden City is located in southwestern Kansas; at the time of the interviews, it had 28,451 residents, 34.7 percent of whom were of Mexican origin. About half of the Mexican-origin population were foreign born. Between roughly 1900 and 1930, Mexican immigrants came to the area to build the railroads and work the sugar beet fields (Avila 1997). Mexican immigrant settlement shifted away from Kansas in the middle of the twentieth century, and there was a roughly forty-year hiatus in Mexican immigration to the state. In 1980, the largest beef-packing plant in the world opened near Garden City, attracting a new wave of Mexican migrants.

Santa Maria is located on the central coast of California; 52.3 percent of its 77,423 inhabitants are of Mexican origin. As in Garden City, roughly half of the Mexican-origin population is foreign born. Unlike in Garden City, however, Mexican migration to Santa Maria was constant throughout the twentieth century, but especially heavy from the early 1990s

on. Agricultural work has always attracted Mexican immigrants to Santa Maria, where they are the primary, if not only, source of agricultural labor. Variation in immigration patterns yielded some differences, but the heavy influx of Mexican immigrants to both cities over the last twenty years suppressed any pronounced differences related to the central research question.

Immigrant Replenishment and Intergroup Boundaries

Mexican Americans in Garden City and Santa Maria exhibit significant socioeconomic, marital, and residential assimilation. Canonical theories of assimilation and ethnic identity would thus predict that they also experience ethnicity as a symbolic and optional aspect of their identity. Instead, Mexican Americans face rigid intergroup boundaries resulting from the presence of a large immigrant population.

Because of their large numbers and high level of unauthorized status, Mexican immigrants are the primary targets of anti-immigrant antipathy, or what John Higham calls nativism: "an intense opposition to an internal minority on the ground of its foreign (i.e., 'un-American') connections" (1955, 4). Non-Mexicans voice nativist sentiments in anti-Mexican terms, tying general antipathy about changes resulting from immigration to Mexicans in particular. Mexican Americans become aware of these nativist expressions through interpersonal encounters and the more public and highly visible expressions of nativism that abound in each city in the study. Indeed, Mexican immigrants are a prism through which nativism refracts into the lives of Mexican Americans.

Nearly all respondents reported witnessing anti-Mexican nativism on the part of non-Mexican friends, peers, coworkers, and strangers. Typical are the experiences of Ryan Bradley, a sixteen-year-old, third- and fourth-generation high school student in Santa Maria, who lives in a large house in the upper-middle-class subsection of the city. He attends a private school, where he is one of a handful of middle-class, later-generation Mexican Americans. Like many respondents, Ryan's ethnic identity becomes important to him when he come up against the rigid intergroup boundaries that nativism animates:

If there's a threat that's apparent on somebody else who is of the same descent that I am, and the other person is being totally racist about it, and it's all just hate of color, that's when my background comes to be more important to me. . . . I have a friend. . . . And he was picking on this guy that I didn't know. And he was Mexican and they were bagging on him because he was Mexican and I'm just sitting there going, "Hey. I'm Mexican too." [He said,] "No, no, no, this doesn't concern you. You're cool. This guy is not." And I'm just like, "Hey back up." And I just totally got in his face because I was getting mad . . . they were calling him a wetback and just totally dissing on him because he was Mexican.

Like Ryan, respondents reported that they hear nativist comments that rely on a language that invokes ethnicity, which sharpens the boundaries that circumscribe all people of Mexican descent.

Respondents reported hearing similar kinds of tirades having to do with the frequent use of Spanish language. As Marcela Muñoz, a nineteen-year-old, third- and fourth-generation college student in Garden City, who works as a customer service agent at a local retail store, recalled:

[W]e have a Spanish recording. And a guest called and she was asking about American flags. [I said,] "No Ma'am. We're not sched-

uled to get any more until July. We're sorry for the inconvenience." . . . But she just opened her mouth and she was like, "Oh and by the way, what is up with that Mexican crap?" Like that. So I of course was like, "Ma'am, over half of our community understands Spanish." And she started going off on me. I was like "Ma'am, I'm Mexican American." And she didn't know what to say! She just hung up.

Here, too, the nativist rant couches discontent about an issue tied to immigration (Spanish-language use) as a problem seemingly related to "Mexicans."

Mexican Americans also become aware of pervasive nativism through more visible proclamations. Established residents use public forums, such as speeches, demonstrations, and the opinion section of local newspapers, to express nativist fears about the ways in which Mexican immigrants have changed each of the study cities and the country. These expressions most often center around the increasing use of Spanish, a perception that immigrants take advantage of misguided multicultural policies, and a belief that immigrants are a drain on public resources. It is not the frequency of these public expressions, but rather their high visibility that accounts for their power to harden intergroup boundaries.

Mexican Americans internalize this nativism as part of their own ethnic identity. Because immigration is a salient part of historical *and* present-day experience, immigration and the struggles of assimilation are central to Mexican American ethnic identity. Nativist expressions directed at Mexican immigrants thus activate respondents' identity as people of Mexican descent. The comments of Mike Fernandez, a nineteen-year-old, third- and fourth-generation community college student in Santa Maria, illustrate how encounters with nativism play a role in the formation of ethnic identity. Mike describes his family as "a white family who is Mexican," because Mexican traditions play only a small role in his family life. Yet immigration as a defining feature of ethnic identity comes to the fore when he encounters the nativist expressions that other respondents mention:

[S]omebody will say something about Mexicans or something like that and it's not said towards me, it's not directed towards me. But at that point, I'll feel myself discriminated against. I'll put the discrimination on myself, feeling that even though they're not directing it towards me, I can't help but feel that it's degrading towards me in some way, when in fact I know it's not meant directly towards me—it's a general comment. But it just kind of makes me uncomfortable. . . . Just because they're speaking about a Mexican family or a Mexican person and I know that, though my family is not in that position, that I know somewhere along down before me, somebody in my family, I'm sure, has been in that position. And although I'm not in it, and probably never will be in that position, I just think that back when my ancestors were in that position and people were the same way towards them.

Although many respondents, like Mike, have only a vague idea about their family's immigrant history, Mexican immigrants are an en vivo representation of their families' historical struggles. Verbal attacks on Mexican immigrants thus become an affront to all people of Mexican descent, both foreign and native-born.

Immigrant Replenishment, Intergroup Boundaries, and the Continuing Significance of Race

Race matters in the lives of Mexican Americans, and the large and continual influx of Mexican immigrants refreshes its salience and imbues it with meaning. The contentious historical relationship between Mexicans and Anglos in the Midwest (García 1996) and West (Almaguer 1994; Camarillo 1996 [1979]) lurks in the background. But it is the large influx of Mexican immigrants that most significantly structures how respondents experience race. In a context of heavy Mexican immigration, notions of race are intimately tied to ancestry, nativity, and even legal status.

Respondents with darker skin report being mistaken for immigrants by people who assume that they are Mexican-born based on their skin color. But race has added meaning in a context of heavy *unauthorized* Mexican immigration. The unauthorized status of more than half of all Mexican immigrants and political attention given to the US-Mexico border only tighten the relationships among race, ancestry, nativity, and even legal status. Take, for example, the experience of Pedro Ramirez, a fifty-two-year-old, third-generation high school teacher. He re-

called the especially troubling experience of being pulled over by an immigration official while driving his pickup truck after doing yard work at a rental property he owns:

It's this guy with a Smokey the Bear hat and wrap around glasses. It's *la migra*. It's the INS, the border patrol! So I get out [of my car] and the guy says "¡vete aquí!" ("come here") I go oh no, and I'm laughing. I come over and say, "May I help you?" He says, "Do you speak English?" I said, "What the hell do you think I just said?" He says, "Do you have some ID?" I go, "What the hell do you want to know if I have ID for? I wasn't going past the speed limit. Besides you're not a cop. You're the Border Patrol. All right, I'll play your game." He said, "Do you have some ID?" So I pull out my driver's license and show him my wallet. "Do you have anything else?" I said, "Yeah." And I showed him my social security card. He wanted to reach for it and I go, "You ain't getting this. Forget that!" He goes, "You have anything else?" I go, "Sure I do." So I pull out my American Express card. And it's green. I said, "Don't leave home without it. This is harassment!" Guilt by association: Mexican needing a haircut and a shave on a Friday afternoon with bandana around his neck, with an old pickup truck loaded with mowers and edgers and stuff like that.

Even if respondents do not have dark skin, they are not entirely immune to stereotypes about Mexicans as foreigners. Non-Mexicans frequently tag respondents who have a Spanish surname as immigrants. Surnames often serve as markers of ethnicity for all groups. They may signal when someone has, for example, Italian, Polish, or Irish ancestry. But when immigration is replenished, surnames mark both ancestry and nativity.

Ethnic Expectations and Intragroup Boundaries

Ethnic identities are not just assigned to groups and individuals; they are also asserted by group members. The heavy influx of immigrants to Garden City and Santa Maria informs ideas about authentic expressions of Mexican ethnicity, giving rise to rigid intragroup boundaries that run through the

Mexican-origin population. Immigrants and second-generation individuals regard Mexican Americans who fail to live up to these expectations as "inauthentic" ethnics.

Many people of Mexican descent, including those in my sample, do not speak Spanish (Rumbaut, Massey, and Bean 2006). But immigrants from Mexico and even young second-generation individuals maintain Spanish-language use as a central component of identity. Interviews abound with reports of experiences in which immigrants or second-generation individuals called into question respondents' authenticity because of their inability to speak the mother tongue of their immigrant ancestors. Consider the experience of Kyle Gil, a thirty-year-old, fourth-generation auto body shop owner. Some Mexican immigrants who come into Kyle's shop react negatively when they realize that he does not speak Spanish: "[T]hey'll come in and they'll look at me [and say], 'You speak Spanish?' [I answer,] 'No, not really.' [They say,] 'You dumb or what? How come you don't speak Spanish?' And it's like I'm not good enough for them because I can't. So you get that reverse. It's tough."

Respondents' inability to satisfy the gatekeepers of ethnic authenticity stems from the fact that their parents and grandparents did not transmit the Spanish language across generations. An ideology of Americanization that forced earlier generations of Mexican Americans to speak only English, combined with the long length of time that their families have been in the United States, means that young respondents are ill-equipped to use Spanish to validate their ethnic roots to others who expect them to do so.

Immigrants and young second-generation individuals also challenge Mexican Americans about their styles of dress, tastes, and choice of friends. In the eyes of those who enforce the criteria for authenticity, Mexican ethnicity and "mainstream" American culture are at odds. Having tastes and styles perceived to be devoid of Mexican overtones fails to meet the expectations about Mexican ethnicity that many immigrants and young second-generation individuals impose.

These intragroup boundaries are drawn down generational lines, with later-generation Mexican Americans falling on one side and those closer to the immigrant generation on the other. The end result is that Mexican Americans cannot symbolically or optionally assert their ethnic identity without being challenged.

Discussion and Conclusion

The duration of an immigrant wave has played at most a marginal role in theories of assimilation and ethnic identity formation. This chapter demonstrates *how* it matters in shaping the salience of group boundaries.

As the experiences of Mexican Americans in Garden City, Kansas, and Santa Maria, California, show, the role of ethnicity as a symbolic and optional aspect of identity is in part a function of immigrant replenishment. Although Mexican Americans exhibit significant signs of assimilation, continuous waves of immigration maintain the rigidity of group boundaries in their lives.

Comparing the case of white ethnics, who today experience virtually no immigrant replenishment, with that of Mexican Americans further illustrates the importance of immigrant replenishment. Even after recognizing differences between Mexican- and European-origin experiences, a central factor differentiating how later-generation Mexican Americans and later-generation white ethnics construct their ethnic identity lies in the extent of immigrant replenishment. Both later-generation Mexican Americans and white ethnics exhibit signs of assimilation, as measured by socioeconomic advancement, intermarriage, and residential mobility though to a lesser degree for Mexican American. Because large-scale European immigration attenuated, so too did the accompanying forms of nativism familiar to European immigrants in the past and to Mexican immigrants today. Without immigrant replenishment, later-generation descendants of these European immigrants negotiate an American society that no longer sees them as belonging to poor, laboring foreign groups that tear at the American economic and social fabric. They are instead seen as American ethnics who have overcome the hardships of assimilation to become fully woven into the American mainstream (Alba 1990).

Race played a central role in the assimilation processes of white ethnics, animating the boundaries between European immigrants and the native-born "white" population (Higham 1955). But the experience of these groups further suggests the link between race and immigration. With the cessation of large-scale European immigration, the racial markers that once served as cues about ancestry and nativity grew weaker in their association with the particular groups from which they originated, and they "became white" (Roediger 2005). This weak association among race, ancestry, and nativity contributed to the later generations' status as "white," freeing them from the racialized foreign status with which their immigrant and second-generation ancestors were all too familiar.

Immigrant replenishment also determines the extent to which ethnicity is an aspect of identity that can be invoked optionally. European-origin ethnicity has thinned in salience to such an extent that white ethnics require nothing more from each other than the claim that their ancestors came from a particular homeland (Waters 1990). Without any replenishment of immigrants, standards for ethnic group authenticity are low, and white ethnics are free to assert their ethnic identity optionally, without challenge, and without running into intragroup boundaries. The Mexican American experience suggests that, had European immigration continued at levels equal to those around the turn of the last century, white ethnics might very well face more stringent criteria for group authenticity. It follows that the duration of immigrant flows is a central factor shaping ethnic identity formation and one for which researchers must account to more fully understand ethnic and racial change.

REFERENECES

Alba, Richard D. 1990. *Ethnic Identity: The Transformation of White America*. New Haven, CT: Yale University Press.

Almaguer, Tomás. 1994. *Racial Fault Lines: The Historical Origins of White Supremacy in California*. Berkeley: University of California Press.

Avila, Henry J. 1997. "Immigration and Integration: The Mexican Americans Community in Garden City, Kansas, 1900–1950." *Kansas History* 20: 22–37.

Camarillo, Albert. 1996 [1979]. *Chicanos in a Changing Society: From Mexican Pueblos to American Barrios in Santa Barbara and Southern California, 1848–1930*. Cambridge, MA: Harvard University Press.

Gans, Herbert J. 1979. "Symbolic Ethnicity: The Future of Ethnic Groups and Cultures in America." *Ethnic and Racial Studies* 2: 1–20.

García, Juan R. 1996. *Mexicans in the Midwest, 1900–1932*. Tucson: University of Arizona Press.

Gordon, Milton M. 1964. *Assimilation in American Life: The Role of Race, Religion, and National Origins*. New York: Oxford University Press.

Higham, John. 1955. *Strangers in the Land: Patterns of American Nativism, 1860–1925*. New Brunswick, NJ: Rutgers University Press.

Roediger, David R. 2005. *Working Toward Whiteness: How America's Immigrants Become White; The Strange Journey from Ellis Island to the Suburbs*. New York: Basic Books.

Rumbaut, Rubén G., Douglas S. Massey, and Frank D. Bean. 2006. "Linguistic Life Expectancies: Immigrant Language Retention in Southern California." *Population and Development Review* 32: 447–460.

Waters, Mary C. 1990. *Ethnic Options: Choosing Identities in America*. Berkeley: University of California Press.

Waters, Mary C., and Tomás R. Jiménez. 2005. "Assessing Immigrant Assimilation: New Empirical and Theoretical Challenges." *Annual Review of Sociology* 31: 105–102.

Discrimination, Prejudice, and Stereotyping

47. Marianne Bertrand and Sendhil Mullainathan*

Are Emily and Greg More Employable Than Lakisha and Jamal?: A Field Experiment on Labor Market Discrimination

Every measure of economic success reveals significant racial inequality in the U.S. labor market. Compared to Whites, African-Americans are twice as likely to be unemployed and earn nearly 25 percent less when they are employed (Council of Economic Advisers, 1998). This inequality has sparked a debate as to whether employers treat members of different races differentially. When faced with observably similar African-American and White applicants, do they favor the White one? Some argue yes, citing either employer prejudice or employer perception that race signals lower productivity. Others argue that differential treatment by race is a relic of the past, eliminated by some combination of employer enlightenment, affirmative action programs and the profit-maximization motive. In fact, many in this latter camp even feel that stringent enforcement of affirmative action programs has produced an environment of reverse discrimination. They would argue that faced with identical candidates, employers might favor the African-American one. Data limitations make it difficult to empirically test these views. Since researchers possess far less data

*Marianne Bertrand and Sendhil Mullainathan. "Are Emily and Greg More Employable Than Lakisha and Jamal? A Field Experiment on Labor Market Discrimination," *The American Economic Review* (September 2004), pp. 991–992, 1006–1007, 1009–1013. Reprinted by permission of The American Economic Review and the author. As published in *Social Stratification: Class, Race, and Gender in Sociological Perspective*, 3rd Edition, by David B. Grusky, copyright © 2009. Reprinted by permission of Westview Press, an imprint of Perseus Books, LLC, a subsidiary of Hachette Book Group, Inc.

than employers do, White and African-American workers that appear similar to researchers may look very different to employers. So any racial difference in labor market outcomes could just as easily be attributed to differences that are observable to employers but unobservable to researchers.

To circumvent this difficulty, we conduct a field experiment that builds on the correspondence testing methodology that has been primarily used in the past to study minority outcomes in the United Kingdom. We send resumes in response to help-wanted ads in Chicago and Boston newspapers and measure callback for interview for each sent resume. We experimentally manipulate perception of race via the name of the fictitious job applicant. We randomly assign very White-sounding names (such as Emily Walsh or Greg Baker) to half the resumes and very African-American-sounding names (such as Lakisha Washington or Jamal Jones) to the other half. Because we are also interested in how credentials affect the racial gap in callback, we experimentally vary the quality of the resumes used in response to a given ad. Higher-quality applicants have on average a little more labor market experience and fewer holes in their employment history; they are also more likely to have an e-mail address, have completed some certification degree, possess foreign language skills, or have been awarded some honors. In practice, we typically send four resumes in response to each ad: two higher-quality and two lower-quality ones. We randomly assign to one of the higher- and one of the lower-quality resumes an African-American-sounding name. In total, we respond to over 1,300 employment ads in the sales, administrative support, clerical, and customer services job categories and send nearly 5,000 resumes. The ads we respond to cover a large spectrum of job quality, from cashier work at retail establishments and clerical work in a mail room, to office and sales management positions.

We find large racial differences in callback rates. Applicants with White names need to send about 10 resumes to get one callback whereas applicants with African-American names need to send about 15 resumes. This 50-percent gap in callback is statistically significant. A White name yields as many more callbacks as an additional eight years of experience on a resume. Since applicants' names are randomly assigned, this gap can only be attributed to the name manipulation.

Race also affects the reward to having a better resume. Whites with higher-quality resumes receive nearly 30-percent more callbacks than Whites with lower-quality resumes. On the other hand, having a higher-quality resume has a smaller effect for African-Americans. In other words, the gap between Whites and African-Americans widens with resume quality. While one may have expected improved credentials to alleviate employers' fear that African-American applicants are deficient in some unobservable skills, this is not the case in our data.

The experiment also reveals several other aspects of the differential treatment by race. First, since we randomly assign applicants' postal addresses to the resumes, we can study the effect of neighborhood of residence on the likelihood of callback. We find that living in a wealthier (or more educated or Whiter) neighborhood increases callback rates. But, interestingly, African-Americans are not helped more than Whites by living in a "better" neighborhood. Second, the racial gap we measure in different industries does not appear correlated to Census-based measures of the racial gap in wages. The same is true for the racial gap we measure in different occupations. In fact, we find that the racial gaps in callback are statistically indistinguishable across all the occupation and industry categories covered in the experiment. Federal contractors, who are thought to be more severely constrained by affirmative action laws, do not treat the African-American resumes more preferentially; neither do larger employers or employers who explicitly state that they are "Equal Opportunity Employers." In Chicago, we find a slightly smaller racial gap when employers are located in more African-American neighborhoods.[1] . . .

Interpretation

Three main sets of questions arise when interpreting the results above. First, does a higher callback rate for White applicants imply that employers are discriminating against African-Americans? Second, does our design only isolate the effect of race or is the name manipulation conveying some other fac-

tors than race? Third, how do our results relate to different models of racial discrimination?

Interpreting Callback Rates

Our results indicate that for two identical individuals engaging in an identical job search, the one with an African-American name would receive fewer interviews. Does differential treatment within our experiment imply that employers are discriminating against African-Americans (whether it is rational, prejudice-based, or other form of discrimination)? In other words, could the lower callback rate we record for African-American resumes *within our experiment* be consistent with a racially neutral review of the *entire pool* of resumes the surveyed employers receive?

In a racially neutral review process, employers would rank order resumes based on their quality and call back all applicants that are above a certain threshold. Because names are randomized, the White and African-American resumes we send should rank similarly on average. So, irrespective of the skill and racial composition of the applicant pool, a race-blind selection rule would generate equal treatment of Whites and African-Americans. So our results must imply that employers use race as a factor when reviewing resumes, which matches the legal definition of discrimination.

But even rules where employers are not trying to interview as few African-American applicants as possible may generate observed differential treatment in our experiment. One such hiring rule would be employers trying to interview a target level of African-American candidates. For example, perhaps the average firm in our experiment aims to produce an interview pool that matches the population base rate. This rule could produce the observed differential treatment if the average firm receives a higher proportion of African-American resumes than the population base rate because African-Americans disproportionately apply to the jobs and industries in our sample.

Some of our other findings may be consistent with such a rule. For example, the fact that "Equal Opportunity Employers" or federal contractors do not appear to discriminate any less may reflect the fact that such employers receive more applications from African-Americans. On the other hand, other key findings run counter to this rule. As we discuss above, we find no systematic difference in the racial gap in callback across occupational or industry categories, despite the large variation in the fraction of African-Americans looking for work in those categories. African-Americans are underrepresented in managerial occupations, for example. If employers matched base rates in the population, the few African-Americans who apply to these jobs should receive a higher callback rate than Whites. Yet, we find that the racial gap in managerial occupations is the same as in all the other job categories. This rule also runs counter to our findings on returns to skill. Suppose firms are struggling to find White applicants but overwhelmed with African American ones. Then they should be less sensitive to the quality of White applicants (as they are trying to fill in their hiring quota for Whites) and much more sensitive to the quality of Black applicants (when they have so many to pick from). Thus, it is unlikely that the differential treatment we observe is generated by hiring rules such as these.

Potential Confounds

While the names we have used in this experiment strongly signal racial origin, they may also signal some other personal trait. More specifically, one might be concerned that employers are inferring social background from the personal name. When employers read a name like "Tyrone" or "Latoya," they may assume that the person comes from a disadvantaged background. In the extreme form of this social background interpretation, employers do not care at all about race but are discriminating only against the social background conveyed by the names we have chosen.

While plausible, we feel that some of our earlier results are hard to reconcile with this interpretation. For example, we found that while employers value "better" addresses, African-Americans are not helped more than Whites by living in Whiter or more educated neighborhoods. If the African-American names we have chosen mainly signal negative social background, one might have expected the estimated name gap to be lower for better addresses. Also, if the names mainly signal social background, one might have expected the name gap to be higher for jobs that rely more on soft skills or require more interpersonal interactions. We found no such evidence.

There is one final potential confound to our results. Perhaps what appears as a bias against African-Americans is actually the result of *reverse discrimination*. If qualified African-Americans are thought to be in high demand, then employers with

average quality jobs might feel that an equally talented African-American would never accept an offer from them and thereby never call her or him in for an interview. Such an argument might also explain why African-Americans do not receive as strong a return as Whites to better resumes, since higher qualification only strengthens this argument. But this interpretation would suggest that among the better jobs, we ought to see evidence of reverse discrimination, or at least a smaller racial gap. However, we do not find any such evidence. The racial gap does not vary across jobs with different skill requirements, nor does it vary across occupation categories. Even among the better jobs in our sample, we find that employers significantly favor applicants with White names.

Relation to Existing Theories

What do these results imply for existing models of discrimination? Economic theories of discrimination can be classified into two main categories: taste-based and statistical discrimination models. Both sets of models can obviously "explain" our average racial gap in callbacks. But can these models explain our other findings? More specifically, we discuss the relevance of these models with a focus on two of the facts that have been uncovered in this [chapter]: (i) the lower returns to credentials for African-Americans; (ii) the relative uniformity of the race gap across occupations, job requirements and, to a lesser extent, employer characteristics and industries.

Taste-based models (Gary S. Becker, 1961) differ in whose prejudiced "tastes" they emphasize: customers, coworkers, or employers. Customer and coworker discrimination models seem at odds with the lack of significant variation of the racial gap by occupation and industry categories, as the amount of customer contact and the fraction of White employees vary quite a lot across these categories. We do not find a larger racial gap among jobs that explicitly require "communication skills" and jobs for which we expect either customer or coworker contacts to be higher (retail sales for example).

Because we do not know what drives employer tastes, employer discrimination models could be consistent with the lack of occupation and industry variation. Employer discrimination also matches the finding that employers located in more African-American neighborhoods appear to discriminate somewhat less. However, employer discrimination models would struggle to explain why African-Americans get relatively lower returns to their credentials. Indeed, the cost of indulging the discrimination taste should increase as the minority applicants' credentials increase.

Statistical discrimination models are the prominent alternative to the taste-based models in the economics literature. In one class of statistical discrimination models, employers use (observable) race to proxy for *unobservable* skills (e.g., Edmund S. Phelps, 1972; Kenneth J. Arrow, 1973). This class of models struggles to explain the credentials effect as well. Indeed, the added credentials should lead to a larger update for African-Americans and hence greater returns to skills for that group.

A second class of statistical discrimination models "emphasize[s] the precision of the information that employers have about individual productivity" (Altonji and Blank, 1999). Specifically, in these models, employers believe that the same observable signal is more precise for Whites than for African-Americans (Dennis J. Aigner and Glenn G. Cain, 1977; Shelly J. Lundberg and Richard Startz, 1983; Bradford Cornell and Ivo Welch, 1996). Under such models, African-Americans receive lower returns to observable skills because employers place less weight on these skills. However, how reasonable is this interpretation for our experiment? First, it is important to note that we are using the same set of resume characteristics for both racial groups. So the lower precision of information for African-Americans cannot be that, for example, an employer does not know what a high school degree from a very African-American neighborhood means (as in Aigner and Cain, 1977). Second, many of the credentials on the resumes are in fact externally and easily verifiable, such as a certification for a specific software.

An alternative version of these models would rely on bias in the observable signal rather than differential variance or noise of these signals by race. Perhaps the skills of African-Americans are discounted because affirmative action makes it easier for African-Americans to get these skills. While this is plausible for credentials such as an employee-of-the-month honor, it is unclear why this would apply to more verifiable and harder skills. It is equally unclear why work experience would be less rewarded since our study suggests that getting a job is more, not less, difficult for African-Americans.

The uniformity of the racial gap across occupations is also troubling for a statistical discrimination interpretation. Numerous factors that should affect the level of statistical discrimination, such as the importance of unobservable skills, the observability of qualifications, the precision of observable skills and the ease of performance measurement, may vary quite a lot across occupations.

This discussion suggests that perhaps other models may do a better job at explaining our findings. One simple alternative model is lexicographic search by employers. Employers receive so many resumes that they may use quick heuristics in reading these resumes. One such heuristic could be to simply read no further when they see an African-American name. Thus they may never see the skills of African-American candidates and this could explain why these skills are not rewarded. This might also to some extent explain the uniformity of the race gap since the screening process (i.e., looking through a large set of resumes) may be quite similar across the variety of jobs we study.

Conclusion

This [chapter] suggests that African-Americans face differential treatment when searching for jobs and this may still be a factor in why they do poorly in the labor market. Job applicants with African-American names get far fewer callbacks for each resume they send out. Equally importantly, applicants with African-American names find it hard to overcome this hurdle in callbacks by improving their observable skills or credentials.

Taken at face value, our results on differential returns to skill have possibly important policy implications. They suggest that training programs alone may not be enough to alleviate the racial gap in labor market outcomes. For training to work, some general-equilibrium force outside the context of our experiment would have to be at play. In fact, if African-Americans recognize how employers reward their skills, they may rationally be less willing than Whites to even participate in these programs.

NOTES

1. For further details on this experiment, see Bertrand and Mullainathan (2004).

REFERENCES

Aigner, Dennis J. and Cain, Glenn G. "Statistical Theories of Discrimination in Labor Markets." *Industrial and Labor Relations Review*, January 1977, 30(1), pp. 175–87.

Altonji, Joseph G. and Blank, Rebecca M. "Race and Gender in the Labor Market," in Orley Ashenfelter and David Card, eds., *Handbook of Labor Economics,* Vol. 30. Amsterdam: North-Holland, 1999, pp. 3143–259.

Arrow, Kenneth J. "The Theory of Discrimination," in Orley Ashenfelter and Albert Rees, eds., *Discrimination in Labor Markets.* Princeton, NJ: Princeton University Press, 1973, pp. 3–33.

Becker, Gary S. *The Economics ofDdiscrimination,* 2nd Ed. Chicago: University of Chicago Press, 1961.

Bertrand, Marianne and Sendhil Mullainathan. "Are Emily and Greg More Employable Than Lakisha and Jamal? A Field Experiment on Labor Market Discrimination." *American Economic Review* 94 (September 2004): 991–1013.

Cornell, Bradford and Welch, Ivo. "Culture, Information, and Screening Discrimination." *Journal of Political Economy,* June 1996, 104(3), pp. 542–71.

Council of Economic Advisers. Changing America: Indicators of social and economic well-being by race and Hispanic origin. September 1998, http://w3.access.gpo.gov/eop/ca/pdfs/ca.pdf.

Lundberg, Shelly J. and Starz, Richard. "Private Discrimination and Social Intervention in Competitive Labor Market." *American Economic Review,* June 1983, 73(3), pp. 340–47.

Phelps, Edmund S. "The Statistical Theory of Racism and Sexism." *American Economic Review,* September 1972, 62(4), pp. 659–61.

48. Devah Pager*

Marked: Race, Crime, and Finding Work in an Era of Mass Incarceration

While stratification researchers typically focus on schools, labor markets, and the family as primary institutions affecting inequality, a new institution has emerged as central to the sorting and stratifying of young disadvantaged men: the criminal justice system. With over two million individuals currently incarcerated, and well over half a million prisoners released each year, the large and growing numbers of

* The ideas, issues, and theories considered in this brief piece are examined in greater depth in the following publication: Devah Pager, "The Mark of a Criminal Record," *American Journal of Sociology* 108 (2003), pp. 937–975, published by the University of Chicago Press. The article as printed here was originally prepared by Devah Pager for *Social Stratification: Class, Race, and Gender in Sociological Perspective,* 3rd Edition by David B. Grusky, pp. 683–690. Copyright © 2009. Reprinted by permission of Westview Press, an imprint of Perseus Books, LLC, a subsidiary of Hachette Book Group, Inc.

men being processed through the criminal justice system raises important questions about the consequences of this massive institutional intervention. Further, large racial disparities in incarceration lead us to question the degree to which mass incarceration has particular implications for stratification along racial lines.

This [chapter] focuses on the consequences of incarceration for the employment outcomes of black and white men. I adopt an experimental audit approach to formally test the degree to which race and criminal background affect subsequent employment opportunities. By using matched pairs of individuals to apply for real entry-level jobs, it becomes possible to directly measure the extent to which contact with the criminal justice system—in the absence of other disqualifying characteristics—serves as a barrier to employment among equally qualified applicants. Further, by varying the race of the tester pairs, it becomes possible to assess the ways in which the effects of race and criminal record interact to produce new forms of labor market inequalities.

Mass Incarceration and the Credentialing of Stigma

Over the past three decades, the number of prison inmates has increased by more than 700 percent, leaving the United States the country with the highest incarceration rate in the world (Bureau of Justice Statistics, 2006; Mauer, 1999). During this time, incarceration changed from a punishment reserved primarily for the most heinous offenders to one extended to a much greater range of crimes and a much larger segment of the population. Recent trends in crime policy have led to the imposition of harsher sentences for a wider range of offenses, thus casting an ever widening net of penal intervention.

For each individual processed through the criminal justice system, police records, court documents, and corrections databases detail dates of arrest, charges, conviction, and terms of incarceration. Most states make these records publicly available, often through online repositories, accessible to employers, landlords, creditors, and other interested parties. With increasing numbers of occupations, public services, and other social goods becoming off-limits to ex-offenders, these records can be used as the official basis for eligibility determination or exclusion. The state, in this way, serves as a credentialing institution, providing official and public certification of those among us who have been convicted of wrongdoing. The "credential" of a criminal record, like educational or professional credentials, constitutes a formal and enduring classification of social status, which can be used to regulate access and opportunity across numerous social, economic, and political domains. As increasing numbers of young men are marked by their contact with the criminal justice system, it becomes a critical priority to understand the costs and consequences of this now prevalent form of negative credential (Pager, 2007a).

Racial Stereotypes in an Era of Mass Incarceration

The expansion of the correctional population has been particularly consequential for blacks. Blacks today represent over 40 percent of current prison inmates relative to just 12 percent of the U.S. population. Over the course of a lifetime, nearly one in three young black men—and well over half of young black high school dropouts—will spend some time in prison. According to these estimates, young black men are more likely to go to prison than to attend college, serve in the military, or, in the case of high school dropouts, to be in the labor market (Bureau of Justice Statistics, 1997; Pettit and Western, 2004). Prison is no longer a rare or extreme event among our nation's most marginalized groups. Rather it has now become a normal and anticipated marker in the transition to adulthood.

There is reason to believe that the implications of these trends extend well beyond the prison walls, with assumptions of criminality among blacks generalizing beyond those directly engaged in crime. Blacks in this country have long been regarded with suspicion and fear, but unlike progressive trends in other racial attitudes, associations between race and crime have changed little in recent years. Survey respondents consistently rate blacks as more prone to violence than any other American racial or ethnic group, with the stereotype of aggressiveness and violence most frequently endorsed in ratings of African Americans (Sniderman and Piazza, 1993; Smith, 1991). The stereotype of blacks as criminals is deeply embedded in the collective consciousness of white Americans, irrespective of the perceiver's level of prejudice or personal beliefs (Devine and Elliot, 1995; Eberhardt et al., 2004; Graham and Lowery, 2004).

While it would be impossible to trace the source of contemporary racial stereotypes to any one factor, the disproportionate growth of criminal justice intervention in the lives of young black men—and corresponding media coverage of this phenomenon, which presents an even more skewed representation—has likely played an important role. Experimental research shows that exposure to news coverage of a violent incident committed by a black perpetrator not only increases punitive attitudes about crime but further increases negative attitudes about blacks generally (Gilliam and Iyengar, 2000). The more exposure we have to images of blacks in custody or behind bars, the stronger our expectations become regarding the race of assailants or the criminal tendencies of black strangers (Cole, 1995).

The consequences of mass incarceration then may in fact extend far beyond the costs to the individual bodies behind bars, and to the families that are disrupted or the communities whose residents cycle in and out. The criminal justice system may itself legitimate and reinforce deeply embedded racial stereotypes, contributing to the persistent chasm in this society between black and white.

Assessing the Impact of Race and Criminal Background

In considering the labor market impacts of race and criminal background, questions of causality loom large. For example, while employment disparities between blacks and whites have been well-established, the causes of these disparities remain widely contested. Where racial discrimination may represent one explanation, a growing number of researchers have pointed instead to individual-level factors such as skill deficits and other human capital characteristics as a key source of racial wage differentials (Neal and Johnson, 1996; Farkas and Vicknair, 1996). Likewise, assessing the impact of incarceration is not altogether straightforward. On the one hand, it's not hard to imagine that a prison record would carry a weighty stigma, with members of the general public (employers included) reluctant to associate or work with former inmates. On the other hand, criminal offenders aren't typically the image of the model employee. It's certainly possible that the poor employment outcomes of ex-offenders stem rather from characteristics of the offenders themselves, as opposed to any consequence of their criminal conviction. Poor work habits, substance abuse problems, or deficient interpersonal skills may be sufficient to explain the employment disadvantages of ex-offenders, and yet these characteristics are difficult to capture using standard data sources.

Given the difficulties inherent to evaluating the impact of race and imprisonment through conventional measures, I set out to investigate this issue by constructing an experiment. I wanted to bracket the range of personal characteristics associated with African Americans and ex-offenders in order to hone in on the causal impact of race and a criminal record. The experimental audit methodology allowed me to do just that. Using this approach, I pose the questions: Given two equally qualified job applicants, how much does a criminal record affect the chances of being selected by an employer? To what extent does race condition employers' responses? In answering these questions, we can begin to understand the ways in which race and criminal background shape and constrain important economic opportunities.

The Audit Methodology

The basic design of an employment audit involves sending matched pairs of individuals (called testers) to apply for real job openings in order to see whether employers respond differently to applicants on the basis of selected characteristics. The current study included four male testers, two blacks and two whites, matched into two teams—the two black testers formed one team, and the two white testers formed a second team.[1] The testers were college students from Milwaukee who were matched on the basis of age, race, physical appearance, and general style of self-presentation. The testers were assigned fictitious resumes that reflected equivalent levels of education and work experience.[2] In addition, within each team, one auditor was randomly assigned a "criminal record" for the first week; the pair then rotated which member presented himself as the ex-offender for each successive week of employment searches, such that each tester served in the criminal record condition for an equal number of cases.[3] By varying which member of the pair presented himself as having a criminal record, unobserved differences within the pairs of applicants were effectively controlled.

Before initiating the fieldwork, testers participated in a common training program to become familiar with the details of their assumed profile and to ensure uniform behavior in job interviews. The training period lasted for one week, during which testers participated in mock interviews with one another and practice interviews with cooperating

employers. The testers were trained to respond to common interview questions in standardized ways, and were well-rehearsed for a wide range of scenarios that emerge in hiring situations. Frequent communication between myself and the testers throughout each day of fieldwork allowed for regular supervision and troubleshooting in the event of unexpected occurrences.

A random sample of entry-level positions (those jobs requiring no previous experience and no education beyond high school) was drawn each week from the Sunday classified advertisement section of the *Milwaukee Journal Sentinel*. The most common job titles included waitstaff, laborers and warehouse, production/operators, customer service, sales, delivery drivers, and cashiers; a handful of clerical and managerial positions were also included. I excluded from the sample those occupations with legal restrictions on ex-offenders, such as jobs in the health care industry, work with children and the elderly, jobs requiring the handling of firearms (e.g., security guards), and jobs in the public sector. Of course, any true estimate of the collateral consequences of incarceration would also need to take account of the wide range of employment fully off-limits to individuals with prior felony convictions.

Each of the audit pairs was randomly assigned fifteen job openings each week. The white pair and the black pair were assigned separate sets of jobs, with the same-race testers applying to the same jobs. One member of the pair applied first, with the second applying one day later (randomly varying whether the ex-offender was first or second). A total of 350 employers were audited during the course of this study: 150 by the white pair and 200 by the black pair. Additional tests were performed by the black pair because black testers received fewer callbacks on average, and there were thus fewer data points with which to draw comparisons. A larger sample size enables the calculation of more precise estimates of the effects under investigation (for a more in-depth discussion of the study design, see Pager, 2003).

This study focused only on the first stage of the employment process, as this is the stage most likely to be affected by the barriers of race and criminal record. Testers visited employers, filled out applications, and proceeded as far as they could during the course of one visit. If testers were asked to interview on the spot, they did so, but they did not return to the employer for a second visit. The primary dependent variable then is the proportion of applications that elicited callbacks from employers. Individual

FIGURE 48.1 The Effects of Race and Criminal Background on Employment

voicemail boxes were set up for each tester to record employer responses.

An advantage of the callback as our key outcome variable—as opposed to a job offer—is that it does not require employers to narrow their selection down to a single applicant. At the job offer stage, if presented with an ex-offender and an equally quali-fied nonoffender, even employers with little concern over hiring ex-offenders would likely select the appli-cant with no criminal record, an arguably safer choice. Equating the two applicants could in fact magnify the impact of the criminal record, as it be-comes the only remaining basis for selection between the two (Heckman, 1998). The callback, by contrast, does not present such complications. Typically em-ployers interview multiple candidates for entry-level positions before selecting a hire. In fact, in a subse-quent survey, employers in this study reported inter-viewing an average of eight applicants for the last entry-level position filled. At the callback stage, then, employers need not yet choose between the ex-offender and nonoffender. If the applicants ap-pear well-qualified, and if the employer does not view the criminal record as an automatic disqualifier, s/he can interview them both.[4]

Hiring Outcomes by Race and Criminal Background

Results are based on the proportion of applications submitted by each tester which elicited callbacks from employers. Three main findings should be noted from the audit results, presented in Figure 48.1. First, there is a large and significant effect of a criminal record for all job seekers. Among whites, for example, 34 percent of those without criminal records received callbacks relative to only 17 percent

of those with criminal records. A criminal record is thus associated with a 50 percent reduction in the likelihood of a callback among whites. Often testers reported seeing employers' levels of responsiveness change dramatically once they had glanced down at the criminal record question on the application form. Many employers seem to use the information as a screening mechanism, weeding out applicants at the initial stage of review.

Second, there is some indication that the magni-tude of the criminal record effect may be even larger for blacks. While the interaction between race and criminal record is not statistically significant, the substantive difference is worth noting. The ratio of callbacks for nonoffenders relative to offenders for whites was two to one (34 percent vs. 17 percent), while this same ratio for blacks is close to three to one (14 percent vs. 5 percent).[5] The estimated effect of a criminal record is thus 40 percent larger for blacks than for whites. The combination of minority status and criminal background appears to intensify employers' negative reactions, leaving few employ-ment prospects for black ex-offenders (200 applica-tions resulted in only 10 callbacks).

Finally, looking at the callback rates for black and white tester pairs side by side, the fundamental im-portance of race becomes vividly clear. Among those without criminal records, black applicants were less than half as likely to receive callbacks compared to equally qualified whites (14 percent vs. 34 percent). This implies that young black men needed to work more than twice as hard (apply to twice as many jobs) to secure the same opportunities as whites with iden-tical qualifications. Even more striking, the powerful effects of race rival even the strong stigma conveyed by a criminal record. In this study, a white applicant *with a criminal record* was just as likely, if not more, to receive a callback as a black applicant with no criminal history (17 percent vs. 14 percent). Despite the fact that the white applicant revealed evidence of a felony drug conviction, and despite the fact that he reported having only recently returned from a year and a half in prison, employers seemed to view this applicant as no more risky than a young black man with no history of criminal involvement. Racial disparities have been documented in many contexts, but here, comparing the two effects side by side, we are confronted with a troubling reality: Being black in America today is just about the same as having a felony conviction in terms of one's chances of finding a job.[6]

The results of this research suggest that both race and criminal background represent extremely powerful barriers to job entry. The matched design allows us to separate speculation about applicant qualifications (supply-side influences) from the preferences or biases of employers (demand-side influences). While this study remains silent on the many supply-side factors that may also contribute to the employment difficulties of blacks and ex-offenders, it speaks loud and clear about the significance of employer demand in shaping the opportunities available to job seekers on the basis of their race or criminal background. Before applicants have an opportunity to demonstrate their capabilities in person, a large proportion are weeded out on the basis of a single categorical distinction.

Discussion

There is serious disagreement among academics, policymakers, and practitioners over the extent to which contact with the criminal justice system—in itself—leads to harmful consequences for employment. The present study takes a strong stand in this debate by offering direct evidence of the causal relationship between a criminal record and employment outcomes. Using matched pairs and an experimentally assigned criminal record, this estimate is unaffected by the problems of selection which plague observational data. While certainly there are additional ways in which incarceration may affect economic outcomes, this study provides convincing evidence that mere contact with the criminal justice system, in the absence of any transformative or selective effects, severely limits subsequent employment opportunities. And while the audit study investigates employment barriers to ex-offenders from a micro-perspective, the implications are far-reaching. The finding that ex-offenders are one-half to one-third as likely to be considered by employers suggests that a

criminal record indeed presents a major barrier to employment. With over two million people currently behind bars and over twelve million people with prior felony convictions, the consequences for labor market inequalities are potentially profound.

Second, the persistent effect of race on employment opportunities is painfully clear in these results. Blacks are less than half as likely to receive consideration by employers relative to their white counterparts, and black nonoffenders fall behind even whites with prior felony convictions. While this research cannot identify the precise source of employers' reluctance to hire blacks, it is important to consider the influence of high incarceration rates among blacks as one possible source of racial bias. Indeed, the available evidence points to the pervasiveness of images associating blacks with crime, and the power of these images to strengthen negative feelings about blacks as a group. It may be the case, then, that increasing rates of incarceration among blacks, and the disproportionate coverage of criminal justice contact among blacks in the media, heighten negative reactions toward African Americans generally, irrespective of their personal involvement in crime.

No longer a peripheral institution, the criminal justice system has become a dominant presence in the lives of young disadvantaged men, playing a key role in the sorting and stratifying of labor market opportunities. The "criminal credential" now represents a common marker among young disadvantaged men, allowing for the easy identification and exclusion of those with a prior arrest or conviction. Further, because blacks are so strongly associated with the population under correctional supervision, it becomes common to assume that any given young black man is likely to have—or to be on his way to acquiring—a criminal record.

At this point in history, it is impossible to tell whether the massive presence of incarceration in today's stratification system represents a unique anomaly of the late twentieth century or part of a larger movement toward a system of stratification based on the official certification of individual character and competence. Whether this process will continue to form the basis of emerging social cleavages remains to be seen.

REFERENCES

Bureau of Justice Statistics. 2002. "Recidivism of Prisoners Released in 1994," edited by Patrick Langan and David Levin. Washington, DC: U.S. Department of Justice.

———. 2006. "Prison and Jail Inmates at Midyear 2005." Washington, DC: U.S. Department of Justice.

Bureau of Justice Statistics Special Report 1997. March. Lifetime Likelihood of Going to State or Federal Prison, by Thomas P. Bonczar and Allen J. Beck. Washington, DC: U.S. Department of Justice.

Cole, David. 1995. "The paradox of race and crime: A comment on Randall Kennedy's 'politics of distinction'." *Georgetown Law Journal* 83:2547–2571.

Devine, P. G., and A. J. Elliot. 1995. "Are Racial Stereotypes Really Fading? The Princeton Trilogy Revisited." *Personality and Social Psychology Bulletin* 21(11): 1139–1150.

Eberhardt, Jennifer L., Phillip Atiba Goff, Valerie J. Purdie, and Paul G. Davies. 2004. "Seeing black: Race, crime, and visual processing." *Journal of Personality & Social Psychology* 87:876–893.

Farkas, George, and Kevin Vicknair. 1996. "Appropriate tests of racial wage discrimination require controls for cognitive skill: Comment on Cancio, Evans, and Maume." *American Sociological Review* 61:557–560.

Freeman, Richard B. 1987. "The Relation of Criminal Activity to Black Youth Employment." *Review of Black Political Economy* 16(1–2): 99–107.

Gilliam, Franklin D., and Shanto Iyengar. 2000. "Prime suspects: The influence of local television news on the viewing public." *American Journal of Political Science* 44:560–573.

Graham, Sandra, and Brian S. Lowery. 2004. "Priming unconscious racial stereotypes about adolescent offenders." *Law and Human Behavior* 28:483–504.

Heckman, James J. 1998. "Detecting discrimination." *The Journal of Economic Perspectives* 12:101–116.

Heckman, James, and Peter Seligman. 1993. "The Urban Institute Audit Studies: Their Methods and Findings." In Michael Fix and Raymond J. Struyk (eds.), *Clear and Convincing Evidence: Measurement of Discrimination in America*. Washington, DC: Urban Institute Press.

Mauer, Marc. 1999. *Race to Incarcerate*. New York: New Press.

Neal, Derek, and William Johnson. 1996. "The Role of Premarket Factors in Black-White Wage Differences." *Journal of Political Economy* 104(5): 869–895.

Pager, Devah. 2003. "The Mark of a Criminal Record." *American Journal of Sociology* 108(5): 937–975.

———. 2007a. *Marked: Race, Crime, and Finding Work in an Era of Mass Incarceration*. Chicago: University of Chicago Press.

———. 2007b. "The Use of Field Experiments for Studies of Employment Discrimination: Contributions, Critiques, and Directions for the Future." *Annals of the American Academy of Political and Social Science* 609: 104–133.

Pager, Devah, and Bruce Western. 2005. "Discrimination in Low Wage Labor Markets: Evidence from New York City." Paper presented at Population Association of America. Philadelphia, PA.

Pettit, Becky, and Bruce Western. 2004. "Mass Imprisonment and the Life Course: Race and Class Inequality in U.S. Incarceration." *American Sociological Review* 69: 151–169.

Sampson, Robert J., and John H. Laub. 1993. *Crime in the Making: Pathways and Turning Points Through Life*. Cambridge, MA: Harvard University Press.

Schwartz, Richard, and Jerome Skolnick. 1962. "Two Studies of Legal Stigma." *Social Problems*, Fall: 133–142.

Smith, Tom W. 1991. "Ethnic Images. General Social Survey Technical Report, 19." Chicago: National Opinion Research Center, University of Chicago.

Sniderman, Paul M., and Thomas Piazza. 1993. *The Scar of Race*. Cambridge, MA: Harvard University Press.

Travis, Jeremy, Amy Solomon, and Michelle Waul. 2001. *From Prison to Home: The Dimensions and Consequences of Prisoner Reentry*. Washington, DC: Urban Institute Press.

Uggen, Christopher. 2000. "Work as a Turning Point in the Life Course of Criminals: A Duration Model of Age, Employment, and Recidivism." *American Sociological Review* 65(4): 529–546.

Uggen, Christopher, Jeff Manza, and Melissa Thompson. 2006. "Citizenship and Reintegration: The Socioeconomic, Familial, and Civic Lives of Criminal Offenders." *The Annals of the American Academy of Social and Political Science* 605:281–310.

Western, Bruce. 2002. "The Impact of Incarceration on Wage Mobility and Inequality." *American Sociological Review* 67(4): 526–546.

Western, Bruce, and Katherine Beckett. 1999. "How Unregulated Is the U.S. Labor Market? The Penal System as a Labor Market Institution." *American Journal of Sociology* 104(4): 1030–60.

Wilson, William Julius. 1996. *When Work Disappears: The World of the New Urban Poor*. New York: Vintage Books.

NOTES

1. The two teams were sent to different employers in order to minimize suspicion that might otherwise arise from two similar applicants with similar criminal backgrounds applying within a short time interval. In the present design, the criminal record effect is estimated as a within-team effect while race is measured as a between-team effect. While the latter is less efficient, the comparison should be unbiased. Black and white testers used *identical* resumes (something that would not have been possible had they visited the same employers) and were selected and trained to present comparable profiles to employers. Likewise, employers were randomly assigned across tester pairs, minimizing heterogeneity in employer characteristics by team.

2. Testers presented themselves as high school graduates with steady work experience in entry-level jobs.

3. The criminal record in all cases was a drug felony, possession with intent to distribute (cocaine), and eighteen months of prison time. Testers presented the information to employers by checking the box "yes" in answer to the standard application question, "Have you ever been convicted of a crime?" As additional cues, testers also reported work experience in the correctional facility and listed their parole officer as a reference (see Pager, 2003 for a more in-depth discussion of these issues).

4. A more in-depth discussion of methodological concerns, including limits to generalizability, representativeness of testers, sample restrictions, and experimenter effects is presented in Pager (2007a), appendix 4A.

5. While not significant in the full sample, this interaction becomes significant when analyzed specifically for suburban employers or among employers with whom the testers had extended personal contact (see Pager, 2007a, chap. 7).

6. These results do not appear to be specific to Milwaukee. Other audit studies have revealed effects of similar magnitude (see Pager, 2007b for a summary); and a replication of the present study in New York City comes to similar conclusions (Pager and Western, 2005).

---

49. Claude Steele*

Stereotype Threat and African-American Student Achievement

Over the past four decades African-American college students have been more in the spotlight than any other American students. This is because they aren't just college students; they are a cutting edge in America's effort to integrate itself in the nearly forty years since the passage of the Civil Rights Act. These students have borne much of the burden for our national experiment in racial integration. And to a significant degree the success of the experiment will be determined by their success.

Nonetheless, throughout the 1990s the national college dropout rate for African-Americans has been 20 to 25 percent higher than that for whites. Among

*From "Young, Gifted, and Black" by Claude Steele, Asa Hilliard, Theresa Perry. Copyright © 2003 by Theresa Perry, Asa Hilliard III, and Claude Steele. Reprinted by permission of Beacon Press, Boston. As published in *The Inequality Reader: Contemporary and Foundational Readings in Race, Class, and Gender*, 2nd Edition, by David B. Grusky and Szonja Szelenyi, copyright © 2011. Reprinted by permission of Westview Press, an imprint of Perseus Books, LLC, a subsidiary of Hachette Book Group, Inc.

those who finish college, the grade point average of Black students is two-thirds of a grade below that of whites. . . .

Virtually all aspects of underperformance—lower standardized test scores, lower college grades, lower graduation rates—persist among students from the African-American middle class. This situation forces on us an uncomfortable recognition: that beyond class, something racial is depressing the academic performance of these students.

Some time ago two of my colleagues, Joshua Aronson and Steven Spencer, and I tried to see the world from the standpoint of African-American students, concerning ourselves less with features of theirs that might explain their troubles than with features of the world they see. A story I was told recently depicts some of these. The storyteller was worried about his friend, a normally energetic Black student who had broken up with his longtime girlfriend and had since learned that she, a Hispanic, was now dating a white student. This hit him hard. Not long after hearing about his girlfriend, he sat through an hour's discussion of *The Bell Curve* in his psychology class, during which the possible genetic inferiority of his race was openly considered. Then he overheard students at lunch arguing that affirmative action allowed in too many underqualified Blacks. By his own account, this young man had experienced very little of what he thought of as racial discrimination on campus. Still, these were features of his world. Could they have a bearing on his academic life?

My colleagues and I have called such features "stereotype threat"—the threat of being viewed through the lens of a negative stereotype, or the fear of doing something that would inadvertently confirm that stereotype. Everyone experiences stereotype threat. We are all members of some group about which negative stereotypes exist, from white males and Methodists to women and the elderly. And in a situation where one of those stereotypes applies—a man talking to women about pay equity, for example, or an aging faculty member trying to remember a number sequence in the middle of a lecture—we know that we may be judged by it.

Like the young man in the story, we can feel mistrustful and apprehensive in such situations. For him, as for African-American students generally, negative stereotypes apply in many situations, even personal ones. Why was that old roommate unfriendly to him? Did that young white woman who has been so nice to him in class not return his phone call because she's afraid he'll ask her for a date? Is it because of his race or something else about him? He cannot know the answers, but neither can his rational self fully dismiss the questions. Together they raise a deeper question: Will his race be a boundary to his experience, to his emotions, to his relationships? . . .

Measuring Stereotype Threat

Can stereotype threat be shown to affect academic performance? And if so, who would be most affected—stronger or weaker students? Which has a greater influence on academic success among Black college students—the degree of threat or the level of preparation with which they enter college?

As we confronted these questions in the course of our research, we came in for some surprises. We began with what we took to be the hardest question: Could something as abstract as stereotype threat really affect something as irrepressible as intelligence? Ours is an individualistic culture; forward movement is seen to come from within. Against this cultural faith one needs evidence to argue that something as "sociological" as stereotype threat can repress something as "individualistic" as intelligence.

To acquire such evidence, Joshua Aronson and I (following a procedure developed with Steven Spencer) designed an experiment to test whether the stereotype threat that Black students might experience when taking a difficult standardized test could depress their performance on the test to a statistically reliable degree. We brought white and Black Stanford students into the laboratory and gave them, one at a time, a very difficult thirty-minute section of a Graduate Record Exam subject test in English literature. Most of these students were sophomores, which meant that the test—designed for graduating seniors—was particularly hard for them—precisely the feature, we reasoned, that would make this simple testing situation different for our Black participants than for our white participants, despite the fact that all the participants were of equal ability levels measured by all available criteria. (The difficulty of the test guaranteed that both Black and white students would find the test frustrating. And it is in these situations that members of ability-stereotyped groups are most likely to experience the extra burden of stereotype threat. First, the experience of frustration with the test gives credibility to the limitation alleged in the stereotype. For this reason, frustration can be especially stinging and disruptive for test-takers to whom the stereotype is relevant. Second, it is on a demanding test that one can least afford to be bothered by the thoughts that likely accompany stereotype threat.)

A significant part of the negative stereotype about African Americans concerns intellectual ability. Thus, in the stereotype threat conditions of the experiments in this series, we merely mentioned to participants that the test was a measure of verbal ability. This was enough, we felt, to make the negative stereotype about African Americans' abilities relevant to their performance on the test, and thus to put them at risk of confirming, or being seen to confirm, the negative stereotype about their abilities. If the pressure imposed by the relevance of a negative stereotype about one's group is enough to impair an important intellectual performance, then Black participants should perform worse than whites in the "diagnostic" condition of this experiment but not in the "nondiagnostic" condition. As Figure 49.1 depicts, this is precisely what happened: Blacks performed a full standard deviation lower than whites under the stereotype threat of the test being "diagnostic" of their intellectual ability, even though we had statistically matched the two groups in ability level. Something other than ability was involved; we believed it was stereotype threat.

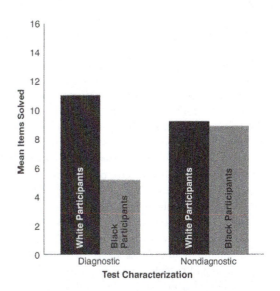

FIGURE 49.1 White and Black Participants' Score (Controlled for SAT) on a Difficult English Test as a Function of Characterization of the Test

But maybe the Black students performed less well than the white students because they were less motivated or because their skills were somehow less applicable to the advanced material of this test. We needed some way to determine if it was indeed stereotype threat that depressed the Black students' scores. We reasoned that if stereotype threat had impaired their performance on the test, then reducing this threat would allow their performance to improve. We presented the same test as a laboratory task that was used to study how certain problems are generally solved. We stressed that the task did not measure a person's level of intellectual ability. A simple instruction, yes, but it profoundly changed the meaning of the situation. In one stroke, "spotlight anxiety," as the psychologist William Cross once called it, was turned off—and the Black students' performance on the test rose to match that of equally qualified whites (see Figure 49.1). In the nonstereotype threat conditions, we presented the same test as an instrument for studying problem solving that was "nondiagnostic" of individual differences in ability—thus making the racial stereotype irrelevant to their performance.

Aronson and I decided that what we needed next was direct evidence of the subjective state we call stereotype threat. To seek this, we looked into whether simply sitting down to take a difficult test of ability was enough to make Black students mindful of their race and stereotypes about it. This may seem unlikely. White students I have taught over the years have sometimes said that they have hardly any sense of even having a race. But Blacks have many experiences with the majority "other group" that make their race salient to them.

We again brought Black and white students in to take a difficult verbal test. But just before the test began, we gave them a long list of words, each of which had two letters missing. They were told to complete the words on this list as fast as they could. We knew from a preliminary survey that twelve of the eighty words we had selected could be completed in such a way as to relate to the stereotype about Blacks' intellectual ability. The fragment "—ce," for example, could become "race." If simply taking a difficult test of ability was enough to make Black students mindful of stereotypes about their race, these students should complete more fragments with stereotype-related words. That is just what happened. When Black students were told that the test would measure ability, they completed the fragments with significantly more stereotype-related words than

when they were told that it was not a measure of ability. Whites made few stereotype-related completions in either case. . . .

How Stereotype Threat Affects People Differently

Is everyone equally threatened and disrupted by a stereotype? One might expect, for example, that it would affect the weakest students most. But in all our research the most achievement-oriented students, who were also the most skilled, motivated, and confident, were the most impaired by stereotype threat. This fact had been under our noses all along—in our data and even in our theory. A person has to care about a domain in order to be disturbed by the prospect of being stereotyped in it. That is the whole idea of disidentification—protecting against stereotype threat by ceasing to care about the domain in which the stereotype applies. Our earlier experiments had selected Black students who identified with verbal skills and women who identified with math. But when we tested participants who identified less with these domains, what had been under our noses hit us in the face. None of them showed any effect of stereotype threat whatsoever.

These weakly identified students did not perform well on the test: once they discovered its difficulty, they stopped trying very hard and got a low score. But their performance did not differ depending on whether they felt they were at risk of being judged stereotypically.

This finding, I believe, tells us two important things. The first is that the poorer college performance of Black students may have another source in addition to the one—lack of good preparation, and perhaps, of identification with school achievement—that is commonly understood. This additional source—the threat of being negatively stereotyped in the environment—has not been well understood. The distinction has important policy implications: different kinds of students may require different pedagogies of improvement.

The second thing is poignant: what exposes students to the pressure of stereotype threat is not weaker academic identity and skills, but stronger academic identity and skills. They may have long seen themselves as good students—better than most. But led into the domain by their strengths, they pay an extra tax on their investment—vigilant worry that their future will be compromised by society's perception and treatment of their group.

This tax has a long tradition in the Black community. The Jackie Robinson story is a central narrative of Black life, literature, and journalism. *Ebony Magazine* has run a page for fifty years featuring people who have broken down one or another racial barrier. Surely the academic vanguard among Black college students today knows this tradition—and knows, therefore, that the thing to do, as my father told me, is to buckle down, pay whatever tax is required, and disprove the damn stereotype.

That, however, seems to be precisely what these students are trying to do. In some of our experiments we administered the test of ability by computer, so that we could see how long participants spent looking at different parts of the test questions. Black students taking the test under stereotype threat seemed to be trying too hard rather than not hard enough. They reread the questions, reread the multiple choices, rechecked their answers, more than when they were not under stereotype threat. The threat made them inefficient on a test that, like most standardized tests, is set up so that thinking long often means thinking wrong, especially on difficult items like the ones we used. . . .

In the old song about the "steel-drivin' man," John Henry races the new steam-driven drill to see who can dig a hole faster. When the race is over, John Henry has prevailed by digging the deeper hole—only to drop dead. The social psychologist Sherman James uses the term "John Henryism" to describe a psychological syndrome that he found to be associated with hypertension in several samples of North Carolina Blacks: holding too rigidly to the faith that discrimination and disadvantage can be overcome with hard work and persistence. Certainly this is the right attitude. But taken to extremes, it can backfire. A deterioration of performance under stereotype threat by the skilled, confident Black students in our experiments may be rooted in John Henryism.

This last point can be disheartening. Our research, however, offers an interesting suggestion about what can be done to overcome stereotype threat and its detrimental effects. The success of Black students may depend less on expectations and motivation—things that are thought to drive academic performance—than on trust that stereotypes about their group will not have a limiting effect in their school world.

Putting this idea to the test, Joseph Brown and I asked, "How can the usual detrimental effect of stereotype threat on the standardized-test performance of these students be reduced? By strengthening students' expectations and confidence, or by strengthening their trust that they are not at risk of being judged on the basis of stereotypes?" In the ensuing experiment we strengthened or weakened participants' confidence in their verbal skills, by arranging for them to have either an impressive success or an impressive failure on a test of verbal skills, just before they took the same difficult verbal test we had used in our earlier research. When the second test was presented as a test of ability, the boosting or weakening of confidence in their verbal skills had no effect on performance: Black participants performed less well than equally skilled white participants. What does this say about the common sense idea that black students' academic problems are rooted in lack of self-confidence?

What did raise the level of black students' performance to that of equally qualified whites was reducing stereotype threat—in this case by explicitly presenting the test as racially fair. When this was done, Blacks performed at the same high level as whites even if their self-confidence had been weakened by a prior failure.

These results suggest something that I think has not been made clear elsewhere: when strong Black students sit down to take a difficult standardized test, the extra apprehension they feel in comparison with whites is less about their own ability than it is about having to perform on a test and in a situation that may be primed to treat them stereotypically. We discovered the extent of this apprehension when we tried to develop procedures that would make our Black participants see the test as "race-fair." It wasn't easy. African Americans have endured so much bad press about test scores for so long that, in our experience, they are instinctively wary about the tests' fairness. We were able to convince them that our test was race-fair only when we implied that the research generating the test had been done by Blacks. When they felt trust, they performed well regardless of whether we had weakened their self-confidence beforehand. And when they didn't feel trust, no amount of bolstering of self-confidence helped.

REFERENCES

Aronson, J. 1997. *The Effects of Conceptions of Ability on Task Valuation.* Unpublished manuscript, New York University.

———. 1999. *The Effects of Conceiving Ability as Fixed or Improvable on Responses to Stereotype Threat.* Unpublished manuscript, New York University.

Brown, J. L., and C. M. Steele. 2001. *Performance Expectations Are Not a Necessary Mediator of Stereotype Threat in African American Verbal Test Performance.* Unpublished manuscript, Stanford University.

Cross, W. E., Jr. 1991. *Shades of Black: Diversity in African-American Identity.* Philadelphia: Temple University Press.

Spencer, S. J., E. Iserman, P. G. Davies, and D. M. Quinn. 2001. *Suppression of Doubts, Anxiety, and Stereotypes as a Mediator of the Effect of Stereotype Threat on Women's Math Performance.* Unpublished manuscript, University of Waterloo.

Spencer, S. J., C. M. Steele, and D. M. Quinn. 1999. "Stereotype Threat and Women's Math Performance." *Journal of Experimental Social Psychology* 35: 4–28.

Steele, C. M. 1975. "Name-Calling and Compliance." *Journal of Personality and Social Psychology* 31: 361–69.

———. 1992. "Race and the Schooling of Black Americans." *Atlantic Monthly* 269: 68–78.

———. 1997. "A Threat in the Air: How Stereotypes Shape Intellectual Identity and Performance." *American Psychologist* 52: 613–29.

———. 1999. "Thin Ice: Stereotype Threat and Black College Students." *Atlantic Monthly* 248: 44–54.

Steele, C. M., and J. Aronson. 1995. "Stereotype Threat and the Intellectual Test Performance of African Americans." *Journal of Personality and Social Psychology* 69: 797–811.

Steele, C. M., S. J. Spencer, and J. Aronson. 2002. "Contending with Group Image: The Psychology of Stereotype and Social Identity Threat." In *Advances in Experimental Social Psychology*, vol. 34, ed. M. Zanna. Academic Press.

Steele, C. M., S. J. Spencer, P. G. Davies, K. Harber, and R. E. Nisbett. 2001. *African American College Achievement: A "Wise" Intervention.* Unpublished manuscript, Stanford University.

Steele, S. 1990. *The Content of Our Character: A New Vision of Race in America.* New York: St. Martin's.

Race and Ethnicity in the 21st Century and Beyond

50. William Julius Wilson*
The Declining Significance of Race: Blacks and Changing American Institutions

Race relations in America have undergone fundamental changes in recent years, so much so that now the life chances of individual blacks have more to do with their economic class position than with their day-to-day encounters with whites. In earlier years, the systematic efforts of whites to suppress blacks were obvious to even the most insensitive observer. Blacks were denied access to valued and scarce resources through various ingenious schemes of racial exploitation, discrimination, and segregation, schemes that were reinforced by elaborate ideologies of racism. But the situation has changed. However determinative such practices were for the previous efforts of the black population to achieve racial equality, and however significant they were in the creation of poverty-stricken ghettoes and a vast underclass of black proletarians—that massive population at the very bottom of the social class ladder plagued by poor education and low-paying, unstable jobs—they do not provide a meaningful explanation of the life chances of black Americans today. The traditional patterns of interaction between blacks and whites, particularly in the labor market, have been fundamentally altered.

In the antebellum period, and in the latter half of the nineteenth century through the first half of

the twentieth century, the continuous and explicit efforts of whites to construct racial barriers profoundly affected the lives of black Americans. Racial oppression was deliberate, overt, and is easily documented, ranging from slavery to segregation, from the endeavors of the white economic elite to exploit black labor to the actions of the white masses to eliminate or neutralize black competition, particularly economic competition.[1] As the nation has entered the latter half of the twentieth century, however, many of the traditional barriers have crumbled under the weight of the political, social, and economic changes of the civil rights era. A new set of obstacles has emerged from basic structural shifts in the economy. These obstacles are therefore impersonal but may prove to be even more formidable for certain segments of the black population. Specifically, whereas the previous barriers were usually designed to control and restrict the entire black population, the new barriers create hardships essentially for the black underclass; whereas the old barriers were based explicitly on racial motivations derived from intergroup contact, the new barriers have racial significance only in their consequences, not in their origins. In short, whereas the old barriers bore the pervasive features of racial oppression, the new barriers indicate an important and emerging form of class subordination.

It would be shortsighted to view the traditional forms of racial segregation and discrimination as having essentially disappeared in contemporary America; the presence of blacks is still firmly resisted in various institutions and social arrangements, for example, residential areas and private social clubs. However, in the economic sphere, class has become more important than race in determining black access to privilege and power. It is clearly evident in this connection that many talented and educated blacks are now entering positions of prestige and influence at a rate comparable to, or in some situations, exceeding that of whites with equivalent qualifications. It is equally clear that the black underclass is in a hopeless state of economic stagnation, falling further and further behind the rest of society. . . .

Three Stages of American Race Relations

My basic thesis is that American society has experienced three major stages of black-white contact and that each stage embodies a different form of racial stratification structured by the particular arrangement of both the economy and the polity. Stage one coincides with antebellum slavery and the early postbellum era and may be designated the period of *plantation economy and racial-caste oppression.* Stage two begins in the last quarter of the nineteenth century and ends at roughly the New Deal era and may be identified as the period of *industrial expansion, class conflict, and racial oppression.* Finally, stage three is associated with the modern, industrial, post–World War II era, which really began to crystallize during the 1960s and 1970s, and may be characterized as the period of *progressive transition from racial inequalities to class inequalities.* For the sake of brevity I shall identify the different periods respectively as the preindustrial, industrial, and modern industrial stages of American race relations.

Although this abbreviated designation of the periods of American race relations seems to relate racial change to fundamental economic changes rather directly, it bears repeating that the different stages of race relations are structured by the unique arrangements and interactions of the economy and the polity. Although I stress the economic basis of structured racial inequality in the preindustrial and industrial periods of race relations, I also attempt to show how the polity more or less interacted with the economy either to reinforce patterns of racial stratification or to mediate various forms of racial conflict. Moreover, for the modern industrial period, I try to show how race relations have been shaped as much by important economic changes as by important political changes. Indeed, it would not be possible to understand fully the subtle and manifest changes in race relations in the modern industrial period without recognizing the dual and often reciprocal influence of structural changes in the economy and political changes in the state. Thus, my central argument is that different systems of production and/or different arrangements of the polity have imposed different constraints on the way in which racial groups have interacted in the United States, constraints that have structured the relations between racial groups and

that have produced dissimilar contexts not only for the manifestation of racial antagonisms but also for racial group access to rewards and privileges.

In contrast to the modern industrial period in which fundamental economic and political changes have made economic class affiliation more important than race in determining Negro prospects for occupational advancement, the preindustrial and industrial periods of black-white relations have one central feature in common, namely, overt efforts of whites to solidify economic racial domination (ranging from the manipulation of black labor to the neutralization or elimination of black economic competition) through various forms of juridical, political, and social discrimination. Since racial problems during these two periods were principally related to group struggles over economic resources, they readily lend themselves to the economic class theories of racial antagonisms that associate racial antipathy with class conflict. A brief consideration of these theories, followed by a discussion of their basic weaknesses, will help to raise a number of theoretical issues that will be useful for analyzing the dynamics of racial conflict in the preindustrial and industrial stages of American race relations. However, in a later section of this chapter, I shall attempt to explain why these theories are not very relevant to the modern industrial stage of American race relations.

Economic Class Theories

Students of race relations have paid considerable attention to the economic basis of racial antagonism in recent years, particularly to the theme that racial problems in historical situations are related to the more general problems of economic class conflict. A common assumption of this theme is that racial conflict is merely a special manifestation of class conflict. Accordingly, ideologies of racism, racial prejudices, institutionalized discrimination, segregation, and other factors that reinforce or embody racial stratification are seen as simply part of a superstructure determined and shaped by the particular arrangement of the class structure.[2] However, given this basic assumption, which continues to be the most representative and widely used economic class argument,[3] proponents have advanced two major and somewhat divergent explanations of how class conflicts actually shape and determine racial relations—the orthodox Marxist theory of capitalist exploitation,[4] and the *split labor-market theory* of working-class antagonisms.[5] The orthodox Marxist theory, which is the most popular variant of the Marxists' explanations of race,[6] postulates that because the ultimate goal of the capitalist class is to maximize profits, efforts will be made to suppress workers' demands for increased wages and to weaken their bargaining power by promoting divisions within their ranks. The divisions occur along racial lines to the extent that the capitalist class is able to isolate the lower-priced black labor force by not only supporting job, housing, and educational discrimination against blacks, but also by developing or encouraging racial prejudices and ideologies of racial subjugation such as racism. The net effect of such a policy is to insure a marginal working class of blacks and to establish a relatively more privileged position for the established white labor force. Since discrimination guarantees a situation where the average wage rate of the black labor force is less than the average wage rate of the established white labor force, the probability of labor solidarity against the capitalist class is diminished.

At the same time, orthodox Marxists argue the members of the capitalist class benefit not only because they have created a reserved army of labor that is not united against them and the appropriation of surplus from the black labor force is greater than the exploitation rate of the white labor force,[7] but also because they can counteract ambitious claims of the white labor force for higher wages either by threatening to increase the average wage rate of black workers or by replacing segments of the white labor force with segments of the black labor force in special situations such as strikes. The weaker the national labor force, the more likely it is that it will be replaced by lower-paid black labor especially during organized strikes demanding wage increases and improved working conditions. In short, orthodox Marxists argue that racial antagonism is designed to be a "mask for privilege" that effectively conceals the efforts of the ruling class to exploit subordinate minority groups and divide the working class.

In interesting contrast to the orthodox Marxist approach, the split labor-market theory posits the view that rather than attempting to protect a segment of the laboring class, business "supports a liberal or *laissez faire* ideology that would permit all workers to compete freely in an open market. Such open competition would displace higher paid labor. Only under duress does business yield to a labor aristocracy [i.e., a privileged position for white workers]."[8] The central hypothesis of the split labor-market theory is that racial antagonism first develops in a labor market split along racial lines. The term "antagonism" includes all aspects of intergroup conflict, from beliefs and ideologies (e.g., racism), to overt behavior (e.g., discrimination), to institutions (e.g., segregationist laws). A split labor market occurs when the price of labor for the same work differs for at least two groups, or would differ if they performed the same work. The price of labor "refers to labor's total cost to the employer, including not only wages, but the cost of recruitment, transportation, room and board, education, health care (if the employer must bear these), and the cost of labor unrest."[9] There are three distinct classes in a split labor market: (1) business or employers; (2) higher-paid labor; and (3) cheaper labor. Conflict develops between these three classes because of different interests. The main goal of business or employers is to maintain as cheap a labor force as possible in order to compete effectively with other businesses and to maximize economic returns. Employers will often import laborers from other areas if local labor costs are too high or if there is a labor shortage. Whenever a labor shortage exists, higher-paid labor is in a good bargaining position. Accordingly, if business is able to attract cheaper labor to the market place, the interests of higher-paid labor are threatened. They may lose some of the privileges they enjoy, they may lose their bargaining power, and they may even lose their jobs. Moreover, the presence of cheaper labor in a particular job market may not only represent actual competition but potential competition as well. An "insignificant trickle" could be seen as the beginning of a major immigration. If the labor market is split along ethnic lines, for example, if higher-paid labor is white and lower-paid labor is black, class antagonisms are transformed into racial antagonisms. Thus, "while much rhetoric of ethnic antagonism concentrates on ethnicity and race, it really in large measure (though probably not entirely) expresses this class conflict."[10] In some cases, members of the lower-paid laboring class, either from within the territorial boundaries of a given country or from another country, are drawn into or motivated to enter a labor market because they feel they can improve their standard of living. As Edna Bonacich points out, "the poorer the economy of the recruits, the less the inducement needed for them to enter the new labor market."[11] In other cases, individuals are forced into a new labor-market situation, such as the involuntary migration of blacks into a condition of slavery in the United States. In this connection, the greater the employer's control over lower-priced labor, the more threatening is lower-paid labor to higher-paid labor.

However, if more expensive labor is strong enough, that is, if it possesses the power resources to preserve its economic interests, it can prevent being replaced or undercut by cheaper labor. On the one hand it can exclude lower-paid labor from a given territory. "Exclusion movements clearly serve the interests of higher-paid labor. Its standards are protected, while the capitalist class is deprived of cheaper labor."[12] On the other hand, if it is not possible for higher-paid labor to rely on exclusion (cheaper labor may be indigenous to the territory or may have been imported early in business-labor relations when higher-paid labor could not prevent the move) then it will institutionalize a system of ethnic stratification which could (1) monopolize skilled positions, thereby ensuring the effectiveness of strike action; (2) prevent cheaper labor from developing the skills necessary to compete with higher-paid labor (for example, by imposing barriers to equal access to education); and (3) deny cheaper labor the political resources that would enable them to undercut higher-paid labor through, say, governmental regulations. "In other words, the solution to the devastating potential of weak, cheap labor is, paradoxically, to weaken them further, until it is no longer in business' immediate interest to use them as replacement."[13] Thus, whereas orthodox Marxist arguments associate the development and institutionalization of racial stratification with the motivations and activities of the capitalist class, the split labor-market theory traces racial stratification directly to the powerful, higher-paid working class.

Implicit in both of these economic class theories is a power-conflict thesis associating the regulation of labor or wages with properties (ownership of land or capital, monopolization of skilled positions) that determine the scope and degree of a group's ability to influence behavior in the labor market. Furthermore, both theories clearly demonstrate the need to focus on the different ways and situations in which various segments of the dominant racial group perceive and respond to the subordinate racial group. However, as I examine the historical stages of race relations in the United States, I find that the patterns of black/white interaction do not consistently and sometimes do not conveniently conform to the propositions outlined in these explanations of racial antagonism. In some cases, the orthodox Marxian explanation seems more appropriate; in other instances, the split labor-market theory seems more

appropriate; and in still others, neither theory can, in isolation, adequately explain black-white conflict.

If we restrict our attention for the moment to the struggle over economic resources, then the general pattern that seems to have characterized race relations in the United States during the preindustrial and industrial stages was that the economic elite segments of the white population have been principally responsible for those forms of racial inequality that entail the exploitation of labor (as in slavery), whereas whites in the lower strata have been largely responsible for those forms of imposed racial stratification that are designed to eliminate economic competition (as in job segregation). Moreover, in some situations, the capitalist class and white workers form an alliance to keep blacks suppressed. Accordingly, restrictive arguments to the effect that racial stratification was the work of the capitalist class or was due to the "victory" of higher-paid white labor obscure the dynamics of complex and variable patterns of black-white interaction.

However, if we ignore the more categorical assertions that attribute responsibility for racial stratification to a particular class and focus seriously on the analyses of interracial contact in the labor market, then I will be able to demonstrate that, depending on the historical situation, each of the economic class theories provides arguments that help to illuminate race relations during the preindustrial and industrial periods of black-white contact. By the same token, I hope to explain why these theories have little application to the third, and present, stage of modern industrial race relations. My basic argument is that the meaningful application of the arguments in each theory for any given historical period depends considerably on knowledge of the constraints imposed by the particular systems of production and by the particular laws and policies of the state during that period, constraints that shape the structural relations between racial and class groups and which thereby produce different patterns of intergroup interaction. . . .

The Influence of the System of Production

The term "system of production" not only refers to the technological basis of economic processes or, in Karl Marx's terms, the "forces of production," but it also implies the "social relations of production," that is, "the interaction (for example, through employment and property arrangement) into which men enter at a given level of the development of the forces of production."[14] As I previously indicated, different systems of production impose constraints on racial group interaction. In the remainder of this section I should like to provide a firmer analytical basis for this distinction as it applies specifically to the three stages of American race relations, incorporating in my discussion relevant theoretical points raised in the foregoing sections of this chapter.

It has repeatedly been the case that a non-manufacturing or plantation economy with a simple division of labor and a small aristocracy that dominates the economic and political life of a society has characteristically generated a paternalistic rather than a competitive form of race relations, and the antebellum South was no exception.[15] Paternalistic racial patterns reveal close symbiotic relationships marked by dominance and subservience, great social distance and little physical distance, and clearly symbolized rituals of racial etiquette. The southern white aristocracy created a split labor market along racial lines by enslaving blacks to perform tasks at a cheaper cost than free laborers of the dominant group. This preindustrial form of race relations was not based on the actions of dominant-group laborers, who, as we shall see, were relatively powerless to effect significant change in race relations during this period, but on the structure of the relations established by the aristocracy. Let me briefly amplify this point.

In the southern plantation economy, public power was overwhelmingly concentrated in the hands of the white aristocracy. This power was not only reflected in the control of economic resources and in the development of a juridical system that expressed the class interests of the aristocracy, but also in the way the aristocracy was able to impose its viewpoint on the larger society.[16] This is not to suggest that these aspects of public power have not been disproportionately controlled by the economic elite in modern industrialized Western societies; rather it indicates that the hegemony of the southern ruling elite was much greater in degree, not in kind, than in these societies. The southern elite's hegemony was embodied in an economy that required little horizontal or vertical mobility. Further, because of the absence of those gradations of labor power associated with complex divisions of labor, white workers in the antebellum and early postbellum South had little opportunity to challenge the control of the aristocracy. Because white laborers lacked power resources in the southern plantation economy, their influence on the form and quality of racial stratification was minimal throughout the antebellum and early

postbellum periods. Racial stratification therefore primarily reflected the relationships established between blacks and the white aristocracy, relationships which were not characterized by competition for scarce resources but by the exploitation of black labor.[17] Social distance tended to be clearly symbolized by rituals of racial etiquette: gestures and behavior reflecting dominance and subservience. Consequently, any effort to impose a system of public segregation was superfluous. Furthermore, since the social gap between the aristocracy and black slaves was wide and stable, ideologies of racism played less of a role in the subordination of blacks than they subsequently did in the more competitive systems of race relations following the Civil War. In short, the relationship represented intergroup paternalism because it allowed for "close symbiosis and even intimacy, without any threat to status inequalities."[18] This was in sharp contrast to the more competitive forms of race relations that accompanied the development of industrial capitalism in the late nineteenth century and first few decades of the twentieth century (the industrial period of American race relations), wherein the complex division of labor and opportunities for greater mobility not only produced interaction, competition, and labor-market conflict between blacks and the white working class, but also provided the latter with superior resources (relative to those they possessed under the plantation economy) to exert greater influence on the form and content of racial stratification.

The importance of the system of production in understanding race relations is seen in a comparison of Brazil and the southern United States during the post-slavery periods. In the United States, the southern economy experienced a fairly rapid rate of expansion during the late nineteenth century, thereby creating various middle level skilled and unskilled positions that working-class whites attempted to monopolize for themselves. The efforts of white workers to eliminate black competition in the South generated an elaborate system of Jim Crow segregation that was reinforced by an ideology of biological racism. The white working class was aided not only by its numerical size, but also by its increasing accumulation of political resources that accompanied changes in its relation to the means of production.

As white workers gradually translated their increasing labor power into political power, blacks experienced greater restrictions in their efforts to achieve a satisfactory economic, political, and social life. In Brazil, on the other hand, the large Negro and mulatto population was not thrust into competition with the much smaller white population over access to higher-status positions because, as Marvin Harris notes, "there was little opportunity for any member of the lower class to move upward in the social hierarchy."[19] No economic class group or racial group had much to gain by instituting a rigid system of racial segregation or cultivating an ideology of racial inferiority. Racial distinctions were insignificant to the landed aristocracy, who constituted a numerically small upper class in what was basically a sharply differentiated two class society originally shaped during slavery. The mulattoes, Negroes, and poor whites were all in the same impoverished lower-ranking position. "The general economic stagnation which has been characteristic of lowland Latin America since the abolition of slavery," observes Marvin Harris, "tends to reinforce the pattern of pacific relationships among the various racial groups in the lower ranking levels of the social hierarchy. Not only were the poor whites out-numbered by the mulattoes and Negroes, but there was little of a significant material nature to struggle over in view of the generally static condition of the economy."[20] Accordingly, in Brazil, segregation, discrimination, and racist ideologies failed to crystallize in the first several decades following the end of slavery. More recently, however, industrialization has pushed Brazil toward a competitive type of race relations, particularly the southern region (for example, São Paulo) which has experienced rapid industrialization and has blacks in economic competition with many lower-status white immigrants.[21] Whereas the racial antagonism in the United States during the period of industrial race relations (such as the Jim Crow segregation movement in the South and the race riots in northern cities) tended to be either directly or indirectly related to labor-market conflicts, racial antagonism in the period of modern industrial relations tends to originate outside the economic order and to have little connection with labor-market strife. Basic changes in the system of production have produced a segmented labor structure in which blacks are either isolated in the relatively non-unionized, low-paying, basically undesirable jobs of the noncorporate sector, or occupy the higher-paying corporate and government industry positions in which job competition is either controlled by powerful unions or is restricted to the highly trained and educated, regardless of race. If there is a basis for labor-market conflict in the modern industrial period, it is most probably related to

the affirmative action programs originating from the civil rights legislation of the 1960s. However, since affirmative action programs are designed to improve job opportunities for the talented and educated, their major impact has been in the higher-paying jobs of the expanding government sector and the corporate sector. The sharp increase of the more privileged blacks in these industries has been facilitated by the combination of affirmative action and rapid industry growth. Indeed, despite the effectiveness of affirmative action programs, the very expansion of these sectors of the economy has kept racial friction over higher-paying corporate and government jobs to a minimum.

Unlike the occupational success achieved by the more talented and educated blacks, those in the black underclass find themselves locked in the low-paying and dead-end jobs of the noncorporate industries, jobs which are not in high demand and which therefore do not generate racial competition or strife among the national black and white labor force. Many of these jobs go unfilled, and employers often have to turn to cheap labor from Mexico and Puerto Rico. As Nathan Glazer has pointed out, "Expectations have changed, and fewer blacks and whites today will accept a life at menial labor with no hope for advancement, as their fathers and older brothers did and as European immigrants did."[22] Thus in the modern industrial era neither the corporate nor government sectors nor the noncorporate low-wage sector provide the basis for the kind of interracial competition and conflict that has traditionally plagued the labor market in the United States. This, then, is the basis for my earlier contention that the economic class theories which associate labor-market conflicts with racial antagonism have little application to the present period of modern industrial race relations.

The Polity and American Race Relations

If the patterned ways in which racial groups have interacted historically have been shaped in major measure by different systems of production, they have also been undeniably influenced by the changing policies and laws of the state. For analytical purposes, it would be a mistake to treat the influences of the polity and the economy as if they were separate and unrelated. The legal and political systems in the antebellum South were effectively used as instruments of the slaveholding elite to strengthen and legitimate the institution of slavery. But as industrialization altered the economic class structure in the postbellum South, the organizing power and political consciousness of the white lower class increased and its members were able to gain enough control of the political and juridical systems to legalize a new system of racial domination (Jim Crow segregation) that clearly reflected their class interests.

In effect, throughout the preindustrial period of race relations and the greater portion of the industrial period the role of the polity was to legitimate, reinforce, and regulate patterns of racial inequality. However, it would be unwarranted to assume that the relationship between the economic and political aspects of race necessarily implies that the latter is simply a derivative phenomenon based on the more fundamental processes of the former. The increasing intervention, since the mid-twentieth century, of state and federal government agencies in resolving or mediating racial conflicts has convincingly demonstrated the political system's autonomy in handling contemporary racial problems. Instead of merely formalizing existing racial alignments as in previous periods, the political system has, since the initial state and municipal legislation of the 1940s, increasingly created changes leading to the erosion of traditional racial alignments; in other words, instead of reinforcing racial barriers created during the preindustrial and industrial periods, the political system in recent years has tended to promote racial equality.

Thus, in the previous periods the polity was quite clearly an instrument of the white population in suppressing blacks. The government's racial practices varied, as I indicated above, depending on which segment of the white population was able to assert its class interests. However, in the past two decades the interests of the black population have been significantly reflected in the racial policies of the government, and this change is one of the clearest indications that the racial balance of power has been significantly altered. Since the early 1940s the black population has steadily gained political resources, and with the help of sympathetic white allies, has shown an increasing tendency to utilize these resources in promoting or protecting its group interests.

By the mid-twentieth century the black vote had proved to be a major vehicle for political pressure. The black vote not only influenced the outcome of national elections but many congressional, state, and municipal elections as well. Fear of the Negro vote

produced enactment of public accommodation and fair employment practices laws in northern and western municipalities and states prior to the passage of federal civil rights legislation in 1964. This political resurgence for black Americans increased their sense of power, raised their expectations, and provided the foundation for the proliferation of demands which shaped the black revolt during the 1960s. But there were other factors that helped to buttress Negro demands and contributed to the developing sense of power and rising expectations, namely, a growing, politically active black middle class following World War II and the emergence of the newly independent African states.

The growth of the black middle class was concurrent with the growth of the black urban population. It was in the urban areas, with their expanding occupational opportunities, that a small but significant number of blacks were able to upgrade their occupations, increase their income, and improve their standard of living. The middle-class segment of an oppressed minority is most likely to participate in a drive for social justice that is disciplined and sustained. In the early phases of the civil rights movement, the black middle class channeled its energies through organizations such as the National Association for the Advancement of Colored People, which emphasized developing political resources and successful litigation through the courts. These developments were paralleled by the attack against traditional racial alignments in other parts of the world. The emerging newly independent African states led the assault. In America, the so-called "leader of the free world," the manifestation of racial tension and violence has been a constant source of embarrassment to national government officials. This sensitivity to world opinion made the national government more vulnerable to pressures of black protest at the very time when blacks had the greatest propensity to protest.

The development of black political resources that made the government more sensitive to Negro demands, the motivation and morale of the growing black middle class that resulted in the political drive for racial equality, and the emergence of the newly independent African states that increased the federal government's vulnerability to civil rights pressures all combined to create a new sense of power among black Americans and to raise their expectations as they prepared to enter the explosive decade of the 1960s. The national government was also aware of this developing sense of power and responded to the pressures of black protest in the 1960s with an unprecedented series of legislative enactments to protect black civil rights.

The problem for blacks today, in terms of government practices, is no longer one of legalized racial inequality. Rather the problem for blacks, especially the black underclass, is that the government is not organized to deal with the new barriers imposed by structural changes in the economy. With the passage of equal employment legislation and the authorization of affirmative action programs, the government has helped clear the path for more privileged blacks, who have the requisite education and training, to enter the mainstream of American occupations. However, such government programs do not confront the impersonal economic barriers confronting members of the black underclass, who have been effectively screened out of the corporate and government industries. And the very attempts of the government to eliminate traditional racial barriers through such programs as affirmative action have had the unintentional effect of contributing to the growing economic class divisions within the black community.

Class Stratification and Changing Black Experiences

The problems of black Americans have always been compounded because of their low position in both the economic order (the average economic class position of blacks as a group) and the social order (the social prestige or honor accorded individual blacks because of their ascribed racial status). It is of course true that the low economic position of blacks has helped to shape the categorical social definitions attached to blacks as a racial group, but it is also true that the more blacks become segmented in terms of economic class position, the more their concerns about the social significance of race will vary.

In the preindustrial period of American race relations there was of course very little variation in the economic class position of blacks. The system of racial-caste oppression relegated virtually all blacks to the bottom of the economic class hierarchy. Moreover, the social definitions of racial differences were heavily influenced by the ideology of racism and the doctrine of paternalism, both of which clearly assigned a subordinate status for blacks vis-à-vis whites. Occasionally, a few individual free blacks would emerge and accumulate some wealth or property, but they were the overwhelming exception. Thus the uniformly low economic class position of blacks reinforced, and in the eyes of most whites, substantiated the social definitions that asserted Negroes were culturally and biogenetically inferior to whites. The uniformly low economic class position of blacks also removed the basis for any meaningful distinction between race issues and class issues within the black community.

The development of a black middle class accompanied the change from a preindustrial to an industrial system of production. Still, despite the fact that some blacks were able to upgrade their occupation and increase their education and income, there were severe limits on the areas in which blacks could in fact advance. Throughout most of the industrial period of race relations, the growth of the black middle class occurred because of the expansion of institutions created to serve the needs of a growing urbanized black population. The black doctor, lawyer, teacher, minister, businessman, mortician, excluded from the white community, was able to create a niche in the segregated black community. Although the income levels and lifestyles of the black professionals were noticeably and sometimes conspicuously different from those of the black masses, the two groups had one basic thing in common: a racial status contemptuously regarded by most whites in society. If E. Franklin Frazier's analysis of the black bourgeoisie is correct, the black professionals throughout the industrial period of American race relations tended to react to their low position in the social order by an ostentatious display of material possessions and a conspicuous effort to disassociate themselves from the black masses.[23] Still, as long as the members of the black middle class were stigmatized by their racial status; as long as they were denied the social recognition accorded their white counterparts; more concretely, as long as they remained restricted in where they could live, work, socialize, and be educated, race would continue to be a far more salient and important issue in shaping their sense of group position than their economic class position. Indeed, it was the black middle class that provided the leadership and generated the momentum for the civil rights movement during the mid-twentieth century. The influence and interests of this class were clearly reflected in the way the race issues were defined and articulated. Thus, the concept of "freedom" quite clearly implied, in the early stages of the movement, the right to swim in certain swimming pools, to eat in certain restaurants, to attend certain movie theaters, and to have the same voting privileges as whites. These basic concerns were reflected in the 1964 Civil Rights Bill which helped to create the illusion that, when the needs of the black middle class were met, so were the needs of the entire black community.

However, although the civil rights movement initially failed to address the basic needs of the members of the black lower class, it did increase their awareness of racial oppression, heighten their expectations about improving race relations, and increase their impatience with existing racial arrangements. These feelings were dramatically manifested in a series of violent ghetto outbursts that rocked the nation throughout the late 1960s. These outbreaks constituted the most massive and sustained expression of lower-class black dissatisfaction in the nation's history. They also forced the political system to recognize the problems of human survival and de facto segregation in the nation's ghettoes—problems pertaining to unemployment and underemployment, inferior ghetto schools, and deteriorated housing.

However, in the period of modern industrial race relations, it would be difficult indeed to comprehend the plight of inner-city blacks by exclusively focusing on racial discrimination. For in a very real sense, the current problems of lower-class blacks are substantially related to fundamental structural changes in the economy. A history of discrimination and oppression created a huge black underclass, and the technological and economic revolutions have combined to insure it a permanent status.

As the black middle class rides on the wave of political and social changes, benefiting from the growth of employment opportunities in the growing corporate and government sectors of the economy, the black underclass falls behind the larger society in every conceivable respect. The economic and political systems in the United States have demonstrated remarkable flexibility in allowing talented blacks to fill positions of prestige and influence at the same time that these systems have shown persistent rigidity in handling the problems of lower-class blacks. As a result, for the first time in American history class, issues can meaningfully compete with race issues in the way blacks develop or maintain a sense of group position.[24]

Conclusion

The foregoing sections of this chapter present an outline and a general analytical basis for the arguments that will be systematically explored [elsewhere].[25] I have tried to show that race relations in American society have been historically characterized by three major stages and that each stage is represented by a unique form of racial interaction which is shaped by the particular arrangement of the economy and the polity. My central argument is that different systems of production and/or different policies of the state have imposed different constraints on the way in which racial groups interact—constraints that have structured the relations between racial groups and produced dissimilar contexts not only for the manifestation of racial antagonisms but also for racial-group access to rewards and privileges. I emphasized in this connection that in the preindustrial and industrial periods of American race relations, the systems of production primarily shaped the patterns of racial stratification and the role of the polity was to legitimate, reinforce, or regulate these patterns. In the modern industrial period, however, both the system of production and the polity assume major importance in creating new patterns of race relations and in altering the context of racial strife. Whereas the preindustrial and industrial stages were principally related to group struggles over economic resources as different segments of the white population overtly sought to create and solidify economic racial domination (ranging from the exploitation of black labor in the preindustrial period to the elimination of black competition for jobs in the industrial period) through various forms of political, juridical, and social discrimination; in the modern industrial period fundamental economic and political changes have made economic class position more important than race in determining black chances for occupational mobility. Finally, I have outlined the importance of racial norms or belief systems, especially as they relate to the general problem of race and class conflict in the preindustrial and industrial periods.

My argument that race relations in America have moved from economic racial oppression to a form of class subordination for the less-privileged blacks is not meant to suggest that racial conflicts have disappeared or have even been substantially reduced. On the contrary, the basis of such conflicts have shifted from the economic sector to the sociopolitical order and therefore do not play as great a role in determining the life chances of individual black Americans as in the previous periods of overt economic racial oppression.

NOTES

1. See William J. Wilson, *Power, Racism and Privilege: Race Relations in Theoretical and Sociohistorical Perspectives* (New York: The Free Press, 1973).

2. In Marxist terminology, the "superstructure" refers to the arrangements of beliefs, norms, ideologies, and non-economic institutions.

3. However, not all theorists who emphasize the importance of economic class in explanations of race relations simply relegate problems of race to the superstructure. The Marxist scholars Michael Burawoy and Eugene Genovese recognize the reciprocal influence between the economic class structure and aspects of the superstructure (belief systems, political systems, etc.), a position which I also share and which is developed more fully in subsequent sections of this chapter. See Eugene D. Genovese, *Roll, Jordan, Roll: The World the Slaves Made* (New York: Pantheon, 1974); idem, *In Red and Black: Marxian Explorations in Southern and Afro-American History* (New York: Vintage Press, 1971); and Michael Burawoy, "Race, Class, and Colonialism," *Social and Economic Studies* 23 (1974): 521–50.

4. Oliver C. Cox, *Caste, Class and Race: A Study in Social Dynamics* (Garden City, New York: Doubleday, 1948); Paul A. Baran and Paul M. Sweezy, *Monopoly Capital: An Essay on the American Economic and Social Order* (Harmondsworth: Penguin, 1966); Michael Reich, "The Economics of Racism," in *Problems in Political Economy,* ed. David M. Gordon (Lexington, Mass.: Heath, 1971); and M. Nikolinakos, "Notes on an Economic Theory of Racism," *Race: A Journal of Race and Group Relations* 14 (1973): 365–81.

5. Edna Bonacich, "A Theory of Ethnic Antagonism: The Split Labor Market," *American Sociological Review* 37 (October 1972): 547–59; idem, "Abolition, the Extension of Slavery and the Position of Free Blacks: A Study of Split Labor Markets in the United States," *American Journal of Sociology* 81 (1975): 601–28.

6. For examples of alternative and less orthodox Marxist explanations of race, see Eugene D. Genovese, *The Political Economy of Slavery: Studies in the Economy and Society of the Slave South* (New York: Pantheon, 1966); idem, *The World the Slaveholders Made: Two Essays in Interpretation* (New York: Pantheon, 1969); idem, *In Red and Black;* idem, *Roll, Jordan, Roll;* and Burawoy, "Race, Class, and Colonialism."

7. "Exploitation," in Marxian terminology, refers to the difference between the wages workers receive and the value of the goods they produce. The size of this difference, therefore, determines the degree of exploitation.

8. Bonacich, "A Theory of Ethnic Antagonism," p. 557.

9. Ibid., p. 549.

10. Ibid., p. 553.

11. Ibid., p. 549.

12. Ibid., p. 555.

13. Ibid., p. 556.

14. Neil J. Smelser, *Karl Marx on Society and Social Change* (Chicago: University of Chicago Press, 1974), p. xiv. According to Smelser, Marx used the notions "forces of production" and "social relations of production" as constituting the "mode of production." However, in Marx's writings the mode of production is often discussed as equivalent only to the "forces of production." To avoid confusion, I have chosen the term "system of production" which denotes the interrelation of the forces of production and the mode of production.

15. Pierre L. van den Berghe, *Race and Racism: A Comparative Perspective* (New York: John Wiley and Sons, 1967), p. 26.

16. See, for example, Genovese, *Roll, Jordan, Roll.*

17. An exception to this pattern occurred in the cities of the antebellum South, where non-slaveholding whites played a major role in the development of urban segregation. However, since an overwhelming majority of the population resided in rural areas, race relations in the antebellum southern cities were hardly representative of the region.

18. van den Berghe, *Race and Racism,* p. 27.

19. Marvin Harris, *Patterns of Race in the Americas* (New York: Walker, 1964), p. 96.

20. Ibid., p. 96.

21. van den Berghe, *Race and Racism,* p. 28.

22. Nathan Glazer, "Blacks and Ethnic Groups: The Difference, and the Political Difference It Makes," in *Key Issues in the Afro-American Experience,* ed. Nathan I. Huggins, Martin Kilson, and Daniel M. Fox (New York: Harcourt Brace Jovanovich, 1971), 2: 209.

23. E. Franklin Frazier, *Black Bourgeoisie* (New York: The Free Press, 1957). See also Nathan Hare, *Black Anglo-Saxons* (New York: Collier, 1965).

24. The theoretical implications of this development for ethnic groups in general are discussed by Milton Gordon under the concept "ethclass." See Milton M. Gordon, *Assimilation in American Life* (New York: Oxford University Press, 1964).

25. See William Julius Wilson, *The Declining Significance of Race: Blacks and Changing American Institutions* (Chicago and London: University of Chicago Press, 1978).

51. Reanne Frank, Ilana Redstone Akresh, and Bo Lu*

How Do Latino Immigrants Fit into the Racial Order?

"The problem of the twentieth-century is the problem of the color-line" (Du Bois 1903, 3). A century later, scholars are revisiting W. E. B. Du Bois's famous proclamation and labeling it this century's biggest puzzle. There is increased uncertainty about the issue of the color line and its meaning for US society (Lee and Bean 2007a, 2007b; Lewis, Krysan, and Harris 2004). Over the past fifty years the arrival of unprecedented numbers of immigrants from Latin America, in particular from Mexico, has radically changed the racial/ethnic mix of the United States and has challenged the continued relevance of the traditional black/white model of race relations.

This chapter addresses a two-part question about US racial boundaries and the place of the Latino immigrant population therein. First, how do Latinos see themselves fitting into the US racial order; that is, how do Latino immigrants define themselves when confronted with the US system of racial classification? Second, on the flip side, how are Latino immigrants influenced by the existing system of racial stratification in the United States? In particular, does the US color-based system of stratification affect Latino immigrants, even though they themselves may not readily identify with an existing racial group?

Boundary Construction

In investigating the puzzle of the US color line and the place of Latinos therein, we follow the tradition of Barth (1969) and, more recently, Wimmer (2008b), who suggest that racial/ethnic boundaries are not given divisions of human populations to which all members of society ascribe. Rather, these

*The ideas, issues, and theories considered in this brief commissioned piece are examined in greater depth in the following publication: Reanne Frank, Ilana Redstone Akresh, and Bo Lu, "Latino Immigrants and the U.S. Racial Order: How and Where Do They Fit In?" *American Sociological Review* 75 (June 2010), pp. 940–963, published by Sage Publications. The article printed here was originally prepared by Reanne Frank, Ilana Redstone Akresh, and Bo Lu for the fourth edition of *Social Stratification: Class, Race, and Gender in Sociological Perspective*, edited by David B. Grusky. Copyright © 2014 by Westview Press.

divisions are conceptualized as products of classificatory struggles in which "individuals and groups struggle over who should be allowed to categorize, which categories are to be used, which meanings they should imply and what consequences they should entail" (Wimmer 2007, 11).

In the language of a boundary-centered framework, a social boundary occurs when two different schemas, one categorical and the other behavioral, coincide (Wimmer 2008b). According to Wimmer (2008b), the categorical dimension of a given boundary divides the world into social groups: "us" and "them." For the purposes of this chapter, we evaluate the categorical dimension of a possible racial boundary forming around Latinos using immigrant racial self-identification practices. The behavioral dimension of social boundaries involves the everyday action scripts that dictate how individuals interact with those labeled "us" and "them" (Wimmer 2008b). We address this aspect of racial boundary formation through a matching exercise that evaluates the effect of skin-color-based discrimination on Latino immigrants' annual earnings.

We investigate where Latinos fit into the existing US racial order by first examining racial self-identification, one aspect of a boundary's categorical dimension. Current federal policy in the United States says that individuals can belong to one or more racial groups. Significantly, Hispanics and Latinos have been set apart as an ethnic group and are instructed to choose the race that best describes them (Tafoya 2005). This forces Latino immigrants to place themselves along a sharply drawn color line that separates blacks and whites and has remained relatively inflexible over time (Davis 1991).

A boundary-centered framework suggests that actors may pursue several options in reaction to existing categorical boundaries dictated by the state (Wimmer 2008a). From the immigrant vantage point, one possible reaction to an existing racial boundary is to reject the available choices and instead promote other nonracial modes of classification and social practice (Kusow 2006; Wimmer 2008a). This process, labeled "boundary contraction," can be seen in the case of West Indian immigrants who have made concerted efforts to resist the US racialization process by stressing their cultural and national identity (Foner 1987). By asserting an alternative category not recognized in the United States, members of this group attempt to position themselves in an intermediate racial category between black and white (Landale and Oropesa 2002).

A second option for Latino immigrants is to racially identify in a way that challenges existing racial boundaries. Many researchers interpret the high number of Latino respondents in the 1990 and 2000 Census who marked "some other race" as a blurring of existing racial boundaries (Wimmer 2008b). This has led some authors to argue that although Latinos are undoubtedly aware of the black/white color line in the United States, they are asserting a distinct Hispanic/Latino racial classification by marking "some other race" (Logan 2003; Michael and Timberlake 2008) and rejecting the federal distinction between race and ethnicity (Hitlin, Brown, and Elder 2007; Campbell and Rogalin 2006). According to one Mexican American respondent interviewed on the subject of US Census racial categories, "I think we are big enough to be our own race, especially now that we are growing" (Dowling 2004, 101).

Other researchers focus less on the large number of other race Latinos in the US Census and instead study the slightly larger number of Latino respondents who select white as their race (Rodriguez 2000). Instead of attempting to modify the topography of racial boundaries by expanding existing options, choosing "white" may reflect a process whereby the meanings associated with particular racial boundaries are modified. Illustrative remarks come from a Mexican American woman living in Texas who, when asked which race she chose on the US Census form, responded: "White . . . there's no such thing as a brown race. They call Hispanic people brown, right? But we are White. . . . Ignorance is the only thing that would cause anybody to check anything else but White, because that's what we are. . . . There is no such thing as brown . . . we've been here too long. We're just Americans" (Dowling 2004, 92).

The debate over who should be allowed to categorize, and which categories should be used in the formation of a social boundary, is important because categories coincide with "scripts of action" that determine how individual members of particular groups are treated by others. Whether a boundary can be crossed, altered, or redefined depends not only on those attempting to renegotiate it, but also on actors on the other side who may reject the newcomers. One of the most tenacious forms of racism in the United States is discrimination by skin tone (Hochschild 2005). If some Latino immigrants are discriminated against on the basis of their skin color, we may expect an increasingly sharper racial boundary to form around them and their descendants (Hersch 2008).

Data

The data come from the 2003 cohort of the New Immigrant Survey (NIS), which was originally pilot tested with a 1996 sample cohort of immigrants. The sampling frame for the NIS 2003 was immigrants age eighteen and older who were granted legal permanent residency between May and November 2003 (see Jasso et al., forthcoming). The sample includes new arrivals in the United States and individuals who had adjusted their visa status.

Among the NIS respondents, 2,729 self-identified as Latino. A total of 1,539 observations are available for the first part of the analysis predicting racial identification. Most of the remaining 1,190 cases were lost because of missing information on the skin color chart, primarily because interviews were done over the phone and therefore precluded an interviewer assessment of skin color. The NIS skin color scale (developed by Massey and Martin [2003]) instructs interviewers to rate a respondent's skin color as closely as possible using the shades shown in an array of ten progressively darker hands (1 is lightest, 10 is darkest). In the second part of this chapter, where our dependent variable is annual earnings, we restrict the sample to Latinos who are members of the labor force and have valid skin color information (N = 954).

Racial Self-Identification

We first focus on Latino immigrants' responses to federally mandated racial identification choices by predicting racial identification in three categories: (1) white, (2) nonwhite (including those who chose Native American/Alaska Native, Black, Asian, and Native Hawaiian/Pacific Islander), and (3) refused to answer. By focusing on these patterns of refusal alongside the federally mandated racial category choices, we evaluate the ways in which Latinos are either accepting, challenging, or expanding federally validated racial boundaries and what this means for the future of the US color line. Skin color is measured, as noted previously, using the NIS skin color scale.

We present five multinomial regression models predicting the log odds of either a white or a nonwhite racial self-identification as compared to not choosing any racial identification category. We add variable sets sequentially.

Table 51.1 presents the results from the multinomial logistic regression modeling of racial self-identification. For each specification, two columns present es-

TABLE 51.1 Multinomial Regression Predicting Racial Self-Identification as White or Nonwhite Compared to None

	Model 1		Model 2		Model 3		Model 4		Model 5	
	White	Nonwhite	White	Nonwhite	White	Nonwhite	White	Nonwhite	White	Nonwhite
Skin Color, 1 to 10, Light–>Dark	−.24**	.01	−.21**	.03	−.21**	.03	−.22**	.03	−.22**	.06
	(.05)	(.07)	(.05)	(.07)	(.05)	(.07)	(.05)	(.07)	(.05)	(.07)
Cuba [Mexico]			1.45*	.84	1.53*	.92	1.52*	.87	.88	−.23
			(.60)	(.78)	(.60)	(.79)	(.61)	(.79)	(.65)	(.87)
Dominican Republic			−.56*	−.57	−.44	−.40	−.51	−.47	−.89*	−2.20**
			(.28)	(.47)	(.29)	(.48)	(.29)	(.49)	(.41)	(.61)
Central America			−.11	−.21	−.03	−.13	−.03	−.12	−.13	−.30
			(.17)	(.27)	(.17)	(.27)	(.18)	(.27)	(.19)	(.30)
South America			.55*	.37	.59*	.43	.59*	.38	.21	−.75
			(.27)	(.39)	(.28)	(.39)	(.28)	(.41)	(.32)	(.47)
Age					.01	.00	.01	.00	.00	−.00
					(.01)	(.01)	(.01)	(.01)	(.01)	(.01)
Married					.41*	.49	.42**	.50*	.48**	.48
					(.16)	(.25)	(.16)	(.25)	(.17)	(.26)
Female					.20	.06	.12	−.01	.14	−.01
					(.15)	(.23)	(.16)	(.24)	(.16)	(.25)
Earnings (logged)							−.15*	−.12	−.13	−.06
							(.07)	(.10)	(.07)	(.11)
Occ. Prestige							−.00	−.00	−.00	.00
							(.01)	(.01)	(.01)	(.01)
Years of Education							.00	.01	.01	.04
							(.02)	(.03)	(.02)	(.03)
HH < 18									−.56**	−.32
									(.18)	(.26)
Years in United States									.01	−.03
									(.01)	(.02)
English Proficient									−.47*	−.60*
									(.19)	(.30)
Northeast [Southwest]									.37	1.57**
									(.29)	(.38)
Midwest									.10	.50
									(.41)	(.57)
South									.83*	1.19**
									(.37)	(.50)
West									.00	−.40
									(.43)	(.83)
Constant	2.84**	−.63	2.67**	−.67+	1.94**	−1.13*	3.51**	−.07	3.86**	−.33
	(.23)	(.35)	(.25)	(.38)	(.34)	(.53)	(.80)	(1.16)	(.83)	(1.21)
Observations	1,539	1,539	1,539	1,539	1,539	1,539	1,539	1,539	1,539	1,539

Note: Standard errors in parentheses.

*p < .05; **p < .01.

timates of choosing white or nonwhite, respectively, as compared to not choosing a racial category.

Model 1 shows the relationship between skin color and racial identification. Latino immigrants who identify as white have significantly lighter skin tone than those who do not racially identify. There are no significant differences in skin color between respondents who identify as nonwhite and those who do not racially identify.

Model 2 tests for national origin differences in racial classification. Even after accounting for variation in racial phenotype, Cubans and South Americans are more likely to choose a white racial category, and Dominicans have the highest odds of not choosing a racial category. These results point to the significant influence wielded by racial categorization systems prevalent in immigrants' origin countries, which predict racial self-identification in the United States above and beyond individual skin tone.

Model 3 adds demographic controls. Currently married respondents are more likely to identify as white or nonwhite than to not racially identify, although the latter effect is only significant once the socioeconomic controls are added in Model 4. This finding supports the role the mate selection process may play in racial identity formation.

Model 4 accounts for the role of socioeconomic factors in explaining differences in racial identification. Respondents with higher incomes are more likely to not report a race than to identify as white. This effect runs counter to past evidence that suggests a positive relationship between increased economic attainment and a white racial self-classification (Tafoya 2005). Instead, it suggests that once the effect of skin color is accounted for, individuals who earn more money are less likely to identify as white and more likely to refuse to racially identify.

Model 5 adds a set of measures intended to evaluate whether exposure to the United States alters one's racial self-identification. English-proficient respondents are significantly more likely to not racially identify than to identify as white or nonwhite. The presence of children in a household is associated with an increased likelihood of not choosing a racial category compared with choosing a white racial category. These findings suggest that Latinos with more exposure to the United States—in terms of time spent in the country, language facility, or exposure to schools and other parents—are more likely to eschew federally mandated racial categories.

We find that individuals living in the South are more likely than those in the Southwest to choose a racial designation, either white or nonwhite. Individuals in the Northeast have higher odds of choosing a nonwhite racial category. These findings confirm that local-level interpretations of the US racial categorization scheme influence Latino immigrants and how they self-identify. Latinos in the Southwest, where a Latino racial identity may be more salient, are more likely than those in the South to opt out of traditional options. An alternative interpretation suggests that in the South, where the black/white divide has historically been more explicit, Latino immigrants are more likely to identify racially. Residence in the Northeast, where Latinos experience more external racialization as black, results in a stronger identification with a nonwhite self-classification than in the Southwest (Itzigsohn, Giorguli-Saucedo, and Vazquez 2005; Logan 2003).

Discrimination and Earned Income

Next we investigate the other side of immigrants' perceptions of racial categories: whether Latinos are subject to effects of a racial stratification system based on phenotype. Here we acknowledge the multi-actor nature of racial boundary formation. Not only do Latino immigrants confront new racial boundaries, but they may also be subject to effects of the existing racial boundaries. We approach this possibility by testing whether Latino immigrants experience discrimination in annual earnings based on their racial phenotype. Several methodological challenges complicate such a test; to address them we offer an alternative approach through propensity score matching with doses methodology (Lu, Hornik, and Rosenbaum 2001; Rosenbaum and Rubin 1983). With propensity score matching, the analysis is based on a balanced covariate distribution rather than assuming a certain functional form of the covariates, which allows for a more robust inference regarding the causal effect than would be true with standard regression techniques. We use multivariate matching with doses to conduct a more thorough test of whether racial phenotype is related to earned income through the hypothesized mechanism of discrimination based on skin color.

Matching with doses differs from the conventional form of matching with treated subjects and untreated controls, because all subjects are exposed to treatment, but the doses vary. It is particularly useful in practical scenarios when there are no clearly defined dichotomous treatment and control groups.

Instead, participants are exposed to the treatment at numerous levels.

Because we have multiple ordinal dose levels, we use an ordinal logit regression model to estimate the propensity score. A propensity score represents the conditional probability of membership in a dose group given a vector of observed covariates. Once estimated, the propensity score is used to compare relatively lighter- and darker-skinned individuals with the same observed characteristics. We use an optimal nonbipartite matching algorithm to create 477 pairs among four dose groups (Lu, Greevy, and Xu 2008). We restrict the sample to Latinos who are members of the labor force and have valid skin color information (N = 954).

Table 51.2 presents the results from the post-matching analysis. Comparing earned annual income across the matched pairs, we find an average difference of $2,435.63 between lighter- and darker-skinned individuals. This difference can be interpreted to mean that, after accounting for relevant differences between any two dose groups, Latino immigrants with darker skin earn, on average, $2,500 less per year than their lighter-skinned counterparts. We also explored the possibility of a dose response relationship, but we did not find evidence that the relationship was associated with dose. Instead, it appears that the relative nature of racial phenotype is important (i.e., relatively darker-skinned individuals earn less than relatively lighter-skinned individuals). To the extent that this difference represents an actual difference in earnings by racial phenotype, net of measured premigration differences, it suggests that skin color is related to earnings via discrimination against Latino immigrants. This finding suggests that Latino immigrants are not all treated equally upon arrival in the United States; individuals with darker skin are more likely to face discrimination.

TABLE 51.2 Postmatching Analysis of Earned Income and Skin Tone Among 477 Matched Pairs of Latino Immigrants

Group	Observations	Mean Income
Low Dose	477	$22,294.29 ($20,738.48; $23,850.10)
High Dose	477	$19,858.66 ($18,329.94; $21,387.38)
Lighter Skin–Darker Skin Contrast	954	$2,435.63 ($257.22; $4614.03)

Discussion

The US racial landscape continues to undergo dramatic changes; demographers predict that the Latino population will increase and the non-Hispanic white population will become the minority in the near future. These forecasts have sparked debate over the definition of whiteness and the future of the US color line. This chapter focused on one dimension of these debates, addressing the question of where the Latino immigrant population stands in the existing US racial order.

Our findings support the possibility that the US racial boundary system is changing. According to a boundary-centered approach to racial/ethnic divisions, a social boundary is created when two dimensions, one categorical and the other behavioral, coincide. Essentially, a social boundary forms when "ways of seeing the world correspond to ways of acting in the world" (Wimmer 2008b, 975). Our analysis supports the possibility that a new racial boundary is forming around Latino immigrants. Not all Latinos, however, will be defined by this new boundary. Some, in particular those with lighter skin, will probably be successful in their attempts to expand the boundary of whiteness (Gans 1999; Lee and Bean 2007a).

Other findings, however, call into question the likelihood that whiteness will expand again to incorporate all new Latino immigrants (Bonilla-Silva and Dietrich 2008). First, and most importantly, we find evidence that Latino immigrants experience skin-color-based discrimination in the workplace. The finding that Latino immigrants, regardless of how many self-identify as white, are not immune from penalties associated with darker skin in the United States, is a compelling argument against the possibility that all newcomers will simply be accepted as white. Instead, we find that for Latino immigrants, skin color continues to maintain its role in producing and maintaining stratification (Montalvo and Codina 2001).

In addition, we found that respondents who were Dominican immigrants or who had more exposure to the United States, either by having children with them in the United States, being more fluent in English, or having higher levels of economic assimilation, were more likely to opt out of choosing an existing racial category than to choose a racial category that does not fit well or is stigmatized. We interpret this finding as evidence that some Latino immigrants are attempting to engage in boundary change, which could represent a process of boundary blurring, that is, failure to choose a racial category as a way of emphasizing nonracial ways of belonging. Alternatively, it could also represent an attempt to emphasize an alternative racial self-classification (i.e., Latino).

Returning to the predictions laid out at the beginning of the chapter, our findings support those who argue that the US racial structure is changing. Although some Latinos will be included within the white racial boundary, our evidence is at odds with past predictions that all or most Latinos will be successful in their bid for whiteness (Yancey 2003). Although Latinos can choose their racial identification, our findings show that this choice is constrained by the color of their skin and skin-color-based discrimination (Golash-Boza and Darity 2008).

Measuring fluctuating classification systems is by definition speculative (Bailey 2008). The evidence presented here suggests that at present the burden of race does not fall equally on all members of the contemporary Latino immigrant population (Alba 2009). Instead of a uniform racial boundary, a boundary is solidifying around only some Latino immigrants, specifically those with darker skin who have more experience with the US racial stratification system. Light-skinned Latinos and those less integrated into the United States are likely to continue to test the flexibility of the white racial boundary (Alba 2005). Whether this strategy will prove successful, and the degree to which boundaries will become stabilized and institutionalized over time, is necessarily left for the future. Foreign-born immigrants inevitably set the stage for determining how US racial boundaries will be redrawn to fit Latinos, but it is native-born offspring who will ultimately set the future course.

REFERENCES

Alba, Richard. 2005. "Bright vs. Blurred Boundaries: Second-Generation Assimilation and Exclusion in France, Germany, and the United States." *Ethnic & Racial Studies* 28: 20–49.

———. 2009. *Blurring the Color Line: The New Chance for a More Integrated America*. Cambridge, MA: Harvard University Press.

Bailey, Stanley R. 2008. "Unmixing for Race Making in Brazil." *American Journal of Sociology* 114: 577–614.

Barth, Fredrik. 1969. *Ethnic Groups and Boundaries: The Social Organization of Culture Difference*. London: George Allen & Unwin.

Bonilla-Silva, Eduardo, and David R. Dietrich. 2008. "The Latin Americanization of Racial Stratification in the U.S." In *Racism in the 21st Century*, edited by R. E. Hall, 151–170. New York: Springer.

Campbell, Mary E., and Christabel L. Rogalin. 2006. "Categorical Imperatives: The Interaction of Latino and Racial Identification." *Social Science Quarterly* 87: 1030–1052.

Davis, F. J. 1991. *Who Is Black: One Nation's Definition*. State College: Pennsylvania State University Press.

Dowling, Julie Anne. 2004. "The Lure of Whiteness and the Politics of 'Otherness': Mexican American Racial Identity." PhD diss., Department of Sociology, University of Texas at Austin.

Du Bois, W. E. B. 1903. *The Souls of Black Folk*. New York: Barnes and Nobles Classics.

Foner, Nancy. 1987. "The Jamaicans: Race and Ethnicity Among Migrants in New York City." In *New Immigrants in New York City*, edited by N. Foner, 195–217. New York: Columbia University Press.

Gans, Herbert J. 1999. "The Possibility of a New Racial Hierarchy in the Twenty-first Century United States." In *The Cultural Territories of Race*, edited by M. Lamont, 371–390. New York: Russell Sage Foundation.

Golash-Boza, Tanya, and William Darity. 2008. "Latino Racial Choices: The Effects of Skin Colour and Discrimination on Latinos' and Latinas' Racial Self-Identifications." *Ethnic & Racial Studies* 31: 899–934.

Hersch, Joni. 2008. "Profiling the New Immigrant Worker: The Effects of Skin Color and Height." *Journal of Labor Economics* 26: 345–386.

Hitlin, Steven, J. Scott Brown, and Glen H. Elder Jr. 2007. "Measuring Latinos: Racial vs. Ethnic Classification and Self-Understandings." *Social Forces* 86: 587–611.

Hochschild, Jennifer L. 2005. "Looking Ahead: Racial Trends in the United States." *Daedalus* (Winter): 70–81.

Itzigsohn, Jose, Silvia Giorguli-Saucedo, and Obed Vazquez. 2005. "Incorporation, Transnationalism, and Gender: Immigrant Incorporation and Transnational Participation as Gendered Processes." *International Migration Review* 39: 895–920.

Jasso, G., D. S. Massey, M. R. Rosenzweig, and J. P. Smith. Forthcoming. "The U.S. New Immigrant Survey: Overview and Preliminary Results Based on the New-Immigrant Cohorts of 1996 and 2003." In *Immigration Research and Statistics Service Workshop on Longitudinal Surveys and Cross-Cultural Survey Design: Workshop Proceedings*, edited by B. Morgan and B. Nicholson. London: Crown Publishing.

Kusow, Abdi. 2006. "Migration and Racial Formations Among Somali Immigrants in North America." *Journal of Ethnic & Migration Studies* 32: 533–551.

Landale, Nancy S., and R. S. Oropesa. 2002. "White, Black or Puerto Rican? Racial Self-Identification among Mainland and Island Puerto Ricans." *Social Forces* 81: 231–254.

Lee, Jennifer, and Frank D. Bean. 2007a. "Redrawing the Color Line?" *City & Community* 6: 49–62.

———. 2007b. "Reinventing the Color Line: Immigration and America's New Racial/Ethnic Divide." *Social Forces* 86: 561–586.

Lewis, Amanda E., Maria Krysan, and Nakisha Harris. 2004. "Assessing Changes in the Meaning and Significance of Race and Ethnicity." In *The Changing Terrain of Race and Ethnicity*, edited by M. Krysan and A. E. Lewis, 1–10. New York: Russell Sage Foundation.

Logan, John. 2003. "How Race Counts for Hispanic Americans." Report, Lewis Mumford Center for Comparative and Urban Regional Research, the University of Albany, SUNY, July 14. http://mumford.albany.edu/census/BlackLatinoReport/BlackLatino01.htm.

Lu, Bo, Robert Greevy, and Xinyi Xu. 2008. "Optimal Nonbipartite Matching and Its Statistical Applications." Working Paper, Department of Biostatistics, The Ohio State University, Columbus.

Lu, Bo, Robert Hornik, and Paul R. Rosenbaum. 2001. "Matching with Doses in an Observational Study of a Media Campaign Against Drug Abuse." *Journal of the American Statistical Association* 96: 1245–1253.

Massey, Doug S., and Jennifer Martin. 2003. "The NIS Skin Color Scale." Office of Population Research, Princeton University, Princeton, NJ.

Michael, Joseph, and Jeffrey M. Timberlake. 2008. "Are Latinos Becoming White? Determinants of Latinos' Racial Self-Identification in the U.S." In *Racism in Post-Race America: New Theories, New Directions*, edited by C. A. Gallagher, 107–122. Chapel Hill, NC: Social Forces.

Montalvo, Frank F., and G. Edward Codina. 2001. "Skin Color and Latinos in the United States." *Ethnicities* 1: 321–341.

Rodriguez, Clara E. 2000. *Changing Race: Latinos, the Census, and the History of Ethnicity in the United States.* New York: New York University Press.

Rosenbaum, P. R., and D. B. Rubin. 1983. "The Central Role of the Propensity Score in Observational Studies for Causal Effects." *Biometrika* 70: 41–55.

Tafoya, Sonya M. 2005. "Shades of Belonging: Latinos and Racial Identity." *Harvard Journal of Hispanic Policy* 17: 58–78.

Wimmer, Andreas. 2007. "How (Not) to Think about Ethnicity in Immigrant Societies." Oxford Centre on Migration, Policy and Society Working Paper Series 07-44, 1–38.

———. 2008a. "Elementary Strategies of Ethnic Boundary Making." *Ethnic & Racial Studies* 31 (6): 1025–1055.

———. 2008b. "The Making and Unmaking of Ethnic Boundaries: A Multilevel Process Theory." *American Journal of Sociology* 113: 970–1022.

Yancey, George. 2003. *Who Is White? Latinos, Asians, and the New Black/Nonblack Divide.* Boulder, CO: Lynne Rienner.

52. Mary Pattillo*

Black Picket Fences: Privilege and Peril Among the Black Middle Class

Even though America is obsessed with race, some policymakers and even more average citizens act as if race no longer matters. . . . Not even forty years since separate water fountains—which, in the scheme of Jim Crow prohibitions, were much less onerous than the exclusion of African Americans from libraries, museums, schools, and jobs—many Americans would now like to proceed as if the slate is clean and the scale is balanced. . . . Even though the facts say differently, such perceptions partially rest on the visible progress that African Americans have made over the last half-century. The upward strides of many African Americans into the middle class have given the illusion that race cannot be the barrier that some make it out to be. The reality, however, is that even the black and white *middle classes* remain separate and unequal.

Much of the research and media attention on African Americans is on the black poor. . . . With more than one in four African Americans living below the official poverty line (versus approximately one in nine whites), this is a reasonable and warranted bias. But rarely do we hear the stories of the other three-fourths, or the majority of African Americans, who may be the office secretary, the company's computer technician, a project manager down the hall, or the person who teaches our children. The growth of the black middle class has been hailed as one of the major triumphs of the civil rights movement, but if we have so little information on who makes up this group and what their lives are like, how can we be so sure that triumphant progress is the full story? The optimistic assumption of the 1970s and 1980s was that upwardly mobile African Americans were quietly integrating formerly all-white occupations, businesses, neighborhoods, and social clubs. The black middle class dropped from the policy agenda, even though basic evidence suggests that celebration of black middle-class ascendance has perhaps been too hasty.

*From *Black Picket Fences: Privilege and Peril among the Black Middle Class,* Second Edition, by Mary Pattillo, pp. 1-12 (with edits). Published by the University of Chicago. © 1999, 2013 by the University of Chicago Press.

We know, for example, that a more appropriate socioeconomic label for members of the black middle class is "lower middle class." The one black doctor who lives in an exclusive white suburb and the few African American lawyers who work at a large firm are not representative of the black middle class overall (but neither are their experiences identical to those of their white colleagues). And although most white Americans are also not doctors or lawyers, the lopsided distribution of occupations for whites does favor such professional and managerial jobs, whereas the black middle class is clustered in the sales and clerical fields. Because one's occupation affects one's income, African Americans have lower earnings. Yet the inequalities run even deeper than just income. Compound and exponentiate the current differences over a history of slavery and Jim Crow, and the nearly fourteen-fold wealth advantage that whites enjoy over African Americans—regardless of income, education, or occupation—needs little explanation.

We also know that the black middle class faces housing segregation to the same extent as the black poor. African Americans are more segregated from whites than any other racial or ethnic group. In fact, the black middle class likely faces the most blatant racial discrimination, in that many in its ranks can actually afford to pay for housing in predominantly white areas. . . . Racial segregation means that racial inequalities in employment, education, income, and wealth are inscribed in space. Predominantly white neighborhoods benefit from the historically determined and contemporarily sustained edge that whites enjoy.

Finally, we know that middle-class African Americans do not perform as well as whites on standardized tests (in school or in employment); are more likely to be incarcerated for drug offenses; are less likely to marry, and more likely to have a child without being married; and are less likely to be working. . . . For middle-class blacks, who ostensibly do not face the daily disadvantages of poverty, it is even more difficult to explain why they do not measure up to whites. To resolve this quandry, it is essential to continuously refer back to the ways in which the black middle class *is not equal* to the white middle class.

[I focus on one realm] of the black middle-class experience—the neighborhood context—by investigating how racial segregation, economic structures, and black poverty affect the residential experience of black middle-class families, and especially youth. To accomplish this goal, [I report] on over three years of research in Groveland, a black middle-class neighborhood on Chicago's South Side. . . . Groveland's approximately ninety square blocks contain a population of just under twelve thousand residents, over 95 percent of whom are African American. . . . By income and occupational criteria, as well as the American dream of homeownership, Groveland qualifies as a "middle-class neighborhood." Yet this sterile description does not at all capture the neighborhood's diversity, which is critical to correctly portraying the neighborhood context of the black middle class.

Groveland's unemployment rate is 12 percent, which is higher than the citywide rate, but *lower* than the percentage of unemployed residents in the neighborhoods that border Groveland. Twelve percent of Groveland's families are poor, which again makes it a bit *more* advantaged than the surrounding areas, but worse off than most of Chicago's predominantly white neighborhoods. The geography of Groveland is typical of black middle-class areas, which often sit as a kind of buffer between core black poverty areas and whites. Contrary to popular discussion, the black middle class has not out-migrated to unnamed neighborhoods outside of the black community. Instead, they are an overlooked population still rooted in the contemporary "Black Belts" of cities across the country. Some of the questions about why middle-class blacks are not at parity with middle-class whites can be answered once this fact is recognized.

The mix of residents in Groveland and in Chicago's predominantly black South Side defines the experiences and exposures of black middle-class youth. Groveland residents like twenty-one-year-old Ray Gibbs most insightfully describe this heterogeneous environment:

If a family wanted to feel the different spectrum of life, I think this would probably be a' ideal place to raise children. I mean, you know, you go outside in the suburbs, it's la-di-da-di. Trouble, stuff like that, don't happen. If you want somebody to see probably everything that could happen, you'd move here. Some days you'll have your good days where everything'll be perfect. Then you might have your bad days when yo' kid might have a fight. You know, you'll get to see all the makings of all different type of people. That's to me, that's what this neighborhood is.

Ray Gibbs put a positive spin on the range of activities and incidents that characterize black middle-class neighborhoods. But parents who desire to shield their children from negative influences are less enamored by what Ray seems to think is exciting. Many parents actively attempt to curtail their children's attraction to the less savory aspects of neighborhood life—most significantly, the gangs and the drug dealing.

Privileges and Perils

By the end of my research tenure in Groveland, I had seen three groups of eighth-graders graduate to high school, high school kids go on to college, and college graduates start their careers. I also heard too many stories and read too many obituaries of the teenagers who were jailed or killed along the way. The son of a police detective in jail for murder. The grandson of a teacher shot while visiting his girlfriend's house. The daughter of a park supervisor living with a drug dealer who would later be killed at a fast-food restaurant. These events were jarring, and all-too-frequent discontinuities in the daily routine of Groveland residents. Why were some Groveland youth following a path to success, while others had concocted a recipe for certain failure? After all, these are not the stories of poor youth caught in a trap of absent opportunities, low aspirations, and harsh environments. Instead, Groveland is a neighborhood of single-family homes, old stately churches, tree-lined streets, active political and civic organizations, and concerned parents trying to maintain a middle-class way of life. . . .

African American social workers and teachers, secretaries and nurses, entrepreneurs and government bureaucrats are in many ways the buffer between the black poor and the white middle class. . . . More than thirty years after the civil rights movement, racial segregation remains a reality in most American cities. Middle-income black families fill the residential gap between the neighborhoods that house middle-class whites and the neighborhoods where poor African Americans live. Unlike most whites, middle-class black families must contend with the crime, dilapidated housing, and social disorder in the deteriorating poor neighborhoods that continue to grow in their direction.

Residents attempt to fortify their neighborhoods against this encroachment, and limit their travel and associations to other middle-class neighborhoods in the city and suburbs. Yet even with these efforts, residents of black middle-class neighborhoods share schools, grocery stores, hospitals, nightclubs, and parks with their poorer neighbors, ensuring frequent interaction within and outside the neighborhood.

The in-between position of the black middle class sets up certain crossroads for its youth. This peculiar limbo begins to explain the disparate outcomes of otherwise similar young people in Groveland. The right and wrong paths are in easy reach of neighborhood youth. Working adults are models of success. Some parents even work two jobs, while still others combine work and school to increase their chances of on-the-job promotions. All of the positive knowledge, networking, and role-model benefits that accrue to working parents are operative for many families in Groveland. But at the same time, the rebellious nature of adolescence inevitably makes the wrong path a strong temptation, and there is no shortage of showy drug dealers and cocky gang members who make dabbling in deviance look fun. Youth walk a fine line between preparing for success and youthful delinquent experimentation, the consequences of which can be especially serious for black youth. . . .

To [understand] the various obstacles and pressures that black middle-class families and youth face, [we have to look to] the economic, spatial, and cultural contexts that influence decision-making, life transitions, and outcomes for Groveland residents, especially the youth.

The economy: First, the post-1970s economy stunted the previously impressive growth of the black middle class. . . . Groveland's first generation came of age during a period of sustained and rapid economic growth, fostering optimism for themselves, for their children, and for African Americans generally. The adolescents and young adults in today's Groveland—the second and third generations—are facing the uncertainties of changing technologies, stronger demands for an educated workforce, and the rising costs of higher education. There are myriad local effects of these broad economic shifts. Because of downward intergenerational mobility, housing maintenance suffers as inheritors lack the means to keep up their parents' investment. Older adolescents and young adults remain in their parents' homes well into their thirties in order to make ends meet, finish school, or sustain their youthful irresponsibility. And for some, the fast money promised by the ever-present underground economy is difficult to refuse when legitimate economic success is uncertain.

Segregation: Second, the segregated geography of urban America has ramifications for the spatial context of the black middle class. Social ties across class lines, across lifestyles, and across the law exist partly because of the assignment of most African Americans to "the black side of town." . . . Some families have four generations living within the neighborhood's boundaries, and others have developed kin-like relationships with their longtime neighbors. [These] networks promote easy access to both criminal and positive opportunities. The relationships between teachers and gang leaders, or preachers and drug dealers, highlight the appropriateness of the "crossroads" imagery in describing the neighborhood experiences of black middle-class youth. . . .

The cultural context: The cultural context is also distinctive. Groveland youth are targets and consumers of, and active participants in, mass cultural styles that, while imaginative and entertaining, also provide a fashion and behavioral manual for deviance. Groveland youth are placed within the very American cultural context of mass-media "gangstas." While there are autonomous cultural productions in Groveland, much of youth style—what is said, done, worn, and sung—is the local translation of mass cultural products received through magazines, television, movies, and radio. The popular cultural productions favored by Groveland's youth glamorize the hard life of poverty and scoff at the ordinariness of middle-classdom. . . .

The black middle class is connected to the black poor through friendship and kinship ties, as well as geographically. Policies that hurt the black poor will ultimately negatively affect the black middle class. At the same time, the black middle class sits at the doorstep of middle-class privilege. Continued affirmative action, access to higher education, a plan to create real family-wage jobs, and the alleviation of residential segregation should be at the forefront of policy initiatives to support the gains already made by the black middle class.

53. Jennifer Lee*
Tiger Kids and the Success Frame

In early 2011, *The Wall Street Journal* published "Why Chinese Mothers are Superior" by Yale Law professor Amy Chua in advance of the release of her memoir, *Battle Hymn of the Tiger Mother*. Chua's argument that Eastern parenting is superior to Western parenting (and more likely to produce "successful kids," "math whizzes," and "music prodigies") set off a firestorm of controversy.

In Chua's view, there's a simple formula for raising Tiger Kids: place an uncompromising value on education, then reinforce it with hard work, strict discipline, and practice, practice, and more practice. By contrast, she believes Western parents guide their children through positive reinforcement and ask them only to "try their best." . . .

It would be easy to dismiss Chua's argument as little more than a reification of racial, ethnic, and cultural stereotypes—but by doing so, we'd miss an opportunity to engage in a real discussion. Specifically, how *do* we explain the academic achievement of Asians, especially when the patterns defy traditional status attainment models?

For example, some second-generation Chinese and Vietnamese have immigrant parents who arrive to the United States with only an elementary school education, no English language skills, and little financial capital, yet graduate as high school valedictorians, gain admission into elite universities, and pursue graduate degrees. Their achievement is vexing; previous research has shown that even when controlling for family background, ethnicity remains significant, and being Chinese, Korean, or Vietnamese gives immigrant children an advantage in educational attainment. But while we know ethnicity matters, we rarely talk about *how* it matters.

Sociologists have shied away from invoking cultural arguments, worried they might shift the attention from structural inequalities to individual and cultural deficiencies (an either/or argument, instead of a both/and). However, the absence of a strong social science voice in this large-scale discussion has left the door open for scholars like Amy Chua to invoke essentialist cultural arguments (like that of the Tiger Mother) that reach a wide, even international, audience—and resonate.

My aim [is] to bring ethnicity and culture more analytically into the debate about second-generation educational outcomes. Based on analyses of the Immigrant and Intergenerational Mobility in Metropolitan Los Angeles survey data (IIMMLA) as well as 140 in-depth interviews with 1.5- and second-generation Mexicans, Chinese, and Vietnamese respondents, I address two main questions.

First, how do 1.5- and second-generation Chinese and Vietnamese exhibit high academic outcomes, even when controlling for socioeconomic factors like parental education, occupation, and income? Second, is there something about being Asian or about Asian culture that confers advantage?

Bridging literature in immigration, culture, and social psychology, I illustrate how ethnicity and culture can operate as a tool kit of resources for some children. More specifically, I explain how immigrant parents and their children frame success, and show how frames are supported by ethnic and institutional resources. These resources cut vertically across class lines, thereby making them available to *both* middle- and working-class ethnics; this, in turn, helps second-generation Chinese and Vietnamese from poor and working-class backgrounds overcome their disadvantaged class background in their quest to get ahead.

LA's Chinese, Vietnamese, and Mexicans

[The] IIMMLA survey data reveals distinctive patterns among Chinese, Vietnamese, and Mexicans in Los Angeles. First, Chinese immigrant parents are the most educated of the three groups, reflecting the high selectivity of Chinese immigration to LA (61 percent of Chinese immigrant fathers and 42 percent of Chinese immigrant mothers have a BA or higher).

On the other end of the educational attainment spectrum are Mexican immigrant parents, the majority of whom have not graduated from high school; close to 60 percent of Mexican immigrant fathers and mothers have less than a high school education. The Vietnamese immigrant parents (especially mothers) fall in between, with lower educational attainment than both native-born whites and blacks.

Turning to their children (the 1.5 and second generation), Chinese Americans exhibit the highest levels of educational attainment, reflecting the intergenerational transmission of advantage of high parental human capital; 63 percent have graduated from college, and of this group, 22 percent have also attained graduate degrees. None of the 1.5- and second-generation Chinese students in our study has dropped out of high school.

While Mexicans exhibit the lowest level of educational attainment, what often gets lost in presenting cross-sectional, inter-group comparisons is the enormous *inter*generational mobility Mexicans have achieved within just one generation. For example, while nearly 60 percent of Mexican immigrant parents did not graduate from high school, this figure drops to 14 percent within one generation. . . . When measuring attainment *inter*generationally, the children of Mexican immigrants exhibit the greatest mobility of the three groups.

Another notable pattern is the educational attainment of the 1.5- and second-generation Vietnamese, whose educational attainment surpasses both native-born blacks and whites; nearly half (48 percent) of 1.5- and second-generation Vietnamese has attained a college degree or more, and only 1 percent has failed to complete high school. Their educational mobility is exceptional given their relatively low parental human capital. . . . That poor parental human capital does not obstruct their mobility (as the traditional status attainment model would predict) suggests ethnicity and culture may affect outcomes in ways that immigration researchers have not fully examined. . . .

Frames and Ethnic Resources

In the vast literature on culture, I found the concept of *frames* particularly useful in understanding second-generation outcomes. Following in the footsteps of sociologist Erving Goffman, I define a frame as an analytical tool by which people observe, interpret, and make sense of their social life. Most plainly, frames are ways of understanding how the world works. By untangling the frames people adopt in their decision-making process, we may begin to understand variation in behavior.

Based on in-depth interviews of 1.5- and second-generation Mexicans, Chinese, and Vietnamese, I was able to tease out different frames for "success" and "a good education." Some frame a "good education" as graduating from high school, attending a local community college, and earning an occupational certificate. Others adopt a frame that involves graduating as the high school valedictorian, gaining admission into an elite university, and going to law or medical school. In other words, it's not that some groups *value* education more than others (the essentialist interpretation of culture), but that groups construct remarkably different ideas of what "a good education" means depending on which frames are accessible to them and which they adopt. Ethnicity matters because the frame that members of the 1.5- and second-generation adopt is shaped by the immigrant selectivity (how immigrants differ from non-migrants in their countries of origin), the average socioeconomic status of an ethnic group, and the group's capacity to mobilize resources.

Because group resources are ethnic resources (they are preferentially available to members of an ethnic group), second-generation ethnics from poor and working-class backgrounds have access to these resources to help override their disadvantage. In this way, ethnic resources can help children whose Chinese and Vietnamese immigrant parents have not graduated from high school, do not speak English, and work in Chinatown's restaurants and factories compensate for their parents' low level of human capital and access a group's ethnic capital instead.

"The Success Frame"

One of the most striking findings from our interviews was the consistency with which 1.5- and second-generation Chinese and Vietnamese framed "success" and "a good education," regardless of parental human capital, migration history, and class background. Across the board, these kids told us high school is mandatory, college is an expectation, and only an advanced degree will gain kudos. Caroline, a thirty-five-year-old, second-generation Chinese woman explained:

> The idea of graduating from high school for my mother was not a great, congratulatory day. I was happy, but you know what? My mother was very blunt, she said, "This is a good day but it's not that special." . . . She finds it absurd that graduating from high school is made into a big deal because you should graduate high school; everyone should. . . . It's a further obligation that you go to college and get a bachelor's degree. Thereafter, if you get a Ph.D. or a Master's, that's the big thing; that's the icing on the cake with a cherry on top, and that's what she values.

For people like Caroline, "doing well in school" was narrowly framed as getting straight A's, graduating as valedictorian or salutatorian, getting into a top UC (University of California school), and pursuing graduate education to work in one of the "four professions": doctor, lawyer, engineer, or pharmacist. So exacting is the frame that second-generation Chinese and Vietnamese described grades as "A is for average, and B is an Asian fail." . . .

When we asked Maryann, a twenty-four-year-old, second-generation Vietnamese woman who grew up in the housing projects in downtown LA how she defined success, she relayed, "getting into one of the top schools" (by her account, "UCLA, Berkeley, Yale, Harvard, Princeton, and Stanford") and then working in one of the "top professions" such as "doctor or lawyer." When we asked Maryann how she knew the top schools and top professions, she said: "Other parents who have kids. We know a few families who have kids who've gone to Yale, and they're doctors now, and they're doing really well for themselves."

Maryann's Vietnamese parents had arrived as refugees to the United States with only a sixth-grade education. They do not speak English, they work in Chinatown's garment factories, and they have raised their family in the projects. In spite of Maryann's class disadvantage and residential segregation from more privileged immigrants, she recounted a success frame that mirrored that of her middle-class peers. . . . Because the 1.5- and second-generation Chinese and Vietnamese turn to high-achieving coethnics as their reference group, those who do not fit the narrow frame for success feel like outliers, and in some cases, failures. But rather than rejecting the constricting frame, they are more likely to reject their ethnic and racial identities, claiming that they do not feel Chinese, Vietnamese, or even Asian because their outcomes differ from "the norm" for Asians.

The Importance of Resources

Simply adopting a frame for academic success can't ensure a particular outcome; for frames to be effective, they need institutional support and resources. Chinese and Vietnamese immigrant parents support the success frame in a number of ways. First, they buy homes or rent apartments in neighborhoods based on the strength of the public school district. Second, they demand that their children be placed in the Honors or Advanced Placement tracks in high school, and provide supplementary education and tutoring to make sure they get in. Third, Chinese and Vietnamese immigrant parents point to high-achieving coethnic role models to show that the success frame is realistic and attainable. And finally, they acquire information about schools, neighborhoods, and supplementary education programs through ethnic channels. In these ways, ethnicity cuts vertically across class lines and operates as a group resource that's most beneficial to those with poor parental human capital.

Consider Jason. He's a twenty-five-year-old, second-generation Chinese who attended elementary school in a working-class neighborhood of Long Beach. As soon as his parents could, they moved to a modest home in Cerritos because they learned from the *"Chinese Yellow Book"* that Cerritos High School "ranks in the teens." The *Chinese Yellow Book* is a 3 1/2" thick, 2,500-page directory that provides a list of the area's ethnic businesses, as well as the rankings of southern California's public high schools and the country's best universities.

LA's Chinese Yellow Pages

When Jason first moved to Cerritos for seventh grade, he was placed in the school's "regular" academic track. Dismayed, Jason's parents immediately enrolled him in an after-school Chinese academy. When Jason took the exam for high school, he was placed in the AP track. He graduated in the top 10 percent of his class and later graduated from UCLA. Now he's in his third year of law school.

Jason's parents did not graduate from high school, had little understanding of the American school system, and couldn't help their son with his schoolwork. But, they *were* able to rely on ethnic resources to compensate, thereby helping their son attain intergenerational mobility. They weren't alone in providing supplemental education for their children; supplemental education was such an integral part of the Chinese and Vietnamese students' adolescence that they hardly characterized it as "supplemental." . . .

An important caveat is that supplemental education is not unique to second-generation Asian ethnic groups. Sociologists Annette Lareau and Sean Reardon find that higher-income families use their class resources to invest more money and time in their children than ever before; this translates into more extracurricular classes, activities, and tutors. However, *ethnic resources* differ from *class resources* in that they're not limited to middle-class and affluent students. The availability of ethnic resources across class

lines is what gives second-generation Chinese and Vietnamese from poor and working-class backgrounds a leg up.

Beyond the Tiger Mom

I began this [chapter] by engaging the controversy in which Amy Chua . . . reduced the educational attainment of high-achieving Asians to the East Asian cultural values. And it's true: culture matters, but not in the essentialist way that Chua claims. While all second-generation groups in the US value education, groups frame a "good education" and "success" differently depending on immigrant selectivity, the average socioeconomic status of an ethnic group, and the group's capacity to mobilize resources conducive to upward mobility. Importantly, the success frame is supported by ethnic resources that help compensate for individual family disadvantages.

In this particular frame, academic success becomes the pragmatic goal in itself. Chinese and Vietnamese immigrant parents perceive education as the *only* sure path to a better life—and this frame fits squarely into the US context in which education is touted as the route to a bright future.

This is not, however, the case in other countries. Among the second-generation in Spain, the Chinese exhibit the *lowest* educational aspirations and expectations of all second-generation groups, including Ecuadorians, Central Americans, Dominicans, and Moroccans. Nearly 40 percent of second-generation Chinese expect to complete only basic secondary school—roughly the equivalent of tenth grade in the US. Given the perception of a closed opportunity structure in Spain—especially for visible minorities—Chinese immigrants have no faith that a post-secondary education or a university degree will lead to a professional job, so they've turned to entrepreneurship and encouraged their children to do the same. Hence, Spain's Asian immigrants adopt an entirely different success frame, in which entrepreneurship—rather than education—is the mobility strategy. Their frame is supported by ethnic business associations, much like education is supported by a supplementary education system in the United States.

This simple counterfactual illustrates that it's not something essential about Chinese or Asian culture that promotes exceptional educational outcomes. It also reminds us that what may be most exceptional about "Asian-American exceptionalism" is actually "American exceptionalism."

PART VII

GENDER, SEXUALITY, AND INEQUALITY

In our introductory essay, we noted that modernization theory assumed that all forms of ascription were fated to wither away because (a) they rested on an inefficient allocation of labor that ignored considerations of merit and talent, and (b) they were inconsistent with our moral commitment to running an equal-opportunity society. By this logic, the ascription that persists to this day is but a residual holdover, with the twin forces of efficiency and egalitarianism slowly but gradually wearing them down.

When one examines the long-run trend in the percentage of married mothers who are employed, the simple and elegant modernization account would appear to have some merit. Between the mid-1960s and 1995, we indeed see nothing short of a gender revolution: The percentage of married mothers who were employed nearly doubled over this period. This revolution was partly driven by demand-side changes in the willingness of employers to hire women for jobs that, in the past, were seen as exclusively the province of men. It was also partly driven by supply-side changes in the aspirations and human capital investments of women.

If the period up to 1995 played out roughly as a modernization theorist would have it, the period thereafter most surely did not. In the last fifteen to twenty years, we have instead witnessed a surprising stalling-out in many important indicators of gender equality, including the pay gap, the labor force participation of married women, and the segregation of women and men into different occupations (see England, Ch. 63; Ridgeway, Ch. 64).

What accounts for this stalling out? The readings in this section take on just this question by exploring the sources of the revolution in the late 20th century as well as the many forms of backlash that may have undermined or offset those sources. These analyses suggest that, contrary to a simple modernization account, there are important differences between class, gender, and racial forms of ascription. Although each type has its own peculiarities, the gender form is especially distinctive by virtue of playing out so prominently within families. Because we watch "up close and personal" the gender division of labor in our own families, we are under special pressure to believe essentialist stories justifying that division of labor, stories that represent women as especially suited for nurturing, social interaction, and socioemotional support. These stories legitimate and perpetuate an essentialist division of labor and thus impart a special staying power to gender-based ascription.

For this and many other reasons, we might expect gender inequality to evolve under a logic that differs from that governing racial, ethnic, or class inequalities. The main purpose of this section is to explore precisely what that distinctive logic might be. The readings examine whether women are "opting out" of the workplace, whether there is much discrimination against women, mothers, and gay men, whether there are "glass ceilings" and other forms of workplace hypersegregation, whether the gender gap in wages can be explained away with occupational and other variables, and whether race, class, and gender interact and intersect in complicated ways (see Percheski, Ch. 57; Goldin and Rouse, Ch. 59; Correll, Benard, and In Paik, Ch. 60; Tilcsik, Ch. 62; Levanon and Grusky, Ch. 58; Andersen and Collins, Ch. 61).

These readings rest heavily on the classic sociological insight that a strict demarcation of women from men (i.e., the "gender binary") is, just like the black-white binary, a categorization that may be treated as natural and obvious but is in fact socially constructed (see Lorber, Ch. 54). The stalling-out narrative, which developed in response to the slowdown in labor market equalization, does not seem to hold equally in the domain of gender identity and categorization. It is difficult, in other words, to reconcile the evidence of stalling-out on many objective measures of labor market inequality with our ever-growing willingness to challenge the legitimacy of the gender binary. There is at least a superficial parallel here with the corresponding decline of the black-white binary. That is, just as the black-white binary has been complicated by rising intermarriage and new immigration streams, so too the female-male binary is being called into question as gender and sexuality are no longer so routinely conflated (see Pascoe and Bridges, Ch. 55). Although the undoing of these two binaries is driven by seemingly different forces, it is surely worth asking whether there is any larger sociological force that stands behind both. The continuing spread of egalitarianism, especially when tied to a commitment to the sanctity of the individual (as unfettered by any constraints), may well underlie both lines of challenge and ultimately lead to a world in which strict and simple categorizations are replaced by more fluid and continuous dimensions.

Gender and Sexuality as a Social Construct

54. Judith Lorber*
The Social Construction of Gender

Talking about gender for most people is the equivalent of fish talking about water. Gender is so much the routine ground of everyday activities that questioning its taken-for-granted assumptions and presuppositions is like thinking about whether the sun will come up. Gender is so pervasive that in our society we assume it is bred into our genes. Most people find it hard to believe that gender is constantly created and re-created out of human interaction, out of social life, and is the texture and order of that social life. Yet gender, like culture, is a human production that depends on everyone constantly "doing gender" (West and Zimmerman 1987).

And everyone "does gender" without thinking about it. Today, on the subway, I saw a well-dressed man with a year-old child in a stroller. Yesterday, on a bus, I saw a man with a tiny baby in a carrier on his chest. Seeing men taking care of small children in public is increasingly common—at least in New York City. But both men were quite obviously stared at—and smiled at, approvingly. Everyone was doing gender—the men who were changing the role of fathers and the other passengers, who were applauding them silently. But there was more gendering going on that probably fewer people noticed. The baby was wearing a white crocheted cap and white clothes. You couldn't tell if it was a boy or a girl. The child in the stroller was wearing a dark blue T-shirt and dark print pants. As they

started to leave the train, the father put a Yankee baseball cap on the child's head. "Ah, a boy," I thought. Then I noticed the gleam of tiny earrings in the child's ears, and as they got off, I saw the little flowered sneakers and lace-trimmed socks. Not a boy after all. Gender done.

Gender is such a familiar part of daily life that it usually takes a deliberate disruption of our expectations of how women and men are supposed to act to pay attention to how it is produced. Gender signs and signals are so ubiquitous that we usually fail to note them—unless they are missing or ambiguous. Then we are uncomfortable until we have successfully placed the other person in a gender status; otherwise, we feel socially dislocated. In our society, in addition to man and woman, the status can be *transvestite* (a person who dresses in opposite-gender clothes) and *transsexual* (a person who has had sex-change surgery). Transvestites and transsexuals carefully construct their gender status by dressing, speaking, walking, gesturing in the ways prescribed for women or men—whichever they want to be taken for—and so does any "normal" person.

For the individual, gender construction starts with assignment to a sex category on the basis of what the genitalia look like at birth. Then babies are dressed or adorned in a way that displays the category because parents don't want to be constantly asked whether their baby is a girl or a boy. A sex category becomes a gender status through naming, dress, and the use of other gender markers. Once a child's gender is evident, others treat those in one gender differently from those in the other, and the children respond to the different treatment by feeling different and behaving differently. As soon as they can talk, they start to refer to themselves as members of their gender. Sex doesn't come into play again until puberty, but by that time, sexual feelings and desires and practices have been shaped by gendered norms and expectations. Adolescent boys and girls approach and avoid each other in an elaborately scripted and gendered mating dance. Parenting is gendered, with different expectations for mothers and for fathers, and people of different genders work at different kinds of jobs. The work adults do as mothers and fathers and as low-level workers and high-level bosses, shapes women's and men's life experiences, and these experiences produce different feelings, consciousness, relationships, skills—ways of being that we call feminine or masculine. All of these processes constitute the social construction of gender.

Gendered roles change—today fathers are taking care of little children, girls and boys are wearing unisex clothing and getting the same education, women and men are working at the same jobs. Although many traditional social groups are quite strict about maintaining gender differences, in other social groups they seem to be blurring. Then why the one-year-old's earrings? Why is it still so important to mark a child as a girl or a boy, to make sure she is not taken for a boy or he for a girl? What would happen if they were? They would, quite literally, have changed places in their social world.

To explain why gendering is done from birth, constantly and by everyone, we have to look not only at the way individuals experience gender but at gender as a social institution. As a social institution, gender is one of the major ways that human beings organize their lives. Human society depends on a predictable division of labor, a designated allocation of scarce goods, assigned responsibility for children and others who cannot care for themselves, common values and their systematic transmission to new members, legitimate leadership, music, art, stories, games, and other symbolic productions. One way of choosing people for the different tasks of society is on the basis of their talents, motivations, and competence—their demonstrated achievements. The other way is on the basis of gender, race, ethnicity—ascribed membership in a category of people. Although societies vary in the extent to which they use one or the other of these ways of allocating people to work and to carry out other responsibilities, every society uses gender and age grades. Every society classifies people as "girl and boy children," "girls and boys ready to be married," and "fully adult women and men," constructs similarities among them and differences between them, and assigns them to different roles and responsibilities. Personality characteristics, feelings, motivations, and ambitions flow from these different life experiences so that the members of these different groups become different kinds of people.

The process of gendering and its outcome are legitimated by religion, law, science, and the society's entire set of values. . . .

Western society's values legitimate gendering by claiming that it all comes from physiology—female and male procreative differences. But gender and sex are not equivalent, and gender as a social construction does not flow automatically from genitalia and reproductive organs, the main physiological differences of females and males. In the construction of ascribed social statuses, physiological differences such as sex, stage of development, color of skin, and size are crude markers. They are not the source of the social statuses of gender, age grade, and race. Social statuses are carefully constructed through prescribed processes of teaching, learning, emulation, and enforcement. Whatever genes, hormones, and biological evolution contribute to human social institutions is materially as well as qualitatively transformed by social practices. . . .

For Individuals, Gender Means Sameness

Although the possible combinations of genitalia, body shapes, clothing, mannerisms, sexuality, and roles could produce infinite varieties in human beings, the social institution of gender depends on the production and maintenance of a limited number of gender statuses and of making the members of these statuses similar to each other. Individuals are born sexed but not gendered, and they have to be taught to be masculine or feminine. As Simone de Beauvoir said: "One is not born, but rather becomes, a woman. . . ; it is civilization as a whole that produces this creature . . . which is described as feminine." (1952, 267).

Children learn to walk, talk, and gesture the way their social group says girls and boys should. Ray Birdwhistell, in his analysis of body motion as human communication, calls these learned gender displays *tertiary* sex characteristics and argues that they are needed to distinguish genders because humans are a weakly dimorphic species—their only sex markers are genitalia (1970, 39–46). Clothing, paradoxically, often hides the sex but displays the gender.

In early childhood, humans develop gendered personality structures and sexual orientations through their interactions with parents of the same and opposite gender. As adolescents, they conduct their sexual behavior according to gendered scripts. Schools, parents, peers, and the mass media guide young people into gendered work and family roles.

As adults, they take on a gendered social status in their society's stratification system. Gender is thus both ascribed and achieved (West and Zimmerman 1987). . . .

For human beings there is no essential femaleness or maleness, femininity or masculinity, womanhood or manhood, but once gender is ascribed, the social order constructs and holds individuals to strongly gendered norms and expectations. Individuals may vary on many of the components of gender and may shift genders temporarily or permanently, but they must fit into the limited number of gender statuses their society recognizes. In the process, they re-create their society's version of women and men: "If we do gender appropriately, we simultaneously sustain, reproduce, and render legitimate the institutional arrangements. . . . If we fail to do gender appropriately, we as individuals—not the institutional arrangements—may be called to account (for our character, motives, and predispositions)" (West and Zimmerman 1987, 146).

The gendered practices of everyday life reproduce a society's view of how women and men should act (Bourdieu [1980] 1990). Gendered social arrangements are justified by religion and cultural productions and backed by law, but the most powerful means of sustaining the moral hegemony of the dominant gender ideology is that the process is made invisible; any possible alternatives are virtually unthinkable (Foucault 1972; Gramsci 1971).

For Society, Gender Means Difference

The pervasiveness of gender as a way of structuring social life demands that gender statuses be clearly differentiated. Varied talents, sexual preferences, identities, personalities, interests, and ways of interacting fragment the individual's bodily and social experiences. Nonetheless, these are organized in Western cultures into two and only two socially and legally recognized gender statuses, "man" and "woman."[1] In the social construction of gender, it does not matter what men and women actually do; it does not even matter if they do exactly the same thing. The social institution of gender insists only that what they do is *perceived* as different.

If men and women are doing the same tasks, they are usually spatially segregated to maintain gender separation, and often the tasks are given different job titles as well, such as executive secretary and administrative assistant (Reskin 1988). If the differences between women and men begin to blur, society's

"sameness taboo" goes into action (G. Rubin 1975, 178). At a rock-and-roll dance at West Point in 1976, the year women were admitted to the prestigious military academy for the first time, the school's administrators "were reportedly perturbed by the sight of mirror-image couples dancing in short hair and dress gray trousers," and a rule was established that women cadets could dance at these events only if they wore skirts (Barkalow and Raab 1990, 53). Women recruits in the US Marine Corps are required to wear makeup—at a minimum, lipstick and eye shadow—and they have to take classes in makeup, hair care, poise, and etiquette. This feminization is part of a deliberate policy of making them clearly distinguishable from men Marines. Christine Williams quotes a twenty-five-year-old woman drill instructor as saying: "A lot of the recruits who come here don't wear makeup; they're tomboyish or athletic. A lot of them have the preconceived idea that going into the military means they can still be a tomboy. They don't realize that you are a *Woman* Marine" (1989, 76–77).

If gender differences were genetic, physiological, or hormonal, gender bending and gender ambiguity would occur only in hermaphrodites, who are born with chromosomes and genitalia that are not clearly female or male. Since gender differences are socially constructed, all men and all women can enact the behavior of the other, because they know the other's social script: "'Man' and 'woman' are at once empty and overflowing categories. Empty because they have no ultimate, transcendental meaning. Overflowing because even when they appear to be fixed, they still contain within them alternative, denied, or suppressed definitions" (J. W. Scott 1988, 49). . . .

Gender as Process, Stratification, and Structure

As a social institution, gender is a process of creating distinguishable social statuses for the assignment of rights and responsibilities. As part of a stratification system that ranks these statuses unequally, gender is a major building block in the social structures built on these unequal statuses.

As a *process*, gender creates the social differences that define "woman" and "man." In social interaction throughout their lives, individuals learn what is expected, see what is expected, act and react in expected ways, and thus simultaneously construct and maintain the gender order: "The very injunction to be a given gender takes place through discursive routes: to be a good mother, to be a heterosexually desirable object, to be a fit worker, in sum, to signify a multiplicity of guarantees in response to a variety of different demands all at once" (J. Butler 1990, 145). Members of a social group neither make up gender as they go along nor exactly replicate in rote fashion what was done before. In almost every encounter, human beings produce gender, behaving in the ways they learned were appropriate for their gender status, or resisting or rebelling against these norms. Resistance and rebellion have altered gender norms, but so far they have rarely eroded the statuses.

Gendered patterns of interaction acquire additional layers of gendered sexuality, parenting, and work behaviors in childhood, adolescence, and adulthood. Gendered norms and expectations are enforced through informal sanctions of gender-inappropriate behavior by peers and by formal punishment or threat of punishment by those in authority should behavior deviate too far from socially imposed standards for women and men.

Everyday gendered interactions build gender into the family, the work process, and other organizations and institutions, which in turn reinforce gender expectations for individuals.[2] Because gender is a process, there is room not only for modification and variation by individuals and small groups, but also for institutionalized change (J. W. Scott 1988, 7).

As part of a *stratification* system, gender ranks men above women of the same race and class. Women and men could be different but equal. In practice, the process of creating difference depends to a great extent on differential evaluation. As Nancy Jay (1981) says: "That which is defined, separated out, isolated from all else is A and pure. Not-A is necessarily impure, a random catchall, to which nothing is external except A and the principle of order that separates it from Not-A" (45). From the individual's point of view, whichever gender is A, the other is Not-A; gender boundaries tell the individual who is like him or her, and all the rest are unlike. From society's point of view, however, one gender is usually the touchstone, the normal, the dominant, and the other is different, deviant, and subordinate. In Western society, "man" is A, "wo-man" is Not-A. (Consider what a society would be like where woman was A and man Not-A.)

The further dichotomization by race and class constructs the gradations of a heterogeneous society's stratification scheme. Thus, in the United States,

white is A, African American is Not-A; middle class is A, working class is Not-A, and "African-American women occupy a position whereby the inferior half of a series of these dichotomies converge" (P. H. Collins 1990, 70). The dominant categories are the hegemonic ideals, taken so for granted as the way things should be that white is not ordinarily thought of as a race, middle class as a class, or men as a gender. The characteristics of these categories define the Other as that which lacks the valuable qualities the dominants exhibit.

In a gender-stratified society, what men do is usually valued more highly than what women do because men do it, even when their activities are very similar or the same. In different regions of southern India, for example, harvesting rice is men's work, shared work, or women's work: "Wherever a task is done by women it is considered easy, and where it is done by [men] it is considered difficult" (Mencher 1988, 104). A gathering and hunting society's survival usually depends on the nuts, grubs, and small animals brought in by the women's foraging trips, but when the men's hunt is successful, it is the occasion for a celebration. Conversely, because they are the superior group, white men do not have to do the "dirty work," such as housework; the most inferior group does it, usually poor women of color (Palmer 1989). . . .

Societies vary in the extent of the inequality in social status of their women and men members, but where there is inequality, the status "woman" (and its attendant behavior and role allocations) is usually held in lesser esteem than the status "man." Since gender is also intertwined with a society's other constructed statuses of differential evaluation—race, religion, occupation, class, country of origin, and so on—men and women members of the favored groups command more power, more prestige, and more property than the members of the disfavored groups. Within many social groups, however, men are advantaged over women. The more economic resources, such as education and job opportunities, are available to a group, the more they tend to be monopolized by men. In poorer groups that have few resources (such as working-class African Americans in the United States), women and men are more nearly equal, and the women may even outstrip the men in education and occupational status (Almquist 1987).

As a *structure*, gender divides work in the home and in economic production, legitimates those in authority, and organizes sexuality and emotional life (Connell 1987, 91–142). As primary parents, women significantly influence children's psychological development and emotional attachments, in the process reproducing gender. Emergent sexuality is shaped by heterosexual, homosexual, bisexual, and sadomasochistic patterns that are gendered—different for girls and boys, and for women and men—so that sexual statuses reflect gender statuses.

When gender is a major component of structured inequality, the devalued genders have less power, prestige, and economic rewards than the valued genders. In countries that discourage gender discrimination, many major roles are still gendered; women still do most of the domestic labor and child rearing, even while doing full-time paid work; women and men are segregated on the job and each does work considered "appropriate"; women's work is usually paid less than men's work. Men dominate the positions of authority and leadership in government, the military, and the law; cultural productions, religions, and sports reflect men's interests.

In societies that create the greatest gender difference, such as Saudi Arabia, women are kept out of sight behind walls or veils, have no civil rights, and often create a cultural and emotional world of their own (Bernard 1981). But even in societies with less rigid gender boundaries, women and men spend much of their time with people of their own gender because of the way work and family are organized. This spatial separation of women and men reinforces gendered differentness, identity, and ways of thinking and behaving (Coser 1986).

Gender inequality—the devaluation of "women" and the social domination of "men"—has social functions and a social history. It is not the result of sex, procreation, physiology, anatomy, hormones, or genetic predispositions. It is produced and maintained by identifiable social processes and built into the general social structure and individual identities deliberately and purposefully. The social order as we know it in Western societies is organized around racial ethnic, class, and gender inequality. I contend, therefore, that the continuing purpose of gender as a modern social institution is to construct women as a group to be the subordinates of men as a group. The life of everyone placed in the status "woman" is "night to his day—that has forever been the fantasy. Black to his white. Shut out of his system's space, she is the repressed that ensures the system's functioning" (Cixous and Clément [1975] 1986, 67).

NOTES

1. Other societies recognize more than two categories, but usually no more than three or four (Jacobs and Roberts 1989).

2. On the "logic of practice," or how the experience of gender is embedded in the norms of everyday interaction and the structure of formal organizations, see Acker 1990; Bourdieu [1980] 1990; Connell 1987; Smith 1987.

BIBLIOGRAPHY

Acker, Joan. 1990. "Hierarchies, Jobs, and Bodies: A Theory of Gendered Organizations." *Gender and Society* 4: 139–58.

Almquist, Elizabeth M. 1987. "Labor Market Gendered Inequality in Minority Groups." *Gender and Society* 1:400–14.

Barkalow, Carol, with Andrea Raab. 1990. In *The Men's House*. New York, NY: Poseidon Press.

Bernard, Jessie. 1981. *The Female World*. New York, NY: Free Press.

Birdwhistell, Ray L. 1970. *Kinesics and Context: Essays on Body Motion Communication*. Philadelphia: University of Pennsylvania Press.

Bourdieu, Pierre. [1980] 1990. *The Logic of Practice*. Stanford, California: Stanford University Press.

Butler, Judith. 1990. *Gender Trouble: Feminism and the Subversion of Identity*. New York and London: Routledge.

Cixous, Hélène and Catherine Clément. [1975] 1986. *The Newly Born Woman*, translated by Betsy Wing. Minneapolis: University of Minnesota Press.

Collins, Patricia Hill. 1990. *Black Feminist Thought: Knowledge, Consciousness, and the Politics of Empowerment*. Boston: Unwin Hyman.

Connell, R. W. 1987. *Gender and Power: Society, the Person, and Sexual Politics*. Stanford, California: Stanford University Press.

Coser, Rose Laub. 1986. "Cognitive Structure and the Use of Social Space." *Sociological Forum* 1:1–26.

De Beauvoir, Simone. 1953. *The Second Sex*, translated by H. M. Parshley. New York, NY: Knopf.

Foucault, Michel. 1972. *The Archeology of Knowledge and the Discourse on Language*, translated by A. M. Sheridan Smith. New York, NY: Pantheon.

Gramsci, Antonio. 1971. Selections from the *Prison Notebooks*, translated and edited by Quintin Hoare and Geoffrey Nowell Smith. New York, NY: International Publishers.

Jacobs, Sue-Ellen and Christine Roberts. 1989. "Sex, Sexuality, Gender, and Gender Variance." In *Gender Anthropology*, edited by Sandra Morgen. Washington, DC: American Anthropological Association.

Jay, Nancy. 1981. "Gender and Dichotomy." *Feminist Studies* 7: 38–56.

Mencher, Joan. 1988. "Women's Work and Poverty: Women's Contribution to Household Maintenance in

South India. In *A Home Divided: Women and Income in the Third World*, edited by Daisy Dwyer and Judith Bruce. Stanford, CA: Stanford University Press.

Palmer, Phyllis. 1989. *Domesticity and Dirt: Housewives and Domestic Servants in the United States, 1920–1945.* Philadelphia: Temple University Press.

Reskin, Barbara F. 1988. "Bringing the Men Back In: Sex Differentiation and the Devaluation of Women's Work." *Gender and Society* 2:58–81.

Rubin, Gayle. 1975. "The Traffic in Women: Notes on the Political Economy of Sex." In *Toward an Anthropology of Women*, edited by Rayna R. Reiter. New York, NY: Monthly Review Press.

Scott, Joan Wallach. 1988. *Gender and the Politics of History.* New York, NY: Columbia University Press.

Smith, Dorothy. 1987. The *Everyday World as Problematic: A Feminist Sociology.* Toronto: University of Toronto Press.

West, Candace and Don Zimmerman. 1987. "Doing Gender." *Gender and Society* 1:125–51.

Williams, Christine L. 1989. *Gender Differences at Work: Women and Men in Nontraditional Occupations.* Berkeley, CA: University of California Press.

55. C.J. Pascoe and Tristan Bridges*

Fag Discourse in a Post-Homophobic Era

"There's a faggot over there! There's a faggot over there! Come look!" yelled Brian, a senior at River High School, to a group of ten-year-old boys. Following Brian, the ten-year-olds dashed down a hallway. At the end of the hallway Brian's friend, Dan, pursed his lips and began sashaying towards the ten-year-olds. He minced down the hall, swinging his hips exaggeratedly and wildly waving his arms. To the boys Brian yelled, "Look at the faggot! Watch out! He'll get you!" In response the ten-year-olds

---

* The ideas, issues, and theories considered in this brief contributed piece are examined in greater depth in the following publications: Pascoe, C.J. 2005. "'Dude, You're a Fag': Adolescent Masculinity and the Fag Discourse." *Sexualities* 8(3): 329–346, and Bridges, Tristan and C.J. Pascoe. 2016. "Masculinities and Post-Homophobias." Pp. 412–424 in *Exploring Masculinities*, edited by C.J. Pascoe and Tristan Bridges. New York: Oxford University Press. The article printed here was originally prepared by C.J. Pascoe and Tristan Bridges for this first edition of *Inequality in the 21st Century: A Reader*, edited by David B. Grusky and Jasmine Hill. Copyright © 2017 by Westview Press.

raced back down the hallway screaming in terror. (From C.J. Pascoe's field notes.)**

As scholars of gender have demonstrated, gender is accomplished through day-to-day interactions (Fine, 1987; Hochschild, 1989; West and Zimmerman, 1991; Thorne, 1993). Homophobia is central to young men's daily enactments of gender. In fact, young men's homophobia is a primary mechanism through which they socialize each other into normatively masculine behaviors, practices, attitudes, and dispositions (Pascoe 2007). However, this interactional homophobia has as much (if not more) to do with masculinity as it does with actual fear of gay men (Corbett 2001; Kimmel 1994). Homophobic insults are levied against boys who are not masculine, if only momentarily, *and* boys who identify (or are identified by others) as gay. The specter of the "faggot" so provocatively invoked by Brian in the above example symbolizes this particular form of gendered homophobia, something I came to call a "fag discourse," when researching young men at River High School. A *fag discourse* is a gendered and sexualized practice, policing selves and others into acceptably masculine identities, dispositions, relations, and enactments. A fag discourse consists of jokes, taunts, imitations, and threats on which young men rely to publicly signal their rejection of that which they considered unmasculine.

What, however, does a fag discourse look like in an era when anti-gay prejudice is declining and in which heterosexual men are increasingly showing support for sexual equality? Examining young heterosexual men's use of homophobic epithets, as well as their pro-gay and pro-feminist activism, indicates that a fag discourse is flexible and diffuse enough to be mobilized by men attempting to challenge the relationship between masculinity and homophobia. These *hybrid masculine* practices (Bridges and Pascoe 2014) illustrate the tenacity of gender and sexual inequality even in the face of significant challenges to them.

Who Is a Fag?

"Since you were little boys you've been told, 'hey, don't be a little faggot,'" explained Darnell, an African-American football player, as we sat on a bench next to the athletic field. Indeed, both the boys and

---

** The examples in the first portion of the paper draw extensively on Pascoe's fieldwork. As such, first person pronouns are used throughout this section.

girls I interviewed told me that "fag" was the worst epithet one guy could direct at another. Jeff, a slight white sophomore, explained to me that boys call each other fag because "gay people aren't really liked over here and stuff." Jeremy, a Latino junior told me that this insult literally reduced a boy to nothing, "To call someone gay or fag is like the lowest thing you can call someone. Because that's like saying that you're nothing."

Most guys explained their or other's dislike of fags by claiming that homophobia is just part of what it means to be a guy. For instance Keith, a white soccer-playing senior, explained, "I think guys are just homophobic." Several students told me that these homophobic insults only applied to boys and not girls. For example, while Jake, a handsome white senior, told me that he didn't like gay people, he quickly added, "Lesbians, okay that's good." In this sense it is not strictly homophobia, but a gendered homophobia that constitutes adolescent masculinity in the culture of this school. However, it is clear, according to these comments, that lesbians are "good" because of their place in heterosexual male fantasy, not necessarily because of some enlightened approach to same-sex relationships. It does, however, indicate that using only the term homophobia to describe boys' repeated use of the word "fag" might be a bit simplistic and misleading.

Some boys took pains to say that "fag" is not about sexuality. J.L., a white sophomore at Hillside High, asserted "Fag, seriously, it has nothing to do with sexual preference at all. You could just be calling somebody an idiot you know?" I asked Ben, a quiet, white sophomore who wore heavy metal t-shirts to auto-shop each day, "What kind of things do guys get called a fag for?" Ben answered, "Anything . . . literally, anything. Like you were trying to turn a wrench the wrong way, 'dude, you're a fag.' Even if a piece of meat drops out of your sandwich, 'you fag!'"

While Ben might rightly feel like a guy could be called a fag for "anything . . . literally, anything," there are actually specific behaviors which, when enacted by most boys, can render him more vulnerable to a fag epithet. In this instance Ben's comment highlights the use of "fag" as a generic insult for incompetence, which in the world of River High, is central to a masculine identity. A boy could get called a fag for exhibiting any sort of behavior defined as non-masculine (although not necessarily behaviors aligned with femininity): being stupid, incompetent, dancing, caring too much about clothing, being too emotional or expressing interest (sexual or platonic) in other guys. However, given the extent of its deployment and the laundry list of behaviors that could get a boy in trouble it is no wonder that Ben felt like a boy could be called "fag" for "anything."

One-third (thirteen) of the boys I interviewed told me that, while they may liberally insult each other with the term, they would not actually direct it at a homosexual peer. Jabes, a Filipino senior, told me,

I actually say it [fag] quite a lot, except for when I'm in the company of an actual homosexual person. Then I try not to say it at all. But when I'm just hanging out with my friends I'll be like, 'shut up, I don't want to hear you any more, you stupid fag.'

Similarly J.L. compared homosexuality to a disability, saying there is "no way" he'd call an actually gay guy a fag because,

There's people who are the retarded people who nobody wants to associate with. I'll be so nice to those guys and I hate it when people make fun of them. It's like, 'bro do you realize that they can't help that?' And then there's gay people. They were born that way.

According to this group of boys, gay is a legitimate, if marginalized, social identity. If a man is gay, there may be a chance he could be considered masculine by other men (Connell, 1995). In other words, the possibility exists, however slight, that a boy can be gay and masculine. But, to be a "fag" is, by definition, the opposite of masculine. In explaining this to me, Jamaal, an African-American junior, cited the explanation of popular rap artist, Eminem,

Although I don't like Eminem, he had a good definition of it. It's like taking away your title. In an interview they were like, 'you're always capping on gays, but then you sing with Elton John.' He was like 'I don't mean gay as in *gay*.'

While it is not necessarily acceptable to be gay, at least a man who is gay can do other things that render him acceptably masculine. A fag, by the very definition of the word, indicated by students' usages at River High, cannot be masculine.

Becoming a Fag

"The ubiquity of the word faggot speaks to the reach of its discrediting capacity" (Corbett, 2001:4). It is almost as if boys cannot help but shout it out on a regular basis – in the hallway, in class, across campus as a greeting, or as a joke. In my fieldwork, I was amazed by the ways the word seemed to pop uncontrollably out of boys' mouths in all kinds of situations. To quote just one of many instances from my field notes:

Two boys walked out of the P.E. locker room and one yelled 'fucking faggot!' at no one in particular.

Boys invoked the fag in two ways: through humorous imitation and through lobbing the epithet at one another. Boys at River High imitated the fag by acting out an exaggerated "femininity" and/or by pretending to sexually desire other boys. In imitative performances a fag discourse functions as a constant reiteration of the fag's existence, affirming that it is out there; at any moment a boy can become one. At the same time, these performances demonstrate that the boy who is invoking the epithet is not a fag, often by immediately becoming masculine again after the performance. They mock their own performed femininity and/or same-sex desire, assuring themselves and others that such an identity is one deserving of derisive laughter.

Boys also consistently tried to put another in the fag position by lobbing the fag epithet at each other. Going through the junk-filled car in the auto-shop parking lot, Jay poked his head out and asked, "Where are Craig and Brian?" Neil, responded with, "I think they're over there," pointing, then thrusting his hips and pulling his arms back and forth to indicate that Craig and Brian might be having sex. The boys in auto-shop laughed.

This sort of joke temporarily labels both Craig and Brian as faggots. However, these are not necessarily identities that stick. Nobody actually thinks Craig and Brian are homosexuals. Rather, the fag identity is a fluid one—certainly an identity that no boy wants, but one that a boy can escape, usually by engaging in some sort of discursive contest to turn another boy into a fag. "Fag" becomes a hot potato that no boy wants to be left holding.

Racing the Fag

The fag trope is not deployed consistently or identically across social groups at River High. Differences between white boys' and African-American boys'

meaning making around clothes and dancing reveal ways in which the fag as the abject position is racialized.

Clean, oversized, carefully put together clothing is central to a hip-hop identity for African-American boys who identify with hip-hop culture. Richard Majors calls this presentation of self a "cool pose" consisting of "unique, expressive and conspicuous styles of demeanor, speech, gesture, clothing, hairstyle, walk, stance and handshake," developed by African-American men as a symbolic response to institutionalized racism (Majors, 2001:211). This amount of attention and care given to clothing for white boys not identified with hip-hop culture would certainly cast them into an abject, fag position. White boys are not supposed to appear to care about their clothes or appearance, because only fags care about how they look. Ben illustrates this:

Ben walked in to the auto-shop classroom from the parking lot where he had been working on a particularly oily engine. Grease stains covered his jeans. He looked down at them, made a face and walked toward me with limp wrists, laughing and lisping in a high pitch sing-song voice 'I got my good pants all dirty!'

Ben draws on indicators of a fag identity, such as limp wrists, as do the boys in the introductory vignette to illustrate that a masculine person certainly would not care about having dirty clothes. However, African-American boys involved in hip-hop culture talk frequently about whether or not their clothes, specifically their shoes, are dirty.

Monte, River High's star football player echoed this concern about dirty shoes when looking at the fancy red shoes he had lent to his cousin the week before, told me he was frustrated because after his cousin used them, the "shoes are hella scuffed up." Clothing, for these boys, does not indicate a fag position, but rather defines membership in a certain cultural and racial group (Perry, 2002).

Dancing is another arena that carries distinctly fag-associated meanings for white boys and masculine meanings for African-American boys who participate in hip-hop culture. White boys often associate dancing with "fags." J.L. told me that guys think "'NSync's gay" because they can dance. 'NSync is an all-white male singing group known for their dance moves. At dances white boys frequently held their female dates tightly, locking their hips together. The boys never danced with one another, unless engaged in a round of "hot potato." White boys often jokingly danced together in order to embarrass each other by making someone else into a fag:

> Lindy danced behind her date, Chris. Chris's friend, Matt, walked up and nudged Lindy aside, imitating her dance moves behind Chris. As Matt rubbed his hands up and down Chris's back, Chris turned around and jumped back startled to see Matt there instead of Lindy. Matt cracked up as Chris turned red.

Dancing, however, does not carry this sort of sexualized gender meaning for all boys at River High. For African-American boys, dancing demonstrates membership in a cultural community (Best, 2000). African-American boys frequently danced together in single-sex groups, teaching each other the latest dance moves, showing off a particularly difficult move, or making each other laugh with humorous dance moves.

Students recognized K.J. as the most talented dancer at the school. K.J. was extremely popular. Girls hollered his name as they walked down the hall and thrust urgently written love notes folded in complicated designs into his hands as he sauntered to class. When he danced at assemblies, the room reverberated with screamed chants of "Go K.J.! Go K.J.! Go K.J.!" Because dancing for African-American boys places them within a tradition of masculinity, they are not at risk of becoming a fag for this particular gendered practice. Nobody called K.J. a fag. In fact, in several of my interviews, boys of multiple racial/ethnic backgrounds spoke admiringly of K.J.'s dancing abilities.

Gendered Meanings of the Fag Epithet

It may be tempting to think of this usage of homophobic language as something that is unique to the young people at River High. However, survey research indicates otherwise. One study asked 111 Canadian undergraduate men, "if you were to call a straight man a 'fag' or 'faggot' would you seriously be suggesting that you really and truly believe the man is gay?" (Brown and Alderson 2010). *Not a single respondent answered yes,* but most did affirm that they used homophobic epithets when referring to other men. In other words, the gendered homophobia of a

fag discourse is not limited to the young men at River High.

The fag epithet, when hurled at other boys, may or may not have explicit sexual meanings, but it always has gendered and often racialized meanings. When a boy calls another boy a fag, it means he is not a man, not necessarily that he is a homosexual. The boys in this study know that they are not supposed to call gay men "fags" because that is mean. This has been the limited success of the mainstream gay rights movement. The message absorbed by some of these teenage boys is that "gay men can be masculine, just like you." Instead of challenging gender inequality, this particular discourse of gay rights has reinscribed it. Indeed, this assimilation narrative has the effect of shoring up not only a normative gender order, but an unequal racial order as well.

Perhaps due to the effect of this particular assimilationist narrative, it seems, young men also understand how to participate in a fag discourse without ever uttering the word, "fag." Consider Bridges' (2010) research on "Walk a Mile in Her Shoes" marches—an event in which men gather in a public space to walk one mile in high heels to raise awareness about gender and sexual violence. Dominated by straight men, the participants in the marches Bridges observed participated in behavior not so different from Pascoe's (2007) high school boys. Consider the following interaction:

> At the marches, men often commented on each other's bodies in a way that was interactionally understood as jokingly gay. "Whoa!" commented one man, "You guys have some nice legs," elongating the *i* in "nice." Another friend chuckled and responded, "I don't like the idea of you lookin' at my legs, man." As he said this, he covered his behind with both hands and jokingly sped up, insinuating that he was protecting himself. *He was literally pretending to protect himself from sexual assault in jest during a march protesting sexual assault.* The audience laughed as the first man pretended to chase him, holding up both arms, wrists cocked, taking quick dainty steps. The surrounding crowd cheered and laughed as the men put on this show for everyone.

No one used the word "fag." No one even said "gay." And the interaction involved men in their early 30s. But, it's the same kind of behavior Brian and Dan enacted with the ten-year-old boys. As the marchers' jokes about "nice legs" illustrates, a fag discourse and the connections between masculinity and homophobia are not only about language. A fag discourse is malleable enough that it can be invoked subtly, even by men who are seemingly working for gender and sexual equality.

Masculinities and Post-Homophobias?

In recent years, we have witnessed recent changes in responses from heterosexual men to homosexuality that make it hard to understand the role that gendered homophobia plays in contemporary understandings of masculinity. Take, for instance, the reaction to Jason Collins, a professional basketball player who came out after his first year playing in the NBA. While his story made front-page news, prominent basketball stars, politicians, and other public figures responded with support and praise. Or the calendar assembled by the Warwick University men's rowing team. Since 2009 they have posed nude together in a series of photos that they sell to benefit their team as well as to donate to anti-homophobia and anti-bullying organizations. Similarly, straight, white hip-hop artist Ben Haggerty (Macklemore) scored popular acclaim upon the release of his hit song, "Same Love" (2012), a ballad of support for gay and lesbian rights, in which he affirms his own heterosexual identity by stating that he's "loved girls since before pre-k."

In perhaps a less well-known illustration of straight, white male support for gay rights, two fans of Chick-fil-A, Skyler Stone and Mike Smith, found themselves disturbed by the company's public stance opposing same-sex marriage. The two men wanted to continue to visit the restaurant chain, but did not want to compromise deeply held values about equality and civil rights for all. So they decided to stage a protest at their local Chick-fil-A. Theirs was not the usual protest featuring signs, urging boycotts, or presenting a list of demands. Instead, their protest consisted of showing exactly how far two straight guys were willing to go in support of both gay rights and the love of Chick-fil-A: they staged a kiss-in . . . with each other. While cameras rolled, these two handsome twenty-something heterosexual-identifying men called their girlfriends to secure permission, washed their mouths with mouthwash, and asked gay men for kissing advice. Duly prepared, the pair walked up to a Chick-fil-A "take out" window, placed their order, and passionately embraced—kissing (with overdramatic use of tongue and leg movements) in full view of a gathered crowd and restaurant employees.

That a protest by two straight men in support of gay rights even happened, much less involved a same-sex kiss, signifies that important social transformations are underway. On first read, these changes seem to challenge understandings of homophobia as a central component of masculinity in the West (e.g., Kimmel 1994). If homophobia is so central to contemporary constructions of masculinity, these examples implicitly ask, why are straight, normatively masculine men kissing each other in public in support of gay rights?

One critically important aspect of the two young men who protested at Chick-fil-A is that they did so humorously. Their protest was undertaken in a way that ensured (throughout the protest) that no one could mistake them as *actually* gay. They signaled that they were explicitly not gay in a variety of ways: asking their girlfriends for permission (situating each of them within heterosexual relationships), asking gay men for advice (underscoring the fact that authentically straight men could not accomplish kissing each other successfully without expert advice), cleaning their mouths out with mouthwash in ways that one usually would not for a kiss, and finally kissing in a manner that looked more like they were attacking each other than engaging in something erotic, passionate, tender, or loving. Their intentions merit celebration, to be sure. But Stone and Smith's protest accomplished something else: they made a big display of exactly how *straight* they are while making a joke about same-sex desire, all in support of gay rights. How in the world could these men be making a homophobic joke while supporting gay rights?

Arguably, Stone and Smith were engaging in a form of a fag discourse, albeit unintentionally. They strategically framed their kiss, for instance, as a stereotype of gay masculinity. They performed gay masculinity, but framed that performance as "straight." To fully appreciate this process as well as its relationship with gender and sexual inequality necessitates a discussion of what Bridges (2014) refers to as "sexual aesthetics." *Sexual aesthetics* refer to the cultural and stylistic distinctions utilized to delineate boundaries between gay and straight cultures and individuals. A focus on sexual aesthetics complicates the face-value interpretation of changes in masculine practice as indicative of a transformation in gender and sexual relations. Although men's actions are often laudable, these new practices and performances often have the less visible consequence of shoring up particular masculine identities while obscuring this process as it occurs. Heterosexual men's comfort with and adoption of "gay aesthetics" are practices associated with emergent forms of homophobia. They illustrate the tenacity of gender *inequality* behind a façade of gender and sexual equality.

For instance, in the pro-feminist group of men in Northern Virginia that Bridges (2014) studied ethnographically for just over a year, it was common for men in the group to claim that they were "mistaken for gay" and to identify with aspects of gay culture in the process. Like Stone and Smith, one member of the group—Shane—claims to strategically mobilize a symbolic protest against sexual inequality: "I take it as an opportunity to help gay people…. I'll usually say something like, 'Because I'm stylish? Or because I'm nice to people? … What? Because I'm healthy and care about my clothes and the way I look?' You know? Like, 'Oh, because I have good taste in music?'" On the face of it, Shane is actively resisting heterosexism and attempting to emphatically illustrate to others that he is not homophobic. He may also be attempting to critique heteronormative configurations of masculinity if being "nice," "clean," "healthy," and "stylish" call men's (hetero)sexuality into question.

Much like Stone and Smith, Shane is also relying on a fag discourse—but in a way that is qualitatively different from the young men at River High. A fag discourse works in ways that establish and reinforce clear boundaries between gay and straight. This is why young men feel comfortable flirting with the boundary: their performances rely on and reproduce the belief that this boundary exists. And although Shane might appear to be calling the boundaries between "gay" and "straight" into question by illustrating that a straight man can look and act "gay" too, he also participates in (re)defining those behaviors, interests, and qualities as "gay" in the first place. When others in the group discussed having been mistaken for gay, it wasn't uncommon for them to joke about how to avoid a similar kind of mistake in the future. For instance, Ben, a school counselor in the group, shared that students mistake him for gay. He shared, "Maybe I'll put a car engine in [my office]. Or like hang some porn on my wall." Similarly, Jacob, a bank teller who loves to wear extremely colorful, fitted clothes, shared that his clothing has caused others to question his sexuality. In response, he joked, "Would it make you more comfortable if I

looked like some oppressive Bible salesman, like telling women to get back in the kitchen?"

Shane, Ben, and Jacob are all doing something similar here. As feminist-identifying men, they strategically rely on gay aesthetics to symbolically distance themselves from masculinities that have earned a bad reputation among feminists. Their gendered performances and discussions often appear to be a sort of anti-fag discourse. That is, they wear being read as sexually illegible as a badge of honor rather than an insult. These stories are traded as a form of masculine capital, validating specific masculinities by implicitly "Othering" masculinities that fail to meet the criteria they interactionally define as worthy of status and respect. In doing so, however, they underscore exactly how straight they actually are.

Hybrid Masculinities

The gendered practices involved in these protests mobilize a discourse that enables men to create distance between themselves and configurations of gender more easily situated as responsible for gender and sexual inequality than those, for instance, enacted by the teenage boys at River High. The (primarily white) men protesting homophobia and sexism are enacting "hybrid masculinities"—configurations of gender practice that strategically borrow from marginalized and subordinated groups (such as gay men) in ways that obscure many heterosexual men's enduring positions of gendered, raced, classed, and sexualized power even as they call those positions into question (Bridges and Pascoe 2014). Thus, when examining shifts in the relationship between masculinity and homophobia, it is imperative to continue to investigate the elasticity of a fag discourse and its multiple expressions than assuming all challenges to gender and sexual inequality are equally effective.

In this chapter we suggest a way to reconcile the seeming contradiction posed by twin trends – young men invoking a fag discourse to shore up masculine identities and straight men's increasing support for gay rights and gender equality. Rather than suggesting that homophobia is *either* still a bedrock of masculinity *or* that it is in decline, we suggest that both of these trends are occurring simultaneously. To understand how homophobia can *both* remain a foundation of contemporary Western masculinity *and* that men's homophobic attitudes can be drastically changing, we need to understand two issues. First, we need to understand sexuality as something that does not necessarily reside in particular bodies, but as gendered discursive practice (exemplified by a fag discourse). Second, we need to understand that there are multiple ways to measure and express homophobia; some may be declining, others remaining, and still others emerging (Bryant and Vidal-Ortiz 2008). The iterations of homophobia we address here do not necessitate the fear or hatred of gay men. New forms of gender and sexual inequality materialize even as others are called into question. Indeed—as with masculinity—it is more appropriate to speak of "homophobias" than the singular homophobia. Hybrid masculine practices, such as engaging in a fag discourse and deploying particular sexual aesthetics, have the potential to challenge some forms of gender and sexual inequality while simultaneously shoring up others.

REFERENCES

Best, Amy. 2000. *Prom Night: Youth, Schools and Popular Culture.* New York: Routledge.

Bridges, Tristan S. 2010. "Men Just Weren't Made to Do This: Performances of Drag at 'Walk a Mile in Her Shoes' Marches." *Gender & Society* 24 (1): 5–30.

Bridges, Tristan. 2014. "A Very 'Gay' Straight?: Hybrid Masculinities, Sexual Aesthetics, and the Changing Relationship between Masculinity and Homophobia." *Gender & Society* 28 (1): 58–82.

Bridges, Tristan, and C. J. Pascoe. 2014. "Hybrid Masculinities: New Directions in the Sociology of Men and Masculinities." *Sociology Compass* 8 (3): 246–258.

Brown, Tyler L., and Kevin G. Alderson. 2010. "Sexual Identity and Heterosexual Male Students' Usage of Homosexual Insults: An Exploratory Study." *Canadian Journal of Human Sexuality* 19 (1/2): 27–42.

Bryant, Karl, and Salvador Vidal-Ortiz. 2008. "Introduction to Retheorizing Homophobias." *Sexualities* 11 (4): 387–396.

Connell, Raewyn. 1995. *Masculinities.* Berkeley: University of California Press.

Corbett, Ken. 2001. "Faggot = Loser." *Stuies in Gender and Sexuality* 2 (1):3-28.

Fine, Gary Alan. 1987. *With the Boys: Little League Baseball and Preadolescent Culture.* Chicago: University of Chicago Press.

Hochschild, Arlie. 1989. *The Second Shift.* New York: Avon.

Kimmel, Michael. 1994. "Masculinity as Homophobia." Pp. 119-141 in *Theorizing Masculinities*, edited by Harry Brod and Michael Kaufman. Thousand Oaks, CA: Sage.

Majors, Richard. 2001. "Cool Pose: Black Masculinity and Sports." Pp. 209-217 in *The Masculinities Reader*, edited by Stephen Whitehead and Frank Barrett Cambridge, Polity. 209-217

Pascoe, C. J. 2007. "Dude, You're a Fag": *Masculinity and Sexuality in High School.* Berkeley: University of California Press.

Perry, Pamela. 2002. *Shades of White: White Kids and Racial Identities in High School.* Durham: Duke University Press.

West, Candace and Zimmerman, Don. 1987 "Doing Gender." *Gender & Society* 1(2): 125-151.

Thorne, Barrie. 1993. *Gender Play: Boys and Girls in School.* New Brunswick: Rutgers University Press

The Division of Labor

56. Arlie Russell Hochschild*

The Time Bind: When Work Becomes Home and Home Becomes Work

It is 6:45 A.M. on a fine June day in the midwestern town of Spotted Deer. At a childcare center in the basement of the Baptist church, Diane Caselli, a childcare worker in blue jeans and loose shirt, methodically turns over small upended chairs that rest on a Lilliputian breakfast table. She sets out small bowls, spoons, napkins, and a pitcher of milk around a commanding box of Cheerios. The room is cheerful, clean, half-asleep. Diane moves slowly past neatly shelved puzzles and toys, a hat rack hung with floppy, donated dress-up hats and droopy pocketbooks, a tub filled with bits of colored paper. Paintings of swerving trains and tipsy houses are taped to the wall.

At seven A.M., a tall, awkward-looking man peers hesitantly into the room, then ventures a few steps forward looking for Diane. His son Timmy tromps in behind him. Diane walks over, takes Timmy's hand, and leads him to the breakfast table, where she seats him and helps him pour cereal and

milk into his bowl. Timmy's dad, meanwhile, hurries toward the door.

One wall of the room has four large windows that overlook a sidewalk. In front of the second window is a set of small wooden steps children climb to wave good-bye to their departing parents. It's called "the waving window." Timmy dashes from the breakfast table, climbs up the wooden steps, and waits.

His dad, an engineer, briskly strides past the first window toward his red Volvo parked down the street. He stops for a moment in front of the waving window, tilts his head, eyebrows lifted clownishly, then walks on without a backward glance. Timmy returns to his cereal, sighs, and declares excitedly, "My Dad sawed me wave!" . . .

At 7:40 A.M., four-year-old Cassie sidles in, her hair half-combed, a blanket in one hand, a fudge bar in the other. "I'm late," her mother explains to Diane. "Cassie wanted the fudge bar so bad, I gave it to her," she adds apologetically—though Diane has said nothing. Gwen Bell is a sturdy young woman, with short-cropped dark hair. Lightly made-up and minimally adorned with gold stud earrings, she is neatly dressed in khaki slacks and jacket. Some Amerco mothers don business suits as soldiers don armor while a few wear floral dresses suggesting festivity and leisure. But Cassie's mother is dressed in a neutral way, as if she were just getting the job of self-presentation done.

"Pleeese, can't you take me with you?" Cassie pleads.

"You know I can't take you to work," Gwen replies in a tone that suggests she's heard this request before. Cassie's shoulders droop in defeat. She's given it a try, but now she's resigned to her mother's imminent departure, and she's agreed, it seems, not to make too much fuss about it. Aware of her mother's unease about her long day at childcare, however, she's struck a hard bargain. Every so often she gets a morning fudge bar. This is their deal, and Cassie keeps her mother to it. As Gwen Bell later explained to me, she continually feels that she owes Cassie

*Excerpt from "The Waving Window" from the book *THE TIME BIND: When Work Becomes Home and Home Becomes Work* by Arlie Russell Hochschild. Copyright © 1997 by Arlie Russell Hochschild. Reprinted by permission of Henry Holt and Company, LLC. All rights reserved. Adapted from "Time in the Balance" by Arlie Russell Hochschild. Copyright © 1994 by Arlie Russell Hochschild. Originally appeared in *The Nation* (May 26, 1994). Reprinted by permission of Georges Borchardt, Inc. on behalf of the author. As published in *Social Stratification: Class, Race, and Gender in Sociological Perspective*, 3rd edition, by David Grusky, copyright © 2009. Reprinted by permission of Westview Press, an imprint of Perseus Books, LLC, a subsidiary of Hachette Book Group, Inc.

more time than she actually gives her. She has a time-debt to her daughter. If many busy parents settle such debts on evenings or weekends when their children eagerly "collect" promised time, Cassie insists on a morning down payment, a fudge bar that makes her mother uneasy but saves her the trouble and embarrassment of a tantrum. Like other parents at the center, Gwen sometimes finds herself indulging her child with treats or softened rules in exchange for missed time together. Diane speaks quietly to Cassie, trying to persuade her to stop sulking and join the others.

The center works on "child time." Its rhythms are child-paced, flexible, mainly slow. Teachers patiently oversee the laborious task of tying a shoelace, a prolonged sit on the potty, the scrambled telling of a tall tale. In this and other ways it is an excellent childcare center, one of a dozen islands of child time I was to discover in my three summers of field research at Amerco, a Fortune 500 company headquartered in Spotted Deer.[1] Scattered throughout the town, such islands—a playground, a pediatrician's waiting room, the back of a family van—stand out against the faster paced, more bureaucratically segmented blocks of adult work time. . . .

At the Spotted Deer Childcare Center, the group of young breakfasters gradually expands, early arrivals watching the entertainment provided by yet more newcomers. Sally enters sucking her thumb. Billy's mother carries him in even though he's already five. Jonathan's mother forgets to wave, and soon after, Jonathan kicks the breakfast table from below, causing milk to spill and children to yell. Marie ushers him away to dictate a note to his mother explaining that it hurts his feelings when she doesn't wave.

Cassie still stands at the front door holding her fudge bar like a flag, the emblem of a truce in a battle over time. Every now and then, she licks one of its drippy sides while Diane, uncertain about what to do, looks on disapprovingly. The cereal eaters watch from their table, fascinated and envious. Gwen Bell turns to leave, waving goodbye to Cassie, car keys in hand. By our prior arrangement, I am her shadow for this day, and I follow her out the door and into the world of Amerco.

Arriving at her office, as always, exactly at 7:50 A.M., Gwen finds on her desk a cup of coffee in her personal mug, milk no sugar (exactly as she likes it), prepared by a coworker who has managed to get in ahead of her. The remaining half of a birthday cake has been left on a table in the hall outside her office by a dieting coworker who wants someone else to

eat it before she does. Gwen prepares materials for her first meeting (having e-mailed messages to the other participants from home the previous night), which will inaugurate her official 8 A.M. to 5:45 P.M. workday. As she does so, she nibbles at a sliver of the cake while she proofreads a memo that must be Xeroxed and handed out at a second meeting scheduled for 9 A.M.

As the assistant to the head of the Public Relations Office, Gwen has to handle Amerco's responses to any press reports that may appear about the company. This time the impending media attention is positive, and her first meeting has been called to discuss how to make the most of it. As the members of the publicity team straggle into her office and exchange friendly greetings, she sighs. She's ready.

Gwen loves her job at Amerco, and she is very good at it. Whatever the daily pressures, she also feels remarkably at home there. Her boss, a man who she says reminds her of the best aspects of her father, helps her deal with work problems and strongly supports her desire to rise in the company. In many ways, her "Amerco dad" has been better to her than her own father, who, when she was small, abruptly walked out on her mother and her. She feels lucky to have such a caring boss, and working for him has reinforced her desire to give her all to work—insofar as she can. She and her husband need her salary, she tells me, since his job, though more lucrative than hers, is less steady.

Gradually, over the last three years, Gwen's workday has grown longer. She used to work a straight eight-hour day. Now it is regularly eight and a half to nine hours, not counting the work that often spills over into life at home. Gwen is not happy about this. She feels Cassie's ten-hour day at Spotted Deer is too long, but at the same time she is not putting energy into curbing her expanding workday. What she does do is complain about it, joke about it, compare stories with friends at work. Hers are not the boastful "war stories" of the older men at Amerco who proudly proclaim their ten-hour workdays and biweekly company travel schedules. Rather, Gwen's stories are more like situation comedies: stories about forgetting to shop and coming home to a refrigerator containing little more than wilted lettuce and a jar of olives, stories told in a spirit of hopeless amusement. Gwen is reasonably well-informed about Amerco's flextime and reduced-hours policies, which are available to white-collar employees like her. But she has not talked with her boss about cutting back her hours, nor have her joking coworkers, and her boss hasn't raised the possibility himself. There is just so much to get done at the office.

At 5:45 P.M. on the dot, Gwen arrives back at Spotted Deer. Cassie is waiting eagerly by the door, her coat over her arm, a crumpled picture she has drawn in her hand. Gwen gives Cassie a long, affectionate hug. By the time Gwen and Cassie roll into the driveway of their two-story white frame house, surrounded by a border of unruly shrubs, it is 6:25 P.M. John Bell is already there, having shopped, taken the messages off the phone machine, set the table, and heated the oven. This is one of two days a week he leaves home and returns earlier than his wife. He has eaten an ample lunch, knowing that they usually have a late, light dinner, but this evening he's hungrier than he means to be. He plays with Cassie while Gwen makes dinner.

To protect the dinner "hour"—8:00 to 8:30—Gwen checks that the phone machine is on, and we hear a series of abbreviated rings several times during dinner. John says grace, and we all hold hands. It is time, it seems, to let go and relax. Right after dinner, though, it's Cassie's bath time. Cassie both loves and protests her nightly bath. Gwen has come to expect Cassie to dawdle as she undresses or searches for a favorite bath toy, trying to make a minivacation of it. Gwen lets Cassie linger, scans through her phone messages, and sets them aside.

At 9 P.M., the bath over, Gwen and Cassie have "quality time" or "QT," as John affectionately calls it. This they see as their small castle of time protected from the demands of the outside world. Half an hour later, at 9:30 P.M., Gwen tucks Cassie into bed.

Later, as Gwen and John show me around their home, John points out in passing an expensive electric saw and drill set he bought two years earlier with the thought of building a tree house for Cassie, a bigger hutch for her rabbit Max, and a guest room for visiting friends. "I have the tools," John confides. "I just don't have the time to use them." Once, those tools must have represented the promise of future projects. Now they seemed to be there in place of the projects. Along with the tools, perhaps John has tried to purchase the illusion of leisure they seemed to imply. Later, as I interviewed other working parents at Amerco, I discovered similar items banished to attics and garages. Timmy's father had bought a boat he hadn't sailed all year. Jarod and Tylor's parents had a camper truck they had hardly driven. Others had cameras, skis, guitars, encyclopedia sets,

even the equipment to harvest maple syrup, all bought with wages that took time to earn.

John's tools seemed to hold out the promise of another self, a self he would be "if only I had time." His tools had become for him what Cassie's fudge bar was for her—a magical substitute for time, a talisman.

There were, in a sense, two Bell households: the rushed family they actually were, and the relaxed family they imagined they could be if only they had time. Gwen and Bill complained that they were in a time bind: they wanted more time for life at home than they had. It wasn't that they wanted more small segments of "quality time" added into their over-busy days. They wanted a quality life, and Gwen, at least, worked for a family-friendly company whose policies seemed to hold out hope for just that. So what was preventing them from getting it?

Time in the Balance

We've gotten ourselves into a time bind. Feeling that we are always late, having no free time, trying to adapt as best we can to the confines of our time prisons—these are all symptoms of what has become a national way of life. There are several reasons for this. Over the past two decades, global competition and inflation have lowered the buying power of the male wage. In response, many women have gone to work in order to maintain the family income. But the legacy of patriarchy has given cultural shape to this economic story. As women have joined men at work, they have absorbed the views of an older, male-oriented work world—its views of "an honest day's work"—at a much faster rate than men have absorbed their share of domestic work and culture. One reason women have changed more than men is that the world of "male" work seems more honorable and valuable than the "female" world of home and children.

There is another factor too—we are increasingly anxious about our "culture of care." Where do we turn when we are down and out? This is a question we ask, understandably, even when we are up and in. With recent welfare "reform," the government is cutting off aid to women and the poor. With the growth of the benefit-less contingency labor force, many corporations are doing the same thing to middle-class men. Meanwhile, modern families have grown more ambiguous: It's a little less clear than it once was who's supposed to take care of whom, how much, and for how long. So we've grown more anxious. Given our tradition of individualism, many of us feel alone in this anxiety, and insofar as work is our rock, we cling to it.

In this context, the idea of cutting back the work-day is an idea that seems to have died, gone to heaven, and become an angel of an idea. We dream about it, but it's something we'd never really expect to do. No matter how a movement for work-family balance is structured, in the long run, no such balance will ever take hold if the social conditions that would make it possible—men who are willing to share parenting and housework, supportive communities, and policymakers and elected officials who are prepared to demand family-friendly reforms—remain out of reach. . . .

As my study of Amerco has shown, however, even when the jobs of working parents are secure, pay a sufficient wage, and provide family-friendly programs, many working parents are still reluctant to spend more time at home. American fathers spend less time at home than mothers do, expand their work hours when children are small, and if Amerco is any indication, are reluctant to take paternity leaves. We know from previous research that many men have found a haven at work. This isn't news. The news is that growing numbers of working women are leery of spending more time at home as well. They feel guilty and stressed out by long hours at work, but they feel ambivalent about cutting back on those hours.

Women fear losing their place at work; having such a place has become a source of security, pride, and a powerful sense of being valued. As a survey conducted by Bright Horizons (a Boston-based company that runs on-site daycare centers in twenty-three states) indicates, women are just as likely to feel appreciated as men at the workplace; as likely as men to feel underappreciated at home; and even more likely than men to have friends at work. To cut back on work hours means risking loosening ties to a world that, tension-filled as it is, offers insurance against even greater tension and uncertainty at home. For a substantial number of time-bound working parents, the stripped-down home and the community-denuded neighborhood are simply losing out to the pull of the workplace.

Many women are thus joining men in a flight from the "inner city" of home to the "suburbs" of the workplace. In doing so, they have absorbed the views of an older, male-oriented work world about what a "real career" and "full commitment to the job" really mean. Women now make up nearly half the labor force. The vast majority of them need and want to be there. There is definitely no going back. But women have entered the workplace on "male" terms. It would be less problematic for women to adopt a male model of work—to finally enjoy privileges formerly reserved for men—if the male model of work were one of balance. But it is not.

All this is unsettling news, in part because the children of working parents are being left to adjust to or resist the time bind—and all of its attendant consequences—more or less on their own. It is unsettling because while children remain precious to their parents, the "market value" of the world in which they are growing up has declined drastically. One need not compare their childhoods with a perfect childhood in a mythical past to conclude that our society needs to face up to a serious problem.

NOTES

1. To protect the privacy of the people in this chapter, I have given the company a fictional name and declined to specify what its workers produce or where they live. I've also altered the names, occupations, and defining details of the personal lives of individuals. I have, however, tried to document as accurately as possible their experiences of life at home and at work and to capture the essence of the culture that infuses both worlds.

57. Christine Percheski*
Opting Out?

Women's participation in paid employment has increased substantially in the United States over the past fifty years, particularly among married women and mothers of young children. This occurred without a substantial reorganization of work or family life. Although men perform more housework and child care than in the past, they still spend on

*The ideas, issues, and theories considered in this brief commissioned piece are examined in greater depth in the following publication: Christine Percheski, "Opting Out? Cohort Differences in Professional Women's Employment Rates from 1960 to 2005," *American Sociological Review* 73 (June 2008), pp. 497–517, published by Sage Publications. The article printed here was originally prepared by Christine Percheski for the fourth edition of *Social Stratification: Class, Race, and Gender in Sociological Perspective*, edited by David B. Grusky. Copyright © 2014 by Westview Press.

average far less time engaged in these activities than women do, leaving the gendered nature of family life and childrearing essentially intact. The nature of paid work also remains fundamentally unchanged. Despite the expansion of maternity leave policies and flexible work schedules, the organization of most workplaces is still predicated on a concept of workers as "male" and free of personal responsibilities (Acker 1990). Many working women with children consequently experience significant difficulties because of the competing demands of work and family life. This has prompted questions about the sustainability of high employment rates for women. In this chapter I consider whether recent cohorts of women in professional and managerial occupations are increasing or maintaining high employment rates or are "opting out" of professional employment to stay at home with children.

Whether US women will maintain high employment levels has sparked interest outside of academia. Mainly relying on anecdotal evidence, many media outlets in the United States have run stories either predicting or claiming an exodus of women from professional work (Williams, Manvell, and Bornstein, 2006). One of these articles made a particularly controversial claim: a *New York Times Magazine* article by Belkin (2003) describes an "opt-out revolution" among highly educated professional women and asserts that women's voluntary employment exits to accommodate childrearing account for persistent gender inequalities in employment.

Media attention to "opting out" centers on highly educated women in professional and managerial occupations, and perhaps for good reason. The expansion of women's educational opportunities has yielded more women qualified for historically male-dominated jobs that require advanced schooling. Because professional and managerial occupations confer prestige, social influence, and economic rewards, women's success in these fields may be particularly important for gender equality.

This chapter describes cohort changes in employment patterns of college-educated professional and managerial women in the United States from 1960 to 2010 and evaluates whether recent cohorts are increasingly "opting out" of paid employment.

Theory and Previous Research

Widespread social change—such as the expansion of women's employment opportunities—is experienced differently by birth cohorts who mature under different historical circumstances and are at different stages in the life cycle when change occurs (Ryder 1965). Many societal changes over the past fifty years may have contributed to employment differences across birth cohorts among professional women. Changes that may have increased employment rates include the expansion of employment opportunities and legal protections for women, women's increased control over their fertility owing to technological and legal changes, and an increase in the earnings premiums for higher education and professional work. Other changes may have led to a decline in women's employment rates across cohorts, including a conservative cultural shift, increased time demands of professional occupations, more marriage opportunities for educated women, and a shift toward more mother-intensive parenting practices.

Cohort change can be thought of as having two sources: changes in the composition of the population and changes in the behavior of subgroups of the population. For example, an increase across cohorts in the percentage of professional women who are mothers—a compositional change—could decrease employment rates. Employment rates could similarly decrease if the percentage of mothers stayed the same while the employment rates of mothers decreased—a behavioral change. The changes outlined previously may have impacted the compositional characteristics of professional women, their behaviors, or both.

The evidence on cohort change among women in professional and managerial occupations is limited; in 2008 I found just one study of cohort employment patterns for this group using nationally representative data. Whittington, Averett, and Anderson (2000) examine postpartum employment patterns among married mothers using data from the Panel Study of Income Dynamics (PSID) from 1968 to 1992. They do not find significant cohort differences in models controlling for period effects, but their sample size is small, and their model specification may be inadequate.

Two other studies are particularly relevant to this research question. Goldin's (2006) analysis of women born around 1958 who attended selective colleges finds relatively small employment differences between mothers and childless women. In addition, less than half of the mothers in the sample were out of the labor force for more than six months at a time. Another cohort study considers the fertility and employment patterns of college-educated women born from 1960 to 1979 between ages twenty-two and twenty-seven. Vere (2007) finds modest decreases in cumulative annual employment hours for single-year cohorts born after 1974 and increases in fertility among cohorts born after 1966, but this analysis cannot show whether employment decreases were concentrated among women with children.

Data and Methods

Data

I use the Integrated Public Use Microdata Series (IPUMS) Census data for the 1960 through 2000 Censuses and American Community Survey (ACS) data for 2005 and 2010 (Ruggles et al. 2004). (The original analysis published in the *American Sociological Review* in 2008 included ACS data from 2005; I have used data from 2010 instead of 2005 for most of this updated analysis.) My sample includes college-educated women ages twenty-five to fifty-four in professional or managerial occupations (hereafter referred to as "professional women") in the 1960 General, 1970 Form 2 Metro, 1980 1% Metro B, 1990 1% Metro, 2000 1% Census, and 2005 and 2010 ACS IPUMS samples. For some analyses I consider only women in the prime childbearing years (ages twenty-five to thirty-nine).

Professionals and managers. I define professional women as those with a college degree (or four years of college) and an occupation classified as professional or managerial by the Census Bureau. Specifically, I use the IPUMS code *occ1950*.

Birth cohorts. I divide the sample into seven ten-year cohorts, starting with the birth year 1906 and ending with the year 1975. I use the cohort parameters defined by Sayer, Cohen, and Casper (2004) to facilitate comparisons with their research on women's employment. The final sample, which includes observations from 1960 to 2010, contains 370,713 observations.

Measures of employment. I examine three measures of employment by birth cohorts: labor force participation (LFP), full-time, year-round employment (FTYR), and working more than fifty hours per week (hereafter referred to as "working long hours").

Occupational characteristics. The historical gender composition or sex-type of an occupation captures a broad array of factors that may influence employment rates, including prestige, working conditions,

and salary. In the category of historically male professions, I include doctors and physicians, lawyers and judges, engineers, accountants, college professors and deans, clergy, and dentists. In the category of historically female professions are nurses, social workers, teachers, and librarians.

Family characteristics. In this analysis I consider whether a woman has children and the age of her youngest child. I classify a woman who reports her youngest child's age as five or younger as "having young children," and a woman whose youngest child is between the ages of six and eighteen as "having older children." Women who do not report any of their own children in the household are classified as "without children." This operational definition is likely to slightly underestimate maternal status.

Analysis Plan

To examine changes in professional women's employment over time, I use a cohort analysis approach. First, I show how age-specific rates of LFP, FTYR, and working long hours have changed by cohort. This part of the analysis is similar to Sayer, Cohen, and Casper's (2004) cohort analysis; my analysis differs primarily in the population examined and the number of cohorts considered. Second, I track changes in the composition of professional women across cohorts and in employment rates among subgroups, defined by family characteristics and occupation sex-type. To calculate employment rates for the main childbearing years, I compute single-year, age-specific rates and then average these single-year rates together to compute an average rate for twenty-five- to thirty-nine-year-olds. For data from 1990 and later years, I use weights as suggested by the US Census Bureau. Finally, I describe the characteristics of women who were out of the labor force in the previous year.

Results

Age-Specific Employment Rates

Labor force participation rates. Figure 57.1 shows the trends in labor force participation (LFP) rates for professional women by age and birth cohort. Each line in the figure shows the trend in LFP rates for one five-year age group. The horizontal axis shows birth cohorts. By following each line from left to right, one can see the trend of increasing age-specific rates across cohorts. Steep increases across cohorts

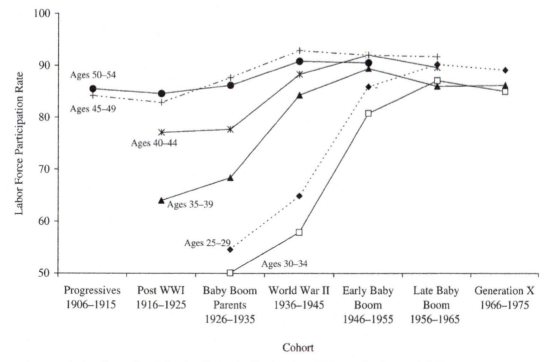

FIGURE 57.1 Labor Force Participation Rates for Professional Women by Age and Cohort

are most pronounced for the youngest age groups, with more modest increases among older women. Many of the age-specific trend lines plateau or slightly dip across the youngest cohorts. For example, the LFP rate for thirty- to thirty-four-year-olds decreased from 87.1 for the Late Baby Boom cohort (1956 to 1965) to 85.0 for Generation X (1966 to 1975). In contrast, a higher percentage of Generation X women in their late thirties and early forties are in the labor force (91.5 percent and 92.6 percent, respectively) than similarly aged women from the Late Baby Boom cohort (86.0 percent and 89.7 percent, respectively).

Full-time, year-round employment rates. The percentage of professional women working full-time, year-round (FTYR) has greatly increased across cohorts. Age-specific rates (not shown) increased across every cohort. For example, the percentage of women ages thirty-five to thirty-nine who were working FTYR increased from 42.7 percent of the Early Baby Boom cohort, to 52.1 percent of the Late Baby Boom cohort, to 64.0 percent of women in the Generation X cohort.

Percentage working long hours. The percentage of professional women working more than fifty hours a week increased from less than 10 percent in each age group for the oldest three cohorts (born before

1935) to over 15 percent for most ages in the youngest two cohorts (born after 1956). For this measure, there is a greater percentage of women ages thirty to thirty-four working long hours in the Generation X cohort (18.0 percent) than in the Late Baby Boom (13.9 percent), but similar percentages of these cohorts work long hours across other age groups.

Compositional Changes Across Cohorts

To better understand what drives cohort change, I examine changes in the composition of cohorts and in the behavior of subgroups within and across cohorts. Table 57.1 shows that the percentage of the total female population who are college educated and in professional and managerial occupations has increased across cohorts, indicating decreased selectivity, which would predict falling employment rates. At the same time, more women in younger cohorts have advanced degrees, suggesting rising employment rates, because highly educated women have higher employment rates than do less educated women. Table 57.1 also shows that the share of professional women in historically male occupations has increased across cohorts. Would this be expected to result in higher or lower employment levels? On the

TABLE 57.1 Cohort Compositional Changes: Educational and Occupational Characteristics of Women Ages 30 to 34 for the Total Female Population and for Professional Women

Birth Cohort	Percent College-Educated Professionals and Managers		Percent with Advanced Degrees		Percent in Historically Male Professions[1]		Percent in Historically Female Professions[2]	
	Total Female Population	Professionals	Total Female Population	Professionals	Total Female Population	Professionals	Total Female Population	Professionals
Baby Boom Parents (1926 to 1935)	4.5 (4.3–4.7)	100	.8 (.69–.82)	12.7 (11.5–13.9)	.2 (.17–.24)	6.4 (5.5–7.3)	3.0 (2.9–3.2)	62.9 (61.1–64.7)
World War II (1936 to 1945)	8.0 (7.7–8.2)	100	1.3 (1.2–1.4)	14.2 (13.2–15.2)	.5 (.46–.58)	7.7 (6.9–8.4)	5.6 (5.4–5.8)	66.6 (65.2–67.9)
Early Baby Boom (1946 to 1955)	13.1 (12.9–13.3)	100	5.0 (4.9–5.2)	30.0 (29.2–30.8)	1.3 (1.2–1.4)	10.2 (9.7–10.8)	7.7 (7.5–7.8)	56.8 (55.9–57.7)
Late Baby Boom (1956 to 1965)	15.4 (15.2–15.6)	100	6.1 (5.9–6.2)	31.3 (30.6–32.0)	2.5 (2.4–2.6)	15.4 (14.8–15.9)	5.7 (5.6–5.9)	39.7 (39.0–40.5)
Generation X (1966 to 1975)	21.2 (21.1–21.4)	100	9.8 (9.7–10.0)	37.7 (37.2–38.1)	3.7 (3.6–3.8)	17.0 (16.6–17.4)	7.1 (7.0–7.3)	34.9 (34.4–35.3)

Source: 1960 to 2000 Census and 2005 ACS microdata from IPUMS.

Note: 95 percent confidence intervals are in parentheses.

1. Historically male professions are accountants, clergy, dentists, doctors, engineers, lawyers, and college professors and deans.
2. Historically female professions are librarians, nurses, social workers, and teachers.

one hand, there is evidence of continuing discrimination against women in some of these professions (Blair-Loy 2001; Kay and Hagan 1995; Roth 2003). On the other hand, these professions confer higher salaries and more prestige, raising the opportunity costs of not working in these fields.

The percentage of professional women ages thirty to thirty-four who have children has decreased across cohorts, reflecting the rising mean age of US mothers at their first birth. However, the majority of professional women between the ages of thirty-five and thirty-nine have children, and this has not varied much across cohorts.

Employment Rates of Population Subgroups

Employment rates by occupation. Differences in labor force participation (LFP) rates by occupational sex-type are small or nonexistent across the cohorts studied. In contrast, rates of FTYR employment vary more across sex-type of occupation. Women work FTYR at much higher rates in historically male unclassified occupations than in female-typed occupations. Working long hours varies even more across occupational types. Among Late Baby Boomers, 24 percent in male-typed occupations work long hours, compared to 17 percent of those in unclassified occupations and 12 percent of those in female-typed occupations. The increase across cohorts in the percentage of professional women in male-typed occupations contributed to rising rates of FTYR and working long hours, but did not affect LFP rates.

Employment rates by maternal status. As Table 57.2 shows, LFP rates among women with young children increased greatly across cohorts, climbing from 33.5 percent for the Baby Boom Parents cohort (1926 to 1935) to 76.2 percent for the Late Baby Boom and 78.4 percent for Generation X (1956 to 1975). The percentage of women who have older children and are in the labor force has also increased across cohorts, and in the youngest cohorts, women with children over age five have LFP rates similar to those of women without children. Not only are mothers in younger cohorts more likely to be working, but they are working more hours. In the early cohorts, FTYR employment among women with young children was quite rare; less than 10 percent of these mothers worked full-time. For the Late Baby Boom and Generation X cohorts (1956 to 1975), FTYR employment among mothers of young chil-

dren is much more common and has become the norm among mothers of older kids.

Despite the overall trend of increasing employment rates, this analysis shows some evidence of a leveling off of employment rates across the youngest cohorts. For all three subgroups defined by maternal status, there were no statistically significant differences in LFP rates between Generation X and the Late Baby Boom cohort. Notably, however, there was a substantial increase in the FTYR rates for women with young children (from 31.6 to 43.8) and for women with older children (51.9 to 63.0). In addition, the percentage of women with young children working more than fifty hours per week increased substantially across the youngest two cohorts (from 7.6 to 10.5).

Percentage Opting Out

Table 57.3 shows the percentage of professional women between the ages of twenty-five and thirty-nine who were not employed or enrolled in school in the previous year. The first column shows that the percentage decreased, from 30.6 for the Baby Boom Parents (1926 to 1935) to 3.8 for Generation X (1966 to 1975). The second and third columns show that the percentage among those with advanced degrees and in historically male professions also decreased across cohorts. Notably, this finding of a continued decrease in the percentage "opting out" between the Late Baby Boom and Generation X cohorts differs from my conclusions published in 2008 based on the 2005 data; using the 2005 data, I found no statistically significant difference in the percentage opting out between the Late Baby Boom and Generation X. Regardless of whether I use 2005 or 2010 data, my conclusion is the same: there is no evidence of a new opt-out phenomenon.

Three characteristics of women who did no paid work in the previous year are particularly striking. First, opting-out seems to be concentrated among women with high-earning husbands. Second, the percentage of nonworking professional women who have children is decreasing. Although the vast majority of these women have children at home, a greater percentage in the younger cohorts do not. Finally, whereas the percentage of women with advanced degrees and in historically male occupations who are not working is decreasing (see Table 57.3), the percentage opting out who hold an advanced degree or work in a historically male profession is increasing across cohorts.

TABLE 57.2 Employment Rates of Professional Women Ages 25 to 39 by Motherhood Status and Age of Youngest Child

Cohort	Labor Force Participation Rates			Full-Time, Year-Round Employment Rates			Percentage Working 50+ hrs./week		
	Without Children	With Young Children[1]	With Older Children[2]	Without Children	With Young Children	With Older Children	Without Children	With Young Children	With Older Children
Baby Boom Parents (1926 to 1935)	88.7	33.5	77.2	33.2	5.6	17.9	7.2	1.3	2.1
World War II (1936 to 1945)	92.3	47.2	78.5	36.9	9.3	19.8	8.5	2.1	6.1
Early Baby Boom (1946 to 1955)	96.0	68.6	91.9	54.0	19.8	40.0	15.3	4.1	7.5
Late Baby Boom (1956 to 1965)	95.9	76.2	92.9	67.6	31.6	51.9	23.8	7.6	11.5
Generation X (1966 to 1975)	95.2	78.4	93.4	70.8	43.8	63.0	24.1	10.5	15.5

Source: 1960 to 2000 Census and 2010 ACS microdata from IPUMS.

Notes: Respondents enrolled in school are excluded from this analysis. Standard errors are the following: less than 2.5 for all LFP rates except for Baby Boom Parents with older children (3.0) and World War II with older children (4.3); less than 2.0 for full-time, year-round rates except for Baby Boom Parents with older children (2.2), Early Baby Boom with older children (2.2), and Generation X with young children (2.1); and less than 1.5 for all estimates of working more than 50 hrs./week.

1. Children 5 years old or younger.
2. Children 6 to 18 years old.

TABLE 57.3 Percentage of Professional Women Ages 25 to 39 Not Enrolled in School and Not Working in the Previous Year

	Percent of All Professional Women	*Percent of Those in Male Professions*	*Percent of Those with Advanced Degrees*
Baby Boom Parents	30.6	29.8	17.2
(1926 to 1935)	(25.7–35.5)	(23.7–35.8)	(13.9–20.4)
World War II	20.7	16.3	9.8
(1936 to 1945)	(15.2–26.2)	(12.2–20.5)	(7.4–12.2)
Early Baby Boom	8.0	6.6	5.1
(1946 to 1955)	(6.4–9.5)	(5.2–8.0)	(4.0–6.1)
Late Baby Boom	6.1	5.3	4.4
(1956 to 1965)	(4.9–7.3)	(3.7–6.9)	(3.4–5.3)
Generation X	3.8	3.5	2.7
(1966 to 1975)	(2.1–5.5)	(1.9–5.1)	(1.5–3.9)

Source: 1960 to 2000 Census and 2010 ACS microdata from IPUMS.
Note: 95 percent confidence intervals reported in parentheses.

Conclusions

I find little evidence that recent cohorts of professional women are opting out of paid work at higher rates than preceding cohorts did. Indeed, the FTYR employment rate of professional women with young children in Generation X is higher than that of any previous cohort. In addition, women in younger cohorts—even those with young children—are more likely to be working long hours than women in older cohorts. Notably, however, labor force participation rates have held relatively constant—instead of continuing to rise—over the last two cohorts of professional women.

If there is no opt-out phenomenon, why have media stories suggesting otherwise garnered so much attention? I suggest three possible reasons. First, the opt-out journalistic account may ring partially true for working mothers in professional occupations. Having children is associated with substantially lower rates of employment, and although professional women are working more now than ever before, a large percentage are not working full-time, year-round.

Second, many people expected greater progress toward gender equality in employment would have been achieved by now. Though it is more feasible for women in younger cohorts to simultaneously pursue a career and raise children than it was for women in older cohorts, professional women with children still work fewer hours than men or women without children.

Finally, there are more professional women now than ever before, so the average person is more likely to know a professional woman who has left the labor force. In addition, although the percentage of women with advanced degrees who are not working is declining across cohorts, the percentage of nonworking women who have an advanced degree is growing, because the entire population is becoming more educated.

"Opting out" does not describe the trend characterizing the employment patterns of recent cohorts of professional women. By most measures, professional women—including mothers with young children—are working more than ever. By narrowly focusing on motherhood as the primary source of women's employment disadvantages, the new opting-out rhetoric pins the explanation for gender inequality on individual choices. This diverts attention from structural and institutional factors that may depress women's employment levels. We need to ask new questions about women's employment—including issues of work-family conflict—but also transcend them if we are to better understand gender inequality in the workplace.

REFERENCES

Acker, Joan. 1990. "Hierarchies, Jobs, Bodies: A Theory of Gendered Organizations." *Gender and Society* 4 (2): 139–158.

Belkin, Lisa. 2003. "The Opt-Out Revolution." *New York Times Magazine*, October 26, 42–47, 58, 85–86.

Blair-Loy, Mary. 2001. "It's Not Just What You Know, It's Who You Know: Technical Knowledge, Rainmaking, and Gender Among Finance Executives." *Research in the Sociology of Work* 10: 51–83.

Goldin, Claudia. 2006. "The Quiet Revolution That Transformed Women's Employment, Education, and Family." *American Economic Review* 96 (2): 1–21.

Kay, Fiona M., and John Hagan. 1995. "The Persistent Glass Ceiling: Gendered Inequalities in the Earnings of Lawyers." *The British Journal of Sociology* 46: 279–310.

Roth, Louise Marie. 2003. "Selling Women Short: A Research Note on Gender Differences in Compensation on Wall Street." *Social Forces* 82 (2): 783–802.

Ruggles, Stephen, Matthew Sobek, Trent Alexander, Catherine Fitch, Ronald Goeken, Patricia Kelly Hall, Miriam King, and Charles Ronnander. 2004. *Integrated Public Use Microdata Series*: Version 3.0 [MRDF]. Minneapolis: Minnesota Population Center [producer and distributor].

Ryder, Norman. 1965. "The Cohort as a Concept in the Study of Social Change." *American Sociological Review* 30 (6): 843–861.

Sayer, Liana C., Philip N. Cohen, and Lynne M. Casper. 2004. *The American People Census 2000: Women, Men, and Work*. New York: Russell Sage Foundation.

US Bureau of the Census. 1950. Alphabetic Index of Occupations and Industries: 1950. Washington, DC: US Government Printing Office.

Vere, James. 2007. "'Having It All' No Longer: Fertility, Female Labor Supply and the New Life Choices of Generation X." *Demography* 44 (4): 821–828.

Whittington, Leslie, Susan Averett, and Donna Anderson. 2000. "Choosing Children over Career? Changes in the Postpartum Labor Force Behavior of Professional Women." *Population Research and Policy Review* 19: 339–355.

Williams, Joan C., Jessica Manvell, and Stephanie Bornstein. 2006. "'Opt-Out' or Pushed Out? How the Press Covers Work/Family Conflict." In *WorkLifeLaw Report*. San Francisco, CA: UC Hastings College of the Law.

58. Asaf Levanon and David B. Grusky*
Why Is There Still So Much Gender Segregation?

The rise of gender egalitarianism over the last half-century, while spectacular and unprecedented, is clearly an incomplete project that faces strong resistance, especially within the workplace (e.g.,

*This chapter draws on material in Levanon, Asaf, and David B. Grusky, 2016, "The Persistence of Extreme Gender Segregation in the Twenty-first Century," *American Journal of Sociology* 122(2), pp. 573-619. Used with permission of the University of Chicago Press.

England 2015; Gerson 2015, 2011; Ridgeway 2014; Correll 2013; Cotter, Hermsen, and Vanneman 2011). There has been much discussion, in particular, of the gender pay gap and how historic declines in this gap have recently stalled (e.g., Blau and Kahn 2016; Blau 2012; Stone 2009). It is equally striking, however, that women and men continue to work in extremely segregated occupations, with women still crowding into a relatively small number of female-typed occupations. It is perhaps surprising that we refer to a "gender revolution" even though a full 53 percent of the employed women in the United States would have to shift to a different occupational category to eliminate all segregation (e.g., Blau and Kahn 2011; Jacobs 2001; Levanon, England, and Allison 2009). The contemporary workplace remains so segregated that it may still be fairly characterized as "hypersegregated" (Charles and Grusky 2011; 2004).

The purpose of this chapter is to develop a new model of occupational segregation that casts light on why sex segregation has been so resistant to change. The foil around which we build our new segregation model is the distinction between essentialist and vertical sources of segregation. As Charles and Grusky (2004) have argued, two distinct cultural principles are interwoven to generate the contemporary pattern of sex segregation, the first being the essentialist presumption that women and men have fundamentally different tastes and proclivities and are accordingly suited for very different types of occupations, and the second being the vertical presumption that men are more competent, committed, and status-worthy than women and accordingly well-suited for positions requiring the most substantial human capital investments (see Cotter, Hermsen, and Vanneman, 2011; Charles and Grusky 2011; Grusky and Levanon 2008; Bridges 2003; Blackburn, Brooks, and Jarman 2001; Blackburn, Jarman, and Brooks 2000). Although a hybrid model of this sort has been proposed frequently, no attempt has been made to develop a comprehensive formulation or to estimate it at a properly detailed level.

We define essentialism as the *belief* that men and women are fundamentally different in their interests and skills (e.g., Charles and Grusky 2011), a belief that both (a) encourages women and men to make investments and choices that reproduce gender inequality (i.e., supply-side essentialism), and (b) encourages employers to allocate occupations in accord with such presuppositions (i.e., demand-side essentialism). If essentialist processes are indeed fundamental in generating such supply-side and demand-side segregation, the simple empirical implication is that women will mainly work in occupations with female-typed traits (e.g., nurturing) and men will mainly work in occupations with male-typed traits (e.g., analytical). Although there are many well-known and frequently-cited examples of such essentialist segregation, it is not known whether the essentialist form fully and completely permeates the nooks and crannies of the labor market.

The future of segregation depends on precisely how extensive such essentialism is. The essentialist form resists change because it embodies the story that (a) women are peculiarly suited for female-typed jobs that just happen to be low in pay and prestige, and (b) men are peculiarly suited for male-typed jobs that just happen to be high in pay and prestige. If the labor market is deeply and resoundingly essentialist, it thus expresses a legitimating story about the sources of segregation and the pay gap, a story that *may* render both resistant to change.

It is entirely possible that much of the segregation now in play has precisely this essentialist backing. It is also possible, however, that contemporary segregation is instead largely vertical in character, meaning that men remain deeply advantaged in securing high-status occupations even after all essentialist effects are purged. We follow Charles and Grusky (2011) and others (e.g., England 2010) in defining vertical segregation as the residual association between gender and status that cannot be explained as the consequence of demand-side and supply-side sorting of women into female-typed tasks and men into male-typed tasks. It thus pertains to a raw form of male advantage that is not legitimated by conventional stories about the types of tasks for which women and men are well-suited.

The sources of such vertical segregation are, like the sources of essentialist segregation, rooted in both supply-side and demand-side processes. It can arise because (a) women are burdened with domestic responsibilities that oblige them to "choose" occupations that are lower in pay, prestige, and workplace demands (i.e., supply-side processes), or because (b) women are allocated to lesser occupations via networks, discrimination, and other employer processes (i.e., demand-side processes). We will not be attempting here to adjudicate between such supply and demand forces because there is much excellent research that addresses their effects and the feedback processes connecting them (e.g.,

Blau and Kahn 2016; Blau 2012; Polachek 2012). As we see it, the logically prior task is to assess to what extent the vertical and essentialist forms are in play, a precursory question that our data are uniquely suited to take on.

The key underlying source of vertical segregation is the *presumption* that, when it comes to carrying out tasks within the formal economy, men are intrinsically more committed and competent than women and hence more deserving of the best positions and the most substantial rewards (e.g., pay, prestige). This presumption has of course been called increasingly into question as egalitarianism spreads (Cotter et al. 2011). Although vertical forms of segregation are likely weakening, we do not know whether they are now a minor residual form or instead are alive and well and loom large in the formal economy. The segregation field has faltered in this regard because, perhaps surprisingly, a comprehensive model of segregation that operationalizes the many forms of essentialism and vertical advantage has not been developed as yet. We turn to that task here.

The main proponents of an essentialist account, such as Charles and Grusky (2011), have operated with an unsatisfying one-parameter representation of essentialism that distinguishes between occupations that are and are not strength-requiring (also see Charles and Grusky 2004; Grusky and Levanon 2008). We are, like Charles and Grusky (2011), impressed with the power of that single parameter. But even so our suspicion is that essentialism extends well beyond the simple presumption on the part of employers that men and women differ in their strength and in their "taste" to engage in strength-requiring pursuits. It is well to bear in mind that Charles and Grusky (2011) treated this physical strength dimension as but an *illustration* of the larger principle of essentialism. We accordingly seek to explore the full reach of an essentialist account by developing a more comprehensive operationalization that distinguishes between its physical, analytic, and interactional variants. The resulting model will capture the effects of the main essentialist processes at play, such as the presumption that women are endowed with fine motor skills, that men are especially well-suited to analytic tasks, that women are skillful nurturers, and that men are skillful leaders. Because we seek to be comprehensive in this way, the resulting model will come closer to exhausting the full reach of essentialism, a critical task in putting the essentialist approach to reasonable test.

The conventional single-parameter operationalization is thus inadequate because it is unlikely to exhaust the forces of essentialism. The further problem with focusing exclusively on strength-based essentialism is that it is one of the relatively rare types that, by virtue of steering women away from low-status and low-paying jobs, may be understood as female-advantaging. By contrast, the presumption that men are suited to analytic tasks is a male-advantaging variant, as occupations that rely on analytic skills are typically higher in status and pay than those that do not. We suspect that the various types of essentialism that have typically been omitted from conventional analyses are likewise male-advantaging in their effects. The simple implication: Although most forms of essentialism are likely to be male-advantaging, the main occupational segregation models on offer ignore such essentialism and hence misrepresent the way in which it operates to produce advantage and disadvantage.

Measuring essentialism and the vertical principle

The two-step strategy behind our analysis entails (a) scaling detailed occupations in terms of three forms of essentialism (i.e., physical, analytic, and interactional) and two vertical dimensions (i.e., pay and prestige), and (b) then modeling cross-occupational differences in the extent of segregation as a function of essentialism and vertical segregation. We discuss each of these two steps in turn.

The centerpiece of our effort to build a comprehensive model of sex segregation is the underused O*NET database of worker attributes and job characteristics (Petersen et al. 1999). As the replacement for the *Dictionary of Occupational Titles* (DOT), O*NET is a rich resource that provides detailed information on worker characteristics (including abilities, interests, and work styles), skill and experience requirements, and work activities and contexts (see US Department of Commerce 2000). We rely here on the O*NET 4.0 ratings produced by occupational analysts and will apply them to the 468 occupations that can be identified in the Standard Occupational Classification (SOC) used in the 2000 US Census. Because both O*NET and the 2000 US Census are based on SOC, the conventional problem of linking two different occupational classification systems, which long plagued DOT users, has now been entirely eliminated. We have opted to use the 2000 US Census data, rather than the 2010 US Census, because the O*NET 4.0 assessments were conducted in 1999 and therefore align especially directly to labor market circumstances in 2000.

The model that we have developed stands or falls on our claim that the core essentialist processes invoked in the contemporary workplace are well-captured. Because gender essentialism is such a sprawling cultural construction, we well appreciate that this is an ambitious claim, if nothing else one that we hope will trigger efforts by others to disconfirm it. We have proceeded by carefully examining the vast literature on sex stereotypes and ferreting out those essentialist dimensions that are likely to be salient in the workplace (e.g., Cejka and Eagly 1999; Deaux and LaFrance 1998; Lueptow, Garovitch-Szabo, and Lueptow 2001; Spence 1993; Williams and Best 1990; Zemora, Fiske, and Kim 2000). In all cases, O*NET includes excellent measurements of the dimensions identified within this literature, and we cannot therefore blame any possible shortcomings of our measurements on problems with data availability. We have an extraordinary (and underused) data resource at our disposal and have fashioned it into an essentialist scheme that we are prepared to represent as comprehensive.

We have developed a nine-dimension scheme in which each dimension is understood as capturing a form of physical, analytic, or interactional essentialism (see Cjeka and Eagly 1999 for a similar set of umbrella categories). As shown in Table 58.1, only two of these nine scales is based on a single O*NET measurement (i.e., manual work, fine motor skills), while the remaining seven are composites that draw on a host of O*NET ratings. The scale for strength, for example, is a composite of five task measurements pertaining to the extent to which the occupation demands (a) general physical activities, (b) explosive strength, (c) dynamic strength, (d) trunk strength, and (e) static strength. The final scheme, as represented in Table 58.1, includes measures of manual work, strength, robustness, mathematical skills, problem-solving skills, technical demands, exercise of authority, fine motor skills, and sociability. The first seven measures pertain to skills or demands that are presumed to be male-typed, while the last two pertain to skills or demands that are presumed to be female-typed (see Cejka and Eagly [1999] for evidence on those presumptions). We applied the factor score weights (as shown in Table 58.1) from our nine-factor confirmatory model to construct the final measures of these nine essentialist dimensions.

TABLE 58.1 Descriptions and Factor Loadings for Gradational and Essentialist Measures

Factor	Indicator	Loading
A. Gradational		
Wage (V1)	Proportion Hourly Earnings > $19.19	1.00
Prestige (V2)	Occupational Prestige	1.00
B. Physical Essentialism		
Manual (E1)	Manual vs. Non-manual	1.00
Strength (E2)	Performing General Physical Activities	.84
	Explosive Strength	.92
	Dynamic Strength	.92
	Trunk Strength	.76
	Static Strength	.91
Robustness (E3)	Outdoors or Exposed to Weather	.68
	Noise Levels Are Distracting	.86
	Very Hot or Cold Temperatures	.88
	Extremely Bright or Inadequate Lighting	.85
	Exposed to Whole Body Vibration	.74
	Exposed to High Places	.59
	Exposed to Hazardous Conditions	.71
	Exposed to Hazardous Equipment	.80
Fine Motor (E4)	Finger Dexterity	1.00
C. Analytical Essentialism		
Mathematical Skills (E5)	Mathematical Reasoning	.95
	Number Facility	.92
	Using Mathematics to Solve Problems	.81
	Processing Information	.71
Problem-Solving Skills (E6)	Critical Thinking	.93
	Judgment and Decision Making	.92
	Systems Analysis	.96
	Systems Evaluation	.96
	Making Decisions and Solving Problems	.82
D. Interactional Essentialism		
Technical (E7)	Equipment Selection	.62
	Installing Equipment	.82
	Equipment Maintenance	.92
	Repairing	.95
	Maintaining Mechanical Equipment	.88
	Maintaining Electronic Equipment	.60
Authority (E8)	Authority	.89
	Management of Personnel Resources	.92
	Coordinating Work of Others	.93
	Developing and Building Teams	.90
	Guiding, Dir., Motivating Subordinates	.94
	Coaching and Developing Others	.87
	Coordinating or Leading Others	.89
Sociability (E9)	Actively Looking for Ways to Help People	.81
	Social Service	.84
	Assisting and Caring for Others	.75
	Social Occupations	.87
	Active Listening	.85
	Talking with Others	.89
	Communicate Outside Org.	.88
	Maintaining Interpersonal Relationships	.87
	Contact with Others	.93
	Working Directly with the Public	.80

Note: The source for all variables, except occupational wages, is O*NET. The occupational wages were calculated with data from the one-percent micro-data sample of the 2000 Census. Factor loadings were obtained from confirmatory factor analysis using maximum likelihood estimation.

The segregation model estimated here also includes two measures of the vertical principle. Although the vertical principle is typically measured unidimensionally (e.g., Charles and Grusky 2011), we have distinguished between pay and prestige on the argument that different gender dynamics potentially underlie these two dimensions. In particular, the conventional argument is that women are more likely than men to trade off pay for prestige, a luxury that becomes possible insofar as women can rely upon their (male) spouses to deliver enough pay to meet household needs (see Rothstein and Rouse 2007; Magnusson 2009; Kleinjans, Krassel, and Dukes 2011). The tradeoff argument of course conditions on the premise that, because men are regarded as primary breadwinners, women have the freedom to consider high-prestige (but comparatively low-pay) occupations. Although the spread of liberal egalitarianism calls that premise increasingly into question, it is important to build a baseline model that allows for the possibility that it is still in play.

We have measured occupational prestige by exploiting a new O*NET scale pertaining to the degree to which occupational incumbents "are looked up to by others in their company and community" (Petersen et al. 1999; see Nakao and Treas 1994 for an overview of the measurement of occupational standing). Because O*NET does not provide good measures of pay, we have constructed our second vertical measure by analyzing the 2000 US Census Public Use Microdata (one-percent sample). We follow Hauser and Warren (1997) and their precursors (e.g., Blau and Duncan 1967) in using a wage threshold defined as the started logit of the percentage of workers (in the employed civilian labor force) within each occupation that earns $19.19 or more per hour.

A multidimensional segregation model

We have used the 2000 US Census Public Use Microdata to construct a 468 × 2 sex segregation array for the employed civilian labor force. We then apply the following association model to this array:

$$m_{ij} = a\beta_i\gamma_j\delta_1^{z_iV_j^1}\delta_2^{z_iV_j^2}\delta_3^{z_iE_j^1} ... \delta_{11}^{z_iE_j^9} \qquad (1)$$

where i refers to gender, j refers to occupation, m_{ij} refers to the expected value in the ij^{th} cell, α refers to the main effect, β_i refers to the marginal effect for

gender, γ_j refers to the marginal effects for occupation, Z_i is an indicator variable for gender (i.e., $Z_1=0$, $Z_2=1$), V^1 and V^2 are the scales for pay and prestige, E^1 through E^9 are the essentialist scales, and δ_1 through δ_{11} are the estimated parameters pertaining to the effects of pay, prestige, and the essentialist scales. The parameter estimates for this model, which are presented in Figure 58.1, have been standardized by fixing the mean of the independent variables at zero and their variance at one (except for the dummy-variable coefficient pertaining to the manual-nonmanual contrast).

We have stressed that there are two very distinct ways in which men may be advantaged in contemporary segregation regimes. If segregation were *entirely* essentialist in form, the tendency of men to secure more desirable occupations (i.e., those high in pay and prestige) would arise because such occupations "happen" to be ones that require attributes (e.g., authoritativeness, analytic skills) that men are understood to be more likely to hold. Although our full essentialist model might conceivably provide this complete account of segregation, it is also possible that, even after applying a full set of essentialist controls, men still have a substantial net advantage that cannot be legitimated in essentialist terms.

The results of Figure 58.1 show that a simple essentialist account is indeed inadequate. That is, we find that women are disadvantaged in terms of prestige as well as pay, with their disadvantage in pay slightly more prominent. But even the effects of prestige are nontrivial: The coefficient for prestige implies that female representation is reduced by a factor of .81 (i.e., $e^{-.21}=0.81$) for every standard deviation increase in occupational prestige (with a standard deviation of prestige equaling, for example, the difference between bank tellers and financial advisors). Taken together, the total disadvantage on the two vertical dimensions is sizable, and our main conclusion must therefore be that segregation is partly driven by vertical processes.

We next ask which forms of essentialism are especially important in generating sex segregation. The estimates of Figure 58.1 reveal that the physical dimension is, just as Charles and Grusky (2004, pp. 15-16) assumed, an extremely strong segregating force, although we also find that this dimension incorporates a wider range of effects than has typically been assumed. The well-appreciated effects of manual skill and strength are indeed quite strong, yet the

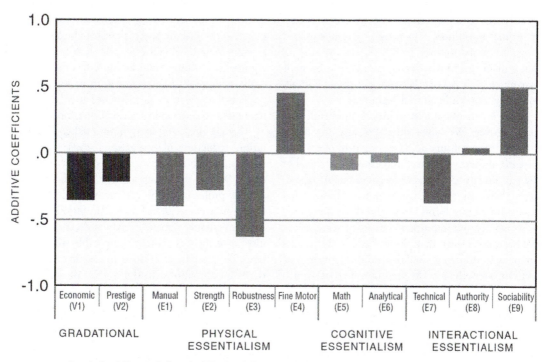

FIGURE 58.1 Analytical Essentialism is Weak while Physical and Interactional Essentialism are Strong

Note: All of the coefficients are significant at α = .01.

effects of robustness and fine motor skills, which are typically ignored, are yet stronger. The results presented in Figure 58.1 also clarify that some types of physical labor are the province of women (i.e., fine motor skills), other types are more integrated (i.e., strength), and yet other types are very much the province of men (i.e., robustness). It is *not* simply the case that men work with their hands and women with their "heart."

The more important point, however, is that the physical dimension hardly exhausts the forces of essentialism. The effects of interactional essentialism, especially sociability, are also quite strong, a result that again has not been properly incorporated into prior quantitative segregation models. The effects of analytic essentialism are, by contrast, surprisingly weak: We find that men are only slightly advantaged in the competition for problem-solving and mathematical occupations. As indicated in Figure 58.1, an increase of a full standard deviation in problem-solving reduces female representation by a factor of only 0.94, a relatively weak effect (i.e., $e^{-.06}=0.94$). Although we cannot of course speak directly to trend, these weak effects for problem-solving and mathematical essentialism are at least consistent with the

argument that, insofar as essentialism has been called into question, it has been a very partial and asymmetric questioning in which women are pursuing *some* male-typed tasks (e.g., problem-solving, mathematical) without men in turn pursuing *any* female-typed tasks (e.g., sociability, fine motor). The weakness of analytic essentialism suggests, then, that at least some forms of essentialism may be vulnerable to egalitarian drift. The analytic variant of essentialism appears to be weakening as some liberal parents encourage their daughters to become mathematicians, engineers, scientists, and other professions that draw heavily on mathematical or problem-solving skills. Within this vanguard population of anti-essentialists, it would appear that daughters are not simply being encouraged to invest heavily in human capital, but additionally they are being encouraged to target such investments in mathematical or problem-solving skills.

Conclusions

We led off this chapter with the promise that our comprehensive model would yield new insights into why occupational sex segregation in the early 21st

century is so extreme even after nearly a half-century of "gender revolution." The foregoing results indeed suggest a partial solution to this puzzle: We suspect that a main reason why segregation is so extreme is that much of it is essentialist in its sources and accordingly more difficult to delegitimate.

Why is our essentialist model so powerful? The main answer: We have taken seriously the many forms of essentialism and have sought to operationalize *all* of them. We have been especially critical of the past literature's exclusive focus on female-advantaging physical essentialism and have shown that male-advantaging forms, especially those pertaining to sociability, are important sources of segregation. We have also shown that physical essentialism takes on many forms that go well beyond the conventional focus on strength (e.g., the presumption that women have fine motor skills).

What are the implications of these results for the future of occupational segregation? As we see it, we are in the midst of two revolutions, the first being a "vertical revolution" that is still far from complete, and the second being an "essentialist revolution" that is yet more unfinished. Despite the current stalling out, our results lead us to believe that both revolutions are, over the *long run*, likely to continue to play out. The balance of this section, which is devoted to laying out this two-revolution account, is necessarily speculative given that our analyses are based on a single point in time.

With that important caveat in mind, we begin by discussing the likely future of the first "vertical revolution," a revolution that our results reveal to be quite incomplete. It is incomplete in the sense that, even when a full constellation of essentialist effects is fit, men still hold a substantial vertical advantage, especially with respect to pay but also for prestige. This result is inconsistent with the claim that sex segregation trends have recently "stalled out" because the easy reductions in vertical discrimination have been completely creamed off and left us with nothing but the more pernicious essentialist variant.

If contemporary segregation were *fully* essentialist in form, the tendency of men to secure more desirable occupations would arise entirely because such occupations were ones requiring skills that men are understood as holding. We have stressed that essentialist segregation is a pernicious form because it matches workers and occupations in ways that can (incorrectly) be presumed to be the outcome of differential tastes and choice (see Cech 2013). The

vertical component to segregation cannot be legitimated in this fashion and may instead be understood as vulnerable to liberal egalitarian critique. By this argument, nothing could be more favorable for the egalitarian project than to find a strong vertical component to segregation, precisely because that component lacks an essentialist legitimation propping it up.

There is, then, ample room for further "first revolution" reductions in segregation because the vertical residual, which remains strong, is vulnerable to critique. When, for example, it is pointed out that physics professors (who are mainly male) are paid more, on average, than biology professors (who are more frequently female), this may lead to "pay equity" investigatory panels, comparable worth initiatives, or other interventions to equalize pay across the two occupations. In the context of our models, these changes in pay practices would (a) initially reduce vertical segregation (by equalizing the pay of biology and physics professors), and (b) ultimately trigger some occupational integration by raising the status and pay of biology and rendering that occupation more attractive to men. The simple upshot: Because our models reveal a large residue of inequality that cannot be justified in liberal-egalitarian terms, it seems likely that conventional liberal-egalitarian efforts to reduce those inequalities will continue apace. If this reasoning is on the mark, it means that the first revolution is far from over and that much headway in reducing vertical inequalities can still be made. At the same time, we cannot rule out the possibility that the recent slowdown arises in part because the remaining vertical inequality, while still substantial, is nonetheless less egregious and obvious than earlier forms.

This suggests that it will become increasingly necessary to rely on a "second revolution" that takes on essentialist segregation. Is there reason to believe that this second revolution can be successfully waged? The standard story here is of course a worrying one. Because the essentialist form involves segregating workers in ways that can be represented as the outcome of gender-specific tastes, it *can* be legitimated in liberal-egalitarian terms and may be protected against efforts to take it on (see Cech 2013). For a liberal egalitarian, one must defend the right of women to freely and fairly compete for any occupation to which they aspire, but there is no corollary obligation to examine how those aspirations were formed or why they may differ from men's. Although radical egalitarians may complain, for example, about the disproportionate number of female pediatricians and their relatively low pay, their concerns are unlikely to gain traction because of the seductive essentialist story that legitimates such segregation as well as the inequality in remuneration that so often goes with it. Namely, liberal egalitarians will understand essentialist segregation as arising, in part, from the exogenous tastes of women, implying that the wage penalty they suffer is compensated by the extra utility they derive from realizing their tastes for sociable or nurturant work.

The results presented here suggest that this standard account can be too strongly put. It ignores the growing popularity of a counter-narrative that represents tastes and aspirations as socially constructed rather than exogenous and wholly beyond the purview of intervention. The case of analytic essentialism is instructive in making this point. For many egalitarian parents, the current fashion is to carefully cultivate the cognitive and analytic abilities of their daughters, a commitment that leads them to press their daughters to become engineers or scientists and thereby call analytic essentialism into question (see Grusky and Levanon 2008). If indeed parents, peers, and other role models are increasingly committed to supporting and even fostering an analytic sensibility among girls, then this is surely inconsistent with a simplistic brand of liberal egalitarianism that treats tastes and capacities as straightforwardly exogenous. There is arguably a new breed of parents, peers, and role models who are under the full sway of a "sociological narrative" about the social construction of tastes and accordingly understand it as their duty and responsibility to cultivate tastes that call conventional forms of essentialism into question.

It is at this point that one might worry that we have reached the limits of this new sociology-informed brand of egalitarianism. The twofold problem in this regard is that (a) analytic essentialism is already very weak and does not allow for much in the way of further change, and (b) the main remaining forms of essentialism that might be undermined (i.e., interactional essentialism) appear to require changes in the socialization of boys rather than girls. The latter changes are of course conventionally regarded as very difficult to secure. As England (2010) has stressed, there is a disturbingly asymmetric structure to contemporary changes in gender inequality, with women adopting stereotypically male roles and men, by contrast, evincing a quite limited inclination to reciprocate by adopting stereotypically

female roles. By this logic, analytic essentialism was readily undermined because it merely required changes in how girls were socialized, whereas interactional essentialism will be more difficult to undermine because doing so requires changing how *boys* are socialized. The delegitimation of analytical essentialism was in this sense an "easy win" and may not presage more widespread changes in other forms of essentialism.

We are not entirely persuaded by these worries. After all, there is no necessary reason why analytic essentialism is fated to simply wither away (i.e., converge to zero), indeed to the contrary it may well reverse sign and come to privilege women. If the payoff to analytic skills remains large despite the influx of women into the analytic skills sector, a sign reversal of this sort would bring about further reductions in the pay gap (see England 2010). This type of change, far from bespeaking the end of essentialism, instead entails the rise of female-advantaging essentialism. If we are right to worry that men may come to eschew disadvantaging definitions of masculinity (based on simple physicality), this sign reversal could nicely counter other declines in female-advantaging essentialism.

There is also good reason to challenge the conventional view that interactional essentialism can only be undermined by inducing men to value sociability and interactional skills. Although there is much to suggest that just such a change is in fact underway within some contemporary subcultures (e.g., "emo boys"), the more important point is that interactional essentialism can decline even in the absence of boy-led change. This decline can also be triggered insofar as egalitarian parents, peers, and teachers come to deemphasize the importance of cultivating nurturing and sociability among girls. If fewer women then come to pursue nurturing jobs (e.g., nurse, childcare worker), the resulting labor shortage will impel employers to raise the wages for such jobs to a level that may be above many men's reservation wage for them. Indeed, insofar as young men continue to face profound employment problems, a woman-led decline in interactional essentialism seems altogether likely.

This is all to suggest that, despite the current stalling out, the *long-term* forces making for a decline in vertical and essentialist segregation are very much in play. The residual of vertical segregation, which is substantial, is still deeply vulnerable because it does not comport well with the liberal egalitarian vision.

We have sought to stress that, because so much vertical segregation remains, there likewise remains much "first revolution" work still to be carried out. Moreover, when the vertical parameter finally begins to approach zero and the first revolution begins to dissipate, it may be overtaken by a second "sociological" revolution that represents tastes, capacities, and aspirations as highly constructed and that therefore delegitimates essentialist-backed segregation. Because so much of contemporary segregation has an essentialist backing, this second revolution has the capacity, once it is unleashed, to bring about especially dramatic change in gender inequality.

REFERENCES

Blackburn, Robert M., Bradley Brooks, and Jennifer Jarman. 2001. "Occupational Stratification: The Vertical Dimension of Occupational Segregation." *Work, Employment and Society* 15: 511–538.

Blackburn, Robert M., Jennifer Jarman, and Bradley Brooks. 2000. "The Puzzle of Gender Segregation and Inequality: A Cross-National Analysis." *European Sociological Review* 16: 119-135.

Blau, Peter and Otis D. Duncan. 1967. https://ssl.haifa.ac.il/ERICWebPortal/search/,DanaInfo=eric.ed.gov+detailmini.jsp?_nfpb=true&_&ERICExtSearch_SearchValue_0=ED066526&ERICExtSearch_SearchType_0=no&accno=ED066526 *The American Occupational Structure*. New York: John Wiley & Sons.

Blau, Francine D., and Lawrence M. Kahn. 2011. "The Gender Pay Gap: Have Women Gone as Far as They Can?" Pp. 549-66 in *The Inequality Reader: Contemporary and Foundational Readings in Race, Class, and Gender*, Edited by David B. Grusky and Szonja Szeléni. Boulder, CO: Westview Press.

Blau, Francine D., and Lawrence M. Kahn. 2016. "The Gender Wage Gap: Extent, Trends, and Explanations." *National Bureau of Economic Research*, Working Paper 21913.

Blau, Francine D. 2012. "The Sources of the Gender Pay Gap." Pp. 189-210 in *The New Gilded Age*, edited by David B. Grusky and Tamar Kricheli-Katz. Stanford: Stanford University Press.

Bridges, William P. 2003. "Rethinking Gender Segregation and Gender Inequality: Measures and Meanings." *Demography* 40: 543–568.

Cech, Erin A. 2013. "The Self-Expressive Edge of Occupational Sex Segregation." *American Journal of Sociology* 119: 747-789.

Cejka, Mary Ann and Alice H. Eagly. 1999. "Gender-Stereotypic Images of Occupations Correspond to the Sex Segregation of Employment." *Personality and Social Psychology Bulletin* 25:413–423.

Charles, Maria and David B. Grusky. 2004. *Occupational Ghettos: the Worldwide Segregation of Women and Men*. Stanford, CA: Stanford University Press.

Charles, Maria, and David B. Grusky. 2011. "Egalitarianism and Gender Inequality." Pp. 327-42 in *The Inequality Reader: Contemporary and Foundational Readings in Race, Class, and Gender*. Boulder, CO: Westview Press.

Correll, Shelley J. 2013. "Gender and Economic Inequality." Pp. 111-121, *Occupy the Future*, edited by David B. Grusky, Doug McAdam, Rob Reich and Debra Satz. Cambridge: MIT Press.

Cotter, David A., Joan M. Hermsen, and Reeve Vanneman. 2011. "The End of the Gender Revolution? Gender Role Attitudes from 1977 to 2008." *American Journal of Sociology* 117: 259-89.

Deaux, Kay and Marianne LaFrance. 1998. "Gender." Pp. 982-1026 in *The Handbook of Social Psychology*, edited by Daniel T. Gilbert, Susan T. Fiske, and Gardner Lindzey. New York: McGraw-Hill.

Paula England. 2015. "The Incomplete Gender Revolution." *Silver Dialogues*. Online at: http://silverdialogues.fas.nyu.edu/page/appointed

England, Paula. 2010. "The Gender Revolution: Uneven and Stalled." *Gender and Society* 24:149-166.

Gerson, Kathleen. 2015. "There's No Such Thing as Having It All: Gender, Work, & Care in an Age of Insecurity." In *Gender (In)equality: Stalled Revolutions and Shifting Terrains in the 21st Century*, edited by Shannon N. Davis, David J. Maume, and Sarah Winslow.

Gerson, Kathleen. 2011. *The Unfinished Revolution: How a New Generation is Reshaping Family, Work, and Gender in America*. Oxford: Oxford University Press.

Grusky David B. and Asaf Levanon. 2008. "Four Gloomy Futures for Sex Segregation." Pp. 812-825 in *Social Stratification: Class, Race, and Gender in Sociological Perspective*, 3rd edition, edited by David B. Grusky, Manwai C. Ku and Szonja Szelényi. Boulder, CO: Westview Press.

Hauser, Robert M. and John Robert Warren. 1997. "Socioeconomic Indexes for Occupations: A Review, Update, and Critique." *Sociological Methodology* 27:177–298.

Jacobs, Jerry A. 2001. "Evolving Patterns of Sex Segregation." Pp. 535-550 in *Sourcebook of Labor Markets: Evolving Structures and Processes*, edited by Ivar Berg and Arne L. Kalleberg New York: Kluwer Academic.

Kleinjans, Kristin J., Karl Fritjof Krassel, and Anthony Dukes. 2011. "Explaining Gender Differences in Occupational Choice: Do Women Place Relatively Less Weight on Wages and More Weight on Social Prestige?" Working paper, Univ. of Southern California, Marshall School of Business.

Levanon, Asaf, Paula England, and Paul Allison. 2009. "Occupational Feminization and Pay: Assessing Causal Dynamics Using 1950-2000 Census Data." *Social Forces* 88: 865–892.

Lueptow, Lloyd B., Lori Garovich-Szabo, and Margaret B. Leuptow. 2001. "Social Change and the Persistence of Sex Typing: 1974-1997." *Social Forces* 80:1–36.

Magnusson, Charlotta. 2009. "Gender, Occupational Prestige, and Wages: A Test of Devaluation Theory." *European Sociological Review* 25: 81–101.

Nakao, Keiko and Judith Treas. 1994. "Updating Occupational Prestige and Socioeconomic Scores: How the New Measures Measure Up." *Sociological Methodology* 24: 1–72.

Peterson, Norman. G. Michael D. Mumford, Walter C. Borman, P Richaerd Jeanneret and Edward A. Fleishman. 1999. *An Occupational Information system for the 21st Century: The Development of O*NET.* Washington, DC: APA Books.

Polachek, Solomon. 2012. "A Human Capital Account of the Gender Pay Gap." Pp. 161-188 in The New Gilded Age, edited by David B. Grusky and Tamar Kricheli-Katz. Stanford: Stanford University Press.

Ridgeway, Cecilia. 2014. "The Persistence of Gender Inequality." *Social Stratification: Class, Race, and Gender in Sociological Perspective*, 4th edition, edited by David B. Grusky and Katherine Weisshaar. Boulder: Westview Press.

Rothstein, J., and C. Rouse. 2007. "Constrained After College: Student Loans and Early Career Occupational Choices." NBER Working Paper 13117.

Spence, Janet T. 1993. "Gender-Related Traits and Gender Ideology: Evidence for a Multifactorial Theory." *Journal of Personality and Social Psychology* 64:624-635.

Stone, Pamela. 2009. "Getting to Equal: Progress, Pitfalls, and Policy Solutions on the Road to Gender Parity in the Workplace." *Pathways* (Spring): 3-7.

Williams, John E. and Deborah L. Best. 1990. *Measuring Sex Stereotypes: a Multination Study.* Newbury Park, CA.: Sage.

Zemore, Sarah E., Susan T. Fiske, and Hyun-Jeong Kim. 2000. "Gender Stereotypes and the Dynamics of Social Interaction." Pp. 207-241 in *The Developmental Social Psychology of Gender*, edited by Thomas Eckes and Hanns M. Trautner. Mahwah, NJ: Lawrence Erlbaum Associates, Publishers.

How Much Discrimination Is There?

59. Claudia Goldin and Cecilia Rouse*

Orchestrating Impartiality: The Impact of "Blind" Auditions on Female Musicians

Sex-biased hiring has been alleged for many occupations but is extremely difficult to prove. The empirical literature on discrimination, deriving from the seminal contributions of Gary Becker (1971) and Kenneth Arrow (1973), has focused mainly on disparities in earnings between groups (e.g., males and females), given differences in observable productivity-altering characteristics. With the exception of various audit studies (e.g., Genevieve Kenney and Douglas A. Wissoker, 1994; David Neumark et al., 1996) and others, few researchers have been able to address directly the issue of bias in hiring practices. A change in the way symphony orchestras recruit musicians provides an unusual way to test for sex-biased hiring.

Until recently, the great symphony orchestras in the United States consisted of members who were largely handpicked by the music director. Although virtually all had auditioned for the position, most of the contenders would have been the (male) students of a select group of teachers. In an attempt to overcome this seeming bias in the hiring of musicians, most major US orchestras changed their audition policies in the 1970s and 1980s, making them more

*Claudia Goldin and Cecilia Rouse. "Orchestrating Impartiality: The Impact of 'Blind' Auditions on Female Musicians," *American Economic Review* 90 (2000), pp. 715–726, 734–738, 740–741. Reprinted by permission of the *American Economic Review* and the authors. As published in *Social Stratification: Class, Race, and Gender in Sociological Perspective*, 3rd edition, by David Grusky, copyright © 2009. Reprinted by permission of Westview Press, an imprint of Perseus Books, LLC, a subsidiary of Hachette Book Group, Inc.

open and routinized. Openings became widely advertised in the union papers, and many positions attracted more than 100 applicants where fewer than twenty would have been considered before. Audition committees were restructured to consist of members of the orchestra, not just the conductor and section principal. The audition procedure became democratized at a time when many other institutions in America did as well.

But democratization did not guarantee impartiality, because favorites could still be identified by sight and through resumes. Another set of procedures was adopted to ensure, or at least give the impression of, impartiality. These procedures involve hiding the identity of the player from the jury. Although they take several forms, we use the terms "blind" and "screen" to describe the group. The question we pose is whether the hiring process became more impartial through the use of blind auditions. Because we are able to identify sex, but no other characteristics, for a large sample, we focus on the impact of the screen on the employment of women.

Screens were not adopted by all orchestras at once. Among the major orchestras, one still does not have any blind round to their audition procedure (Cleveland) and one adopted the screen in 1952 for the preliminary round (Boston Symphony Orchestra), decades before the others. Most other orchestras shifted to blind preliminaries from the early 1970s to the late 1980s. The variation in screen adoption at various rounds in the audition process allows us to assess its use as a treatment.

The change in audition procedures with the adoption of the screen allows us to test whether bias exists in its absence. In both our study and studies using audits, the issue is whether sex (or race or ethnicity), apart from objective criteria (e.g., the sound of a musical performance, the content of a resume), is considered in the hiring process. Why sex might make a difference is another matter. . . .

Sex Composition of Orchestras

Symphony orchestras consist of about 100 musicians and, although the number has varied between ninety and 105, it is rarely lower or higher. The positions, moreover, are nearly identical between orchestras and over time. As opposed to firms, symphony orchestras do not vary much in size and have virtually identical numbers and types of jobs. Thus we can easily look at the proportion of women in an orchestra without being concerned about changes in the composition of occupations and the number of workers. An increase in the number of women from, say, one to ten cannot arise because the number of harpists (a female-dominated instrument) has greatly expanded. It must be because the proportion female within many groups has increased.

Among the five highest-ranked orchestras in the nation (known as the "Big Five")—the Boston Symphony Orchestra (BSO), the Chicago Symphony Orchestra, the Cleveland Symphony Orchestra, the New York Philharmonic (NYPhil), and the Philadelphia Orchestra—none contained more than 12 percent women until about 1980.[1] As can be seen in Figure 59.1A, each of the five lines (giving the proportion female) greatly increases after some point. For the NYPhil, the line steeply ascends in the early 1970s. For the BSO, the turning point appears to be a bit earlier. The percentage female in the NYPhil is currently 35 percent, the highest among all eleven orchestras in our sample after being the lowest (generally at zero) for decades. Thus the increase of women in the nation's finest orchestras has been extraordinary. The increase is even more remarkable because, as we discuss below, turnover in these orchestras is exceedingly low. The proportion of new players who were women must have been, and indeed was, exceedingly high.

Similar trends can be discerned for four other orchestras—the Los Angeles Symphony Orchestra (LA), the San Francisco Philharmonic (SF), the Detroit Symphony Orchestra, and the Pittsburgh Symphony Orchestra (PSO)—given in Figure 59.1B.[2] The upward trend in the proportion female is also obvious in Figure 59.1B, although initial levels are higher than in Figure 59.1A. There is somewhat more choppiness to the graph, particularly during the 1940s. Although we have tried to eliminate all substitute, temporary, and guest musicians, especially during World War II and the Korean War, this was not always possible.

The only way to increase the proportion women is to hire more female musicians and turnover during most periods was low. The number of new hires is graphed in Figure 59.2 for five orchestras. Because "new hires" is a volatile construct, we use a centered five-year moving average. In most years after the late 1950s, the top-ranked orchestras in the group (Chicago and NYPhil) hired about four musicians a year, whereas the other three hired about six. Prior to 1960 the numbers are extremely high for LA and the PSO, because, it has been claimed, their music directors exercised their power to terminate, at will, the employment of musicians. Also of interest is that the number of new hires trends down, even excluding years prior to 1960. The important points to take from Figure 59.2 are that the number of new hires was small after 1960 and that it declined over time.

The proportion female among the new hires must have been sizable to increase the proportion female in the orchestras. Figure 59.3 shows the trend in the share of women among new hires for four of the "Big Five" (Figure 59.3A) and four other orchestras (Figure 59.3B).[3] In both groups the female share of new hires rose over time, at a somewhat steeper rate for the more prestigious orchestras. Since the early 1980s the share female among new hires has been about 35 percent for the BSO and Chicago, and about 50 percent for the NYPhil, whereas before 1970 less than 10 percent of new hires were women.

Even though the fraction of new hires who are female rises at somewhat different times across the orchestras, there is a discernible increase for the group as a whole from the late 1970s to early 1980s, a time when the labor force participation of women increased generally and when their participation in various professions greatly expanded. The question, therefore, is whether the screen mattered in a direct manner or whether the increase was the result of a host of other factors, including the appearance of impartiality or an increased pool of female contestants coming out of music schools. Because the majority of new hires are in their late twenties and early thirties, the question is whether the most selective music schools were producing considerably more female students in the early 1970s. We currently have information by instrument for only the Juilliard School of Music. With the exception of the brass section, the data, given in Figure 59.4, do not reveal any sharp breaks in the fraction of all graduates who are female. Thus, it is not immediately obvious that an expansion in the supply of qualified female

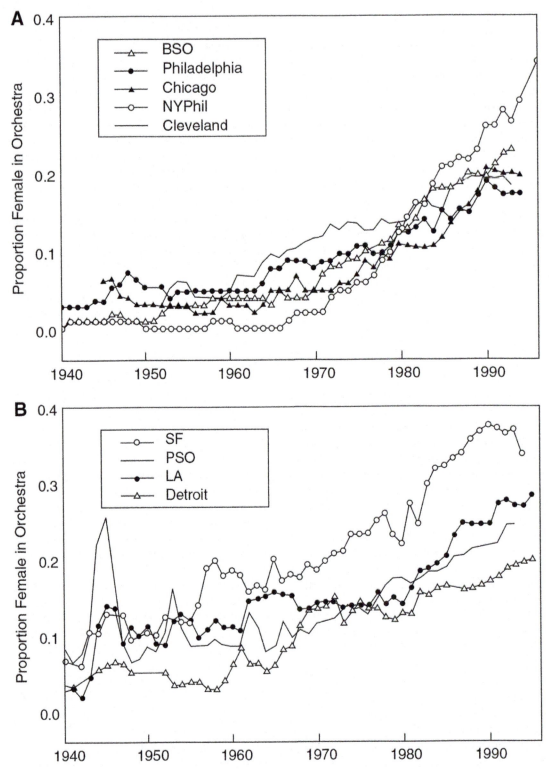

FIGURE 59.1 Proportion Female in Nine Orchestras, 1940 to 1990s. A: The "Big Five"; B: Four Others

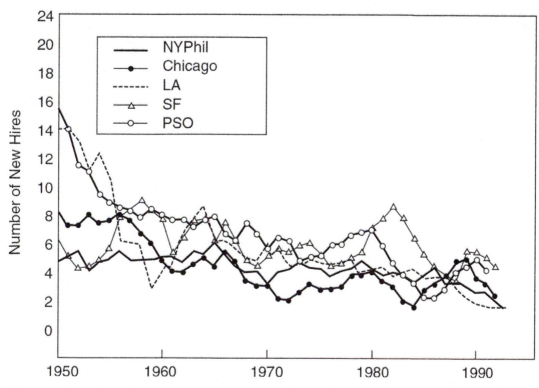

FIGURE 59.2 Number of New Hires in Five Orchestras, 1950 to 1990s

Source: Roster sample. See text.

musicians explains the marked increase in female symphony orchestra members; it could, therefore, be because of changes in the hiring procedures of orchestras.

But why would changes in audition procedures alter the sex mix of those hired? Many of the most renowned conductors have, at one time or another, asserted that female musicians are not the equal of male musicians. Claims abound in the world of music that "women have smaller techniques than men," "are more temperamental and more likely to demand special attention or treatment," and that "the more women [in an orchestra], the poorer the sound."[4] Zubin Mehta, conductor of the Los Angeles Symphony from 1964 to 1978 and of the New York Philharmonic from 1978 to 1990, is credited with saying, "I just don't think women should be in an orchestra."[5] Many European orchestras had, and some continue to have, stated policies not to hire women. The Vienna Philharmonic has only recently admitted its first female member (a harpist). Female musicians, it can be convincingly argued, have historically faced considerable discrimination. Thus a blind hiring procedure, such as a screen that conceals the identity of the musician auditioning, could eliminate the possibility of discrimination and increase the number of women in orchestras.

Orchestral Auditions

To understand the impact of the democratization of the audition procedure and the screen, we must first explain how orchestra auditions are now conducted. After determining that an audition must be held to fill an opening, the orchestra advertises that it will hold an audition. Each audition attracts musicians from across the country and, often, from around the world. Musicians interested in auditioning are required to submit a resume and often a tape of compulsory music (recorded according to specific guidelines) to be judged by members of the orchestra. In some orchestras this prescreening is dispositive; in others the musician has the right to audition live in the preliminary round, even if the audition committee rejects the candidate on the basis of the tape. All candidates are given, in advance, most of the music they are expected to perform at the live audition.

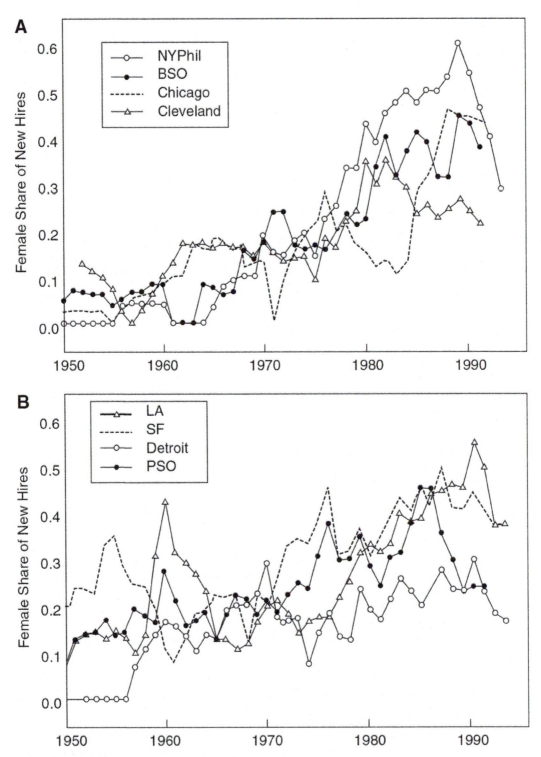

FIGURE 59.3 Female Share of New Hires in Eight Orchestras, 1950 to 1990s. A: Four of the "Big Five"; B: Four Others

Source: Roster sample. See text.

Note: A five-year centered moving average is used. New hires are musicians who were not with the orchestra the previous year, who remain for at least one additional year and who were not substitute musicians in the current year.

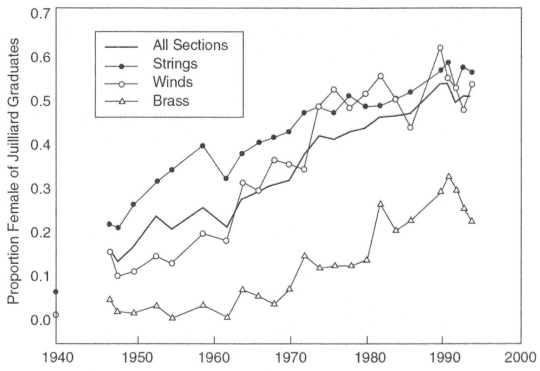

FIGURE 59.4 Proportion Female of Julliard Graduates, Total and by Section, 1947 to 1995
Source: Julliard Music School files.

Live auditions today generally consist of three rounds: preliminary, semifinal, and final. But there is considerable variation. Although all orchestras now have a preliminary round, some have two final rounds and in many there was no semifinal round until the 1980s. The preliminary is generally considered a screening round to eliminate unqualified candidates. As a result, the committee is free to advance as many, or as few, as they wish. Candidates advanced from the semifinal round are generally considered "acceptable for hire" by the audition committee (which does not include the music director, a.k.a. conductor, until the finals). Again, this means that the committee can advance as many as it wishes. The final round generally results in a hire but sometimes does not.

In blind auditions (or audition rounds) a screen is used to hide the identity of the player from the committee. The screens we have seen are either large pieces of heavy (but sound-porous) cloth, sometimes suspended from the ceiling of the symphony hall, or look like large room dividers. Some orchestras also roll out a carpet leading to center stage to muffle footsteps that could betray the sex of the candidate. Each candidate for a blind audition is given a number, and the jury rates the candidate's performance next to the number on a sheet of paper. Only the personnel manager knows the mapping from number to name and from name to other personal information. The names of the candidates are not revealed to the juries until after the last blind round.

Almost all preliminary rounds are now blind. The semifinal round, added as the number of applicants grew, may be blind. Finals are rarely blind and almost always involve the attendance and input of the music director. Although the music director still wields considerable power, the self-governance that swept orchestras in the 1970s has served to contain the conductor's authoritarianism. The music director can ignore the audition committee's advice, but does so at greater peril. Once an applicant is chosen to be a member of an orchestra, lifetime tenure is awarded after a brief probationary period. The basis for termination is limited and rarely used. The positions we are analyzing are choice jobs in the musical world. In 1995 the *minimum starting* base salary for musicians at the BSO was $1,400 per week (for a fifty-two-week year), not including recording contracts, soloist fees, overtime and extra service payments, bonuses, and per diem payments for tours and Tanglewood. . . .

TABLE 59.1 Orchestra Audition Procedure Summary Table

Orchestra	Preliminaries	Semifinals	Finals
A	Blind since 1973	Blind (varies) since 1973	Not blind
B	Blind since at least 1967	Use of screen varies	Blind 1967–1969; since winter 1994
C	Blind since at least 1979 (definitely after 1972)	Not blind: 1991–present Blind: 1984–1987	Not blind
D	Blind since 1986	Blind since 1986; varies until 1993	1st part blind since 1993; 2nd part not blind
E	Use of screen varies until 1981	Use of screen varies	Not blind
F	Blind since at least 1972	Blind since at least 1972	Blind since at least 1972
G	Blind since 1986	Use of screen varies	Not blind
H	Blind since 1970	Not blind	Not blind
I	Blind since 1979	Blind since 1979	Blind since fall 1983
J	Blind since 1952	Blind since 1952	Not blind
K	Not blind	Not blind	Not blind

Notes: The eleven orchestras (A through K) are those in the roster sample described in the text. A subset of eight form the audition sample (also described in the text). All orchestras in the sample are major big-city U.S. symphony orchestras and include the "Big Five."
Sources: Orchestra union contracts (from orchestra personnel managers and libraries), personal conversations with orchestra personnel managers, and our mail survey of current orchestra members who were hired during the probable period of screen adoption.

The audition procedures of the eleven orchestras in the roster sample are summarized in Table 59.1.[6] Although audition procedures are now part of union contracts, that was not the case in the more distant past and the procedures were not apparently recorded in any surviving documents. We gathered information on these procedures from various sources, including union contracts, interviews with personnel managers, archival documents on auditions, and a mail survey we conducted of orchestral musicians concerning the procedures employed during the audition that won them their current position.

An obvious question to ask is whether the adoption of the screen is endogenous. Of particular concern is that more meritocratic orchestras adopted blind auditions earlier, producing the spurious result that the screen increased the likelihood that women were hired.[7] We estimate a probit model of screen adoption by year, conditional on an orchestra's not previously having adopted the screen (an orchestra exits the exercise once it adopts the screen). Two time-varying covariates are included to assess commonly held notions about screen adoption: the proportion female (lagged) in the orchestra, and a measure of tenure (lagged) of then-current orchestra members. Tenure is included because personnel managers maintain the screen was advocated more by younger players.

As the proportion female in an orchestra increases, so does the likelihood of screen adoption in the preliminary round, as can be seen in columns (1) and (2) in Table 59.2, although the effects are very

small and far from statistically significant. We estimate a similar effect when we assess the role of female presence on the adoption of blind finals [see column (3)]. The impact of current tenure, measured by the proportion with less than six years with

TABLE 59.2 Estimated Probit Models for the Use of a Screen

	Preliminaries blind		Finals blind
	(1)	(2)	(3)
(Proportion female) $_{t-1}$	2.744	3.120	0.490
	(3.265)	(3.271)	(1.163)
	[0.006]	[0.004]	[0.011]
(Proportion of orchestra personnel with <6 years tenure) $_{t-1}$	−26.46	−28.13	−9.467
	(7.314)	(8.459)	(2.787)
	[−0.058]	[−0.039]	[−0.207]
"Big Five" orchestra		0.367	
		(0.452)	
		[0.001]	
pseudo R²	0.178	0.193	0.050
Number of observations	294	294	434

Notes: The dependent variable is 1 if the orchestra adopts a screen, 0 otherwise. Huber standard errors (with orchestra random effects) are in parentheses. All specifications include a constant. Changes in probabilities are in brackets. "Proportion female" refers to the entire orchestra. "Tenure" refers to years of employment in the current orchestra. "Big Five" includes Boston, Chicago, Cleveland, New York Philharmonic, and Philadelphia. The data begin in 1947 and an orchestra exits the exercise once it adopts the screen. The unit of observation is an orchestra-year.
Source: Eleven-orchestra roster sample. See text.

the orchestra, is—contrary to general belief—negative and the results do not change controlling for whether the orchestra is one of the "Big Five." In all, it appears that orchestra sex composition had little influence on screen adoption, although the stability of the personnel may have increased its likelihood.

The Role of Blind Auditions on the Audition and Hiring Process

A. Data and Methods

Audition Records. We use the actual audition records of eight major symphony orchestras obtained from orchestra personnel managers and the orchestra archives. The records are highly confidential and occasionally contain remarks (including those of the conductor) about musicians currently with the orchestra. To preserve the full confidentiality of the records, we have not revealed the names of the orchestras in our sample.

Although availability differs, taken together we obtained information on auditions dating from the late 1950s through 1995. Typically, the records are lists of the names of individuals who attended the auditions, with notation near the names of those advanced to the next round. For the preliminary round, this would indicate advancement to either the semifinal or final round. Another list would contain the names of the semifinalists or finalists with an indication of who won the audition. From these records, we recorded the instrument and position (e.g., section, principal, substitute) for which the audition was held. We also know whether the individual had an "automatic" placement in a semifinal or final round. Automatic placement occurs when a musician is already known to be above some quality cutoff and is invited to compete in a semifinal or final round. We also recorded whether the individual was advanced to the next round of the current audition.

We rely on the first name of the musicians to determine sex. For most names establishing sex was straightforward. Sexing the Japanese and Korean names was equally straightforward, at least for our Japanese and Korean consultants. For more difficult cases, we checked the names in three baby books (Connie Lockhard Ellefson, 1990; Alfred J. Kolatch, 1990; Bruce Lansky, 1995). If the name was listed as male- or female-only, we considered the sex known. The gender-neutral names (e.g., Chris, Leslie, and Pat) and some Chinese names (for which sex is indeterminate in the absence of Chinese characters) remained ambiguous. Using these procedures, we were able to determine the sex of 96 percent of our audition sample.

In constructing our analysis sample, we exclude incomplete auditions, those in which there were no women (or only women) competing, rounds from which no one was advanced, and the second final round, if one exists, for which the candidates played with the orchestra. In addition, we generally consider each round of the audition separately. These sample restrictions exclude 294 rounds (199 contained no women) and 1,539 individuals. Our final analysis sample has 7,065 individuals and 588 audition rounds (from 309 separate auditions) resulting in 14,121 person-rounds and an average of 2.0 rounds per musician. . . .

Roster Data. Our second source of information comes from the final results of the audition process, the orchestra personnel rosters. We collected these data from the personnel page of concert programs, one each year for eleven major symphony orchestras. These records are in the public domain, and thus we have used the orchestra names in the graphs containing those data alone. As opposed to the auditionees, we were able to confirm the sex of the players with the orchestra personnel managers and archivists. We considered a musician to be new to the orchestra in question if he or she had not previously been a regular member of that orchestra (i.e., we did not count returning members as new). We excluded, when possible, temporary and substitute musicians, as well as harpists and pianists. Our final sample for 1970 to 1996 has 1,128 new orchestra members. . . .

B. The Effect of the Screen on the Hiring of Women

Using the Audition Sample. We turn now to the effect of the screen on the actual hire and estimate the likelihood an individual is hired out of the initial audition pool.[8] Whereas the use of the screen for each audition round was, more or less, an unambiguous concept, that for the entire process is not and we must define a blind audition. The definition we have chosen is that a blind audition contains all rounds that use the screen. In using this definition, we compare auditions that are completely blind with those that do not use the screen at all or use it for the early rounds only. We divide the sample into auditions that have a semifinal round and those that do

TABLE 59.3 Linear Probability Estimates of the Effect of Blind Auditions on the Likelihood of Being Hired with Individual Fixed Effects

	Without semifinals		With semifinals		All	
	(1)	(2)	(3)	(4)	(5)	(6)
Completely blind	−0.024	0.047	0.001	0.006	0.001	0.005
audition	(0.028)	(0.041)	(0.009)	(0.011)	(0.008)	(0.009)
Completely blind	0.051	0.036	0.001	−0.004	0.011	0.006
audition X female	(0.046)	(0.048)	(0.016)	(0.016)	(0.013)	(0.013)
Year effects?	No	Yes	No	Yes	No	Yes
Other covariates?	No	Yes	No	Yes	No	Yes
R^2	0.855	0.868	0.692	0.707	0.678	0.691
Number of observations	4,108	4,108	5,883	5,883	9,991	9,991

Notes: The unit of observation is person-round. The dependent variable is 1 if the individual is advanced (or hired) from the final round and 0 if not. Standard errors are in parentheses. All specifications include individual fixed effects, whether the sex is missing, and an interaction for sex being missing and a completely blind audition. "Other covariates" are the size of the audition, the proportion female at the audition, the number of individuals advanced (hired), whether a "Big Five" orchestra, the number of previous auditions, and whether the individual had an automatic semifinal or final.
Source: Eight-orchestra audition sample. See text.

not, because the earlier analysis suggested they might differ (Goldin and Rouse 2000).

The impact of completely blind auditions on the likelihood of a woman's being hired is given in Table 59.3, for which all results include individual fixed effects.[9] The impact of the screen is positive and large in magnitude, but only when there is no semifinal round. Women are about 5 percentage points more likely to be hired than are men in a completely blind audition, although the effect is not statistically significant. The effect is nil, however, when there is a semifinal round. The impact for all rounds [columns (5) and (6)] is about 1 percentage point, although the standard errors are large and thus the effect is not statistically significant. Given that the probability of winning an audition is less than 3 percent, we would need more data than we currently have to estimate a statistically significant effect, and even a 1-percentage-point increase is large, as we later demonstrate.

Using the Roster Data. The roster data afford us another way to evaluate the effect of the screen on the sex composition of orchestras. Using the rosters, we know the sex of new hires each year for eleven orchestras, and we also have information (see Table 59.1) on the year the screen was adopted by each orchestra. We treat the orchestra position as the unit of observation and ask whether the screen affects the sex of the individual who fills the position. We model the likelihood that a female is hired in a particular year as a function of whether the orchestra's audition procedure involved a screen, again relying on the variation over time within a particular orches-

tra. Thus, in all specifications, we include orchestra fixed effects and an orchestra-specific time trend.

The roster data extend further back in time than do the audition data and could conceivably begin with the orchestra's founding, although there is no obvious reason to include many years when none used the screen. We report, in Table 59.4, the effects of the screen on the hiring of women from 1970 to 1996 using a probit model. The screen is first defined to include any blind auditions [column (1)]. In column (2) we estimate separate effects for orchestras using blind preliminary (and semifinal) rounds but not blind finals and those with completely blind auditions.

To interpret the probit coefficient, we first predict a base probability, under the assumption that each orchestra does not use a screen. We then predict a new probability assuming the orchestra uses a screen. The mean difference in the probabilities is given in brackets.

The coefficient on blind in column (1) is positive, although not significant at any usual level of confidence. The estimates in column (2) are positive and equally large in magnitude to those in column (1). Further, these estimates show that the existence of any blind round makes a difference and that a completely blind process has a somewhat larger effect (albeit with a large standard error). According to the point estimates in column (1) of Table 59.4, blind auditions increase the likelihood a female will be hired by 7.5 percentage points. The magnitude of the effect must be judged relative to the overall average and, for the period under consideration, it was about

TABLE 59.4 Probit Estimates of the Effect of Blind Auditions on the Sex of the New Members, 1970 to 1996

	Any blind auditions	Only blind preliminaries and/or semifinals vs. completely blind auditions
	(1)	(2)
Any blind auditions	0.238	
	(0.183)	
	[0.075]	
Only blind preliminaries and/or semifinals		0.232
		(0.184)
		[0.074]
Completely blind auditions		0.361
	(0.438)	
	[0.127]	
Section: Woodwinds	−0.187	−0.188
	(0.114)	(0.114)
Brass Percussion	[−0.058]	[−0.058]
	−1.239	−1.237
	(0.157)	(0.157)
	[−0.284]	[−0.284]
	−1.162	−1.164
	(0.305)	(0.305)
	[−0.235]	[−0.235]
p-value of test: only blind preliminaries and/or semifinals = completely blind	0.756	
pseudo R^2	0.106	0.106
Number of observations	1,128	1,128

Notes: The dependent variable is 1 if the individual is female and 0 if male. Standard errors are in parentheses. All specifications include orchestra fixed effects and orchestra-specific time trends. Changes in probabilities are in brackets; see text for an explanation of how they are calculated. New members are those who enter the orchestra for the first time. Returning members are not considered new. The omitted section is strings.
Source: Eleven-orchestra roster sample. See text.

30 percent. Thus blind auditions increased the likelihood a female would be hired by 25 percent.[10] . . .

Conclusion

The question is whether hard evidence can support an impact of discrimination on hiring. Our analysis of the audition and roster data indicates that it can, although we mention various caveats before we summarize the reasons. Even though our sample size is large, we identify the coefficients of interest from a much smaller sample. Some of our coefficients of interest, therefore, do not pass standard tests of statistical significance and there is, in addition, one persistent result that goes in the opposite direction. The weight of the evidence, however, is what we find most persuasive and what we have emphasized. . . .

As in research in economics and other fields on double-blind refereeing (see, e.g., Blank, 1991), the impact of a blind procedure is toward impartiality and the costs to the journal (here to the orchestra) are relatively small. We conclude that the adoption of the screen and blind auditions served to help female musicians in their quest for orchestral positions.

REFERENCES

Arrow, Kenneth. "The Theory of Discrimination," in Orley Ashenfelter and Albert Rees, eds., *Discrimination in labor markets*. Princeton, NJ: Princeton University Press, 1973, pp. 3–33.

Becker, Gary. *The economics of discrimination*, 2nd Ed. Chicago: University of Chicago Press, 1971 [orig. pub. 1957].

Blank, Rebecca. "The Effects of Double-Blind versus Single-Blind Refereeing: Experimental Evidence from the American Economic Review." *American Economic Review*, December 1991, 81(5), pp. 1041–67.

Ellefson, Connie Lockhard. *The melting pot book of baby names*, 2nd Ed. Cincinnati, OH: Better Way Books, 1990.

Goldin, Claudia and Cecilia Rouse. 2000. "Orchestrating Impartiality: The Impact of 'Blind' Auditions on Female Musicians." *American Economic Review* 90 (September): 715–741.

Kenney, Genevieve and Wissoker, Douglas A. "An Analysis of the Correlates of Discrimination Facing Young Hispanic Job-Seekers." *American Economic Review*, June 1994, 84(3), pp. 674–83.

Kolatch, Alfred J. *The Jonathan David dictionary of first names.* New York: Perigee Books, 1990.

Lansky, Bruce. *35,000+ baby names.* New York: Meadowbrook Press, 1995.

Neumark, David (with Bank, Roy and Van Nort, Kyle D.). "Sex Discrimination in Restaurant Hiring: An Audit Study." *Quarterly Journal of Economics*, August 1996, 111(3), pp. 915–41.

Seltzer, George. *Music matters: The performer and the American Federation of Musicians.* Metuchen, NJ: Scarecrow Press, 1989.

NOTES

1. The data referred to, and used in Figures 59.1 to 59.3, are from orchestral rosters, described in more detail below.

2. Our roster sample also includes the Metropolitan Opera Orchestra and the St. Louis Symphony.

3. A centered five-year moving average is also used for this variable.

4. Seltzer (1989), p. 215.

5. Seltzer (1989), p. 215.

6. We identify the orchestras by letter, rather than by name, to preserve confidentiality of the audition sample.

7. Note, however, it is unlikely that the orchestras that sought to hire more women chose to adopt the screen earlier since the best way to increase the number of women in the orchestra is to have not-blind auditions (so that one could be sure to hire more women).

8. The original article (Goldin and Rouse 2000) includes much additional analysis examining the effect of the screen on the likelihood of being advanced through each stage of the audition process.—EDS

9. There are four auditions in which the committee could not choose between two players and therefore asked each to play with the orchestra. We consider both to be winners. The results are not sensitive to this classification. For this analysis we exclude auditions with no women, all women, or no winner; these exclusions do not change the results.

10. In Table 59.3 we are identified off of individuals who competed in auditions that were completely blind *and* those that were not completely blind (that is, *any* one round could not be blind). The unit of observation is the person-round and there are ninety-two fulfilling this criterion for auditions without a semifinal [columns (1) and (2)]; on average these persons competed in 3.6 auditions in this sample. There are 625 person-rounds fulfilling this criterion that included a semifinal [columns (3) and (4)] and on average these persons competed in 3.5 auditions in this sample. Finally, there are 911 person-rounds fulfilling this criterion across all auditions [columns (5) and (6)] and on average these persons competed in 3.5 auditions in this sample. The sample off of which we are identified is larger for all auditions than for the sum of the other two because some individuals auditioned both with and without a semifinal round.

---

60. Shelley J. Correll, Stephen Benard, and In Paik*
Getting a Job: Is There a Motherhood Penalty?

Mothers experience disadvantages in the workplace in addition to those commonly associated with gender. Recent studies show employed mothers in the United States suffer a 5 percent per-child wage penalty on average after controlling for the usual human capital and occupational factors that affect wages (Budig and England 2001; Anderson, Binder, and Krause 2003). The pay gap between mothers and nonmothers under age thirty-five is larger than the pay gap between men and women (Crittenden 2001), and employed mothers now account for most of the "gender gap" in wages (Glass 2004).

The disadvantages are not limited to pay. Describing a consultant as a mother leads evaluators to rate her as less competent than when she is described as not having children (Cuddy, Fiske, and Glick 2004), and visibly pregnant managers are judged as less committed to their jobs, less dependable, less authoritative, but warmer, more emotional, and more irrational than otherwise equal women managers (Halpert, Wilson, and Hickman 1993; Corse 1990). While the pattern is clear, the underlying mechanism remains opaque. Why would being a parent lead to disadvantages in the workplace for women?

*The ideas, issues, and theories considered in this brief piece are examined in greater depth in the following publication: Shelley J. Correll, Stephen Benard, and In Paik, "Getting a Job: Is There a Motherhood Penalty?" *American Journal of Sociology* 112 (March 2007), pp. 1297–1338, published by the University of Chicago Press. The article as printed here was originally prepared for *Social Stratification: Class, Race, and Gender in Sociological Perspective*, 3rd Edition by David B. Grusky, pp. 759–770. Copyright © 2009. Reprinted by permission of Westview Press, an imprint of Perseus Books, LLC, a subsidiary of Hachette Book Group, Inc.

And why might similar disadvantages not occur for men?

This paper presents a laboratory experiment and an audit study. The laboratory experiment evaluates the hypothesis that the "motherhood penalty" occurs because cultural understandings of motherhood lead evaluators to, perhaps unconsciously, expect mothers to be less competent and less committed to their jobs (Blair-Loy 2003; Ridgeway and Correll 2004). As a result, we argue, employers will discriminate against mothers when making hiring, promotion, and salary decisions. We do not expect fathers to experience similar workplace disadvantages since being a good father is not seen in our culture as incompatible with being a good worker (Townsend 2002). By having participants rate job applicants, we expect that applicants presented as women with children will be viewed as less competent and less committed to work, will need to present evidence that they are more qualified for the job, will be rated as less promotable, and will be offered lower starting salaries compared with otherwise similar applicants presented as women without children. While the laboratory experiment isolates and examines the mechanism of discrimination, the audit study provides external validity by evaluating whether actual employers discriminate against mothers.

Wage Penalty for Motherhood

Explanations for the motherhood wage penalty generally can be classified as worker explanations, which seek to identify differences in the traits, skills, and behaviors between mothers and nonmothers, and discrimination explanations, which rely on the differential preference for or treatment of mothers and nonmothers. Empirical evaluations of these explanations have largely focused on the former.

Budig and England (2001) find that interruptions from work, working part-time, and decreased seniority/experience collectively explain no more than about one-third of the motherhood penalty. In addition, "mother-friendly" job characteristics (i.e., differences in the type of jobs chosen) explain very little of the penalty. Similarly, Anderson, Binder, and Krause (2003) find that human capital and occupational and household resource variables (e.g., number of adults in household) collectively account for 24 percent of the total penalty for one child and 44 percent for women with two or more children. As Budig and England (2001) conclude, the remaining wage gap likely arises either because mothers are

somehow less productive at work than nonmothers, or because employers discriminate against mothers (or some combination of the two processes).

Productivity and Discrimination

To distinguish between discrimination and productivity explanations, ideally one would compare the outcomes of employed mothers and nonmothers who have equal levels of workplace productivity. If differences in pay or promotion rates were found between equally productive mothers and nonmothers, this would suggest that discrimination factors were at work. However, the datasets analyzed in the previous studies lack direct measures of worker productivity. One likely reason for this is that it is inherently problematic to specify what makes someone a productive employee. This difficulty leads to another: unexplained gaps in wages between employed mothers and nonmothers can always be attributed to unmeasured productivity differences between the two groups.

To address these problems, we experimentally held constant the workplace performances and other relevant characteristics of a pair of fictitious job applicants and varied only their parental status. By holding constant workplace-relevant characteristics, differences between the ratings of mothers and nonmothers cannot be attributed to productivity or skill differences. While this design cannot rule out the possibility that productivity differences account for part of the wage penalty found in previous studies, the laboratory study will isolate a potential status-based discrimination mechanism by evaluating whether being a parent disadvantages mothers in the workplace even when no productivity differences exist between them and women without children.

Performance Expectations and Evaluations of Workplace Competence

Status Characteristics Theory

The laboratory study evaluates the theoretical claim that motherhood is a "status characteristic" that, when salient, results in biased evaluations of competence and commitment, a stricter standard for evaluating the workplace performances of mothers, and a bias against mothers in hiring, promotion, and salary decisions. A status characteristic is a categorical distinction among people, such as race or occupational status, that has attached to it widely held cultural beliefs associating greater status worthiness and competence with one category of the distinction over others (Berger et al. 1977).

Theory and empirical research suggest that ability standards are stricter for those with lower performance expectations (Foschi 1989). The logic behind this prediction is that good performances are inconsistent with expectations for lower status actors; therefore, when they perform well, their performances are critically scrutinized and judged by a stricter standard compared with higher status actors. Thus, performances of low-status actors—even when "objectively" equal to that of their high-status counterparts—are less likely to be judged as demonstrating task ability or competence (for a comparison of status discrimination and economic theories of statistical discrimination, see Correll and Benard 2006).

Motherhood as a Status Characteristic

To understand how motherhood might function as a devalued status characteristic in workplace settings, it is helpful to broaden the conventional usage of "performance expectations." While researchers typically focus on the anticipated relative *competence* of group members, cultural beliefs about the relative *effort* that social groups exert in task situations can also be the basis for forming differentiated performance expectations. While it is logically difficult to understand why taking on the motherhood role should affect a person's underlying competence, there is considerable evidence that contemporary cultural beliefs assume that employed mothers are less committed to work than nonmothers, and consequently, put less *effort* into it (Ridgeway and Correll 2004). Motherhood affects perceptions of commitment because contradictory schemas govern conceptions of "family devotion" and "work devotion" (Blair-Loy 2003: 5). A cultural norm that mothers should always be on call for their children coexists in tension with another widely held normative belief in our society that the "ideal worker" be unencumbered by competing demands and "always there" for his or her employer (Acker 1990; Hays 1996; Williams 2001; Blair-Loy 2003). The tension between these two roles occurs at the level of normative cultural assumptions, and not necessarily at the level of mothers' own commitment to work. Indeed, Bielby and Bielby (1984) found no differences in the workplace commitment of mothers and nonmothers. Instead it is the *perceived* tension between these

two roles that leads us to suggest that motherhood is a devalued status in workplace settings.

Therefore, we predict that mothers will be rated as less competent, less committed, less suitable for hire and promotion, and deserving of lower starting salaries compared with otherwise equal women who are not mothers. In addition, we expect mothers will be judged by a harsher standard. Since being a good father is not seen as culturally incompatible with being an ideal worker (Townsend 2002), we do not expect that fathers will experience lower workplace evaluations.

The Laboratory Experiment

Paid undergraduate volunteers (84 men and 108 women) rated a pair of equally qualified, same-gender (either male or female), same-race (either African American or white) fictitious job applicants, presented as real, who differed on parental status. Since there were very few significant effects of participant gender or applicant race, we do not discuss these results here.

The Use of Undergraduates

The laboratory setting ensures sufficient control over factors that would interfere with tests of our hypotheses, such as other people in the room to prime other status characteristics, telephones, or other distractions, and it allows us to collect detailed measures to fully test our argument. By necessity we rely on a sample of undergraduates. The theory presented here implies that to the extent that employers share the belief that mothers are less committed to or competent in workplace settings, they too will subtly discriminate against mothers. Qualitative and quantitative research provides some evidence that employers share this belief (Blair-Loy 2003; Crittenden 2001; Kennelly 1999; Cleveland and Berman 1987; Cleveland 1991; Olian and Schwab 1988). The audit study, described below, will provide more direct evidence regarding the extent to which employers discriminate against mothers.

Procedure

Participants read a description of a company that was purportedly hiring for a mid-level marketing position and examined application materials for two equally qualified applicants who differed on parental status. To increase their task orientation, participants were told that their input would impact actual hiring decisions. They then inspected each applicant's file, containing three items: a short memo, a "fact sheet," and a resume. The memos contained notes purportedly from a company human resources staff member who conducted a screening interview with the applicant. The "fact sheet" summarized relevant information about the potential employee (e.g., college GPA) not presented on the resume. The fact sheets and the resumes established that the candidates were equally productive in their past jobs and had equivalent skills and backgrounds. Prior to the actual experiment, pretesting of the two versions of the materials confirmed that the resumes were perceived to be of equivalent quality.

Experimental Manipulations

The race and gender of applicants were manipulated by altering first names on the applicant files (Bertrand and Mullainathan 2003). Parental status was manipulated on the resume and on the human resources memo. The resume described one applicant as an officer in an elementary school Parent-Teacher Association, and the accompanying memo included the following phrase: "Mother/Father to Tom and Emily. Married to John/Karen." The nonparent was presented as married, but with no mention of children.

Dependent Measures

There are eight dependent measures: two that measure competence and commitment, two that measure the ability standard participants used to judge the applicants, and four that serve as our key evaluation measures. The competence measure is a weighted average of participants' ratings of the applicants on seven-point scales ranging from "not at all" to "extremely" capable, efficient, skilled, intelligent, independent, self-confident, aggressive, and organized (alpha = .85). The commitment measure comes from a single-item question that asked participants how committed they thought the applicant would be relative to other employees in similar positions at the company.

There are two ability standard items. Participants were asked: (1) what percentile the applicant would need to score on an exam diagnostic of management ability, and (2) "how many days could this applicant be late or leave early per month before you would no longer recommend him/her for management track?"

We predict that mothers will be required to score in a *higher* percentile than nonmothers before being considered hirable and will be allowed *fewer* days of being late or leaving early.

There are four evaluation measures. Participants were asked: (1) to recommend a *salary* for each applicant, (2) to estimate the likelihood that an applicant would be subsequently *promoted* if hired, (3) to judge whether the applicant, if hired, should be recommended for a *management-training* course designed for those with strong advancement potential, and (4) to decide if they would recommend each applicant for *hire*. We predict that mothers will be offered lower starting salaries, will be rated as less promotable, will be less likely to be recommended for management, and will be less likely to be recommended for hire than nonmothers.

Laboratory Experiment Results

As predicted, mothers were judged significantly less competent and committed than women without children (see Table 60.1, left side) and were held to harsher performance and punctuality standards. They were allowed significantly fewer times of being late to work and needed a significantly higher score on the management exam than nonmothers before being considered hirable. Similarly, the evaluation measures show significant and substantial penalties for motherhood. The recommended starting salary for mothers was $11,000 (7.4 percent) less than that offered nonmothers, a significant difference. Mothers were also rated significantly less promotable and were less likely to be recommended for management. Finally, while participants recommended 84 percent of female nonmothers for hire, they recommended a significantly lower 47 percent of mothers.

Fathers were not disadvantaged, and in fact were advantaged on some of these measures. Relative to nonfathers, fathers were rated significantly more committed to their jobs, allowed to be late to work significantly more times, and offered significantly higher salaries.

Multivariate Analysis

We now turn to multivariate models to evaluate the motherhood penalty hypothesis by estimating the effects of gender of applicant, parental status, and the interaction of gender of applicant with parental status on each of the eight dependent variables. We refer to the interaction term (gender of applicant x parental

TABLE 60.1 Means or Proportions of Status, Standards and Evaluation Variables by Gender and Parental Status of Applicant (Standard Deviation in Parentheses)

	Female Applicants Mothers	Female Applicants Non-mothers	Male Applicants Fathers	Male Applicants Non-fathers
Competence	5.19 (0.73)**	5.75 (0.58)	5.51 (0.68)	5.44 (0.66)
Commitment	67.0 (19.1)**	79.2 (15.2)	78.5** (16.3)	74.2 (18.6)
Days allowed late	3.16 (1.98)**	3.73 (2.01)	3.69** (2.55)	3.16 (1.85)
Percent score required on exam	72.4 (27.5)**	67.9 (27.7)	67.3 (32.7)	67.1 (33.0)
Salary recommended	$137,000** (21,000)	$148,000 (25,000)	$150,000** (23,000)	$144,000 (20,700)
Proportion recommend for management	.691++	.862	.936+	.851
Likelihood of promotion	2.74 (0.65)**	3.42 (0.54)	3.30* (0.62)	3.11 (0.70)
Proportion recommend for hire	.468++	.840	.734+	.617

* p<.1, test for difference in means between parent and non-parents
** p<.05, test for difference in means between parent and non-parents
+ z<.1, test for difference in proportion between parents and non-parents
++ z<.05, test for difference in proportion between parents and non-parents
Notes: 94 participants rated female applicants and 94 rated male applicants. For this table, the data for male and female subjects are pooled, as are the data by race of applicant.

status) as the "motherhood penalty interaction." Applicant race and participant gender are included in all models, and standard errors are clustered by participant ID to take into account the nonindependence of observations that results from asking participants to rate applicants in pairs. Linear regression models are used for the continuous dependent variables. Logistic regression models are estimated for the binary evaluation variables (recommend for management and recommend for hire). Ordered logistic regression, with the proportional odds specification, is used for the ordered categorical evaluation variable, likelihood of promotion. Parental status, gender of applicant, gender of participant, and race of applicant are dummy variables, with parents, females, and African Americans coded as 1.

The estimated regression coefficients are presented in Tables 60.2–4. For all eight dependent variables, the motherhood penalty interaction is significant and in the predicted direction. This result shows strong support for the main prediction that parental status negatively impacts ratings for female, but not male, applicants.

Confirming our prediction, mothers were viewed as less competent than nonmothers. The significant, negative motherhood penalty interaction indicates that being a parent lowers the competence ratings for women, but not men (see left column, Table 60.2). Participants also perceived mothers as less committed than other applicants: the motherhood penalty interaction is significant and negative in the

TABLE 60.2 Estimated Regression Coefficients for the Effects of Gender, Parental Status and Race on Applicant's Perceived Competence and Commitment (Robust Standard Errors in Parentheses, Clustered by Participant ID)

Independent Variables	Competence	Commitment
Parent	0.089 (0.088)	5.15 *** (1.73)
Female applicant	0.376 *** (0.104)	5.68 ** (2.51)
African American	-0.038 (0.090)	-2.01 (2.27)
Female participant	0.060 (0.094)	-2.61 (2.26)
Motherhood interaction^	-0.750 *** (0.132)	-17.3 *** (2.32)
Intercept	5.42 *** (0.100)	75.8 *** (2.55)

^ Parent * Female applicant * p<.1 ** p<.05 *** p<.001
Note: N=188 participants

model predicting commitment ratings (see right column, Table 60.2). The positive and significant main effect for parental status implies that fathers are actually rated as more committed than nonfathers.

Consistent with the status-based discrimination argument, mothers were held to a stricter performance standard (see Table 60.3). The motherhood interaction is significant and positive in the model predicting the required test score, while the main

TABLE 60.3 Estimated Regression Coefficients for the Effects of Gender, Parental Status and Race on Ability Standard Variables (Robust Standard Errors in Parentheses, Clustered by Participant ID)

Independent Variables	Days allowed late	Test score required (%)
Parent	0.515 ***	1.03
	(0.137)	(0.968)
Female applicant	0.572 **	1.25
	(0.294)	(4.52)
African American	-0.361	-4.06
	(0.294)	(4.38)
Female participant	0.234	-9.44 **
	(0.289)	(4.30)
Motherhood interaction^	-1.10 ***	3.56 ***
	(0.213)	(1.21)
Intercept	3.22 ***	73.7 ***
	(0.322)	(4.27)

^Parent * Female applicant * p<.1 ** p<.05 *** p<.001
Note: N=188 participants

effects of gender of applicant and parental status are insignificant, showing that participants require mothers (but not fathers) to score higher on a test of management ability than other applicants before considering them for a job. Mothers are also held to a higher standard of punctuality, being allowed fewer days of being late.

In Table 60.4, the motherhood penalty interaction is significant and negative across all four mod-

els, indicating that mothers, relative to other applicants, are believed to deserve lower salaries and to be less suitable for hiring, promoting, and training for management. In the model predicting likelihood of promotion, the main effect of parental status is marginally significant and positive, while the motherhood penalty interaction is significant and negative, indicating that the negative effect of parental status on perceptions of promotability accrues only to women.

Consistent with previous literature on the motherhood wage penalty, mothers are offered lower starting salaries than other types of applicants, as indicated by the significant, negative coefficient for the motherhood interaction term. Childless men were recommended an average salary of approximately $148,000. Fathers were offered a significantly higher salary of approximately $152,000. Women without children were offered approximately $151,000, whereas mothers were recommended a significantly lower salary of about $139,000, or about 7.9 percent less than otherwise equal childless women.

While the motherhood penalty interaction is significant and its sign is in the predicted direction for each model, to complete our argument, we need to give evidence that motherhood disadvantages job applicants *because* it is a status characteristic. If the theory is correct, then evaluations of competence and commitment should mediate the motherhood penalty.

TABLE 60.4 Estimated Regression Coefficients for the Effects of Gender, Parental Status and Race on Evaluation Variables (Robust Standard Errors in Parentheses, Clustered by Participant ID)

Independent Variables	Promotion likelihood (ordered logistic estimates)	Mgmt training? (binary logistic estimates)	Hire? (binary logistic estimates)	Recommended salary in thousands of dollars (linear estimates)
Parent	1.03 *	0.605 *	0.570	4.47 ***
	(0.545)	(0.321)	(0.366)	(1.84)
Female applicant	0.256	1.009 ***	1.21 ***	2.56
	(0.425)	(0.319)	(0.365)	(3.18)
African American	0.309	-0.211	-0.163	-6.80 **
	(0.299)	(0.218)	(0.197)	(2.94)
Female participant	0.496 *	0.526 **	0.606 ***	0.691
	(0.298)	(0.226)	(0.199)	(2.82)
Motherhood interaction^	-2.14 ***	-2.72 ***	-2.38 ***	-15.9 ***
	(0.651)	(0.426)	(0.548)	(2.42)
Intercept	^^	4.56 ***	0.210	148
		(0.601)	(0.266)	(2.55)

^ Parent *Female applicant ^^ Since ordered logistic regression produces multiple intercepts, we do not present them here.
* p<.1 ** p<.05 *** p<.001
Note: N=188 participants

TABLE 60.5 Estimated Regression Coefficients for the Mediation of Competence and Commitment on the Impact of Parental Status on Workplace Evaluations (Robust Standard Errors in Parentheses, Clustered by Participant ID)

Independent Variables	Promotion likelihood (ordered logistic estimates)	Mgmt training? (binary logistic estimates)	Hire? (binary logistic estimates)	Recommended salary in thousands of dollars (linear estimates)
Competence	0.628 **	1.263 ***	1.21 ***	7.00 ***
	(0.295)	(0.281)	(0.258)	(1.99)
Commitment	0.237 ***	0.206 **	0.308 ***	1.08
	(0.095)	(0.099)	(0.081)	(0.762)
Parent	0.901 *	0.508	0.433	3.23 *
	(0.558)	(0.340)	(0.426)	(1.78)
Female applicant	-0.140	0.661 **	0.755 *	-0.817
	(0.426)	(0.332)	(0.410)	(3.31)
African American	0.374	-0.154	-0.092	-6.30 ***
	(0.319)	(0.237)	(0.244)	(2.86)
Female participant	0.557 *	0.606 ***	0.755 ***	0.512
	(0.316)	(0.236)	(0.254)	(2.81)
Motherhood interaction^	-1.34 **	-1.89 ***	-1.39 **	-8.52 ***
	(0.646)	(0.437)	(0.606)	(2.66)
Intercept	^^	3.64 ***	-2.09 ***	140
		(0.947)	(0.702)	(6.37)
Percent reduction of motherhood penalty	37.4 %	30.5 %	41.6 %	46.4 %

^Parent *Female applicant ^^Since ordered logistic regression produces multiple intercepts, we do not present them here. *p<.1 **p<.05 ***p<.001. *Note*: N=188 participants

When the competence and commitment ratings were added as independent variables to the models (see Table 60.5), the negative effect of motherhood status on workplace evaluations was significantly reduced, by a magnitude of 31–46 percent. Thus, mothers are rated as less hirable, less suitable for promotion and management training, and deserving of lower salaries in part because they are believed to be less competent and less committed to paid work. Having established support for the causal mechanism with the laboratory data, we turn to the audit study to assess whether actual employers discriminate against mothers.

The Audit Study

The audit methodology combines experimental design with real-life settings. As in laboratory experiments, audit studies isolate a characteristic (e.g., race or gender) and test for discriminatory behavior. Distinct from most laboratory studies, audit study participants are the people who make important decisions about actual applicants, such as employers

conducting new employee searches. While laboratory experiments permit closer investigation of social and cognitive processes, audit studies provide greater generalizability of results.

Resumes and cover letters from a pair of fictitious, equally qualified, same-gender applicants were sent to employers advertising for marketing and business job openings in a large, northeastern city newspaper over an eighteen-month period of time. The same-sex pair contained one parent and one nonparent. Job openings were randomly assigned to either the male or female condition. We manipulated parental status on the resume and on the cover letter. We did not manipulate race in this study.

We monitor whether gender and parental status impact the odds that an employer will call back an applicant. Based on the 5–8 percent callback rate found in an audit study of race in hiring (Bertrand and Mullainathan 2003), and to ensure that we had sufficient statistical power to evaluate the effect of parental status, we submitted 1,276 resumes and cover letters to 638 employers.

TABLE 60.6 Proportions of Applicants Receiving Callbacks by Gender and Parental Status

	Callbacks / Total Jobs	Proportion Called Back
Mothers	10 / 320	.0313
Childless women	21 / 320	.0656++
Fathers	16 / 318	.0503
Childless men	9 / 318	.0283

++ $z<.05$ Test for difference in proportions between parents and non-parents. *Notes*: Mothers and childless women applied to the same 320 jobs; fathers and childless men applied to the same 318 jobs.

Results

The results suggest that real employers do discriminate against mothers (see Table 60.6). Childless women received 2.1 times as many callbacks as equally qualified mothers. This finding is similar to the laboratory experiment (see Table 60.1) in which childless women were recommended for hire 1.8 times more frequently than mothers. In the laboratory study, fathers were recommended for hire at a slightly *higher* rate, although the difference was only marginally significant; in the audit study, fathers were called back at a higher rate, although the difference was not significant.

We now consider a multivariate model for the effects of parental status, applicant gender, and the interaction of parental status and applicant gender on the odds that an applicant receives a callback from an employer. Table 60.7 shows the motherhood penalty interaction is significant and negative, while the main effect for parental status is insignificant, and the main effect for the female applicant variable is significant and positive. The significant negative motherhood penalty interaction term indicates that being a parent lowers the odds that a woman, but not a man, will receive a callback from employers. In sum, the audit data show that, compared with their equally qualified childless counterparts, mothers are disadvantaged when actual employers make hiring decisions.

Strengths and Limitations

While the audit study evaluates whether actual employers discriminate against mothers in the hiring process, it does not give us insight into the mechanism underlying discrimination, because it was not possible to collect employers' rankings of commit-

TABLE 60.7 Estimated Binary Logistic Regression Coefficients for the Effects of Parental Status and Gender on the Odds of Receiving a Callback (Robust Standard Errors in Parentheses, Clustered by Job)

Independent Variables	Callback?
Parent	0.598
	(.433)
Female applicant	0.887**
	(.407)
Motherhood interaction^	-1.38**
	(.590)
Intercept	-3.54***
	(.338)

^Parent *Female applicant *$p<.1$ **$p<.05$ ***$p<.001$
Notes: Mothers and childless women applied to the same 320 jobs; fathers and childless men applied to the same 318 jobs, for a total of 1276 applications for 638 jobs.

ment, competence, performance standards, and other relevant variables. These limits mean that while the audit study establishes that actual employers discriminate against mothers, it cannot establish why.

By considering the results of these two companion studies simultaneously, however, we find support for the status-based discrimination mechanism using the laboratory data and see real world implications of the argument with data generated from the audit study. Further, these results are consistent with qualitative work showing that employers discriminate against mothers (Blair-Loy 2003; Crittenden 2001; Kennelly 1999) and with survey research that consistently finds a wage penalty for motherhood (Budig and England 2001; Anderson, Binder, and Krause 2003). Thus, across a wide range of methodological approaches—each of which has its unique strengths and weaknesses—we find evidence that mothers experience disadvantages in workplace settings and that discrimination plays a role in producing these disadvantages.

Summary and Conclusions

This project makes two main contributions. First, it isolates and experimentally evaluates a status-based discrimination mechanism that explains some of the disadvantages mothers experience in the paid labor market. Second, it shows that real employers discriminate against mothers. The results of this study have implications for understanding some of the enduring patterns of gender inequality in paid work.

Studies have documented the motherhood penalty in at least fifteen countries (Harkness and Waldfogel 1999; Misra, Budig, and Moller 2005) and shown its stability over time (Avellar and Smock 2003). This study offers a partial explanation for the mechanism behind a widespread, durable phenomenon with implications for a broad segment of the population.

More generally, a gender gap in wages has persisted despite the vast movement of women into paid labor in the United States since the early 1970s, and employed mothers account for most of this gap (Glass 2004). This study suggests that cultural beliefs about the tension between the motherhood and "ideal worker" roles may play a part in reproducing this pattern of inequality. A second enduring pattern of gender inequality is the so-called "glass ceiling," a metaphor for the barriers that restrict women's movement up the career ladder to the highest positions in organizations and firms. To the extent that employers view mothers as less committed to their jobs and less "promotable," the glass ceiling women face could be, in part, a motherhood ceiling.

Writing for the National Center for Policy Analysis, Denise Venable (2002) reports that among people ages twenty-seven to thirty-three who have never had children, women's earnings approach 98 percent of men's. She concludes, "When women behave in the workplace as men do, the wage gap between them is small." Claims of unequal pay, she continues, "almost always involve comparing apples and oranges." However, since most employed men and employed women have children at some point in their lives, the most illustrative "within fruit" comparison is not the comparison of childless men to childless women, but the comparison of men with children to women with children. As the two studies reported here show, when women "behave as men do," by giving evidence of being a parent, they are discriminated against, while their male counterparts are often advantaged. Far from being an "apples to oranges" comparison, the male and female applicants who were evaluated in these studies were exactly equal by experimental design. That parental status disadvantaged only female applicants is strong evidence of discrimination.

REFERENCES

Acker, Joan. 1990. "Hierarchies, jobs, and bodies: a theory of gendered organizations." *Gender & Society* 4: 139–158.

Anderson, Deborah J., Melissa Binder, and Kate Krause. 2003. "The motherhood wage penalty revisited: Experience, heterogeneity, work effort and work-schedule flexibility." *Industrial and Labor Relations Review* 56: 273–294.

Avellar, Sarah, and Pamela Smock. 2003. "Has the price of motherhood declined over time? A cross-cohort comparison of the motherhood wage penalty." *Journal of Marriage and the Family* 65: 597–607.

Berger, Joseph, Hamit Fisek, Robert Norman, and Morris Zelditch, Jr. 1977. *Status Characteristics and Social Interaction.* New York: Elsevier.

Bertrand, Marianne, and Sendhil Mullainathan. 2003. "Are Emily and Greg more employable than Lakisha and Jamal? A field experiment on labor market discrimination." National Bureau of Economic Research Working Paper Series, Working Paper no. 9873. Retrieved September 2003 (http://www.nber.org/papers/w9873).

Bielby, Denise D., and William T. Bielby. 1984. "Work commitment, sex-role attitudes, and women's employment." *American Sociological Review* 49: 234–247.

Blair-Loy, Mary. 2003. *Competing Devotions: Career and Family Among Women Executives.* Cambridge, MA: Harvard University Press.

Budig, Michelle, and Paula England. 2001. "The wage penalty for motherhood." *American Sociological Review* 66: 204–225.

Cleveland, Jeanette N. 1991. "Using hypothetical and actual applicants in assessing person-organization fit: A methodological note." *Journal of Applied Social Psychology* 21: 1004–1011.

Cleveland, Jeanette N., and Andrew H. Berman. 1987. "Age perceptions of jobs: Agreement between samples of students and managers." *Psychological Reports* 61: 565–566.

Correll, Shelley J., and Stephen Benard. 2006. "Biased estimators? Comparing status and statistical theories of gender discrimination." Pp. 89–116 in *Social Psychology of the Workplace* (Advances in Group Process Volume 23), edited by Shane R. Thye and Edward J. Lawler. New York: Elsevier.

Corse, Sara J. 1990. "Pregnant managers and their subordinates: The effects of gender expectations on hierarchical relationships." *Journal of Applied Behavioral Science* 26: 25–48.

Crittenden, Ann. 2001. *The Price of Motherhood: Why the Most Important Job in the World Is Still the Least Valued.* New York: Metropolitan Books.

Cuddy, Amy J. C., Susan T. Fiske, and Peter Glick. 2004. "When professionals become mothers, warmth doesn't cut the ice." *Journal of Social Issues* 60: 701–718.

Foschi, Martha. 1989. "Status characteristics, standards and attributions." Pp. 58–72 in *Sociological Theories in Progress: New Formulations*, edited by Joseph Berger, Morris Zelditch, Jr., and Bo Anderson. Boston: Houghton Mifflin.

Glass, Jennifer. 2004. "Blessing or curse? Work-family policies and mother's wage growth over time." *Work and Occupations* 31: 367–394.

Halpert, Jane A., Midge L. Wilson, and Julia Hickman. 1993. "Pregnancy as a source of bias in performance appraisals." *Journal of Organizational Behavior* 14: 649–663.

Harkness, Susan, and Jane Waldfogel. 1999. "The family gap in pay: Evidence from seven industrialised countries." CASE paper 29: Centre for Analysis of Social Exclusion.

Hays, Sharon. 1996. *The Cultural Contradictions of Motherhood*. New Haven, CT: Yale University Press.

Kennelly, Ivy. 1999. "That single mother element: How white employers typify black women." *Gender & Society* 13: 168–192.

Misra, Joya, Michelle Budig, and Stephanie Moller. 2005. "Employment, wages, and poverty: Reconciliation policies and gender equity." Paper presented at the Annual Meeting of the American Sociological Association, Philadelphia, PA.

Olian, Judy D., and Donald P. Schwab. 1988. "The impact of applicant gender compared to qualifications on hiring recommendations: A meta-analysis of experimental studies." *Organizational Behavior and Human Decision Processes* 41: 180–195.

Ridgeway, Cecilia, and Shelley J. Correll. 2004. "Motherhood as a status characteristic." *Journal of Social Issues* 60: 683–700.

Townsend, Nicholas W. 2002. *The Package Deal: Marriage, Work and Fatherhood in Men's Lives*. Philadelphia, PA: Temple University Press.

Venable, Denise. 2002. "The wage gap myth." National Center for Policy Analysis, April 12, 2002, Brief Analysis no. 392. Retrieved December 12, 2004 (http://www.ncpa.org/pub/ba/ba392/).

Waldfogel, Jane. 1997. "The effect of children on women's wages." *American Sociological Review* 62: 209–217.

Williams, Joan. 2001. *Unbending Gender: Why Work and Family Conflict and What to Do About It*. Oxford: Oxford University Press.

How Gender Intersects

61. Margaret L. Andersen and Patricia Hill Collins*

Why Race, Class, and Gender Matter

Race, class, and gender matter because they continue to structure society in ways that value some lives more than others. Currently, some groups have more opportunities and resources, while other groups struggle. Race, class, and gender matter because they remain the foundations for systems of power and inequality that, despite our nation's diversity, continue to be among the most significant social facts of people's lives. Thus, despite having removed the formal barriers to opportunity, the United States is still highly stratified along lines of race, class, and gender. . . . For years, social scientists have studied the consequences of race, class, and gender inequality for different groups in society. [We] explore how race, class, and gender operate *together* in people's lives. Fundamentally, race, class, and gender are *intersecting* categories of experience that affect all aspects of human life; thus, they *simultaneously* structure the experiences of all people in this society. At any moment, race, class, or gender may feel more salient or meaningful in a given person's life, but they are overlapping and cumulative in their effects.

[We] emphasize *social structure* in our efforts to conceptualize intersections of race, class, and gender. We [suggest] the approach of a matrix of domination to analyze race, class, and gender. A *matrix of domination* sees social structure as having multiple, interlocking levels of domination that stem from the societal configuration of race, class, and gender relations. This structural pattern affects individual consciousness, group interaction, and group access to

institutional power and privileges (Collins 2000). Within this structural framework, we focus less on comparing race, class, and gender as separate systems of power than on investigating the structural patterns that join them. Because of the simultaneity of race, class, and gender in people's lives, intersections of race, class, and gender can be seen in individual stories and personal experience. In fact, much exciting work on the intersections of race, class, and gender appears in autobiographies, fiction, and personal essays. We do recognize the significance of these individual narratives, but we also emphasize social structures that provide the context for individual experiences.

Second, studying interconnections among race, class, and gender within a context of social structures helps us understand how race, class, and gender are manifested differently, depending on their configuration with the others. Thus, one might say African American men are privileged *as men,* but this may not be true when their race and class are also taken into account. Otherwise, how can we possibly explain the particular disadvantages African American men experience in the criminal justice system, in education, and in the labor market? For that matter, how can we explain the experiences that Native American women undergo—disadvantaged by the unique experiences that they have based on race, class, *and* gender—none of which is isolated from the effects of the others? Studying the connections among race, class, and gender reveals that divisions by race and by class and by gender are not as clear-cut as they may seem. White women, for example, may be disadvantaged because of gender but privileged by race and perhaps (but not necessarily) by class. And increasing class differentiation within racial-ethnic groups reminds us that race is not a monolithic category, as can be seen in the fact that white poverty is increasing more than poverty among other groups, even while some whites hold the most power in society.

Third, the matrix of domination approach to race, class, and gender studies is historically grounded. We [choose] to emphasize the intersections of race, class, and gender as institutional systems that have had a special impact in the United States. Yet race, class, and gender intersect with other categories of experience, such as sexuality, ethnicity, age, ability, religion, and nationality. Historically, these intersections have taken varying forms from one society to the next; within any given society, the connections among them also shift. Thus, race is not inherently more important than gender, just as sexuality is not inherently more significant than class and ethnicity.

Given the complex and changing relationships among these categories of analysis, [it is important to] ground analyses in the historical, institutional context of the United States. Doing so means that race, class, and gender emerge as fundamental categories of analysis in the US setting, so significant that in many ways they influence all of the other categories. Systems of race, class, and gender have been so consistently and deeply codified in US laws that they have had intergenerational effects, on economic, political, and social institutions. For example, the capitalist class relations that have characterized all phases of US history have routinely privileged or penalized groups organized by gender and by race. US social institutions have reproduced economic equalities for poor people, women, and people of color from one generation to the next. Thus, in the United States, race, class, and gender demonstrate visible, long-standing, material effects that in many ways foreshadow more recently visible categories of ethnicity, religion, age, ability, and/or sexuality.

REFERENCES

Collins, Patricia Hill. 2000. *Black Feminist Thought: Knowledge, Consciousness, and Empowerment.* New York: Routledge.

62. András Tilcsik*
Do Openly Gay Men Experience Employment Discrimination?

In recent years the rights of and legal protections for lesbian, gay, bisexual, and transgender (LGBT) people have been at the center of heated debates in the United States. In the absence of a federal law specifically protecting LGBT employees and job seekers, one debate has focused on sexual orientation discrimination in employment; that is, the behaviors and practices—both deliberate and unconscious—that disadvantage individuals of a particular sexual orientation compared to individuals of another sexual orientation in employment contexts. Although scholars have produced a considerable amount of research relevant to this debate, most of the literature has focused on wage inequality and has produced little direct evidence about the difficulties that LGBT people may face in obtaining a job. This is a significant omission, because hiring discrimination is an important inequality-generating mechanism with potentially powerful effects on a job seeker's access to a broad range of opportunities.

I begin to address this lacuna by directly examining hiring discrimination against openly gay men. Limiting the scope of this study to one LGBT group—gay men—was advantageous, because the precise nature of prejudice based on sexual orientation might vary among LGBT groups. By focusing on a single group—and leaving future research to explore discrimination against other LGBT groups—it was possible to delve more deeply into the nature of discrimination against that one group, gay men. To do so, I conducted an audit study. I responded with a pair of fictitious but ostensibly real resumes to 1,769 postings of white-collar, entry-level jobs in seven states, randomly assigning a signal of sexual orientation to each resume. The findings from this study provide evidence about the extent of discrimination as well as the factors that affect the

*The ideas, issues, and theories considered in this brief commissioned piece are examined in greater depth in the following publication: András Tilcsik, "Pride and Prejudice: Employment Discrimination Against Openly Gay Men in the United States," *American Journal of Sociology* 117:2 (2011), pp. 586–626, published by the University of Chicago Press. The article printed here was originally prepared by András Tilcsik for the fourth edition of *Social Stratification: Class, Race, and Gender in Sociological Perspective*, edited by David B. Grusky. Copyright © 2014 by Westview Press.

likelihood of its occurring, including the presence of antidiscrimination laws and the extent to which employers value stereotypically male heterosexual personality traits.

Prior Research and the Audit Approach

Much of the extant literature on sexual orientation discrimination in the United States has focused on compensation. Controlling for human capital, these studies have found that gay men earn 10–32 percent less than heterosexual men (Badgett et al. 2007). Although these studies generated important evidence, they focused on earnings rather than on the hiring decision and were not designed to provide direct evidence about discrimination. Indeed, regression analyses that define discrimination as unexplained income differences may lead to biased estimates of discrimination if differences in employee productivity or preferences are observed incompletely. Another line of research examined employee self-reports and found that many LGBT individuals report experiencing some form of discrimination in the workplace (e.g., Croteau 1996). The generalizability of these studies, however, is limited, because they rely on convenience samples and capture subjective perceptions, rather than the actual incidence, of discrimination. A third approach focused on the number of employment discrimination complaints that LGBT employees filed in states that outlaw sexual orientation discrimination (e.g., Rubenstein 2002). However, like self-reports, complaint rates do not necessarily represent the actual incidence of discrimination.

Seeking more direct evidence about sexual orientation discrimination in the United States, some researchers have adopted an experimental approach. Crow, Fok, and Hartman (1998), for example, asked full-time employees in a southern city to select six out of eight fictitious applicants for an accounting position. Similarly, Horvath and Ryan (2003) instructed undergraduates to rate resumes for which sexual orientation and gender were experimentally manipulated. Taking a somewhat different approach, Hebl and colleagues (2002) conducted a field experiment in which male and female confederates applied for retail jobs in a mall. For each store, the confederates were randomly assigned to wear a baseball hat with the words "Gay and Proud" or "Texan and Proud." Although these experiments were an important first step toward directly measuring hiring discrimination, they had significant limitations.

First, all three experiments were limited to a single context: a single city, university, or mall area. Thus, it is unclear how accurately the results reflect broader patterns of discrimination. Second, in two of these studies the decision-makers knew that they were participating in an experiment and that their choices had no consequences for real hiring outcomes (Crow et al. 1998; Horvath and Ryan 2003). Whether these decision-makers would make the same hiring choices in a real employment context, faced with real incentives and constraints, remains unclear.

To overcome these limitations, I conducted a large-scale correspondence audit, sending pairs of fictitious resumes in response to real job postings and assessing the effect of a randomly assigned signal of sexual orientation on whether a resume elicited an invitation for a job interview. This methodology offers important advantages. By experimentally controlling for human capital factors that might be confounded with minority status, audit studies provide more direct evidence about the causal impact of discrimination than do wage regressions (Bertrand and Mullainathan 2004; Pager 2007). By gathering such evidence in a real employment context from real employers, audit studies are also more generalizable than studies with undergraduate participants and experiments in which participants know that their choices will not affect real hiring outcomes (Correll et al. 2007). To date, however, few studies have taken an audit approach to sexual orientation discrimination (Adam 1981; Hebl et al. 2002; Weichselbaumer 2003; Drydakis 2009), and there has been no large-scale audit of sexual orientation discrimination in the United States.

Discrimination, Regional Variation, and Stereotypes

The likelihood of discrimination against gay men probably varies across geographic areas and jobs. First, differences in the level of tolerance toward gay men and in antidiscrimination laws may lead to geographic variation in the incidence of discrimination. Public opinion polls indicate considerable regional variation in attitudes toward gay men. Whereas almost half of Americans in the Northeast and the West have a favorable view of gay men, only slightly more than a third of respondents express similar views in the Midwest, and even fewer do so in the South (Pew Research Center 2003). The adoption of state laws that prohibit sexual orientation discrimination follows a similar geographic pattern. At the time of this study, twenty states and the District of Columbia prohibited sexual orientation discrimination in the private sector, but most of these states were in the Northeast and the West. The geographic distribution of counties and cities that ban sexual orientation discrimination in private employment was roughly similar, with relatively few antidiscrimination laws in southern cities and counties. Notably, however, such laws have been passed in some major cities in the South and the Midwest, including Atlanta, Austin, Chicago, Dallas, and Detroit.

In addition to geographic differences, we might also observe important variation in the level of discrimination across jobs if stereotypes of gay men play a role in hiring decisions. *Stereotypes* are socially shared sets of implicit or explicit beliefs about the typical characteristics of members of a social group. Because stereotyped judgments simplify and justify social reality, stereotyping has potentially powerful effects on how people perceive and treat one another. However, stereotyping has received relatively little empirical attention in the audit literature. One notable exception is a correspondence test in Austria that compared the callback rates of three fictitious job applicants (a man, a feminine woman, and a masculine woman) for job postings that emphasized different personality traits (e.g., "powerful," "dynamic," "friendly"; Weichselbaumer 2004). This research design made it possible to assess whether employers looking for job candidates with stereotypically masculine traits favored men over women and masculine women over feminine women.

I adopt a similar approach. If stereotyped judgments influence callback decisions, employers should be more likely to engage in discrimination if they value and emphasize attributes that gay men are stereotypically perceived to lack. What might these attributes be? Research suggests that gay men are often perceived to exhibit behaviors associated with "feminine" characteristics; for example, they are commonly seen as sensitive, emotional, gentle, affectionate, and passive. Consequently, gay men are often seen as lacking "toughness" and "masculinity" (Madon 1997). Even a quick perusal of job postings reveals that it is not uncommon for employers to emphasize personality characteristics that are considered typical of heterosexual men, such as decisiveness, assertiveness, and aggressiveness (Bem 1974; Gorman 2005). Searches in online job databases return hundreds of postings in which employers seek, for example, "an aggressive, motivated self-starter," "an assertive associate," or "a decisive, results-

oriented leader." This emphasis on stereotypically male heterosexual characteristics may in turn be associated with a higher likelihood of discrimination against gay men. If stereotypes of gay men—as feminine, passive, gentle, or lacking "toughness"—play a significant role in callback decisions, employers who characterize their ideal job candidate with stereotypically male heterosexual traits should be particularly likely to engage in discrimination.

Methods

Signaling Sexual Orientation

An important challenge in resume-based audit studies is to signal the characteristic of interest without introducing a confounding factor into the analysis. In the present case, for example, employers may perceive openly gay applicants as tactless or lacking business savvy because they list an irrelevant experience on their resumes, apparently "trumpeting" their sexual orientation (Weichselbaumer 2003). In addition, perceiving such applicants as radical or liberal, employers may discriminate against them for their perceived political views and activism, rather than for their sexual orientation (Badgett et al. 2007). Moreover, if the "control organization" that is assigned to the resume of the ostensibly heterosexual applicant is not carefully chosen, it may lead to differences in the applicants' perceived level of human capital, making it difficult to assess the extent of discrimination.

I took several steps to address these issues.[1] First, the fictitious job seekers in this study were graduating college seniors applying for entry-level jobs. For this population of applicants, listing volunteer experiences in political, cultural, ethnic, religious, or other identity-based campus organizations in a resume is a common practice, especially if the experience involves an elected position with important responsibilities. Thus, in the case of college seniors, listing involvement in political or identity-based groups is less likely to be perceived as unprofessional or unusual than it would be if experienced job seekers did so.

Second, to signal homosexual orientation, I chose an experience in a gay community organization that could not be easily dismissed as irrelevant to a job application. Thus, instead of being just a member of a gay and lesbian campus organization, the applicant served as the elected treasurer for several semesters, managing the organization's financial operations.

Accordingly, rather than focusing on the organization's nature or goals, this resume item explicitly emphasized the applicant's managerial and financial skills. Thus the applicant's participation in this organization could be seen as a meaningful, valuable experience with potentially important transferable skills. In other words, omitting this experience from the resume would have meant concealing relevant and important human capital. Given the heavy emphasis on the specific financial and organizational activities associated with the treasurer position on the resume, it would be difficult to dismiss this experience as a social activity or a way of simply trumpeting the applicant's sexual orientation.

Third, I used a control organization to ensure that any observed differences in callbacks could be attributed to antigay discrimination rather than other factors. An important consideration was that participation in a gay organization might be associated with progressive, liberal, or leftist political views. Thus, if I had used an apolitical control organization (or no control organization at all), observed differences in callbacks might have been attributable to discrimination based on either sexual orientation or political affiliation, and it would have been impossible to determine the net effect of sexual orientation. Accordingly, to determine whether there is a "gay penalty" above and beyond the possible effect of political discrimination, I chose a control organization that is associated with leftist or progressive views. At first glance, a campus chapter of college Democrats might seem suitable for this purpose. However, because Democratic campus groups are typically larger than gay and lesbian student groups, leadership experiences in a Democratic organization might seem more valuable than similar experiences in a gay organization. To avoid this problem, the control group was a small left-wing campus organization (the "Progressive and Socialist Alliance").

Resumes, Randomization, and Sample

Over six months in 2005, I sent fictitious resumes, via e-mail, in response to advertisements for full-time, entry-level positions on three recruitment Web sites targeted to college seniors and recent graduates. I sent two resumes in response to each job posting, with one day or less in between. Before sending out each resume pair, I randomly assigned the gay signal to one of the resumes and the control signal to the other. Thus, even though the resumes differed in order to avoid raising suspicion, there was

no systematic relationship between their quality and sexual orientation. Consequently, any significant difference in callback rates could be attributed to the experimental manipulation of the resumes. Importantly, I varied only the name of the treatment organization and the control organization. As a result, the activities of the applicants in their respective groups were not systematically related to sexual orientation. I thus effectively controlled for any differences in the applicants' achievements in the treatment organization and the control organization. For each application, I recorded whether it led to an invitation to a first-round job interview (either an in-person or a telephone interview).

I submitted a total of 3,538 resumes, responding to 1,769 job postings by private employers. The sample included jobs in five occupations and seven states. The five occupations were managers (including management trainees), business and financial analysts, sales representatives, customer service representatives, and administrative assistants. The sampled states included four states in the Northeast and the West (New York, Pennsylvania, California, Nevada) and three states in the Midwest and the South (Ohio, Florida, Texas). These states—and the counties and cities in them—offered an intriguing mosaic of legal environments. California, Nevada, and New York prohibited sexual orientation discrimination in private employment, but the other four states had no such legislation. At the same time, with the exception of Nevada, each state had some cities and counties that banned sexual orientation discrimination.

Findings

The submission of resumes led to a total of 331 interview invitations, an overall callback rate of 9.35 percent. Table 62.1 tabulates callback rates by sexual orientation. Whereas heterosexual applicants had an 11.5 percent chance of being invited for an interview, equally qualified gay applicants had only a 7.2 percent chance of receiving a positive response. This is a difference of 4.3 percentage points, or about 40 percent. This gap is statistically significant ($P < .001$) and implies that a heterosexual job seeker had to apply to fewer than nine different jobs to obtain a positive response, whereas a gay applicant needed to reply to almost fourteen ads to achieve the same result.

The size of the callback gap, however, varied substantially across states. On the one hand, in the southern and midwestern states (Texas, Florida, and

TABLE 62.1 Callback Rates by Sexual Orientation

Sample (n job ads)	% Callback		Difference	
	Not Gay	Gay	Ratio	(P-value)
Total Sample (*n* = 1,769)	11.5	7.2	1.59	4.3 (.000)
California (*n* = 337)	11.0	9.2	1.20	1.8 (.443)
Nevada (*n* = 131)	12.2	6.1	2.00	6.1 (.087)
New York (*n* = 236)	10.2	11.4	0.89	-1.2 (.656)
Pennsylvania (*n* = 201)	12.9	9.4	1.37	3.5 (.268)
Ohio (*n* = 219)	14.1	5.5	2.56	8.6 (.002)
Florida (*n* = 347)	9.5	5.5	2.11	4.0 (.044)
Texas (*n* = 298)	12.0	3.7	3.24	8.3 (.000)
Employers subject to a city, county, or state law that prohibits sexual orientation discrimination:				
Yes (*n* = 983)	11.6	8.7	1.33	2.9 (.037)
No (*n* = 786)	11.3	5.3	2.13	6.0 (.000)
Job postings that require stereotypically male heterosexual traits:				
Yes (*n* = 361)	13.0	3.9	3.33	9.1 (.000)
No (*n* = 1,408)	11.1	8.1	1.37	3.00 (.007)

*Assertiveness, aggressiveness, or decisiveness

Ohio), there was a substantial difference in the callback rates for gay and heterosexual applicants. In Texas and Ohio, for example, the size of the callback gap (8.3 and 8.6 percentage points, respectively) was substantially larger than in the overall sample (4.1 percentage points). By contrast, there was no statistically significant callback gap in any of the western and northeastern states (California, Nevada, Pennsylvania, and New York). Similarly, there was variation in the callback gap across legal environments. In the case of employers subject to a relevant antidiscrimination law at the city, county, or state levels, the callback gap was less than 3 percentage points; in the case of employers not subject to such regulation, the gap was as large as 6 percentage points. In both cases, however, the callback gap was statistically significant.

In addition, as expected the callback gap was particularly large among employers who emphasized the importance of stereotypically male heterosexual traits, particularly assertiveness, aggressiveness, and decisiveness. Notably, however, there was a statistically significant callback gap even within the sample of employers who did not specifically require such traits. Thus, even when these traits were not emphasized, gay applicants suffered significant callback discrimination.

Using logistic regression models, I found that these basic patterns were robust to the inclusion of control variables, including occupation and industry dummies, employer size, and the local unemployment rate, as well as the degree of urban-ness, political conservatism, and level of education characteristic

of the area where the job was located. Under a variety of conditions, these models consistently indicated discrimination overall, as well as variation in the level of discrimination by region and by the traits required in the job postings. Moreover, the effect of geographic differences and the influence of required personality traits were significant even net of each other.

Conclusions

This study shows that openly gay men encounter significant barriers in the hiring process because, at the initial point of contact, employers more readily disqualify openly gay applicants than equally qualified heterosexual applicants. These findings are consistent with less direct indicators of discrimination against LGBT people; taken together, these lines of evidence suggest that sexual orientation discrimination is a prominent feature of many American labor markets.

At the same time, the results indicate dramatic geographic variation in the level of discrimination. What explains this variation? A key finding is that employers in states and counties with a relevant antidiscrimination law were significantly less likely to engage in discrimination. This result, however, does not necessarily imply that lower levels of discrimination were due entirely to antidiscrimination laws. Because public opinion about gay people might affect both the level of discrimination and the probability that an antidiscrimination policy will be adopted, the effect of laws on discrimination may be confounded with the effect of attitudes. Data limitations prevented me from fully untangling these factors in the present study, but the mechanisms behind the observed geographic variation are an important topic for future research.

Moreover, this study has identified stereotyping as a potentially important mechanism underlying hiring discrimination against gay men. Employers who sought applicants with stereotypically male heterosexual traits were much more likely to discriminate against gay applicants than employers who did not emphasize the importance of such traits. This finding suggests that employers' implicit or explicit stereotypes of gay men are inconsistent with the image of an assertive, aggressive, and decisive employee. It seems, therefore, that the discrimination documented in this study is partly rooted in specific stereotypes and cannot be completely reduced to a general antipathy against gay employees.

REFERENCES

Adam, Barry. 1981. "Stigma and Employability: Discrimination by Sex and Sexual Orientation in the Ontario Legal Profession." *Canadian Review of Sociology and Anthropology* 18: 216–221.

Badgett, M. V. Lee, Holning Lau, Brad Sears, and Deborah Ho. 2007. "Bias in the Workplace: Consistent Evidence of Sexual Orientation and Gender Identity Discrimination." Report, Williams Institute, University of California School of Law.

Bem, Sandra. 1974. "The Measurement of Psychological Androgyny." *Journal of Consulting and Clinical Psychology* 42: 155–162.

Bertrand, Marianne, and Sendhil Mullainathan. 2004. "Are Emily and Greg More Employable Than Lakisha and Jamal? A Field Experiment on Labor Market Discrimination." *American Economic Review* 94: 991–1013.

Correll, Shelley J., Stephen Benard, and In Paik. 2007. "Getting a Job: Is There a Motherhood Penalty?" *American Journal of Sociology* 112: 1297–1338.

Croteau, James M. 1996. "Research on the Work Experiences of Lesbian, Gay, and Bisexual People: An Integrative Review of Methodology and Findings." *Journal of Vocational Behavior* 48: 195–209.

Crow, Stephen M., Lillian Y. Fok, and Sandra J. Hartman. 1998. "Who Is at Greatest Risk of Work-Related Discrimination—Women, Blacks, or Homosexuals?" *Employee Responsibilities and Rights Journal* 11: 15–26.

Drydakis, Nick. 2009. "Sexual Orientation Discrimination in the Labour Market." *Labour Economics* 16: 364–372.

Gorman, Elizabeth. 2005. "Gender Stereotypes, Same-Gender Preferences, and Organizational Variation in the Hiring of Women: Evidence from Law Firms." *American Sociological Review* 70: 702–728.

Hebl, Michelle R., Jessica Bigazzi Foster, Laura M. Mannix, and John Dovidio. 2002. "Formal and Interpersonal Discrimination: A Field Study of Bias Toward Homosexual Applicants." *Personality and Social Psychology Bulletin* 28: 815–825.

Horvath, Michael, and Ann Marie Ryan. 2003. "Antecedents and Potential Moderators of the Relationship Between Attitudes and Hiring Discrimination on the Basis of Sexual Orientation." *Sex Roles* 48: 115–130.

Madon, Stephanie. 1997. "What Do People Believe About Gay Males? A Study of Stereotype Content and Strength." *Sex Roles* 37: 663–685.

Pager, Devah. 2007. "The Use of Field Experiments for Studies of Employment Discrimination: Contributions, Critiques, and Directions for the Future." *Annals of the American Academy of Political and Social Science* 609: 104–133.

Pew Research Center. 2003. "Religious Beliefs Underpin Opposition to Homosexuality." http://www.people-press .org/report/197/religious-beliefs-underpin-opposition -to-homosexuality.

Rubenstein, William B. 2002. "Do Gay Rights Laws Matter? An Empirical Assessment." *Southern California Law Review* 75: 65–119.

Tilcsik, András. 2011. "Pride and Prejudice: Employment Discrimination Against Openly Gay Men in the United States." *American Journal of Sociology* 117 (2): 586–626.

Weichselbaumer, Doris. 2003. "Sexual Orientation Discrimination in Hiring." *Labour Economics* 10: 629–642.

———. 2004. "Is It Sex or Personality? The Impact of Sex Stereotypes on Discrimination in Applicant Selection." *Eastern Economic Journal* 30: 159–186.

NOTES

1. For further details on this experiment, the analyses, and robustness checks, see Tilcsik (2011).

A Stalling Out?

63. Paula England*

The Gender Revolution: Uneven and Stalled

We sometimes call the sweeping changes in the gender system since the 1960s a "revolution." Women's employment increased dramatically (Cotter, Hermsen, and England 2008); birth control became widely available (Bailey 2006); women caught up with and surpassed men in rates of college graduation (Cotter, Hermsen, and Vanneman 2004, 23); undergraduate college majors desegregated substantially (England and Li 2006); more women than ever got doctorates as well as professional degrees in law, medicine, and business (Cotter, Hermsen, and Vanneman 2004, 22–23; England et al. 2007); many kinds of gender discrimination in employment and education became illegal (Burstein 1989); women entered many previously male-dominated occupations (Cotter, Hermsen, and Vanneman 2004, 10–14); and more women were elected to political office (Cotter, Hermsen, and Vanneman 2004, 25). As sweeping as these changes have been, change in the gender system has been uneven—affecting some groups more than others and some arenas of life more than others, and change has recently stalled. My goal in this chapter is not to argue over whether we should view the proverbial cup as half empty or half full but, rather, to stretch toward an understanding of why some things change so much more than others. To show the uneven nature of gender change, I will review trends on a number of indicators. While the shape of most of the trends is not in dispute among scholars, the explanations I

offer for the uneven and halting nature of change have the status of hypotheses rather than well-documented conclusions.

I will argue that there has been little cultural or institutional change in the devaluation of traditionally female activities and jobs, and as a result, women have had more incentive than men to move into gender-nontraditional activities and positions. This led to asymmetric change; women's lives have changed much more than men's. Yet in some subgroups and arenas, there is less clear incentive for change even among women; examples are the relatively low employment rates of less educated women and the persistence of traditionally gendered patterns in heterosexual romantic, sexual, and marital relationships.

I also argue, drawing on work by Charles and Bradley, that the type of gender egalitarianism that did take hold was the type most compatible with American individualism and its cultural and institutional logics, which include rights of access to jobs and education and the desideratum of upward mobility and of expressing one's "true self" (Charles 2011; Charles and Bradley 2002, 2009). One form this gender egalitarianism has taken has been the reduction of discrimination in hiring. This has made much of the gender revolution that has occurred possible; women can now enter formerly "male" spheres. But co-occurring with this gender egalitarianism, and discouraging such integration is a strong (if often tacit) belief in gender essentialism—the notion that men and women are innately and fundamentally different in interests and skills (Charles 2011; Charles and Bradley 2002, 2009; Ridgeway 2009). A result of these co-occurring logics is that women are most likely to challenge gender boundaries when there is no path of upward mobility without doing so, but otherwise gender blinders guide the paths of both men and women.

*Paula England. "The Gender Revolution: Uneven and Stalled," *Gender & Society* 24:2 (2010), pp. 149–166. Copyright © 2010 by Sage Publications. Reprinted with Permission by SAGE Publications, Inc.

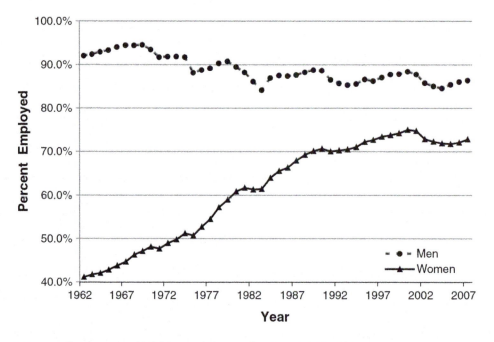

FIGURE 63.1 Percentage of US Men and Women Employed, 1962–2007

Source: Cotter, Hermsen, and Vanneman (2009).

Note: Persons are considered employed if they worked for pay anytime during the year. Refers to adults aged 25 to 54.

Devaluation of "Female" Activities as Asymmetric Incentives for Women and Men to Change

Most of the changes in the gender system heralded as "revolutionary" involve women moving into positions and activities previously limited to men, with few changes in the opposite direction. The source of this asymmetry is an aspect of society's valuation and reward system that has not changed much—the tendency to devalue and badly reward activities and jobs traditionally done by women.

Women's Increased Employment

One form the devaluation of traditionally female activities takes is the failure to treat child-rearing as a public good and support those who do it with state payments. In the United States, welfare reform took away much of what little such support had been present. Without this, women doing child-rearing are reliant on the employment of male partners (if present) or their own employment. Thus, women have had a strong incentive to seek paid employment, and more so as wage levels rose across the decades (Bergmann 2005). As Figure 63.1 shows,

women's employment has increased dramatically. But change has not been continuous, as the trend line flattened after 1990 and turned down slightly after 2000 before turning up again. This turndown was hardly an "opt-out revolution," to use the popular-press term, as the decline was tiny relative to the dramatic increase across forty years (Kuperberg and Stone 2008; Percheski 2008). But the stall after 1990 is clear, if unexplained.

Figure 63.1 also shows the asymmetry in change between men's and women's employment; women's employment has increased much more than men's has declined. There was nowhere near one man leaving the labor force to become a full-time homemaker for every woman who entered, nor did men pick up household work to the extent women added hours of employment (Bianchi, Robinson, and Milkie 2006). Men had little incentive to leave employment.

Among women, incentives for employment vary. Class-based resources, such as education, affect these incentives. At first glance, we might expect less educated women to have higher employment rates than their better-educated peers because they are less likely to be married to a high-earning man. Most marriages are between two people at a similar education level (Mare 1991), so the less educated woman, if she is married, typically has a husband earning less than the husband of the college graduate. Her family would seem to need the money from her employment more than the family headed by two college graduates. Let us call this the "need for income" effect. But the countervailing "opportunity cost" factor is that well-educated women have more economic incentive for employment because they can earn more (England, Garcia-Beaulieu, and Ross 2004). Put another way, the opportunity cost of staying at home is greater for the woman who can earn more. Indeed, the woman who did not graduate from high school may have potential earnings so low that she could not even cover child care costs with what she could earn. It is an empirical question whether the "need for income" or "opportunity cost" effect predominates.

Recent research shows that the opportunity-cost effect predominates in the United States and other affluent nations. England, Gornick, and Shafer (2008) use data from sixteen affluent countries circa 2000 and show that, in all of them, among women partnered with men (married or cohabiting), those with more education are more likely to be employed. Moreover, there is no monotonic relationship between partner's earnings and a woman's employment; at top levels of his income, her employment is deterred. But women whose male partners are at middle income levels are more likely to be employed than women whose partners have very low or no earnings, the opposite of what the "need for income" principle suggests.

In the United States, it has been true for decades that well-educated women are more likely to be employed, and the effect of a woman's own education has increased, while the deterring effect of her husband's income has declined (Cohen and Bianchi 1999). For example, in 1970, 59 percent of college graduate women, but only 43 percent of those with less than a high school education, were employed sometime during the year. In 2007, the figures were 80 percent for college graduates and 47 percent for less than high school (calculated from data in Cotter, Hermsen, and Vanneman 2009).

Women Moving into "Male" Jobs and Fields of Study

The devaluation of and underpayment of predominantly female occupations is an important institutional reality that provides incentives for both men and women to choose "male" over "female" occupa-

tions and the fields of study that lead to them. Research has shown that predominantly female occupations pay less, on average, than jobs with a higher proportion of men. At least some of the gap is attributable to sex composition because it persists in statistical models controlling for occupations' educational requirements, amount of skill required, unionization, and so forth. I have argued that this is a form of gender discrimination—employers see the worth of predominantly female jobs through biased lenses and, as a result, set pay levels for both men and women in predominantly female jobs lower than they would be if the jobs had a more heavily male sex composition (England 1992; Kilbourne et al. 1994; England and Folbre 2005). While the overall sex gap in pay has diminished because more women have moved into "male" fields (England and Folbre 2005), there is no evidence that the devaluation of occupations filled with women has diminished (Levanon, England, and Allison 2009). Indeed, as US courts have interpreted the law, this type of between-job discrimination is not even illegal (England 1992, 225–51; Steinberg 2001), whereas it is illegal to pay women less than men in the same job, unless based on factors such as seniority, qualifications, or performance. Given this, both men and women continue to have a pecuniary incentive to choose male-dominated occupations. Thus, we should not be surprised that desegregation of occupations has largely taken the form of women moving into male-dominated fields, rather than men moving into female-dominated fields.

Consistent with the incentives embedded in the ongoing devaluation of female fields, desegregation of fields of college study came from more women going into fields that were predominantly male, not from more men entering "female" fields. Since 1970, women increasingly majored in previously male-dominated, business-related fields, such as business, marketing, and accounting; while fewer chose traditionally female majors like English, education, and sociology; and there was little increase of men's choice of these latter majors (England and Li 2006, 667–69). Figure 63.2 shows the desegregation of fields of bachelor's degree receipt, using the index of dissimilarity (D), a scale on which complete segregation is 100 and complete integration is 0. It shows that segregation dropped significantly in the 1970s and early 1980s, but has been quite flat since the mid-1980s. Women's increased integration of business fields stopped then as well (England and Li 2006).

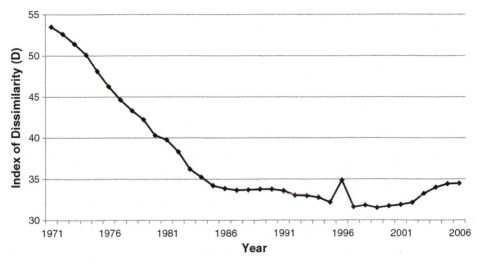

FIGURE 63.2 Sex Segregation of Fields of Study for US Bachelor Degree Recipients, 1971–2006

Source: Author's calculations from the National Center for Education Statistics (NCES) 1971–2003 and NCES 2004–2007.

Women have also recently increased their representation in formerly male-dominated professional degrees, getting MDs, MBAs, and law degrees in large numbers. Women were 6 percent of those getting MDs in 1960, 23 percent in 1980, 43 percent in 2000, and 49 percent in 2007; the analogous numbers for law degrees (JDs) were 3, 30, 46, and 47 percent, and for MBAs (and other management first-professional degrees), 4, 22, 39, and 44 percent (National Center for Education Statistics 2004–2008). There was no marked increase in the proportion of men in female-dominated graduate professional programs such as library science, social work, or nursing (National Center for Education Statistics 2009).

As women have increasingly trained for previously male-dominated fields, they have also integrated previously male-dominated occupations in management and the professions in large numbers (Cotter, Hermsen, and Vanneman 2004, 10–13). Women may face discrimination and coworker resistance when they attempt to integrate these fields, but they have a strong pecuniary incentive to do so. Men lose money and suffer cultural disapproval when they choose traditionally female-dominated fields; they have little incentive to transgress gender boundaries.

The "Personal" Realm

"The personal is political" was a rallying cry of 1960s feminists, urging women to demand equality in private as well as public life. Yet conventions embodying male dominance have changed much less in "the personal" than in the job world. Where they have changed, the asymmetry described above for the job world prevails. For example, parents are more likely to give girls "boy" toys such as Legos than they are to give dolls to their sons. Girls have increased their participation in sports more than boys have taken up cheerleading or ballet. Women now commonly wear pants, while men wearing skirts remains rare. A few women started keeping their birth-given surname upon marriage (Goldin and Shim 2004), with little adoption by men of women's last names. Here, as with jobs, the asymmetry follows incentives, albeit nonmaterial ones. These social incentives themselves flow from a largely unchanged devaluation of things culturally defined as feminine. When boys and men take on "female" activities, they often suffer disrespect, but under some circumstances, girls and women gain respect for taking on "male" activities.

What is more striking than the asymmetry of gender change in the personal realm is how little gendering has changed at all in this realm, especially in dyadic heterosexual relationships. It is still men who usually ask women on dates, and sexual behavior is generally initiated by men (England, Shafer, and Fogarty 2008). Sexual permissiveness has increased, making it more acceptable for both heterosexual men and women to have sex outside committed relationships. But the gendered part of this—the double standard—persists stubbornly;

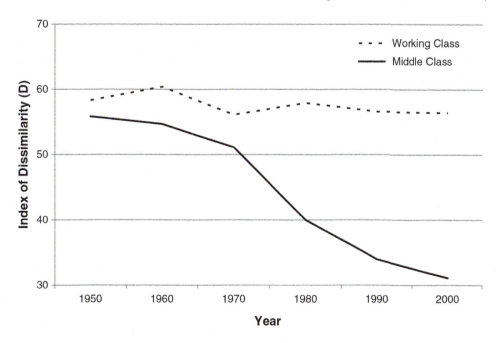

FIGURE 63.3 Sex Segregation of Middle-Class and Working-Class Occupations in the United States, 1950–2000

Source: Cotter, Hermsen, and Vanneman (2004, 14).

Note: Middle-class occupations include professional, management, and nonretail sales. All others are classified as working-class occupations.

women are judged much more harshly than men for casual sex (Hamilton and Armstrong 2009; England, Shafer, and Fogarty 2008). The ubiquity of asking about height in Internet dating Web sites suggests that the convention that men should be taller than their female partner has not budged. The double standard of aging prevails, making women's chances of marriage decrease with age much more than men's (England and McClintock 2009). Men are still expected to propose marriage (Sassler and Miller 2007). Upon marriage, the vast majority of women take their husband's surname. The number of women keeping their own name increased in the 1970s and 1980s but little thereafter, never exceeding about 25 percent even for college graduates (who have higher rates than other women) (Goldin and Shim 2004). Children are usually given their father's surname; a recent survey found that even in cases where the mother is not married to the father, 92 percent of babies are given the father's last name (McLanahan forthcoming). While we do not have trend data on all these personal matters, my sense is that they have changed much less than gendered features of the world of paid work.

The limited change seen in the heterosexual personal realm may be because women's incentive to change these things is less clear than their incentive to move into paid work and into higher-paying "male" jobs. The incentives that do exist are largely noneconomic. For example, women may find it meaningful to keep their birth-given surnames and give them to their children, and they probably enjoy sexual freedom and initiation, especially if they are not judged adversely for it. But these noneconomic benefits may be neutralized by the noneconomic penalties from transgressing gender norms and by the fact that some have internalized the norms. When women transgress gender barriers to enter "male" jobs, they too may be socially penalized for violating norms, but for many this is offset by the economic gain.

Co-Occurring Logics of Women's Rights to Upward Mobility and Gender Essentialism

I have stressed that important change in the gender system has taken the form of women integrating traditionally male occupations and fields of study. But even here change is uneven. The main generalization is shown by Figure 63.3, which divides all occupations by a crude measure of class, calling professional, management, and nonretail sales occupations "middle class," and all others "working class" (including retail sales, assembly work in manufacturing, blue-collar trades, and other nonprofessional service work). Figure 63.3 shows that desegregation has proceeded much farther in middle-class than working-class jobs. Middle-class jobs showed dramatic desegregation, although the trend lessened its pace after 1990. By contrast, working-class jobs are almost as segregated as they were in 1950! Women have integrated the previously male strongholds of management, law, medicine, and academia in large numbers. But women have hardly gained a foothold in blue-collar, male-dominated jobs, such as plumbing, construction, truck driving, welding, and assembly in durable manufacturing industries such as auto and steel (Cotter, Hermsen, and Vanneman 2004, 12–14). This is roughly the situation in other affluent nations as well (Charles and Grusky 2004). This same class difference in trend can be seen if we compare the degree of segregation among those who have various levels of education; in the United States, sex segregation declined much more dramatically since 1970 for college graduates than any other group (Cotter, Hermsen, and Vanneman 2009, 2004, 13–14).

Why has desegregation been limited to high-level jobs? The question has two parts: why women did not integrate blue-collar male jobs in significant numbers, and why women did integrate professional and managerial jobs in droves. Why one and not the other? Many factors were undoubtedly at work, but I will focus on one account, which borrows from Charles and Bradley (Charles 2011; Charles and Bradley 2002, 2009). In the United States and many Western societies today, a certain kind of gender egalitarianism has taken hold ideologically and institutionally. The logic is that individuals should have equal rights to education and jobs of their choice. Moreover, achievement and upward mobility are generally valued. There is also a "postmaterialist" aspect to the culture which orients one to find her or his "true self." The common ethos is a combination of "the American dream" and liberal individualism. Many women, like men, want to "move up" in earnings and/or status, or at least avoid moving down. But up or down relative to what reference group? I suggest that the implicit reference group is typically those in the previous generation (or previous birth cohorts) of one's own social class background and

one's own sex. For example, women might see their mothers or aunts as a reference, or women who graduated with their level of education ten years ago. Persons of the same-sex category are the implicit reference group because of strong beliefs in gender essentialism, that notion that men and women are innately and fundamentally different (Charles 2011; Ridgeway 2009). While liberal individualism encourages a commitment to "free choice" gender egalitarianism (such as legal equality of opportunity), ironically, orienting toward gender-typical paths has probably been encouraged by the emerging form of individualism that stresses finding and expressing one's "true self." Notions of self will in fact be largely socially constructed, pulling from socially salient identities. Because of the omnipresent nature of gender in the culture (Ridgeway 2009; West and Zimmerman 1987), gender often becomes the most available material from which to construct aspirations and may be used even more when a job choice is seen as a deep statement about self (Charles and Bradley 2009).

Given all this, I hypothesize that if women can move "up" in status or income relative to their reference group while still staying in a job typically filled by women, then because of gender beliefs and gendered identities, they are likely to do so. If they cannot move up without integrating a male field, and demand is present and discrimination not too strong, they are more likely to cross the gender boundary. Applying this hypothesis, why would women not enter male blue-collar fields? To be sure, many women without college degrees would earn much more in the skilled blue-collar crafts or unionized manufacturing jobs than in the service jobs typically filled by women at their education levels—jobs such as maid, child care worker, retail sales clerk, or assembler in the textile industry. So they have an economic incentive to enter these jobs. But such women could also move "up" to clerical work or teaching, higher status and better paying but still traditionally female jobs. Many take this path, often getting more education.

In contrast, consider women who assumed they would go to college and whose mothers were in female-dominated jobs requiring a college degree, like teacher, nurse, librarian, or social worker. For these women, to move up in status or earnings from their reference group options requires them to enter traditionally male jobs; there are virtually no heavily female jobs with higher status than these female professions. These are just the women, usually of

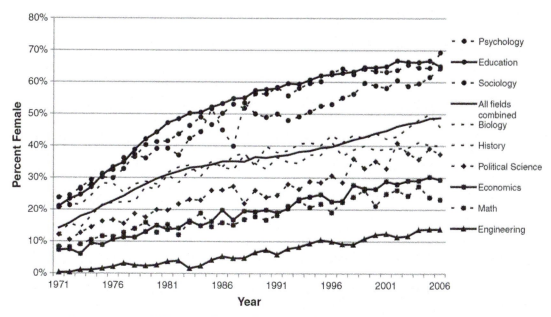

FIGURE 63.4 Percentage of All Doctoral Degree Recipients Who Were Women in Selected Large Fields, 1971–2006

Source: Author's calculations from the National Center for Education Statistics (NCES) 1971–2003 and NCES 2004–2007.

Note: All fields combined refers to all fi elds of doctoral study, not only the nine fields shown here. Engineering refers to doctoral degrees in E.E. Psychology excludes clinical psychology.

middle-class origins, who have been integrating management, law, medicine, and academia in recent decades. For them, upward mobility was not possible within traditional boundaries, so they were more likely to integrate male fields.

In sum, my argument is that one reason that women integrated male professions and management much more than blue-collar jobs is that the women for whom the blue-collar male jobs would have constituted "progress" also had the option to move up by entering higher-ranking female jobs via more education. They thus had options for upward mobility without transgressing gender boundaries not present for their middle-class sisters.

Even women entering male-typical occupations, however, sometimes choose the more female-intensive subfields in them. In some cases, ending up in female-intensive subfields results from discrimination, but in others it may result from the gender essentialism discussed above. An example is the movement of women into doctoral study and into the occupation of "professor." This development brought women into a new arena. But within this arena, there was virtually no desegregation of fields of doctoral study from 1970 on (England et al. 2007, 32). Women have gone from being only 14

percent of those who get doctorates in 1971 to nearly half. But, conditional on getting a doctoral degree, neither women nor men have changed the fields of study they choose much (England et al. 2007). This can be seen in Figure 63.4, which shows the percentage of women in nine large fields of study in each year from 1971 to 2006. The percentage female in every field went up dramatically, reflecting the overall increase in women getting doctorates. But the rank order of fields in their percentage female changed little. The fields with the highest percentage of women today are those that already had a high percentage of women decades ago relative to other fields.

What explains the failure of fields of doctoral study—and thus academic departments—to desegregate? Following the line of argument above, I suggest that the extreme differentiation of fields of academic study allowed many women moving "up" to doctoral study and an academic career to do so in fields that seemed consistent with their (tacitly gendered) notions of their interests and "true selves." Women academics in the humanities and social sciences thus find themselves in the more female subunits (disciplines) of a still largely male-dominated larger unit (the professorate).

Conclusion

Change in the gender system has been uneven, changing the lives of some groups of people more than others and changing lives in some arenas more than others. Although many factors are at play, I have offered two broad explanations for the uneven nature of change.

First, I argued that, because of the cultural and institutional devaluation of characteristics and activities associated with women, men had little incentive to move into badly rewarded, traditionally female activities such as homemaking or female-dominated occupations. By contrast, women had powerful economic incentives to move into the traditionally male domains of paid employment and male-typical occupations; and when hiring discrimination declined, many did. These incentives varied by class, however; the incentive to go to work for pay is much stronger for women who can earn more; thus employment levels have been higher for well-educated women. I also noted a lack of change in the gendering of the personal realm, especially of heterosexual romantic and sexual relationships

Second, I explored the consequences of the co-occurrence of two Western cultural and institutional logics. Individualism, encompassing a belief in rights to equal opportunity in access to jobs and education in order to express one's "true self," promotes a certain kind of gender egalitarianism. It does not challenge the devaluation of traditionally female spheres, but it encourages the rights of women to upward mobility through equal access to education and jobs. To be sure, this ideal has been imperfectly realized, but this type of gender egalitarianism has taken hold strongly. But co-occurring with it, somewhat paradoxically, are strong (if tacit) beliefs in gender essentialism—that men and women are innately and fundamentally different in interests and skills (Charles 2011; Charles and Bradley 2002, 2009; Ridgeway 2009). Almost no men and precious few women, even those who believe in "equal opportunity," have an explicit commitment to undoing gender differentiation for its own sake. Gender essentialism encourages traditional choices and leads women to see previous cohorts of women of their social class as the reference point from which they seek upward mobility. I concluded that the co-occurrence of these two logics—equal opportunity individualism and gender essentialism—make it most likely for women to move into nontraditional fields of study or work when there is no possible female field that constitutes upward mobility from the socially constructed reference point. This helps explain why women integrated male-dominated professional and managerial jobs more than blue-collar jobs. Women from working-class backgrounds, whose mothers were maids or assemblers in nondurable manufacturing, could move up financially by entering blue-collar "male" trades but often decide instead to get more education and move up into a female job such as secretary or teacher. It is women with middle-class backgrounds, whose mothers were teachers or nurses, who cannot move up without entering a male-dominated career, and it is just such women who have integrated management, law, medicine, and academia. Yet even while integrating large fields such as academia, women often gravitate toward the more female-typical fields of study.

While discussing the uneven character of gender change, I noted that the type of gender change with the most momentum—middle-class women entering traditionally male spheres—has recently stalled (Cotter, Hermsen, and Vanneman 2004, 2009). Women's employment rates stabilized, desegregation of occupations slowed down, and desegregation of fields of college study stopped. Erosion of the sex gap in pay slowed as well (Cotter, Hermsen, and Vanneman 2009). While the reason for the stalling is unclear, like the unevenness of change, the stalling of change reminds us how contingent and path-dependent gender egalitarian change is, with no inexorable equal endpoint. Change has been as much unintended consequence of larger institutional and cultural forces as realization of the efforts of feminist organizing, although the latter has surely helped. Indeed, given the recent stalling of change, future feminist organizing may be necessary to revitalize change.

REFERENCES

Bailey, Martha J. 2006. More power to the pill: The impact of contraceptive freedom on women's life cycle labor supply. *Quarterly Journal of Economics* 121:289–320.

Bergmann, Barbara. 2005. *The economic emergence of women.* 2nd ed. New York: Basic Books.

Bianchi, Suzanne, John P. Robinson, and Melissa A. Milkie. 2006. *Changing rhythms of American family life.* New York: Russell Sage Foundation.

Burstein, Paul. 1989. Attacking sex discrimination in the labor market: A study in law and politics. *Social Forces* 67:641–65.

Charles, Maria. 2011. A world of difference: International trends in women's economic status. *Annual Review of Sociology* 37:355–71.

Charles, Maria, and Karen Bradley. 2002. Equal but separate: A cross-national study of sex segregation in higher education. *American Sociological Review* 67:573–99.

———. 2009. Indulging our gendered selves: Sex segregation by field of study in 44 countries. *American Journal of Sociology* 114:924–76.

Charles, Maria, and David B. Grusky. 2004. *Occupational ghettos: The worldwide segregation of women and* men. Stanford, CA: Stanford University Press.

Cohen, Philip N., and Suzanne M. Bianchi. 1999. Marriage, children, and women's employment: What do we know? *Monthly Labor Review* 122:22–31.

Cotter, David A., Joan M. Hermsen, and Paula England. 2008. Moms and jobs: Trends in mothers' employment and which mothers stay home. In *American families: A multicultural reader*, 2nd ed., edited by Stephanie Coontz, with Maya Parson and Gabrielle Raley, 379–86. New York: Routledge.

Cotter, David A., Joan M. Hermsen, and Reeve Vanneman. 2004. *Gender inequality at work*. New York: Russell Sage Foundation.

———. 2009. End of the gender revolution website, http://www.bsos.umd.edu/socy/vanneman/endofgr/default.html (accessed December 14, 2009).

Edin, Kathryn, and Maria Kefalas. 2005. *Promises I can keep: Why poor women put motherhood before marriage*. Berkeley: University of California Press.

England, Paula 1992. *Comparable worth: Theories and evidence*. New York: Aldine.

England, Paula, Paul Allison, Su Li, Noah Mark, Jennifer Thompson, Michelle Budig, and Han Sun. 2007. Why are some academic fields tipping toward female? The sex composition of U.S. fields of doctoral degree receipt, 1971–2002. *Sociology of Education* 80:23–42.

England, Paula, and Nancy Folbre. 2005. Gender and economic sociology. In *The handbook of economic sociology*, edited by N. J. Smelser and R. Swedberg, 627–49. New York: Russell Sage Foundation.

England, Paula, Carmen Garcia-Beaulieu, and Mary Ross. 2004. Women's employment among Blacks, whites, and three groups of Latinas: Do more privileged women have higher employment? *Gender & Society* 18 (4): 494–509.

England, Paula, Janet C. Gornick, and Emily Fitzgibbons Shafer. 2008. Is it better at the top? How women's employment and the gender earnings gap vary by education in sixteen countries. Paper presented at the 2008 annual meeting of the American Sociological Association.

England, Paula, and Su Li. 2006. Desegregation stalled: The changing gender composition of college majors, 1971–2002. *Gender & Society* 20:657–77.

England, Paula, and Elizabeth Aura McClintock. 2009. The gendered double standard of aging in U.S. marriage markets. *Population and Development Review* 35:797–816.

England, Paula, Emily Fitzgibbons Shafer, and Alison C. K. Fogarty. 2008. Hooking up and forming romantic relationships on today's college campuses. In *The gendered society reader*, 3rd ed., edited by Michael Kimmel and Amy Aronson, 531–46. New York: Oxford University Press.

Ferree, Myra Marx. 1976. Working-class jobs: Paid work and housework as sources of satisfaction. *Social Problems* 23 (4): 431–41.

Goldin, Claudia, and Maria Shim. 2004. Making a name: Women's surnames at marriage and beyond. *Journal of Economic Perspectives* 18:143–60.

Hamilton, Laura, and Elizabeth A. Armstrong. 2009. Gendered sexuality in young adulthood: Double binds and flawed options. Gender & Society 23:589–616.

Kilbourne, Barbara Stanek, Paula England, George Farkas, Kurt Beron, and Dorothea Weir. 1994. Returns to skills, compensating differentials, and gender bias: Effects of occupational characteristics on the wages of white women and men. *American Journal of Sociology* 100:689–719.

Kuperberg, Arielle, and Pamela Stone. 2008. The media depiction of women who opt out. *Gender & Society* 2:497–517.

Levanon, Asaf, Paula England, and Paul Allison. 2009. Occupational feminization and pay: Assessing causal dynamics using 1950–2000 census data. *Social Forces* 88:865–92.

Mare, Robert D. 1991. Five decades of educational assortative mating. *American Sociological Review* 56:15–32.

McLanahan, Sara. Forthcoming. Children in fragile families. In *Families in an unequal society, edited by Marcia Carlson and Paula England*. Stanford, CA: Stanford University Press.

McQuillan, Julia, Arthur L. Greil, Karina M. Shreffler, and Veronica Tichenor. 2008. *The importance of motherhood among women in the contemporary United States. Gender & Society* 22:477–96.

Morris, Martina, and Bruce Western. 1999. Inequality in earnings at the close of the twentieth century. *Annual Review of Sociology* 25:623–57.

National Center for Education Statistics. 1971–2003. *Digest of education statistics*. Washington, DC: Government Printing Office.

———. 2004–2007. Table numbers by year: 2004: 253, 2005: 252, 2006: 58, 2007: 264. 2008: 279. http://nces.ed.gov/programs/digest (accessed December 14, 2009).

Percheski, Christine. 2008. Opting out? Cohort differences in professional women's employment rates from 1960 to 2000. *American Sociological Review* 73:497–517.

Ridgeway, Cecilia L. 2009. Framed before we know it: How gender shapes social relations. *Gender & Society* 23:145–60.

Risman, Barbara J. 2009. From doing to undoing: Gender as we know it. *Gender & Society* 23:81–84.

Sassler, Sharon, and Amanda Miller. 2007. Waiting to be asked: Gender, power and relationship progression among cohabiting couples. Presented at the annual meeting of the American Sociological Association, New York, August.

Steinberg, Ronnie J. 2001. Comparable worth in gender studies. In *International encyclopedia of the social and behavioral sciences*, vol. 4, edited by Neil J. Smelser and Paul B. Baltes. Cambridge: Cambridge University Press.

West, Candace, and Donald H. Zimmerman. 1987. *Doing gender. Gender & Society* 1:125–51.

64. Cecilia Ridgeway*
The Persistence of Gender Inequality

How does gender inequality persist in an advanced industrial society like the contemporary United States, in which many economic, legal, institutional, and political forces work against it? In this chapter I argue that people's everyday use of gender as a primary means for organizing their social relations with others is a powerful social process that continually re-creates gender inequality in new forms as society changes (Ridgeway 2011). The use of gender as an initial framing device for relationships with others spreads gendered meanings, including assumptions about inequality embedded in those meanings, beyond contexts associated with sex and reproduction to all spheres of social life that occur through social relationships. Through gender's role in organizing social relations, gender inequality is rewritten into new economic and social arrangements as they emerge, preserving that inequality in modified form throughout socioeconomic transformations.

This persistence process turns on the fact that cultural beliefs about gender change more slowly than

*The ideas, issues, and theories considered in this brief commissioned piece are examined in greater depth in the following publication: Cecilia Ridgeway, *Framed by Gender: How Gender Inequality Persists in the Modern World*, published by Oxford University Press in 2011. The article printed here was originally prepared by Cecilia Ridgeway for the fourth edition of *Social Stratification: Class, Race, and Gender in Sociological Perspective*, edited by David B. Grusky. Copyright © 2014 by Westview Press.

do material arrangements between men and women, even though these beliefs eventually respond to material changes. As a result of this cultural lag, at the edge of social change people confront their new, uncertain circumstances with gender beliefs that are more traditional than those circumstances. As they implicitly draw on the too-convenient cultural frame of gender to help organize their new ways of doing things, they reinscribe trailing cultural assumptions about gender difference and inequality into the new activities, procedures, and forms of organization that they create, in effect reinventing gender inequality for a new era. In the following discussion I explain this argument and some of the evidence behind it.

Gender as a Primary Frame

What do I mean by gender being a primary cultural frame for social relations? We all depend for our very survival on social relations with others, but these relations pose a well-known problem: to relate to another person to accomplish a valued goal, we and the other have to find some way to coordinate our behavior. Classic sociologists like Goffman (1967) and contemporary game theorists (Chwe 2001) have arrived at the same conclusion about what it takes to solve this coordination problem: for you and me to coordinate effectively, we need shared, "common" knowledge, which of course is cultural knowledge, to use as a basis for our joint actions. In particular, we need a shared way of categorizing and defining "who" the self and other are in the situation, so that we can anticipate how each of us is likely to act and coordinate our actions accordingly.

Coordination and Difference

Systems for categorizing and defining things are based on contrast and therefore difference: something is *this* because it is different from *that*. Defining self and other to relate, then, focuses us on finding shared principles of social difference that we can use to categorize and make sense of one another. I argue that the coordination problem inherent in organizing social relations drives populations of people who must regularly relate to one another to develop shared social category systems based on culturally defined standards of difference.

To manage social relations in real time, some of these cultural category systems must be so simplified that they can be quickly applied as framing devices to virtually anyone to start the process of defining self and other in the situation. In fact, studies of social cognition suggest that a very small number of such cultural difference systems, approximately three, serve as the primary categories of person perception in a society (Brewer and Lui 1989; Fiske 1998). These categories define the things a person in that society must know about another person to render that someone sufficiently meaningful to relate to him or her. In the United States, sex, race, and age are primary categories (Schneider 2004, 96).

Social cognition studies show that we automatically and nearly instantly sex categorize any specific person we attempt to relate to (Stangor et al. 1992; Ito and Urland 2003). Our subsequent categorizations of people as, say, bosses or coworkers, are nested in our prior understandings of them as males or females and take on a slightly different meaning as a result, as cognitive research has shown (Brewer and Lui 1989; Fiske 1998; Macrae and Quadflieg 2010). This happens not just in person, but also over the Internet and even in imagination, as we examine a person's resume or think about the kind of person we would like to hire. This initial framing by sex never quite disappears from our understanding of others or of ourselves in relation to them.

Cultural Beliefs About Gender

Primary categories of person perception, including sex category, work as cultural frames for coordinating behavior by associating category membership with widely shared cultural beliefs about how people in one category are likely to behave compared to those in a contrasting category—in other words, stereotypes. We all know common gender stereotypes as cultural knowledge, even though many of us do not personally endorse them (Diekman and Eagly 2000; Glick et al. 2004). Because we think "most people" hold these beliefs, we expect others to judge us according to them. As a result, we must take these beliefs into account in our own behavior even if we do not agree with them. In this way, these shared cultural beliefs act as the "rules" for coordinating public behavior on the basis of gender. And as we would expect from the "rules" for gender, widely shared gender stereotypes have been shown to have a prescriptive as well as descriptive quality (Eagly and Karau 2002; Prentice and Carranza 2002).

The content of our gender stereotypes shows the characteristic pattern of status inequality, in which the higher status group is perceived as more proactive and agentically competent ("from Mars"), and the lower status group is seen as more reactive and emotionally expressive ("from Venus") (Cuddy, Fiske, and Glick 2007; Conway, Pizzamiglio, and Mount 1996; Fiske et al. 2002; Wagner and Berger 1997). Consequently, coordination on the basis of our shared gender beliefs creates social relations of inequality as well as difference.

How Does the Gender Frame Shape Behavior?

Research shows that sex categorization unconsciously primes gender stereotypes in our minds and makes them cognitively available to shape behavior and judgments (Blair and Banaji 1996; Kunda and Spencer 2003). The extent to which they actually do shape our behavior, however, can range from negligible to substantial, depending on the nature of the particular situation and our own motives or interests in it (Macrae and Quadflieg 2010; Wagner and Berger 1997). What matters is the extent to which the information in gender beliefs is diagnostic for us, in that it helps us figure out how to act in the situation.

As part of the primary person frame, the instructions for behavior encoded in gender stereotypes are exceedingly abstract and diffuse. For this very reason they can be applied to virtually any situation, but by the same token, they do not take an actor very far in figuring out exactly how to behave. In contrast, the institutional frameworks that govern the contexts in which most everyday social relations take place are much more specific. They contain defined roles and the expected relationships among them. For individuals, these institutional identities and rules are in the foreground of their sense of who they are and how they should behave in most settings. Gender, in contrast, is almost always a *background identity* for individuals. As a background identity, gender typically acts to bias in gendered directions the performance of behaviors undertaken in the name of more concrete, foregrounded organizational roles or identities. Thus gender becomes a way of acting like a doctor or managing a team project (West and Zimmerman 1987).

A wide variety of research shows that the extent and direction of the biases the background gender frame introduces into our expectations for self and others, our behavior, and our judgments fall into a distinctive pattern (see Ridgeway 2001; Ridgeway and Correll 2004; Ridgeway and Smith-Lovin 1999 for reviews). In mixed-sex settings in which the task or context is relatively gender neutral, cultural beliefs that men are more agentically competent and more worthy of status advantage them over otherwise similar women, but only modestly so. In settings that are culturally typed as masculine, gender beliefs bias judgments and behaviors more strongly in favor of men. In contexts culturally linked with women, biases weakly favor women, except for positions of authority. Men are advantaged for authority in all settings.

The Persistence Process

We can see how this pattern of implicit biases, acting through the everyday social relations that make up the worlds of work and home, reinforces and helps reproduce the structures of gender inequality with which we are familiar: the gender gap in wages and authority (cf. Cotter, Hermsen, and Vanneman 2004), the sex-segregated job structure (cf. Charles and Grusky 2004), and the unequal division of household labor (cf. Bianchi, Robinson, and Milkie 2006). The everyday reproduction of inequality within established institutional structures is an important part of the persistence process. But the future of gender as a principle of inequality lies with sites at the edge of social and technological change, where substantially new forms of work or of heterosexual unions are innovated. Some of these innovations then become blueprints for new industries and ways of life.

I argue that the gender frame, acting through social relations, infuses assumptions about gender inequality even into innovative contexts that are explicitly devoted to doing things differently. Sites of innovation are typically small, interpersonally oriented settings. Also, they are settings in which the determination to do things differently weakens the normally powerful impact of existing institutional schemas as guides to behavior. Both factors increase the likelihood that participants will unconsciously fall back on familiar person-based schemas, like gender, to help organize their inherently uncertain task. The shared gender stereotypes people have to fall back on trail behind changes in the material circumstances they find themselves in.

What is the support for these arguments? First I examine evidence that cultural beliefs about gender lag behind changes in women's material status in society. Then I turn to evidence that lagging beliefs infect sites of innovation.

Do Gender Beliefs Lag Behind?

When changing social circumstances, such as women's growing commitment to the labor force, cause people to have more and more gender-atypical experiences, why would this not simply be reflected in changed gender stereotypes? The answer is that it will eventually, but the impact of atypical experiences is blunted by two processes that slow down changes in stereotypes. At the individual level, gender stereotypes are subject to powerful confirmation biases that cause people to resist noticing gender-inconsistent information or to reinterpret it as consistent (von Hippel, Sekaquaptewa, and Vargas 1995; Dunning and Sherman 1997). Even more importantly, however, is a social process that derives from the use of gender as a frame for coordinating behavior. People's assumption that gender stereotypes are "common knowledge" rules for gendered behavior inhibits the public display of explicitly disconfirming behavior or information (Clark and Kashima 2007; Rudman and Fairchild 2004; Seachrist and Stangor 2001). This further reinforces people's assumption that "most people" hold these stereotypes.

As we would expect, then, evidence suggests that gender stereotypes have lagged behind changes in women's roles in society. Studies show a slight narrowing of the gender gap in instrumental, agentic traits over the last few decades, in that women are now seen as almost the same as men on the softer aspects of agency like "analytical" or "reasoning." Women, however, are still rated much lower than men in the stronger aspects of agency like "aggressive," "forceful," "leaderlike," or "competitive." Women also are still rated much higher than men in communal traits like "warmth" (Cejka and Eagly 1999; Diekman and Eagly 2000; Prentice and Carranza 2002; Spence and Buckner 2000). In common stereotypes, then, men are still from Mars and women are still mostly from Venus, despite massive changes in women's labor force involvement since the 1970s. The next question is, do these lagging stereotypes have an impact on emergent forms of gender relations at sites of social innovation?

Sites of Innovation

Recall that the gender frame produces a distinctive pattern of implicit biases that vary systematically by context. The most telling evidence that the gender frame reestablishes gender inequality at sites of innovation would come from sites for which the argument makes different predictions about the degrees of inequality likely to emerge. An example of such evidence from the work world focuses on high-tech start-ups.

Hi-tech Start-ups

Whittington and Smith-Doerr examined how women scientists fared in innovative start-ups compared to more traditional, established research firms (Smith-Doerr 2004; Whittington 2007; Whittington and Smith-Doerr 2008). Some of the start-ups were biotech firms based in the life sciences. Others were information technology (IT) firms in engineering and the physical sciences. All had adopted a new kind of organizational form in which work is organized in terms of project teams that are often jointly constructed with other firms. Scientists in a firm move flexibly among these project teams, and the hierarchies of control over their activities are relatively flat. Is this informal, flexible, less hierarchical structure advantageous or disadvantageous for women scientists who work in these high-tech firms? The gender frame argument predicts that the answer will be different for biotech firms than for IT firms, even though these firms have the same organizational structure.

Applying the distinctive pattern of biases created by the background gender frame to biotech start-ups, here is what we would expect. The life sciences are no longer strongly sex-typed in contemporary culture. Women earn half the PhDs in this area (England et al. 2007). Therefore, because of the mixed gender composition of the workforce in this field, cultural beliefs about gender should be salient in biotech firms, but only diffusely so, and we would expect these beliefs to create only modest advantages for men in expected competence. Facing only modest biases, women scientists in biotech should have the basic credibility with their coworkers that they need to take effective advantage of the opportunities offered by the flexible structure of innovative firms. In fact, Whittington and Smith-Doerr (2008) find women life scientists do better in these innovative biotech firms in terms of supervisory positions and patents earned than they do in more traditional research organizations like pharmaceutical firms. Even in these innovative firms, however, women attain fewer total patents than comparable men. This disadvantage is not surprising if we remember that background gender biases still modestly favor men even in this innovative biotech context.

In contrast to the life sciences, engineering and the physical sciences are still strongly sex-typed in favor of men. Thus the background gender frame in the IT context is more powerfully relevant and creates stronger implicit biases against women's competence than in biotech settings. In this situation we would expect the informality and flexibility of the innovative firm to be, if anything, a disadvantage for women scientists. Facing strong challenges to their credibility, it will be more difficult for women to effectively take advantage of the flexible structure. Also, in the context of a masculine-typed gender frame, the informal work structure may lead to a "boys' club" atmosphere. Not surprisingly, then, Whittington (2007) found that women physical scientists and engineers were just as disadvantaged in terms of patents in small, flexible start-ups as in traditional industrial research firms. Another study found women engineers actually did better in a traditional, rule-structured aerospace firm than in a more informal start-up, because in the context of a disadvantaging background gender frame, formal rules leveled the playing field to some extent (McIlwee and Robinson 1992).

Since the organizational form of the firms is held constant in these studies, it is especially likely that the varying effects of the gender frame are behind these differing patterns of inequality between the biotech and IT start-ups. Other studies suggest that these initial patterns of gender inequality at the start-up stage of a firm or industry potentially have long-range effects. Gender relations in these start-ups work together with the organizational logic of the firms to shape the workplace practices, routines, and procedures that define work in that firm. These workplace practices and routines then carry the implicit stamp of those founding gender inequalities, and as the practices and routines become institutionalized, they become an independent agent by which the gender regime is reproduced within the firm (Baron et al. 2007). These implicitly gendered procedures also spread to other firms (Phillips 2005). Thus, the way that the background frame of gender infuses gender inequality into the organizational routines of small, pioneering firms potentially has long-range consequences for the future of gender inequality in the workplace as the economy changes and new industries emerge.

Innovative Intimate Unions

The work world is important for the persistence of gender inequality, but so is the world of intimate heterosexual unions. Although there has been less change in the gendered structure of heterosexual unions than in paid work, new, innovative social forms do develop even in this sphere. An example is the way the casual date on college campuses has increasingly been replaced by the explicitly egalitarian "hook-up" (England, Shafer, and Fogarty 2008; Hamilton and Armstrong 2009).

Because of the intensely gendered nature of the hook-up context, the gender frame argument predicts that students will pursue their intended egalitarian goals against a powerful if implicit backdrop of lagging gender stereotypes about gender difference and male status superiority. As students implicitly draw on these stereotypes to make sense of their uncertain encounters, the argument suggests that they will inadvertently rewrite gender inequality into the new cultural norms and practices that they forge for this innovative type of intimate encounter.

Studies of contemporary college students show (Armstrong, England, and Fogarty 2012; England, Shafer, and Fogarty 2008) that women are only slightly less likely than men to initiate the intimate talking and dyadic focus that lead to a hook-up, but men still usually initiate the move to sexual behavior. And both men and women students report that sexual activities during hook-ups are oriented more toward the man's sexual pleasure than the woman's. Furthermore, traditional double standards persist in the social reputations that men and women acquire for having hook-ups with many partners. Despite the increasingly egalitarian material terms on which college men and women encounter one another, lagging cultural beliefs about gender continue to cause substantial inequality in close heterosexual bonds.

Conclusion

In contexts as diverse as high-tech start-ups and college student hook-ups, our everyday use of gender as a basic framing device for social relations is a powerful, if implicit, process by which gender as a principle of social inequality is reinscribed into new forms of social and economic organization as they emerge in society. This persistence dynamic does not mean that gender inequality can never be overcome. After all, powerful economic, legal, and institutional forces, as well as women's own self-interests, all work against gender inequality in the modern world. But this persistence dynamic does mean that the forces for change are not unopposed. As a result, progress toward equality is likely to be both uneven and uncertain.

REFERENCES

Armstrong, Elizabeth A., Paula England, and Alison C. K. Fogarty. 2012. "Accounting for Women's Orgasm and Sexual Enjoyment in College Hookups and Relationships." *American Sociological Review* 77: 435–462.

Baron, James N., Michael T. Hannan, Greta Hsu, and Ozgecan Kocak. 2007. "In the Company of Women: Gender Inequality and the Logic of Bureaucracy in Start-Up Firms." *Work and Occupations* 34: 35–66.

Bianchi, Suzanne M., John P. Robinson, and Melissa Milkie. 2006. *Changing Rhythms of American Family Life.* New York: Russell Sage Foundation.

Blair, Irene V., and Mahzarin R. Banaji. 1996. "Automatic and Controlled Processes in Stereotype Priming." *Journal of Personality and Social Psychology* 70: 1142–1163.

Brewer, Marilynn B., and Layton N. Lui. 1989. "The Primacy of Age and Sex in the Structure of Person Categories." *Social Cognition* 7: 262–274.

Cejka, Mary Ann, and Alice H. Eagly. 1999. "Gender-Stereotypic Images of Occupations Correspond to the Sex Segregation of Employment." *Personality and Social Psychology Bulletin* 25: 413–423.

Charles, Maria, and David Grusky. 2004. Occupational Ghettos: The Worldwide Segregation of Women and Men. Stanford, CA: Stanford University Press.

Chwe, Michael S. 2001. *Rational Ritual: Culture, Coordination, and Common Knowledge.* Princeton, NJ: Princeton University Press.

Clark, Anna E., and Yoshihisa Kashima. 2007. "Stereotypes Help People Connect with Others in the Community: A Situated Functional Analysis of the Stereotype Consistency Bias in Communication." *Journal of Personality and Social Psychology* 93: 1028–1039.

Conway, Michael M., Teresa Pizzamiglio, and Lauren Mount. 1996. "Status, Communality, and Agency: Implications for Stereotypes of Gender and Other Groups." *Journal of Personality and Social Psychology* 71: 25–38.

Cotter, David A., Joan M. Hermsen, and Reeve Vanneman. 2004. "Gender Inequality at Work." In *The American People Census 2000.* New York: Russell Sage Foundation and Population Reference Bureau.

Cuddy, Amy J., Susan T. Fiske, and Peter Glick. 2007. "The BIAS Map: Behaviors from Intergroup Affect and Stereotypes." *Journal of Personality and Social Psychology* 92: 631–648.

Diekman, Amanda B., and Alice H. Eagly. 2000. "Stereotypes as Dynamic Constructs: Women and Men of the Past, Present, and Future." *Personality and Social Psychology Bulletin* 26: 1171–1188.

Dunning, David, and David A. Sherman. 1997. "Stereotypes and Trait Inference." *Journal of Personality and Social Psychology* 73: 459–471.

Eagly, Alice H., and Stephen J. Karau. 2002. "Role Congruity Theory of Prejudice Towards Female Leaders." *Psychological Review* 109: 573–579.

England, Paula, Paul Allison, Su Li, Noah Mark, Jennifer Thompson, Michelle Budig, and Han Sun. 2007. "Why Are Some Academic Fields Tipping Toward Female? The Sex Composition of U.S. Fields of Doctoral Degree Receipt, 1971–2002." *Sociology of Education* 80: 23–42.

England, Paula, Emily Fitzgibbons Shafer, and Alison C. K. Fogarty. 2008. "Hooking-up and Forming Romantic Relationships on Today's College Campuses." In *The Gendered Society Reader*, 3rd ed., edited by M. S. Kimmel and A. Aronson, 531–547. New York: Oxford University Press.

Fiske, Susan T. 1998. "Stereotyping, Prejudice, and Discrimination." In *The Handbook of Social Psychology*, 4th ed., edited by D.T. Gilbert, S.T. Fiske, and G. Lindzey, 357–411. New York: McGraw-Hill.

Fiske, Susan T., Amy J. Cuddy, Peter Glick, and Jun Xu. 2002. "A Model of (Often Mixed) Stereotype Content: Competence and Warmth Respectively Follow from Perceived Status and Competition." *Journal of Personality and Social Psychology* 82: 878–902.

Glick, Peter, Maria Lameiras, Susan T. Fiske, Thomas Eckes, Barbara Masser, Chiara Volpato, Anna Maria Manganelli, Jolynn C. X. Pek, Li-li Huang, Nuray Sakalli-Ugurlu, Yolanda Rodriguez Castro, Maria Luiza D'Avila Pereira, Tineke M. Willemsen, Annetje Brunner, Iris Six-Materna, and Robin Wells. 2004. "Bad But Bold: Ambivalent Attitudes Toward Men Predict Gender Inequality in 16 Nations." *Journal of Personality and Social Psychology* 86: 713–728.

Goffman, Erving. 1967. *Interaction Ritual: Essays on Face-to-Face Behavior*. 1st ed. Garden City, NY: Anchor Books.

Hamilton, Laura, and Elizabeth A. Armstrong. 2009. "Gendered Sexuality in Young Adulthood: Double Binds and Flawed Options." *Gender & Society* 23: 589–616.

Ito, Tiffany A., and Geoffrey R. Urland. 2003. "Race and Gender on the Brain: Electrocortical Measures of Attention to the Race and Gender of Multiply Categorizable Individuals." *Journal of Personality and Social Psychology* 85 (4): 616–626.

Kunda, Ziva, and Steven J. Spencer. 2003. "When Do Stereotypes Come to Mind and When Do They Color Judgment? A Goal-Based Theoretical Framework for Stereotype Activation and Application." *Psychological Bulletin* 129 (4): 522–554.

Macrae, C. Neil, and Susanne Quadflieg. 2010. "Perceiving People." In *Handbook of Social Psychology*, 5th ed., Vol. I, edited by S. T. Fiske, D. T. Gilbert, and G. Lindzey, 428–463. New York: Wiley.

McIlwee, Judith S., and J. Gregg Robinson. 1992. *Women in Engineering: Gender, Power, and Workplace Culture*. Albany: State University of New York Press.

Phillips, Damon J. 2005. "Organizational Genealogies and the Persistence of Gender Inequality: The Case of Silicon Valley Law Firms." *Administrative Science Quarterly* 50: 440–472.

Prentice, Deborah A., and Erica Carranza. 2002. "What Women and Men Should Be, Shouldn't Be, Are Allowed to Be, and Don't Have to Be: The Contents of Prescriptive Gender Stereotypes." *Psychology of Women Quarterly* 26: 269–281.

Ridgeway, Cecilia L. 2001. "Gender, Status, and Leadership." *Journal of Social Issues* 57: 637–655.

———. 2011. *Framed by Gender: How Gender Inequality Persists in the Modern World*. New York: Oxford University Press.

Ridgeway, Cecilia L., and Shelley J. Correll. 2004. "Unpacking the Gender System: A Theoretical Perspective on Cultural Beliefs and Social Relations." *Gender and Society* 18: 510–531.

Ridgeway, Cecilia L., and Lynn Smith-Lovin. 1999. "The Gender System and Interaction." *Annual Review of Sociology* 25: 191–216.

Rudman, Laurie A., and Kimberly Fairchild. 2004. "Reactions to Counterstereotypic Behavior: The Role of Backlash in Cultural Stereotype Maintenance." *Journal of Personality and Social Psychology* 87: 157–176.

Schneider, Donald J. 2004. *The Psychology of Stereotyping*. New York: Guilford Press.

Seachrist, Gretchen B., and Charles Stangor. 2001. "Perceived Consensus Influences Intergroup Behavior and Stereotype Accessibility." *Journal of Personality and Social Psychology* 80: 645–654.

Smith-Doerr, Laurel. 2004. *Women's Work: Gender Equality vs. Hierarchy in the Life Sciences*. Boulder, CO: Lynne Rienner Publishers.

Spence, Janet T., and Camille E. Buckner. 2000. "Instrumental and Expressive Traits, Trait Stereotypes, and Sexist Attitudes: What Do They Signify?" *Psychology of Women Quarterly* 24: 44–62.

Stangor, Charles, Laure Lynch, Changming Duan, and Beth Glass. 1992. "Categorization of Individuals on the Basis of Multiple Social Features." *Journal of Personality and Social Psychology* 62: 207–218.

von Hippel, Willaim, Denise Sekaquaptewa, and Patrick T. Vargas. 1995. "On the Role of Encoding Processes in Stereotype Maintenance." *Advances in Experimental Social Psychology* 27: 177–254.

Wagner, David G., and Joseph Berger. 1997. "Gender and Interpersonal Task Behaviors: Status Expectation Accounts." *Sociological Perspectives* 40: 1–32.

West, Candace, and Don H. Zimmerman. 1987. "Doing Gender." *Gender and Society* 1: 125–151.

Whittington, Kjersten Bunker. 2007. "Employment Sectors as Opportunity Structures: Male and Female: The Effects of Location on Male and Female Scientific Dissemination." PhD diss., Department of Sociology, Stanford University, Stanford, CA.

Whittington, Kjersten Bunker, and Laurel Smith-Doerr. 2008. "Women Inventors in Context: Disparities in Patenting Across Academia and Industry." *Gender and Society* 22: 194–218.

PART VIII

HOW INEQUALITY
SPILLS OVER

We have focused to this point on the task of understanding how various types of inequality (i.e., class, race, gender) are generated and reproduced. We now shift our attention from the sources of inequality to its consequences.

There are two types of consequences that might be examined: (a) the extent to which upper-class people have different lifestyles, political views, or health outcomes than lower-class people (i.e., micro-level consequences); and (b) the extent to which high levels of inequality at the system-level (e.g., the nation-state) have implications for other system-level outcomes (e.g., the viability of democratic governance, the gross national product, the chances of a revolution). The first line of analysis might ask, for example, whether upper-class people are more conservative, raise their children in less authoritarian ways, or lead healthier lifestyles. The second line of analysis, by contrast, asks whether high-inequality countries tend to be less democratic, have lower overall levels of economic output, or face egalitarian revolutions.

This section leads with an especially important example of the macro-level effects of income inequality on segregation (Reardon and Bischoff, Ch. 65). However, because the macro-level approach has been well covered in our earlier sections, we quickly turn to micro-level analyses of how class advantage or disadvantage "spill over" to affect all manner of other life outcomes. We have included chapters examining micro-level effects on voting behavior (Hout and Laurison, Ch. 66), childrearing and socialization practices (Laureau, Ch. 67), and health outcomes (Lutfey and Freese, Ch. 68).

These micro-level effects tend of course to be very strong. In contemporary societies, most everything is marketized and commodified, meaning that one's capacity to access valued goods (e.g., desirable neighborhoods), participate in advantageous networks (e.g., country clubs), or lead a healthy life is directly affected by the capacity to pay for that access. The obvious implication: the muckraking task of demonstrating "class effects" is a bit like shooting fish in a barrel. This conclusion even holds for many so-called "public goods" that are putatively conferred automatically to all members of society but are, in practice, meted out on the basis of race, class, and other dimensions of inequality (e.g., access to voting).

65. Sean F. Reardon and Kendra Bischoff*

Income Inequality and Income Segregation

Introduction

After decreasing for decades, income inequality in the United States has grown substantially in the last forty years.[1] At the same time, income segregation has also increased (Jargowsky 1996; Mayer 2001; Wheeler and La Jeunesse 2006; Watson 2009), although the details of how and why it has grown have been much less thoroughly investigated than those related to income inequality. Common sense and empirical evidence suggest that these trends are linked—greater inequality in incomes implies greater inequality in the housing and neighborhood "quality" that families or individuals can afford—but it is less clear in what specific ways income inequality affects income segregation.

Income segregation—the uneven geographic distribution of income groups within a certain area—is a complex, multidimensional phenomenon. In particular, it may be characterized by the spatial segregation of poverty (the extent to which the lowest-income households are isolated from middle- and upper-income households) and/or the spatial segregation of affluence (the extent to which the highest-income households are isolated from middle- and lower-income households). In addition, income segregation may occur at different geographic scales. High- and low-income households may be physically far apart or may be in economically homogeneous neighborhoods that are close to each other (Reardon et al. 2008). Given the strong correlation between income and race in the United States, income segregation is often empirically entangled with racial segregation, implying the necessity of examining income segregation separately by race as well as for the population as a whole.

Income segregation—and its causes and trends—is of interest to sociologists because it may lead to inequality in social outcomes. It implies, by definition, that lower-income households will live in neighborhoods with lower average incomes than do higher-income households. If the average income of one's neighbors indirectly affects one's own social, economic, or physical outcomes (many sociological theories predict such contextual effects; see, e.g., Jencks and Mayer 1990; Sampson et al. 1997; Leventhal and Brooks-Gunn 2000; Morenoff 2003; Sampson et al. 2008), then income segregation will lead to more unequal outcomes between low- and high-income households than their differences in income alone would predict. In a highly segregated region, then, higher-income households may be advantaged over lower-income households not only by the difference in their own incomes, but also by the differences in their respective neighbors' incomes.

In this chapter we seek to understand if and how variations in income inequality—including among metropolitan areas, between racial groups, and over time—shaped patterns of income segregation between 1970 and 2000. First, we describe a set of trends in average metropolitan area income segregation from 1970 to 2000, including trends for all families, among white and black families separately, and in the segregation of poverty and affluence. We use a rank-order measure of income segregation that avoids the confounding of changes in the income distribution with changes in income segregation. Second, we estimate the effect of metropolitan area income inequality on overall metropolitan area income segregation during this time period. Third, we investigate in more detail how income inequality affects the geographic segregation of poverty and affluence and the extent to which it affects income segregation among white and black families differently.

Background

Income inequality in the United States in the twentieth century exhibited a "U-shaped" trend (Nielsen and Alderson 1997; Ryscavage 1999). The increase in income inequality over the past four decades has been driven largely by the growth of "upper-tail inequality"—dispersion in the relative incomes of those in the upper half of the income distribution—

*The ideas, issues, and theories considered in this brief commissioned piece are examined in greater depth in the following publication: Sean F. Reardon and Kendra Bischoff, "Income Inequality and Income Segregation," *American Journal of Sociology* 116:6 (January 2011), pp. 1934–1981, published by the University of Chicago Press. The article printed here was originally prepared by Sean F. Reardon and Kendra Bischoff for the fourth edition of *Social Stratification: Class, Race, and Gender in Sociological Perspective*, edited by David B. Grusky. Copyright © 2014 by Westview Press.

rather than by growth in "lower-tail inequality" (Piketty and Saez 2003; Autor, Katz et al. 2006, 2008). As we argue in the following discussion, this pattern of growth in income inequality has important implications for its effects on income segregation. There are many mechanisms through which income segregation might affect individual outcomes. The quality of public goods and local social institutions is affected by a jurisdiction's tax base and by the involvement of the community in the maintenance of and investment in these public resources. If high-income households cluster together within a small number of neighborhoods or municipalities, they may be able to collectively better their own outcomes by pooling their extensive financial and social capital to generate resources of which only they can take advantage. High-income neighborhoods, therefore, may have more green space, better-funded schools, better social services, or more of any number of other amenities that affect quality of life. In addition, high- and low-income neighborhoods may differ in their social processes, norms, and social environments (Sampson, Raudenbush et al. 1997; Sampson, Morenoff et al. 1999). Conversely, if high-income households are not clustered together, they may help to fund social services and institutions that serve lower-income populations. Thus the ability of high-income households to self-segregate affects the welfare of poor people and the neighborhoods in which they reside. Not only does this resource problem affect residents' current quality of life and opportunities, but it can also bridge generations—the income distribution in a community may affect the intergenerational transfer of occupational status through investment in locally financed institutions that serve children, such as schools (Durlauf 1996).

The Relationship Between Income Inequality and Income Segregation

Income inequality is a necessary condition for income segregation. By definition, if there were no income inequality, there could be no income segregation. Because all individuals would have the same income and thus all neighborhoods would have the same income distribution. Nonetheless, income inequality alone is not sufficient to create income segregation, which also requires the presence of income-correlated residential preferences, an income-based housing market, and/or housing policies that link income to residential location. Three kinds of income-correlated residential

preferences may lead to income segregation in the presence of income inequality: preferences about the socioeconomic characteristics of one's neighbors, preferences about characteristics of one's neighbors that are correlated with their income (e.g., race/ethnicity or educational levels), and preferences about local public goods (e.g., public school quality, public parks, police services). Even in the presence of sizeable income inequality, however, these income-correlated preferences may be insufficient to produce income segregation. Income segregation also requires the existence of a housing market based on residents' ability to pay or housing policies that sort households by income.

As we suggested previously, income inequality may affect income segregation differently among black and white households because of the variation in housing markets available to each group. Racial discrimination in the housing market has meant that historically, minority households (particularly black households) have had fewer residential options than white households with similar income and wealth. Even if black households had the same preferences and the same level of income inequality as white households, the racially discriminatory aspects of the housing market likely would lead to lower levels of income segregation among black households than among white households. In the period from 1970 to 2000, however, the housing options available to middle-class blacks greatly expanded (though housing discrimination persisted throughout this period; see Farley and Frey 1994; Yinger 1995; Ross and Turner 2005), probably tightening the link between inequality and segregation among blacks over this period.

Data and Methods

To distinguish income *segregation* (the sorting of families by income among census tracts, independent of the income distribution) from income *inequality* (the uneven distribution of income among families), we use the *rank-order information theory index* (*HR*) (Reardon 2011), which relies only on information about the rank-ordering of incomes among families, not on information about actual dollar income amounts. This index ranges from a minimum of 0, indicating there is no income segregation (the income distribution in each local environment, such as the census tract, mirrors that of the region as a whole), to a maximum of 1, indicating there is complete income segregation (there is no income variation in any local environment).[2] We

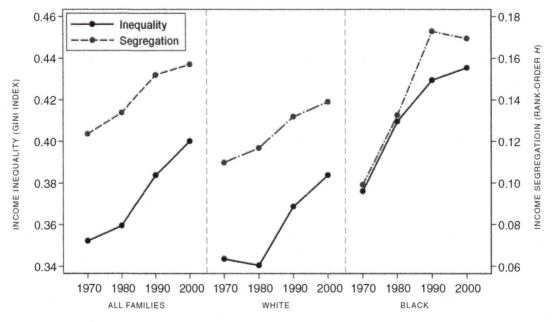

FIGURE 65.1 Trends in Family Income Inequality and Income Segregation, 1970–2000, by Race, 100 Largest Metropolitan Areas

Note: Black trends based on 61 metropolitan areas with at least 10,000 black families in each census year, 1970–2000.

measure income inequality within each race group-metro-year with the Gini index, which measures the extent to which the actual income distribution deviates from a hypothetical distribution in which each person receives an identical share of total income. The measure ranges from 0, indicating perfect equality (each individual receives an identical share of the distribution), to 1, indicating maximum inequality (one individual holds all of the income).

Throughout this study we rely on tract-level family income data from the US Census (GeoLytics 2004; Minnesota Population Center 2004). We include the one hundred metropolitan areas with the largest populations in 2000;[3] however, we retain only cases in which there were at least ten thousand families of a given race group in a given metro area in 1970, 1980, 1990, and 2000.

Results

Patterns and Trends in Income Inequality and Segregation

Figure 65.1 reports the average levels of income inequality and income segregation, by race, for the one hundred largest metropolitan areas in the United States. Overall, metropolitan area income inequality grew from 1970 to 2000, with the greatest increase occurring in the 1980s. Average metropolitan area income inequality increased more rapidly for blacks than whites, particularly in the 1970s, a pattern that reflects the continuing growth of the black middle class that began in the 1960s. Average metropolitan area income segregation followed a similar pattern, growing from 1970 to 2000, with the fastest increase occurring in the 1980s. For black families, income segregation grew rapidly in the 1970s and 1980s, at a rate more than three times faster than the corresponding growth of white income segregation. In fact, average black income segregation was about one-third of a standard deviation *lower* than white income segregation in 1970, but was about one standard deviation *higher* than white income segregation by 1990. These patterns suggest a relationship between income inequality and income segregation; for both black and white families, as well as for the total population, changes in income segregation appear to roughly mirror changes in income inequality.

Although Figure 65.1 shows changes in the average values of the rank-order information theory index from 1970 to 2000, it does not provide details on the extent to which changes in income segregation are attributable to changes in the segregation of

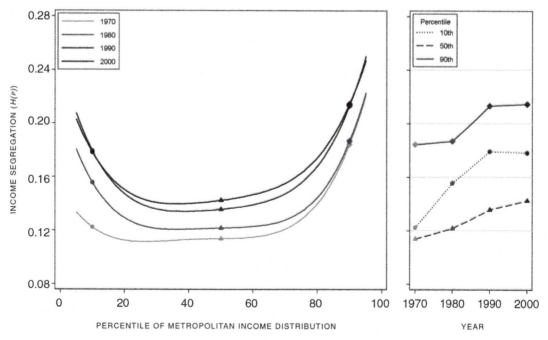

FIGURE 65.2 Trends in Average Metropolitan Area Income Segregation, by Income Percentile, All Families, 100 Largest Metropolitan Areas, 1970–2000

Note: Left panel of figure indicates estimated average between-tract segregation (as measured by the information theory index, H) between families with incomes at or above and below each percentile of the metropolitan-wide family income distribution. Right panel shows trends for between-tract segregation at three specific percentiles.

affluence and poverty. Figure 65.2 shows the average metropolitan area segregation profiles across the one hundred largest metropolitan areas from 1970 to 2000, illustrating the extent to which segregation has changed between the poor and nonpoor and the rich and nonrich, for example.[4] Note that in 1970 the poor were much less segregated from the nonpoor than the rich were from the nonrich. Income segregation between the poor and nonpoor (segregation of poverty) increased sharply between 1970 and 1980, whereas income segregation of the rich and nonrich (segregation of affluence) did not. In the 1980s, however, income segregation grew at all parts of the income distribution. In the 1990s, income segregation increased only modestly, and only between families in the middle part of the income distribution. On average, the segregation of poverty and the segregation of affluence were relatively unchanged in the 1990s.

Figure 65.3 shows the corresponding trends for black families (the trend of income segregation among white families is quite similar to the overall patterns shown in Figure 65.2, because of the size of the white population). Black income segregation grew rapidly in the 1970s and 1980s at all parts of the black income distribution. Not only did low-income black families become more isolated from middle- and higher-income black families, but higher-income blacks also became increasingly segregated from lower- and middle-income black families. In the 1990s this trend ceased abruptly. In fact, the segregation of lower- and moderate-income black families from higher-income black families declined slightly in the 1990s.

Our descriptive analyses reveal several important trends. First, average metropolitan area income inequality and segregation both increased from 1970 to 2000, although the growth in both was much larger for black families than for white ones. Second, income segregation grew at all parts of the income distribution from 1970 to 2000, although at different times and rates for black and white families. Most of the growth in income segregation occurred between 1970 and 1990. Nonetheless, both the segregation of poverty and the segregation of affluence were much higher in 2000 than they had been in 1970, for white and black families alike. Finally, the segregation of affluence is generally greater than the segregation of poverty in the one hundred largest metropolitan areas. The next section of this chapter

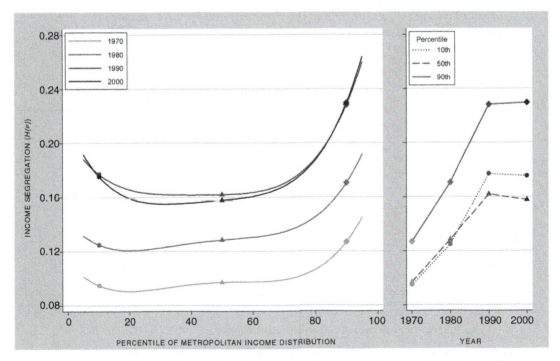

FIGURE 65.3 Trends in Average Metropolitan Area Income Segregation, by Income Percentile, Black Families, 61 Largest Metropolitan Areas with at Least 10,000 Black Families, 1970–2000

Note: Left panel of figure indicates estimated average between-tract segregation (as measured by the information theory index, H) between black families with incomes at or above and below each percentile of the metropolitan-wide family income distribution. Right panel shows trends for between-tract segregation at three specific percentiles.

investigates the extent to which variation in income inequality can explain these patterns.

Estimating the Effects of Income Inequality on Income Segregation

We estimate the effect of income inequality on income segregation using a set of fixed-effects regression models. The models rely on 644 metro-group-year cases. Because each observation in the data corresponds to a specific metropolitan area, decade, and race group, there are three potential sources of variation in income inequality: variation across decades (within each metro-by-group cell), variation among metropolitan areas (within each decade-by-group cell), and variation between race groups (within each metro-by-decade cell).[5] We use three fixed effects models, each relying on a different source of variation in income inequality, to estimate the effects of income inequality on segregation over time, across race groups, and across metropolitan areas, respectively. In addition, we control for metropolitan demographic characteristics, housing market pressures and housing stock, intra- and inter-metropolitan

mobility, population growth, labor market characteristics, and family structure (Wilson 1987; Massey and Eggers 1993; Abramson, Tobin et al. 1995; Jargowsky 1996; Pendall and Carruthers 2003; Wheeler 2006; Watson 2009).

In the first set of regression models (Models 1 and 2), we estimate the effect of changes in inequality on changes in segregation, including both metropolitan area-by-group fixed effects and decade fixed effects. We compute bootstrapped standard errors in all of the regression models to account for the clustered nature of the observations. In the second set of models (Model 3 and 4), we estimate the effect of differences in income inequality between race groups on income segregation, using metropolitan area-by-year fixed effects and group-specific dummy variables. In the final set of models (Model 5 and 6), we estimate the effect of differences in income inequality among racial groups on income segregation, using metropolitan area and group-by-year fixed effects. Because the three models rely on different sources of variation in income inequality, each relies on a different key assumption to support a causal claim about the effect of income inequality

TABLE 65.1 Estimated Effects of Income Inequality on Income Segregation, 1970–2000

	Source of Variation in Income Inequality					
	Temporal Variation Within Metro-by-Race Cells		*Between-Race Variation Within Metro-by-Year Cells*		*Between-Metro Variation Within Race-by-Year Cells*	
	Model 1	Model 2	Model 3	Model 4	Model 5	Model 6
Gini Index	0.385***	0.467***	0.431***	0.783***	0.286**	0.502***
	(0.059)	(0.060)	(0.069)	(0.125)	(0.103)	(0.110)
Year=1980	0.013***	0.029***				
	(0.002)	(0.009)				
Year=1990	0.028***	0.032**				
	(0.003)	(0.012)				
Year=2000	0.026***	0.027				
	(0.003)	(0.015)				
Black			-0.013**	-0.065***		
			(0.005)	(0.015)		
Model Specification						
Metro-Year Covariates		Yes				Yes
Group-Metro-Year Covariates		Yes		Yes		Yes
Metro-x-Group Fixed Effects	Yes	Yes				
Metro-x-Year Fixed Effects			Yes	Yes		
Group-x-Year Fixed Effects					Yes	Yes
Adjusted R²	0.879	0.933	0.691	0.770	0.822	0.883
N	644	644	488	488	644	644

Notes: Bootstrapped standard errors in parentheses. *p<.05; **p<.01; ***p<.001. Sample includes observations from 100 largest metropolitan areas in 2000, excluding black observations from 39 metropolitan areas with fewer than 10,000 black families in 1970. Coefficients on covariates and fixed effects not shown. Metro-year covariates include metro populations, unemployment rate, proportion under age 18, proportion over age 65, porportion with high school diploma, proportion foreign born, proportion female-headed families, per capita income, proportions employed in manufacturing, construction, financial and real estate, professional and managerial jobs, and proportions of housing built within ten, five, and one years. Group-metro-year covariates include race-group-specific population, per capita income, proportion with high school diploma, proportion female-headed families, and unemployment rate.

on income segregation.[6] As a result, many sources of potential bias can be ruled out if the three sets of models produce similar results.

Main Effects of Income Inequality on Income Segregation

Table 65.1 reports the estimates from the models. Of primary interest here are the estimated coefficients on the Gini index in Models 2, 4, and 6, which include the full set of covariates as well as the fixed effects. Model 2 yields an estimated association of 0.467 (*s.e.* = 0.060; *p* < .001) between income inequality and income segregation, net of the model's fixed effects and covariates. In other words, a change of one point in a group's income inequality is associated with a change of roughly half a point in income segregation.

Model 4, which relies on variation in income inequality between white and black families within the same metropolitan area and year, yields an estimated

association between inequality and segregation of 0.783 (*s.e.* = 0.125; *p* < .001), somewhat larger than the estimate from model 2. Finally, Model 6 yields an estimated association between income inequality and income segregation of 0.502 (*s.e.* = 0.110; *p* < .001). Thus, each of the three models yields estimated coefficients on income inequality that imply inequality has a positive effect on income segregation. To get a sense of the magnitude of these effects, note that an effect of 0.500 (roughly that found in Models 2 and 6) implies that the changes in income inequality from 1970 to 2000 shown in Table 65.1 account for roughly 40 percent of the average change in black income segregation, 80 percent of the average change in white income segregation, and 60 percent of the average change in overall income segregation. Put differently, a one-standard deviation change in income inequality leads to roughly one-quarter of a standard deviation change in income segregation.[7]

To ensure that the estimates from Models 2, 4, and 6 are not driven by one particular race group or

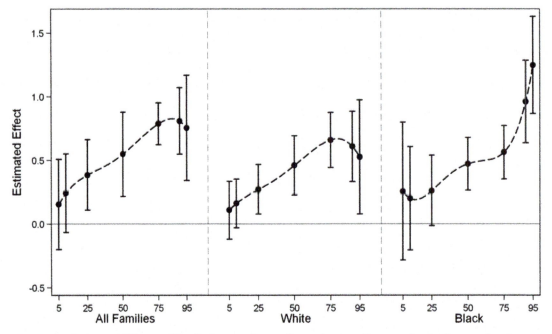

FIGURE 65.4 Estimated Effects of Family Income Inequality on Income Segregation by Percentile of Income Distribution and Race, 100 Largest Metropolitan Areas, 1970–2000

Note: Bars indicate 95 percent confidence interval for estimates. Model specifications and samples are identical to those in columns 1–3 of Table 65.1.

decade, we fit an additional set of models (not shown) for each race group separately and another set of models for each decade separately. In each model, the coefficient on inequality is positive and statistically significant. In the group-specific models, the coefficients range from 0.450 to 0.561; in the decade-specific models, they range from 0.624 to 0.732. Thus, across all the models we find that income inequality has a large and positive association with income segregation, regardless of whether we rely on temporal, between-group, or between-metropolitan-area variation to identify this association, and regardless of which groups or decades we use in the sample.

Effects of Income Inequality on the Segregation of Poverty and Affluence

One advantage of the information theory index is that it enables us to investigate whether income inequality more strongly affects income segregation through the segregation of poverty or the segregation of affluence. To do this, we fit models identical to Models 2, 4, and 6 but using income segregation measured at a set of income percentiles (the 5th,

10th, 25th, 50th, 75th, 90th, and 95th percentiles) rather than the rank-order information theory index as the outcome.

The estimates from these models are reported in the left-hand section of Figure 65.4, which shows that income inequality has little or no significant impact on the segregation of the very poorest families in a metropolitan area from all other families, but has large and significant effects on the segregation of moderate- to high-income families from those with lower incomes. In other words, income inequality appears to be much more strongly linked to the segregation of affluence than to the segregation of poverty.

The same general pattern is true when we investigate the effects of income inequality on income segregation for white and black families separately, as shown in the middle and right-hand sections of Figure 65.4. However, the effect of inequality on the segregation of affluence is much stronger for black families than for white ones. That is, in metropolitan areas and years when black income inequality is largest, the highest-earning 10 percent of black families is much more segregated from the lower 90 percent of black families than when and where black income inequality is low.

Discussion and Conclusions

Our analysis yields three main findings. First, we reproduce the finding in Watson (2009) and Mayer (2001) linking income inequality to income segregation. Using a set of fixed-effects regression models, we show that there is a strong and robust relationship between within-race metropolitan area income inequality and within-race metropolitan area income segregation, net of secular trends, stable between-race differences, and stable differences among metropolitan areas. Our estimates indicate that a one-standard-deviation increase in income inequality leads to a quarter of a standard deviation increase in income segregation, an effect roughly half the size of that found by Watson (2009). Nonetheless, these effects are large enough to be substantially meaningful: they imply that increasing income inequality was responsible for 40–80 percent of the changes in income segregation from 1970 to 2000. The strength and consistency of our results across a wide range of model specifications suggests this is a robust relationship, at least among large metropolitan areas in the period 1970–2000. It is important to keep in mind that this analysis investigates the effect of income inequality in an era of rising inequality. It is not clear to what extent these findings can be generalized to eras of lower, or stable, inequality.

Our second main finding is that income inequality influences income segregation primarily by affecting the segregation of affluence, rather than the segregation of poverty. Although the segregation of poverty increased from 1970 to 2000 for both white and black families, as well as for all families, very little of this change is attributable to changes in income inequality. Given this, we suspect that the segregation of poverty is more a result of housing policy than of income inequality. Throughout the 1980s federal and metropolitan housing policies fostered the development of high-density housing for low-income families. These policies may be responsible for much of the increase in the segregation of poverty during that period. Likewise, the growth in scattered site low-income and mixed-income housing in the 1990s, coupled with the demolition of some large, high-density public housing projects, may account for the stabilization of the segregation of poverty in the 1990s.

Third, we find that the relationship between income inequality and income segregation differs for black and white families. In 1970 income segregation among black families was lower than among white families. This was probably the result of the ghettoization of minorities that took place, particularly in northern and midwestern American cities, during the post–World War II suburbanization boom. Because of housing discrimination, black families were largely denied access to suburban areas, leaving both middle- and lower-income black families living in relative proximity in urban areas. The passage of housing and lending antidiscrimination legislation in the 1970s began to reduce the prevalence of housing discrimination, making a wider range of neighborhood options available to middle-income black families. As a result, income segregation among black families rose steeply from 1970 to 1990, as the growing black middle class was able to move into previously inaccessible suburban areas. Although this increase in income segregation among black families is a result of both the growing black middle class and reductions in housing discrimination—both signs of progress since the 1960s—it nonetheless may have negative consequences. Given high levels of racial segregation in US cities, the growth of income segregation among black families results in the increasing racial and socioeconomic isolation of low-income black families in neighborhoods of concentrated disadvantage (Wilson 1987).

In sum, our analyses show that income inequality has a strong and robust effect on income segregation, but it is more nuanced in form than one might expect. In fact, additional analyses (included in the original, unabridged version of this chapter; see Reardon and Bischoff 2011) show that income inequality appears to be responsible for a specific aspect of income segregation: the large-scale separation of the affluent from lower-income households and families. It does not, however, appear to be responsible for patterns of segregation of poverty (for that, housing policy is probably to blame). Nor is it responsible for patterns of small-scale income segregation, such as those resulting from the gentrification of urban neighborhoods adjacent to poor, nongentrifying neighborhoods.

The macroscale spatial segregation of high-income households from middle- and low-income households may have important and far-reaching consequences, particularly given that the top 10 percent of earners in the United States now receive 45 percent of all income. The segregation of these high-income households in communities physically far from lower-income households may reduce the likelihood that high-income residents will have social, or even casual, contact with lower-income residents. This in turn may make it less likely that they will be willing to invest in metropolitan-wide public resources that would benefit residents of all income levels, such as transportation networks, utilities, parks, services, and cultural amenities. Moreover, the separation of the affluent and poor implies that there will be few opportunities for disadvantaged families to benefit from local spillover of public goods. The distance between affluent and lower-income communities makes it unlikely that disadvantaged families will be able to take advantage of the local schools, parks, and services in which affluent communities invest. Although most sociological theory and research on the spatial distribution of income has focused on the effects of concentrated *poverty* on residents of poor neighborhoods, the findings here suggest that a better understanding of the effects of concentrated *affluence* on residents far from affluent communities is also needed. The segregation of affluence may directly affect the resources available to residents of both poor and low-income neighborhoods.

REFERENCES

Abramson, A. J., M. S. Tobin, et al. 1995. "The Changing Geography of Metropolitan Opportunity: The Segregation of the Poor in U.S. Metropolitan Areas, 1970 to 1990." *Housing Policy Debate* 6 (1): 45–72.

Autor, D. H., L. H. Katz, et al. 2006. "The Polarization of the U.S. Labor Market." *American Economic Review* 95 (2): 189–194.

Autor, D. H., L. H. Katz, et al. 2008. "Trends in U.S. Wage Inequality: Revising the Revisionists." Review of Economics and Statistics 90 (2): 300–323.

Durlauf, S. 1996. "A Theory of Persistent Income Inequality." *Journal of Economic Growth* 1: 75–93.

Farley, R., and W. H. Frey. 1994. "Changes in the Segregation of Whites from Blacks During the 1980s: Small Steps Toward a More Integrated Society." *American Sociological Review* 59 (February): 23–45.

GeoLytics. 2004. *Neighborhood Change Database.* East Brunswick, NJ, GeoLytics, Inc.

Jargowsky, P. A. 1996. "Take the Money and Run: Economic Segregation in U.S. Metropolitan Areas." *American Sociological Review* 61 (6): 984–998.

Jencks, C., and S. Mayer. 1990. "The Social Consequences of Growing Up in a Poor Neighborhood." In *Inner-city Poverty in the United States*, edited by L. E. Lynn Jr. and M. G. H. McGeary, 111–186. Washington, DC: National Academy Press.

Leventhal, T., and J. Brooks-Gunn. 2000. "The Neighborhoods They Live in: The Effects of Neighborhood Residence on Child and Adolescent Outcomes." *Psychological Bulletin* 126 (2): 309–337.

Massey, D. S., and M. L. Eggers. 1993. "The Spatial Concentration of Affluence and Poverty During the 1970s." *Urban Affairs Quarterly* 29: 299–315.

Mayer, S. E. 2001. "How the Growth in Income Inequality Increased Economic Segregation." Joint Center for Poverty Research Working Paper 230.

Minnesota Population Center. 2004. National Historical Geographic Information System: Pre-release Version 0.1. Minneapolis: University of Minnesota.

Morenoff, J. D. 2003. "Neighborhood Mechanisms and the Spatial Dynamics of Birth Weight." *American Journal of Sociology* 108 (5): 976–1017.

Nielsen, F., and A. S. Alderson. 1997. "The Kuznets Curve and the Great U-turn: Income Inequality in U.S. Counties, 1970 to 1990." *American Sociological Review* 62 (1): 12–33.

Pendall, R., and J. I. Carruthers. 2003. "Does Density Exacerbate Income Segregation? Evidence from U.S. Metropolitan Areas, 1980 to 2000." *Housing Policy Debate* 14 (4): 541–589.

Piketty, T., and E. Saez. 2003. "Income Inequality in the United States, 1913–1998." *Quarterly Journal of Economics* 118 (1): 1–39.

Reardon, S. F. 2011. "Measures of Income Segregation." Working paper, Stanford Center for Education Policy Analysis.

Reardon, S. F., and K. Bischoff. 2011. "Income Inequality and Income Segregation." *American Journal of Sociology* 116 (4): 1092–1153.

Reardon, S. F., S. A. Matthews, et al. 2008. "The Geographic Scale of Metropolitan Racial Segregation." *Demography* 45: 489–514.

Ross, S. L., and M. A. Turner. 2005. "Housing Discrimination in Metropolitan America: Explaining Changes Between 1989 and 2000." *Social Problems* 52: 152–180.

Ryscavage, P. 1999. *Income Inequality in America: An Analysis of Trends.* New York: M. E. Sharpe.

Sampson, R. J., J. D. Morenoff, et al. 1999. "Beyond Social Capital: Spatial Dynamics of Collective Efficacy for Children." *American Sociological Review* 64 (5): 633–660.

Sampson, R. J., S. W. Raudenbush, et al. 1997. "Neighborhoods and Violent Crime: A Multilevel Study of Collective Efficacy." *Science* 277: 918–924.

Sampson, R. J., P. Sharkey, et al. 2008. "Durable Effects of Concentrated Disadvantage on Verbal Ability Among African-American Children." Proceedings of the National Academy of Sciences 105 (3): 845–852.

Watson, T. 2009. "Inequality and the Measurement of Residential Segregation by Income." *Review of Income and Wealth* 55 (3): 820–844.

Wheeler, C. H. 2006. *Urban Decentralization and Income Inequality: Is Sprawl Associated with Rising Income Segregation Across Neighborhoods?* St. Louis, MO: Federal Reserve Bank of St. Louis.

Wheeler, C. H., and E. A. La Jeunesse. 2006. *Neighborhood Income Inequality*. St. Louis, MO: Federal Reserve Bank of St. Louis.

Wilson, W. J. 1987. *The Truly Disadvantaged: The Inner City, the Underclass, and Public Policy*. Chicago: University of Chicago Press.

Yinger, J. 1995. *Closed Doors, Opportunities Lost: The Continuing Costs of Housing Discrimination*. New York: Russell Sage Foundation.

NOTES

1. http://www.census.gov/hhes/www/income/histinc/p60no231_tablea3.pdf (accessed September 2, 2009).

2. Refer to Reardon and Bischoff (2011) for more details about this measure.

3. These 100 metropolitan areas together were home to 173 million residents in 2000, 62 percent of the total U.S. total population, including 70 percent of non-Hispanic blacks (23.6 million), 78 percent of Hispanics (27.6 million), and 89 percent of Asians (9 million). The metropolitan areas range in population from 561,000 (Scranton–Wilkes-Barre, PA) to 11.3 million (New York–White Plains, NY-NJ).

4. The income segregation profile shows the extent of segregation of those below a given income percentile from those above that percentile. The curved "profile" traces this value for all income percentiles. So, for example, the leftmost dots on the curves indicate the segregation of the bottom 10 percent of families from the top 90 percent; dots in the middle of the curves indicate the segregation level of those with below-median income from those with above-median income. For a full description of the income segregation profiles, see the unabridged version of this chapter (Reardon and Bischoff 2011).

5. Only sixty-one of the 100 metropolitan areas have this latter variation, because we include observations for black families in the sample only for the sixty-one metropolitan areas where there are at least 10,000 black families in each of the four Census years.

6. The models that include metro-by-group fixed effects rely on the assumption that changes in income inequality within a metropolitan area and race group over time are exogenous, conditional on secular trends common to all groups and metropolitan areas and the set of included covariates in the model. The models that include metro-by-year fixed effects rely on the assumption that differences between white and black income inequality within the same metropolitan area and decade are exogenous, once we have accounted for differences in income inequality between white and black families that are common across metropolitan areas and time and differences in inequality that are associated with differences in the covariates included in the model. Finally, the models that include group-by-year and metropolitan area fixed effects rely on the assumption that differences in income inequality within a given year and for a given race group are exogenous, once we have accounted for stable differences among metropolitan areas and differences associated with the covariates in the model. None of these three assumptions is likely to be perfectly true, but each model is somewhat insulated against threats to any other.

7. These are computed from the 1970–2000 changes in inequality and segregation shown in Table 65.2. For example, income inequality among all families grew by 0.048 from 1970 to 2000. If the effect of income inequality on segregation were 0.500, this would imply a change in income segregation of 0.048 · 0.5=0.024, which is roughly 70 percent of the observed total change (0.033) in income segregation from 1970 to 2000. Likewise, the standard deviation of income inequality within a given year was roughly 0.025, on average, whereas the standard deviation of income segregation was roughly 0.050. This implies that an effect of 0.500 corresponds to an effect size of 0.25.

66. Michael Hout and Daniel Laurison*
The Realignment of U.S. Presidential Voting

Introduction

American presidential elections since the 1960s have supplied ample material for study by political scientists and political sociologists, who have contended that the stable class politics of the industrial era— roughly 1932–1964 (or perhaps as late as 1976)— gave way to new, "postmaterial" politics (e.g., Inglehart 1977; Lipset 1981; Clark and Lipset 1991). Scholars who subscribe to this viewpoint to newer cleavages based on gender, identity, concern for the environment, and family values, which they argue have displaced class from its central place in American politics. When Democrats appeal to middle-class voters and the British Labour Party touts a

*This commissioned piece was prepared by Michael Hout and Daniel Laurison for the fourth edition of *Social Stratification: Class, Race, and Gender in Sociological Perspective*, edited by David B. Grusky. Copyright © 2014 by Westview Press. The article updates the work of Hout, Brooks, and Manza (1995). The authors owe a huge debt to Jeff Manza and Clem Brooks, who established the research templates used in this work and to Benjamin Moodie, who coauthored the 2006 update. In addition, they thank the participants of the 2005 Stanford-Berkeley Inequality Colloquium, especially Annette Lareau, for helpful discussion.

"third way" in twenty-first-century politics, some of these ideas ring true.

Other scholars have countered the postmaterialists. Hout, Brooks, and Manza (1995) noted that political cleavages need not sum to zero. Voters typically balance many facets of their political identity when they vote, including class, race, gender, religion, and region. Nothing in the political arithmetic of social cleavages mandates that the emergence of a new factor lowers the weight given to others. The empirical evidence supports this insight. Research has shown that nearly all those factors that were important for voting in US presidential elections in the 1960s were more important in the 2000s, even as gender and church attendance emerged as new cleavages (Greeley and Hout 2006, ch. 3; Bartels 2008). In Britain, class voting fluctuated without trend (Goldthorpe 1999). In the United States, classes realigned (Hout, Brooks, and Manza 1995), and the effects of income on the vote increased (Bartels 2008). In a six-country comparison of elections from the 1960s to the 1990s, Brooks, Nieuwbeerta, and Manza (2006) found small but significant changes in overall cleavage—increases in the United States and Australia, decreases in Germany and Britain—that made politics in the six countries more similar in the 1990s than in the 1960s.

Class Voting and Class Politics

Interest in class voting goes back to the dawn of modern understandings of class, to the grand theorists of the nineteenth century. The roots of contemporary debates about class voting, however, are planted in data, not in class theory. The national election surveys that have been taken in many countries since the 1960s and the World Values Surveys that began in the 1970s yielded a harvest of class-voting time series. Findings through the early 1970s showed a strong, if variable, relationship between class (as indicated by occupation) and voters' choices of candidates and parties (Lipset 1981; Alford 1963; Rose 1974). Lipset and Rokkan's (1967) influential synthesis of the empirical record pointed to two nineteenth-century revolutions, the national revolution and the Industrial Revolution, which they argued initiated processes of social differentiation and conflict everywhere. As democracy spread, the four axes of social differentiation—(1) churches versus the secular state, (2) dominant versus subject subcultures, (3) rural areas versus cities, and (4) employers versus workers—came to influence voting behavior. The details varied from country to country, depending on history, the

presence and influence of churches and minority subcultures, and timing. But everywhere the advance of industrialization pushed the first three axes to the side and the fourth—class—to the fore.

In many Western European nations (and Australia) the cleavage structure was "frozen" in the dominance of class-based political parties (see Rose and Urwin 1970; Mair 1999; Lipset and Rokkan 1967). Where this happened, it makes sense to speak of "class politics" (Mair 1999). Elsewhere the association between class and voting behavior is better thought of as "class voting." Without a party structure that freezes both classes and voters in place, we face the prospect of shifting alliances, new coalitions, and realignment. In the United States, the lack of explicit links between classes and parties frees voters to weigh each party's appeal and frees each party to revise its strategies from time to time.

This process has been explicit in US presidential elections since 1992. First Bill Clinton and then John Kerry dropped the Democrats' familiar appeals to "working people" in favor of direct calls to the middle class. Barack Obama has maintained that emphasis, even while touting the revival of auto manufacturing in Michigan and Ohio. Most American blue-collar workers still identify with the working class when surveyed, but many Americans have trouble describing their class position; modest correlations among education, occupation, and income ($r \approx 0.4$) mean many people can easily justify more than one answer (Hout 2006). So the broader appeal to middle-class values and interests has been effective for Democrats in the last twenty years. Rhetoric aside, the working class is too small in postindustrial America to be an effective political base; even winning every working-class vote would not add up to victory (Manza and Brooks 1999).

Unions used to bind blue-collar Americans to a Democratic Party that mimicked labor party features. From 1936 to 1968 (and again in 1984) Democrats gave unions an important voice in the selection of candidates. In exchange, the unions delivered their share of the working-class vote to the Democrats. That link was snapped by electoral reforms in the 1970s. The popular party primary system of selecting candidates moved politics from back rooms to TV screens, and unions lost out. At the same time, they were losing membership and the trust of members and nonmembers alike (Lipset and Schneider 1983; Hout, Manza, and Brooks 1999). In the age of Jimmy Hoffa, identification with unions became more a political liability than an asset, and unions never regained the clout they once had at the ballot box. Union members still lean strongly toward Democratic candidates (Hout, Manza, and Brooks 1999), but the heyday of identification between the Democrats and the labor movement is over. Unions are not exclusively working-class anymore, either. The teachers' unions have been essential to Democrats, at least since Jimmy Carter's campaign in 1976.

As unions declined, Republican appeals to a "right to work" and less industrial regulation attracted blue-collar voters. From Reagan to Romney, Republican candidates' promises of relief from regulations and taxes appealed to a growing minority of blue-collar workers as well as to managers and the self-employed. In particular, lower taxes and less regulation made the greatest inroads among small businesspeople and manual workers who were not in unions. To these people, Reagan's firing of striking air-traffic controllers in 1981 may have seemed like a dramatic rebuke to special pleaders who wanted to dodge the apparently inexorable economic changes that everyone else was facing. If we are reading these signs correctly, the persistence of union membership as a factor in American politics is as likely to be a reflection of rightward tilt among people without union protection as a reflection of leftward stance among those with it.

Following Hout, Brooks, and Manza (1995), we distinguish between "traditional" and "total" class voting and use statistical models appropriate to each. Traditional class voting hinges on the correspondence between the working class and parties of the Left and the middle classes and parties of the Center or Right. This correspondence can be embedded in statistical models of class voting that identify a "natural" party for each class (Weakliem 1995). A slightly weaker version of the traditional approach is to array classes and parties as ordered points on latent continua and examine the strength of association between the two latent variables (Weakliem and Heath 1999). However the researcher approaches the data, the traditional model is really only appropriate for understanding the historically significant but specific identification of classes and parties.

Total class voting, on the other hand, is not tied to any specific correspondence of classes and parties. This fact is useful and informative when traditional class voting alliances may not be the strongest or most evident. For example, the recent emergence of affinities between Democrats and teachers may be as strong and significant as the former links between

Democrats and blue-collar workers were. Throw in trial lawyers, college professors, nurses, and half of the doctors, and the Democrats' courting of professionals yields more votes than traditional appeals to blue-collar workers could. A traditional approach would miss this kind of class voting; a total approach can capture it. As long as traditional class voting is but one of several patterns of association between classes and parties, the total approach is to be preferred for its flexibility. In previous work the total approach allowed us to see the class *realignment* in US presidential politics, whereas the traditional approach miscast the same trends as *dealignment* (see Hout, Manza, and Brooks 1999).

Another advantage of the total class voting approach is that it incorporates the class differentials in turnout as well as class differences in votes. Middle-class Americans are more likely to vote than working- or lower-class Americans (Schlozman, Verba, and Brady 2012). The class skew in participation is likely to affect the party system and public policy (Piven and Cloward 1986; Rosenthal 2004). Setting it aside, as the traditional class voting approach does, leaves out an important element of class politics per se. Because of space limitations, we cannot explore this advantage in this chapter; it is sufficient to note that our turnout equation shows no significant change in class differences in turnout since the 1992 election; the patterns Hout, Brooks, and Manza (1995) describe for 1992 are still evident in the data on the 2008 election.

Our distinction between traditional and total class voting is related to Mair's (1999) distinction between "class politics" and "class voting." According to Mair, class politics signifies the kind of institutionalized class alliances that we call traditional. Class voting, for Mair, signifies a tendency for classes to ally themselves with parties in a more ad hoc endorsement for a specific election. The deal, far from being institutionalized in party structure, must be renegotiated for each election cycle. Total class voting, as we have defined it, only requires class voting, not class politics.

Our class voting perspective has supplanted the traditional class politics approach since 1995. Most contemporary research assumes the class voting perspective and treats traditional class politics as a special case, if at all (Jansen, Evans, and de Graaf 2012).

Data and Methods

The data used are from the General Social Survey (GSS), a succession of cross-sectional surveys dating from 1972 (Smith, Marsden, and Hout 2011). The GSS is a full-probability sample of households representative of the English-speaking adult US population through 2002 and the English- or Spanish-speaking adult population since. Sample sizes range from 4,100 to 6,700 respondents per election, except for 2008, which has a sample size of 1,882.

The dependent variable for our analysis is self-reported vote for president in the most recent election, recoded to four categories: (1) the Democratic candidate, (2) the Republican candidate, (3) some other candidate, and (4) did not vote. Self-reports exaggerate turnout but reproduce the partisan split very well (e.g., Abramson, Aldrich, and Rhode 1994).

We include election, class, family income, education, gender, racial ancestry, age, region, and religion as independent variables. Income (recoded to constant dollars and logged), education, and attendance at religious services are treated as scores; the other variables are coded in conventional categories, using dummy variables.[1]

The class scheme used by Hout, Brooks, and Manza (1995) is applied; homemakers and retirees are assigned the class of their most recent occupation.[2] The six substantive classes are (1) professionals, (2) managers, (3) routine white-collar workers (mostly clerical, sales, and white-collar service workers), (4) self-employed (other than professional and blue collar), (5) skilled blue-collar workers, and (6) less-skilled blue-collar workers (including manual service workers).

We test for changes across elections in the association between vote and the independent variables by generating interaction effects between the election and each of the independent variables. Following Hout, Brooks, and Manza (1995), we fit the following model as a multinomial logistic regression:

$$y_{ij} = \ln\left(\frac{p_{ij}}{p_{i1}}\right)$$

$$= \beta_0 + \sum_{k=1}^{14} \beta_k T_{ki} + \sum_{k=15}^{20} \beta_k X_{(k-14)i} + \sum_{k=21}^{P+20} \beta_k Z_{(k-20)i}$$

$$+ \sum_{k=1}^{6} \sum_{k'=1}^{14} \gamma_{kk'} \, {}' X_{ki} T_{k'i} + \sum_{k=1}^{6} \sum_{k'=1}^{14} \delta_{kk'} \, {}' Z_{ki} T_{k'i}$$

for $i = 1, \ldots, N$ indexes persons; $j = 1, \ldots, 4$ indexes outcomes [1 = Republican, 2 = Democrat, 3 = other, 4 = did not vote]; $T_1 \ldots T_{10}$ are dummy variables for elections, $X_1 \ldots X_6$ are dummy variables for

classes, $Z_1 \ldots Z_p$ are continuous or dummy variables for other independent variables, $\beta_0 \ldots \beta_{P+21}$, $\gamma_1 \ldots \gamma_6$, and $\delta_{1,1} \ldots \delta_{10,P}$ are parameters to be estimated. For identification, we constrain

$$\sum_{k=1}^{10} \beta_k = \sum_{k=11}^{16} \beta_k = \sum_{k=1}^{6} \sum_{k'=1}^{10} \gamma_{kk'} = 0$$

For comparison, we also fit two logit regression models in which the dependent variables were Democrat versus any other vote and Republican versus any other vote (excluding nonvoters as missing data). Because the two logit models implied the same substantive conclusions as the more comprehensive multinomial model, we only report multinomial results here. For statistical efficiency, we dropped interaction effects that failed to reach the conventional significance level ($p < .05$) from further calculations after checking to see if a simpler set of time contrasts might be significant. For income that proved to be the case, so we estimated only three income effects: the main effect, an interaction for the 1980s, and a second interaction for elections in the 1990s or 2000s.

The Realignment of Class Voting

By Barack Obama's election in 2008, professionals were supporting Democrats by a significant margin, the self-employed were supporting Republicans by a nearly identical margin, and managers were almost as strongly Republican as the self-employed were. White-collar and blue-collar workers clustered in the middle, giving Obama an edge over McCain within sampling error of his edge among the electorate as a whole.

That class voting pattern was substantially different from the one in the 1970s, when it was blue-collar workers who were strong Democrats and professionals were in the middle, and even more different from the 1950s, when professionals were strong Republicans (Hout, Brooks, and Manza 1995). The traditional pattern of class voting held in US presidential elections from 1948 to 1960, then gave way to one dominated by a cleavage separating business and the professions, with white-collar and blue-collar voters up for grabs. Figure 66.1 summarizes the realignment of class voting across the presidential elections covered by the GSS. The dots show our statistical estimates in each election, and the lines emphasize the long-term trend.

Figure 66.1 displays all these trends. Each data point in the figure is the value of $\beta_k + \gamma_{kk}$, for all

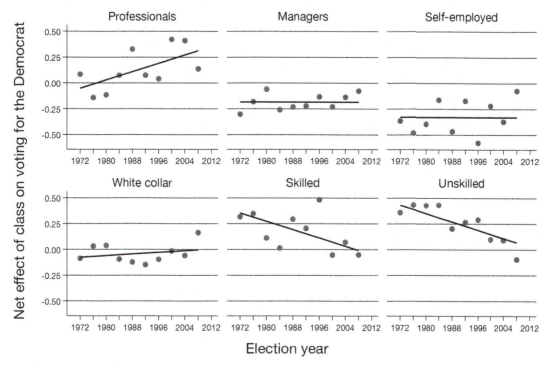

FIGURE 66.1 Net Correlation of Class with Partisan Choice by Election Year, Class, and Model: Persons 25 Years of Age and Older, 1972–2008

Note: Points in these graphs represent multinomial logistic regression coeffi cients, normed to sum to zero within election year. The four sloping lines show the simple regression of those coefficients on time; the two flat lines show the mean of the coefficients. The models control for election, family income, education, gender, racial ancestry, age, region, religion, and statistically signifi cant changes in the correlations between vote and those factors.

Source: Authors' calculations from General Social Surveys, 1973–2010.

possible combinations of $k = 1, \ldots, 6$ and $k' = 1, \ldots, 10$, divided into six panels (one for each value of k'). The lines in most panels were fit by ordinary least squares. For managers and the self-employed, the lines were very nearly flat, so we simply drew horizontal lines at the mean $\beta_k + \gamma_{kk}$ in those two panels.

The most significant feature of these trends for political sociology is the reversed role of the professions and the working class since the 1960s. From the 1960s to the 1990s, professionals switched from being the mainstay of the Republican coalition to being that of the Democratic coalition; from the 1960s to the 2000s, skilled and unskilled blue-collar workers went from being the Democratic mainstay to splitting between Democrats and Republicans. Brooks and Manza (1997) and Brooks (2000) provide convincing evidence that professionals' rising commitments to civil rights for blacks (and to some extent for other groups) prompted their partisan shift. Professionals, when picking candidates, began

to give greater weight to issues of equal opportunity than they had in the past, even bypassing their personal economic interests to do so. Working-class disaffection with federal spending (especially welfare spending), a preference for a tougher approach in criminal justice, and support for the military are possible explanations for the blue-collar shift to the middle (Manza and Brooks 2012). Parties mimicked these preferences and adapted their appeals to the new reality (Jansen, Evans, and de Graaf 2012).

In one sense the triumph of civil rights (and civil liberties and the environment) over personal material interests is a point in favor of postmaterialist accounts of electoral change. But the postmaterialists assert that class no longer correlates with vote. The correlation is evident here; it just departs significantly from the traditional middle-class versus working-class cleavage and rhetoric. Here we see that a class moved from one party to another in response to these rising concerns and did so *as a class*.

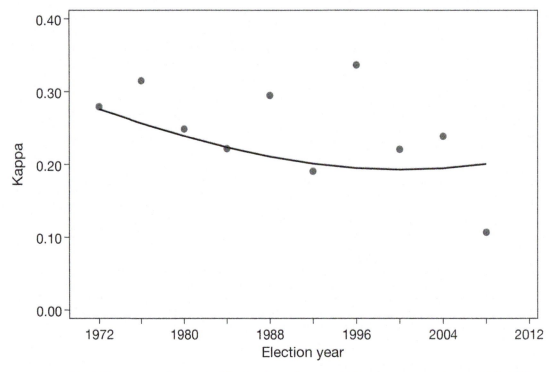

FIGURE 66.2 Total Class Voting (Kappa) by Election Year: Persons 25 Years of Age and Older, 1972–2008

Note: Points show calculation based on points in Figure 66.1; line shows calculation based on lines in Figure 66.1.
Source: Authors' calculations from coefficients in Figure 66.1.

Less challenging to political sociology is the way "traditional," that is, self-interested, class voting appears in much of the rest of the data. Managers voted in recent elections more or less as they did in the 1970s. They changed their attitudes toward civil rights throughout the 1970s, but unlike professionals, their changing attitudes failed to influence their votes (Brooks and Manza 1997). Personal and class interest in cutting taxes and deregulating the economy proved to be more crucial to how they voted. Similarly, the voting pattern of the self-employed maintained a steady preference for Republicans. In the 1950s the self-employed were evenly divided between Democrats and Republicans. They moved strongly toward the Republicans in the 1960s and were their most reliable supporters throughout the 1972–2008 period under observation here. We suspect that some of the change reflects issues and some reflects a shift in composition; farmers were a more significant share of the self-employed in 1952 than by 1980.

All of these changes might suggest that total class voting may have disappeared. That is not the case. The kappa measure, introduced by Hout, Brooks,

and Manza (1995), declined from 1972 to 1992, but has leveled off since then. The dots in Figure 66.2 show that there are substantial fluctuations, but recalculating kappa for the data with linear trends shows twenty years at roughly 0.20 after a 25 percent decline from 1972 to 1992.

Income and Voting

Most discussion of class and voting in political sociology focuses on the role of occupation in defining social class. This reflects the sociologist's proclivity to privilege the source over the amount of income when considering class and class-based behavior and attitudes. Yet as Bartels (2008) and others have shown, family income has long been a significant factor in American political behavior; it became even more important during the Reagan era (roughly the 1980s) and has been so since then (see also Greeley and Hout 2006, 50–54).

Figure 66.3 quantifies the trend toward a steeper income cleavage in American politics. The proportion voting Democratic (adjusted for other correlates) decreased as income increased in each of the three

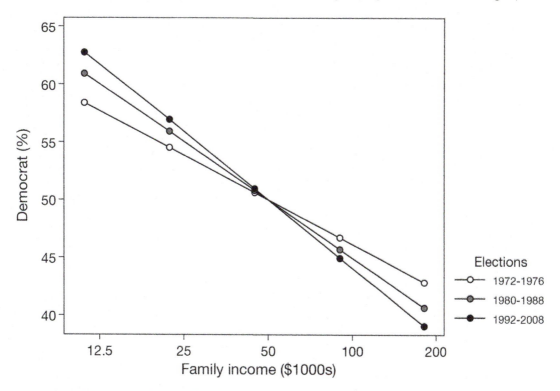

FIGURE 66.3 Relationship Between Family Income and Partisan Choice by Election: Persons 25 Years of Age and Older, 1972–2008

Note: Incomes adjusted for inflation and shown on ratio scale; that is, each value displayed is double the previous one.
Source: Authors' calculations from General Social Surveys, 1972–2010.

political eras shown, but it dropped significantly more in the last five elections than in earlier ones. All else being equal, we expect roughly 60 percent of voters from families with incomes around $12,000 per year to pick the Democrats in a very close election, whereas less than 40 percent of those from families with incomes approaching $200,000 per year would do so. That 20 percentage point income gap in voting is significantly larger than the 15 percentage point gap in the 1970s. The adjustments mean that the income patterns statistically control for occupation, education, gender, race, age, church attendance, region, and differences among elections.

Conclusions

American class coalitions realigned after the civil rights movement in the 1960s. Voters changed their expectations of presidential politics, and parties changed what they promised. The Republican platform of lower taxes and deregulation deepened the loyalty of managers and won over the half of the self-employed who used to back the Democrats.

Blue-collar workers also prefer low taxes. Republicans courted and won their votes in most elections after 1972. But Democrats countered with strong plays for professionals' interests in many kinds of social spending and their commitment to civil rights. "New Democrats"—most notably Clinton—appealed directly to middle-class voters and shored up support among professionals by balancing the budget in the 1990s. On net, the Republicans gained and the Democrats lost among employed people. But Democrats' defense of Social Security and Medicare allowed them to gain support among retirees and pensioners, who are out of the labor force and thus outside this analysis. These changes helped balance the political arithmetic.

We do not have enough evidence to determine whether the class voting realignment in American politics is a general trend that extends to other Western democracies or another instance of "American exceptionalism." We note that English and German parties have started to adopt some American-style appeals. In Britain "New Labour's" platform is known as "the third way"; Schröder moved the German Social Democrats in that direction also. The statistical evidence makes us cautious. In Tony Blair's first win, he drew proportionally higher support in each class, leading to no change in the association between class and vote in Britain (Goldthorpe 1999; Brooks, Nieuwbeerta, and Manza 2006).

The 2012 election probably continued these trends. Discussion of the so-called 1 percent, the video of Romney dismissing the "47 percent," and Obama's promise to extend the Bush tax cuts only for families making less than $250,000 made class issues the most salient element of presidential politics in recent memory. Data published by the *New York Times* show that 62 percent of voters whose incomes fell below $30,000 voted for Obama, compared to 44 percent of voters whose incomes exceeded $100,000—an eighteen-point gap in line with our estimates of the class voting gap (no data on occupations are available yet).

NOTES

1. The age categories are less than twenty-five years, twenty-five to thirty-four, thirty-five to forty-four, forty-five to fifty-four, fifty-five to sixty-four, sixty-five to seventy-four, and seventy-five years and over.

2. People with no labor force experience and those whose occupational report could not be coded are excluded.

REFERENCES

Abramson, P. R., J. H. Aldrich, and D. W. Rhode. 1994. *Change and Continuity in the 1992 Elections.* Washington, DC: Congressional Quarterly Press.

Alford, R. 1963. *Party and Society: The Anglo-American Democracies.* Westport, CT: Greenwood Press.

Bartels, L. M. 2008. *Unequal Democracy.* Princeton, NJ: Princeton University Press.

Brooks, C. 2000. "Civil Rights Liberalism and the Suppression of a Republican Political Realignment in the United States, 1972–1996." *American Sociological Review* 65: 483–505.

Brooks, C., and J. Manza. 1997. "Class Politics and Political Change in the United States, 1952–1992." *Social Forces* 76: 397–408.

Brooks, C., P. Nieuwbeerta, and J. Manza. 2006. "Cleavage-based Voting Behavior in Cross-national Perspective: Evidence from Six Postwar Democracies." *Social Science Research* 35: 88–128.

Clark, T. N., and S. M. Lipset. 1991. "Are Social Classes Dying?" *International Sociology* 6: 397–410.

Goldthorpe, J. H. 1999. "The Persistence of Class Voting in Recent British Elections." In *The End of Class Politics?*, edited by Geoffrey Evans, 63–82. Oxford: Oxford University Press.

Greeley, A. M., and M. Hout. 2006. *The Truth About Conservative Christians.* Chicago: University of Chicago Press.

Hout, M. 2006. "How Class Works: Subjective Aspects of Social Class Since the 1970s." In *Social Class: How Does It Work?*, edited by A. Lareau and D. Conley, 25–64. New York: Russell Sage Foundation.

Hout, M., C. Brooks, and J. Manza. 1995. "The Democratic Class Struggle in U.S. Presidential Elections." *American Sociological Review* 60: 805–828.

Hout, M., J. Manza, and C. Brooks. 1999. "Classes, Unions, and the Realignment of U.S. Presidential Voting, 1952–1992." In *The End of Class Politics?*, edited by G. Evans, 83–95. Oxford: Oxford University Press.

Inglehart, R. 1977. *The Silent Revolution: Changing Values and Political Styles Among Western Publics.* Princeton, NJ: Princeton University Press.

Jansen, Giedo, Geoffrey Evans, and Nan Dirk deGraaf. 2012. "Class Voting and Left–Right Party Positions: A Comparative Study of 15 Western Democracies, 1960–2005." *Social Science Research* 42: 376–400.

Lipset, S. M. 1981. *Political Man: Second, Expanded Edition.* Baltimore, MD: Johns Hopkins University Press.

Lipset, S. M., and S. Rokkan. 1967. "Cleavage Structures, Party Systems, and Voter Alignments." In *Party Systems and Voter Alignments*, edited by S. M. Lipset and S. Rokkan, 1–64. New York: Free Press.

Lipset, S. M., and W. S. Schneider. 1983. *The Confidence Gap: Business, Labor, and Government in the Public Mind.* New York: Free Press.

Mair, P. 1999. "Critical Commentary." In *The End of Class Politics?*, edited by Geoffrey Evans, 308–312. Oxford: Oxford University Press.

Manza, J., and C. Brooks. 1999. "Group Size, Turnout, and Alignments in the Making of U.S. Party Coalitions, 1960–1992." *European Sociological Review* 15: 369–390.

———. 2012. "How Sociology Lost Public Opinion: A Genealogy of a Missing Concept in the Study of the Political." *Sociological Theory* 30: 89–113.

Piven, F. F., and R. A. Cloward. 1986. *Why Americans Don't Vote.* New York: Pantheon.

Rose, R., ed. 1974. *Electoral Behavior: A Comparative Handbook.* New York: Free Press.

Rose, R., and D. Urwin. 1970. "Persistence and Change in Western Party Systems Since 1945." *Political Studies* 18: 287–319.

Rosenthal, H. 2004. "Politics, Public Policy, and Inequality: A Look Back at the 20th Century." In *Social Inequality*, edited by Kathryn Neckerman. New York: Russell Sage Foundation.

Schlozman, K. L., S. Verba, and H. E. Brady. 2012. *The Unheavenly Chorus: Unequal Political Voice and the Broken Promise of American Democracy.* Princeton, NJ: Princeton University Press.

Smith, T. W., P. V. Marsden, and M. Hout. 2011. *General Social Survey Cumulative Codebook*, 1972–2010. Storrs CT: Roper Center.

Weakliem, D. 1995. "Two Models of Class Voting." *British Journal of Political Science* 25: 254–270.

Weakliem, D., and A. F. Heath. 1999. "The Secret Life of Class Voting: Britain, France, and the United States Since the 1930s." In *The End of Class Politics?*, edited by Geoffrey Evans, 97–136. Oxford: Oxford University Press.

67. Annette Lareau*
Unequal Childhoods: Class, Race, and Family Life

There are many studies that tell us of the detrimental effects of poverty on children's lives, but it is less clear what the mechanisms are for the transmission of class advantage across generations.

I suggest that social class has an important impact on the cultural logic of childrearing (see Lareau 2003 for details). Middle-class parents, both white *and* black, appear to follow a cultural logic of childrearing that I call "concerted cultivation." They enroll their children in numerous age-specific organized activities that come to dominate family life and create enormous labor, particularly for mothers. Parents see these activities as transmitting important life skills to children. Middle-class parents also stress language use and the development of reasoning. Talking plays a crucial role in the disciplinary strategies of middle-class parents. This "cultivation" approach results in a frenetic pace for parents, creates a cult of individualism within the family, and emphasizes children's performance.

Among white and black working-class and poor families, childrearing strategies emphasize the "accomplishment of natural growth." These parents believe that as long as they provide love, food, and safety, their children will grow and thrive. They do

* The ideas, issues, and theories considered in this brief commissioned piece are examined in greater depth in the following publication: Annette Lareau, *Unequal Childhoods: Class, Race, and Family Life*, published by the University of California Press in 2003. The article printed here was originally prepared by Annette Lareau for inclusion in *The Inequality Reader: Contemporary and Foundational Readings in Race, Class, and Gender*, First Edition, edited by David B. Grusky, pp. 537–548. Copyright © 2006 by Westview Press. Reprinted by permission of Westview Press, an imprint of Perseus Books, LLC, a subsidiary of Hachette Book Group, Inc.

not focus on developing the special talents of their individual children. Working-class and poor children have more free time and deeper and richer ties within their extended families than the middle-class children. Some participate in organized activities, but they do so for different reasons than their middle-class counterparts. Working-class and poor parents issue many more directives to their children, and in some households, place more emphasis on physical discipline than do middle-class parents.

The pattern of concerted cultivation, with its stress on individual repertoires of activities, reasoning, and questioning, encourages an *emerging sense of entitlement* in children. Of course, not all parents and children are equally assertive, but the pattern of questioning and intervening among the white and black middle-class parents in the study contrasts sharply with the definitions of how to be helpful and effective observed among the white and black working-class and poor families. The pattern of the accomplishment of natural growth, with its emphasis on child-initiated play, autonomy from adults, and directives, encourages an *emerging sense of constraint*. Members of these families, adults as well as children, tend to be deferential and outwardly accepting (with sporadic moments of resistance) in their interactions with professionals such as doctors and educators. At the same time, however, compared to their middle-class counterparts, the white and black working-class and poor families are more distrustful of professionals in institutions. These are differences with long-term consequences. In a historical moment where the dominant society privileges active, informed, assertive clients of health and educational services, the various strategies employed by children and parents are not equally valuable. In sum, differences in family life lie not only in the advantages parents are able to obtain for their children, but also in the skills being transmitted to children for negotiating their own life paths.

Methodology

Study Participants

The study is based on interviews and observations of children eight to ten years of age and their families. A team of graduate research assistants and I collected the data. The first phase involved observations in third-grade public school classrooms, mainly in a metropolitan area in the Northeast. The schools serve neighborhoods in a white suburban area and two urban locales—one a white working-class

TABLE 67.1 Argument of Unequal Childhoods: Class Differences in Childrearing

	Childrearing Approach	
	Concerted Cultivation	*Accomplishment of Natural Growth*
Key Elements	Parent actively fosters and assesses child's talents, opinions, and skills	Parent cares for child and allows child to grow
Organization of Daily Life	*multiple child leisure activities orchestrated by adults	*child "hangs out" particularly with kin
Language Use	*reasoning/directives *child contestation of adult statements *extended negotiations between parents and child	*directives *rare for child to question or challenge adults *general acceptance by child of directives
Interventions in Institutions	*criticisms and interventions on behalf of child *training of child to take on this role	*dependence on institutions *sense of powerlessness and frustrations *conflict between childrearing practices at home and at school
Consequences	Emerging sense of entitlement on the part of the child	Emerging sense of constraint on the part of the child

neighborhood, and the other a nearby poor black neighborhood. About one-half of the children are white and about one-half are black. One child is interracial. The research assistants and I carried out individual interviews (averaging two hours each) with all of the mothers and most of the fathers (or guardians) of eighty-eight children, for a total of 137 interviews. We also observed children as they took part in organized activities in the communities surrounding the schools. The most intensive part of the research, however, involved home observations of twelve children and their families. Nine of the twelve families came from the classrooms I observed, but the boy and girl from the two black middle-class families and the boy from the poor white family came from other sites. Most observations and interviews took place between 1993 and 1995, but interviews were done as early as 1990 and as late as 1997. This chapter focuses primarily on the findings from the observations of these twelve families since the key themes discussed here surfaced during this part of the fieldwork. I do include some information from the larger study to provide a context for understanding the family observations. All names are pseudonyms.

Intensive Family Observations

The research assistants and I took turns visiting the participating families daily, for a total of about twenty visits in each home, often in the space of one month. The observations were not limited to the home. Fieldworkers followed children and parents as they took part in school activities, church services and events, organized play, kin visits, and medical appointments. Most field observations lasted about three hours; sometimes, depending on the event (e.g., an out-of-town funeral, a special extended family event, or a long shopping trip), they lasted much longer. In most cases, there was one overnight visit. We often carried tape recorders with us and used the audiotapes for reference in writing up field notes. Families were paid $350, usually at the end of the visits, for their participation.

A Note on Class

My purpose in undertaking the field observations was to develop an *intensive*, realistic portrait of family life. Although I deliberately focused on only twelve families, I wanted to compare children across gender and race lines. Adopting the fine-grained differentiation of categories characteristic of current neo-Marxist and neo-Weberian empirical studies was not tenable. My choice of class categories was further limited by the school populations at the sites I had selected. Very few of the students were children of employers or of self-employed workers. I decided to concentrate exclusively on those whose parents were employees. Various criteria have been proposed to differentiate within this heterogeneous group, but authority in the workplace and "credential barriers" are the two most commonly used. I assigned the families in the study to a working-class or middle-class category based on discussions with each of the employed adults. They provided extensive information about the work they did, the nature of the organization that employed them, and their educational credentials. I added a third category: families not involved in the labor market (a population traditionally excluded from social class groupings) because in the first school I studied, a substantial number of children were from households supported by public assistance. To ignore them would have restricted the scope of the study arbitrarily. The final subsample contained four middle-class, four working-class, and four poor families.

Children's Time Use

In our interviews and observations of white and black middle-class children, it was striking how busy they were with organized activities. Indeed, one of the hallmarks of middle-class children's daily lives is a set of adult-run organized activities. Many children have three and four activities per week. In some families, every few days, activities conflict, particularly when one season is ending and one is beginning. For example in the white middle-class family of the Tallingers, Garrett is on multiple soccer teams—the "A" traveling team of the private Forest soccer club and the Intercounty soccer team—he also has swim lessons, saxophone lessons at school, private piano lessons at home, and baseball and basketball. These organized activities provided a framework for children's lives; other activities were sandwiched between them.

These activities create labor for parents. Indeed, the impact of children's activities takes its toll on parents' patience as well as their time. For example, on a June afternoon at the beginning of summer vacation, in a white-middle-class family, Mr. Tallinger comes home from work to take Garrett to his soccer game. Garrett is not ready to go, and his lackadaisical approach to getting ready irks his father:

Don says, "Get your soccer stuff—you're going to a soccer game!" Garrett comes into the den with white short leggings on underneath a long green soccer shirt; he's number 16. He sits on an armchair catty-corner from the television and languidly watches the World Cup game. He slowly, abstractedly, pulls on shin guards, then long socks. His eyes are riveted to the TV screen. Don comes in: "Go get your other stuff." Garrett says he

can't find his shorts. Don: "Did you look in your drawer?" Garrett nods. . . . He gets up to look for his shorts, comes back into the den a few minutes later. I ask, "Any luck yet?" Garrett shakes his head. Don is rustling around elsewhere in the house. Don comes in, says to Garrett, "Well, Garrett, aren't you wearing shoes?" (Don leaves and returns a short time later): "Garrett, we HAVE to go! Move! We're late!" He says this shortly, abruptly. He comes back in a minute and drops Garrett's shiny green shorts on his lap without a word.

This pressured search for a pair of shiny green soccer shorts is a typical event in the Tallinger household. Also typical is the solution—a parent ultimately finds the missing object, while continuing to prod the child to hurry. The fact that today's frenzied schedule will be matched or exceeded by the next day's is also par:

Don: (describing their day on Saturday) Tomorrow is really nuts. We have a soccer game, then a baseball game, then another soccer game.

This steady schedule of activity—that none of the middle-class parents reported having when they were a similar age—was not universal. Indeed, while we searched for a middle-class child who did not have a single organized activity, we could not find one, but in working-class and poor homes, organized activities were much less common and there were many children who did not have any. Many children "hung out." Television and video games are a major source of entertainment but outdoor play can trump either of these. No advanced planning, no telephone calls, no consultations between mothers, no drop-offs or pickups—no particular effort at all—is required to launch an activity. For instance, one afternoon, in a black working-class family, Shannon (in 7th grade) and Tyrec (in 4th grade) walk out their front door to the curb of the small, narrow street their house faces. Shannon begins playing a game with a ball; she soon has company:

(Two boys from the neighborhood walk up.) Shannon is throwing the small ball against the side of the row house. Tyrec joins in the game with her. As they throw the ball against the wall, they say things they must do with the ball. It went something like this: Johnny Crow wanted to know. . . . (bounces ball against the wall), touch your knee (bounce), touch your toe (bounce), touch the ground (bounce), under the knee (bounce), turn around (bounce). Shannon and Tyrec played about four rounds.

Unexpected events produce hilarity:

At one point Shannon accidentally threw the ball and it bounced off of Tyrec's head. All the kids laughed; then Tyrec, who had the ball, went chasing after Shannon. It was a close, fun moment—lots of laughter, eye contact, giggling, chasing.

Soon a different game evolves. Tyrec is on restriction. He is supposed to remain inside the house all day. So, when he thinks he has caught a glimpse of his mom returning home from work, he dashes inside. He reappears as soon as he realizes that it was a false alarm. The neighborhood children begin an informal game of baiting him:

The kids keep teasing Tyrec that his mom's coming—which sends him scurrying just inside the door, peering out of the screen door. This game is enacted about six times. Tyrec also chases Shannon around the street, trying to get the ball from her. A few times Shannon tells Tyrec that he'd better "get inside"; he ignores her. Then, at 6:50 [P.M.] Ken (a friend of Tyrec's) says, "There's your mom!" Tyrec scoots inside, then says, "Oh, man. You were serious this time."

Informal, impromptu outdoor play is common in Tyrec's neighborhood. A group of boys approximately his age, regularly numbering four or five but sometimes reaching as many as ten, play ball games together on the street, walk to the store to get treats, watch television at each other's homes, and generally hang out together.

Language Use

In addition to differences by social class in time use, we also observed differences in language use in the home. As others have noted (Bernstein, 1971; Heath, 1983) middle-class parents used more reasoning in their speech with children while working-class and poor parents used more directives. For example, in observations of the African American home of Alex

Williams, whose father was a trial lawyer and mother was a high-level corporate executive, we found that the Williamses and other middle-class parents use language frequently, pleasurably, and instrumentally. Their children do likewise. For example, one January evening, Alexander is stumped by a homework assignment to write five riddles. He sits at the dinner table in the kitchen with his mother and a fieldworker. Mr. Williams is at the sink, washing the dinner dishes. He has his back to the group at the dinner table. Without turning around, he says to Alex, "Why don't you go upstairs to the third floor and get one of those books and see if there is a riddle in there?"

Alex [says] smiling, "Yeah. That's a good idea! I'll go upstairs and copy one from out of the book." Terry turns around with a dish in hand, "That was a joke—not a valid suggestion. That is not an option." He smiled as he turned back around to the sink. Christina says, looking at Alex: "There is a word for that you know, plagiarism." Terry says (not turning around), "Someone can sue you for plagiarizing. Did you know that?" Alex: "That's only if it is copyrighted." They all begin talking at once.

Here we see Alex cheerfully (though gently) goading his father by pretending to misunderstand the verbal instruction to consult a book for help. Mr. Williams dutifully rises to the bait. Ms. Williams reshapes this moment of lightheartedness by introducing a new word into Alexander's vocabulary. Mr. Williams goes one step further by connecting the new word to a legal consequence. Alex upstages them both. He demonstrates that he is already familiar with the general idea of plagiarism and that he understands the concept of copyright, as well.

In marked contrast to working-class and poor parents, however, even when the Williamses issue directives, they often include explanations for their orders. Here, Ms. Williams is reminding her son to pay attention to his teacher:

I want you to pay close attention to Mrs. Scott when you are developing your film. Those chemicals are very dangerous. Don't play around in the classroom. You could get that stuff in someone's eye. And if you swallow it, you could die.

Alex chooses to ignore the directive in favor of instructing his misinformed mother:

Alex corrects her, "Mrs. Scott told us that we wouldn't die if we swallowed it. But we would get very sick and would have to get our stomach pumped." Christina does not follow the argument any further. She simply reiterates that he should be careful.

Possibly because the issue is safety, Ms. Williams does not encourage Alex to elaborate here, as she would be likely to do if the topic were less-charged. Instead, she restates her directive and thus underscores her expectation that Alex will do as she asks.

Although Mr. and Ms. Williams disagreed on elements of how training in race relations should be implemented, they both recognized that their racial and ethnic identity profoundly shaped their and their son's everyday experiences. They were well aware of the potential for Alexander to be exposed to racial injustice, and they went to great lengths to try to protect their son from racial insults and other forms of discrimination. Nevertheless, race did not appear to shape the dominant cultural logic of childrearing in Alexander's family or in other families in the study. All of the middle-class families engaged in extensive reasoning with their children, asking questions, probing assertions, and listening to answers. Similar patterns appeared in interviews and observations with other African American middle-class families.

A different pattern appeared in working-class and poor homes where there was simply less verbal speech than we observed in middle-class homes. There was also less speech between parents and children, a finding noted by other observational studies (Hart and Risley, 1995). Moreover, interspersed with intermittent talk are adult-issued directives. Children are told to do certain things (e.g., shower, take out the garbage) and not to do others (e.g., curse, talk back). In an African American home of a family living on public assistance in public housing, Ms. McAllister uses one-word directives to coordinate the use of the single bathroom. There are almost always at least four children in the apartment and often seven, plus Ms. McAllister and other adults. Ms. McAllister sends the children to wash up by pointing to a child, saying, "Bathroom," and handing him or her a washcloth. Wordlessly, the designated child gets up and goes to the bathroom to take a shower.

Children usually do what adults ask of them. We did not observe whining or protests, even when adults assign time-consuming tasks, such as the hour-long process of hair-braiding Lori McAllister is told to do for the four-year-old daughter of Aunt Dara's friend Charmaine:

Someone tells Lori, "Go do [Tyneshia's] hair for camp." Without saying anything, Lori gets up and goes inside and takes the little girl with her. They head for the couch near the television; Lori sits on the couch and the girl sits on the floor. [Tyneshia] sits quietly for about an hour, with her head tilted, while Lori carefully does a multitude of braids.

Lori's silent obedience is typical. Generally, children perform requests without comment. For example, at dinner one night, after Harold McAllister complains he doesn't like spinach, his mother directs him to finish it anyway:

Mom yells (loudly) at him to eat: "EAT! FINISH THE SPINACH!" (No response. Harold is at the table, dawdling.) Guion and Runako and Alexis finish eating and leave. I finish with Harold; he eats his spinach. He leaves all his yams.

The verbal world of Harold McAllister and other poor and working-class children offers some important advantages as well as costs. Compared to middle-class children we observed, Harold is more respectful towards adults in his family. In this setting, there are clear boundaries between adults and children. Adults feel comfortable issuing directives to children, which children comply with immediately. Some of the directives that adults issue center on obligations of children to others in the family ("don't beat on Guion" or "go do [her] hair for camp"). One consequence of this is that Harold, despite occasional tiffs, is much nicer to his sister (and his cousins) than the siblings we observed in middle-class homes. The use of directives and the pattern of silent compliance are not universal in Harold's life. In his interactions with peers, for example on the basketball "court," Harold's verbal displays are distinctively different than inside the household, with elaborated and embellished discourse. Nevertheless, there is a striking difference in linguistic interaction between adults and children in poor and working-class families when compared to that observed in the home of Alexander Williams. Ms. McAllister has the benefit of being able to issue directives without having to justify their decisions at every moment. This can make childrearing somewhat less tiring.

Another advantage is that Harold has more autonomy than middle-class children in making important decisions in daily life. As a child, he controls his leisure schedule. His basketball games are impromptu and allow him to develop important skills and talents. He is resourceful. He appears less exhausted than ten-year-old Alexander. In addition, he has important social competencies, including his deftness in negotiating the "code of the street."[1] His mother has stressed these skills in her upbringing, as she impresses upon her children the importance of "not paying no mind" to others, including drunks and drug dealers who hang out in the neighborhoods which Harold and Alexis negotiate.

Still, in the world of schools, health care facilities, and other institutional settings, these valuable skills do not translate into the same advantages as the reasoning skills emphasized in the home of Alexander Williams and other middle-class children. Compared to Alexander Williams, Harold does not gain the development of a large vocabulary, an increase of his knowledge of science and politics, a set of tools to customize situations outside the home to maximize his advantage, and instruction in how to defend his argument with evidence. His knowledge of words, which might appear, for example, on future SAT tests, is not continually stressed at home.

In these areas, the lack of advantage is *not* connected to the intrinsic value of the McAllister family life or the use of directives at home. Indeed, one can argue raising children who are polite and respectful children and do not whine, needle, or badger their parents is a highly laudable childrearing goal. Deep and abiding ties with kinship groups are also, one might further argue, important. Rather, it is the specific ways that institutions function that end up conveying advantages to middle-class children. In their standards, these institutions also permit, and even demand, active parent involvement. In this way as well, middle-class children often gain an advantage.

Intervention in Institutions

Children do not live their lives inside of the home. Instead, they are legally required to go to school, they go to the doctor, and many are involved in church and other adult-organized activities. In children's institutional lives, we found differences by social class in how mothers monitored children's institutional experiences. While in working-class and poor families, children are granted autonomy to make their own way in organizations, in the mid-

dle-class homes, most aspects of the children's lives are subject to their mother's *ongoing* scrutiny.

For example, in an African American middle-class home, where both parents are college graduates and Ms. Marshall is a computer worker and her husband a civil servant, their two daughters have a hectic schedule of organized activities including gymnastics for Stacey and basketball for Fern. When Ms. Marshall becomes aware of a problem, she moves quickly, drawing on her work and professional skills and experiences. She displays tremendous assertiveness, doggedness, and, in some cases, effectiveness in pressing institutions to recognize her daughters' individualized needs. Stacey's mother's proactive stance reflects her belief that she has a duty to intervene in situations where she perceives that her daughter's needs are not being met. This perceived responsibility applies across all areas of her children's lives. She is no more (or less) diligent with regard to Stacey and Fern's leisure activities than she is with regard to their experiences in school or church or the doctor's office. This is clear in the way she handles Stacey's transition from her township gymnastics classes to the private classes at an elite private gymnastic program at Wright's:

Ms. Marshall describes Stacey's first session at the club as rocky:

> The girls were not warm. And these were little . . . eight and nine year old kids. You know, they weren't welcoming her the first night. It was kinda like eyeing each other, to see, you know, "Can you do this? Can you do that?"

More importantly, Ms. Marshall reported that the instructor is brusque, critical, and not friendly toward Stacey. Ms. Marshall cannot hear what was being said, but she could see the interactions through a window. A key problem is that because her previous instructor had not used the professional jargon for gymnastic moves, Stacey does not know these terms. When the class ends and she walks out, she is visibly upset. Her mother's reaction is a common one among middle-class parents: She does not remind her daughter that in life one has to adjust, that she will need to work even harder, or that there is nothing to be done. Instead, Ms. Marshall focuses on Tina, the instructor, as the source of the problem:

> We sat in the car for a minute and I said, "Look, Stac," I said. She said, "I-I," and she

started crying. I said, "You wait here." The instructor had come to the door, Tina. So I went to her and I said, "Look." I said, "Is there a problem?" She said, "Aww . . . she'll be fine. She just needs to work on certain things." Blah-blah-blah. And I said, "She's really upset. She said you-you-you [were] pretty much correcting just about everything." And [Tina] said, "Well, she's got—she's gotta learn the terminology."

Ms. Marshall acknowledges that Stacey isn't familiar with specialized and technical gymnastics terms. Nonetheless, she continues to defend her daughter:

I do remember, I said to her, I said, "Look, maybe it's not all the student." You know, I just left it like that. That, you know, sometimes teaching, learning and teaching, is a two-way proposition as far as I'm concerned. And sometimes teachers have to learn how to, you know, meet the needs of the kid. Her style, her immediate style was not accommodating to—to Stacey.

Here Ms. Marshall is asserting the legitimacy of an individualized approach to instruction. She frames her opening remark as a question ("Is there a problem?"). Her purpose, however, is to alert the instructor to the negative impact she has had on Stacey ("She's really upset."). Although her criticism is indirect ("Maybe it's not all the student . . ."), Ms. Marshall makes it clear that she expects her daughter to be treated differently in the future. In this case, Stacey does not hear what her mother says, but she knows that her wishes and feelings are being transmitted to the instructor in a way that she could not do herself.

Although parents were equally concerned about their children's happiness, in working-class and poor homes we observed different patterns of oversight for children's institutional activities. For example, in the white working-class home of Wendy Driver, Wendy's mother does not nurture her daughter's language development like Alexander Williams' mother does her son's. She does not attempt to draw Wendy out or follow up on new information when Wendy introduces the term mortal sin while the family is sitting around watching television. But, just like Ms. Williams, Ms. Driver cares very much about her child and just like middle-class parents she wants to help her daughter

succeed. Ms. Driver keeps a close and careful eye on her Wendy's schooling. She knows that Wendy is having problems in school. Ms. Driver immediately signs and returns each form Wendy brings home from school and reminds her to turn the papers in to her teacher.

Wendy is "being tested" as part of an ongoing effort to determine why she has difficulties with spelling, reading, and related language-based activities. Her mother welcomes these official efforts but she did not request them. Unlike the middle-class mothers we observed, who asked teachers for detailed information about every aspect of their children's classroom performance and relentlessly pursued information and assessments outside of school as well, Ms. Driver seems content with only a vague notion of her daughter's learning disabilities. This attitude contrasts starkly with that of Stacey Marshall's mother, for example. In discussing Stacey's classroom experiences with fieldworkers, Ms. Marshall routinely described her daughter's academic strengths and weaknesses in detail. Ms. Driver never mentions that Wendy is doing grade-level work in math but is reading at a level a full three years below her grade. Her description is vague:

She's having problems. . . . They had a special teacher come in and see if they could find out what the problem is. She has a reading problem, but they haven't put their finger on it yet, so she's been through all kinds of special teachers and testing and everything. She goes to Special Ed, I think it's two classes a day . . . I'm not one hundred percent sure—for her reading. It's very difficult for her to read what's on paper. But then—she can remember things. But not everything. It's like she has a puzzle up there. And we've tried, well, they've tried a lot of things. They just haven't put their finger on it yet.

Wendy's teachers uniformly praise her mother as "supportive" and describe her as "very loving," but they are disappointed in Ms. Driver's failure to take a more active, interventionist role in Wendy's education, especially given the formidable nature of her daughter's learning problems. From Ms. Driver's perspective, however, being actively supportive means doing whatever the teachers tell her to do.

Whatever they would suggest, I would do. They suggested she go to the eye doctor, so I did that. And they checked her and said there was nothing wrong there.

Similarly, she monitors Wendy's homework and supports her efforts to read:

We listen to her read. We help her with her homework. So she has more attention here in a smaller household than it was when I lived with my parents. So, we're trying to help her out more, which I think is helping. And with the two [special education] classes a day at the school, instead of one like last year, she's learning a lot from that. So, we're just hoping it takes time and that she'll just snap out of it.

But Ms. Driver clearly does not have an *independent* understanding of the nature or degree of Wendy's limitations, perhaps because she is unfamiliar with the kind of terms the educators use to describe her daughter's needs (e.g., a limited "sight vocabulary," underdeveloped "language arts skills"). Perhaps, too, her confidence in the school staff makes it easier for her to leave "the details" to them: "Ms. Morton, she's great. She's worked with us for different testing and stuff." Ms. Driver depends on the school staff's expertise to assess the situation and then share the information with her:

I think they just want to keep it in the school till now. And when they get to a point where they can't figure out what it is, and then I guess they'll send me somewhere else. . . .

Her mother is not alarmed, because "the school" has told her not to worry about Wendy's grades:

Her report card—as long as it's not spelling and reading—spelling and reading are like F's. And they keep telling me not to worry, because she's in the Special Ed class. But besides that, she does good. I have no behavior problems with her at all.

Ms. Driver wants the best possible outcome for her daughter and she does not know how to achieve that goal without relying heavily on Wendy's teachers:

I wouldn't even know where to start going. On the radio there was something for children having problems reading and this and that,

call. And I suggested it to a couple different people, and they were like, wait a second, it's only to get you there and you'll end up paying an arm and a leg. So I said to my mom, "No, I'm going to wait until the first report card and go up and talk to them up there."

Thus, in looking for the source of Ms. Driver's deference toward educators, the answers don't seem to lie in her having either a shy personality or underdeveloped mothering skills. To understand why Wendy's mother is accepting where Stacey Marshall's mother would be aggressive, it is more useful to focus on social class position, both in terms of how class shapes worldviews and how class affects economic and educational resources. Ms. Driver understands her role in her daughter's education as involving a different set of responsibilities from those perceived by middle-class mothers. She responds to contacts from the school—such as invitations to the two annual parent-teacher conferences—but she does not initiate them. She views Wendy's school life as a separate realm, and one in which she, as a parent, is only an infrequent visitor. Ms. Driver expects that the teachers will teach and her daughter will learn and that, under normal circumstances, neither requires any additional help from her as a parent. If problems arise, she presumes that Wendy will tell her; or, if the issue is serious, the school will contact her. But what Ms. Driver fails to understand, is that the educators expect her to take on a pattern of "concerted cultivation" where she actively monitors and intervenes in her child's schooling. The teachers asked for a complicated mixture of deference and engagement from parents; they were disappointed when they did not get it.

Conclusions

I have stressed how social class dynamics are woven into the texture and rhythm of children and parents' daily lives. Class position influences critical aspects of family life: time use, language use, and kin ties. Working-class and middle-class mothers may express beliefs that reflect a similar notion of "intensive mothering," but their behavior is quite different. For that reason, I have described sets of paired beliefs and actions as a "cultural logic" of childrearing. When children and parents move outside the home into the world of social institutions, they find that these cultural practices are not given equal value. There are signs that middle-class children benefit, in ways that are invisible to them and to their parents, from the degree of similarity between the cultural repertoires in the home and those standards adopted by institutions.

REFERENCES

Anderson, Elijah. 1999. *Code of the Street.* New York, NY: W. W. Norton.

Bernstein, Basil. 1971. *Class, Codes, and Control: Theoretical Studies Towards a Sociology of Language.* New York, NY: Schocken.

Hart, Betty and Todd R. Risley. 1995. *Meaningful Differences in the Everyday Experiences of Young American Children.* New Haven: Yale University Press.

Heath, Shirley Brice. 1983. *Ways with Words: Language, Life, and Work in Communities and Classrooms.* Cambridge: Cambridge University Press.

Lareau, Annette. 2003. *Unequal Childhoods: Class, Race, and Family Life.* Berkeley, CA: University of California Press.

NOTES

1. Elijah Anderson, *Code of the Street,* New York: W. W. Norton (1999).

68. Karen Lutfey and Jeremy Freese*
The Fundamentals of Fundamental Causality

Weber's ([1921] 1968) concept of "life chances" highlights both the *diverse* consequences of social standing and their *probabilistic* character. The most poignant kind of life chance affected by socioeconomic standing may also be the most literal: the probability of staying alive or dying. Lower socioeconomic status (SES) is associated with worse health and higher mortality rates at virtually every age

*The ideas, issues, and theories considered in this brief commissioned piece are examined in greater depth in the following publication: Karen Lutfey and Jeremy Freese, "Toward Some Fundamentals of Fundamental Causality: Socioeconomic Status and Health in the Routine Clinic Visit for Diabetes," *American Journal of Sociology* 110:5 (March 2005), pp. 1326–1372, published by the University of Chicago Press. The article printed here was originally prepared by Karen Lutfey and Jeremy Freese for the fourth edition of *Social Stratification: Class, Race, and Gender in Sociological Perspective,* edited by David B. Grusky. Copyright © 2014 by Westview Press.

(Robert and House 1994), and this association has persisted across historical periods in which risk factors and disease profiles have changed radically (Link et al. 1998). We use ethnographic data to examine the association between SES and adverse health outcomes among persons with diabetes.

We draw specifically on Link and Phelan's (1995; Phelan, Link, and Tehranifar 2010) concept of SES as a "fundamental cause" of health. Fundamental causality is not just about what causes an outcome like ill-health, but about what *causes the causes* of ill-health. That is, the concept is not about the *specific proximate mechanisms* responsible for a persistent association, but rather about the fact that some *metamechanism(s)* are responsible for the generation of multiple concrete mechanisms that reproduce a particular relationship in different places and times. The metamechanism provides what we refer to as a *durable narrative* (Freese and Lutfey 2011) about why the SES-health relationship should be robust to changes in health threats and treatments—an explanation of why a similar association would be observed in diverse sociohistorical contexts.

A fundamental relationship between two variables such as SES and health implies the potential for a *massive multiplicity* of mechanisms connecting the two. No individual mechanism is so dominant that it alone is responsible for the bulk of the observed association between SES and health. Rather, as proximate causes of health change, the standing conjecture is that these will, on balance, sustain the overall relationship between SES and health. Differential resources provide a possible metamechanism (Link and Phelan 1995). The ways resources can influence health are flexible and varied, allowing the possibility that, when one uses ethnographic methods to consider in a concrete setting how different resources might lead to different outcomes, many potential mechanisms will be revealed.

Diabetes

Diabetes is a major cause of morbidity and mortality in the United States, and its prevalence is increasing dramatically (Centers for Disease Control and Prevention 2011). Diabetes incidence, complications (Booth and Hux 2003; Robbins et al. 2001), and mortality have all been shown to be related to SES. Because diabetes complications are known to be linked to average glucose levels (Diabetes Control and Complications Trial Research Group

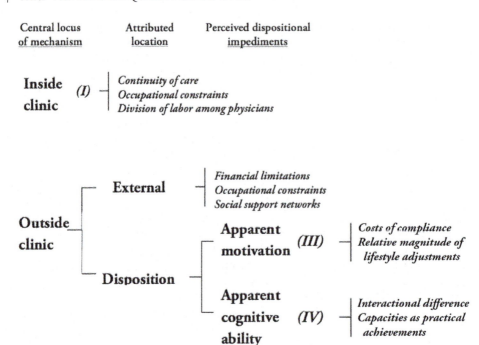

FIGURE 68.1 "Location" of Mechanisms as an Organizing Device

1993), identifying potential mechanisms within an ethnographic inquiry is simplified. Conditions that probabilistically affect patients' capacities for controlling glucose levels can be expected to likewise probabilistically affect long-term health outcomes. More aggressive treatment regimens—increasing in complexity and potential glucose control—may be employed as patients become more adept at managing diabetes, whereas concessionary regimens—decreasing in complexity and effectively accepting that patients will have weaker glucose control and greater risk of long-term complications—may be deployed to accommodate any of several sources of resistance to implementing more effective regimens.

Data and Analytic Strategy

Data are from a yearlong ethnographic study conducted by the first author in 1997–1998. The fieldwork sites were two weekly, four-hour endocrinology clinics at two hospitals that are both part of the same university-based medical center located in a large, midwestern city. The clinics were selected to provide an optimal contrast of the socioeconomic diversity of persons with diabetes: "Park" Hospital serves a primarily white, upper- and middle-class population, whereas "County" Hospital has a largely minority,

working-class, and underinsured clientele. Our data include approximately 250 hours of observation at these clinics and semi-structured interviews conducted with twenty-five practitioners. We pursue systematic connections between the regimen design we observed in the clinics and the socioeconomic conditions of patients' lives. We organize our results around different senses of the "location" of the mechanism, including physical location of the clinic, factors inside and outside the clinic, and those internal and external to individual patients (see Figure 68.1).

Differences Between Park and County Clinics

Because Park clinic serves a much higher SES clientele than the County clinic, we begin by considering whether differences in the organization of the two clinics may affect regimen design. Any differences that place County clinic patients at a systematic, probabilistic disadvantage relative to Park clinic patients can be considered potential mechanisms by which differential access to health care may contribute to preserving the fundamental cause relationship among diabetes patients. Although several such differences are discussed in Lutfey and Freese (2005), here we focus on one key finding related to Park clinic offering higher continuity of care than County clinic does.

Park clinic is similar to many private medical organizations in that the continuity of care—the extent to which patients see the same providers over time—is extremely high. Park has two endocrinologists and one nurse practitioner who see most patients, and all diabetes education occurs in a separate center housing several full-time educational staff. By contrast, County clinic is usually supervised by four attending physicians, but with residents playing a large role. Diabetes education occurs through a certified diabetes educator who attends the clinic weekly on a volunteer basis.

High continuity of care enables providers to become much more familiar with patients' medical histories and their family and work situations. One physician complained that the low continuity of care at County required physicians to rely too heavily on objective indicators, which though important are limited and even potentially deceptive without a broader array of information:

> The outcome [should not be] based on a single test. Nor a single blood sugar, nor a single week, nor a single visit, nor a single anything. . . . The outcome [should be] based on the totality of the things that you assess over the period of time that you see the patient. The focus that you see in the clinic like we have [County] is that the totality of the assessment comes down to "What's your last Hemoglobin A1c [a test estimating average glucose levels over the previous three months]?" Which doesn't mean jack.

A hemoglobin A1c result can be potentially misleading, insofar as it can produce results that make it appear the diabetes has been well controlled when actually the patient has undergone extreme highs and lows. In one example from our field notes, residents at County were pleased by one patient with a seemingly reasonable hemoglobin A1c, but additional probing by a suspicious attending physician revealed that this patient regularly had severe episodes of hypoglycemia because he drank a six-pack of beer every night. For avoiding risks associated with hypoglycemia, hemoglobin A1c may not provide all the information physicians need. High continuity of care may thus allow the physicians at Park to better assemble a "totality" of information, which

in turn allows them to provide more helpful treatment recommendations.

Continuity of care also facilitates open patient-provider communication, increasing the likelihood that useful information is obtained during the visit. Providers in County have much less opportunity to personally monitor or follow patients they treat. One County physician we interviewed complained about having to make regimen decisions while knowing virtually nothing about how the patient would behave outside the clinic. Another explained:

> You have to glean everything from the chart. You don't get a nice letter written to you [about a patient's status], it's a note on a chart, and depending on how busy the [providers who saw the patient last] are in the clinic, they write a longer or shorter note, usually a shorter one because everybody's pretty busy. And that's sometimes a little bit of a struggle to really get a comprehensive picture of what [a patient's] complication status is and what other doctors who are taking care of them are thinking about how their med[ication]s should be adjusted and these kinds of things.

Beyond the challenges of interpreting information from patients' charts, low continuity of care generates the additional problem of learning about a patient's habits and how those habits are connected to his or her diabetes management, as another County physician described:

> I think that's where continuity of care is important, because the more you know somebody's habits—and there's so many different habits to learn about with diabetes, exercise, how much do each of those things vary, how sensitive are they to exercise and to diet, how compliant are they with their diet, how much does their diet vary from day to day. . . . You can address that a lot more effectively with continuity or follow-up over a longer period of time than to try and just see a patient cold and do all that on one visit.

Under these circumstances, providers in County often favored conservative treatment regimens, which they regarded as the safest option in the absence of close follow-up. *In the aggregate, because these regimens afford only weaker glucose control, they might be expected to increase the risk of long-term complications and thus preserve the fundamental relationship.*

External Constraints on Regimen Design

Although we observed two very different diabetes clinics, we do not suggest that all mechanisms would be eliminated if the patients we observed were treated at the same clinic. On the contrary, a series of additional phenomena would preserve the negative relationship between SES and health outcomes. Next we consider occupational influences on regimen design (see Lutfey and Freese 2005 for supplementary discussion of finances and social networks).

Apart from having less money, low SES patients might also be more likely to work at jobs that are less hospitable to implementing effective plans for managing glucose. Physicians noted that patients working swing shifts have schedules that make it very difficult to implement a regimen that permits tight control, because they are sleeping during the day. Manual labor jobs pose additional challenges, because these patients often use glucose somewhat intensely and irregularly while working and so are much more likely to have problems with hypoglycemia. Worse, they are more likely to be in physical danger if they do become hypoglycemic, especially if operating heavy machinery or working alone, and may be at risk for losing operating licenses. To accommodate these risks, regimens for these people usually favor higher glucose levels (and therefore higher risk of complications) to avoid hypoglycemia but preserve daily functioning.

People working in white-collar jobs in offices were seen as better able to maintain regular eating and exercising schedules, to be at lower risk of physical danger, and to be better candidates to receive assistance from nearby and knowledgeable coworkers in the event of hypoglycemia. As one physician attests:

> Some patients don't wanna have more than one or two shots a day. For example, if you have a truck driver . . . you may be able to convince them if they're local drivers to take a shot at bedtime, but they [are] hardly ever going to have more than two shots a day and

they are not gonna adjust their insulin dose while they're on the road. . . . [By contrast,] I've got patients that have a predictable lifestyle . . . they go to the office and they come back and they have their lunch times. They can handle complex regimens much better.

(Apparent?) Motivation

Next we consider the influence of perceived patient motivation on regimen design and the strong SES character we observed in assessments of motivation. For low SES patients, *the relative costs of complying* with particular features of treatment regimens are often greater than for high SES patients, yet providers often attribute these differences to psychological differences in patient motivation.

Showing up for appointments might seem the simplest expectation of all. Practitioners regarded missed visits as strong indicators that patients were probably not following their treatment regimens well. For poorer patients, however, the personal costs of making a clinic visit often may be higher than for middle-class patients. In terms of time, County patients usually had to wait sixty to ninety minutes for their appointments, whereas Park patients usually waited less than ten minutes. Because County Hospital patients were always seen by either a resident or fellow before the attending physician, their actual appointments were also much longer. Patients reported differences in flexibility for taking time off work for appointments, whether such time off is paid (and the personal need for such pay), and the availability of a personal vehicle for driving to appointments compared to time-consuming use of public transportation.

Patients were also often viewed as unmotivated if they allowed prescriptions to lapse. The social program subsidizing medications for many County patients required them to fill their prescriptions at the hospital pharmacy, whereas patients with private insurance could not only use their regular local pharmacies but also call in refills beforehand. As one County physician complained:

> If you gave a businessman a prescription that had to be refilled every month, and he had to stop what he was doing and go to the store and stand there in front of a pharmacist for thirty minutes, forty minutes, he'd say, "Either you give me something that's appropri-

ate, or I'm firing you as my physician." And here [at County] we give patients their prescription and say, "Come back every month and stand here. Come back on the bus and get your prescriptions filled." Gimme a break. If that doesn't interfere with compliance, I don't know what does.

Patients' apparent motivation to comply with medical instructions may also be affected by the immediacy and transparency of *benefits* associated with compliant behavior. For example, the more discretion patients have over their insulin dosage (as in sophisticated regimens), the more incentive there is to maintain a log, because that information is critical for determining dosages. In contrast, patients with basic regimens were directed to check their glucose levels but do nothing other than write them down for the doctor. Consequently, with the cost of glucose testing approaching $2.00–3.00/day, the point of keeping a log may be obscured for patients with simple regimens, especially since—unlike missing a shot of insulin—it has no immediately observable effect on their actual health.

Discussion

This chapter articulates some mechanisms by which the inverse relationship between SES and health outcomes might be produced among persons with diabetes. Comparing patients in two clinics that serve very different clienteles, we identify numerous ways in which SES influences the design or successful implementation of a regimen. That we can specify such a large number of candidate mechanisms is consistent with the animating idea of fundamental causality: that durable relationships between encompassing variables like SES and health may represent an accumulation of many small, pervasive advantages that can be expected to be renewed as the particulars of disease treatment change over time.

We view this compendium of potential mechanisms as a contribution to the social epidemiology of diabetes in its own right. An ethnographic approach to fundamental cause relationships also illustrates the value of describing concrete causal pathways with a depth of observational detail. Apart from generating proposals about specific causal pathways that might be tested using quantitative methods, ethnographic investigations like ours may also expand social epidemiology's understanding of the multiplicity of mechanisms that can underlie the causal role of single variables, such as "continuity of care."

We have purposely limited the scope of our inquiry to capitalize on the strengths of our data and of ethnographic methods—to articulate the concrete experiences of people with the health care system in ways that elude large-scale statistical analyses. As is common in ethnography, we reap these benefits of depth at the expense of generalizability. By restricting our study to patients whose regimens include insulin and who are treated in subspecialty clinics, the average case we observed is more serious than the average case among the general population of diabetes patients. A fuller treatment of diabetes would require much broader observations. Obviously diabetes is only one kind of chronic disease, and chronic diseases are not the only health outcomes for which an inverse relationship between SES and health is observed. An eventual goal might be a comprehensive schematic that draws connections and contrasts among many conditions, but that is far in the future and will require many additional studies of specific conditions by other investigators.

REFERENCES

Booth, Gillian L., and Janet E. Hux. 2003. "Relationship Between Avoidable Hospitalizations for Diabetes Mellitus and Income Level." *Archives of Internal Medicine* 163: 101–106.

Centers for Disease Control and Prevention. 2011. "National Diabetes Fact Sheet: National Estimates and General Information on Diabetes and Prediabetes in the United States." Atlanta, GA: U.S. Department of Health and Human Services, Centers for Disease Control and Prevention.

The Diabetes Control and Complications Trial Research Group. 1993. "The Effect of Intensive Treatment of Diabetes on the Development and Progression of Long-Term Complications in Insulin-Dependent Diabetes Mellitus." *New England Journal of Medicine* 329: 977–986.

Freese, Jeremy, and Karen E. Lutfey. 2011. "Fundamental Causality: Challenges of an Animating Concept for Medical Sociology." In *Handbook of Medical Sociology*, edited by B. Pescosolido, J. Martin, J. McLeod, and A. Rogers, 67–81. New York: Springer.

Link, Bruce G., Mary E. Northridge, Jo C. Phelan, and Michael L. Ganz. 1998. "Social Epidemiology and the Fundamental Cause Concept: On the Structuring of Effective Cancer Screens by Socioeconomic Status." *Milbank Quarterly* 76 (3): 375–402.

Link, Bruce G., and Jo C. Phelan. 1995. "Social Conditions as Fundamental Causes of Disease." Journal of Health and Social Behavior (Extra Issue): 80–94.

Lutfey, Karen E., and Jeremy Freese. 2005. "Toward Some Fundamentals of Fundamental Causality: Socioeconomic Status and Health in the Routine Clinic Visit for Diabetes." *American Journal of Sociology* 110 (5): 1326–1372.

Nicolucci, Antonio, Fabrizio Carinci, and Antonio Ciampi. 1998. "Stratifying Patients at Risk of Diabetic Complications." *Diabetes Care* 21: 1439–1444.

Phelan, Jo C., Bruce G. Link, and Parisa Tehranifar. 2010. "Social Conditions as Fundamental Causes of Health Inequalities: Theory, Evidence, and Policy Implications." *Journal of Health and Social Behavior* 51: S28–S40.

Robert, Stephanie A., and James S. House. 1994. "Socioeconomic Status and Health Across the Life Course." In *Aging and Quality of Life*, edited by R. P. Abeles, H. C. Gift, and M. G. Ory, 253–274. New York: Springer.

Robbins, J., V. Vaccarino, H. Zhang, and S. Kasl. 2001. "Socioeconomic Status and Type 2 Diabetes in African American and Non-Hispanic White Women and Men: Evidence from the Third National Health and Nutrition Examination Survey." *American Journal of Public Health* 91: 76–84.

Weber, Max. [1921] 1968. *Economy and Society*. Translated and edited by Guenther Roth and Claus Wittich. New York: Bedminster Press.

PART IX

MOVING TOWARD EQUALITY?

It is useful to conclude by discussing how various forms of inequality, especially poverty, might be reduced. Because the "interventions industry" is so large and sprawling, we cannot of course do justice to it here. We instead proceed by offering up a simple frame that may be used to classify the many proposals in play. This frame, which draws very directly on the work of Michelle Jackson (Ch. 74), entails making a sharp distinction between (a) relatively narrow-gauge interventions, and (b) more substantial institutional reform.

By "interventions," we mean relatively minor reforms that are tacked-on to existing institutions, reforms that do not address the underlying sources of the disadvantage but instead try to ameliorate with a compensatory program. It has become almost instinctive to turn to such compensatory programs: We tack on "home visiting" programs because we worry that poor mothers are not receiving high-quality prenatal care; we tack on Head Start programs because we worry that poor children do not have access to adequate preschools; and we tack on new tax credits or loan programs because we worry that college is just too expensive for poor families. These interventions leave existing labor market, educational, and neighborhood institutions intact and attempt to overcome the problems they create with initiatives that might offset them.

Why do Americans typically opt for the tack on? It is partly because it is all we can do. That is, major institutional reform is exceedingly difficult to undertake, hence most politicians and others pick battles that, as Jonathan Kozol once put it, are "big enough to matter, small enough to win." This instinct is so well-developed, however, that we sometimes forget that in principle we could reform our institutions themselves rather than just tack on side-programs that work to counter them. We could integrate our neighborhoods; we could pull back on incarceration; we could equalize opportunities for high-quality schooling; we could reduce unemployment with a government jobs program, a more aggressive stimulus package, or by investing in research and development; or we could make college free and thereby reduce the size of the "reserve army" of low-skilled workers chasing after the few low-skill jobs available.

The simple point here: We have two very different pathways from which to choose. We can either (a) engage in fundamental institutional reform that increases opportunities for the poor, or (b) opt for the business-as-usual approach of leaving our labor market, educational, and social institutions intact and then attempt to overlay on them the usual array of compensatory anti-poverty programs. It may be useful to organize the proposals on offer in Part IX by asking which of these two approaches has been taken and whether that decision, typically an implicit one, is nonetheless a well-considered one.

459

69. James J. Heckman*

Skill Formation and the Economics of Investing in Disadvantaged Children

Four core concepts important to devising sound social policy toward early childhood have emerged from decades of independent research in economics, neuroscience, and developmental psychology (*1*). First, the architecture of the brain and the process of skill formation are influenced by an interaction between genetics and individual experience. Second, the mastery of skills that are essential for economic success and the development of their underlying neural pathways follow hierarchical rules. Later attainments build on foundations that are laid down earlier. Third, cognitive, linguistic, social, and emotional competencies are interdependent; all are shaped powerfully by the experiences of the developing child; and all contribute to success in the society at large. Fourth, although adaptation continues throughout life, human abilities are formed in a predictable sequence of sensitive periods, during which the development of specific neural circuits and the behaviors they mediate are most plastic and therefore optimally receptive to environmental influences.

A landmark study concluded that "virtually every aspect of early human development, from the brain's evolving circuitry to the child's capacity for empathy, is affected by the environments and experiences that are encountered in a cumulative fashion, beginning in the prenatal period and extending throughout the early childhood years" (*2*). This principle stems from two characteristics that are intrinsic to the nature of learning: (i) early learning confers value on acquired skills, which leads to self-reinforcing motivation to learn more, and (ii) early mastery of a range of cognitive, social, and emotional competencies makes learning at later ages more efficient and therefore easier and more likely to continue.

Early family environments are major predictors of cognitive and noncognitive abilities. Research has documented the early (by ages four to six) emergence and persistence of gaps in cognitive and noncognitive skills (*3, 4*). Environments that do not stimulate the young and fail to cultivate these skills at early ages place children at an early disadvantage.

Disadvantage arises more from lack of cognitive and noncognitive stimulation given to young children than simply from the lack of financial resources.

This is a source of concern because family environments have deteriorated. More US children are born to teenage mothers or are living in single parent homes compared with forty years ago (*5*). Disadvantage is associated with poor parenting practices and lack of positive cognitive and noncognitive stimulation. A child who falls behind may never catch up. The track records for criminal rehabilitation, adult literacy, and public job training programs for disadvantaged young adults are remarkably poor (*3*). Disadvantaged early environments are powerful predictors of adult failure on a number of social and economic measures.

Many major economic and social problems can be traced to low levels of skill and ability in the population. The US will add many fewer college graduates to its workforce in the next twenty years than it did in the past twenty years (*6, 7*). The high school dropout rate, properly measured with inclusion of individuals who have received general educational development (GED) degrees, is increasing at a time when the economic return of schooling has increased (*8*). It is not solely a phenomenon of unskilled immigrants. Over 20% of the US workforce is functionally illiterate, compared with about 10% in Germany and Sweden (*9*). Violent crime and property crime levels remain high, despite large declines in recent years. It is estimated that the net cost of crime in American society is $1.3 trillion per year, with a per capita cost of $4,818 per year (*10*). Recent research documents the importance of deficits in cognitive and noncognitive skills in explaining these and other social pathologies (*11*).

Noncognitive Skills and Examples of Successful Early Interventions

Cognitive skills are important, but noncognitive skills such as motivation, perseverance, and tenacity are also important for success in life. Much public policy, such as the No Child Left Behind Act, focuses on cognitive test score outcomes to measure the success of interventions in spite of the evidence on the importance of noncognitive skills in social success. Head Start was deemed a failure in the 1960s because it did not raise the intelligence quotients (IQs) of its participants (*12*). Such judgments are common but miss the larger picture. Consider the Perry Preschool Program (*13*), a two-year

*James J. Heckman. "Skill Formation and the Economics of Investing in Disadvantaged Children," *Science* 312, issue 5782 (June 2006), pp. 1900–1902. Reprinted with permission from AAAS.

TABLE 69.1 Economic Benefits and Costs of the Perry Preschool Program

	Perry Preschool
Child care	$986
Earnings	$40,537
K–12	$9184
College/adult	$–782
Crime	$94,065
Welfare	$355
Abuse/neglect	$0
Total benefits	$144,345
Total costs	$16,514
Net present value	$127,831
Benefits-to-costs ratio	8.74

All values are discounted at 3% and are in 2004 dollars. Earnings, Welfare, and Crime refer to monetized value of adult outcomes (higher earnings, savings in welfare, and reduced costs of crime). K–12 refers to the savings in remedial schooling. College/adult refers to tuition costs. (27)

experimental intervention for disadvantaged African American children initially ages three to four that involved morning programs at school and afternoon visits by the teacher to the child's home. The Perry intervention group had IQ scores no higher than the control group by age ten. Yet, the Perry treatment children had higher achievement test scores than the control children because they were more motivated to learn. In follow-ups to age forty, the treated group had higher rates of high school graduation, higher salaries, higher percentages of home ownership, lower rates of receipt of welfare assistance as adults, fewer out-of-wedlock births, and fewer arrests than the controls (13). The economic benefits of the Perry Program are substantial (Table 69.1). Rates of return are 15 to 17% (14). (The rate of return is the increment in earnings and other outcomes, suitably valued, per year for each dollar invested in the child.) The benefit-cost ratio (the ratio of the aggregate program benefits over the life of the child to the input costs) is over eight to one.

Perry intervened relatively late. The Abecedarian program, also targeted toward disadvantaged children, started when participants were four months of age. Children in the treatment group received child care for six to eight hours per day, five days per week, through kindergarten entry; nutritional supplements, social work services, and medical care were provided to control group families. The program was found to permanently raise the IQ and the noncognitive skills of the treatment group over the control group. However, the Abecedarian program was in-

tensive, and it is not known whether it is the age of intervention or its intensity that contributed to its success in raising IQ (15–17).

Reynolds et al. present a comprehensive review of early childhood programs directed toward disadvantaged children and their impact (18). Similar returns are obtained for other early intervention programs (19, 20), although more speculation is involved in these calculations because the program participants are in the early stages of their life cycles and do not have long earnings histories.

Schools and Skill Gaps

Many societies look to the schools to reduce skills gaps across socioeconomic groups. Because of the dynamics of human skill formation, the abilities and motivations that children bring to school play a far greater role in promoting their performance in school than do the traditional inputs that receive so much attention in public policy debates. The Coleman Report (21) as well as recent work (22, 23) show that families and not schools are the major sources of inequality in student performance. By the third grade, gaps in test scores across socioeconomic groups are stable by age, suggesting that later schooling and variations in schooling quality have little effect in reducing or widening the gaps that appear before students enter school (4, 24). Figure 69.1 plots gaps in math test scores by age across family income levels. The majority of the gap at age twelve appears at the age of school enrollment. Carneiro and Heckman performed a cost-benefit analysis of classroom size reduction on adult earnings (3). Although smaller classes raise the adult earnings of students, the earnings gains received by students do not offset the costs of hiring additional teachers. The student-teacher achievement ratio (STAR) randomized trial of classroom size in Tennessee shows some effect of reduced classroom size on test scores and adult performance, but most of the effect occurs in the earliest grades (25, 26). Schools and school quality at current levels of funding contribute little to the emergence of test score gaps among children or to the development of the gaps.

Second Chance Programs

America is a second chance society. Our educational policy is based on a fundamental optimism about the possibility of human change. The dynamics of human skill formation reveal that later

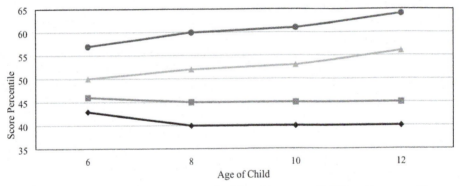

FIGURE 69.1 Average Percentile Rank on Peabody Individual Achievement Test–Math Score by Age and Income Quartile

Income quartiles are computed from average family income between the ages of 6 and 10. Adapted from (3) with permission from MIT Press.
Heckman, James J., and Alan B. Krueger. edited by Benjamin M. Friedman. introduction by Benjamin M. Friedman., *Inequality in America: What Role for Human Capital Policies?*, Figure 2.6a, p. 91 and Figure 2.9a, p. 130, © 2004 Massachusetts Institute of Technology, by permission of The MIT Press.

compensation for deficient early family environments is very costly (*4*). If society waits too long to compensate, it is economically inefficient to invest in the skills of the disadvantaged. A serious trade-off exists between equity and efficiency for adolescent and young adult skill policies. There is no such trade-off for policies targeted toward disadvantaged young children (*28*).

The findings of a large literature are captured in Figure 69.2. This figure plots the rate of return, which is the dollar flow from a unit of investment at each age for a marginal investment in a disadvantaged young child at current levels of expenditure. The economic return from early interventions is high, and the return from later interventions is lower. Remedial programs in the adolescent and young adult years are much more costly in producing the same level of skill attainment in adulthood. Most are economically inefficient. This is reflected in Fig. 69.2 by the fact that a segment of the curve lies below the opportunity cost of funds (the horizontal line fixed at *r*). The opportunity cost is the return from funds if they were invested for purposes unrelated to disadvantaged children.

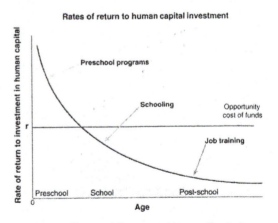

FIGURE 69.2 Rates of Return to Human Capital Investment in Disadvantaged Children

The declining figure plots the payout per year per dollar invested in human capital programs at different stages of the life cycle for the marginal participant at current levels of spending. The opportunity cost of funds (r) is the payout per year if the dollar is invested in financial assets (e.g., passbook savings) instead. An optimal investment program from the point of view of economic efficiency equates returns across all stages of the life cycle to the opportunity cost. The figure shows that, at current levels of funding, we overinvest in most schooling and post-schooling programs and underinvest in preschool programs for disadvantaged persons. Adapted from (3) with permission from MIT Press.

Conclusions

Investing in disadvantaged young children is a rare public policy initiative that promotes fairness and social justice and at the same time promotes productivity in the economy and in society at large. Early interventions targeted toward disadvantaged children have much higher returns than later interventions such as reduced pupil-teacher ratios, public job training, convict rehabilitation programs, tuition subsidies, or expenditure on police. At current levels of resources, society overinvests in remedial skill investments at later ages and underinvests in the early years.

Although investments in older disadvantaged individuals realize relatively less return overall, such investments are still clearly beneficial. Indeed, the advantages gained from effective early interventions are sustained best when they are followed by continued high-quality learning experiences. The technology of skill formation shows that the returns on school investment and postschool investment are higher for persons with higher ability, where ability is formed in the early years. Stated simply, early investments must be followed by later investments if maximum value is to be realized.

REFERENCES AND NOTES

1. E. I. Knudsen, J. J. Heckman, J. Cameron, J. P. Shonkoff, Proc. Natl. Acad. Sci. U.S.A., in press.

2. J. P. Shonkoff, D. Phillips, *From Neurons to Neighborhoods: The Science of Early Child Development* (National Academies Press, Washington, DC, 2000).

3. P. Carneiro, J. J. Heckman, in *Inequality in America: What Role for Human Capitol Policies?* J. J. Heckman, A. B. Krueger, B. Friedman, Eds. (MIT Press, Cambridge, MA, 2003), ch. 2, pp. 77–237.

4. F. Cunha, J. J. Heckman, L. J. Lochner, D. V. Masterov, in *Handbook of the Economics of Education*, E. A. Hanushek, F. Welch, Eds. (North Holland, Amsterdam, 2006).

5. J. J. Heckman, D. V. Masterov, "The productivity argument for investing in young children" (Working Paper No. 5, Committee on Economic Development, Washington, DC, 2004).

6. J. B. DeLong, L. Katz, C. Goldin, in *Agenda for the Nation,* H. Aaron, J. Lindsay, P. Nivola, Eds. (Brookings Institution Press, Washington, DC, 2003), pp. 17–60.

7. D. T. Ellwood, in *The Roaring Nineties: Can Full Employment Be Sustained?* A. Krueger, R. Solow, Eds. (Russell Sage Foundation, New York, 2001), pp. 421–489.

8. J. J. Heckman, P. LaFontaine, J. Lab. Econ., in press.

9. International Adult Literacy Survey, 2002: User's Guide, Statistics Canada, Special Surveys Division, National Literacy Secretariat, and Human Resources Development Canada (Statistics Canada, Ottawa, Ontario, 2002).

10. D. A. Anderson, *J. Law Econ.* 42, 611 (1999).

11. J. J. Heckman, J. Stixrud, S. Urzua, *J. Lab. Econ.,* in press.

12. Westinghouse Learning Corporation and Ohio University, *The Impact of Head Start: An Evaluation of the Effects of Head Start on Children's Cognitive and Affective Development,* vols. 1 and 2 (Report to the Office of Economic Opportunity, Athens, OH, 1969).

13. L. J. Schweinhart et al., *Lifetime Effects: The High/Scope Perry Preschool Study Through Age 40* (High/Scope, Ypsilanti, MI, 2005).

14. A. Rolnick, R. Grunewald, "Early childhood development: Economic development with a high public return" (Tech. rep., Federal Reserve Bank of Minneapolis, Minneapolis, MN, 2003).

15. C. T. Ramey, S. L. Ramey, *Am. Psychol.* 53, 109 (1998).

16. C. T. Ramey, S. L. Ramey, *Prev. Med.* 27, 224 (1998).

17. C. T. Ramey et al., *Appl. Dev. Sci.* 4, 2 (2000).

18. A. J. Reynolds, M. C. Wang, H. J. Walberg, *Early Childhood Programs for a New Century* (Child Welfare League of America Press, Washington, DC, 2003).

19. L. A. Karoly et al., Investing in *Our Children: What We Know and Don't Know About the Costs and Benefits of Early Childhood Interventions* (RAND, Santa Monica, CA, 1998).

20. L. N. Masse, W. S. Barnett, *A Benefit Cost Analysis of the Abecedarian Early Childhood Intervention* (Rutgers University, National Institute for Early Education Research, New Brunswick, NJ, 2002).

21. J. S. Coleman, Equality of Educational Opportunity (U.S. Department of Health, Education, and Welfare, Office of Education, Washington, DC, 1966).

22. S. W. Raudenbush, "Schooling, statistics and poverty: Measuring school improvement and improving schools" (Inaugural Lecture, Division of Social Sciences, University of Chicago, Chicago, IL, 22 February 2006).

23. J. J. Heckman, M. I. Larenas, S. Urzua, unpublished data.

24. D. A. Neal, in *Handbook of Economics of Education*, E. Hanushek, F. Welch, Eds. (Elsevier, Amsterdam, 2006).

25. B. Krueger, D. M. Whitmore, *Econ. J.,* 111, 1 (2001).

26. B. Krueger, D. M. Whitmore, in *Bridging the Achievement Gap,* J. E. Chubb, T. Loveless, Eds. (Brookings Institution Press, Washington, DC, 2002).

27. W. S. Barnett, Benefit-Cost *Analysis of Preschool Education,* 2004 (http://nieer.org/resources/files/Barnett-Benefits.ppt).

28. F. Cunha, J. J. Heckman, J. *Hum. Resour.,* in press.

29. This paper was generously supported by NSF (grant nos. SES-0241858 and SES-0099195), National Institute of Child Health and Human Development (NIH grant no. R01HD043411), funding from the Committee for Economic Development, with a grant from the Pew Charitable Trusts and from the Partnership for America's Economic Success. This research was also supported by the Children's Initiative project at the Pritzker Family Foundation and a grant from the Report to the Nation of America's Promise. The views expressed in this paper are those of the author and not necessarily those of the sponsoring organizations. See our Web site (http://jenni.uchicago.edu/econ_neurosci) for more information.

70. Carol S. Dweck*
Why Late Investments Can Work

James Heckman has done an extraordinary service by bringing psychological research on early interventions to the attention of a broad audience. His review of the scientific evidence is compelling and makes the case that parental training and educational enrichment in the early years have critical and lasting effects on children. . . .

Arguing that allocating funds for early education programs is preferable to funding programs that deal with the aftermath of poor early environments, Heckman introduces the idea of the equity-efficiency tradeoff: although the latter programs are equitable, the return on investment is low and they are thus not economically efficient.

I strongly support early interventions, but Heckman's comparisons can be misleading. First, he compares early programs that foster non-cognitive skills to later remedial programs such as adult literacy programs or public job training programs, which address mostly specific cognitive or job skills. . . . Wouldn't the proper comparison be adolescent and adult programs that focus on non-cognitive skills? Second, and even more important, he compares the very costly early interventions to very costly later interventions. What if there were interventions for adolescents that addressed non-cognitive factors and were both inexpensive and effective?

In fact, there are. My colleagues and I have conducted interventions with adolescents in which they learn that their brains and intellect are malleable. They discover that when they stretch themselves to learn new things, their neurons form new connections and they can, over time, enhance their intellectual skills. Compared to a control group that learned only study skills, these students showed marked improvements in motivation, and their declining grades were sharply reversed. Researchers Catherine Good and Joshua Aronson have found similar effects. In studies led by David Yeager, high school students who were taught a malleable view of their intellectual and social skills showed positive changes in their grades, stress level, conduct (including aggression), and health

that lasted over the course of the school year. Gregory Walton and Geoffrey Cohen have spearheaded interventions that address adolescents' sense of their social and academic belonging in school, enhancing students' motivation and resilience, and leading to a substantial and enduring decrease in the racial achievement gap. None of these treatments required more than eight short sessions, and most required less.

Interventions for adolescents can be inexpensive and efficient. . . . Although I wouldn't claim that these short non-cognitive interventions in adolescence can obliterate a problematic childhood, they do go a long way toward closing the achievement gap between disadvantaged and advantaged adolescents. And they work well for students with no prior enrichment; indeed, they often work best for those who are faring worst. This means that later interventions targeted at non-cognitive factors can achieve impressive gains with remarkable efficiency.

The success of the adolescent interventions derives from their laser-like focus on particular non-cognitive factors and the beliefs that underlie them—knowledge stemming from psychological theory. Such psychological precision needs to be brought to all aspects of early interventions. For example, my colleagues and I recently tested a hypothesis derived from psychological theory and showed that the type of praise a mother directs at her baby predicts the child's desire for challenging tasks five years later. The early interventions Heckman discusses, although groundbreaking, have been massive and non-specific. For example, the Abecedarian Project was a year-round, full-day intervention that started at around four months of age and continued through age five. Other interventions involved lengthy home visits. For early interventions to become feasible on a large scale, we need to make them more efficient—we need to isolate their critical components and focus on them.

Early interventions are of tremendous importance for the future of our society, but so are focused, psychologically potent interventions with older children and adolescents. Our goal should be to use psychological research to make all of our interventions as efficient and potent as possible so that we do not have to decide who will be the haves and who will be the have-nots.

*Dweck, Carol S., "Don't Forget Teens," first published in *Boston Review*, Sept./Oct. 2012. Used by permission of the American Economic Association.

71. Joshua Cohen and Charles Sabel*

Flexicurity

Ten years ago, the stylized story about poverty and inequality went something like this:

> You can be the United States, with lots of income inequality, very flexible labor markets, and very high levels of employment; or you can be Germany, with not so much inequality, rigid labor markets, and lots of unemployment; or you can be Sweden, with pretty low levels of inequality and unemployment. But you can be Sweden only if you employ lots of workers (especially women) in an expanded public sector providing services to families, as inflexible labor market rules keep private sector firms from expanding employment.

Given these options, our system did not seem so bad. Sober analysts acknowledged the costs of American inequality and poverty, especially for African Americans. But sobriety also compelled recognition of the benefits of the great American jobs machine: creating lots of low-wage work was a large compensation, not least to middle-class families who could afford to hire domestic workers to provide some of the services provided publicly in Sweden. It was hard to see an alternative, as we lacked Sweden's cultural homogeneity, its solidaristic political culture, and the associated willingness to maintain outsized public employment.

And really: How could there have been an alternative with better results for low-wage workers, given our deeply rooted concern that the protections provided by rigid labor markets or substantial public employment ultimately limit the life chances of the vulnerable by undermining their sense of personal responsibility? Short-term gains in security sound good, but aren't they overwhelmed by the long-term risks of dependency? Low unemployment with high levels of labor force participation and high growth rates; greater income equality and reduced poverty; and a sense of personal responsibility resistant to the moral hazards of solidaristic subsidies: That mix is

nice work if you can get it, and good for the utopian fantasies that some call "political philosophy." But such a package is simply unrealistic here, and probably impossible (except in a Sweden) given the hard trade-offs that life imposes and that grown-ups understand.

That was then, this is now. The grown-ups who managed the miracle of global finance have been sent to their (generously appointed) rooms. Leading policymakers look openly to Japan for lessons about anti-deflationary policy when interest rates hover just above the "zero bound" and to Sweden for lessons about how to nationalize, revitalize, and reprivatize a financial system after a bad-mortgage binge. Fears are great, but hopes are also high. And the idea that the United States might have something to learn about public policy from the rest of the world seems a little less like the carping of academics constitutionally incapable of appreciating what awed the rest of the world about this country, and a little more like the thing that sensible adults do when they are having "issues."

As it happens, when it comes to addressing inequality and poverty, there is something to learn from the far reaches of Old Europe.

Consider the case of Denmark. In the early 1990s, facing high unemployment, low growth, a public sector nearly immobilized in the face of economic decline, and a long-smoldering revolt against an apparently incapacitated state, Denmark reconfigured its welfare state to create a system called *flexicurity*. The essential idea of flexicurity—conveyed by the name—is to combine high *flexibility* in labor markets with high levels of *security* for workers. The flexibility includes both wage flexibility and relative ease for firms in laying off workers, with much lower levels of job protection than other OECD countries. The security comes from a mix of high levels of unemployment insurance—a considerably higher "replacement rate," or ratio of average weekly benefits to average weekly earnings, than any other OECD country—and an active labor market policy providing education and training. This training ensures successful integration into the labor market for younger and older workers, and it offers life-long learning. The idea, in a slogan, is: *Employment security, not job security*. It means a career at varied, increasingly skilled work, not a lifetime climbing the job ladder in a single firm.

The cumulative effect of flexicurity for individuals, moreover, is to encourage an economy-wide shift

*Joshua Cohen and Charles Sabel, "Flexicurity," *Pathways* (Spring 2009), pp. 9, 10–14.

in favor of more skilled jobs, as well as innovative firms that can make use of them. Low unemployment rates and rising skill levels give the most skilled, desirable workers (who are, of course, likely to be the ones most attentive to skill acquisition) their pick of jobs. Employers have to attract them with work that is not only interesting, but offers the prospect of further learning. Firms can afford to offer such jobs only if they undertake projects that make productive and well-remunerated use of these workers—and such projects, being the opposite of routine, will naturally require innovative exploration of new possibilities. The robust, adaptable security of individuals fosters the adaptive robustness of the whole economy.

Two other features of flexicurity, not built into the name, are essential to its success. In contrast with our conventional picture of public goods as (by their nature) standardized for broad categories of recipients (e.g., primary education for children ages, say, five to ten), flexicurity is individualized. The guiding assumption—based on many recent studies of life on Earth—is that individuals have distinct lives, and that (especially when people are experiencing troubles) those lives cannot easily or constructively be compartmentalized into discrete pieces—work, family, education, training, income, health, transportation, housing—addressed by distinct policies. On the contrary, family problems are likely to aggravate, or be aggravated by, problems in school or work; addressing any one of these effectively requires attention to at least some of the others. So, support for younger and older adult jobseekers requires not just *customized* services, but *bundles* of customized services adjusted to the needs of individuals and meshing with one another.

Moreover, because education and training require the engagement of workers in ways that simple income support (or in-kind assistance) does not, there is also an important role for *personal responsibility*. Customized services are effective only if those to whom the services are directed participate actively in their production—indeed, that participation is required for the services to be customized to particular needs in the first place. Flexicurity is not what a "nanny state" does when it is taking charge of its responsibility-challenged, incapacitated wards; it is not what a sadder-but-wiser, postnanny welfare state does when it compensates citizens for some hard luck in youth before sending them out to face the tough, cold world. It is what a

democracy does to ensure the continuing inclusion of all its equal members, in a world where we face, individually and collectively, the continuing risks of economic, social, and political exclusion thrown up by rapidly changing labor markets in largely open economies.

This low-resolution description of flexicurity focuses on design principles rather than specific policies and corresponding institutions. But this level of description is entirely faithful to the self-understandings of actors in the system (especially to some of the leading social democrats, such as Mogens Lykketoft, who helped create Danish flexicurity in the 1990s, and the many local and regional actors who customize services today) and of the many outsiders who have tried to learn from the Danish experience. As the appeal of flexicurity has spread from Denmark to Ireland, Finland, and the Netherlands, and become a focus of EU debate over labor market policy, participants in that debate have come to understand that flexicurity takes different forms in different settings. Jeremy Bentham once wrote a constitutional code with a blank space left for the name of the country. The participants in the debate about flexicurity are less abstractly universal in their thinking. As they understand it, the right way to think about flexicurity's broader dispersion is not to simply take a Danish operating manual, translate, enter another country's name, and apply. Instead, the point is to adapt the five design principles just described—flexibility in employment and compensation, robust security for workers, lifelong learning, customization, and personal responsibility to make use of changing opportunities—then pursue mutual comparisons across different versions of flexicurity (first internationally, then domestically) for improvement. Thus, a sixth principle of flexicurity is its adaptability—to changes in Denmark, and, at least potentially, to settings in other countries.

Transforming flexibility and security from competing goods to mutually supportive complements is immensely appealing in an age of deep uncertainty. This appeal has made flexicurity the active subject of EU discussion in recent years, as the European Commission has urged other countries to adopt their own versions of the Danish system. The main European debate acknowledges the merits of the scheme as applied in Denmark, which has experienced persistently low unemployment, high labor force participation, and low inequality. (Some critics have argued that Denmark's strong economic performance is not a result of flexicurity. They point to very slight reductions in labor supply resulting from high replacement rates and the detailed rules covering short-term unemployment. But they ignore what appear to be the significant structural benefits of increased mobility and skill acquisition to the economy.) The concern has been whether the essentials of the system, including its adaptability to changing domestic conditions, can translate across national boundaries, especially because of different regulatory institutions (and associated capacities to sustain active labor market policy), varying levels of trust and solidarity (e.g., how much can people be trusted not to game the unemployment insurance system), and different traditions of labor market flexibility and volatility.

Some of the concerns that have been raised in the European portability debate arguably carry over to the United States, with even greater force:

• The Danes have trust and solidarity; the United States, in contrast, is a famously fractious place, with an abstractly constitutional patriotism, not the deeper ethno-national solidarities needed to provide the assurances against cheating on which flexicurity depends.

• Americans have an exceptionally passionate attachment to individual responsibility. Yes, we like our equality of opportunity, too: Indeed, that value lies at the heart of our shared civic convictions. But the conventional idea of mixing equal opportunity and responsibility is to ensure equality at life's starting gate, whether through initial education and training, or—as in the post-nanny welfare state Bruce Ackerman and Anne Alstott proposed—a wealth gift for each citizen at age twenty-one that he or she can use to fund a career, or through some other form of early equalization, after which responsibility kicks in and (but for occasions of personal disaster) individuals are the agents of their own failure and success.

• The Danes like to pay taxes: They have 50 percent tax rates. We don't like taxes. But you have to like them some to support the customized system of lifelong learning.

• The Danes have unions; the United States' unionization rate is about one-tenth Denmark's. How can a country run an active labor market policy with high levels of security and flexibility if it lacks unions with the local knowledge to help ensure the flexibility, or the national power to help guard the state's commitment to security?

These concerns are all forceful, but we are living through unusual times, and we wonder whether we should let ourselves be guided by a knee-jerk invocation of American exceptionalism. All four criticisms remind us that a move to flexicurity would require a sharp departure from past practice, freeing ourselves from the tight grip of the past's famously cold, dead hand. But just a few quick reminders: In November 2008, the country elected a black president, defying conventional expectations. And we are now passing through the largest economic crisis in seventy-five years, a crisis that looks like it will issue in some entirely unanticipated shifts in national policy. We have already thrown caution to the winds. It would be a tragic mistake to think we could do that, yet remain otherwise as constrained as we often take ourselves to be.

These general observations about unusual circumstances and possibilities apply with particular force to the first concern—the sufficiency of national trust and solidarity. Who knows how much trust and solidarity are really essential to make flexicurity work, or how much we can muster?

As for the second, personal responsibility plays, as we have said, a large and essential role in flexicurity. While it is not about finger-wagging, it does accept that a person's success and failure in life depend importantly on her aspirations and efforts. Flexicurity is about lifelong learning in a public policy system that does not deny personal responsibility (you cannot learn without playing an active role), but rather reconceptualizes the conventional notion that we are victims of (a slightly corrigible) fate until eighteen or twenty-one, and nearly self-sufficient thereafter.

What about taxes? One pertinent observation is that no one loves taxes, not even the Danes. In fact, flexicurity was, in part, a reaction to a Danish tax revolt dating to the 1970s. That revolt was animated by a simple idea: Taxes are fine if they are used for good purposes (Danes, like the rest of us, are allergic to throwing money away). But aren't things different in the United States? Doesn't the American allergy extend even to taxes that are used efficiently for public purposes? Isn't the point here to keep "our own money"?

Maybe. But maybe not. In his interesting book *Why Trust Matters*, Mark Hetherington argues that variations in willingness to spend on social welfare in the United States since the 1960s are explained not by shifts to an ideological conservativism, but by shifts in trust, particularly in the government's capacity to make good use of tax resources: "When government programs require people to make sacrifices, they need to trust that the result will be a better future for everyone. Absent that trust, people will deem such sacrifices as unfair, even punitive, and, thus, will not support the programs that require them" (p. 4). Hetherington's argument is that the relevant kinds of trust declined after the mid-1960s. His case is hardly conclusive, but his point has considerable force, at least against the knee-jerk idea that intense tax allergies here make an otherwise attractive labor market policy—good for growth and for distribution—ineligible.

As for unions, we are not expecting a large expansion in American unionization rates. But we need to be careful about the role of unions in the flexicurity system. Danish unions helped push for innovations in the system of lifelong learning, and they play an important part in managing regional services (especially at the plant level). But the national unions are not, at the moment, active in extending or further adapting the system at the national level, and they have been reluctant to encourage too much local initiative for fear of authorizing a decentralization that they would be unable to control. That said, the power of unions to protect workers from employer offensives helps create a political environment in which employers and government are more inclined to look for a reasonable social bargain that does not impose large burdens on workers. A balance of power helps public reason work its magic.

But even here, the lessons for the United States may not be as dim as the point suggests. The last election and the current crisis are creating possibilities that do not exist in more normal times, and there is broad agreement that larger investments in worker training are important. With some foresight and a great deal of good fortune, it might be possible to improve the balance of power here, too, in a way that gives a reinvigorated labor movement a role in constructing a national framework for lifelong learning and contributing to that framework's local adaptability.

The Republicans are accusing President Obama of wanting to turn the United States into a northern European "welfare state." When it comes to flexicurity—with its embrace of equality, dynamic efficiency, and a sensible understanding of responsibility—we hope they are right.

72. Harry J. Holzer*
Reducing Poverty the Democratic Way

The factors that limit success among the poor are pretty clear. The most important are their low education levels and weak skills; the low pay for unskilled work in the United States, the correspondingly reduced incentive for many to remain in the job market, and the difficulty in finding or keeping jobs; and various "group-specific" barriers, such as growing up in a very poor family or neighborhood, having a criminal record, being a noncustodial parent, or having a disability.

The foregoing diagnosis leads directly to the prescription. What we need—very simply—are policies that will:

- Raise education and skills among poor children, youth, and adults.
- "Make work pay" for the unskilled, and make more jobs available to them when needed.
- Address the specific problems of such groups as ex-offenders, noncustodial parents, children in very poor families or neighborhoods, and people with disabilities.

The good news here is that decades of research suggest what works and what doesn't when trying to accomplish the above goals. . . .

Raising Education and Skills among the Poor

Over the long-term, the most important policy for lowering poverty and raising opportunity is to improve the education and skills of low-income children, youth, and adults. If anything, the gaps in schooling between poor children and others are rising.[1] In an economy that values and rewards education more than ever before, these gaps must be closed.

But two additional points need to be addressed by any skill-growing policy. First, many poor youth, as well as adults, now enroll in college, especially community or for-profit colleges. Many have Pell Grants to pay all or most of their tuition. The fundamental problem is that their completion rates are very low, reflecting weaker academic preparation in

* Holzer, Harry J. 2016. "Reducing Poverty the Democratic Way." *Pathways Magazine* (Winter), pp. 18-21.

the K–12 years and other challenges. Second, even when they do successfully attain credentials like associate (AA) degrees, too few are in fields that the labor market rewards. The challenge, then, is to ramp up the amount of training for the poor in strong "career pathways" and high-demand sectors *and* to ensure that they complete such training.

Given this range of problems, an appropriate set of policies is needed to expand access to high-quality training, ensure retention, and ensure that training is targeted to high-demand sectors. Such policies would include:

- Expanding the availability of high-quality pre-K programs for low-income children.
- Increasing the number of effective teachers in strong science/ technology/engineering/math (STEM) programs in poor school districts, and enabling more low-income children to choose and attend schools that have them.
- In high school, making sure that more high-quality career and technical education (CTE) and work-based learning is available.
- Rewarding public colleges with more funding if they raise completion rates and earnings among poor students.
- Making it easier for poor students to use their Pell Grants in short-term or non-credit programs that clearly have labor market value, or for apprenticeships and other forms of work-based learning.

This is *not* a laundry list. It is a targeted set of programs that address the key problems and exploit what we know about what works and what doesn't. There are, it should be stressed, notable omissions here: I am somewhat less interested, for example, in universal pre-K and am more interested in assuring access to high-quality pre-K programs for all low-income children.[2] This is because spending very scarce public resources to pay for pre-K for middle- and upper-income children makes little sense to me. Also, poor children can have access to good math and science instruction in a variety of ways, through traditional public schools, as well as in the best charter programs.

High-quality CTE, unlike old-fashioned vocational education, does not track students away from college and lock them into dead-end jobs. The best CTE programs—like Career Academies or apprenticeships—give students strong academic skills, plus more specific occupational training and work-based learning, providing them with both post-secondary education and career options after high school.[3]

As for higher education, we must help the public institutions that most poor students attend—especially community colleges—by providing more resources and clearer incentives to spend those resources cost-effectively. Basing additional public subsidies to these institutions on the academic and job market outcomes of their poor students is warranted.[4] And making it easier for them to use their Pell Grants in certificate programs that have labor market rewards would help as well.

I do not think that free community college should be an immediate top priority. Again, subsidizing college attendance for middle- and upper-income students in a world of very scarce resources makes less sense than targeting these resources to the practices and services that will best serve low-income students successfully and prepare them for the future.

Making Work Pay and Jobs More Available

When people with low skills work, their pay in the United States is usually very low. This not only means that they struggle to support their families, but it also discourages many workers who expected to have higher wages and benefits, which then leads some to drop out of the workforce. Indeed, falling labor force participation, especially among those well below retirement age, threatens the productive capacity of the US economy, as well as the families and communities in which these workers reside. We have two prominent ways of "making work pay": raising the minimum wage and expanding the Earned Income Tax Credit (EITC). Regarding the minimum wage, we should certainly raise it, but only to levels that do not greatly threaten job loss among the young and less-educated. In my view, a moderate increase—perhaps to $10 or so—would meet this objective.[5]

On the EITC, one group of poor adults now benefits very little from it: childless adults, especially noncustodial parents. A childless adult EITC (in the amount of $1,500–$2,000) should raise their incentives to accept and keep low-wage jobs, as well as their ability to support families.[6]

But some poor youth or adults have great difficulty finding or keeping employment. This is especially so when recessions occur, if they live in depressed regions of the country, or if their work-readiness is very limited. Making sure that they have access to employment is critical. At the same time, public service jobs for the poor are very expensive and often have little long-term impact on their earnings; and tax credits to employers for hiring the poor also have little positive impact over time.

Instead, the government should build on its relatively successful experience during the Great Recession of subsidizing jobs for poor and unemployed workers through its Emergency TANF program, in which about 250,000 such jobs were created quickly in the private and public sectors.[7] These subsidized jobs should be made available even in good times in depressed regions, while even more should be created when the economy weakens.

Helping Specific Groups

The final task is helping particular groups that face more specific problems. Besides raising skills, making work pay, and ensuring job availability, particular groups of low-income children and adults face specific problems and barriers that need specific solutions. Several are pervasive enough or critical enough that they clearly merit attention in any effort to fight poverty and improve opportunity.

For instance, low-income men, especially among African Americans, frequently have criminal records, as well as child support orders for noncustodial children on which they are behind in payment (or in "arrears"). The criminal records strongly deter employers from hiring them, and the high taxes on the earnings of those in arrears often deter these men from formally taking and keeping low-wage jobs.[8]

A range of policies and programs are needed to deal with these problems. Some focus on prevention, including alternatives to criminalizing drug use or jailing minor parole violators and policies to encourage responsible use of contraception to prevent unwed fatherhood. Others encourage states to reduce legal barriers to employment for offenders and offer arrears management. Expanding public funding for effective "transitional jobs" and fatherhood programs should also be in the mix. People with disabilities present a different problem. Currently, the federal disability insurance (DI) program encourages those who meet its eligibility requirements to never work again, thus limiting opportunity for these individuals and their families. A range of reforms that encourage and reward workers and employers for maintaining employment, rather than entering permanent non-employment, have been proposed, and these deserve to be carefully evaluated.[9] Even programs like the Supplemental Nutrition Assistance Program (SNAP, formerly known as the Food Stamp Program), which does not appear to discourage much work *per se*, might do more to help recipients regain employment. But all of this needs to be done without punishing those who truly cannot work and need income support.

Children growing up in families with very low incomes also need more help, especially in the summer months (when they lose access to school breakfasts and lunch) and in periods when their parents and guardians lose employment. Strengthening income support and basic services for children in these circumstances is essential.

Finally, children growing up in impoverished neighborhoods also need help. Recent research by Raj Chetty and Nathaniel Hendren proves beyond a doubt that children who reside in poor neighborhoods have more limited opportunity for upward mobility than those growing up elsewhere.[10] A range of policies to help these children have been proposed and tested over time. Some involve helping them and their families move to less-poor neighborhoods; others seek to improve their access to better schools and jobs in their regions; and still others involve strengthening the communities in which they live and the services provided there.[11] All of these approaches merit further experimentation and evaluation, before being implemented on a broader scale.

Conclusion

Poverty rates in America remain much too high, and opportunities for upward mobility among those raised in poverty remain much too low. . . . An agenda that sensibly combines improving skills, making work pay, ensuring job availability, and addressing group-specific barriers at modest budgetary cost can meet these requirements.

NOTES

1. AEI/Brookings Working Group on Poverty and Opportunity. 2015. *Opportunity, Responsibility and Securi-*

ty: *A Consensus Plan for Reducing Poverty and Restoring the American Dream.* Washington, D.C.: American Enterprise Institute for Public Policy Research and Brookings Institution.

2. Cascio, Elizabeth, and Diane Whitmore Schanzenbach. 2014. "Expanding Preschool Access for Disadvantaged Children." In M. Kearney and B. Harris, eds., *Policies to Address Poverty in America.* Washington, D.C.: The Hamilton Project, Brookings Institution.

3. Holzer, Harry J., Dane Linn, and Wanda Monthey. 2013. *The Promise of High-Quality Career and Technical Education.* New York: The College Board.

4. Holzer, Harry J. 2014. "Improving Employment Outcomes for Disadvantaged Students." In M. Kearney and B. Harris, eds., *Policies to Address Poverty in America.* Washington, D.C.: The Hamilton Project, Brookings Institution.

5. Congressional Budget Office (CBO). 2014. *The Effects of a Minimum Wage Increase on Employment and Family Income.* Washington, D.C.: CBO.

6. MDRC. 2015. *Paycheck Plus: Making Work Pay for Low-Income Single Adults.* New York: MDRC.

7. Roder, Anne, and Mark Elliott. 2013. *Stimulating Opportunity: The Effects of the ARRA Emergency Jobs Program.* New York: Economic Mobility Corporation, Inc.

8. Edelman, Peter, Harry J. Holzer, and Paul Offner. 2006. *Reconnecting Disadvantaged Young Men.* Washington, D.C.: Urban Institute Press.

9. Liebman, Jeffrey, and Jack Smalligan. 2012. *An Evidence-Based Path to Disability Insurance Reform.* Washington, D.C.: The Hamilton Project, Brookings Institution.

10. Chetty, Raj, and Nathaniel Hendren. 2015. *The Impact of Neighborhoods on Intergenerational Mobility.* Cambridge, MA: National Bureau of Economic Research.

11. Reeves, Richard, and Allegra Pocinki. 2015. *Space, Place, Race: Six Policies to Improve Social Mobility.* Washington, D.C.: Brookings Institution.

73. Lucian A. Bebchuk and Jesse M. Fried*

Tackling the Managerial Power Problem: The Key to Improving Executive Compensation

Executive pay continues to attract much attention from investors, financial economists, regulators, the media, and the public at large. The dominant paradigm for economists' study of executive compensa-

*Bebchuk, Lucian A. and Jesse M. Fried, "Tackling the Managerial Power Problem: The Key to Improving Executive Compensation," *Pathways* (Summer 2010), pp. 10–12.

tion has long been that pay arrangements are the product of arm's-length bargaining—bargaining between executives attempting to get the best possible deal for themselves and boards seeking only to serve shareholder interests. According to this "official story," directors can be counted on to act as guardians of shareholders' interests. This assumption has also been the basis for corporate rules governing compensation in publicly traded firms.

But the actual pay-setting process has deviated far from this arm's-length model. Managerial power and influence have played a key role in shaping the amount and structure of executive compensation. Directors have had various economic incentives to support, or at least go along with, arrangements favorable to the company's top executives. Collegiality, team spirit, a natural desire to avoid conflict within the board, and sometimes friendship and loyalty have also pulled board members in that direction. Although many directors own shares in their firms, their financial incentives to avoid arrangements favorable to executives have been too weak to induce them to take the personally costly, or at the very least unpleasant, route of haggling with their CEOs.

The inability or unwillingness of directors to bargain at arm's length has enabled executives to obtain pay that is higher and more decoupled from performance than would be expected under arm's-length bargaining. Indeed, there is a substantial body of evidence indicating that pay has been higher, or less sensitive to performance, when executives have more power over directors. Executives have less power over directors when shareholders are larger or more sophisticated and thus can more easily exert influence over the board. Not surprisingly, executive pay is lower and better tied to performance when there is a large outside shareholder or a greater concentration of institutional owners. Conversely, executive pay increases significantly after the adoption of anti-takeover provisions that give managers more power. Executive pay is also higher when the compensation committee chair has been appointed under the current CEO and may feel some obligation or gratitude toward that CEO.

One of the main constraints on executives' ability to extract even more value from boards is fear of shareholder outrage. Boards thus aggressively "camouflage" the amount and performance-insensitivity of executive pay in an attempt to reduce such outrage. Before 1992, for example, firms were required to disclose executive pay but were not told how they had to disclose it. Many firms thus chose to provide shareholders with long, dense narratives in which any dollar amounts were spelled out rather than expressed in numbers. A shareholder would need to spend a considerable amount of time just to find the dollar amounts, and there was generally not enough information provided to accurately add up the executive's total compensation. In 1992, the SEC required firms to disclose most compensation elements in a standardized, easy-to-read "Summary Compensation Table." Firms responded to the new disclosure requirements by coming up with pay arrangements, such as Supplemental Executive Retirement Plans (SERPs), that did not have to be reported in the table. In 2006, the SEC revised disclosure requirements to better capture the value of such "stealth compensation." But history has shown that compensation designers will try to develop other schemes to deliver pay to executives under shareholders' radar screens.

The desire to camouflage executive pay can explain the widespread practice of backdating executives' option grants, which came to light a few years ago. Most firms grant options to executives that are at-the-money: the exercise price is set to the grant-date stock price. The executive profits to the extent that the sale-date stock price exceeds the exercise price. It turns out that thousands of firms covertly backdated option grants to dates when the stock price was lower. This backdating secretly lowered the exercise price on executives' stock options and boosted the value of their option grants. Backdating also enabled firms to report lower compensation for executives than they actually received.

The existing flaws in compensation arrangements impose substantial costs on shareholders. First, there is the excess pay that managers receive as a result of their power—that is, the difference between what managers' influence enables them to obtain and what they would get under arm's-length contracting. The excess amounts paid to executives come directly at shareholders' expense, and these amounts are not mere pocket change. Second, and perhaps more important, executives' influence leads to compensation arrangements that dilute and distort executives' incentives. In particular, the decoupling of pay from performance reduces executives' incentives to make value-creating decisions and may even lead them to take steps that generate short-term gains at the expense of long-term shareholder value. In our view, the reduction in shareholder value caused by these inefficiencies—rather

than that caused by excessive managerial pay—could well be the biggest cost arising from managerial influence over compensation.

The Need for Shareholder-Serving Directors

The problems of executive compensation arrangements are rooted in boards' failure to bargain at arm's length with executives. Greater transparency, improved board procedures, additional shareholder approval requirements, and a better understanding by shareholders of the desirability of various compensation arrangements can all help improve the situation. But these remedies cannot substitute completely for effective decision making by directors striving to serve shareholder interests.

The problems of executive compensation would be best addressed by improving directors' incentives. We need to turn the "official story" of executive compensation and board governance—which portrays directors as faithfully serving shareholders' interests—from fiction into reality.

Directors who safeguard shareholder interests are needed not only to address executive compensation problems but also to tackle the myriad corporate governance problems that would continue to arise even if compensation arrangements were optimized. For example, having such directors is essential for our ability to rely on boards to prevent managers from engaging in empire-building or from impeding acquisition offers that would benefit shareholders. The foundation of our board-monitoring system of corporate governance is the existence of directors who select, supervise, and compensate executives with shareholders' interests in mind. Shareholders' ability to rely on such directors is, so to speak, the Archimedean point on which this system stands. The critical question, then, is how to make directors more focused on shareholder interests.

The Limits of Director Independence

The main way that the corporate governance system has responded to perceived governance problems over the years is by trying to bolster board independence. Reforms have sought to make nominally independent directors more independent and expand the presence and role of such independent directors on the board. Strengthened director independence is now widely believed to be key to the effectiveness of the board-monitoring model. Attributing past governance problems to insufficient director independence, many believe that strengthened independence will prevent such governance problems in the future.

We agree that director independence is likely to be beneficial. But director independence cannot by itself ensure that boards properly carry out their critical role. Rules governing director independence cannot deliver nearly as much as their enthusiastic supporters claim.

A fundamental limitation of independence requirements is that they fail to provide affirmative incentives for directors to enhance shareholder value. These requirements merely reduce, and do not fully eliminate, directors' incentives and inclinations to favor executives. Thus, any residual tendency among directors to favor executives may still have a substantial impact in the absence of any countervailing incentives to enhance shareholder value. What we need, then, is to provide directors with *affirmative* incentives to focus on shareholder interests.

Invigorating Corporate Elections

In our view, the most effective way to improve board performance is to increase the power of shareholders vis-à-vis directors. We should make directors not only more independent from executives but also less independent from shareholders. The appointment of directors should substantially depend on shareholders, not only in theory but in practice. Such dependence would give directors better incentives to serve shareholder interests.

Making directors dependent on shareholders could counter some of the factors that incline directors to pursue their own interests or those of executives rather than those of shareholders. Such dependence could make the desire for re-election a positive force rather than a negative one. It could also provide directors with an incentive to develop reputations for serving shareholders. And lastly, it could help instill in directors a sense of loyalty toward shareholders, especially if institutional investors take an active role in putting directors on boards.

For all of these reasons, we support the removal of barriers that have historically insulated directors from shareholders. Because of shareholders' collective action problems, increasing shareholder power vis-à-vis directors would hardly be a perfect solution. But movement in this direction has substantial

potential for improving the incentives and performance of boards.

Shareholders' power to replace directors plays a critical role in the corporation. Although this power is not supposed to be used routinely, it should provide a critical fail-safe. "If the shareholders are displeased with the action of their elected representatives," emphasized the Delaware Supreme Court in its well-known opinion in the case of *Unocal Corp. v. Mesa Petroleum Co.*, "the powers of corporate democracy are at their disposal to turn the board out."

In reality, however, this safety valve is weak. Attempts by shareholders to replace incumbents with a team that would do a better job—the kind of action referred to in the *Unocal* opinion above—face considerable impediments. To make directors more focused on shareholder interests, it would be desirable to reduce these impediments.

To begin, shareholders should get access to the corporate ballot. Under existing rules, only incumbents' nominees are placed on the corporate ballot, and outside challengers have to bear the costs of distributing and collecting proxies supporting challengers' nominees. When a significant group of shareholders wishes to run a candidate, this candidate should simply be placed on the corporate ballot.

Beyond providing shareholders with easier access to the corporate ballot, additional measures to strengthen electoral threats should be adopted. Under existing rules of corporate law, incumbents' "campaign" costs are fully covered by the company—providing them with a great advantage over outside candidates, who must pay their own way. To lower the financial barrier for challengers, companies should be required to reimburse reasonable costs incurred by such nominees when they garner sufficient support in the ultimate vote.

Such reimbursement arrangements could be opposed, of course, on grounds that they would be costly to shareholders. But an improved corporate elections process would be in the interests of both companies and shareholders. The proposed measures would not expend corporate resources on nominees whose initial support and chances of winning are negligible; the limited amounts expended on serious challenges would be a small and worthwhile price to pay for an improved system of corporate governance.

Incumbent directors are currently protected from removal not only by the substantial cost to challengers of putting forward a competing slate, but also by staggered boards. In a staggered board, only one-third of the members come up for election each year. As a result, no matter how dissatisfied shareholders are, they must prevail in two annual elections in order to replace a majority of the incumbents and take control away from current management. A substantial fraction of public companies have such an arrangement.

The entrenching effect of staggered boards is costly to shareholders. Companies with a charter-based staggered board have a significantly lower value than other companies, controlling for relevant differences. Legal reforms that would require or encourage firms to have all directors stand for election together could thus contribute significantly to shareholder wealth.

Another way to reduce directors' ability to ignore shareholder interests is to remove the board's veto power over changes to the company's basic governance arrangements. These arrangements are set forth either in the rules of the state in which the company is incorporated or in the company's charter. Under longstanding corporate law, only the board—not a group of shareholders, however large—can initiate and bring to a shareholder vote a proposal to change the state of incorporation or to amend the corporate charter.

Federal securities laws give shareholders the power to express their sentiments in precatory shareholder resolutions, but these resolutions are nonbinding. In recent years, shareholders of companies with staggered boards have increasingly initiated proposals recommending annual election of all directors. However, boards often choose to ignore these proposals, even when they attract a majority of the shareholder vote.

Directors' control over the corporate agenda is often justified on grounds that the US corporation is a completely "representative democracy," in which shareholders can act only through their representatives, the directors. In theory, if shareholders could easily replace directors, that power would be sufficient to induce directors not to stray from shareholders' wishes on major corporate issues.

As we have seen, however, the removal of directors is rather difficult under existing arrangements. It would be far from easy even under a reformed system of corporate elections. Furthermore, shareholders may be pleased with management's general performance but still wish to put in place governance arrangements that restrict management's power or discretion in certain ways. Shareholders should be able to make a change in governance arrangements without concurrently having to replace the board.

The absence of shareholder power to initiate and approve changes in firms' basic corporate governance arrangements has, over time, tilted these arrangements excessively in management's favor. As new issues and circumstances have arisen, firms have tended to adopt charter amendments that address these changes efficiently only when the amendments were favored by management. Additionally, states seeking to attract incorporating and reincorporating firms have had incentives to give substantial weight to management preferences, even at the expense of shareholder interests.

Giving shareholders the power to initiate and approve by vote a proposal to reincorporate or to adopt a charter amendment could produce, in one bold stroke, a substantial improvement in the quality of corporate governance. Shareholder power to change governance arrangements would reduce the need for intervention from outside the firm by regulators, exchanges, or legislators.

Indeed, if shareholders had the power to set the ground rules of corporate governance, they could use it to address some of the problems we have discussed above. Shareholders could establish rules that dismantle staggered boards or invigorate director elections. Shareholders could also adopt charter amendments that improve the process by which executive pay is set or place whatever limits they deem desirable on pay arrangements.

Executive pay problems reflect underlying flaws in corporate governance. To fix these problems, the structure of corporate governance arrangements must be reformed. The power of the board and the weakness of shareholders are often viewed as an inevitable corollary of the modern corporation's widely dispersed ownership. But this weakness is partly due to the legal rules that insulate management from shareholder intervention. Changing these rules would reduce the extent to which boards can stray from shareholder interests and would much improve corporate governance—including flawed executive pay arrangements.

74. Michelle Jackson*

We Need to Have a Second Conversation

We live in a country that, despite being very rich, seems quite willing to tolerate unusually high rates of dire poverty. As Kathryn Edin and H. Luke Shaefer have recently shown, there is real $2/day poverty in the United States, and much of it.[1]

It is perhaps a puzzle that a country so rich is seemingly so untroubled by poverty. It is not that high rates of poverty are altogether ignored: We of course have all manner of poverty reform discussions, poverty conferences, and poverty commissions. The poverty reform business is hardly a small one. But it is striking that we enter into poverty reform discussions with such circumscribed objectives and such narrow-gauge proposals for reform. We assume that the best we can do is contain the problem, and we seldom even consider the idea that we might actually solve it.

This is surprising. When the problem is big, one might imagine that the policy response would likewise be big. But in fact, sweeping reform is rarely contemplated and of course is never enacted. This quiescence is especially strange given that the US is a country that prides itself on viewing institutions as perfectible, as humanly created, and as the proper objects of ceaseless recasting as we attempt to bring them into closer alignment with our principles.

In this essay, rather than advocating for one particular type of policy or another, I will instead argue for the need for two conversations about reducing poverty. Although it is important and valuable to continue on with our usual "poverty reform" conversation, there is also a need for a more assertive strategy. The articles in this book provide important beginnings for that strategy, but I want to suggest that there is room for an even more aggressive conversation. I do not pretend to know exactly where that conversation should go. I will only suggest that we need to begin it.

Conversation One

At present, one conversation dominates the academic and policy discourse: A precisely focused,

*Jackson, Michelle. 2017. "We Need to Have a Second Conversation." *Pathways Magazine*.

science-based conversation that identifies social problems and offers specific, evidence-informed solutions. I focus on a single problem—the reduced educational investments of poor children—to illustrate how "Conversation One" works.

The substantial and persistent inequalities in educational attainment across time and countries are well-documented. For example, much research demonstrates that test score inequalities are present early in life, and that by the time children reach kindergarten, those from high-income backgrounds are many years ahead of those raised in poverty.[2] There is strong evidence to show that income inequalities in test scores have substantially increased over the past sixty years or so, even while inequalities related to race have declined.[3] Socioeconomic inequalities in college access, selective college access, and college completion are similarly ubiquitous, and there is again evidence that such inequalities have only grown larger in recent decades.[4] These findings—and many others—have led to a growing consensus that if we wish to prevent the transmission of poverty across generations, we might look first and foremost at eliminating inequalities in educational attainment.

The very same academics who document inequalities are increasingly likely to propose and test interventions designed to reduce them. This is all to the good. For example, recent research demonstrating that low-income students are under-represented in college partly because they do not always receive the financial aid to which they are entitled was paired with the development of an intervention in which (1) such students were given information about post-secondary education options, and (2) their college financial aid applications were filled out automatically from tax returns.[5] This intervention substantially increased the likelihood of poor students enrolling in college, and if taken to scale, would be expected to reduce the income gap in college enrollment. Other research has pointed to a phenomenon known as "summer melt," wherein graduating high school seniors with a confirmed college placement fail to enroll in college at the end of the summer. Experiments have shown that sending a series of text messages to these graduating seniors significantly reduces the number of students who drop out over the summer months.[6] Given that low-income students are at particular risk of summer melt, this intervention would again be expected to reduce inequalities in college enrollment.

In Conversation One, narrow solutions are proposed to overcome tightly defined problems, where the problem being solved may be but one manifestation of a much wider inequality. An extreme version of Conversation One is perhaps best summed up in the "nudge" philosophy, originating in behavioral economics, which is particularly influential in the current policy discourse. What are nudges? For Thaler and Sunstein, "A nudge, as we will use the term, is any aspect of the choice architecture that alters people's behavior in a predictable way without forbidding any options or significantly changing their economic incentives. To count as a mere nudge, the intervention must be easy and cheap to avoid. Nudges are not mandates. Putting fruit at eye level counts as a nudge. Banning junk food does not."[7] The FAFSA and text messaging interventions described above are both examples of nudges that have been influential in the policy debate around inequalities in college access.

The nudge is of course an especially extreme rendition of our more general tendency to prefer the incremental reform. But it is indicative of our very circumscribed discourse and our preference for tailored interventions: We tinker with different ways to increase the take-up of "food stamps" (i.e., Supplemental Nutritional Assistance Program); we tinker with different ways of delivering home visiting programs; and we tinker with the effects of different types of qualifying work requirements in the context of existing welfare programs (i.e., Temporary Assistance to Needy Families, or TANF). It is of course good that we try to make our existing institutions operate more effectively. But when tinkering with existing institutions fails – in a context of growing poverty and inequality – we should at least consider throwing in the towel and casting new institutions. For this to be feasible, we must encourage and foster what I am labeling "Conversation Two."

Conversation Two

It is perhaps to be expected that contemporary social science should come to be associated with a program of small incisions. An increasing scientism within social science disciplines alongside an emphasis on evidence-informed policy generates pressure to catalog precise mechanisms that address small parts of the puzzle of inequality. This is all to the benefit of human knowledge; a hallmark of science is that it relies upon the accumulation of knowledge across a great many individual scientists and research projects. But by focusing only on the fragmented impact of inequality across many small domains, the larger story is lost. The simple, profound, crushing impact of poverty and inequality on educational attainment or on life chances more generally is missed. At worst, Conversation One may divert our attention from the root problem that the carefully delineated interventions are designed to address.

It is uncontroversial to state that the elimination of poverty would require far-reaching institutional reforms. What is more controversial perhaps is the suggestion that social scientists are likely to undermine the aim of eliminating poverty if Conversation One is the only conversation in which we engage. And yet the very roots of the word "intervention" betray its concerns—the idea is to step in between the process and the outcome.[8] The methods, usually experimental, by which we test interventions rely on the idea that we change just one thing and keep everything else the same. But if we become so inured to the extent of poverty that our only response is to ameliorate its effects through interventions, we are in danger of treating the symptoms of the disease and not the cause. Alongside Conversation One, therefore, we must also engage in Conversation Two.

Conversation Two insists that in addition to any discussion about expedient, small-scale interventions, we have a wider discussion about where poverty comes from and what types of larger-scale changes might be needed to eradicate it. This is a difficult conversation for social scientists to have because when asked what it would take to eradicate poverty, we feel immediately constrained by the self-censoring that occurs when we ask whether or not it *can* be done. In addition, it is problematic to advocate for large-scale institutional reform from a social-scientific standpoint, given the difficulty of testing in advance what the effects of such reform might be. An unanticipated effect of the current mantra on "evidence-based" policy is that we have become exceedingly circumscribed in our policy options. We only contemplate narrow changes, and we thereby forego bold moves that might yield big returns.

This is not to suggest that aggressive policy change is necessarily "evidence-free." We *do* have examples of alternative institutional arrangements that might serve as models for reform. These alternatives take the form of institutional arrangements that are already in place in other countries.

Let us return, by way of example, to the field of education. Here, alternative institutional arrangements abound. In some countries, there have been important steps toward breaking the relationship between neighborhood and school quality. In the US, school socioeconomic segregation is seen as a natural consequence of neighborhood segregation, which affects both the quality of schools (because schools in poor areas have a smaller tax base from which to draw) and the student composition of schools. Neighborhood segregation is less extreme in many countries, but there have been attempts to mitigate its effects on educational outcomes. From a cross-national perspective, it is in fact rare to tie school funding so closely to neighborhood wealth: In the majority of European Union countries, for example, the level of resources provided for teaching staff and operational costs is determined by a centralized funding formula.[9]

This is but one example. If we were to insist on retaining our decentralized funding practices, we could instead follow the lead of countries that attempt to break the relationship between neighborhood and school quality by assigning school placement through a lottery. South Korea instituted a lottery for upper secondary academic schools in large cities in the 1970s, and researchers have reported a greater degree of socioeconomic diversity within schools and increased equality in school outcomes for those areas with such lottery assignment.[10] Cross-national variation at the college level is also substantial. Most notably, in many countries, college is free for all who wish to attend.[11]

In other domains, substantial reforms to the economy and labor market could be implemented along the lines of flexicurity, a labor market system initially developed in Denmark, and which is now one of the central planks of EU labor market policy. In flexicurity systems, flexible employment relationships, employment security, and a high minimum wage exist alongside possibilities for lifelong learning and re-training.[12] Perhaps most relevant for poverty policy, flexicurity tackles long-term unemployment by committing to continuous retraining, increasing financial support for the unemployed, and thus reducing the length of unemployment spells. Flexicurity is doubtless a characteristically European policy, but advocates such as Cohen and Sabel have made a powerful case that the United States should adopt the approach, even if this "would require a sharp departure from past practice, freeing ourselves from the tight grip of the past's famously cold, dead hand."[13] I offer up flexicurity as but one example of big-R reform. We might equally consider new laws that eliminate all intergenerational transfers, that dramatically ramp up unions, that eliminate race-biased incarceration, and that outlaw residential segregation (by race and income). This is but a partial list.

It is sometimes argued that nothing is more sacred in the US than the presumption that only low-income *workers* deserve our help (via, for example, the EITC). The American love affair with work is of course deep. But we must also appreciate that some individuals cannot work and that all individuals, even nonworkers, deserve to be treated with dignity. Edin and Shaefer exposed the desperate situation of American families existing only on state support of less than $2 per day, where welfare state policies focused on work have locked out those with precarious positions in the labor market. In addressing non-working poverty, we might draw on alternative conceptions of welfare states that offer support to those both in and out of the labor market. To be sure, these alternative visions require different types of tax regimes, but it bears noting that tax regimes that would be routinely dismissed as unworkable in one country are implemented unproblematically in others.[14]

In considering the institutional arrangements of other countries as possible models, it is important to acknowledge that we have already moved away from the most radical form of Conversation Two: A conversation rooted in *what might be* rather than merely *what is*. It is, I confess, already bold to ask Americans to consider how other countries "do poverty." It is asking far more that they also consider institutional reforms that are limited only by the imagination. In academic and policy circles, such a sentiment is most likely to be met with an eye-roll, the weary response of the battle-hardened. But there are two important reasons why social scientists should have this radical form of Conversation Two ready and available. First, science requires us to be honest and upfront about the extent of reform that would be required to eliminate poverty. Discussions about the overwhelming and far-reaching effects of poverty and inequality are only undermined by the suggestion that small, or even moderate, tweaks to policy might be able to substantially counter their effects.

The second reason to open up to truly radical reform is yet more important. Namely, what is considered to be a palatable and feasible reform by the public may change, and it may change quickly. Sunstein identifies the phenomenon of a "norm cascade," in which there is a rapid change in what is seen as deviant or acceptable from one moment to the next; this often occurs because there is a disjuncture between what people feel privately and what they are willing to express publicly.[15] In societies with very high levels of socioeconomic inequality and where most are relatively disadvantaged, it is probably unwise to assume that private beliefs about inequality and deprivation will always match the current normative, public expressions. If contemporary norms around poverty and the appropriate institutional responses to poverty were to change rapidly, social science would need to be ready to weigh in on the viability of alternative institutional arrangements.

If there are any doubters on this point, I need only note the rapid, unexpected, and overwhelming change in support for marriage equality. If it can happen there, a realm that many treated as the third rail of conservative politics, then surely it can happen too in discussions of poverty. This sea change may well be underway already: It was not so long ago, after all, that presidential candidates would not even venture the word "inequality." Now it is a word bandied about by Republicans and Democrats alike.

Conclusion

To be sure, social scientists in the United States have made the case for institutional reform, and a call for a stronger form of Conversation Two should not undermine those efforts. The clearest example is to be found in the discussion around early childhood education. This was once a radical conversation: After all, early childhood interventions are predicated in part on the view that we cannot rely on the family for early training and that only by re-allocating that function to other institutions can a substantial reduction in poverty be achieved. The same willingness to undertake significant reform should be ported to the other major institutions of our time. The simple question to be applied to each and every one of our institutions is: What needs to be changed to guarantee that it does not generate or reproduce inequality?

The second conversation is one that ensures that large-scale institutional reform is always on the table. Marx is famous for writing, "Philosophers have hitherto only interpreted the world in various ways; the point is to change it."[16] Since the moment it was committed to print, this phrase has doubtless been perceived as naïve and idealistic, but in fact it encapsulates precisely the naïveté that is seen, at least by some, as the essence of the American experiment. If we do not include Conversation Two alongside the smaller interventions that we think might just have a chance, we are in danger of leaving a legacy of nudges without any real, systemic change.

NOTES

1. Edin, Kathryn J., and H. Luke Schaefer. 2015. *$2.00 a Day: Living on Almost Nothing in America.* New York: Houghton Mifflin Harcourt.

2. See, for example, Heckman, James J. 2007. "The Economics, Technology, and Neuroscience of Human Capability Formation." *Proceedings of the National Academy of Sciences*, 104, 13250–13255; Duncan, Greg J., and Katherine A. Magnuson. 2011. "The Long Reach of Early Childhood Poverty." *Pathways*, Stanford Center for the Study of Poverty and Inequality.

3. Reardon, Sean F. 2011. "The Widening Academic Achievement Gap Between the Rich and the Poor: New Evidence and Possible Explanations". In Greg J. Duncan and Richard J. Murnane, *Whither Opportunity: Rising Inequality, Schools, and Children's Life Chances.* New York: Russell Sage Foundation.

4. Bastedo, Michael N., and Ozan Jaquette. 2011. "Running in Place: Low-Income Students and the Dynamics of Higher Education Stratification." *Educational Evaluation and Policy Analysis*, 33, 318–339; Karen, David. 2002. "Changes in Access to Higher Education in the United States: 1980–1992." *Sociology of Education*, 75, 191–210.

5. Bettinger, Eric P., Bridget Terry Long, Philip Oreopoulos, and Lisa Sanbonmatsu. 2012. "The Role of Application Assistance and Information in College Decisions: Results from the H&R Block FAFSA Experiment". *The Quarterly Journal of Economics*, 127(3), 1205–1242.

6. Castleman, Benjamin L., Karen D. Arnold, and Katherine L. Wartman. 2012. "Stemming The Tide of Summer Melt: An Experimental Study of the Effects of Post-High School Summer Intervention on College Enrollment." *The Journal of Research on Educational Effectiveness*, 5(1), 1–18; Castleman, Benjamin L., and Lindsay C. Page. 2014. *Summer Melt: Supporting Low-Income Students through the Transition to College.* Cambridge, MA: Harvard Education Press.

7. Page 6 of Thaler, Richard H., and Cass Sunstein. 2009. *Nudge: Improving Decisions about Health, Wealth, and Happiness.* New York: Penguin.

8. "Intervention" originates in the Latin words *inter* (between) and *venire* (come).

9. European Commission/EACEA/Eurydice. 2014. *Financing Schools in Europe: Mechanisms, Methods and Criteria in Public Funding. Eurydice Report.* Luxembourg: Publications Office of the European Union.

10. Byun, Soo-Yong, Kyung-Keun Kim, and Hyunjoon Park. 2012. "School Choice and Educational Inequality in South Korea." *Journal of School Choice*, 6(2), 158–183.

11. For a proposal to guarantee American students two free years of college, see Goldrick-Rab, Sara, and Nancy Kendall. 2014. *Redefining College Affordability: Securing America's Future with a Free Two Year College Option.* Indianapolis, IN: Lumina Foundation.

12. For a critique of a narrow vision of higher education as four-year college, and a discussion of alternative visions for the United States, see Stevens, Mitchell L. 2014. "College for Grown-Ups." *New York Times*, December 11, 2014. See also Kirst, Michael W., and Mitchell L. Stevens. 2015. *Remaking College: The Changing Ecology of Higher Education.* Stanford, CA: Stanford University Press.

13. Cohen, Joshua, and Charles Sabel. 2009. "Flexicurity." *Pathways.* Stanford, CA: Stanford Center for the Study of Poverty and Inequality.

14. It is notable that two influential books on income inequality make the case for tax reform as a basis for increasing equality. See Piketty, Thomas. 2014. *Capital in the Twenty-First Century.* Cambridge, MA: Belknap Press; and Atkinson, Anthony B. 2015. *Inequality: What Can be Done?* Cambridge, MA: Harvard University Press.

15. Sunstein, Cass R. 1996. "Social Norms and Social Roles." *Columbia Law Review*, 96(4), 903–968

16. The eleventh of the *Theses on Feuerbach*.

ABOUT THE EDITORS

David B. Grusky is the Barbara Kimball Browning Professor in the Humanities and Sciences, professor of sociology at Stanford University, and director of the Stanford Center on Poverty and Inequality. His recent books include *Occupy the Future, The New Gilded Age, The Great Recession, The Inequality Reader, Social Stratification, The Inequality Puzzle, The Declining Significance of Gender?*, and *Occupational Ghettos*.

Jasmine Hill is a Ph.D. candidate in sociology at Stanford University. Prior to arriving at Stanford, she graduated from the University of California, Los Angeles. Her research focuses on race, class conflict, and social mobility and examines how families find pathways into the middle class and how these processes vary by race and class background.

INDEX

CPSIA information can be obtained
at www.ICGtesting.com
Printed in the USA
LVOW03s1400060217
523329LV00001B/1/P